VISUAL QUICKSTART GUIDE

MACROMEDIA FLASH MX

FOR WINDOWS AND MACINTOSH

Katherine Ulrich

 Peachpit Press

Visual QuickStart Guide
Macromedia Flash MX for Windows and Macintosh
Katherine Ulrich

Peachpit Press

1249 Eighth Street
Berkeley, CA 94710
510/524-2178
800/283-9444
510/524-2221 (fax)

Published by Peachpit Press, a division of Pearson Education.
Find us on the Web at www.peachpit.com.
To report errors, please send a note to errata@peachpit.com.
Published in association with Macromedia Press.

Copyright ©2002 by Katherine Ulrich

Editor: Cliff Colby, Wendy Sharp
Production Coordinator: Lisa Brazieal, Myrna Vladic
Copyeditor: Kathy Simpson
Compositor: Magnolia Studio
Indexer: Joy Dean Lee
Cover Design: The Visual Group

ISBN 0-201-79481-0

9 8 7 6 5

Printed and bound in the United States of America

Dedication

To Perry Whittle, who continues to offer both moral and technical support, who helps me keep it all in perspective, and who downplays my failings and promotes my successes shamelessly.

Thank You:

Special thanks to my editor Cliff Colby for juggling this book with the arrival of his second son; to Wendy Sharp for tucking in loose ends and helping the project out the door; to Kathy Simpson, for catching all my over-used words and misplaced punctuation; to Lisa Brazieal for whipping the pages into shape; to Victor Gavenda, for updating the appendix of keyboard shortcuts; to Jonathan Duran for tracking down tough questions and giving the whole book a technical review; to Bentley Wolfe for answering those pesky last-minute questions; to Brad Bechtel and Janice Pearce for dealing with my OS X woes; and to Erika Burback, Jeremy Clark, Peter Alan Davy, Jane DeKoven, Erica Norton, and Lisa Young for additional technical advice with previous editions. And finally, thank you to Marjorie Baer, Peachpit Executive Editor, for bringing me to this project in the first place.

CONTENTS AT A GLANCE

TABLE OF CONTENTS

Chapter 3:   **Modifying Simple Graphics**   **85**

TABLE OF CONTENTS

TABLE OF CONTENTS

Introduction

Back when the Web was emerging from its academic cocoon and spreading its wings into the consciousness of the wide world, the Internet was drab. Any splash of color, any graphic image, was a refreshing oasis in a vast desert of text against plain gray backgrounds. As the Web grew and its focus shifted, Web sites became vehicles for personal expression, for instruction, for commerce. Web designers longed to expand the graphic content of their sites. Many designers simply forged ahead, adding bitmaps with abandon. Unfortunately, in the process, these designers abandoned their viewers to endless waiting.

Although the bitmap formats that are standard for Web graphics—JPEG, GIF, and PNG—provide compression to make the images as small and fast to download as possible, download times for sites containing lots of images can slow to an audience-losing crawl. Web designers craved a better, more efficient way to send graphics over the Internet. Macromedia Flash provides that efficiency.

What Makes Flash a Special Web-Design Tool?

Flash satisfies designers' cravings for more graphics and more control over those graphics by providing a way to deliver vector images over the Web. Vector images keep file sizes down, and they are scaleable, which means that you can maintain control of what a Web site looks like when your viewer resizes the browser window, for example, making the whole thing stay in proportion as the window grows or shrinks. In addition, Flash provides streaming capability. Streaming allows some elements to display immediately upon download while more information continues to arrive over the Internet.

Animation in Flash is not limited to cartoon characters like Bugs Bunny and The Simpsons. Flash animations also encompass navigation elements, such as buttons and menus. And Flash doesn't limit you to creating animation only for the Web. You can license Flash Player and distribute Flash movies on CD-ROM. You can create stand-alone projectors and distribute them via e-mail or on disk. You can export Flash to other formats, such as QuickTime or Windows .AVI movies. But Web-site creation and enhancement is Flash's primary focus.

Although this book can't teach you to create a complete user interface for your Web site, what it will teach you about using Flash to create graphics, animation, and interactivity will go a long way toward helping you develop expressive, creative, exciting Web sites. Whether you need a banner ad that grabs the viewer's attention, a button for moving around within your site or linking to other URLs, or a fun animated cartoon, this book will get you started quickly, helping you use Flash's tools to add activity and interactivity to your Web site.

What Is Streaming?

Most viewers lack the patience to wait for an entire site to download, especially one that has big bitmaps or sounds. Flash streams the content of your Web site over the Internet. Streaming means that once some of the vector art of your site has downloaded, Flash can display it while the rest of your data continues to download. As Flash plays the first frames of your movie, subsequent frames keep coming into your viewer's computer, and Flash feeds them out at the specified frame rate. If you plan your movie right, the frames coming in never catch up to the frames being displayed, and your viewer sees only a continuous flow of images.

About Flash

Flash began life as Future Splash Animator, a nifty little program for creating and animating vector art. In 1997, Macromedia acquired Future Splash, changed the name to Flash, and promoted the program as a tool for creating graphic content for the World Wide Web. Flash excels as a Web-site-design tool because it provides all the tools you need: tools for creating graphics; tools for animating those graphics; tools for creating interface elements and interactivity; and tools for writing the HTML necessary to display your graphics, animations, and interface elements as a Web page via a browser.

Standard illustration programs, such as Macromedia FreeHand and Adobe Illustrator, rely on Bézier curves to create vector shapes. Flash offers similar tools but also provides natural drawing tools that let you deal with vectors in a more immediate way, without manipulating curve handles or special points on a line. Flash's natural drawing tools provide a spontaneity that appeals to many artists. Flash's natural drawing tools also appeal to nonartists—those of us who can't draw a straight line to save our lives.

Flash helps beginners create simple animated graphics, but anyone who is familiar with animation can use Flash's tools to create quite complex animations. Flash's scripting language, ActionScript, provides assisted modes that help beginners to add simple interactive elements. ActionScript is powerful enough, however, that serious scripters can create highly sophisticated interterface and application designs. Flash's ability to incorporate sounds and video make it easy to bring even more life to your sites.

With each new generation of Flash, Macromedia has added features and functions that expand the program's capabilities as an animation machine and interactivity creator while preserving the easy-to-use drawing tools and assisted animation and interactivity features.

How Flash Animates

Flash uses standard animation techniques to create the illusion of movement. You create a series of still images, each slightly different from the next. By displaying the images rapidly, one after another, you simulate continuous movement. Flash's animation tools help you create, organize, and synchronize the animation of multiple graphic elements, sounds, and video clips.

Flash Movie Formats

Flash is both an authoring environment for creating animation and a playback system for making that content viewable on a local computer or in a Web browser. You create animation and interactivity in Flash-format files. In the Windows world, these files have the extension .fla. To create viewable movies, you convert the authoring files to Flash Player format; these files have the extension .swf. Another name for the playable format is SWF (pronounced *swif*).

How Flash Delivers

Flash's publishing feature creates the necessary HTML code to display your animation in a Web browser. The publishing feature also lets you choose alternative methods of delivering your movie—as animated GIF images, for example, or as a QuickTime movie—and then creates those alternate image files.

Vectors Versus Bitmaps

The data that creates vector graphics and the data that creates bitmapped graphics are similar, in that they are both mathematical instructions to the computer about where and how to create images on-screen. Bitmaps, however, are lengthier and result in a less versatile graphic; vector graphics are compact and fully scaleable.

Bitmap instructions break a whole graphic into little dots and must tell the computer about each dot; vector instructions describe the graphic mathematically as a series of lines and arcs (**Figure i.1**). Picture a 1-inch black horizontal line on a field of white. For a bitmap, the instructions would go something like this: Make a white dot, make a white dot, make a black dot, make a black dot, make a black dot, make a black dot, and so on. These instructions would repeat until you'd strung together enough black dots to make a 1-inch line. Then the white-dot instructions would start again and continue until the rest of the screen was filled with white dots. The vector instructions would simply be a mathematical formula for a straight line, plus the coordinates that define the line's position on-screen.

Figure i.1 For a computer to draw a bit-mapped graphic, it must receive a set of instructions for each dot (each bit of data) that makes up the image. Instructions for a vector graphic describe lines and curves that make up the image mathematically. The bitmapped line (left) appears much rougher than the vector line (right). You can't enlarge the bit-mapped line without losing quality. But you can make the vector line as big as you like; it retains its solid appearance.

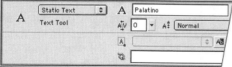

Figure i.2 The new context-sensitive Property Inspector displays different information according to which element or tool you have selected.

Flash MX: What's New?

Flash MX sports an updated interface that brings Flash closer in look and feel to other Macromedia products. The addition of a context-sensitive Property Inspector streamlines Flash's panel set. New frame-selection options make it easier to manipulate frames in the Timeline. Exciting new features include the ability to embed video clips within a movie for playback in Flash Player, the ability to use ActionScript to make movie clips behave like buttons, the ability to customize the ActionScript editor, and more. The following section lists some new features that will be of particular interest to beginning and intermediate users of Flash.

Interface Enhancements

The addition of a context-sensistive Property Inspector means fewer Flash panels overall, reducing the number of items you need to keep open on the desktop (**Figure i.2**). The panels you do have open come out from behind their Flash 5 tabs, and can dock together, expanding and collapsing within a single panel window. The Timeline offers more predictable span-based or frame-based selection styles. The category folders in the Actions Toolbox (in the Actions panel) have been reorganized and divided into subfolders to group actions logically. The new Reference panel puts the ActionScript dictionary right on your desktop. Color-creation and selection functions are now consolidated in the Color Mixer and Color Swatches panels.

Library Enchancements

Flash MX lets you import assets directly to a library and drag and drop library folders between documents while preserving the folder structure. As you bring assets into a movie, Flash MX warns about assset conflicts for items that have the same name but different content, letting you decide whether or not to replace the existing assets. Dragging a graphic element from the Stage to the Library window now opens the dialog box for converting the graphic to a symbol.

Free-Transform Tool

Previously associated with the arrow tool, the Scale and Rotate modifiers have moved to the new free-transform tool, which also offers two new modifers: Distort, for creating perspective effects, and Envelope, for manipulating the Bézier handles and anchor points of a group of selected graphics or text elements (**Figure i.3**)

Document Templates

The new template-document feature lets you capture reusable work in .fla files that are accessible from a single template location (**Figure i.4**). Flash MX comes with numerous templates, that you can use, for example, in creating ads, presentations, slideshows, and quizzes.

Distribute to Layers

The Distribute to Layers command makes quick work of placing graphics on separate layers for motion tweening. Combined with the Break Apart command's new ability to turn selected text into a series of single-character text boxes, the Distribute to Layers command makes it easy to animate editable type.

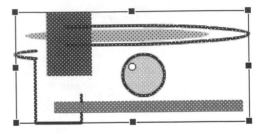

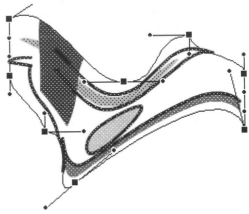

Figure i.3 The free-transform tool's Envelope modify gives you the ability to modify a group of selected graphics using Bézier curves.

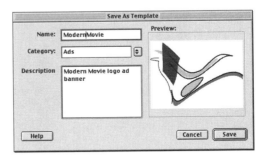

Figure i.4 Flash MX comes with numerous template documents to streamline your work on common projects, such as ads or presentations. You can also set up your own templates.

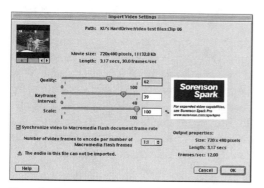

Figure i.5 Sorenson Media's Spark codec helps you make the most of imported video clips' quality while keeping their size down. Embedded video runs directly in Flash Player 6.

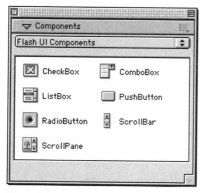

Figure i.6 Built-in components help you create common user-interface elements for your Flash sites.

Editable Vertical Text

To better support foreign languages, Flash MX allows you to create vertical text boxes with live, editable text. You can also control whether text reads left to right or right to left. Text in Flash Player 6 files is now encoded in both UTF-8 and UTF-16 format to better support foreign-language fonts.

Embedded Video Clips

Macromedia has licensed and incorporated Sorenson Media's Spark codec into Flash. Spark lets you import video clips and embed them in Flash, for playback within Flash Player 6 (**Figure i.5**). You can control video clips with ActionScript, just as you would other Flash objects.

Components

Built-in user-interface elements, such as scrolling text or image boxes and radio buttons, come in their own panel (**Figure i.6**). For anyone familiar with Flash 5, these are a new generation of SmartClips.

Movie-Delivery Enhancements

For the first time, Flash gives you the ability to save .fla files as a previous version: Flash 5. As always, you can create .swf files for playback in any of the Flash Player versions (1 through 6). A new HTML setting creates .swf files that won't scale in the browser window, even if viewers resize the window. Flash's Accessibility panel enables you to create descriptions of movie elements for use with screen-reader technology to make Web sites more useful for people with vision impairments.

New OS Support

Flash MX runs natively under Macintosh OS X and Windows XP.

How to Use This Book

Like all Visual QuickStart Guides, this book seeks to take you out of the passive reading mode and help you get started working in the program. The exercises in the book teach you to use Flash's features. The book is suitable for beginners who are just starting to use Flash and for intermediate-level Flash designers. The initial chapters cover the basics of creating graphic elements by using Flash's unique set of drawing tools. Next, you learn how to turn graphic elements into animations. After that, you learn the basics of using ActionScript, sounds, and video to make your movies interactive. Finally, you learn to use Flash's Publish feature to create the HTML that you need to put your Flash movies on the Web.

Cross-Platform Issues

Macromedia designed Flash's authoring environment to have, as much as possible, the same interface on the Macintosh platform (including OS X) as it has on the Windows platform. Still, differences exist where the user interfaces of the platforms diverge. When these differences are substantial, this book describes the procedures for all three platforms. Illustrations of dialog boxes come from all three platforms, but generally, there is no special indication as to which platform is shown. If a given feature differs greatly between platforms, the variations are illustrated. If a feature is available only on one platform, that is noted in the text. Originally Macintosh computers required Macintosh keyboards and some key names were unique to that keyboard, for example, Return (instead of Enter) and Delete (instead of backspace). This book generally uses Enter and Delete for these two key names.

Keyboard Shortcuts

Most of Flash's menu-based commands have a keyboard equivalent. That equivalent appears in the menu next to the command name. When this book first introduces a command, it also describes the keyboard shortcut. In subsequent mentions of the command, however, the keyboard shortcut usually is omitted. You'll find a complete list of these commands in Appendix A.

Contextual Menus

Both the Macintosh and Windows platforms offer contextual menus. To access one of these contextual menus, Control-click (Mac) or right-click (Windows) an element in the Flash movie. You'll see a menu of commands that are appropriate for working with that element. For the most part, these commands duplicate commands in the main menu; therefore, this book does not generally note them as alternatives for the commands described in the book. The book does point out when using the contextual menu is particularly handy or when a contextual menu contains a command that is unavailable from the main menu bar.

The Artwork

The Flash graphics in this book are simple and easy to draw. In most cases, the examples are based on simple geometric shapes, which means that you can spend your time seeing the Flash features in action instead of re-creating fancy artwork. To make it even easier for you to follow along, Flash files containing the graphic elements that you need for each task are available on the Peachpit Web site *http://www.peachpit.com/vqs/flashmx/*.

System Requirements

You can create Flash MX content on the Macintosh and Windows platforms. As a Flash author, you must consider not only the requirements for creating and viewing Flash movies on your own system but also the requirements for viewers of your movie. The following sections list the system requirements for both activities.

To create and edit Flash MX movies on a Macintosh:

Processor: Power Macintosh

Operating system: Mac OS 9.1 or later; Mac OS X 10.1 or later

Free RAM: 64 MB (128 MB recommended)

Free disk space: 85 MB

Monitor: 16-bit (thousands of colors), 1024-by-768 resolution

To create and edit Flash MX movies in Windows:

Processor: 200 MHz Intel Pentium (or equivalent)

Operating system: Windows 98 SE, ME; NT 4.0, 2000, or XP

Free RAM: 64 MB (128 MB recommended)

Free disk space: 85 MB

Monitor: 16-bit (thousands of colors), 1024-by-768 resolution

To view Flash MX content (in Flash Player 6) via browser:

For Macintosh OS 8.6 through 9.2: Netscape 4.5 or later, Netscape 6.2 or later, Microsoft Internet Explorer 5.0 or later, or Opera 5

For Macintosh OS X (version 10.1 or later): Netscape 6.2 or later, or Opera 5

For Windows 95, 98, Me; NT, 2000, XP, or later: Netscape 4.0 or later, Netscape 6.2 or later (with standard install defaults), Internet Explorer 4.0 or later, AOL 7, Opera 6; in addition, Windows 2000 and XP using CompuServe 7 can display Flash Player 6 content

About Flash Player

Early on, the need for viewers of Flash content to use a player was considered to be a drawback to creating Web content with Flash. Designers feared that users would be reluctant to spend time downloading another helper application for their browsers. But Flash has become the de facto standard for vector art and animation on the Web, and Flash Player is now widely distributed. Macromedia estimates that more than 400 million people are equipped to use some version of Flash Player to view Web sites.

THE FLASH AUTHORING TOOL

Before you get started drawing and creating animations in Macromedia Flash MX, it's helpful to take a look around the authoring environment and begin to recognize and manipulate its components. When you open Flash, you enter the Flash authoring environment, and Flash creates a new blank document. Each document consists of three basic items: a Timeline, a record of every frame, layer, and scene that make up your movie; a Stage, the actual area in which your movie displays; and a work area, a space that surrounds the stage during authoring but doesn't appear in the final, published movie. In addition, Flash offers various panels, libraries, and tools that help you accomplish your work.

What does the Flash authoring environment look like? And how do you access tools and different views? This chapter presents a quick tour of the elements you see when you open a Flash document. Subsequent chapters explain in more detail what is what as you really get into using each element.

Understanding Flash Basics

The way Flash works—in terms of installing the application, creating new documents, closing documents, and saving files—presents nothing unusual to the experienced computer user. The Flash installation software guides you through each step of the installation process, and the procedures for launching the application and creating and saving documents are all standard. Because the Macintosh OS 9, OS X, and Windows platforms offer users a variety of ways to organize their computers and workflow—such as using shortcuts (Windows), using aliases (Mac), and creating your own hierarchical setup for storing applications and data—it's impossible to cover all the ways you might set up and access files on your computer. But here are the basics of setting up Flash.

To install Flash from a CD:

1. Insert the Flash MX CD.

   The Flash MX CD icon appears on the Desktop.

2. Double-click the CD icon.

   A window, containing the Flash MX installer, appears (**Figure 1.1**).

3. Double-click the installer icon.

   The installer window opens to a splash screen for Flash MX (**Figure 1.2**).

4. Click the Continue button.

   The installation software walks you through all the necessary steps for installing Flash. The installer asks you to read and accept a licensing agreement and to tell it where to place the working software on your system. Don't forget that you need the serial number to install the program. Keep that serial number in a safe place; you will have to reenter it should you ever need to reinstall Flash.

Figure 1.1 The icon of the Flash MX installer.

Figure 1.2 The opening screen of the Flash MX installer software.

Figure 1.3 The Flash MX application icon.

Figure 1.4 To create a new document in Flash, choose File > New.

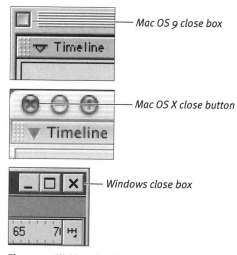

Mac OS 9 close box

Mac OS X close button

Windows close box

Figure 1.5 Clicking the close box or button closes a Flash document.

To launch Flash:

1. In the Finder (Mac) or from the desktop (Windows), navigate to the Flash icon (**Figure 1.3**).

2. Double-click the Flash icon.

   Flash launches and opens a new blank document.

To create a new document:

◆ With Flash active, from the File menu, choose New (**Figure 1.4**).

   Flash opens a new blank document.

To open an existing document:

1. With Flash active, from the File menu, choose Open.

   The Open dialog box appears.

2. Navigate to the file you want to open.

3. Select the file.

4. Click Open.

To close a document:

◆ In the top-left corner of the open document, click the close box (Mac OS 9) or the close button (Mac OS X).

   or

◆ In the top-right corner of the document (Windows), click the close box (**Figure 1.5**).

To save changes to a document:

◆ From the File menu, choose Save.

If you work repeatedly with one type of Flash document—you create banner ads of a specific size with a consistent background or elements, for example—you can save that basic document as a template.

UNDERSTANDING FLASH BASICS

To create a template document:

1. Open the document that you want to turn into a template.

2. From the File menu, choose Save As Template.

   The Save As Template dialog box appears, showing a preview of your document (**Figure 1.6**).

3. In the Name field, enter a name for the template.

4. To specify a category; *do one of the following:*

   ▲ To select an existing category, from the Category pop-up menu, choose the desired category.

   ▲ To create a new category, in the Category field, enter a name.

5. In the Description field, enter a brief summary or reminder of what the template is for.

   Flash limits you to 255 words, but it's still a good idea to give some indication of the intended uses for the template or what its special features are.

6. Click Save.

   Flash saves the document with the other templates in the Templates folder (Macromedia\Flash MX\Configuration Templates) inside the Application Support (Mac) or Application Data (Windows) folder on the drive where you've installed Flash.

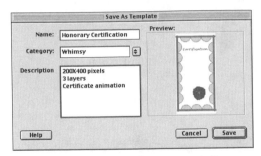

Figure 1.6 The Save As Template command allows you to save Flash documents for reuse. You can save templates in your own special categories, name them, and provide a brief description.

To open a new document from a template document:

1. From the File menu, choose New from Template.

   The New Document dialog box appears, listing categories of templates and the various templates within a selected category (**Figure 1.7**). This dialog box also displays a preview of what the selected document's first frame looks like and a brief description of the template, if available.

2. From the Category list, choose the appropriate category.

3. From the Category Items list, choose the template you want to use.

4. Click Create.

   Flash opens a new document with all the contents of the template.

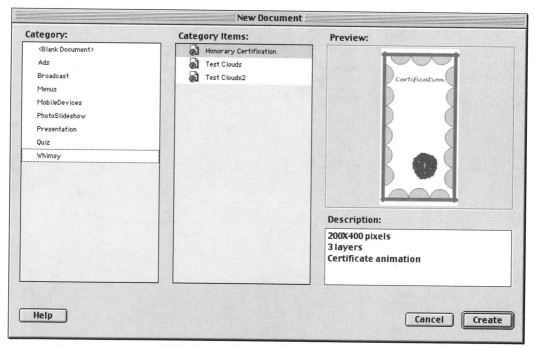

Figure 1.7 Choose File > New from Template to access your template documents. In the New Document dialog box, a preview and description (when available) appear for the item selected in the Category and Name lists.

Touring the Flash Authoring Environment

A Flash document consists of a Timeline, which holds your movie's frames, layers, and scenes; a Stage, where your movie is displayed; and a work area, which extends beyond the Stage on all sides but remains outside the visible frame of the final movie as it plays (**Figure 1.8**).

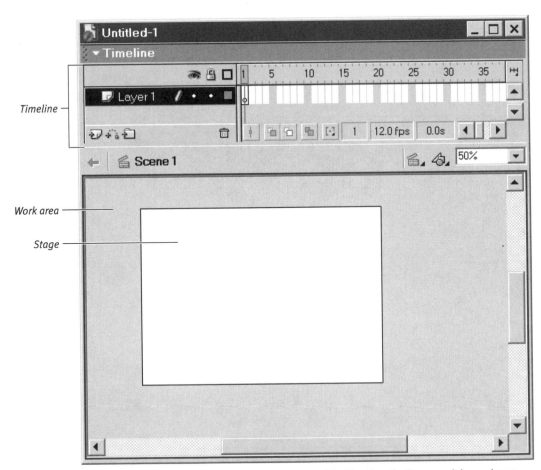

Figure 1.8 A new document opened in Flash consists of the Timeline, the Stage, and the work area.

About the Timeline

If you think of your Flash movie as a book, the Timeline would be its interactive table of contents: Each scene is like a chapter; each frame is like a page. Imagine that you could point to Chapter 10 in the table of contents, and the book would flip open to the first page of that chapter. In Flash, when you click a frame in the Timeline (or when the play-head enters a frame), that frame appears in your document window.

A Flash movie is much more complex than a book, of course. Each movie "page" may actually be several transparent sheets stacked one on top of another. Flash keeps track of these "sheets" in what it calls *layers*. And the whole "book" appears to be in motion as you move through the table of contents, with some unseen hand flipping the pages.

The Timeline is a vital, complex organizational and navigational tool. You will use it extensively when you create animations. Then you'll need to go more deeply into its components. For now, you only need to understand the Timeline generally; you'll learn more about it in Chapter 8.

Figure 1.9 identifies the major Timeline elements. You can dock the Timeline to any side of a Flash window or float it as a separate window.

To undock the Timeline window:

1. Position the pointer over the textured area on the left side of the title bar at the top of the Timeline.

   The pointer changes to the grabber hand (Mac) or move icon (Windows).

2. Click and drag away from the document window (**Figure 1.10**).

   A dotted line represents the Timeline window's position.

3. Release the mouse button where you want the Timeline to sit.

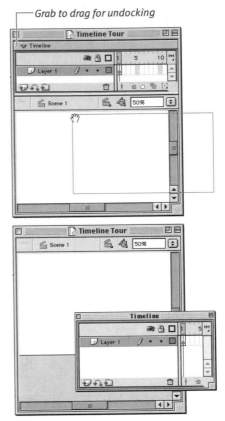

Grab to drag for undocking

Figure 1.10 Drag the Timeline by the textured portion of its title bar (top) and then release the mouse button. The Timeline floats in its own window (bottom).

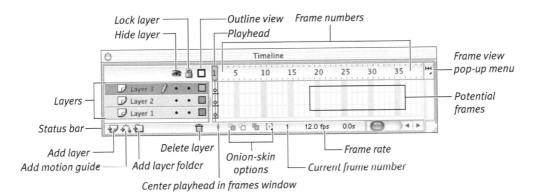

Figure 1.9 The Timeline is the complete record of your movie. It represents each scene, frame, and layer that make up the movie. Frames appear in chronological order. Clicking any frame in the Timeline takes you directly to that frame and displays its contents on the Stage.

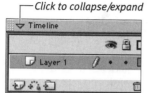

Click to collapse/expand

Figure 1.11 Click the triangle, the name, or anywhere to the right of the name in the title bar to collapse or expand the Timeline window.

To dock the Timeline:

1. Position the pointer over the textured area on the left side of the title bar at the top of the Timeline window.

The pointer changes to the grabber hand (Mac) or move icon (Windows).

2. Click and drag the Timeline to any of the four edges of the document window.

3. Release the mouse button when the pointer is at the edge of the window.

The Timeline resizes to fit the window.

✔ Tip

■ Docking the Timeline vertically (at the left or right edge of the document window) gives you easy access to several layers at a time. Docking the Timeline horizontally increases the number of easily accessible frames.

The Timeline appears in any new document you create, but you can hide the Timeline to give the Stage more room.

To hide the Timeline:

◆ From the View menu, choose Timeline; or press Option-⌘-T (Mac) or Ctrl-Alt-T (Windows) to toggle between hiding and showing the Timeline.

✔ Tips

■ To hide a floating Timeline quickly, simply click the close box (Mac OS 9 or Windows) or the close button (Mac OS X) to close the Timeline as you would any window.

■ You can collapse the Timeline window. Clicking the arrow to the left of the name *Timeline*, the name itself, or anywhere to the right of the name in the title bar toggles between the collapsed and expanded Timeline view (**Figure 1.11**).

ABOUT THE TIMELINE

About the Stage

The Stage is the area containing all the graphic elements that make up a Flash movie. Think of it as being the screen on which you will project your movie. At your local movie house, the screen is whatever size the management could afford to buy for the available space. In Flash, you control how big the screen is, and what color it is, through the Document Properties dialog box. You can also set some document properties in the Property Inspector. You'll learn more about using the Property Inspector later in this chapter.

To access the Document Properties dialog box:

Do one of the following:

◆ From the Modify menu, choose Document; or press ⌘-J (Mac) or Ctrl-J (Windows).

◆ In the Timeline's status bar, double-click the frame-rate display (**Figure 1.12**).

The Document Properties dialog box appears (**Figure 1.13**).

✔ Tip

■ The Document Property Inspector also contains a shortcut to the Document Properties dialog box. Just click the Size button. You'll learn more about the Property Inspector later in this chapter.

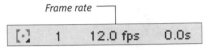

Frame rate

Figure 1.12 Double-clicking the frame-rate box in the status bar is a quick way to access the Document Properties dialog box.

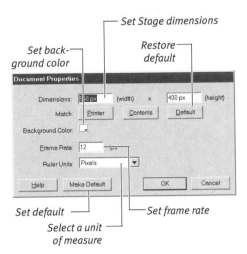

Set Stage dimensions

Set background color

Restore default

Set default

Select a unit of measure

Set frame rate

Figure 1.13 The Document Properties dialog box is where you set all the parameters for viewing the Stage. Selecting a unit of measure for the rulers resets the unit measurement for all the Stage's parameters. Clicking the color box pops up the current set of colors and lets you choose one. Clicking Save Default sets the parameters for all new documents you create.

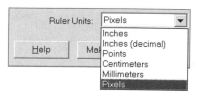

Figure 1.14 Choose a unit measurement from the Ruler Units pop-up menu.

To set the units of measure:

1. In the Document Properties dialog box, click the Ruler Units pop-up menu.
   A list of units appears (**Figure 1.14**).

2. Select the units you prefer to work in.
   Flash uses these units to calculate all measured items on the Stage: rulers, grid spacing, and dimensions.

3. Click OK.

✔ Tip

■ If you want a banner that's 1 inch tall and 5 inches wide but don't know what that size is in pixels (the standard units of measure used for working on the Web), Document Properties can figure it out for you. First, set Ruler Units to inches. Enter 1 in the Width field and 5 in the Height field. Then return to Ruler Units and choose pixels. Flash does the math for you and sets the Stage dimensions. (Note that Flash uses screen pixels in its calculations, which means that an inch in your movie may differ from an inch in the real world, depending on the resolution of the monitor on which you vicw the Flash movie.)

ABOUT THE STAGE

You have three options for setting the size of your Stage.

To set the size of your Stage:

1. To set your own dimensions for the Stage, open the Document Properties dialog box, and enter values for Width and Height in the appropriate fields of the Dimensions section (**Figure 1.15**).

2. Click OK.

   Flash automatically assigns the units of measure currently selected in Ruler Units (see "To set the units of measure" earlier in this chapter).

   or

1. To create a Stage big enough to cover all the elements in your movie, in the Match section of the Document Properties dialog box, click the Contents button (**Figure 1.16**).

2. Click OK.

   Flash calculates the minimum Stage size required to cover all the elements in the movie and enters those measurements in the Width and Height fields of the Dimensions section.

   or

1. To set the Stage size to the maximum print area currently available, in the Match section of the Document Properties dialog box, click the Printer button.

2. Click OK.

   Flash gets the paper size from the Page Setup dialog box, subtracts the current margins, and puts the resulting measurements in the Width and Height fields of the Dimensions section.

✔ Tip

- When you click the Stage, it becomes the active area. When you click the Timeline, it becomes active. Flash gives the active area a highlighted outline.

Figure 1.15 To assign new proportions to your Stage, enter a width and height in the Dimensions section of the Document Properties dialog box.

Figure 1.16 To make your Stage just big enough to enclose the objects in your movie, click the Contents button in the Match section of the Document Properties dialog box.

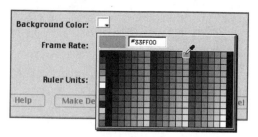

Figure 1.17 To assign your Stage a new color, choose one from the Background Color pop-up menu in the Document Properties dialog box.

To set the background color:

1. In the Background Color section of the Document Properties dialog box, click the color box to pop up your choices (**Figure 1.17**).

2. Select a color.

   The color you select appears in the color box.

3. Click OK.

   The Stage now appears in this color in your current document.

Frames are the lifeblood of your animation, and the *frame rate* is the heart that keeps that blood flowing at a certain speed. Flash's default setting is 12 frames per second—a good setting for work viewed over the Web. (By comparison, the standard frame rate for film movies is double that speed.) You'll learn more about frame rates in Chapter 8.

✔ Tip

- The Document Property Inspector also contains a color box pop-up for selecting the movie's background color. You'll learn more about the Property Inspector later in this chapter.

To set the frame rate:

1. In the Frame Rate section of the Document Properties dialog box, type a value (**Figure 1.18**).

2. Click OK.

To save your settings as the default:

◆ In the Document Properties dialog box, click the Make Default button.

The current settings in the Document Properties dialog box become the defaults for any new documents.

✔ Tip

■ If you've changed a document's properties, you can apply all of the default properties quickly by accessing the Document Properties dialog box and then clicking the Default button.

Figure 1.18 Enter a frame rate for your movie in the Frame Rate section of the Document Properties dialog box.

Touring the Info Bar

At the top of the Stage, you'll find the info bar. The info bar lets you know what mode you are working in (editing your movie, or editing a symbol or group within the movie). The info bar's pop-up menus give you the power to switch scenes, to choose a symbol to edit and immediately switch to symbol-editing mode, and to change the magnification for viewing the Stage. When you are editing symbols or groups, the info bar displays information about the elements you are editing (**Figure 1.19**). To learn about working with groups, see Chapter 4; for symbols, see Chapter 6; for scenes, see Chapter 11.

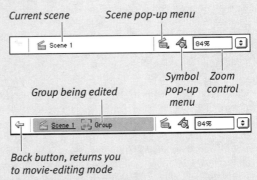

Figure 1.19 The info bar is located at the top of the Stage. You can use it to access symbols and scenes and to change magnification. In symbol-editing mode (bottom), the info bar displays the name of the symbol you are editing. Clicking the Back button returns you to movie-editing mode (top).

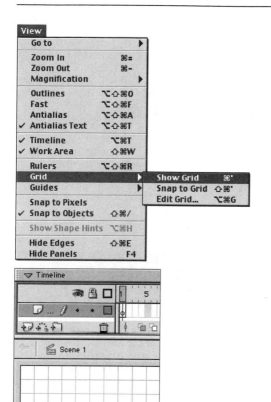

Figure 1.20 Choosing View > Grid > Show Grid (left) makes the grid lines visible on the Stage (right).

Using Grids

A *grid* is a set of crisscrossing vertical and horizontal lines that acts as a guide for drawing and positioning elements, the way that graph paper functions in the nondigital world. Flash also uses the grid to align objects when you activate the Snap to Grid feature. The grid does not appear in your final movie.

To make grids visible:

Do one of the following:

◆ From the View menu, choose Grid > Show Grid.

◆ Press ⌘-apostrophe (') (Mac) or Ctrl-apostrophe (') (Windows).

A check indicates that this feature is on. Flash displays a set of crisscrossing lines as part of the Stage (**Figure 1.20**).

To set grid color:

1. From the View menu, choose Grid > Edit Grid, or press Option-⌘-G (Mac) or Ctrl-Alt-G (Windows).

   The Grid dialog box appears (**Figure 1.21**).

2. Click the Color box.

   The pointer changes to an eyedropper, and a pop-up box of swatches appears (**Figure 1.22**).

3. Position the eyedropper pointer over a color swatch or over an item on the Stage.

   (For more information on selecting colors, see Chapter 3.)

4. Click the swatch or the item on the Stage.

   The color beneath the pointer when you click appears in the Color box. Flash uses the selected color to create the grid lines on the Stage.

5. Click OK.

To set grid spacing:

1. Follow step 1 of the preceding exercise to open the Grid dialog box.

2. Enter a value in the Width field.

3. Enter a value in the Height field (**Figure 1.23**).

   The width and height values define the spacing of the grid. Note that the grid need not consist of perfect squares.

4. Click OK.

✔ Tip

■ In the Grid dialog box, click the Save Default button to make your settings for grids the default for all new documents.

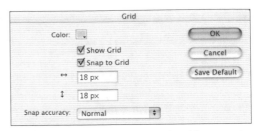

Figure 1.21 Choose View > Grid > Edit Grid to open the Grid dialog box and change grid parameters.

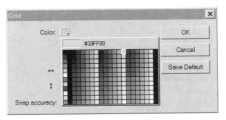

Figure 1.22 To select a new grid color, with the eyedropper pointer, click anywhere in the pop-up set of swatches or on the Stage. The pop-up color-swatch menu displays the currently selected color set.

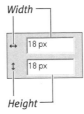

Figure 1.23 Enter values in the Width and Height fields to set grid spacing.

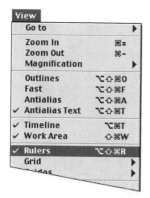

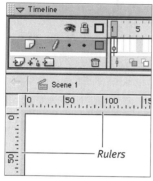

Figure 1.24 Choosing View > Rulers (top) makes rulers visible on the Stage (bottom).

Figure 1.25 As you drag a guide line from the ruler bar, a direction indicator appears next to the arrow tool.

Figure 1.26 You can position individual vertical and horizontal guides anywhere you want on the Stage.

Using Rulers and Guides

Rulers and guides aid you in drawing objects with precise sizes, shapes, and positions on the Stage.

To display rulers:

◆ From the View menu, choose Rulers, or press Option-Shift-⌘-R (Mac) or Ctrl-Alt-Shift-R (Windows).

Ruler bars appear on the left side and top of the Stage (**Figure 1.24**). To change ruler units, see "To set the units of measure" earlier in this chapter.

To hide rulers:

◆ With rulers visible on the Stage, choose View > Rulers, or press Option-Shift-⌘-R (Mac) or Ctrl-Alt-Shift-R (Windows).

To place a guide:

1. With rulers visible, position the pointer over the vertical or horizontal ruler bar.

   If you are using a tool other than the arrow tool, the pointer changes to the arrow.

2. Click and drag the pointer onto the Stage.

   As you click, a small directional arrow appears next to the pointer, indicating which direction to drag (**Figure 1.25**).

3. Release the mouse button.

   Flash places a vertical or horizontal line on the Stage (**Figure 1.26**).

To reposition a guide:

1. From the Toolbox, select the arrow tool.

2. On the Stage, position the arrow tool over the guide you want to reposition.

   The direction arrow appears next to the arrow pointer, indicating that the guide can be dragged.

3. Click and drag the guide to a new location.

4. Release the mouse button.

✔ Tips

- To remove a guide, drag it completely off the Stage.

- To avoid repositioning guides accidentally, choose View > Guides > Lock Guides, or press Option-⌘-semicolon (;) (Mac) or Ctrl-Alt-semicolon (;) (Windows). The directional arrow no longer appears next to the arrow tool when you place it over a guide line, and the guides cannot be moved. To unlock the guides, choose View > Guides > Lock Guides or press the keyboard shortcut again.

To set guide color:

1. From the View menu, choose Guides > Edit Guides, or press Option-Shift-⌘-G (Mac) or Ctrl-Alt-Shift-G (Windows).

   The Guides dialog box appears.

2. Click the Color box.

   The pointer changes to an eyedropper, and a pop-up box of swatches appears (**Figure 1.27**).

3. Using the eyedropper pointer, click a color swatch or an item on the Stage to select a new guide color.

4. Click OK.

   Flash applies that color to any existing guides and uses it for creating new guides.

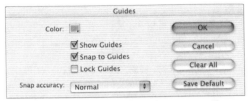
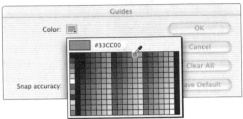

Figure 1.27 To choose the color for guides, in the Guides dialog box, click the color box to access swatches for the currently loaded color set. With the eyedropper pointer, select one of the swatches, or click an element on the Stage to sample its color.

✔ Tips

- If you've placed numerous guides in your document, dragging them from the Stage may get tedious. To remove them all at once, access the Guides dialog box and click the Clear All button.

- You can also lock or unlock guides and set their visibility by selecting or deselecting checkboxes in the Guides dialog box.

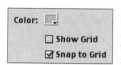

Figure 1.28 In the Grid dialog box, check the Snap to Grid checkbox to turn on snapping.

Working with Snapping

Flash's snapping feature helps you align objects as you position them on the Stage. With Snap turned on, Flash forces the edge or center of an object to sit directly on top of a user-defined grid or guide line as soon as you position the object within a user-specified distance from that line. Flash can also snap objects to other objects or to the intersections of a 1-pixel-by-1-pixel grid.

To snap objects to user-defined grids:

◆ From the View menu, choose Grid > Snap to Grid, or press Shift-⌘-apostrophe (') (Mac) or Ctrl-Shift-apostrophe (') (Windows).

   or

1. Choose View > Grid > Edit Grid, or press Option-⌘-G (Mac) or Ctrl-Alt-G (Windows).

   The Grid dialog box appears.

2. Check the Snap to Grid checkbox (**Figure 1.28**).

3. Click OK.

   A check appears next to the Snap to Grid command in the menu.

   As you drag an object near a grid line, Flash highlights potential snap points by enlarging the snap ring—the circle that appears under the arrow tool as you drag an object.

✔ Tip

■ The snap ring corresponds roughly to the place where the arrow tool connects with the object you are dragging. Flash can snap an object only by its center point or a point on its perimeter, however. If you have trouble seeing the snap ring, try grabbing the object nearer to its center, an edge, or a corner.

WORKING WITH SNAPPING

To set parameters for snapping to the grid:

1. Choose View > Grid > Edit Grid.

2. In the Grid dialog box, choose a parameter from the Snap Accuracy pop-up menu (**Figure 1.29**).

3. Click OK.

To snap objects to guides:

◆ From the View menu, choose Guides > Snap to Guides, or press Shift-⌘-semi-colon (;) (Mac) or Ctrl-Shift-semicolon (;) (Windows).

   or

1. Choose View > Guide > Edit Guides, or press Option-Shift-⌘-G (Mac) or Ctrl-Alt-Shift-G (Windows).

   The Guides dialog box appears (**Figure 1.30**).

2. Check the Snap to Guides checkbox.

3. Click OK.

To set parameters for snapping to guides:

1. Choose View > Guides > Edit Guides.

2. In the Guides dialog box, choose a parameter from the Snap Accuracy pop-up menu.

3. Click OK.

To turn off snapping to grids:

◆ Choose View > Grids > Snap to Grids.
   or

1. Choose View > Grid > Edit Grid.
   The Grid dialog box appears.

2. In the Grid dialog box, uncheck the Snap to Grid checkbox.

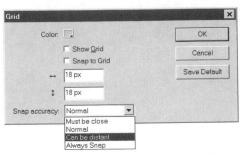

Figure 1.29 Choose a Snap Accuracy setting to determine how close an object must be to the grid before Flash snaps the object to the grid line. Choosing Always Snap forces the edge or center of an object to lie directly on a grid line.

Figure 1.30 In the Guides dialog box, you can set the color and visibility of guides, their status as locked or unlocked and how close items must be before they will snap to the guides.

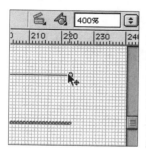

Figure 1.31 At magnifications of 400 percent or greater, the pixel grid used by Flash's Snap to Pixels feature becomes visible. You can use this mode for precise positioning of graphic elements.

To turn off snapping to guides:

◆ Choose View > Guides > Snap to Guides.

or

1. Choose View > Guides > Edit Guides. The Guide dialog box appears.

2. Uncheck the Snap to Guides checkbox.

3. Click OK.

To snap objects to objects:

◆ From the View menu, choose Snap to Objects, or press Shift-⌘-/ (Mac) or Ctrl-Shift-/.

or

◆ With the arrow tool selected, in the options section of the Toolbox, click the magnet icon.

To snap objects to pixels:

◆ From the View menu, choose Snap to Pixels.

Flash creates a grid whose squares measure 1 pixel by 1 pixel. To see the grid, you must set the Stage's magnification to at least 400 percent (**Figure 1.31**). You'll learn more about magnified views in "Viewing Graphics at Various Magnifications" later in this chapter.

About the Toolbox

The Toolbox contains Flash's drawing tools and other tools you'll need to create and manipulate graphics for animation. The Mac and Windows operating systems handle the Toolbox slightly differently. In Windows, you can dock the Toolbox on either side of the application window. In the Mac OS, the Toolbox always floats as a separate window.

To view the Toolbox:

◆ From the Window menu, choose Tools. A check indicates that the Toolbox window is open. The Toolbox window appears on the desktop (**Figure 1.32**).

To hide the Toolbox:

With the Tools window active, *do one of the following*:

◆ From the Window menu, choose Tools. This menu command toggles the Tools window view.

◆ Click the close box (Mac OS 9 and Windows) or close button (Mac OS X).

Figure 1.32 To access Flash's drawing tools, choose Window > Tools (left). The Toolbox window appears on your desktop (right).

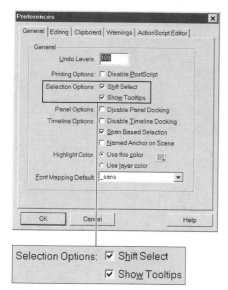

Figure 1.33 Turn on tooltips by checking Show Tooltips in the General tab of the Preferences dialog box.

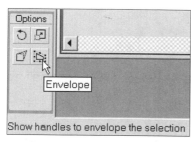

Figure 1.34 When the tooltips feature is on, a label appears whenever the pointer rests over an icon for a few seconds.

Figure 1.35 In Windows, additional tooltip information appears at the bottom of the application window when you activate the status bar (choose Window > Toolbars > Status).

To relocate the Toolbox:

1. Click the bar at the top of the Toolbox window, and hold down the mouse button.

2. Drag the Toolbox to the desired location.

To turn on tooltips:

1. From the Edit menu (Mac OS 9 and Windows) or from the Flash menu (Mac OS X), choose Preferences.

2. In the Preferences dialog box, select the General tab.

3. Check the Show Tooltips checkbox (**Figure 1.33**).

   When the tooltips feature is on (as it is by default), Flash pops up an identifying label whenever you position the pointer over a tool icon and don't click it (**Figure 1.34**).

✔ Tip

- In Windows, you can display additional tooltip information at the bottom of the application window by displaying the status bar. Choose Window > Toolbars > Status (**Figure 1.35**).

To create a floating Toolbox (Windows):

1. Click anywhere in the docked Toolbox that's not actually a tool icon, and hold down the mouse button.

2. Drag the Toolbox away from the edge of the window.

   An outline version of the floating Toolbox appears.

ABOUT THE TOOLBOX

To dock the Toolbox (Windows):

◆ When the Toolbox is floating, drag it to the right or left edge of the application window.

Flash snaps the Toolbox to the edge of the application window (**Figure 1.36**).

✔ Tip

■ Double-clicking the title bar of a floating Toolbox automatically docks it to the side of the window where it was last docked.

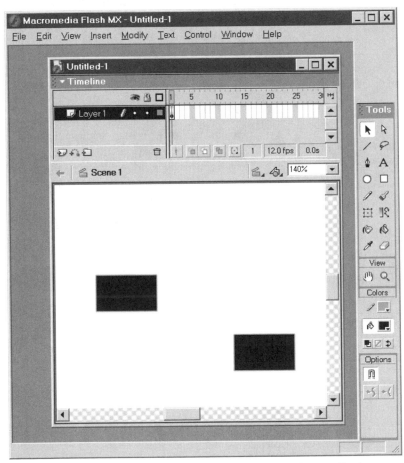

Figure 1.36 In Windows, you can drag the Toolbox to either side of the application window to dock it.

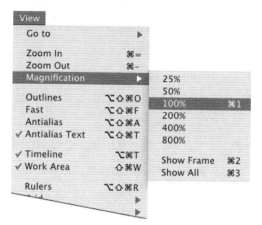

Figure 1.37 Choose 100% magnification to display graphics at the size they will be in the final movie.

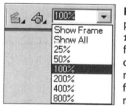

Figure 1.38 Enter a percentage greater than 100 in the Zoom Control field to magnify objects on the Stage. The pop-up menu to the right of the field offers several common magnification levels.

Viewing Graphics at Various Magnifications

Flash offers several ways to adjust the magnification of elements on the Stage.

To view objects at actual size:

◆ From the View menu, choose Magnification > 100% (**Figure 1.37**), or press ⌘-1 (Mac) or Ctrl-1 (Windows).

or

◆ In the Zoom Control field at the right end of the Stage's info bar, enter **100%**. Press Enter.

At 100%, Flash displays objects as close as possible to the size they will be in the final movie. (Some monitors and video cards may display slightly different sizes.)

To zoom in or out on the Stage:

1. In the Zoom Control field, enter the desired percentage of magnification.

   To zoom in, enter a percentage larger than 100. To zoom out, enter a percentage smaller than 100 (**Figure 1.38**).

2. Press Return (Mac) or Enter (Windows).

✔ Tip

■ Click the triangle next to the Zoom Control field to open a menu that duplicates the View > Magnification submenu. Choose a percentage from this menu to change magnification immediately. This menu also lets you choose Show Frame and Show All modes. Choose Show Frame to display the full Stage area in the current window; choose Show All to display just the elements on the Stage.

VIEWING GRAPHICS AT VARIOUS SIZES

To zoom in on specific areas of the Stage:

1. In the Toolbox, select the magnifier tool (or press M or Z on the keyboard).

The pointer changes to a magnifying glass.

2. Choose the Enlarge modifier.

3. Move the pointer over the Stage, and *select the area to magnify in one of two ways:*

▲ Click the area or element you want to enlarge.

Flash doubles the percentage of magnification in the Zoom Control field and places the spot you clicked at the center of the viewing window.

▲ Click and drag to create a selection rectangle that encloses the element you want to view.

Flash fills the window with your selected area (**Figure 1.39**).

To zoom out:

1. In the Toolbox, select the magnifier tool.

2. Choose the Reduce modifier.

3. Move the pointer over the Stage, and click the element or the area you want to see more of (or view at a smaller size).

Flash halves the percentage of magnification specified in the Zoom Control field.

✔ Tips

■ To switch the magnifier tool temporarily from Enlarge to Reduce, and vice versa, hold down the Option (Mac) or Alt (Windows) key.

■ In Reduce mode, dragging a selection rectangle creates a magnified view.

■ To access the magnifier tool in Enlarge mode temporarily, press ⌘-spacebar (Mac) or Ctrl-spacebar (Windows). To access the tool in Reduce mode, press ⌘-Shift-spacebar (Mac) or Ctrl-Shift-spacebar (Windows).

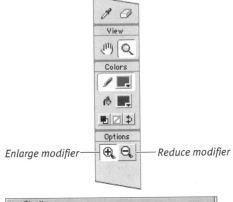

Enlarge modifier — ⊕ ⊖ — Reduce modifier

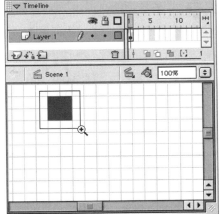

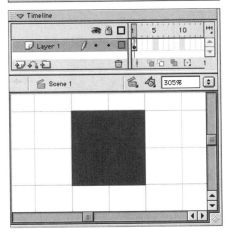

Figure 1.39 Use the magnifier tool (top) to draw a selection rectangle around an element (middle). Flash places the element at the center of the enlarged view (bottom).

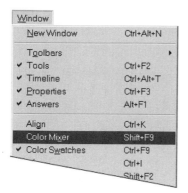

Figure 1.40 The Window menu contains a list of panels.

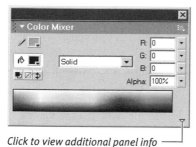

Click to view additional panel info

Figure 1.41 This panel window contains the Color Mixer.

About Panels

In addition to the Toolbox, Flash puts authoring tools in *panels*—windows that can stay open on the desktop for quick access as you work. Some panels, such as the Color Mixer, let you set attributes to be used in creating new elements or modifying existing elements. Others, such as the Movie Explorer and Scenes panels, help you organize and navigate your Flash document. One crucial panel, the Property Inspector, lets you get information about selected elements and modify them. You'll learn to use individual panels in later chapters of this book. For now, you will learn general features of panels and how to manage the panel environment.

To open a panel window:

◆ From the Window menu, choose the desired panel—for example, Color Mixer (**Figure 1.40**).

Flash opens a window containing that panel (**Figure 1.41**).

✔ Tip

■ The preceding technique works to open a panel that is not open or to expand a panel if it is collapsed. If a panel is already open and expanded, using this technique closes the panel.

To close a panel window:

◆ Click the panel window's close box (Mac OS 9 and Windows) or close button (Mac OS X).

or

◆ From the panel's Options menu, choose Close Panel.

or

◆ Control-click (Mac) or right-click (Windows) the panel's title bar, and choose Close Panel from the contextual menu.

✔ Tips

■ To close all the open panel windows, choose Window > Close All Panels, or Alt-click (Windows) any panel window's close box.

■ To hide all the open panel windows (including the Toolbox, Property Inspector, and any open Library windows), press the Tab key. Press Tab again to show the windows.

To collapse or expand a panel window:

◆ Click the triangle to the left of the panel title.

To reposition a panel window:

◆ Click the bar at the top of the panel window, and drag the window to a new location.

✔ Tip

■ When you position one panel window so that one of its edges lies right next to the edge of another panel window, Flash docks the two windows. It's not a permanent connection, but it ensures that the two take up as little space together as possible. In the Windows operating system, you can also dock panels at edges of the application window.

To resize a panel window:

◆ Click and drag the bottom-right corner of the window (Windows) or the resize handle (Mac).

ABOUT PANELS

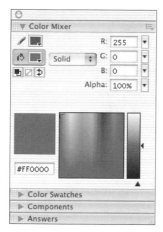

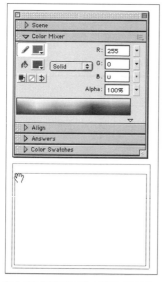

Figure 1.42
Choosing Flash's default panel set opens four frequently used panels in a single window on the right side of the desktop.

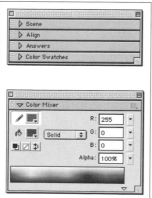

Figure 1.43
To separate one panel from a group, drag the panel's title bar away from the window until you see the outline of the panel (top); then release the mouse button to create a separate panel window (bottom).

Working with Grouped Panels

You can group several panels in one window to save space on your desktop. Each panel within the window can be collapsed or expanded individually. Flash provides seven sets of pregrouped panels, some geared to designers and some to developers.

To open the default panel set:

◆ From the Window menu, choose Panel Sets > Default Layout.

Flash opens the Toolbox and Property Inspector, plus one panel window containing four other panels (**Figure 1.42**).

To separate panels:

1. Follow the preceding steps to open the default panel set.

2. In the grouped panel window, click the textured area at the left side of one panel's title bar.

The pointer changes to the grabber hand.

3. Drag the panel away from the main panel window.

Flash displays an outline of the panel as you drag.

4. Release the mouse button.

The panel appears in its own window (**Figure 1.43**).

WORKING WITH GROUPED PANELS

To combine panels in one window:

1. With two or more panel windows open on the desktop, click the textured area on the left side of the panel's title bar.

   The pointer changes to the grabber hand.

2. Drag the panel on top of another open panel window.

   Flash highlights the target panel window.

3. Release the mouse button.

   The panel you dragged now appears in the destination window in expanded mode (**Figure 1.44**).

✔ Tips

- You determine where in the target panel window Flash adds the new panel. Watch the way Flash highlights the target panel window. A double line indicates the spot where Flash will insert the added panel. Drag up or down in the target window to move the double-line highlight to the correct position.

- To collapse and expand individual panels within the panel window, click the triangle to the left of the panel's title.

- To collapse or expand the entire window of grouped panels, double-click the bar at the top of the panel window, or click the minimize button in the window's top-right corner (Mac OS 9).

- To expand one panel and collapse all the others in that panel window, from the panel's Options menu, choose Maximize Panel. (To access the Options menu, you must have the panel in expanded mode.)

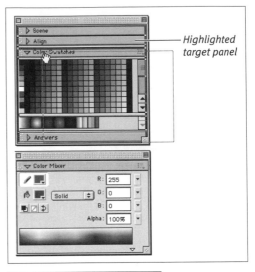

Highlighted target panel

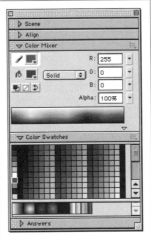

Figure 1.44 To group panels, drag one panel over another. When the target panel window highlights (top), release the mouse button. The new panel appears in the target window (bottom).

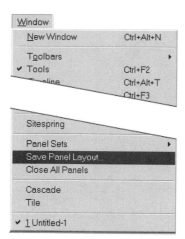

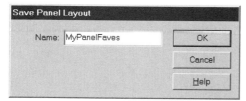

Figure 1.45 Choose Window > Save Panel Layout to create a custom panel set.

Figure 1.46 Enter a name for your custom layout in the Save Panel Layout dialog box.

The Mysterious Persistence of Panel-Group Memory

Flash appears to have a selective memory when it comes to panel groups. If you have grouped panels, and you close the group by clicking the panel window's close box (Mac OS 9 or Windows) or close button (OS X), the next time you choose any of the grouped panels from the Window menu, Flash opens the whole group together in its window. If, however, you closed the group by choosing Windows > Close All Panels, the next time you choose one of the panels from the Window menu, Flash opens that panel in its own window.

Using Custom Panel Sets

Flash lets you save and restore any number of customized panel configurations. A custom panel layout stores information about which panels are open, which are grouped, how large each panel or group window should be, and where to place those windows on the desktop.

To create a custom panel layout:

1. Open the panels you want to work with.

2. Group, resize, and reposition the panels as you desire.

3. From the Window menu, choose Save Panel Layout (**Figure 1.45**).

   The Save Panel Layout dialog box appears.

4. Enter a name for your layout (**Figure 1.46**).

5. Click OK.

   Flash saves the current panel configuration and makes it available in the Panel Sets submenu. Whenever you launch Flash, it opens the panel set that was active during your previous work session.

✔ Tips

- Assign a custom keyboard shortcut to the panel layouts you use most frequently (see "Customizing Keyboard Shortcuts" later in this chapter).

- If you discover a useful panel layout, you can share it with your friends and co-workers. Flash stores panel-set information in a text file that lives in the Panel Sets folder (Macromedia\Flash MX\Configuration\Panel Sets), which you'll find inside the Application Support folder (Mac) or Application Data folder (Windows) on the drive where you've installed Flash.

To invoke a custom panel set:

1. From the Window menu, choose Panel Sets.

A submenu appears, listing Default Layout, layouts for designers and developers (optimized for different monitor resolutions), and any custom panel layouts you have saved (**Figure 1.47**).

2. From the submenu, choose the desired custom set.

Flash closes whatever panels you have open and configures your desktop with the custom setup.

To remove a custom panel set:

1. In the Finder (Mac) or on the desktop (Windows), navigate to the Panel Sets folder (Macromedia\Flash MX\Configuration\Panel Sets), which you'll find inside the Application Support folder (Mac) or Application Data folder (Windows) on the drive where you've installed Flash.

2. Delete the file that bears the name of the panel set you want to remove.

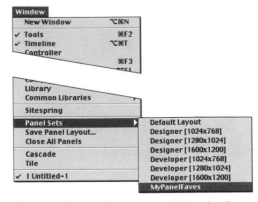

Figure 1.47 Choose Window > Panel Sets to invoke a custom panel configuration or to reestablish one of the panel layouts that come with Flash.

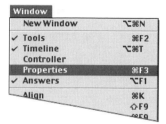

Figure 1.48 To access the Property Inspector, choose Window > Properties.

Entering Values in the Property Inspector

In many modes, the Property Inspector requires you to enter a value in a field to change a parameter. You can always type a new value. When modifying selected items, you usually must press Enter to apply the new value to selected items.

A small triangle to the right of an entry field indicates the presence of a pop-up slider for entering values quickly. Often, a slider previews new values interactively. The following methods work for most sliders:

◆ **Click and drag.** Click the small triangle, and hold down the mouse button; you can start dragging the slider's lever right away. Release the mouse button. Flash enters the current slider value in the field and—in most cases—applies that value to selected objects automatically.

◆ **Click and click.** Click the small triangle, and release the mouse button right away; the slider pops up and stays open. You can drag the slider's lever or click various locations on the slider to choose a new value. Flash enters the value in the field. To apply the value to selected items, you must click somewhere off the slider. Click another entry field, click elsewhere on the panel, or click the Stage.

About the Property Inspector

In Flash 5, you set most properties and attributes of elements and tools (such as fill color, stroke style, and font) in panels. Panels still exist in Flash MX, but one special panel— the Property Inspector—has taken on several tasks formerly carried out by separate panels. The Property Inspector is context-sensitive, and changes constantly to reflect your selections. You'll learn more about the many specific versions of the Property Inspector as they become relevant in later chapters. For now, just learn its general rules of operation.

To access the Property Inspector:

◆ From the Window menu, choose Properties (**Figure 1.48**).

Flash opens the Property Inspector.

In the Windows operating system, the Property Inspector docks to the bottom of the application window by default, but you can make it float as a separate panel.

To create a floating Property Inspector (Windows):

◆ Click the textured area in the top-left corner of the Property Inspector, and drag the panel away from the edge of the window.

To dock the Property Inspector (Windows):

◆ When the Property Inspector is floating, click the bar on the left side of the panel, and drag the panel to the top or bottom edge of the application window.

Flash snaps the Property Inspector to the edge of the application window.

To collapse or expand the docked Property Inspector (Windows):

◆ To collapse or expand the Property Inspector vertically, click the triangle in the top-left corner of the panel (**Figure 1.49**).

◆ To show or hide the bottom half of the panel, click the triangle in the bottom-right corner of the panel.

To collapse or expand the floating Property Inspector:

◆ To collapse or expand the Property Inspector horizontally, click the minimize button in the bottom-left corner of the window (Mac OS 9), or double-click the bar on the left side of the window (Mac OS 9 and Windows) (**Figure 1.50**).

◆ To show or hide the lower half of the panel, click the triangle in the bottom-right corner of the window.

To close the Property Inspector:

◆ If the Property Inspector is open, from the Window menu, choose Properties. Flash closes the Property Inspector panel.

◆ If the Property Inspector is floating, click the close box (Mac OS 9 and Windows) or close button (OS X).

◆ If the Property Inspector is docked (Windows), from the Options menu in the top-right corner, choose Close Panel (**Figure 1.51**).

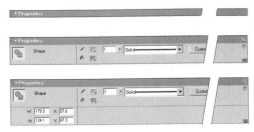
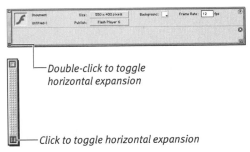

Figure 1.49 You can collapse and expand the docked Property Inspector (Windows) by clicking the minimize/maximize triangle (top). In some modes, the Property Inspector displays more information when you expand the lower portion of the panel (bottom).

Double-click to toggle horizontal expansion

Click to toggle horizontal expansion

Figure 1.50 In Mac OS 9, and in Windows when the Property Inspector is floating, you can collapse or expand the Property Inspector horizontally by double-clicking the bar on the left side of the panel. In Mac OS 9, you can also click the minimize button.

Figure 1.51 To close a docked Property Inspector, from the panel's Options menu, choose Close Panel.

The Power of the Property Inspector

Think of the Property Inspector as being a context-sensitive superpanel—a panel that changes to reflect whatever item you have selected. It displays information about the active Flash document, a selected tool, a selected graphic element (a shape, grouped shape, or symbol; a text block; a bitmap or video clip), or a selected frame.

The Property Inspector is also the place for setting many tools' parameters and for changing the attributes of selected elements.

Select the line tool, for example, and the Property Inspector becomes the Line Tool Property Inspector (**Figure 1.52**). In this incarnation, the Property Inspector presents all the line tool's parameters for you to set: color, thickness, and style. Select a line on the Stage, and the Property Inspector becomes the Shape Property Inspector. Because the selected shape is a line, the Property Inspector displays the same parameters as the Line Tool Property Inspector; change the parameters in the Property Inspector, and Flash changes the selected line to match.

Click a blank area of the Stage, and you'll see the Document Property Inspector, which gives you access to various document settings. Select a symbol instance on the Stage, and the Property Inspector reveals the instance's heritage (which master symbol it came from), as well as what its height, width, and Stage position are. Change those settings in the Property Inspector, and Flash makes those changes in the selected symbol instance.

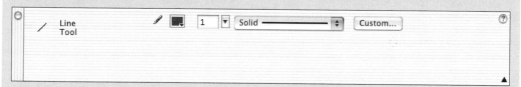

Figure 1.52 The Property Inspector displays information about selected items and allows you to modify them. In its Line Tool mode, for example, the Property Inspector lets you set the color, thickness, and style for lines that the line tool creates.

ABOUT THE PROPERTY INSPECTOR

Customizing Keyboard Shortcuts

Flash MX's default shortcut set (the Macromedia Standard set) lets you access the drawing tools and most menu commands from the keyboard quickly. But what if your favorite operation lacks a shortcut or uses a key combination that you find awkward? You can create your own set of combinations, add shortcuts to items that lack them, and change the assigned key commands.

Flash comes with five additional shortcut sets that let you implement the same keyboard shortcuts as Macromedia's Flash 5, Fireworks 4, FreeHand 10, or Adobe's Illustrator 10 and Photoshop 6.

To switch among shortcut sets:

1. From the Edit menu (Mac OS 9 and Windows) or the Flash application menu (Mac OS X), choose Keyboard Shortcuts. The Keyboard Shortcuts dialog box appears.

2. From the Current Set menu, choose one of the listed shortcut sets (**Figure 1.53**).

3. Click OK.
   Flash loads the new shortcuts. The new key combinations appear in menus and tooltips.

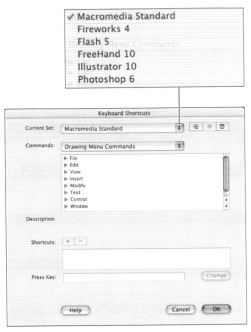

Figure 1.53 Use the Current Set pop-up menu in the Keyboard Shortcuts dialog box to switch to a different set of shortcuts.

Figure 1.54 When creating custom shortcuts, you must work on a copy of one of the sets that comes with Flash. Click the Duplicate Set button to copy the set displayed in the Current Sets pop-up menu.

Figure 1.55 In the Duplicate dialog box, enter a name for your new shortcut set.

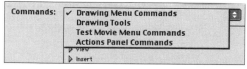

Figure 1.56 The Commands menu in the Keyboard Shortcuts dialog box offers four categories of items to which you can assign keyboard shortcuts.

To create a custom shortcut set:

1. Follow the steps in the preceding exercise to select a set of keyboard shortcuts.

   The selected set forms the basis of your new set.

2. In the Keyboard Shortcuts dialog box, click the Duplicate Set button in the top-right corner of the keyboard shortcuts dialog box (**Figure 1.54**).

   The Duplicate dialog box appears.

3. Enter a name for your custom shortcut set (**Figure 1.55**).

4. Click OK.

   Flash makes the new set available in the scrolling Commands list. Now you can add more shortcuts and delete existing ones.

To assign a new shortcut:

1. From the Edit menu (Mac OS 9 and Windows) or the Flash application menu (Mac OS X), choose Keyboard Shortcuts.

   The Keyboard Shortcuts dialog box appears.

2. From the Current Sets pop-up menu, choose the set you want to modify.

3. From the Commands pop-up menu, choose one of the following options (**Figure 1.56**):

   ▲ To modify a command used in Flash's authoring environment, choose Drawing Menu Commands.

   ▲ To modify a command used in Flash's movie-testing environment, choose Test Movie Menu Commands.

   ▲ To modify a command that accesses a drawing tool, choose Drawing Tools.

   (continues on next page)

▲ To modify a command for use in creating ActionScripts, Flash's scripting language, choose Actions Panel Commands. (You'll learn about ActionScripting in chapters 12, 13, and 15.)

A scrolling list of the selected commands and their current assigned keyboard shortcuts appears in the Commands window.

4. In the Commands window, select the name of the command or tool you want to modify.

An overview of the selected command appears in the Description area of the dialog box (**Figure 1.57**). Any existing shortcuts for that item appear in the scrolling Shortcuts list and in the Press Key field.

5. Click the Add Shortcut button.

Flash enters <empty> in the Shortcuts window, in the Press Key field, and in the Commands window (**Figure 1.58**).

6. On the keyboard, press the keys you want to use as a shortcut to access the item.

Flash enters the shortcut in the Press Key field.

7. Click the Change button to update the shortcut set.

Flash replaces <empty> with the key combination in the Shortcuts and Commands windows (**Figure 1.59**).

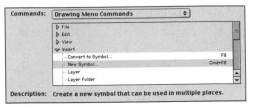

Figure 1.57 Menu-related commands appear in a hierarchical list. To expand or collapse entries in the list, click the triangle to the left of each menu name.

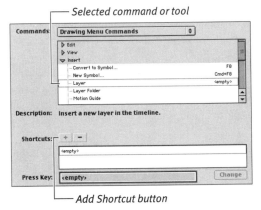

Selected command or tool

Add Shortcut button

Figure 1.58 Select a command or tool in the Commands window to see its description. Click the Add Shortcut button to define a new shortcut.

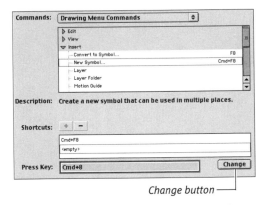

Change button

Figure 1.59 After entering a new shortcut, click the Change button to confirm the new key combination.

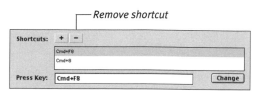

Figure 1.60 Clicking the Remove Shortcut button deletes a selected shortcut.

✔ Tips

- Shortcut keys for menu commands must be function keys or must include the ⌘ character (Mac) or the Ctrl character (Windows).

- You can assign multiple shortcuts to a single command or tool.

- You cannot alter Flash's default shortcuts set directly. To customize Flash's standard set of keyboard commands, first duplicate the set named Macromedia Standard and then add and remove shortcuts in the duplicate set.

To remove a shortcut:

1. Follow steps 1 through 4 of the preceding exercise.

2. Click the Remove Shortcut button (**Figure 1.60**).

   Flash removes the shortcut from the Shortcuts and Commands windows.

✔ Tip

- To change an existing shortcut for a selected command or tool, select the shortcut name in the Shortcuts window, select the shortcut characters in the Press Key field, enter a new key combination, and click the Change button.

CREATING
SIMPLE GRAPHICS

2

This chapter teaches you to use Macromedia Flash MX's drawing tools to create basic shapes from lines and areas of color—in Flash terminology, *strokes* and *fills.*

Flash also lets you import graphics from other programs. If you create graphics in a program such as Macromedia FreeHand or Adobe Illustrator, you can import them into Flash for animation (see Chapter 7).

Flash offers the option of using its original natural-style drawing tools or using a pen tool to create Bézier curves. Flash's natural drawing tools allow you to sketch freely with various levels of drawing assistance. Flash can help you, for example, by changing a basically straight line that bobbles a bit into one that's perfectly straight. Flash also can smooth curves so that they flow beautifully instead of in jaggy fits and starts. The pen tool works similarly to the Bézier tool featured in other graphics programs.

You can edit all shapes, even those drawn with the natural drawing tools, with the Bézier subselection tool. You also can correct a shape by tugging on its outline. (To learn about editing shapes, see Chapter 3.)

Touring the Toolbox

The Flash MX Toolbox holds two new tools: the free transform tool and the fill transform tool (**Figure 2.1**). Actually, these tools are reincarnations and extensions of functions that were available only as modifiers of other tools in previous versions of Flash. Transformation functions that used to be an option for the selection arrow tool are now consolidated in the free-transform tool. The paint bucket's former transform-fill modifier has transmogrified into the fill-transform tool. As a tool in the Toolbox, with modifiers of its own, the free-transform tool is easier to access and more powerful than its antecedents. The tool's Distort modifier allows you to distort shapes freely to simulate 2D and 3D perspective. The Envelope modifier enables you to reshape the bounding box of a selection by using Bézier curves.

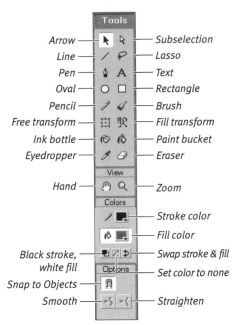

Figure 2.1 The Toolbox contains tools for drawing, editing, and manipulating graphic elements in Flash. The Colors section allows you to assign stroke and fill colors. The Options section displays modifiers appropriate to the currently selected tool.

What Are Strokes and Fills?

Stroke and *fill* are two terms you will encounter often in graphics programs, and Flash is no exception. What do these terms mean? Basically, a stroke is an outline, and a fill is a solid shape. Picture a coloring book in pristine condition, with simple black lines creating the pictures: Those lines are strokes. When you fill in the areas outlined by strokes—say, with crayon—that colorful area is the fill. In a coloring book, you always start with an outline and create the fill inside it. In Flash, you can work the other way around—start with a solid shape and then create the outline around it as a separate object.

Flash's oval and rectangle tools allow you to create an element that's just a stroke or just a fill or to create the stroke and fill elements simultaneously. The line tool, as you might guess, creates only strokes. The pen tool can create both strokes and fills.

The concept of fills and strokes is a bit trickier to grasp in relation to the brush tool. This tool creates fills. Though these fills may look like lines or brush strokes, they are really shapes you can outline with a stroke. Flash provides special tools for adding, editing, and removing strokes and fills: the ink bottle, the paint bucket, and the faucet eraser. Chapter 3 discusses these tools in greater detail.

Figure 2.2 Click the line icon in the Toolbox to select the line tool.

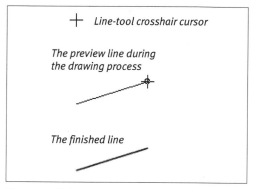

+ Line-tool crosshair cursor

The preview line during the drawing process

The finished line

Figure 2.3 Click and drag with the line tool's crosshair cursor. Flash previews the line as you draw. Release the mouse button, and the line takes on the attributes currently assigned to the strokes.

✔ Tips

■ The line is not set until you release the mouse button. You can shorten, lengthen, and reorient the line's direction or angle by dragging until you release the mouse button.

■ Holding down the Shift key as you draw a line constrains it to the vertical, horizontal, or 45-degree angle position.

■ If you're using a narrow line thickness, you may need to zoom in to see it accurately on-screen. On-screen, thin lines may look identical to slightly thicker lines unless you zoom in; they will print accurately, though.

Using the Line Tool

Flash offers a tool that does nothing but draw perfectly straight-line segments. By putting together several line segments, you can create a shape made of several straight sides, such as a pentagon or star.

To draw line segments:

1. In the Toolbox, select the line tool by clicking the line icon, or press N (**Figure 2.2**).

2. Move the pointer to the spot on the Stage where you want your line to begin.

    The pointer changes to a crosshair as it moves over the Stage area.

3. Click and drag to pull a line segment out from your starting point (**Figure 2.3**).

    Flash displays an outline preview of the line—a simple form that doesn't show the line's color, style, and weight settings. A circle beneath the pointer indicates the line's endpoint.

4. Release the mouse button when the line is the right length and in the right position.

    Flash draws a line segment on the Stage, using the current stroke-color, stroke-style, and stroke-height settings (see "Setting Stroke Attributes" later in this chapter).

Setting Stroke Attributes

A line has three attributes: color, thickness (also known as *weight* or, in Flash, *stroke height*), and style. You can set all three in the Property Inspector for any tool that creates or modifies strokes (the line, pen, oval, rectangle, and ink-bottle tools). In addition, you can set stroke color from the Toolbox or from the Color Mixer panel.

To access the Property Inspector:

◆ If the Property Inspector is not open, from the Window menu, choose Properties (**Figure 2.4**).

The Property Inspector appears on the desktop. Note that the Property Inspector displays the attributes for lines only when you have selected a line-related tool in the Toolbox or you have selected lines on the Stage. (You learn to use line-related tools in the following exercises; you learn to use the Property Inspector with selections in Chapter 3.)

To set stroke color via the Property Inspector:

1. With the Property Inspector open, choose the line tool.

   The Line Tool Property Inspector appears, showing the current settings for the three attributes for strokes.

2. In the Property Inspector, click the stroke-color box.

   The pointer changes to an eyedropper, and a set of swatches appears (**Figure 2.5**).

3. To select a color, *do one of the following:*

   ▲ To select the color directly below the tip of the eyedropper, with the eyedropper tool, click a swatch or an item on the Stage.

   ▲ In the hexadecimal-color field, enter a value.

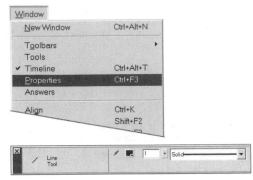

Figure 2.4 Choose Window > Properties (top) to display the Property Inspector (bottom).

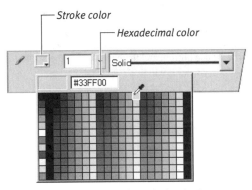

Figure 2.5 Clicking the stroke-color box in the Property Inspector opens a set of color swatches and provides the eyedropper tool for selecting a new color.

SETTING STROKE ATTRIBUTES

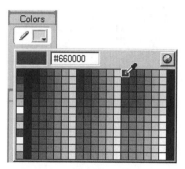

Figure 2.6 Click the stroke-color box in the Toolbox to open a set of color swatches similar to those available in the Property Inspector.

✔ Tips

- You can also set stroke color in the Color Mixer panel. Choose Window > Color Mixer to open the Color Mixer panel, click the stroke-color box, and select a color as described in step 3 of the preceding exercise.

- You can set stroke color without opening any panels. In the Toolbox, with any tool selected, click the stroke-color box. The eyedropper tool and a set of swatches appear (**Figure 2.6**). Select a color; Flash updates all the stroke-color boxes, and tools that create strokes will use that color.

- The trio of small buttons at the bottom of the Colors section of the Toolbox allows you to set the stroke color (and fill color) to black, white, or none quickly. To set stroke color to black (and fill color to white), with the stroke-color box selected, click the leftmost button of the trio: the Black and White button. Click the rightmost button to make the current stroke and fill colors change places. (The middle button lets you set fill or stroke to no color when you use the oval and rectangle tools, which you'll learn about later in this chapter.)

  The selected color appears in the stroke-color box in the Property Inspector, the Color Mixers, and the Toolbox. Flash uses that color to create lines when you use the line tool or any other tool that creates strokes.

To set a line weight:

1. With the Property Inspector open, select the line tool.

   You can also select one of the other tools that work with strokes, pencil, pen, oval, rectangle, and ink bottle. You'll learn to use the pencil, pen, oval, and rectangle tools later in this chapter, the ink bottle, in Chapter 3.

2. In the Line Tool Property Inspector's stroke-height field, enter a number between 0.25 and 10 (**Figure 2.7**).

   Flash uses that stroke height to create lines when you use the line tool or any other tool that creates strokes.

✔ Tips

■ For easy entry of line weights, click the triangle to the right of the stroke-height field. A slider pops open. Drag the slider's lever to choose a value between 0.25 and 10 points. Click elsewhere in the panel window or on the Stage to close the slider and apply the new line weight.

■ For even quicker changes, just drag the slider triangle. When you release the slider's lever, Flash applies the new weight immediately.

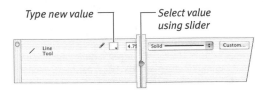

Type new value   Select value
                      using slider

Figure 2.7 Entering a new value in the stroke-height field sets the thickness for strokes created by tools that draw strokes.

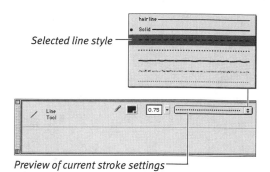

Selected line style

Preview of current stroke settings

Figure 2.8 Choose a line style from the pop-up menu in the Property Inspector.

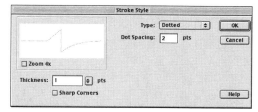

Figure 2.9 Click the Custom button in the Property Inspector to access the Stroke Style dialog box.

Figure 2.10 The Stroke Style dialog box contains a pop-up menu for selecting the type of line you want to customize. The dialog box shown here is for dotted lines.

To select a line style:

1. In the Line Tool Property Inspector, click the Stroke Style pop-up menu (**Figure 2.8**).

   A list of seven styles (hairline, solid, dashed, dotted, ragged, stippled, and hatched) appears.

2. Select a style.

   A graphic representation of that style appears in the stroke-style menu. Flash now applies that style to any new lines you create.

✔ Tip

- In Flash, the hairline setting is considered to be a line style, not a line weight. (Use the Stroke Style pop-up menu to get the hairline setting.) In symbols, hairlines do not change thickness when you resize the symbol. Other lines in symbols grow thicker or thinner as you scale them up or down. (To learn about symbols, see Chapter 6.)

You can modify line styles—creating, for example, a custom dotted line with lots of space between dots or a stippled line with a highly random pattern.

To customize a line style:

1. In the Line Tool Property Inspector, click the Custom button (**Figure 2.9**).

   The Stroke Style dialog box appears.

2. From the Type menu, choose a style—for example, Dotted.

   The parameters appropriate to the currently selected stroke style appear in the dialog box (**Figure 2.10**).

   (continues on next page)

3. In the Dot Spacing box, enter a number between 1 and 20.

This value specifies the amount of space (in points) that appears between the dots in the dotted line.

4. To select a thickness value, do one of the following:

   ▲ Enter a value from 1 to 10 in the Thickness field.

   ▲ Choose a value from the pop-up menu.

5. If you want Flash to place a dot at the tip of each corner when you draw a line, choose Sharp Corners.

6. Click OK.

A preview of your custom dotted-line style appears in the Stroke Style menu in the Property Inspector. Any tools that create strokes are now set to use that style.

✔ Tips

■ Custom stroke-style settings remain in effect until you customize that style again or quit Flash. Define a custom dashed line that has really long dashes, and you'll get the same long dashes the next time you choose the dashed line from the Stroke Style menu in the Property Inspector.

■ Changing the stroke height doesn't affect any other custom settings you've applied. If you want to use your customized long dashes with a thinner line, just enter a new stroke-height value directly in the Property Inspector; you don't need to choose Custom and go back to the Line Style dialog box.

SETTING STROKE ATTRIBUTES

Figure 2.11 Choose Window > Color Mixer (top) to open the Color Mixer panel, where you can set fill attributes (bottom).

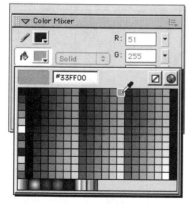

Figure 2.12 Click the fill-color box to access the eyedropper tool and swatches for selecting a new fill color. To define a color that's not in the swatch set, enter values in the RGB (or HSB) fields or click the color-picker bar.

✔ Tip

■ You can set fill color without opening the Color Mixer panel. In the Toolbox, with any tool selected, click the fill-color box. The eyedropper tool and a set of swatches appear. Select a color; Flash updates the fill-color box in the Toolbox, the Color Mixer panel, and the Property Inspector.

Setting Fill Attributes

Flash offers five fill styles: none, solid, linear gradient, radial gradient, and bitmap. You can set the fill style, color, and transparency in the Color Mixer panel. You can also choose some fills from the Toolbox and from fill-related Property Inspectors, such as the one that accompanies the rectangle tool. The following exercises deal with solid fills; you'll learn about gradients and bitmaps in Chapter 3.

To access the Color Mixer panel:

◆ If the Color Mixer panel is not open, from the Window menu, choose Color Mixer. The Color Mixer panel appears (**Figure 2.11**).

To select a fill style:

◆ From the Color Mixer panel's Fill Style menu, choose a fill type—Solid, for example. The attributes for that fill appear in the panel.

To select a solid fill color from the Color Mixer panel:

1. In the Color Mixer panel, with Solid selected as the fill style, click the fill-color box. The pointer changes to an eyedropper, and a set of swatches appears (**Figure 2.12**).

2. To select a color, *do one of the following:*
   ▲ To select the color directly below the tip of the eyedropper, click a swatch or an item on the Stage.
   ▲ Enter values in the color RGB (or HSB) fields.
   ▲ To define a color that's not in the swatch set, click the color-picker bar. (For more information on defining colors, see Chapter 3.)

   The new color appears in the fill-color box and will be used by any of the tools that create fills.

Using the Oval and Rectangle Tools

Flash provides separate tools for drawing ovals and rectangles. The tools work quite similarly; both can draw a shape as an outline (just a stroke) or as a solid object (a fill). You can also create an object with a fill and a stroke simultaneously.

To draw an oval outline:

1. In the Toolbox, select the oval tool, or press O (**Figure 2.13**).

2. To activate the fill-color box, in the Colors section of the Toolbox, select the paint-bucket icon.

3. To set fill color to none, *do one of the following:*
   - ▲ Click the fill-color box, and in the set of swatches that appears, click the No Color button (**Figure 2.14**).
   - ▲ In the Colors section of the Toolbox, click the No Color button (**Figure 2.15**).

4. Use the current stroke color and line weight or select new ones (see "Setting Stroke Attributes" earlier in this chapter).

5. Move the pointer over the Stage.
   The pointer turns into a crosshair.

6. Click and drag to create an oval of the size and proportions you want (**Figure 2.16**). Flash displays an outline preview of the oval as you drag.

7. Release the mouse button.
   Flash draws an oval outline.

✔ Tip

- ■ To draw a perfect circle, hold down the Shift key while you drag the crosshair cursor. Flash makes the oval grow with the proportions of a perfect circle.

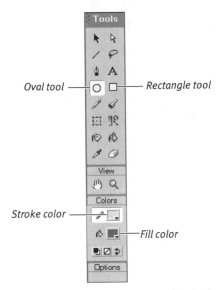

Oval tool · Rectangle tool · Stroke color · Fill color

Figure 2.13 The Toolbox with the oval tool selected.

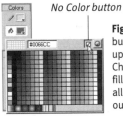

No Color button

Figure 2.14 The No Color button appears in the pop-up set of fill swatches. Choosing No Color as the fill color with the oval tool allows you to create oval outlines.

No Color button

Figure 2.15 When the fill-color box is selected in the Colors section of the Toolbox, clicking the No Color button allows whatever tool you select to create a shape with no fill.

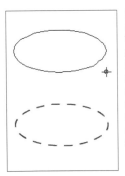

Figure 2.16 Click the Stage, and drag to create an oval. You see a preview outline of your shape (top). Release the mouse button, and Flash creates an oval outline, using the current color, thickness, and style settings. In this case, the oval tool is set to black stroke color, no fill, dotted line style, and a stroke height of 1 point (bottom).

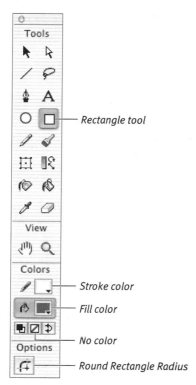

Tools

Rectangle tool

View

Colors

Stroke color

Fill color

No color

Options

Round Rectangle Radius

Figure 2.17 Select the rectangle tool in the Toolbox; the Round Rectangle Radius modifier appears. Use the modifier to create rectangles with blunt corners.

Corner-radius value

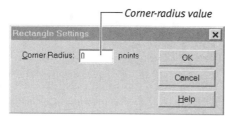

Figure 2.18 Enter a value of o in the Rectangle Settings dialog box to create a rectangle with sharp corners. Enter a larger value to round the corners of your rectangle.

To draw a rectangular fill:

1. In the Toolbox, select the rectangle tool, or press R (**Figure 2.17**).

2. To set a stroke color, in the Colors section of the Toolbox, click the pencil icon.

3. To set stroke color to none, *do one of the following:*

   ▲ Click the stroke-color box, and in the swatch window, click the No Color button.

   ▲ In the Colors section of the Toolbox, click the No Color button.

4. Use the current fill color or select a new one (see "Setting Fill Attributes" earlier in this chapter).

5. To open the Rectangle Settings dialog box, do one of the following:

   ▲ In the Options section of the Toolbox, click the Round Rectangle Radius button.

   ▲ Double-click the rectangle tool.

   The Rectangle Settings dialog box appears (**Figure 2.18**).

6. Enter a value of 0 points.

   This setting creates a rectangle with sharp 90-degree angles at the corners.

7. Click OK to close the dialog box.

8. Move the pointer over the Stage.

   The pointer changes to a crosshair.

9. Click and drag to create a rectangle of the size and proportions you want.

   Flash displays an outline preview of the rectangle as you drag.

   (continues on next page)

USING THE OVAL AND RECTANGLE TOOLS

10. Release the mouse button.

Flash draws a rectangular fill, using the currently selected fill color (**Figure 2.19**).

✔ Tip

- To create a perfect square, hold down the Shift key as you draw your rectangle. Flash constrains the rectangle to the proportions of a perfect square.

To draw a rounded rectangle with fill and stroke:

1. In the Toolbox, select the rectangle tool.

2. Make sure that you have selected a fill and stroke color other than No Color (see "Setting Stroke Attributes" and "Setting Fill Attributes" earlier in this chapter).

3. Click the Round Rectangle Radius button to open the Rectangle Settings dialog box.

4. Enter the desired corner-radius setting, and click OK.

5. Click and drag on the Stage with the crosshair cursor to create a rectangle.

6. Release the mouse button.

Flash creates a filled rectangle, using the currently selected fill color, and gives the rectangle a stroke with the currently selected color, thickness, and style (**Figure 2.20**).

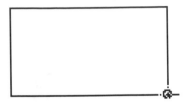

Figure 2.19 As you drag the rectangle tool, Flash creates an outline preview of a rectangle (top). To complete the fill shape, release the mouse button (bottom).

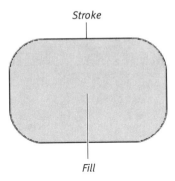

Stroke

Fill

Figure 2.20 A rounded rectangle with stroke and fill.

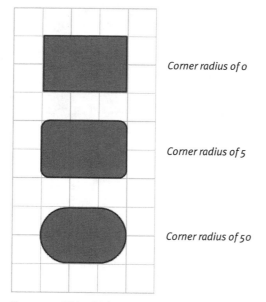

Corner radius of 0

Corner radius of 5

Corner radius of 50

Figure 2.21 With a higher corner-radius setting, the rectangle tool creates a more-rounded corner.

✔ Tips

- Flash accepts corner-radius settings ranging from 0 to 999 points (integers only). This value equals the radius of the imaginary circle that creates the rounded corner. A larger value creates a more-rounded corner (**Figure 2.21**).

- To reset the rectangle tool's corner radius to 0 quickly, Shift-double-click the rectangle tool or Shift-click the Round Rectangle Radius button.

- You can change a rectangle's corner radius as you draw. Drag on the Stage with the rectangle tool to create your shape. Before releasing the mouse button, press the up-arrow key to reduce the corner-radius value; press the down-arrow key to increase it. The preview rectangle changes interactively as you press the arrow keys. Release the mouse button to complete your shape.

- The Round Rectangle modifier of the rectangle tool makes it easy to draw capsule shapes in Flash. Use a large corner-radius setting—say, 300 points. This high setting ensures that a smooth arc connects the two shorter sides of the rectangle and that the longer sides remain flat. Note that if you draw four sides of equal length using this high corner-radius setting, you'll wind up with something more like a circle than a square.

USING THE OVAL AND RECTANGLE TOOLS

Using the Pencil Tool with Assistance

Flash's pencil tool offers two freeform line-drawing modes—Straighten and Smooth—that help you draw smooth, neat shapes.

Straighten mode eliminates the small blips and tremors that can mar quick hand sketches. Straighten refines your line into straight-line segments and regular arcs. This mode also carries out what Flash calls shape recognition. In Straighten mode, Flash evaluates each rough shape you draw, and if the shape comes close enough to Flash's definition of an oval or rectangle, Flash turns your rough approximation into a version of the shape neat enough to please your high-school geometry teacher.

Smooth mode helps you by transforming your rough drawing into one composed of smooth, curved line segments.

To use Straighten mode for freeform drawing:

1. In the Toolbox, select the pencil tool.
   The pencil-tool's modifiers appear at the bottom of the Toolbox (**Figure 2.22**).

2. From the Pencil Mode pop-up menu, choose Straighten.

3. Move the pointer over the Stage.
   The pointer turns into the pencil tool.

4. Click and draw a squiggle (**Figure 2.23**).
   Flash previews your rough line.

5. Release the mouse button.
   Flash recasts the line you've drawn, turning it into a set of straight-line segments and regular curves.

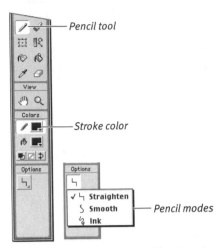

Figure 2.22 When the pencil tool is selected, the Toolbox displays a pop-up menu of pencil modes.

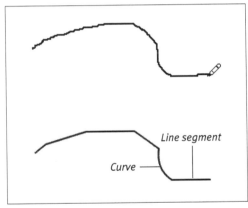

Figure 2.23 With the pencil in Straighten mode, when you draw a squiggle, Flash previews it for you. When you release the mouse button, Flash applies straightening, turning your rough squiggle (top) into a set of straight-line segments and smooth curves (bottom).

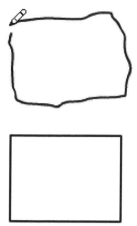

Figure 2.24 In the pencil tool's Straighten mode, when you draw a rough rectangle (top) and release the mouse button, Flash turns your shape into a rectangle with straight sides and sharp corners. You can also rough out oval shapes and have Flash fix them the same way.

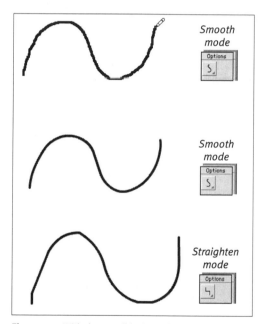

Figure 2.25 With the pencil in Smooth mode, when you draw a wavy line (top), Flash turns it into a series of smooth curves (middle). Compare a similar shape drawn with the pencil set to Straighten mode (bottom).

To use Straighten mode for drawing rectangles and ovals:

1. With the pencil tool in Straighten mode, click and quickly draw a rectangle or circle (**Figure 2.24**).

   You don't need to close the shape completely; leave a slight gap between the first and last points of your line.

2. Release the mouse button.

   Flash recognizes the shape and creates a perfect rectangle or oval, connecting the ends of your line and completing the shape for you.

✔ Tip

- Tolerance settings are all-important here. You can set Flash to change almost anything ovoid into a circle and anything slightly more oblong into a rectangle. Take a little time to play around with the settings in the Editing tab of the Preferences dialog box (see "Controlling the Amount of Assistance You Get" later in this chapter) to find the degree of accuracy that's right for you.

Smooth mode does not recognize shapes or connect line segments; it simply smoothes out the curves you draw.

To draw smooth curves:

1. With the pencil tool selected, choose Smooth from the Pencil Mode pop-up menu.

2. Move the pointer over the Stage; then click and draw a wavy line.

3. Release the mouse button.

   Flash eliminates any vectors that aren't needed to define the basic shape (**Figure 2.25**).

   Notice that Flash turns your line into a set of smooth curved segments instead of straight-line segments.

USING THE PENCIL TOOL WITH ASSISTANCE

Controlling the Amount of Assistance

Flash helps you by straightening line segments, recognizing shapes, and smoothing curves as you draw them with the various pencil-tool modifiers discussed in the preceding sections. The degree of assistance depends on the settings you pick in the Editing tab of the Preferences dialog box. The settings are relative to the resolution of your monitor and the amount of magnification you're using to view the Stage. At 100 percent magnification with the setting Can Be Distant, for example, Flash recognizes and closes an oval that has a gap of 5 pixels between its beginning and ending points. But bump the magnification to 400 percent, and Flash refuses to close a gap of 5 pixels. You must get the shape's end points within around 1 pixel of each other before Flash will recognize the gap and close the shape for you.

To set the degree of assistance:

1. From the Edit menu (Mac OS 9 and Windows) or from the Flash application menu (Mac OS X), choose Preferences. The Preferences dialog box appears.

2. Choose the Editing tab of the Preferences dialog box (**Figure 2.26**).

3. In the Drawing Settings section of the dialog box, choose an option from each of the five pop-up menus (**Figure 2.27** through **Figure 2.31**).

   Your choices range from turning the feature off to having Flash give you the highest degree of assistance.

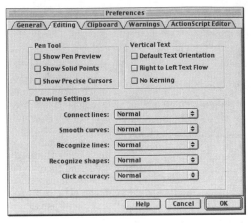

Figure 2.26 Choose Edit > Preferences (Mac OS 9 and Windows) or Flash > Preferences (Mac OS X), and select the Editing tab to set the amount of assistance Flash gives you in smoothing and recognizing shapes.

Figure 2.27 Connect Lines controls how close the beginning and ending points of an oval or rectangle must be before Flash closes them for you.

Figure 2.28 Smooth Curves determines how much Flash alters the curve you've drawn to make it smoother.

Figure 2.29 Recognize Lines determines how close to straight a line must be before Flash removes all curves and changes it to a straight-line segment.

Figure 2.30 Recognize Shapes determines how nearly ovoid or rectangular a shape must be for Flash to transform it to a perfect oval or rectangle.

Figure 2.31 Click Accuracy determines how close you must get to a line segment with the arrow pointer to select that segment.

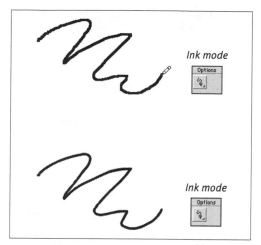

Ink mode

Ink mode

Figure 2.32 Flash turns a squiggle drawn in the pencil's Ink mode (top) into a vector graphic (bottom), with minimal smoothing and straightening of curves and line segments.

Using the Pencil Tool Without Assistance

The pencil tool's Ink mode allows you to bypass the assistance features and draw without correction or shape recognition. Ink mode leaves all the little bumps, twists, and turns of your rough sketch intact.

To use Ink mode to draw irregular, unsmoothed lines:

1. With the pencil tool selected, from the Pencil Mode pop-up menu, choose Ink.

2. Move the pointer over the Stage; then click and draw a squiggle (**Figure 2.32**).

3. Release the mouse button.

   Flash recasts the line you've drawn so that it looks less jaggy, but Flash does not straighten lines or smooth curves.

Using the Pen Tool: Straight Lines

With most Flash tools, the math goes on behind the scenes. You draw a line or a shape, and Flash takes care of placing points that define the line segments and curves that make up that shape. The pen tool brings the process to center stage. The pen tool lets you place defining points (called *anchor points*) and adjust the curvature of the lines connecting them (using controllers called *Bézier handles*). You learn more about curves and handles in the following section of this chapter and in Chapter 3.

The *path*—the series of points and connecting lines created by the pen tool— is the skeleton of your object. When you've completed a path, Flash fleshes it out by applying a stroke to it.

For the following exercises, set the pen tool to show previews as you create your path. Choose Edit > Preferences (Mac OS 9 and Windows) or Flash > Preferences (Mac OS X) to open the Preferences dialog box, select the Editing tab, and check the Show Pen Preview checkbox (**Figure 2.33**).

To draw straight-line segments with the pen tool:

1. In the Toolbox, select the pen tool, or press P (**Figure 2.34**).

2. Set the stroke attributes for your path.

3. Move the pointer over the Stage.

   The pen tool appears with a small *x* next to it (**Figure 2.35**). The *x* indicates that you are ready to place the first point of a path.

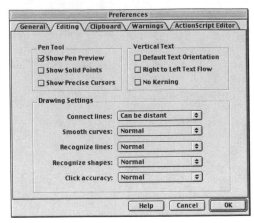

Figure 2.33 In its default mode, Flash's pen tool previews a curve segment only after you place both of the curve's defining anchor points. For these exercises, choose Edit > Preferences (Mac OS 9 and Windows) or Flash > Preferences (Mac OS X), select the Editing tab, and check the Show Pen Preview checkbox. This setting allows you to preview the curve as you position the pointer before clicking to set the second defining anchor point.

Figure 2.34 Select the pen tool to create paths.

Figure 2.35 The *x* next to the pen tool indicates that you are about to start a new path. Click to place the first anchor point.

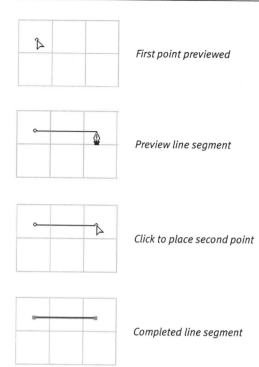

First point previewed

Preview line segment

Click to place second point

Completed line segment

Figure 2.36 Flash previews points as you place them (top) and it adds a stroke to the path as soon as you complete a segment (bottom).

4. Click where you want your line segment to begin.

The pointer changes to a hollow arrowhead; a small circle indicates the location of the anchor point on the Stage.

5. Reposition the pen tool where you want your line segment to end.

Flash extends a preview of the line segment from the first point to the tip of the pen as you move around the Stage.

6. Click.

Flash completes the line segment, using the selected stroke attributes. The anchor points appear as solid squares (**Figure 2.36**).

7. Repeat steps 5 and 6 to draw a series of connected line segments.

To end an open path:

To end a line segment or series of segments, *do one of the following*:

◆ Double-click the last point in your path.

◆ In the Toolbox, click the pen tool (or any other tool).

◆ From the Edit menu, choose Deselect All, or press ⌘-Shift-A (Mac) or Ctrl-Shift-A (Windows).

◆ On the Stage, ⌘-click (Mac) or Ctrl-click (Windows) away from your path.

USING THE PEN TOOL: STRAIGHT LINES

To create a closed path:

1. With the pen tool selected, click three areas on the Stage to place three anchor points in a triangular layout.

   Flash completes two legs of your triangle with strokes.

2. Position the pointer over your first anchor point.

   Flash previews a line segment for the third side of the triangle. A small hollow circle appears next to the pen tool (**Figure 2.37**).

3. Click.

   Flash closes the shape, adding a stroke to the triangle's third side and filling the triangle with the currently selected fill color.

4. Move the pointer away from your anchor points.

   A small *x* appears next to the pen tool, indicating that you are free to place the first anchor point of a new path.

✔ Tip

- You can close a path anywhere along a line (or curve) segment. Position the pen over the path between anchor points. (A small circle appears next to the pen tool.) Click, and Flash closes the path, creating a stroke with no fill. To close the path and fill the resulting shape, double-click just inside the path (**Figure 2.38**).

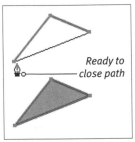

Figure 2.37 To close a path, position the pen tool over an existing anchor point (top). A circle next to the pen tool indicates that you are directly on top of the path. Click to complete the path (bottom).

Figure 2.38 You can close a path by clicking between anchor points. Click once directly on the path (top) to create just a stroke (middle). Double-click just inside the path to create a filled closed shape (bottom).

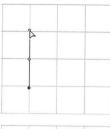

Click and drag upward
—the direction in which
the curve should bulge

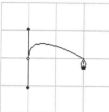

Preview of curve before
placing second point

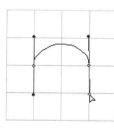

Click to place second
point; drag away from
the curve's bulge

Completed line segment

Figure 2.39 To create an upward curve, when placing the first anchor point, click and drag toward the top of the Stage. Before you click and drag your second point, the preview looks lopsided. You adjust the curvature as you drag the Bézier handle. Drag toward the bottom of the Stage.

Using the Pen Tool: Curved Line Segments

In the preceding exercise, you clicked to lay down anchor points, and Flash created straight-line segments connecting those points. To create curved segments, you must activate the points' Bézier handles. Do this by clicking and dragging when you place a point. As you drag, the handles extend out from the anchor point. As you learn to create curves with the pen tool, it helps to have a grid visible on the Stage. To display the grid, choose View > Show Grid.

To draw an upward curve with the pen tool:

1. With the pen tool selected, move the pointer over the Stage.

   The pen icon appears with a small *x* next to it. The *x* indicates that you are ready to place the first point of a path.

2. Click the grid intersection where you want your curve segment to begin, and hold down the mouse button.

   Flash places a preview point on the Stage; the pointer changes to a hollow arrowhead.

3. Drag the pointer in the direction in which you want your curve to bulge.

   Two handles extend from the anchor point, growing in opposite directions as you drag.

4. Release the mouse button, and reposition the pointer to the right of your original point.

   The pen tool returns, and Flash previews the curve you are drawing.

5. Click and drag in the opposite direction from the curve's bulge.

   As you drag, the preview of the curve changes.

(continues on next page)

6. When the curve preview looks the way you want, release the mouse button.

Flash completes your curve segment with a stroke (**Figure 2.39**).

You can end the path here (as described in the preceding section) or repeat steps 2 through 6 to add more curves to your path.

To draw an S curve with the pen tool:

1. Follow steps 1 and 2 of the preceding exercise.

2. Drag the pointer in the direction in which you want the left side of the curve to bulge.

3. Release the mouse button, and reposition the pointer to the right of your original point.

4. Click and drag in the same direction you went in step 2.

Flash creates a horizontal S shape centered between the anchor points you placed (**Figure 2.40**).

✔ Tips

■ When you create symmetrical curves, use grid lines to help position anchor points and Bézier handles.

■ Don't worry about fine-tuning each curve as you draw; just get down the basic outlines. It's often easier to adjust points and curves when you have a rough version of the object to work on. You learn to modify paths in Chapter 3.

■ One of the tricks of drawing with the pen tool is visualizing the way a shape's curves and lines must look before you place points and adjust handles. To get the hang of it, try creating paths that trace existing objects. Lock the layer that contains your template shapes. Add a new layer, and practice re-creating the shapes, using the locked layer as a guide. (You learn about using layers in Chapter 5.)

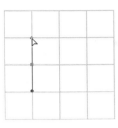

Click and drag upward—the direction in which the first half of the S curve should bulge

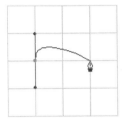

Preview of curve before placing second point

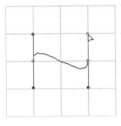

Click to place second point; drag in same direction as for first point

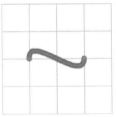

Completed curve segment

Figure 2.40 Click and drag your first point upward to start an S curve. Click and drag your second point in the same direction. Release the mouse button to finish the curve.

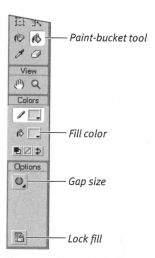

Paint-bucket tool

Fill color

Gap size

Lock fill

Figure 2.41 The paint-bucket tool and its modifiers.

Figure 2.42 The hot spot on the paint-bucket tool is the little drip at the end of the spilling paint. The hot spot changes to white when you move the paint bucket over a darker color.

Figure 2.43 Clicking inside an outline shape with the paint bucket (top) fills the shape with the currently selected color (bottom).

Using the Paint Bucket

The paint-bucket tool lets you fill the inside of a closed shape with a solid color. You can also use the paint bucket to change the color of an existing fill. The oval and rectangle tools automatically create closed shapes that are easy to fill. If you draw a shape yourself, it may have some small gaps. You can have Flash ignore these gaps and fill the basic shape anyway.

In addition to filling with solid colors, the paint-bucket tool can fill shapes with gradients or bitmapped patterns (see Chapter 3).

To fill an outline shape with a solid color:

1. In the Toolbox, select the paint-bucket tool by clicking the paint-bucket icon, or press K.

   The paint-bucket icon is highlighted in the Toolbox, and the Gap Size menu and Lock fill modifier appear in the Options section of the Toolbox (**Figure 2.41**).

2. From the Toolbox's fill-color box, the Color Mixer panel, or the Property Inspector, select a fill color.

3. Place the paint bucket's hot spot (the tip of the drip of paint) somewhere inside an outline shape, and click (**Figure 2.42**).

   The shape fills with the currently selected fill color (**Figure 2.43**).

To set gap closure:

1. With the paint bucket selected, from the Gap Size menu in the Options section of the Toolbox, choose a setting (**Figure 2.44**).

   Flash presents four options for filling gaps.

2. Choose the amount of assistance you want.

   If you draw your shapes precisely, medium or small gap closure serves you best; you don't want Flash to fill areas that are not meant to be shapes. If your drawings are rougher, choose Close Large Gaps. This setting enables Flash to recognize less-complete shapes.

✔ Tips

- You may be unaware that your shape has any gaps. If nothing happens when you click inside a shape with the paint bucket, try changing the Gap Size setting.

- Gap-closure settings are relative to the amount of magnification you're using to view the Stage. If the paint bucket's largest gap-closure setting fails at your current magnification, try again after reducing magnification (**Figure 2.45**).

Figure 2.44 The Gap Size pop-up menu controls Flash's capability to fill shapes that aren't fully closed.

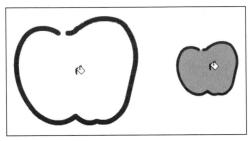

Figure 2.45 The paint bucket cannot fill this apple shape with the setting of Close Large Gaps and a magnification of 100 percent (left). But in a 50 percent view, the paint bucket with the same large-gap closure setting recognizes this shape as complete and fills it.

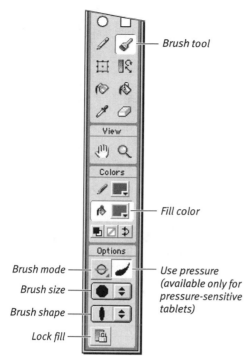

Brush tool

Fill color

Brush mode ——— Use pressure
(available only for
pressure-sensitive
tablets)

Brush size ———

Brush shape ———

Lock fill ———

Figure 2.46 The brush tool and its modifiers.

✓ Paint Normal
  Paint Fills
  Paint Behind
  Paint Selection
  Paint Inside

Figure 2.47 The Brush Mode pop-up menu with Paint Normal selected.

Using the Brush Tool in Normal Mode

Flash's brush tool offers a way to create free-flowing swashes of color. These shapes are actually freeform fills drawn without a stroke. The brush tool enables you to simulate the type of artwork you'd create in the real world with a paintbrush or marking pen. A variety of brush sizes and tip shapes helps you create a painterly look in your drawings.

If you have a pressure-sensitive drawing tablet, the brush can interact with it to create lines of varying thickness as you vary the pressure in your drawing stroke, simulating real-world brush work.

To create freeform fill shapes:

1. In the Toolbox, select the brush tool or press B.

   The various brush modifiers appear at the bottom of the Toolbox (**Figure 2.46**).

2. From the Toolbox's fill-color box, the Color Mixer panel, or the Property Inspector, select a fill color.

   Use the default settings for Brush Size and Brush Shape for now. You'll learn how to change them in the next task.

3. From the Brush Mode pop-up menu in the Options section of the Toolbox, choose Paint Normal (**Figure 2.47**).

   The other paint modes allow your paint strokes to interact in various ways with other lines and shapes on the Stage. You learn more about using these modes in Chapter 4.

   (continues on next page)

4. Move the pointer over the Stage.

   The pointer changes to reflect the current brush size and shape.

5. Click and draw on the Stage.

   Flash previews your brushwork in the currently selected fill color (**Figure 2.48**).

6. When you complete your shape, release the mouse button.

   Flash creates the final shape.

To change the brush size:

1. With the brush tool selected in the Toolbox, click the Brush Size pop-up menu.

   A list of eight circles representing brush sizes appears (**Figure 2.49**).

2. Select the size you want.

3. Release the mouse button.

   A circle the size you selected appears in the Brush Size box in the Toolbox. This circle is the size Flash will use as you work with the brush tool.

✔ Tip

■ You can change the size of your brush stroke by changing the magnification at which you view the Stage. To create a fat stroke without changing your brush-tip settings, set the Stage view to a small percentage. To switch to a thin stroke, zoom out to a higher percentage (**Figure 2.50**). Be sure to check your work in 100% view.

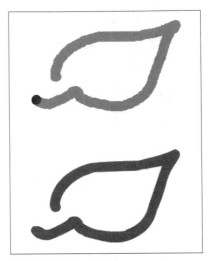

Figure 2.48 Drawing with the brush creates a preview of your shape (top); Flash recasts the shape as a vector graphic with the currently selected fill color.

Figure 2.49 The Brush Size pop-up menu offers eight brush sizes to choose among.

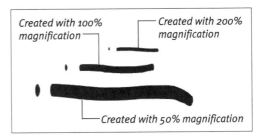

Created with 100% magnification

Created with 200% magnification

Created with 50% magnification

Figure 2.50 Flash created these three brushstrokes with exactly the same brush size—only the magnification level of the Stage changed for each stroke.

Figure 2.51 The Brush Shape pop-up menu.

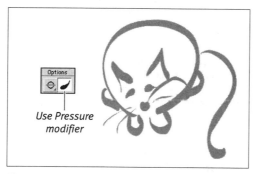

Figure 2.52 Selecting the brush tool's Use Pressure modifier activates the pressure-sensitive capabilities of a connected pressure-sensitive pen and graphics tablet. Then you can produce lively lines of varying thickness simply by applying more or less pressure as you draw. Flash created all the lines in this cat with a single brush size and shape.

To change the brush shape:

1. With the brush tool selected in the Toolbox, click the Brush Shape pop-up menu.

    A list of nine tip shapes appears (**Figure 2.51**).

2. Select the shape you want.

    The shape you picked appears in the Brush Shape box in the Toolbox. This shape is the tip Flash will use as you work with the brush tool.

If you have a Flash-compatible pressure-sensitive drawing tablet attached to your computer, the Toolbox displays an additional brush modifier that lets you take advantage of your tablet.

To use a pressure-sensitive tablet:

◆ With the brush tool selected in the Toolbox, click the Use Pressure modifier. The modifier is highlighted.

You have activated the pressure-sensitive capabilities of your pen, and you can draw lines that vary in thickness according to the amount of pressure you use (**Figure 2.52**). Applying more pressure makes your brush stroke fatter; applying less pressure keeps the brush stroke thin. Note that Flash will not create a brush stroke fatter than the currently selected brush size.

Using the Text Tool

The text tool creates blocks of editable text. You can set the text to read horizontally or vertically. You can also apply a variety of text attributes to text—including text and paragraph styles. Editable text can later be turned into raw shapes.

To create a single line of text for use as a graphic element:

1. In the Toolbox, select the text tool or press T (**Figure 2.53**).

   For this task, use the current settings for type and paragraph styles. You learn to change these settings in upcoming tasks.

2. Move the pointer over the Stage.

   The pointer turns into a crosshair with a letter *A* in the bottom-right corner (**Figure 2.54**).

3. Click the Stage at the spot where you want your text to start.

   Flash creates a text box with a round resize handle and a blinking insertion point, ready for you to enter text (**Figure 2.55**).

4. Start typing to enter your text.

   The text box grows to accommodate whatever you type (**Figure 2.56**).

5. When you finish typing, click elsewhere on the Stage (if you want to create another piece of text) or change tools.

   Flash hides the text box, leaving just the text visible. When you click this text with the arrow tool, Flash selects the text box automatically so that you can reposition it or change the text's attributes directly.

Text tool

Figure 2.53 Select the text tool in the Toolbox to start creating text boxes on the Stage.

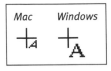

Mac   Windows

Figure 2.54 The text-tool pointer.

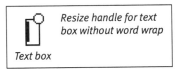

Resize handle for text box without word wrap

Text box

Figure 2.55 Click the Stage with the text tool to create a text box. The round resize handle indicates that the text box does not have word wrap turned on.

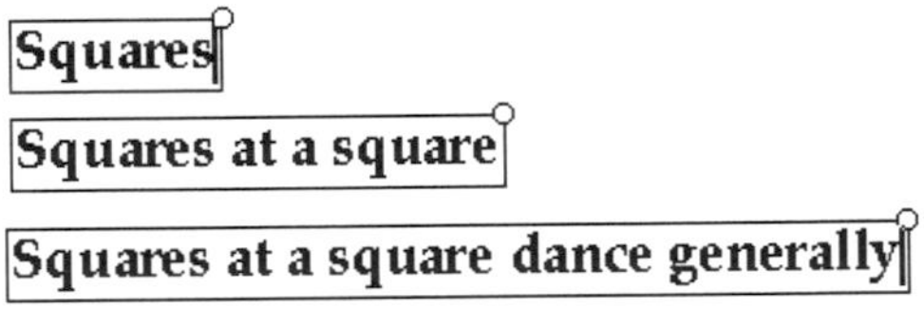

Squares

Squares at a square

Squares at a square dance generally

Figure 2.56 As you type, the box grows horizontally to accommodate your text. The text will not wrap.

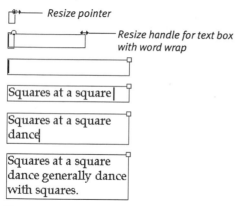

Resize pointer

Resize handle for text box with word wrap

Squares at a square|

Squares at a square dance|

Squares at a square dance generally dance with squares.

Figure 2.57 Click and drag the resize handle to create a text box with a specific width. The handle changes to a square, indicating that the text you enter will wrap to fit the column width of the text box. The text box continues to grow in length—but not width—as you enter more text.

What Is Editable Text?

The term *editable text* has two meanings in Flash. First, you can modify text within the Flash authoring environment. As you create text elements for your movie, you can go back and change your font, pick a new text color, select another font size, fix typos—you name it. Flash calls this type of text *static text*.

Second, text can be modified in a movie playing in the Flash Player. Through the use of actions and variables, your movie can retrieve user input and put it to work in various ways. Flash calls such text *input text*. Or you, the creator, can use editable text fields to update and provide new information in a movie. Flash calls such text *dynamic text*.

In this chapter, you learn about using static text, which is strictly a graphic element in the final movie. To find out more about input text and dynamic text, check out Chapter 15.

To create a text box with set width and word wrap:

1. With the text tool selected in the Toolbox, click the Stage at the spot where you want your text to start.

   Flash creates a text box with a round resize handle.

2. Move the pointer over the resize handle. The pointer changes to a double-headed arrow.

3. Click and drag the handle until your text box is as wide as you want it (**Figure 2.57**). The resize handle changes to a square.

4. Release the mouse button.

   The blinking insertion point appears in the text box.

5. Enter your text.

   Flash wraps the text horizontally to fit inside the column that the text box defines. The box automatically grows taller (not wider) to accommodate your text.

✔ Tips

- To reposition a text box with the text tool active, position the pointer along the edge of the text box. The pointer changes to the selection arrow. Now you can drag the text box to a new location.

- If you enter so much text on one line that the end of the text box starts to disappear off the Stage, you can fix the problem. Either drag the text box to the left with the selection arrow or choose View > Work Area (Shift-⌘ W [Mac], Ctrl-Shift-W [Windows]) and reduce magnification until you can see the resize handle. Then you can force the text to wrap by resizing the text box.

Working with Vertical Text

In previous versions of Flash, the only way to set columns of vertical characters was to create a text box that was one character wide. To make vertical text read across several columns, you needed a separate box for each column. Flash MX lets you change the direction in which text flows in static text boxes to create vertical text that flows automatically from column to column. You determine whether the columns read left to right (as they do in English) or vice versa (as required for, say, Japanese text).

You set the text-flow direction in the Property Inspector.

To access the Property Inspector:

◆ If the Property Inspector is not open, from the Window menu, choose Property Inspector.

To create vertical columns of text:

1. With the text tool selected and the Property Inspector open, in the Property Inspector, click the Change Direction of Text button (**Figure 2.58**).

   A pop-up menu of text directions appears.

2. To create a vertical text box, *do one of the following:*

   ▲ To make text columns read from the left side of the box to the right, choose Vertical, Left to Right.

   ▲ To make text columns read from the right side of the box to the left, choose Vertical, Right to Left.

3. Click the Stage at the spot where you want your text to start.

   Flash creates a vertical text box with a round resize handle. Notice that the blinking insertion pointer is lying on its side (**Figure 2.59**).

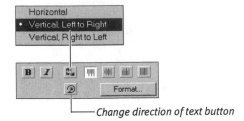

Change direction of text button

Figure 2.58 When you have selected the text tool or a text box, the Property Inspector displays a text-direction button. Clicking it opens a menu of options for setting the direction in which your text flows.

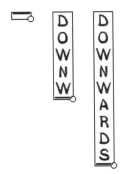

Figure 2.59 With text direction set to vertical, clicking the Stage with the text tool gives you an insertion point lying on its side (top). As you type, you enter a column of single characters (middle). The text box grows in length to accommodate all the text you enter (bottom).

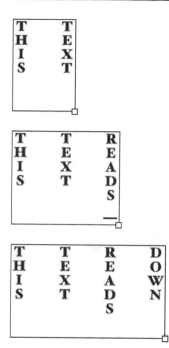

Figure 2.60 When text direction is set to Vertical, Left to Right, a fixed-height text box creates columns of downward-reading characters that flow from column to column automatically.

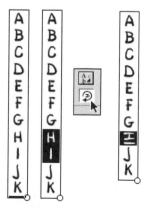

Figure 2.61 Select characters within a vertical text column (left); then click the Rotation button in the Property Inspector (middle) to rotate the characters and create a word that reads horizontally down (right).

4. Click and drag the resize handle.

5. When your text box is the desired height, release the mouse button.

   The resize handle changes to the square word-wrap handle.

6. Enter your text.

   Flash places one character below another till the text reaches the bottom edge of the box. Then text jumps to the next column and continues flowing vertically (**Figure 2.60**). You can force text to flow to the next column by adding a paragraph return.

7. When you finish typing, click elsewhere on the Stage or change tools.

✔ Tips

- If you want to create a single column of vertical text, you can start typing as soon as you click the Stage to create the text box. As in the first task in the preceding exercise, the text box continues to grow in length as long as you type.

- In some Asian languages whose text is set in vertical columns, it is common to set words borrowed from foreign languages that are set in Latin characters so that they can be read as a unit instead of character by character. You can make any selected text characters read horizontally down as a unit by clicking the Rotation button in the Property Inspector (**Figure 2.61**).

- When the text tool is set to create vertical text, you'll see the horizontal I-beam cursor as soon as you click the Stage. But how can you tell which direction the text will flow without opening the text-direction menu in the Property Inspector? If the resize handle appears on the bottom-right corner, the columns flow left to right. If the resize handle is on the bottom-left corner, the columns flow right to left.

If most of your text work demands vertical text columns, you can make that setting your default.

To make vertical text the default:

1. From the Edit menu (Mac OS 9 and Windows) or from the Flash menu (Mac OS X), choose Preferences.

   The Preferences dialog box appears (**Figure 2.62**).

2. Click the Editing tab.

3. In the Vertical Text section, select the Default Text Orientation checkbox.

4. Click OK.

   The text tool is now set to create vertical text boxes and columns that flow left to right by default. You can always choose a new text flow and orientation from the Change Direction of Text pop-up menu in the Property Inspector.

✔ Tip

- If you work with languages that read right to left, you can set that direction as a default in the Preferences dialog box's Vertical Text section as well.

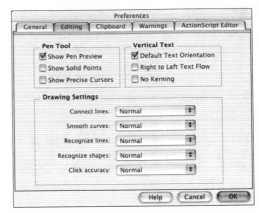

Figure 2.62 The Editing tab of the Preferences dialog box contains options for making vertical text boxes the default style.

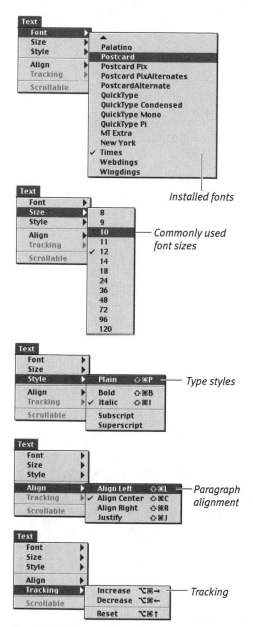

Installed fonts

Commonly used font sizes

Type styles

Paragraph alignment

Tracking

Figure 2.63 The Text menu presents several options for applying type attributes to selected text.

Setting Text Attributes via Menu

Flash offers two ways to set text attributes: the Text menu and the text-related Property Inspector. From the Text menu, you can set the font, size, style, paragraph alignment, and tracking of selected text. You learn to use the Property Inspector to make specific settings in subsequent exercises.

To set attributes via the Text menu:

1. Following the steps in the preceding exercises, create a text block on the Stage.

2. Use the text tool to select some or all of your text.

3. From the Text menu, choose the attribute you want to modify (**Figure 2.63**).
   Flash applies the new setting to your type.

✔ Tip

■ Flash changes all the settings in the text-related Property Inspector to match the attributes of selected text, which means that by selecting text, you load the text tool with that text's attributes. Keep blocks of text with formatting you use often in the work area and just click to re-create their settings for the text tool.

Setting Character Attributes via the Property Inspector

The text-related Property Inspector allows you to set all the attributes you set via menu in the preceding exercise: the typeface, font size, style, and spacing between letters. You can also define text as superscript or subscript, set line spacing, set text color, and create live links between text and URLs in this panel.

You can set character attributes in advance so that as you type, the text tool applies them automatically, or you can apply character attributes to existing text. The text tool always uses whatever settings currently appear in the Text Tool Property Inspector (**Figure 2.64**).

For the following exercises, keep the Property Inspector open (choose Window > Property Inspector if it's not already open).

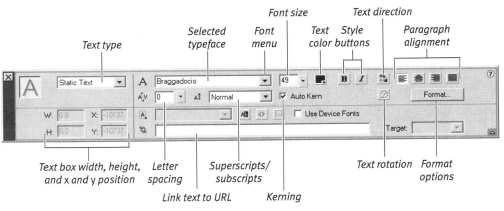

Figure 2.64 When you have selected the text tool in the Toolbox (or a text block on the Stage), the Property Inspector displays the type attributes to be created by the text tool (or applied to the current text selection).

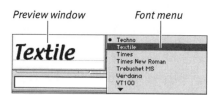

Preview window   Font menu

Textile

Figure 2.65 As you move the pointer through the font list in the Property Inspector, you see a preview of each font installed on your system.

To select text to apply character attributes:

Do one of the following:

◆ With the text tool selected, drag over existing text to highlight just a portion of text.

◆ With the arrow tool selected, click a text box to select all the text within it.

✔ Tip

■ You can select multiple text boxes with the arrow tool and modify them at the same time. (You learn more about selections in Chapter 3.)

The following exercises assume that you have selected text to modify.

To choose an installed typeface:

1. In the Property Inspector, click the scroll arrows to the right of the Font field.

   A scrolling list of your installed fonts appears, together with a font-preview window (**Figure 2.65**).

2. Move the pointer over a font name.

   The preview window displays the name in the selected font.

3. Click to select the currently highlighted font.

   The selected font name appears in the Font field.

4. Press Enter or click outside the Font field to confirm the new font and close the scrolling list.

SETTING CHARACTER ATTRIBUTES

To enter a font by name:

1. In the Property Inspector, double-click (or click and drag) in the Font field to highlight the current font name.

2. Enter the name of the font you want to use.

3. Press Enter or click outside the Font field to confirm the new font and close the scrolling list.

   You can enter the names of fonts that are not installed on your system. Flash will substitute the current system default font for any missing fonts. (The font name appears in parentheses in your list of fonts followed by the words *System Default Font.*) You'll learn more about working with missing fonts and choosing substitute fonts in Chapter 16.

✔ Tip

■ Although the Font field is not case-sensitive, you do need to type accurately. If you make a mistake in typing the name of an installed font, Flash assumes that it's dealing with a missing font and substitutes the system default font.

To set font size:

1. In the Property Inspector, double-click (or click and drag) in the Font Size field to highlight the current value.

2. Enter the desired point size.

3. Press Enter.

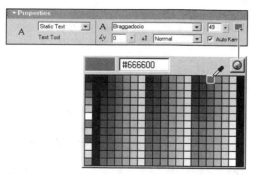

Figure 2.66 Choose a color for text created with the text tool from the Property Inspector's text (fill)-color box.

✔ Tips

■ For easy entry of new font sizes, click the triangle to the right of the Font Size field. A slider pops open. Drag the slider's lever to choose a value between 8 and 96 points. Flash previews the changes on the Stage as you drag the slider lever. Click outside the slider to confirm the new font size.

■ For even quicker changes, just click and drag the slider triangle. When you release the slider's lever, Flash confirms the new font size automatically.

■ To enter font sizes outside the slider's range, you must type the value in the Font Size field.

To choose a text color:

1. In the Property Inspector, click the text-color box (note that text in Flash is considered to be a fill).

   The pointer changes to an eyedropper, and a set of swatches appears (**Figure 2.66**).

2. To select a color, *do one of the following:*

   ▲ To select the color directly below the tip of the eyedropper, with the eyedropper tool, click a swatch or an item on the Stage.

   ▲ Enter a value in the hexadecimal-color field.

   ▲ To define a new color, click the Color Picker button. (For more information on defining colors, see Chapter 3.)

To choose a type style:

In the Property Inspector, *do one of the following:*

◆ To create boldface type, click the Bold button (**Figure 2.67**).

◆ To create italic type, click the Italic button.

◆ To create type that is both boldface and italic, click the Bold and Italic buttons.

◆ When creating bold and italic styles, Flash simply modifies the current typeface; Flash doesn't select a bold or italic typeface in the family of fonts you've chosen.

✔ Tip

■ You can also toggle boldface type by pressing Shift-⌘-B (Mac) or Shift-Ctrl-B (Windows). To toggle italic, press Shift-⌘-I (Mac) or Shift-Ctrl-I (Windows).

Flash allows you to control *tracking*—the amount of space between letters and words in a chunk of selected text.

To apply tracking:

1. Within a text box in a Flash document, select the text to track.

2. In the Property Inspector's Character Spacing field, enter the desired point size.

   A negative value reduces the space between the letters; a positive value increases it (**Figure 2.68**).

3. Press Enter.

Figure 2.67 Access bold and italic styles by clicking the Bold and Italic buttons in the text related Property Inspector.

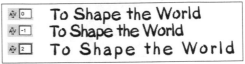

Figure 2.68 Enter a negative tracking value to bring characters closer together. Enter a positive value to space characters out. Enter 0 to use a font's built-in tracking value.

✔ Tips

- To change tracking interactively, in the Property Inspector's Character Spacing field, click the triangle to the right of the field. A slider pops open. Drag the slider's lever to a value between –59 and 59. Flash previews the changes on the Stage as you drag the slider lever. Then press Enter.

- For even quicker changes, just click and drag the slider triangle. When you release the slider's lever, Flash confirms the new tracking value; you don't need to press Enter.

- You can increase tracking of selected text in 0.5-point increments by choosing Text > Tracking > Increase or by pressing ⌘-Option-right arrow (Mac) or Alt-Ctrl-right arrow (Windows).

- To decrease tracking in 0.5-point increments, press ⌘-Option-left arrow (Mac) or Alt-Ctrl-right arrow (Windows).

- Add the Shift key to the keyboard shortcuts for narrower and wider tracking; this method increases or decreases space in 2-pixel increments.

- You can also track interactively by using the keyboard shortcuts. The space between letters continues to expand or contract as long as you hold down the key combination.

- To reset the font's original letter spacing, choose Text > Tracking > Reset or press ⌘-Shift-up arrow (Mac) or Alt-Ctrl-up arrow (Windows)

What Is Kerning?

While *tracking* affects the space between characters and words in an entire line or paragraph of text, *kerning* affects the space between a pair of letters. Because of the way fonts are constructed, with each letter being a separate element, some pairs of letters look oddly spaced when you type them. The space between a capital *T* and a lowercase *o*, for example, may seem too large because of the white space below the crossbar of the *T*. To make the characters look better, you can reduce the space between them, or *kern in* the pair. Some letters may seem to be too close together—say, a *t* and an *i*. You can *kern out* the pair so that it looks better.

Font designers often build into their fonts special information about how to space troublesome pairs of letters. Flash takes advantage of that embedded kerning information when you check the Auto Kern checkbox in the text-related Property Inspectors. It's a good idea to turn kerning on to make your type look its best.

You can kern manually in Flash instead of using the embedded kerning or in addition to it. Select the character pair that you want to kern; then use Flash's Tracking feature to bring the letters closer together or move them farther apart.

SETTING CHARACTER ATTRIBUTES

Setting Paragraph Attributes

Flash allows you to work with paragraph formatting much as you would in a word processor. The text-related Property Inspector allows you to set right and left margins, a first-line indent, line spacing, and alignment (flush left, flush right, centered, or justified) (**Figure 2.69**). You can set paragraph attributes in advance so that as you type, the text tool applies them automatically. And you can apply paragraph attributes to existing text. The text tool uses whatever settings currently appear in the Property Inspector.

In the following exercises, you learn to modify existing text; keep the Property Inspector open. (Choose Window > Property Inspector if it's not already open.)

To select paragraphs to modify:

Do one of the following:

◆ With the text tool selected, click anywhere within the paragraph you want to modify.

◆ With the text tool selected, click and drag to select multiple paragraphs within one text box.

◆ With the arrow tool, click the text box to select all the paragraphs within the box.

To set paragraph alignment:

1. Using the methods in the preceding exercise, select the paragraphs you want to modify.

2. In the Property Inspector, *do one of the following* (**Figure 2.70**):

   ▲ To align horizontal text on the left (vertical text on the top), click the first alignment button.

   ▲ To center horizontal or vertical text, click the second alignment button.

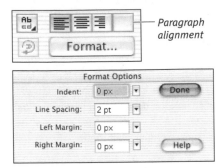

Paragraph alignment

Figure 2.69 Click the format button (top) to access a dialog box for setting the text-related Property Inspector attributes such as alignment, indents, margins, and space between lines of text (bottom).

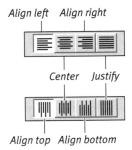

Align left   Align right

Center   Justify

Align top   Align bottom

Figure 2.70 The paragraph-alignment buttons allow you to format the text of a paragraph in four ways. A graphic representation of the selected paragraph alignment style appears on each button in the Paragraph panel.

Left/top margin

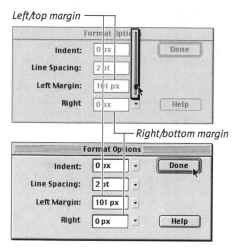

Right/bottom margin

Figure 2.71 You can enter a value for right and left margins (horizontal text) or top and bottom margins (vertical text) directly in the appropriate box (top) or use the slider to select a value (bottom).

▲ To align horizontal text on the right (vertical text on the bottom), click the third alignment button.

▲ To justify text (force all lines except the last line of a paragraph to fill the full column width), click the fourth alignment button.

✔ Tip

■ To select all the paragraphs within a text block, click with the text tool anywhere inside the text block; then choose Edit > Select All. Flash highlights the entire text block.

To set margins:

1. In the Property Inspector, click the Format button.

The Format Options dialog box appears.

2. In the Left Margin or Right Margin field, enter the desired margin size.

The units of measure used for the margin are the ones set in the Document Properties dialog box (see Chapter 1).

3. Click the Done button (**Figure 2.71**).

Flash uses the values that you enter to create margins from the left and right sides of the text box. Your audience will not see the margins unless you are creating text that they can edit, in which case you can make the border of the text box visible.

✔ Tips

■ For easy entry of new values when you have the text tool selected, click the triangle to the right of the Margin field. A slider pops open. Drag the slider's lever to choose a value between 0 and 720 pixels. Click the away from the slider to confirm the new margin value.

■ Flash incorporates the current margin settings into text boxes as you create them. With margins set to the default (0 pixels), clicking the text tool on the Stage creates a small text box, just large enough for the blinking insertion point. If you get a longer text box than you expect when you click the Stage with the text tool, check your margin settings in the Property Inspector and adjust them as needed.

To set a first-line indent:

◆ In the Indent field, use the value-entry techniques described in the preceding exercise to enter a value for indenting the first line of text in the paragraph.

Flash calculates the indent from the left margin; when the left margin is set to 0, Flash measures the indent from the left edge of the text box.

To set line spacing:

◆ In the Line Spacing field, use the value-entry techniques described earlier in this chapter to enter a value for the amount of space you want between lines of text.

If your text contains various point sizes, Flash bases the spacing between two lines on the larger font (**Figure 2.72**).

✔ Tip

■ Points are the most common unit of measure for working with type, and regardless of what units you've set in the Document Properties dialog box, Flash always enters the line-spacing value with the abbreviation pt (for points).

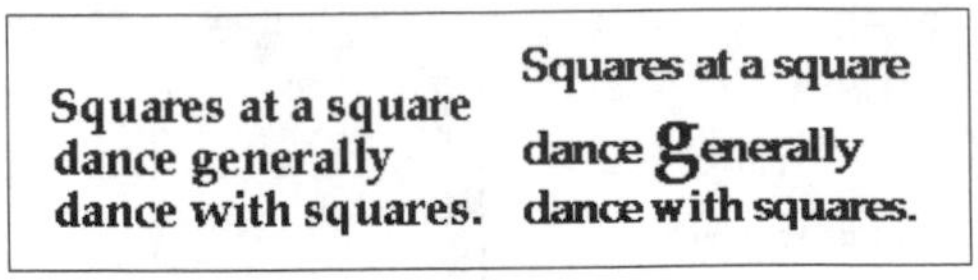

Figure 2.72 The line spacing for the text block on the left is set to 0 points. The space you see between lines is the space included as part of the font. Because the text is all one size, the spacing above and below the middle line of text is the same. In the text block on the right—with the same 0-point line spacing—one letter is a larger point size. Flash increases the space between lines to make room for the larger text.

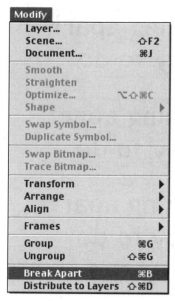

Figure 2.73 Choose Modify > Break Apart to place each letter of a text block in its own text box.

Breaking Apart Text

Flash allows you to *break apart* text—that is, divide one text block containing multiple editable characters into multiple blocks, each containing one editable character. This feature allows you to scale, reposition, or distort individual letters. (You learn to make these kinds of modifications to graphic elements in Chapter 3.) The ability to place letters in separate text boxes also comes in handy for animating text. (You learn more about animation techniques in chapters 8 through 11.)

To divide text blocks into single-letter text boxes:

1. Using the techniques from the preceding exercises, create a block of text.

2. While the text tool's blinking insertion point is still in the text box, choose Modify > Break Apart (**Figure 2.73**).

   Flash places each letter in its own text box and selects all the text boxes. Each text box is just wide enough to hold one letter. Each letter is fully editable on its own, though the group is no longer linked.

You can use the Break Apart command to transform single letters into graphic objects.

✔ Tip

■ You don't have to break text apart immediately after creating it. You can reactivate a text box by clicking it with the text tool. Or you can simply select the text box with the arrow tool and then choose Modify > Break Apart.

To transform letters into raw shapes:

1. Follow the steps in the preceding exercise to place letters in individual text boxes.

2. From the Modify menu, choose Break Apart.

   This second Break Apart command transforms the editable letters into raw shapes on the Stage (**Figure 2.74**). You can edit them as you would any other fill, but you can no longer change their text attributes with the text tool.

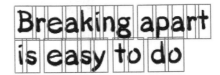

Figure 2.74 Applying the Break Apart command once transforms selected text (top) into single-letter text boxes (middle); applying the command again creates raw fill shapes out of the indivdual letters (bottom).

Modifying Simple Graphics

One way to modify Macromedia Flash XP graphics is to select one or more shapes and edit them by changing their attributes (such as color, size, and location) in the Property Inspector or in the appropriate panels.

You can also modify the shape of an element. Some operations—such as straightening lines, adjusting Bézier curves, and assigning new attributes—require that the element be selected. Other operations, such as reshaping a line segment or curve with the arrow tool, require the element to be deselected. A few operations allow you to edit the element whether it is selected or not—using the paint-bucket tool to change a fill color, for example.

This chapter covers using the arrow, lasso, and subselection tools to select and modify the elements you learned to make in Chapter 2. You also learn about using the Property Inspector and panels to modify elements' attributes.

Setting Selection Preferences

Flash allows you to select elements in several ways. You can click an element with the arrow tool or draw a selection outline. When you click to select an element by using the arrow tool, selecting an entire line can take you several selection actions, because each segment and curve of a line is a separate element that you must select. Adding to a selection is a common operation, and Flash gives you two ways to do it: Shift selection and additive selection.

Flash's default setting has Shift Select turned on. (You set the selection method in the General tab of the Preferences dialog box.) In Shift Select mode, you use the Shift key as a modifier while selecting an item to add it to any selection that is already active on the Stage. When you turn off Shift Select mode, selections become *additive*, which means that any new selections get added to current selections.

You always remove individual items from a selection by Shift-clicking.

To set a selection method for the arrow tool:

1. From the Edit menu (Mac OS 9 and Windows) or from the Flash application menu (Mac OS X), choose Preferences.

    The Preferences dialog box appears.

2. Choose the General tab (**Figure 3.1**).

3. In the Selection Options section, check or uncheck the Shift Select checkbox.

4. Click OK.

In Shift Select mode (Flash's default setting), you must Shift-click to add items to the current selection. With Shift Select turned off, each new item you click with the arrow tool gets added to the current selection.

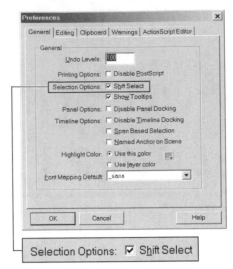

Figure 3.1 Select the General tab of the Preferences dialog box to choose a selection method.

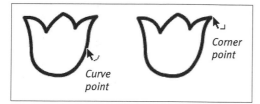

Figure 3.2 As you prepare to select a line, Flash indicates what kind of point the pointer is located over.

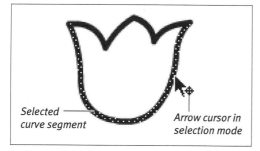

Figure 3.3 When you click the line to select it, Flash highlights that line segment (top). If you have the Property Inspector open, you can see information about your selected line, such as its color, thickness, and position on the Stage.

Selecting Lines with the Arrow Tool

Using the arrow tool to select lines and outline shapes may be a bit confusing at first. What you think of as being a single element—say, a swooping squiggly line or a square—may actually be several connected segments. Flash divides lines that you draw with the pencil tool into curves and segments that it defines as vectors. This means you may need to make multiple selections to select a single item with the arrow tool.

Flash covers selections with a pattern of tiny dots. Make sure that all the parts of the line or outline you intend to select display this pattern.

To select a single line segment:

1. In the Toolbox, select the arrow tool, or press V on the keyboard.

2. Move the pointer over a portion of the line (**Figure 3.2**).

Flash appends a little arc or a little right-angle icon to the arrow. These icons indicate that the arrow is over a point in a line segment and show what type of point it is: a curve or a corner point. (For more information about points, see "Reshaping Lines" later in this chapter).

3. Click to select the line.

Flash highlights the selected segment (**Figure 3.3**).

To select multiple line segments:

1. In the Toolbox, select the arrow tool.

2. To select the segments you want to include, *do one of the following:*

   ▲ If you are using Flash's default selection style (Shift Select), Shift-click each segment you want to select. Flash adds each new segment to the highlighted selection (**Figure 3.4**).

   ▲ If you turned off the Shift Select option in the Preferences dialog box, click each segment you want to include. Flash adds each new segment to the highlighted selection.

To select multiple connected line segments as a unit:

1. In the Toolbox, select the arrow tool.

2. Double-click any segment in the series of connected line segments.

   Flash highlights all the segments (**Figure 3.5**).

✔ Tip

■ To switch to the arrow tool temporarily while using another tool, press ⌘ (Mac) or Ctrl (Windows). The arrow tool remains in effect as long as you hold down the modifier key.

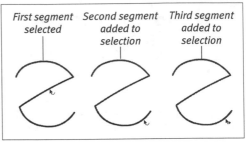

First segment selected   Second segment added to selection   Third segment added to selection

Figure 3.4 This graphic element consists of three segments. To select the entire element, you can click (or Shift-click, depending on your Preferences setting) each segment. Note that the line segments need not be connected, as they are in this example; they can be anywhere on the Stage.

Figure 3.5 After single-clicking (top), you select one segment of this outline. After double-clicking (bottom), you select the entire shape.

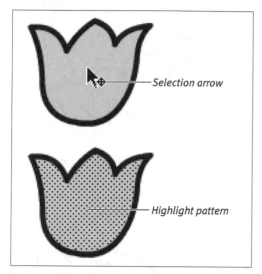

— Selection arrow

— Highlight pattern

Figure 3.6 When the pointer sits above a filled area, it changes into the selection arrow. Click the fill to select it. A dot pattern in a contrasting color highlights the selected fill.

Edit	
Undo	⌘Z
Redo	⌘Y
Cut	⌘X
Copy	⌘C
Paste	⌘V
Paste in Place	⇧⌘V
Clear	⌫
Duplicate	⌘D
Select All	⌘A
Deselect All	⇧⌘A
mes	⌥⌘X

Figure 3.7 Choose Edit > Select All, or press ⌘-A (Mac) or Ctrl-A (Windows), to select everything on the Stage.

Selecting Fills with the Arrow Tool

You can select filled areas the same way you select lines.

To select multiple filled areas:

1. In the Toolbox, select the arrow tool.

2. Position the pointer over the fill you want to select.

   The selection icon appears next to the arrow pointer.

3. Click the fill.

   Flash highlights the selected fill with a dot pattern (**Figure 3.6**).

4. To select additional fills, *do one of the following:*

   ▲ If you are using Flash's default selection style (Shift Select), Shift-click each additional fill you want to select.

   ▲ If you turned off the Shift Select option in the Preferences dialog box, click each fill you want to include.

   Flash adds each newly selected fill to the highlighted selection.

✔ Tip

■ To select everything that's currently on the Stage, from the Edit menu, choose Select All, or press ⌘-A (Mac) or Ctrl-A (Windows) (**Figure 3.7**).

Using a Selection Rectangle

Flash allows you to select several elements (or parts of elements) in a single operation by drawing a special rectangle around them. The rectangle is not a graphic element; it just defines the boundaries of your selection.

To create a selection rectangle:

1. In the Toolbox, select the arrow tool.

2. Click and drag to pull out a selection rectangle (**Figure 3.8**).

3. Continue dragging until the rectangle encloses all the elements you want to select.

   Be sure to start dragging at a point that allows you to enclose the elements you want within a rectangle drawn from that point.

4. Release the mouse button.

   Flash highlights whatever falls inside the selection rectangle.

✔ Tip

- If, as you drag out your selection rectangle, you realize that it won't include all the elements you want to select, and you don't want to add to the selection, drag back toward your starting point and release the mouse button when the rectangle encloses nothing. Then you can start over at a new point.

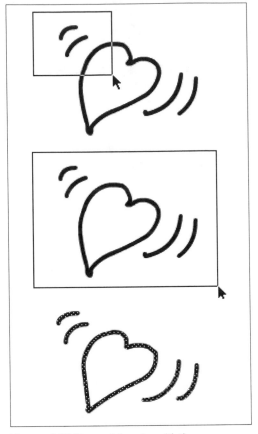

Figure 3.8 Clicking and dragging with the arrow tool creates a selection rectangle (top). Be sure to start from a point that allows you to enclose all the elements you want to select within the rectangle (middle). Release the mouse button, and you've selected those elements (bottom).

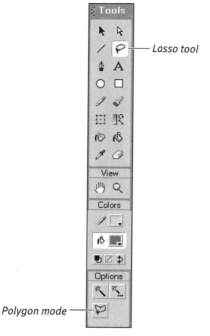

Lasso tool

Polygon mode

Figure 3.9 Use the lasso tool to select an irregular area.

Using the Lasso Tool

If the lines or shapes you want to select are located close to other lines, you may have difficulty selecting just the items you want with a rectangle. The lasso tool lets you create an irregular selection outline.

To select elements with the lasso tool:

1. In the Toolbox, select the lasso tool, or press L (**Figure 3.9**).

2. Click and draw a freeform line around the elements you want to select (**Figure 3.10**).

3. Close the selection outline by bringing the lasso pointer back over the point where you began the selection line.

4. Release the mouse button.
   Flash highlights whatever falls inside the shape you drew with the lasso.

✔ Tip

■ Flash draws a straight line between the starting point of your lasso line and the point at which you release the mouse button. You can skip the step of closing the shape if you're sure that Flash's closing will include the elements you want.

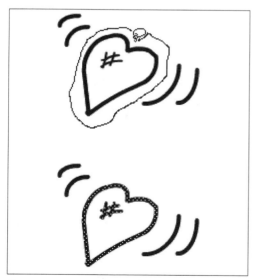

Figure 3.10 The lasso tool lets you select elements that are oddly shaped or too near other elements to allow use of the selection rectangle (top). Whatever falls within the area you outline with the lasso becomes highlighted and selected when you release the mouse button.

USING THE LASSO TOOL

For complex shapes, you may find it difficult to hold down the mouse button and draw the correct shape with the lasso. For these cases, Flash provides Polygon mode. In Polygon mode, the lasso allows you to define the selection area with a series of connected straight-line segments.

To select elements with the lasso tool in polygon mode:

1. With the lasso tool selected, in the Toolbox, select Polygon mode.

2. Click your way around the shape or elements you want to select.

   Each time you click, the polygon lasso finishes one line segment and adds a new point from which to start another connected line segment (**Figure 3.11**).

3. Close the shape by double-clicking.

   Flash draws a straight line from wherever you double-clicked to the point where you started creating the selection outline. To be sure you get all the elements you want, double-click directly over your beginning point.

✔ Tip

■ You can combine the regular lasso tool with the polygon lasso in creating a single selection outline. To access Polygon mode temporarily, hold down Option (Mac) or Alt (Windows) as you click.

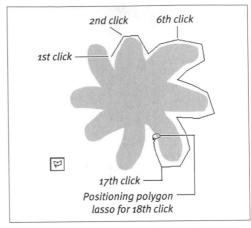

Figure 3.11 In Polygon mode, the lasso tool creates a series of connected line segments to outline whatever element you want to select. Double-clicking finishes the shape by drawing a line from the point where you double-clicked to the starting point.

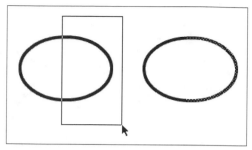

Figure 3.12 You can use the arrow tool to create a selection rectangle that selects a portion of a shape.

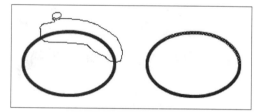

Figure 3.13 The lasso tool gives you greater freedom to select a particular arc of the oval.

Selecting Partial Elements

Sometimes, you want to select just a portion of a line segment, curve, or shape. You can use the arrow tool to draw a rectangle that selects just a slice of an element. The lasso tool is particularly good for this task, because it can select portions of various shapes.

To select part of a line or outline:

1. Select the arrow or lasso tool.

2. To make a selection, *do one of the following:*

   ▲ With the arrow tool, click and drag out a rectangle that encloses just a piece of the line or outline; then release the mouse button (**Figure 3.12**).

   ▲ With the lasso, draw a shape that encloses just a piece of the line or outline (**Figure 3.13**).

   ▲ With the lasso set to Polygon mode, create a series of line segments that enclose just a piece of the line or outline, and double-click to close the shape.

   Flash highlights only what was inside the rectangle or the shape drawn with the lasso.

To select part of a fill:

1. Select the arrow or lasso tool.

2. To make a selection, *do one of the following:*

   ▲ With the arrow tool, click and drag out a rectangle that encloses a slice of the element; then release the mouse button (**Figure 3.14**).

   ▲ With the lasso, draw a shape that encloses part of the line or outline (**Figure 3.15**).

   ▲ With the lasso in Polygon mode, create a series of line segments that enclose part of the line or outline, and double-click to close the shape (**Figure 3.16**).

   Flash highlights only what was inside the rectangle or the shape drawn with the lasso.

✔ Tip

■ You can define a single selection area that encompasses multiple elements or parts of multiple elements. The lasso and polygon lasso tools offer the most flexibility for grabbing different elements.

Figure 3.14 The arrow tool cuts a swath through this ribbon-shaped fill, selecting just part of each zigzag.

Figure 3.15 The lasso tool selects just a portion of the ribbon shape.

Figure 3.16 In Polygon mode, the lasso can select disparate areas of the ribbon easily.

Figure 3.17 With the arrow tool selected, position the pointer over the element you want to remove from the selection (left). Shift-click the item to deselect it (middle). Repeat the process to deselect another item (right).

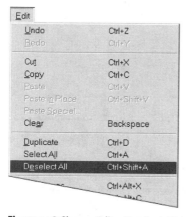

Figure 3.18 Choose Edit > Deselect All to remove selection highlighting from all the graphic elements on the stage.

Deselecting Elements

No matter what method you use to select items, there is just one way to deselect individual elements when you have several selected: You must Shift-click with the arrow tool to remove items from a selection.

To deselect individual items:

1. In the Toolbox, select the arrow tool.

2. Hold down the Shift key.

3. Click any highlighted lines or fills you want to remove from the current selection.

   Flash removes the highlighting from the item you just clicked (**Figure 3.17**).

To deselect everything:

◆ From the Edit menu, choose Deselect All, or press Shift-⌘-A (Mac) or Shift-Ctrl-A (Windows) (**Figure 3.18**).

✔ Tip

■ To deselect all elements quickly, click the arrow tool in an empty area of the Stage or work area.

Repositioning Elements Manually

If you aren't happy with the position of an element, you can always move it.

To reposition an element with the arrow tool:

1. Position the arrow tool over the element you want to move.

   The element doesn't need to be selected, although it can be. The arrow tool displays the selection icon as it hovers over the element.

2. Click the element, and drag it to the desired location (**Figure 3.19**).

   An outline preview appears to help you position the element as you drag it.

3. Release the mouse button.

   The element is now selected and in its new location.

✔ Tip

■ Turn on rulers (View > Rulers) to help you position your element. As you drag the element around the Stage, guide lines indicating the height and width of the element's bounding box (see the sidebar "How Flash Tracks Elements") appear in the ruler area (**Figure 3.20**).

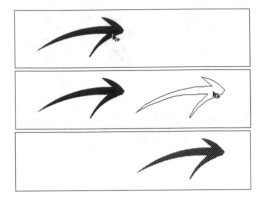

Figure 3.19 Use the arrow tool to select and drag an element to a new location.

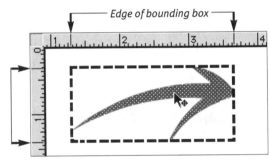

Figure 3.20 The longer lines in the ruler area indicate the edges of the element you are dragging.

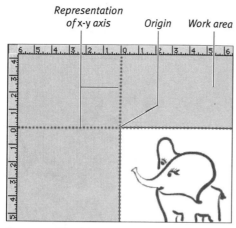

Figure 3.21 The dotted line here represents the *x-y* axis of the Stage. The origin—the o point both horizontally and vertically—is the top-left corner of the Stage.

To reposition an element with the arrow keys:

1. In the Toolbox, select the arrow tool.

2. Select the element you want to move.

3. Use one of the four arrow keys on the keyboard to move the element in 1-pixel increments.

The up-arrow key moves the element toward the top of the Stage. The down-arrow key moves the element toward the bottom of the Stage. The right-arrow key moves the element toward the right side of the Stage. The left-arrow key moves the element toward the left side of the Stage.

✔ Tip

■ To beef up the arrow keys' capability to move an element, hold down the Shift key. Each press of Shift-arrow moves a selected element 10 pixels.

How Flash Tracks Elements

To keep track of an element's size and position on the Stage, Flash encloses each element in a *bounding box*—an invisible rectangle just big enough to enclose the element. Flash then treats the Stage as a giant graph, with the top-left corner of the Stage as the center of the *x* and *y* axis (**Figure 3.21**). Flash locates elements by means of *x* and *y* coordinates on that graph. The units of measure for the graph are the ones currently selected in the Document Property dialog box (to learn more about document property, see Chapter 1). The Shape Property Inspector and the Info panel show you the *x* and *y* coordinates for an element's current position and also display the height and width of the element's bounding box. Flash calculates an element's position on the Stage either from the top-left corner of the element's bounding box or from the element's center point (the point at the exact center of the bounding box).

By entering new *x* and *y* coordinates for Height and Width in the Shape Property Inspector or the Info panel, you can change an element's position and size. (For more information on resizing elements, see "Changing the Size of Graphic Elements" later in this chapter.)

Repositioning Elements Numerically

Flash allows you to reposition a selection numerically by specifying a precise Stage location in x and y coordinates. You can enter the x and y coordinates in either the Shape Property Inspector or the Info panel.

To reposition an element via the Shape Property Inspector:

1. With the Property Inspector open, on the Stage, select an element.

   The coordinates for the element's current position appear in the x and y fields of the Shape Property Inspector (**Figure 3.22**).

2. To position the element, *do one of the following:*

   ▲ Enter a new x coordinate for the element's position along the horizontal axis.

   ▲ Enter a new y coordinate for the element's position along the vertical axis.

   Flash changes the element's horizontal position as soon as you click the y field.

3. Press Enter to confirm the new y coordinate value.

   The element moves to its new position (**Figure 3.23**).

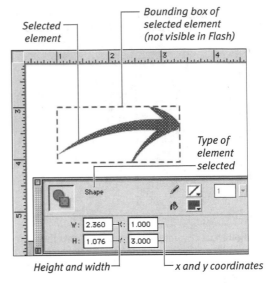

Selected element
Bounding box of selected element (not visible in Flash)
Type of element selected
Height and width
x and y coordinates

Figure 3.22 With a shape selected on the Stage, the Property Inspector reveals attributes of that shape, including the x and y coordinates of the shape's bounding box. This element is located 1 inch to the right along the horizontal axis and 3 inches down the vertical axis.

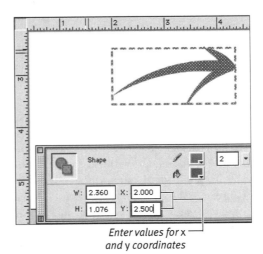

Enter values for x and y coordinates

Figure 3.23 Changing the x and y coordinates in the Shape Property Inspector changes the location of the selected element. This arrow is now located 2 inches to the right along the horizontal axis and 2.5 inches down the vertical axis.

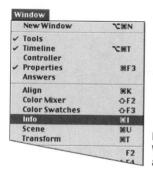

Figure 3.24 Choose Window > Info to access the Info panel.

Selected object

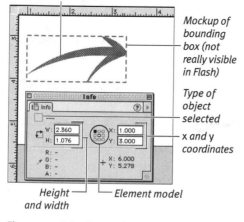

Mockup of bounding box (not really visible in Flash)

Type of object selected

x and y coordinates

Height and width — Element model

Figure 3.25 Selecting an element puts that element's information in the Info panel (bottom).

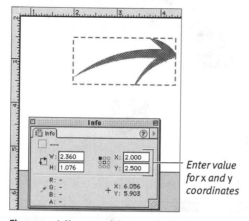

Enter value for x and y coordinates

Figure 3.26 Changes of the coordinates in the Info panel work just like changes of the coordinates in the Shape Property Inspector. The selected shape has moved to the right and down.

To access the Info panel:

◆ If the Info panel is not open, from the Window menu, choose Info (**Figure 3.24**). The Info panel appears.

To reposition an element via the Info panel:

1. With the Info panel open, on the Stage, select the element you want to reposition.

   The coordinates for the element's current position appear in the *x* and *y* fields of the Info panel (**Figure 3.25**).

2. To select the point Flash uses to position the element, *do one of the following:*

   ▲ To position your element by its center point, select the center square in the Info panel's element model.

   ▲ To position your element by its top-left corner, select the top-left square in the Info panel's element model.

3. Enter a new *x* coordinate for the element's position along the horizontal axis.

4. Enter a new *y* coordinate for the element's position along the vertical axis.

   Flash changes the element's horizontal position as soon as you click the *y* field.

5. Press Enter to confirm the new *y* coordinate value.

   The element moves to its new position (**Figure 3.26**).

✔ Tip

■ If you change multiple values in the Info panel (as in the preceding task), Flash confirms each change when you click the next entry field. To confirm the last new value quickly, click any other field in the panel or click the Stage.

Basic Editing Tasks: Cut, Copy, Paste

Flash supports the standard cut, copy, and paste operations and also provides some special operations tailored for working with animated graphics.

To delete a selection:

1. Select the elements you want to remove.

2. From the Edit menu, choose Clear (**Figure 3.27**), or press the Delete key.

   Flash removes the selected items.

To cut a selection:

1. Select the elements you want to cut.

2. From the Edit menu, choose Cut (**Figure 3.27**), or press ⌘-X (Mac) or Ctrl-X (Windows).

   Flash copies the selected items to the Clipboard and removes them from the Stage.

To copy a selection:

1. Select the elements you want to copy.

2. From the Edit menu, choose Copy (**Figure 3.27**), or press ⌘-C (Mac) or Ctrl-C (Windows).

   Flash copies the selected items to the Clipboard.

   After you cut or copy an item, it resides in the Clipboard until your next cut or copy operation. You can retrieve the Clipboard's contents with the Paste command.

To paste the Clipboard's contents in the center of the window:

◆ From the Edit menu, choose Paste, or press ⌘-V (Mac) or Ctrl-V (Windows).

   Flash pastes the Clipboard's contents in the center of the current view (**Figure 3.28**).

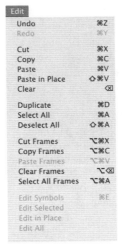

Figure 3.27 The Edit menu offers all the basic cut, copy, and paste commands, as well as some special ones for working with graphics and animations.

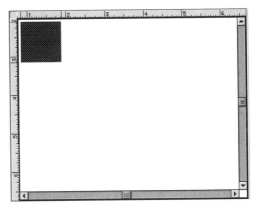

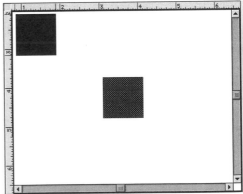

Figure 3.28 Copy a selected graphic element (top) and then choose the Paste command. Flash pastes a copy of the element from the Clipboard to the center of the current view (bottom).

Figure 3.29 The Duplicate command offsets a copy of the element from the original. The duplicate is the selected element.

To paste Clipboard contents in their original location:

◆ From the Edit menu, choose Paste in Place, or press Shift-⌘-V (Mac) or Shift-Ctrl-V (Windows).

Flash pastes the Clipboard contents back into their original location on the Stage. The value of this command will become more apparent when you get into working with layers and animation, when it can be crucial to have elements appear in precisely the same spot but on a different layer or frame.

To duplicate a selection:

1. Select the elements you want to copy.

2. From the Edit menu, choose Duplicate, or press ⌘-D (Mac) or Ctrl-D (Windows).

Flash creates a copy of the selected items. The duplicate appears on the Stage, offset from the original item (**Figure 3.29**). The duplicate is selected so that it doesn't interact with the original. (For more information on interaction between elements, see Chapter 4.) The Duplicate command doesn't change the contents of the Clipboard.

✔ Tip

■ With the arrow or lasso tool active, you can Option-click (Mac) or Ctrl-click (Windows) and drag any selected element to create a copy.

BASIC EDITING TASKS: CUT, COPY, PASTE

Editing Existing Elements with Assistance

Rather than have Flash assist you with everything you draw, you may prefer the flexibility of simply sketching with the pencil tool's freeform Ink mode. Flash can always recognize shapes and apply smoothing and straightening after you draw them.

To smooth an existing line:

1. Select the line with curves you want to smooth.

2. To smooth the curves, *do one of the following*:

   ▲ With the Arrow tool selected, in the Toolbox, click the Smooth button (**Figure 3.30**).

   ▲ From the Modify menu, choose Smooth (**Figure 3.31**).

   Flash smoothes the curves in the selected line according to the tolerances currently set in the Editing tab of the Preferences dialog box. By repeated clicking, you can smooth the curves further and ultimately reduce the number of curve segments in the line.

To straighten an existing line:

1. Select the line you want to straighten.

2. To straighten the line, *do one of the following*:

   ▲ With the arrow tool selected, in the Toolbox, click the Straighten button (**Figure 3.32**).

   ▲ From the Modify menu, choose Straighten.

   Flash straightens the selected line according to the tolerances currently set in the General tab of the Preferences dialog box (see Chapter 2).

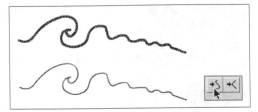

Figure 3.30 With your line selected on the Stage (top) and the arrow tool selected in the Toolbox, click the Smooth button. Flash smoothes the line (bottom).

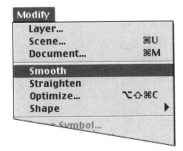

Figure 3.31 Choose Modify > Smooth to smooth curves selected on the Stage.

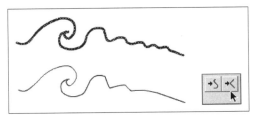

Figure 3.32 With your line selected on the Stage (top) and the arrow tool selected, in the Toolbox, click the Straighten button. Flash straightens the line (bottom).

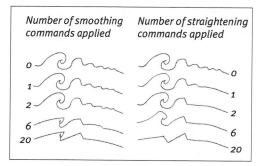

Figure 3.33 Invoking the Smooth and Straighten commands several times can change the appearance of a line dramatically.

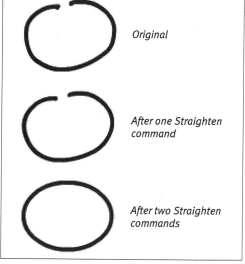

Figure 3.34 Use the Straighten command to recognize a shape.

✔ Tip

■ If the line still looks too rough after your first attempt, apply the Smooth or Straighten command again. Repeated smoothing eventually flattens your curves; repeated straightening eventually turns curve segments into straight-line segments (**Figure 3.33**).

To make Flash recognize existing shapes:

1. Select your rough version of an oval or rectangle.

2. To make Flash recognize your shape, *do one of the following*:

   ▲ With the arrow tool selected, in the Toolbox, click the Straighten button.

   ▲ From the Modify menu, choose Straighten.

   If the shape is recognizable under the tolerances currently set in the General tab of the Preferences dialog box (see Chapter 2), Flash recasts the shape as a perfect oval or rectangle.

✔ Tip

■ If at first Flash fails to recognize your rough shape, try again. Often, the newly straightened shape falls within the parameters Flash needs to recognize it (**Figure 3.34**).

Moving End Points with the Arrow Tool

You can use the arrow tool to change the length of straight-line and curve segments. Simply grab and reposition the segment's end points.

When you use the arrow tool, the segment you want to modify must not be selected. If the segment is selected, the arrow tool simply moves the segment as a unit. Always note what kind of icon the arrow pointer is displaying as it hovers over the line you want to modify (**Figure 3.35**).

For the following exercises, make sure that the item you want to modify is deselected.

To reposition the end of a line segment with the arrow tool:

1. Position the pointer over the end point of the line.

   The corner-point modifier appears.

2. Reposition the end point.

   The arrow tool now operates like the straight-line tool (the line segment changes to preview mode). Dragging away from the existing line lengthens it; dragging toward the existing line shortens it (**Figure 3.36**).

3. Release the mouse button.

   Flash redraws the line segment.

To reposition the end point of a curve with the arrow tool:

1. Position the pointer over the end point of a curve.

   The corner-point modifier appears.

2. Click and drag the end point to the desired location.

3. Release the mouse button.

   Flash redraws the end of the curve (**Figure 3.37**).

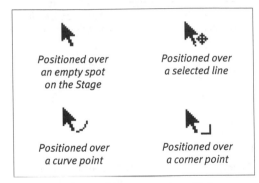

Figure 3.35 The small icons appearing with the arrow pointer indicate what type of graphic element lies beneath the pointer.

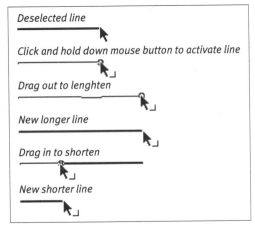

Figure 3.36 You can use the arrow tool to change a line segment's length.

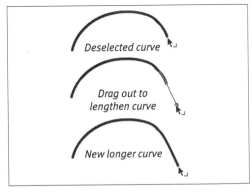

Figure 3.37 You can use the arrow tool to change a curve's length.

Figure 3.38 Use the subselection tool to modify the path of a line segment.

Figure 3.39 When a solid square appears next to the subselection tool, the tool is ready to select the entire path (left). When a hollow square appears (right), the tool is ready to select and manipulate a single anchor point.

Moving Points with the Subselection Tool

The subselection tool allows you to reveal and manipulate the anchor points that define a line segment or curve. Then you can grab and reposition these points to modify lines and curves.

To view a path and anchor points:

1. In the Toolbox, choose the subselection tool (**Figure 3.38**).

The pointer changes to a hollow arrow.

2. On the Stage, click the line or curve you want to modify.

Flash selects and highlights the entire path. In Flash's default editing mode, anchor points appear as solid squares in a contrasting highlight color.

To manipulate a particular point, you must select it directly.

To select an anchor point:

1. With the subselection tool active, position the pointer over the point you want to move.

The anchor-point modifier (a small hollow square) appears next to the hollow-arrow icon (**Figure 3.39**).

2. Click the anchor point.

Flash highlights the selected point. At Flash's default setting, selected corner points appear as hollow squares; selected curve points appear as hollow circles with Bézier handles.

MOVING POINTS WITH THE SUBSELECTION TOOL

✔ Tips

- If you know where a point is in your element, you can skip the step of clicking the path to highlight all the anchor points. To select the point directly, double-click it.

- You can select multiple points on a path directly with the subselection tool. Draw a selection rectangle that includes the points you want to select. Flash highlights the entire path and selects any points that fall within the rectangle.

- To view anchor points as hollow squares and selected points as solid, you need to change Flash's editing preferences. From the Edit menu (Mac OS 9 and Windows) or the Flash menu (Mac OS X), choose Preferences to open the Preferences dialog box. Click the Editing tab, and uncheck the Show Solid Points checkbox.

To reposition anchor points with the subselection tool:

- ◆ With the subselection tool active, click and drag the desired anchor point to a new location.

  Flash redraws the path (**Figure 3.40**).

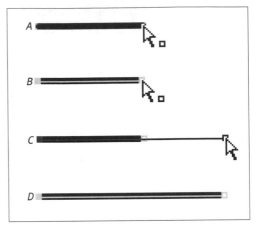

Figure 3.40 When you've selected an anchor point (A), Flash highlights the entire path (B). You can drag the anchor point to lengthen or shorten the path (C). The path and anchor points remain highlighted when you're done (D).

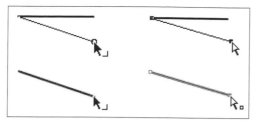

Figure 3.41 Using the arrow tool (left) or subselection tool (right), click the line's end point and drag it to a new position. You can pivot the line and change its angle as you would when creating a line with the straight-line tool. Flash redraws the line. With the subselection tool, when you release the mouse button, the path is selected, and its anchor points are highlighted.

Reshaping Lines

Flash makes drawing easy by allowing you to reshape every line or element you create. The arrow tool lets you simply grab a point and give it a tug. The subselection tool gives you precise control of reshaping by allowing you to manipulate anchor points and Bézier control handles directly.

To change the direction of a line segment (arrow or subselection tool):

1. Using the arrow or subselection tool, position the pointer over the line segment's end point.

The corner-point modifier appears with the arrow tool.

The anchor-point modifier appears with the subselection tool.

2. Click and drag the end point to a new location that changes the line's direction (**Figure 3.41**).

3. Release the mouse button.

Flash redraws the line.

About Curve and Corner Points

Flash's arrow and pen/subselection tools let you modify an element's curves and lines. The subselection tool lets you do so by moving the curve and corner points that define the elements and by rearranging the curves' Bézier handles. When you highlight a path with the subselection tool, Flash reveals any curve points' Bézier handles. (Corner points have no handles.)

When you use the arrow tool, Flash hides all the technical stuff. You simply pull on a line to reshape it. Still, the arrow tool does have its own hidden version of curve and corner points, which are evident only in the changing icons that accompany the tool as it interacts with a line or curve.

For the arrow tool, corner points appear at the end of a segment or at the point where two segments join to form a sharp angle. All those other in-between points—even if they fall in the middle of a line segment that happens to be completely flat—are curve points. When you tug on a curve point with the arrow tool, you pull out a range of points in a tiny arc. When you tug on a corner point with the arrow tool, you pull out a single point.

RESHAPING LINES

Reshaping Curves with the Arrow Tool

You can reshape a curve, or change a straight-line segment into a curve, by using the arrow tool to push and pull on the curve. You can also reshape curves by using the pen and subselection tools in combination (see "Reshaping Curves with the Subselection Tool" later in this chapter).

In the following exercises for the arrow tool, make sure that the line or curve you want to reshape is deselected when you start each exercise.

To reposition the end of a curve with the arrow tool:

1. Position the arrow tool's pointer over the end point of the curve.

   The corner-point modifier appears.

2. Click and drag the end point to a new location.

   As you drag, the end of the line changes to a small circle, showing that the line is active for modifications. The last segment of the curve changes direction depending on where you locate the end point. Flash previews the new curve segment as you drag (**Figure 3.42**).

To reshape a curve with the arrow tool:

1. Position the arrow tool's pointer over the middle of a curve segment.

   The curve-point modifier appears.

2. Click and drag the curve to reshape it (**Figure 3.43**).

   Flash previews the curve you're drawing.

3. Release the mouse button.

   Flash redraws the curve.

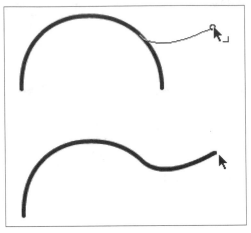

Figure 3.42 Using the arrow tool, click the curve's end point and drag it to a new position. Flash reshapes the end of the curve.

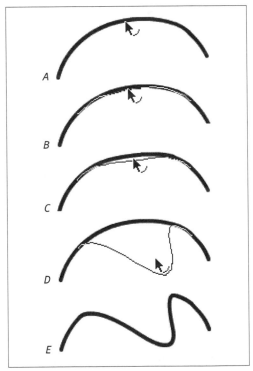

Figure 3.43 Click the middle of a curve (A). Flash activates the curve segment (B). Drag the curve to a new position (C, D). When you release the mouse button, Flash redraws the curve (E).

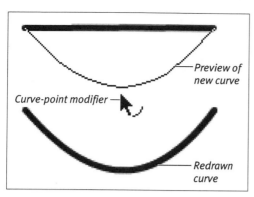

Figure 3.44 Although this line doesn't look curved (top), Flash considers all its middle points to be curve points. Drag one of those points to create a line that looks like a curve (bottom).

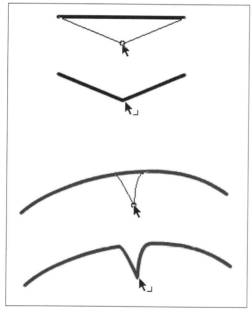

Figure 3.45 Option-click (Mac) or Ctrl-click (Windows) to create a new corner point for editing your line. Dragging a corner point from a straight-line segment creates a sharp *V* (top). Dragging a corner point from a curve creates a *V* with curving sides that comes to a sharp point (bottom).

To turn a straight-line segment into a curve segment with the arrow tool:

1. Position the arrow tool's pointer over the middle of a line segment.

   The curve-point modifier appears.

2. Click and drag the line to reshape it (**Figure 3.44**).

   Flash previews the curve that you're drawing.

3. Release the mouse button.

   Flash redraws the line, giving it the curve you defined.

To create new corner points with the arrow tool:

1. Position the arrow tool's pointer over the middle of a line or curve segment.

   The curve-point modifier appears.

2. Option-click (Mac) or Ctrl-click (Windows).

   After a brief pause, the arrow tool's modifier disappears, and a circle appears where the pointer intersects the line. The circle indicates that you are activating a corner point.

3. Drag to modify the line or curve segment and add a new corner point (**Figure 3.45**).

Reshaping Curves with the Subselection Tool

The subselection tool lets you manipulate a point's Bézier handles to modify the slope and depth of the curve. You can add and delete points and convert existing curve points to corner points, or vice versa, with the pen tool (see "Converting, Removing, and Adding Points," later in this chapter).

One way to reshape a curve is to change the location of the anchor points that define the curve.

To move a curve point:

1. In the Toolbox, choose the subselection tool.

2. Click a path to select it.
   Flash highlights the entire path of the selected element.

3. Position the pointer over a curve point.
   The anchor-point modifier appears.

4. Click and drag the point to a new location.
   Flash previews the new curve as you drag (**Figure 3.46**).

   After you move a curve point, the path remains selected, and the Bézier control handles of the point you moved become active so that you can further manipulate the curve.

To reshape a curve with the Bézier handles:

1. With the subselection tool, click the curve you want to modify.

2. Click one of the two anchor points that define the curve you want to modify.
   Bézier handles appear.

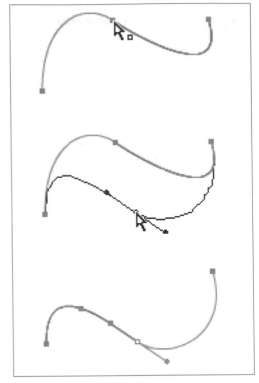

Figure 3.46 One way to modify a curved path is to reposition anchor points with the subselection tool.

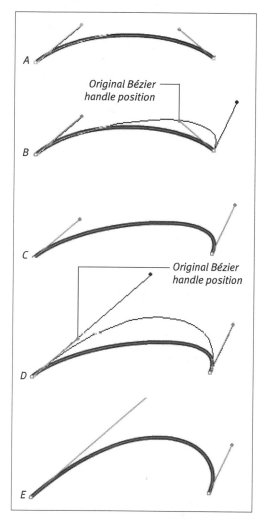

Figure 3.47 When you select anchor points, their Bézier handles appear (A). Leaning a Bézier handle away from a curve (B) makes that curve segment more pronounced (C). Leaning the handle toward the curve flattens that part of the curve. Dragging the Bézier handle away from its anchor point (D) makes the curve deeper (E); dragging the handle toward the anchor point makes the curve shallower.

3. Click and drag one of the Bézier handles. The pointer changes to an arrowhead.

4. To modify the curve, *do one or more of the following:*

▲ To make the curve more pronounced, position the Bézier handle farther from the curve in the direction in which the curve bulges.

▲ To make the curve flatter, position the Bézier handle closer to the curve.

▲ To make the curve bulge in the opposite direction, move the Bézier handle past the existing curve, in the opposite direction from the current bulge.

▲ To make the curve deeper, position the Bézier handle farther from the anchor point.

▲ To make the curve shallower, position the Bézier handle closer to the anchor point.

Flash previews the new curve as you manipulate the Bézier handle (**Figure 3.47**).

✔ Tips

■ To select an anchor point and activate its Bézier handles quickly, use the subselection tool to draw a selection rectangle around the curve you want to modify. Even if the path was not highlighted, Flash selects any anchor points that fall within the section and activates their handles.

■ You can move selected anchor points with the arrow keys. To move in larger increments, press Shift-arrow key.

■ When you have multiple anchor points selected, using the arrow keys moves the selected points as a unit. Dragging one of those points with the subselection tool repositions just that point.

Converting, Removing, and Adding Points

In some graphics programs, you select pen modifiers to convert, remove, and add points. In Flash, the pen tool automatically turns into a modifier as it hovers over a path or an anchor point. The subselection tool can change corner points to curve points. The pen tool can add new points between existing curve points, can reduce a curve point to a corner point, and can reduce a corner point to no point at all.

To convert corner points to curve points:

1. Using the subselection tool, click the path you want to modify.

   Flash highlights the path and its anchor points.

2. Position the hollow-arrow pointer over a corner point.

   The anchor-point modifier appears.

3. Click the anchor point to select it.

4. To pull Bézier handles out of the point, Option-drag (Mac) or Alt-drag (Windows) away from the selected corner point.

   Flash converts the corner point to a curve point (**Figure 3.48**).

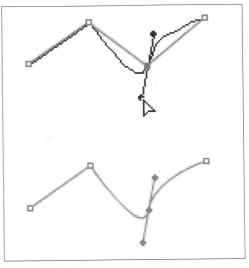

Figure 3.48 To change a corner point into a curve point (one with Bézier handles), use the subselection tool to Option-drag (Mac) or Alt-drag (Windows) a selected corner point (top). You actually pull a Bézier handle out of the point instead of relocating the point. When you release the mouse button, Flash redraws the curve (bottom).

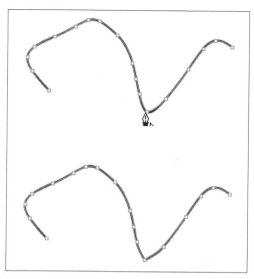

Figure 3.49 When you position the pen tool over a curve point, a small caret appears next to the pointer (top). With the caret modifier active, click the curve point to reduce it to a corner point (bottom). Flash redraws the path accordingly.

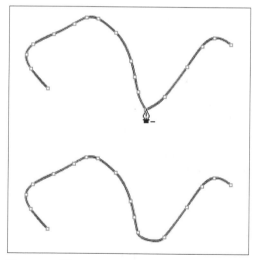

Figure 3.50 When you position the pen tool over a corner point, a small minus sign appears next to the pointer (top). With the minus-sign modifier active, click the corner point to reduce it to no point at all (bottom). Flash redraws the path accordingly.

To convert curve points to corner points:

1. With the path you want to modify selected, in the Toolbox, choose the pen tool.

2. Position the pen pointer over a curve point.

   The convert-to-corner-point modifier (a small caret) appears next to the pen icon.

3. Click the curve point.

   Flash converts the curve point to a corner point and flattens the curved path (**Figure 3.49**).

To delete anchor points:

1. With the path you want to modify selected, in the Toolbox, choose the pen tool.

2. Position the pen pointer over a corner point.

   The remove-point modifier (a minus sign) appears next to the pen icon.

   (Note that if the point you want to delete is currently a curve point, you must follow the steps in the preceding exercise to convert it to a corner point.)

3. Click the corner point.

   Flash removes the anchor point and reshapes the path to connect the remaining points (**Figure 3.50**).

✔ Tip

- You can also delete one or more anchor points by selecting them with the subselection tool and pressing Delete.

To add new anchor points to a curve segment:

1. With the path you want to modify selected, in the Toolbox, choose the pen tool.

2. Position the pen pointer over the path between two curve points.

   The add-point modifier (a plus sign) appears next to the pen icon.

3. Click the path.

   Flash adds a new curve point (**Figure 3.51**).

✔ Tips

■ If you need to add points to a straight-line segment, first convert the corner points that define the segment to curve points. Then you'll be able to add another curve point between them.

■ To add points to the end of an open path, position the pen pointer over the end of the path. When the *x* to the right of the pen pointer disappears, click the last anchor point and then continue clicking to add more points.

■ You can select an open path with the pen tool by clicking the anchor point at either end of the path. Flash won't convert or delete the end anchor point; it just highlights the path the same way that the subselection tool would.

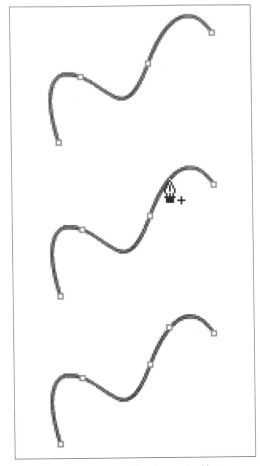

Figure 3.51 When you position the pen tool between existing curve points, a small plus sign appears next to the pointer (middle). With the plus-sign modifier active, click the curve to add a new curve point (bottom). Note that the pen tool cannot add points between corner points.

Figure 3.52 When you position the pointer over the edge of a fill shape, the arrow tool displays either the curve-point or corner-point modifier. If you then click the edge of the fill, Flash activates part of the outline for reshaping.

Before   *After*

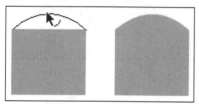

Pull out a curve point

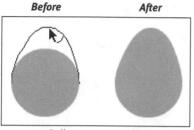

Pull out a curve point

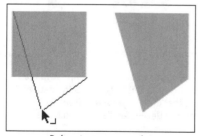

Relocate a corner point

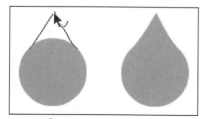

Create a new corner point

Figure 3.53 Take some time to play around with reshaping fills. You can pull points out to create protrusions or move points in to create indentations. You can reshape the fill pretty much any way you want.

Reshaping Fills

Although you can't see the outlines of filled shapes unless you give them a stroke, fills do have outlines that act just like any other line. This means you can use the arrow, pen, and subselection tools to reshape fills the same way that you reshaped lines and paths in the previous tasks.

To reshape a fill with the arrow tool:

1. With nothing selected, position the arrow tool's pointer over the edge of your filled shape.

   The curve point or corner-point modifier appears (**Figure 3.52**).

2. Click and drag the curve point or corner point to reshape the fill (**Figure 3.53**).

   Flash previews the new outline.

3. Release the mouse button.

   Flash creates the new fill shape.

To reshape a fill with the subselection and pen tools:

1. In the Toolbox, choose the subselection tool.

2. Position the hollow-arrow pointer over the edge of your filled shape.

3. Click.

   Flash highlights the path and anchor points that define the fill shape (**Figure 3.54**).

4. Add, remove, and reposition anchor points and Bézier handles with the pen and subselection tools, as described earlier in this section.

✔ Tip

- To select an entire fill path quickly, use the subselection tool to drag a selection rectangle over any portion of the fill. Unlike the arrow tool, the subselection tool selects the whole shape even if you include just a small portion of it within the selection rectangle. Any curve points that fall within the rectangle display their Bézier handles.

Figure 3.54 Select the edge of a fill shape with the subselection tool, and Flash highlights the path and anchor points that outline the shape (top). Reposition anchor points and Bézier handles to modify the fill shapes (bottom).

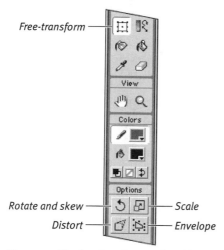

Free-transform

Rotate and skew — *Scale*
Distort — *Envelope*

Figure 3.55 The free-transform tool enables you to select and scale elements interactively.

Changing the Size of Graphic Elements

Flash gives you several ways to resize, or scale, graphic elements. You can scale selected elements interactively on the Stage, or you can set specific scale percentages or dimensions for your element via menu commands, panels, or the Property Inspector.

To resize a graphic element interactively:

1. In the Toolbox, select the free-transform tool (**Figure 3.55**).

2. On the Stage, click the element you want to resize.

   Flash selects and highlights the element, and places transformation handles on all four sides and at the corners of the element's bounding box.

3. In the Toolbox, choose the Scale modifier.

4. Position the pointer over a handle.

   The pointer changes to a double-headed arrow, indicating the direction in which the element will grow or shrink as you pull or push on the handles.

5. To change the graphic element's width, click and drag one of the side handles.

   Dragging toward the center of the element narrows it; dragging away widens it (**Figure 3.56**).

   (continues on next page)

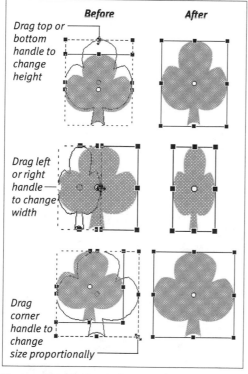

Before   **After**

Drag top or bottom handle to change height

Drag left or right handle to change width

Drag corner handle to change size proportionally

Figure 3.56 Activating the free-transform tool's Scale modifier places a set of handles around a selected element. Click and drag the handles to change the size of the element.

6. To change the element's height, click and drag the top or bottom handle.

Dragging toward the center of the element shortens it; dragging away makes it taller.

7. To change the size of the element proportionately, click and drag one of the corner handles.

Dragging toward the center of the element reduces it; dragging away enlarges it.

✔ Tips

■ If you have made a selection with the arrow tool, you can activate transformational handles for the selection by choosing Modify > Transform > Scale. Flash chooses the free-transform tool and its Scale modifier in the Toolbox. Or you can just click the free-transform tool and its Scale modifier directly in the Toolbox yourself.

■ In the default scaling mode, the selection scales from the control point opposite the one you are dragging. When you drag the center handle of a square's right side, the left side of the square stays fixed. As you pull, the right side moves away from the left to make a rectangle. To scale relative to the center of a selection, hold down the Option key (Mac) or Alt key (Win) as you drag. The left- and right-side handles both move away from the center of the selection as you drag.

■ With one exception, you can select a whole graphic element, part of an element, or multiple elements to scale with any of the selection methods discussed at the beginning of this chapter. You cannot use the subselection tool to select an element by its path, because choosing the free-transform tool automatically deselects the selected path.

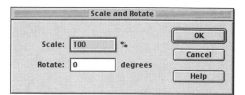

Figure 3.57 You can enter a specific percentage of enlargement or reduction in the Scale and Rotate dialog box.

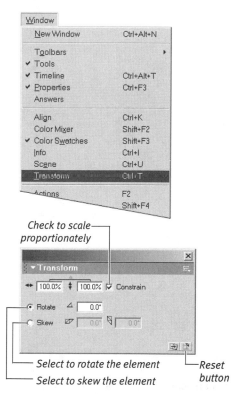

Check to scale proportionately

Select to rotate the element

Select to skew the element

Reset button

Figure 3.58 Choose Window > Transform (top) to access the Transform panel, where you can enter values for scaling, rotating, and skewing selected elements (bottom).

To resize a graphic element with the Scale and Rotate command:

1. Select the element you want to resize.

2. From the Modify menu, choose Transform > Scale and Rotate.

   The Scale and Rotate dialog box appears (**Figure 3.57**).

3. To resize the element, *do one of the following:*

   ▲ To make the element smaller, in the Scale field, enter a value less than 100%.

   ▲ To make the element larger, in the Scale field, enter a value greater than 100%.

4. Click OK.

   Flash resizes the element relative to its center point.

✔ Tip

■ You can resize an element relative to its top-left corner by changing the element's width and height in the Info panel. But you need to do the math yourself to preserve the element's aspect ratio, the ratio between the height and width.

You can also resize elements by using the Transform panel.

To access the Transform panel:

◆ If the Transform panel is not open, from the Window menu, choose Transform.

   The Transform panel appears (**Figure 3.58**).

To resize an element proportionately by using the Transform panel:

1. With the Transform panel open, on the Stage, select the element you want to resize.

   A value of 100% appears in the Width and Height fields of the Transform panel.

2. Check the Constrain checkbox next to the Width and Height fields.

3. Enter a new value in either field.

   A value less than 100% shrinks the element; a value greater than 100% enlarges the element. As you enter the value in one field, Flash automatically updates the other field.

4. Press Enter.

   Flash resizes the element.

✔ Tip

- After you've applied a transformation to an element, you can undo it quickly— by clicking the Reset button in the bottom-right corner of the Transform panel—provided that you have not deselected the element.

To resize the width and height of an element separately by percentage:

1. With the Transform panel open, on the Stage, select the element you want to resize.

2. In the Transform panel, uncheck the Constrain checkbox.

3. Enter a new percentage in the Scale Width field.

4. Enter a new percentage in the Scale Height field.

5. Press Enter.

   Flash resizes the element.

✔ Tips

- You can scale several elements at the same time. Select all the elements and then use any of the scaling methods described earlier in this section. The bounding box that contains the elements scales relative to its center point, and the entire selection grows or shrinks to fit the new box.

- You can transform a copy of the element by clicking the Copy and Apply Transform button in the Transform panel.

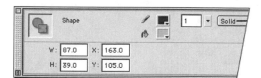

Figure 3.59 The Shape Property Inspector displays the width and height of the bounding box of the selected element. Enter new values to resize the element.

Element model

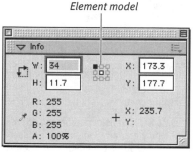

Figure 3.60 You can enter precise dimensions for an element's width and height in the Info panel. The element model shows whether changes will be relative to the center or to the top-left corner of the element's bounding box. To apply the values you entered in the panel to the selected graphic element, click the Stage or press Enter.

You can also specify precise measurements for a selected element in the Shape Property Inspector or in the Info panel.

To specify width and height via the Property Inspector:

1. Open the Property Inspector

If the Property Inspector panel is not open, choose Window > Property.

2. On the Stage, select the element you want to resize.

The Shape attributes, including the width and height of the selected element, appear in the Shape Property Inspector (**Figure 3.59**).

3. In the Shape Property Inspector's Width of Instance field, enter a new value for the element's width.

4. In the Height of Instance field enter a new value for the element's height.

5. Press Enter.

Flash resizes the element.

✔ Tip

■ You can also enter specific width and height values for a selected element in the Info panel (**Figure 3.60**). The panel contains no option to constrain the width and height. To preserve the current aspect ratio, you'll have to do the math yourself. But you can determine whether the element changes size relative to the center of the object or the top-left corner of its bounding box. Click the appropriate point on the element model in the Info panel.

Reorienting Graphic Elements

Flash lets you rotate, flip, and skew selected elements. You can either manipulate elements freely with the free-transform tool's Rotate and Skew modifier or use a variety of commands to do the job with more precision.

To flip a graphic element:

1. Select the element you want to flip.

2. To reorient the element so that it spins 180 degrees around its vertical central axis like a weathervane, from the Modify menu, choose Transform > Flip Horizontal (**Figure 3.61**).

3. To reorient the element so that it spins 180 degrees around its horizontal central axis like a Rolodex file, from the Modify menu, choose Transform > Flip Vertical. **Figure 3.62** shows the results of the two types of flipping.

✔ Tip

■ You can flip and scale elements simultaneously by using the free-transform tool's Scale modifier. With the selected element in Scale mode, drag one handle all the way across the bounding box and past the handle on the other side. To flip a selected element vertically and horizontally, for example, drag the handle in the bottom-right corner diagonally upward, past the handle in the top-left corner (**Figure 3.63**). The flipped element starts small and grows as you continue to drag away from the element's top-left corner. Flash previews the flipped element; release the mouse button when the element is the size you want.

Rotate 90 degrees clockwise

Rotate 90 degrees counter-clockwise

Flip 180 degrees like a Rolodex card file

Flip 180 degrees like a weathervan

Figure 3.61 The Modify > Transform submenu offers commands for flipping graphic elements vertically and horizontally. It also offers commands for rotating an element in 90-degree increments, both clockwise and counterclockwise.

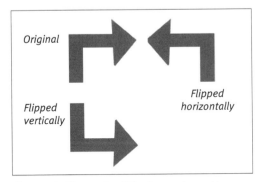

Original

Flipped horizontally

Flipped vertically

Figure 3.62 The results of flipping an element by using the Flip commands in the Modify > Transform submenu.

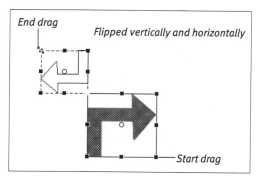

End drag

Flipped vertically and horizontally

Start drag

Figure 3.63 The free-transform tool's Scale modifier can flip and scale an element simultaneously. Here, the Scale modifier is flipping the element both vertically and horizontally.

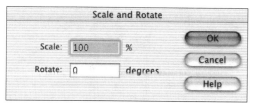

Figure 3.64 The Scale and Rotate dialog box lets you rotate graphic elements in precise increments. Positive values rotate the element clockwise; negative values rotate it counterclockwise.

To rotate an element in 90-degree increments:

1. Select the element you want to rotate.

2. To rotate the element, *do one of the following:*

   ▲ To rotate the element counterclockwise 90 degrees, from the Modify menu, choose Transform > Rotate 90° CCW.

   ▲ To rotate the element clockwise 90 degrees, from the Modify menu, choose Transform > Rotate 90° CW.

   Flash rotates the element 90 degrees. You can repeat the command to rotate the element 180 and 270 degrees or back to its starting point.

To rotate an element by a user-specified amount:

1. From the Modify menu, choose Transform > Scale and Rotate, or press ⌘-Option-S (Mac) or Ctrl-Alt-S (Windows). The Scale and Rotate dialog box appears (**Figure 3.64**).

2. To specify the direction and amount of rotation, *do one of the following:*

   ▲ To rotate the element counterclockwise, enter a negative value (–1 to –360) in the degree field.

   ▲ To rotate the element clockwise, enter a positive value (1 to 360).

3. Click OK.

   Flash rotates the selected element by the amount you specified.

✔ Tip

■ You can also rotate a selected element via the Transform panel. Click the Rotate button, and enter a value in the Rotate field.

REORIENTING GRAPHIC ELEMENTS

To skew an element by using the Transform panel:

1. With the Transform panel open, select the element you want to skew.

2. In the Transform panel, choose Skew.

3. Enter the desired skew values in the horizontal and vertical fields (**Figure 3.65**).

4. To complete the transformation, press Enter.

✔ Tip

■ To skew a copy of the selected element, in the Transform panel, click the Copy and Apply Transform button.

To rotate an element interactively:

1. Select the element you want to rotate.

2. In the Toolbox, select the free-transform tool; then click the Rotate and Skew modifier (**Figure 3.66**).

   Solid square handles appear on all four sides and at the corners of the element's bounding box.

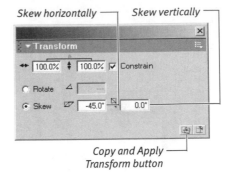

Skew horizontally — Skew vertically —

Copy and Apply — Transform button

Figure 3.65 Use the Transform panel to skew selected elements. You can set separate values for horizontal and vertical skewing.

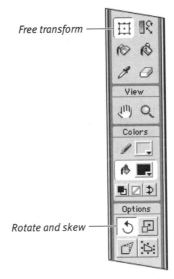

Free transform —

Rotate and skew —

Figure 3.66 Select the free-transform tool's Rotate and Skew modifier to access handles for rotating or skewing a selected element interactively.

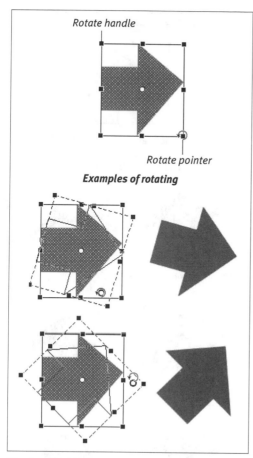

Rotate handle

Rotate pointer

Examples of rotating

Figure 3.67 With the free-transform tool's Rotate and Skew modifier selected, you can drag one of the corner handles of a selected element's bounding box to rotate that element.

3. Position the pointer over one of the corner handles.

The pointer changes to a circular arrow. Drag clockwise to rotate the element clockwise; drag counterclockwise to rotate the element counterclockwise. Flash spins the element around its center point, previewing the rotation as you drag (**Figure 3.67**).

4. Release the mouse button.

Flash redraws the rotated element.

✔ Tips

- You can rotate an element around one of its corners instead of its center point by pressing Option (Mac) or Alt (Windows) while dragging. The handle diagonally across from the one you are manipulating becomes the point of rotation.

- You don't have to choose the Scale modifier or the Rotate and Skew modifier to make those manipulations. You can just select an object with the free-transform tool and watch carefully as you move the pointer near the handles. If you pause directly on top of a corner handle, the icon changes to the double-headed arrow that allows you to scale the object. Move the pointer slightly away from the corner handle, and the icon changes to the rotation arrow. Now you can click and drag to rotate the object.

REORIENTING GRAPHIC ELEMENTS

To skew an element interactively:

1. With the free-transform tool selected in the Toolbox and its modifier set to Rotate and Skew, select the element you want to skew.

2. Position the pointer over one of the side handles of the element's bounding box.

   The pointer changes to a two-way arrowhead indicating that the element will skew as you drag that handle.

3. Click and drag the side handle in the direction you want to skew the element.

   Flash previews the skewing as you drag (**Figure 3.68**).

4. Release the mouse button.

   Flash redraws the skewed element.

✔ Tip

■ The Rotate and Skew modifier creates a constrained skew. You can drag only in a straight line along the edge of the selected element. You can create a freeform skew by using the Distort modifier, which you'll learn about later in this chapter.

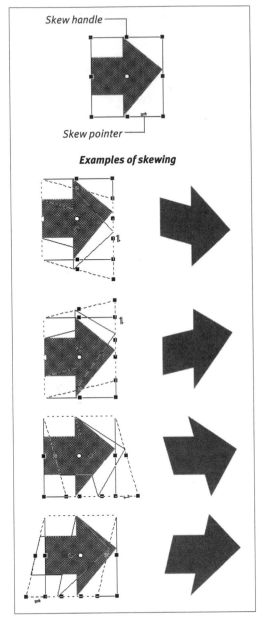

Skew handle

Skew pointer

Examples of skewing

Figure 3.68 To skew a selected element with the free-transform tool, choose the Rotate and Skew modifier; then drag one of the side handles of the element's bounding box.

Free transform

View

Colors

Options

Distort

Figure 3.69 Choose the free-transform tool's Distort modifier to reposition the corner points of your selection independently.

Distorting Graphic Elements

The free-transform tool allows you to distort a graphic element by changing the shape of its bounding box. You can reposition one or more corners of the box individually; you can manipulate paired corner handles simultaneously to turn the rectangular box into a trapezoid; and you can stretch, shrink, and/or skew the box by moving the side handles of the bounding box. The selected element(s) stretch or shrink to fit the new bounding box. Distortion works only on raw shapes, not on grouped elements or symbols, which you'll learn about in chapters 4 and 6.

To distort an element freely:

1. Using the free-transform tool, select the element you want to distort.

   A bounding box with transformational handles appears.

2. In the Toolbox, select the Distort modifier (**Figure 3.69**).

(continues on next page)

Distorted Perspective

As beginning art students discover, it's not too hard to add depth to objects made up of rectangular shapes. You simply adjust the appropriate edges to align with imaginary "parallel" lines that converge at a distant point on the horizon—the vanishing point. This creates the illusion that the objects recede into the distance. Adding perspective to nonrectangular shapes takes a bit more experience and the ability to imagine the way that those shapes should look. The Distort modifier of Flash's free-transform tool helps you because it encloses your selected shape—circle, oval, or squiggle—within a rectangular bounding box. All you need to do is adjust that box as you would a rectangular shape.

Beginning art students learn about 1-point, 2-point, and 3-point perspective. The "points" here refer to the vanishing point—the spot in the distance where parallel lines seem to converge. By selecting elements in your artwork carefully, and by using the distort tools to make the edges of the bounding box seem to line up with those "converging" lines, you can add perspective to objects even if they do not contain the parallel lines that would make it easy for you to fake the depth perception you want.

Note that the center point of your selection disappears, indicating that you are in Distort mode.

3. Position the pointer over one of the transformational handles.

The pointer changes to a hollow arrowhead.

4. To change the shape of the bounding box, *do one of the following:*

▲ To relocate one corner of the element's bounding box, position the pointer over one of the corner handles; then click and drag the handle to the desired location. You can position each of the four corner handles independently (**Figure 3.70**).

▲ To skew the element, position the pointer over one of the side handles; then drag the handle to the desired position. The element skews toward the direction you drag.

▲ To stretch the element as you skew it, move the selected side handle away from the element's center (**Figure 3.71**).

▲ To shrink the element as you skew it, move the selected side handle toward the element's center.

5. Release the mouse button.

Flash redraws the selection to fill the new bounding-box shape.

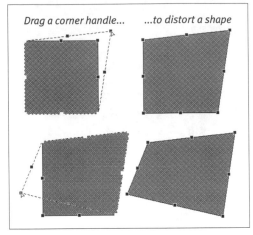

Figure 3.70 Use the free-transform tool's Distort modifier to redefine the shape of an element's bounding box. You can drag each corner handle separately.

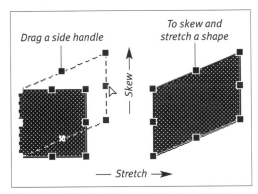

Figure 3.71 When the Distort modifier is selected, dragging the side handles of a selected element's bounding box skews the element. To enlarge (or shrink) the element at the same time, move the side handle away from (or in toward) the center of the original shape.

✔ Tips

■ You can use the free-transform tool to distort multiple graphic elements. Select the elements you want to modify. Then, using the Distort modifier of the free-transform tool, redefine the shape of the bounding box that surrounds the set of elements. The elements change as a unit.

■ If you want to make multiple changes to distort an element, such as repositioning all the corner handles, you should make those changes one after another without deselecting the element. When you deselect the element, the transformational bounding box that you created disappears. If you select the element again, you get a new, rectangular bounding box that encompasses the distorted shape. If this happens when you don't intend it, choose Edit > Undo to restore your selection with the modified bounding box; then select the Distort modifier again and continue your changes.

To distort graphic elements symmetrically:

1. Follow steps 1 and 2 of the preceding exercise to prepare an element for distorting.

2. To taper the element, *do one of the following.*

   ▲ To make the top of the bounding box narrower than the other sides, Shift-click and drag the top-right corner handle toward the top-left corner handle, or vice versa (**Figure 3.72**).

   ▲ To make the top of the bounding box wider than the other sides, Shift-click and drag the top-right corner handle away from the top-left corner handle, or vice versa.

   As you drag, the two corner handles move in tandem, coming together if you drag in or moving apart if you drag out.

3. Release the mouse button.

   Flash redraws the bounding box and its contents. If you dragged in, the box appears to taper toward the top. If you dragged out, the box appears to taper toward the bottom. You can follow these procedures for the sides or bottom of the bounding box, thereby tapering the box in any direction.

✔ Tip

■ To access the Free Transform tool's hollow-arrowhead pointer temporarily without selecting the Distort modifier, press ⌘ (Mac) or Ctrl (Win). Then you can drag or Shift-drag to distort selected elements.

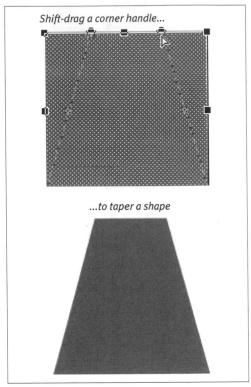

Shift-drag a corner handle...

...to taper a shape

Figure 3.72 Using the Distort modifier of the free-transform tool, Shift-click and drag a corner handle to taper selected elements.

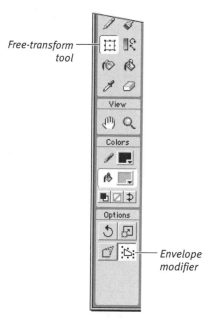

Free-transform tool

View

Colors

Options

Envelope modifier

Figure 3.73 The free transform tool's Envelope modifier allows you to reshape a selection by manipulating the Bézier curves that make up the selection's bounding box.

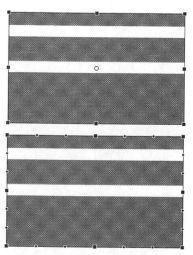

Figure 3.74 When you select multiple graphic elements with the free-transform tool, a single transformational bounding box surrounds all of them (top). Choosing the Envelope modifier hides the selection's center point and makes the box's Bézier handles available for manipulation (bottom).

Changing the Envelope of Selected Elements

Earlier in this chapter, you learned to use the subselection tool to manipulate the anchor points and Bézier curves that make up the path of a selected element. The free-transform tool's Envelope modifier lets you manipulate the anchor points and Bézier curves that make up the path of the transformational bounding box of a selection. That selection could be one element or several, but it must contain raw shapes. The Envelope modifier does not work with grouped elements or symbols, which you'll learn about in chapters 4 and 6

To reshape a selection's bounding box by using Bézier curves:

1. Using the free-transform tool, select the element(s) you want to transform.

   A bounding box with transformational handles appears.

2. In the Toolbox, select the Envelope modifier (**Figure 3.73**).

   The center point of your selection disappears, and anchor points with Bézier handles appear on the bounding box, indicating that you are in Envelope mode (**Figure 3.74**).

(continues on next page)

3. To reshape the bounding box, *do one of the following:*

▲ Position the pointer over a Bézier handle. The hollow-arrowhead pointer appears. Then click and drag the handle to redefine the curve (**Figure 3.75**).

▲ Position the pointer over an anchor point. The hollow-arrowhead pointer appears. Then click and drag the anchor point to a new location.

For more details about modifying Bézier curves, see "Reshaping Curves with the Subselection Tool" earlier in this chapter.

4. Release the mouse button.

Flash redraws the curves, and all the selected elements transform together.

✔ Tips

■ When you're manipulating Bézier handles, it's quite easy to deselect your selection accidentally. If you do, the transformational bounding box that you were working on disappears. If you select the elements again, you get a new, rectangular bounding box. To restore the bounding box that's in progress, choose Edit > Undo immediately. Then choose the free-transform tool's Envelope modifier to continue your changes.

■ If your selection consists of grouped elements or symbols, the Envelope modifier becomes inactive in the Toolbox, because Envelope doesn't work on groups or symbols. If your selection mixes raw shapes with groups or symbols, however, the Envelope modifier becomes available again. Selecting this modifier lets you see and manipulate a bounding box that includes the groups or symbols in your selection, but the changes you make have no effect on these items. The raw shapes are the only things that change.

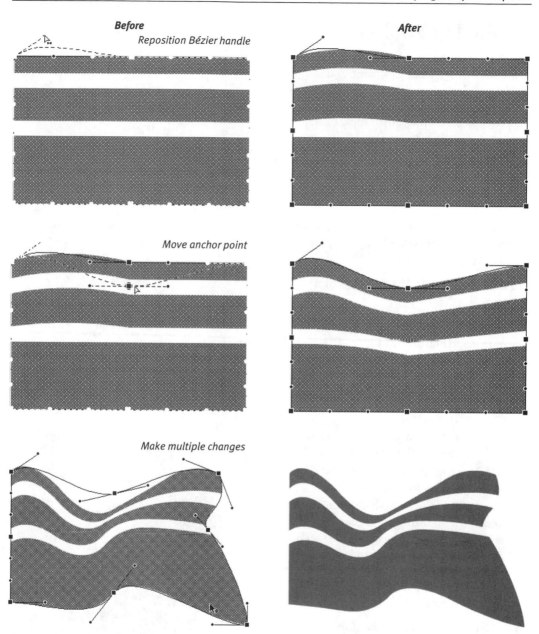

Before   **After**

Reposition Bézier handle

Move anchor point

Make multiple changes

Figure 3.75 You can use the free-transform tool in Envelope mode to reposition Bézier handles and move anchor points. All of the elements transform together.

Modifying Strokes

Flash provides two methods for modifying the stroke of an existing element: You can select the element and change its stroke attributes in the Property Inspector, or you can use the ink-bottle tool to apply the current stroke settings to unselected elements. Certain modifications, however, you can make only with the ink bottle. To add a stroke to an element that currently lacks one, for example, you must use the ink bottle.

For the following exercises, keep the Property Inspector open (choose Window > Property if it's not open).

To add a stroke to the outside of a shape:

1. In the Toolbox, select the ink-bottle tool or press S (**Figure 3.76**).

2. In the Property Inspector, *set any of the following attributes:*

   ▲ From the Stroke Style pop-up menu, choose a new style.

   ▲ In the stroke-height field, enter a value for the thickness of the stroke.

   ▲ Click the stroke-color box, and choose a new color from the swatch set.

   The stroke-color boxes in the Toolbox and Property Inspector display the selected color, and the ink-bottle tool is ready to apply the other stroke attributes you set in the Property Inspector. (For more details about setting stroke attributes, see Chapter 2.)

3. Move the pointer over the Stage.

   The pointer appears as a little ink bottle spilling ink.

Figure 3.76 The ink-bottle tool applies all the stroke attributes currently set in the Ink Bottle Property Inspector.

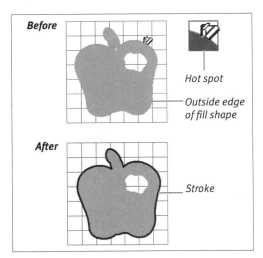

Figure 3.77 As you move the ink bottle over a filled shape, the hot spot appears as a white dot at the end of the ink drip that's spilling out of the bottle. To add a stroke around the outside edge of your fill shape, position the hot spot along that edge (top) and then click. Flash adds a stroke with the current attributes set in the Ink Bottle Property Inspector (bottom).

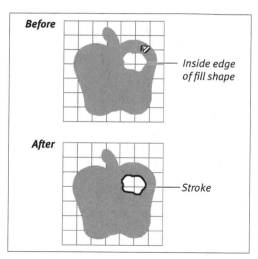

Figure 3.78 Position the ink bottle's hot spot along the inside edge of your fill shape (top) and then click. Flash uses the current line attributes set in the Toolbox or Property Inspector to outline the hole in your shape (bottom).

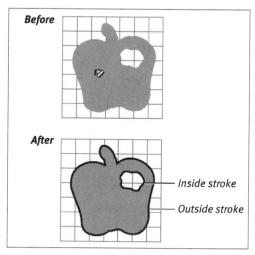

Figure 3.79 Position the ink bottle's hot spot in the middle of your fill shape (top) and then click. Flash uses the current stroke attributes to add a stroke around the outside and inside of your shape (bottom).

4. With the ink bottle's hot spot, click the outside edge of the shape (**Figure 3.77**).

Flash adds a stroke around your shape, using the color, thickness, and style settings from the Property Inspector. Note that you must click near the outside edge to add the stroke to the shape's outside.

When a shape has a hole in it, you can outline the shape of the hole.

To add a stroke to the inside of a shape:

1. Follow steps 1 through 3 of the preceding exercise.

2. With the ink bottle's hot spot, click near the inside edge of the shape.

Flash outlines the hole (the inside edge of the shape), using the current stroke settings. Be sure to click inside the shape but near the hole to outline the inside edge. (**Figure 3.78**).

✔ Tip

■ Sometimes, you want to outline both the outside of a shape and the hole inside the shape. The ink-bottle tool does both simultaneously when you click the ink bottle's hot spot in the middle of the shape (**Figure 3.79**).

To modify existing strokes with the ink bottle:

1. In the Toolbox, select the ink-bottle tool.

2. In the Property Inspector, set the attributes for color, stroke height, and stroke style.

3. Click the ink bottle's hot spot on the stroke you want to modify.

   When you click a stroke directly to modify it, the stroke can be selected or deselected.

✔ Tips

- If you leave an element fully deselected, or if you select the whole element (both fill and stroke), you won't need to position the ink bottle's hot spot so carefully. Clicking anywhere in the graphic element modifies its stroke. **Figure 3.80** shows the way that the ink bottle interacts with selections.

- To apply new attributes to the inside and outside strokes of a graphic element, click the middle of the shape with the ink bottle's hot spot.

- Remember that lines you've created with the straight-line tool and the pencil are also strokes. To change the attributes of an existing line, set the stroke attributes as described earlier in this section and then use the ink-bottle tool to click the line you want to modify. The line can be selected or deselected.

- You don't have to modify an entire stroke. You can select just a piece of a stroke and use the ink bottle to apply changes to just that piece.

- You can modify multiple strokes at the same time. Select all the strokes you want to change; then click any selected stroke with the ink bottle to modify them all in one fell swoop.

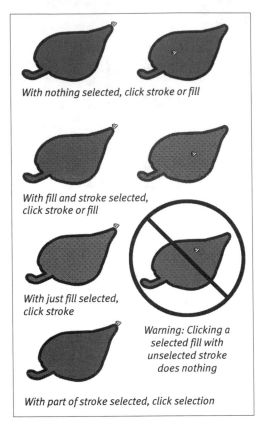

With nothing selected, click stroke or fill

With fill and stroke selected, click stroke or fill

With just fill selected, click stroke

Warning: Clicking a selected fill with unselected stroke does nothing

With part of stroke selected, click selection

Figure 3.80 You don't have to select a stroke to change its attributes; just click the stroke or the unselected fill with the ink bottle. Warning: If you have the fill selected, you must click the stroke itself; you can't click the selected fill to change an unselected stroke.

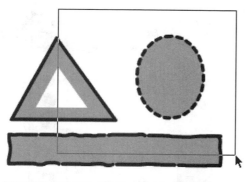

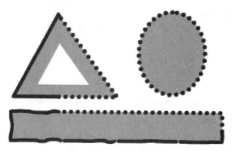

Figure 3.81 Select one or more strokes for modification (top). Set new attributes in the Property Inspector (middle). Flash applies the attributes to all the strokes in your selection (bottom).

To modify selected strokes by using the Property Inspector:

1. Using the arrow tool, select one or more strokes on the Stage.

2. Set the attributes for color, stroke height, and stroke style in the Property Inspector.

   Flash changes all selected strokes as you enter each new attribute in the Property Inspector (**Figure 3.81**).

✔ Tips

- When a line is selected, it can be difficult to see certain line styles. The stipple and hatched styles, for example, are obscured by the selection highlighting. If you apply a new line style, but the line seems not to change, deselect it to see the new style in place. Or choose View > Hide Edges. Just don't forget to turn the feature off later; otherwise, you won't be able to see any selections.

- You cannot modify the stroke attributes of a selected path (one selected with the subselection tool). You can, however, modify the stroke attributes of selections created with any other selection methods.

- You can modify the color of a selected stroke without using the ink bottle or opening the Property Inspector. Click the stroke-color box in the Toolbox, and choose a new color. Any selected strokes update to the new color.

Using the Eraser Tool in Normal Mode

The eraser tool has five modes that interact with fills and strokes in a variety of ways. This chapter describes using the eraser in Normal mode; the other modes will become more important when you handle complex graphics with multiple elements (see Chapter 4).

In Normal mode, the eraser acts pretty much as you'd expect. When you click and drag it over the Stage, the tool removes any line or fill in its path.

To erase all strokes and fills (Erase Normal):

1. In the Toolbox, select the eraser tool, or press E (**Figure 3.82**).

   The eraser modifiers appear in the Options portion of the Toolbox.

2. From the Eraser Mode pop-up menu, choose Erase Normal.

   A check appears by that mode in the menu, and the Erase Normal icon appears in the Toolbox.

3. From the Eraser Shape pop-up menu, choose a size and shape for the eraser.

   The icon for the selected eraser shape appears in the Toolbox.

4. Move the pointer over the Stage.

   The pointer has the size and shape you selected.

5. Click and drag, or scrub back and forth as you would with an ordinary eraser (**Figure 3.83**).

   Flash removes all the lines and fills you erase.

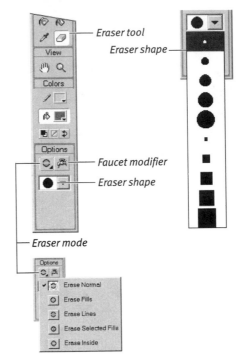

Figure 3.82 Use the eraser tool and its modifiers to remove all or part of strokes and fills.

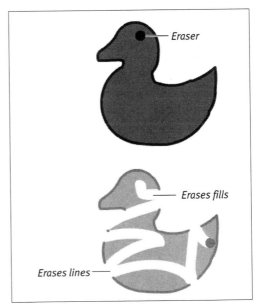

Figure 3.83 Click and drag with the eraser tool in Erase Normal mode to erase all lines and fills.

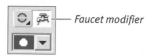

Faucet modifier

Figure 3.84 The eraser tool's Faucet modifier lets you erase entire lines or fills with a single click.

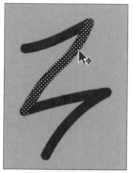

Figure 3.85 This squiggly line contains multiple curve segments, as the selections indicate (top). You can delete the whole line by using the eraser tool's faucet modifier. Click the hot spot of the water drip anywhere on the deselected line (middle); Flash deletes the entire line (bottom).

Using the Faucet Modifier

To speed the erasing of lines and fills, Flash provides the faucet modifier for the eraser tool. The faucet erases an entire fill shape or an entire line with a single click.

To erase a line:

1. In the Toolbox, with the eraser tool selected, click the Faucet modifier (**Figure 3.84**).

   The pointer changes to a dripping-faucet icon.

2. Place the faucet's hot spot (the drop of water) over the line you want to remove (**Figure 3.85**).

   The line should not be selected.

3. Click.

   Flash deletes the entire line, even if it's made up of several line segments.

To erase a fill:

1. Select the eraser tool's Faucet modifier.

2. Place the faucet's hot spot over the fill you want to remove.

3. Click.

   Flash deletes the fill.

✔ Tip

■ In the Toolbox, double-click the eraser tool to delete the entire contents of the Stage.

Modifying Fill Colors

Flash provides two methods for modifying the color of an existing fill. You can use the paint-bucket tool to apply the current fill settings to an unselected fill shape, or you can select the fill shape on the Stage and then choose a new fill color via the fill-color box in the Color Mixer panel, the Toolbox, or the Property Inspector.

To change fill color with the paint-bucket tool and Color Mixer panel:

1. In the Toolbox, select the paint-bucket tool, or press K.

   Modifiers for fills appear in the Options section of the Toolbox (**Figure 3.86**).

2. In the Color Mixer panel, *set the following attributes:*

   ▲ From the Fill Style menu, choose Solid.

   ▲ Click the fill-color box, and choose a new color from the swatch set.

   The fill-color boxes in both the Color Mixer and the Toolbox display the selected color, and the paint bucket is ready to apply the new fill color.

3. Click the paint bucket's hot spot (the tip of the drip of paint) somewhere inside the fill you want to change.

   The shape fills with the new color (**Figure 3.87**).

✔ Tip

■ When you click the fill-color box once, the currently loaded set of color swatches pops up, and you can choose one with the eyedropper tool. If you click the fill-color box and hold the mouse button down, you can move the eyedropper anywhere over your desktop, within Flash or outside it, to pick up a color. You could use this method to match colors with artwork you're creating in another graphics program.

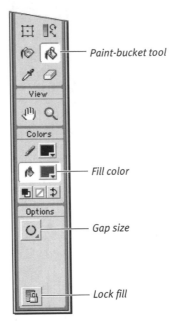

Figure 3.86 The paint-bucket tool lets you modify fills without first selecting them.

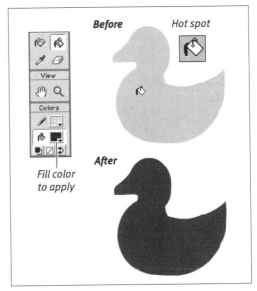

Figure 3.87 Clicking a fill with the paint bucket applies whatever color is selected in the fill-color box. Use this technique to change existing unselected fills.

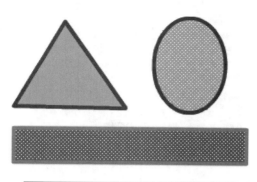

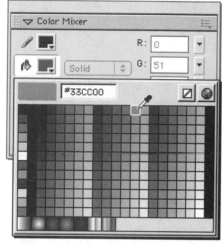

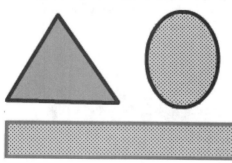

Figure 3.88 Select one or more fills for modification (top). Choose a new color from the Color Mixer panel's fill-color box (middle). Flash changes the color of all the fills in your selection (bottom).

To modify selected fills with the Color Mixer panel:

1. Using the arrow tool, select one or more fills on the Stage.

2. In the Color Mixer panel, click the fill-color box, and choose a new color from the swatch set.

Flash changes all selected fills to whatever color you chose in the Color Mixer panel (**Figure 3.88**).

✔ Tips

■ The Color Mixer panel is not the only place where you can choose a new fill color. For either of the preceding methods of applying new colors to fill shapes, you can choose a new color from the fill-color box in the Toolbox or the Property Inspector. If the fill-color icon in any of these areas is selected, you can simply choose a new color from the Color Swatches panel.

■ Note that changes made with the methods described in this section have no effect on selected strokes. You can safely include strokes in your selection even if you don't want to change them.

Creating Solid Colors: Color Mixer Panel

You can define new solid colors for fills and strokes in the Color Mixer panel. You can do so visually (by clicking a graphic representation of a color space—all the available colors in a given color-definition system) or numerically (by entering specific values for color components). Always choose the type of color—fill or stroke—before you start defining. Flash updates all the related color boxes with the new color. If you define a new fill color, for example, that color becomes the setting for all the tools that use fills. You can also set a color's transparency in the Color Mixer panel.

To access the Color Mixer panel:

◆ If the Color Mixer panel is not open, from the Window menu, choose Color Mixer (**Figure 3.89**) or press Shift-F9.

The Color Mixer panel appears.

To access solid-color attributes in the Color Mixer panel:

1. Open the Color Mixer panel.

2. From the Fill Style menu, choose Solid.

3. To choose a color space, from the panel's Options menu, *do one of the following:*

   ▲ To define colors as mixtures of red, green, and blue, choose RGB.

   ▲ To define colors by percentage of hue, saturation, and brightness, choose HSB (**Figure 3.90**).

4. To determine where Flash applies the new color, *do one of the following:*

   ▲ To sct a new stroke color, click the pencil icon.

   ▲ To set a new fill color, click the paint-bucket icon.

Figure 3.89 To access the Color Mixer panel, choose Window > Color Mixer.

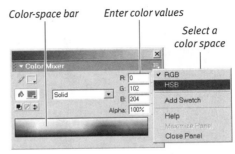

Figure 3.90 The Color Mixer panel lets you choose a color from the color-space bar or enter values directly to define a color in the RGB or HSB color space.

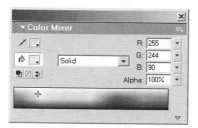

Figure 3.91 Click the color-space bar to choose a new color visually.

To define a new color visually in the Color Mixer panel:

1. With the Color Mixer panel open, choose a color space.

2. Position the pointer over the desired hue in the color-space bar.

3. Click.

The crosshair cursor appears, and Flash selects the color within the crosshairs (**Figure 3.91**).

✔ Tips

■ If you fail to click exactly the right color, keep holding down the mouse button and dragging around within the color bar. When the color you want appears in the color box, release the mouse button. Flash enters the values for that color in the appropriate fields.

■ Even if you have set your monitor resolution to 640 by 480, that color-space bar is awfully tiny. Click the small triangle near the bottom-right corner of the panel to expand the panel. The expanded panel contains a larger Color Picker, a color-preview window that compares the original color with the new color, a luminosity/lightness slider, and a text field for entering the precise hex value of a color.

■ You can access a variety of Color Pickers from any color box (see "Creating Solid Colors: Color Picker" later in this chapter).

■ To match the color of something outside Flash, such as a color from an image file that's open on your desktop, pick up the color with the color box's eyedropper. In the Color Mixer, click the fill- or stroke-color box, and hold down the mouse button. Then position the eyedropper over the area that shows the color you want. Release the mouse button. Specs for that color appear in the Color Mixer panel.

To define a new color numerically in the Color Mixer panel:

1. With the Color Mixer panel open, choose a color space.

2. To define a new color, *do one of the following*:

   ▲ For RGB colors, enter values for red, green, and blue in the R, G, and B fields (**Figure 3.92**).

   ▲ For HSB, enter values for hue, saturation, and brightness in the H, S, and B fields.

To define a color's transparency:

1. With the Color Mixer panel open, define a color.

2. Enter a value in the Alpha field (**Figure 3.93**).

   A percentage of 100 results in a completely solid color; a percentage of 0 results in a completely transparent color.

Figure 3.92 Enter RGB values to specify the amount of red, green, and blue that make up the color. Enter HSB values to specify the color by hue, saturation, and brightness. The new color appears in the selected color box.

Figure 3.93 Enter an Alpha value of less than 100 percent to define a transparent color.

What Are Hex Colors?

The term *hex color* is short for *hexadecimal color*, which is a fancy way of saying "a color defined by a number written in base 16." Hexadecimal coding is the language of bits and bytes that computers speak; it's also the coding you use to specify color in HTML.

If you remember studying bases in high-school math, you'll recall that the decimal system is base 10, represented by the numbers 0 through 9. In hex color, to get the extra six digits, you continue coding with letters A through F.

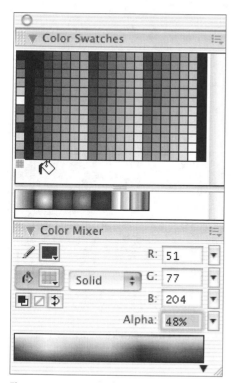

Figure 3.94 Positioning the pointer over the gray area in the Color Swatches panel lets you access the paint-bucket tool. Click the gray area to add a swatch for whatever color is currently defined in the Color Mixer panel.

After you define a new color, you may want to add it to the Color Swatches panel so that you can use it again. (For more information about the Color Swatches panel, see "Creating Color Sets" later in this chapter.)

To add a color to the Color Swatches panel:

1. Use any of the techniques described earlier in this section to define a new color in the Color Mixer panel.

2. From the Color Mixer panel's Options menu, choose Add Swatch.

   Flash appends the new color to the solid-colors section of the Color Swatches panel.

✔ Tips

- You can add new colors to the Color Swatches panel even if it is closed. But if you want to get the feedback when you add a swatch, open the Color Swatches panel in its own window. Resize the panel so that a bit of gray space appears below the existing swatches. You'll see the new swatch come in.

- If the Color Swatches panel is open, you can add your newly defined color with a single click. Position the pointer over the gray area at the bottom of the set of swatches in the Color Swatches panel. The pointer changes to the paint-bucket tool. Click anywhere in the gray area, and Flash adds the new color swatch (**Figure 3.94**).

Creating Solid Colors: Color Picker

In addition to creating colors in the Color Mixer panel, you can create colors in the Color Picker window (Mac) or Color window (Windows). In the Macintosh operating systems, this window offers a variety of Color Pickers. In Mac OS 9, you can choose among CMYK, Crayon (a set of swatches that look like crayons), HLS (hue, lightness, and saturation), HSV (hue, saturation, and value), HTML, and RGB. OS X offers CMYK, Crayon, HSV, Name (a set of swatches keyed to hex colors), and RGB.

To access the Color Picker:

1. In the Toolbox or Color Mixer panel, click the fill-color or stroke-color box.

   A set of color swatches pops up.

2. Click the Color Picker button (**Figure 3.95**).

   The Color Picker (Mac) or Color (Windows) window appears (**Figure 3.96**).

✔ Tip

■ If you open a color box and can't seem to find the Color Picker button, keep this tip in mind: The fill- and stroke-color boxes in the Toolbox and in the Color Mixer panel provide access to the Color Picker window, but the fill- and stroke-color boxes that appear in the Property Inspector do not.

Click to access Color Picker (Mac) or Color (Windows) window

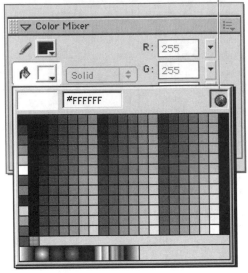

Figure 3.95 The Color Picker button appears in most of the swatch sets that you access via the fill- or stroke-color box.

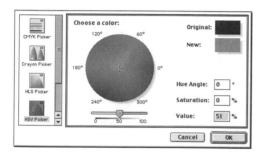

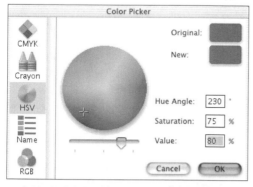

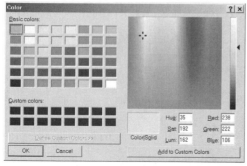

Figure 3.96 Mac OS 9's Color Picker window (top) offers six Color Pickers. Mac OS X's offers five (middle). Each picker has a set of sliders and value boxes or visual representations of the color space. In Windows, you define a color by entering HLS and RGB values or selecting colors from the color-space window in the Color window (bottom).

To define a new fill color with the HSV Picker (Mac):

1. Access the Color Picker from a fill-color box.

2. From the scrolling list on the left side of the window, choose HSV Picker.

   The main portion of the window displays a circular representation of the HSV color space, as well as the appropriate sliders and fields.

3. To set a new value, *do one of the following:*

   ▲ Drag the Value slider to a percentage larger than 0.

   ▲ Enter a number greater than 0 in the Value field.

4. To define the new color, *do one of the following:*

   ▲ Enter new values in the Hue Angle, Saturation, and Value fields.

   ▲ Click and drag the crosshair cursor in the color space.

5. Click OK.

   Flash updates the fill-color box in the Toolbox and relevant panels.

✔ Tip

■ The color that is current in the fill-color box is the color that appears in the Color Picker (Mac) or Color (Windows) window that you open. If that fill-color box is set to black, the color space or color preview will appear as solid black. To see hues in the window, you must change the appropriate setting

In the HSV Picker (Mac), for example, you must change the Value setting. In the Color window (Windows), you must change the Luminosity setting. A similar problem occurs in the Color window (Windows) if white is the selected color when you access the Color window.

CREATING SOLID COLORS: COLOR PICKER

147

To define a new fill color in the Color window (Windows):

1. Access the Color window from a fill-color box.

2. To set luminosity, *do one of the following:*

   ▲ Drag the luminosity slider at the right side of the color-space window to the desired luminosity.

   ▲ Enter a value in the Lum field.

3. To define a new color, *do one of the following:*

   ▲ To define a new color numerically, in the Hue and Saturation (or Red, Green, and Blue) fields, enter the values for your new color.

   ▲ To define a new color visually, click the color-space window. The crosshair cursor moves to the spot you clicked, and Flash updates the color values in the HLS and RGB fields.

4. Click OK.

   Flash updates the fill-color box in the Toolbox and relevant panels..

CREATING SOLID COLORS: COLOR PICKER

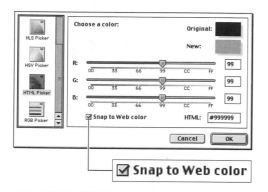

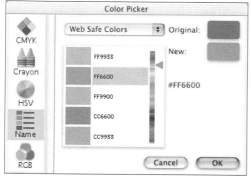

✔ Tip

- You can ensure that your new color is safe for Web use. In Mac OS 9, define the color by using the HTML Picker in the Color Picker window. Check Snap to Web Color. Flash finds the nearest match for your color from the 216 Web-safe colors (**Figure 3.97**). In Mac OS X, choose the Name Color Picker in the Color Picker window. You get a scrolling list of Web-safe swatches. In Windows, set your monitor to display 256 colors. The Color window then displays the current color in a split window; half of the window shows a dithered swatch, and the other half shows a solid swatch. Double-click the solid swatch to force Flash to make the color solid—in other words, Web-safe.

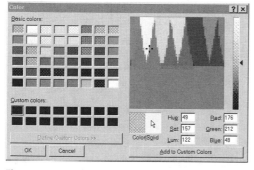

Figure 3.97 In Mac OS 9, define a new Web-safe color by using the HTML Picker in the Color Picker window (top). When Snap to Web Color is checked, Flash restricts the sliders to creating Web-safe combinations. In Mac OS X, use the Name color picker; all the choices are Web safe (middle). In Windows, define Web-safe colors in the Color window (bottom). Double-clicking the Solid area of the current-color swatch forces the crosshair to the nearest color that can be represented without dithering.

Creating New Gradients

In addition to solid colors, Flash works with *gradients*—bands of color that blend into each other. Gradients can be linear (parallel bars of color) or radial (concentric rings of color). Gradients can create interesting visual effects and are useful for adding shading—to make a circle look like a sphere, for example.

Flash defines each gradient with a set of markers, called *gradient pointers*, that indicate which color goes where in the lineup of color bands. You define the color for each pointer. By positioning the pointers on the gradient-definition bar, you control how wide each band of color is. Each gradient can contain as many as eight colors.

You define new gradients in the Color Mixer panel.

To create a three-color linear gradient:

1. Open the Color Mixer panel.

2. From the Color Mixer panel's Fill Style menu, choose Linear.

    The tools for defining gradients—a color-proxy box (a set of swatches for setting a gradient pointer's color) and a gradient-definition bar—appear (**Figure 3.98**).

3. Click the triangle in the bottom-right corner of the panel.

    The HSL Color Picker and gradient-preview window appear (**Figure 3.99**).

4. Position the pointer on or below the gradient-definition bar.

    Flash adds a plus sign to the pointer, indicating that you can add a new gradient pointer in this area.

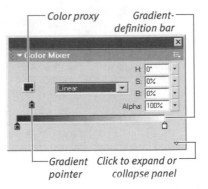

Figure 3.98 Choose Linear from the Fill Style menu to access the tools for defining linear gradients.

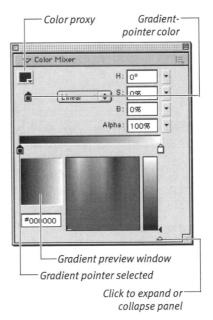

Figure 3.99 Expand the Color Mixer panel to access the gradient-preview window and HSL Color Picker.

Gradient starts with white and blends first to gray and then to black; black fills out the gradient

Move pointers in to increase width of outside bands

Click to add pointers

Figure 3.100 Choose a color for each gradient pointer. The colors and positions of the pointers on the bar define a gradient's color transitions.

5. To add a new pointer, click anywhere along the gradient-definition bar.

Flash adds a new gradient pointer containing the color currently specified in the Color Mixer.

6. To change the leftmost pointer's color, select it and then *do one of the following:*

▲ Click the color-proxy box in the top half of the Color Mixer panel, and choose a color from the set of swatches that appears.

▲ Enter new values in the Alpha and/or RGB or HSB fields.

▲ Choose a new color in the HSL Color Picker.

▲ Enter a new value in the Hex field.

7. Repeat step 6 for the middle and right-most pointers.

8. Drag the pointers to position them on the gradient-definition bar (**Figure 3.100**).

Place pointers closer together to make the transition between colors more abrupt; place them farther apart to spread the transition out over more space.

As you modify the gradient, your changes appear in the Toolbox's fill-color box. The new gradient also appears in the Property Inspector for any tools that create a fill—say, the oval tool. Those tools are now loaded and ready to create shapes using that gradient.

✔ Tips

- During each work session, the first time you define a gradient fill, the default two-color gradient appears in the Color Mixer panel: black on the left, blending to white on the right. You can add up to six additional colors.

- To reduce the number of colors in a gradient, with the gradient selected in the Color Mixer, drag one or more gradient pointers downward, away from the gradient-definition bar. The pointer disappears as you drag. The gradient changes to blend the colors in the remaining gradient pointers.

- When a gradient pointer is set to black, the Color Picker's Luminosity setting gets set to 0% (for white, Luminosity gets set to 100%). That setting means that the color-proxy window is going to show a solid black (or solid white) square even if you enter new RGB values or use the crosshair cursor to choose a new color. To change the color of a pointer that's set to black (or white), you must choose a new color from the color-proxy window's pop-up swatch set, reposition the Luminosity slider (on the right side of the Color Picker window), or enter a new Brightness value.

- To modify an existing gradient, choose it in the Color Swatches panel. Flash switches the Color Mixer panel to gradient mode and displays the selected gradient. Now you can make any changes you need.

- To reverse the direction of a gradient's color transition, drag one gradient pointer over another. In a white-to-black gradient (a white pointer on the left and a black pointer on the right), drag the white pointer to the right past the black one. Your gradient goes from black to white.

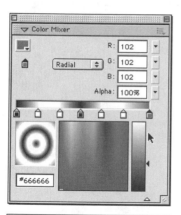

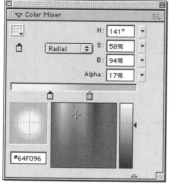

Figure 3.101 Choose Radial from the Fill Style menu to create a circular gradient. The preview window translates the horizontal gradient-definition bar into the appropriate circular color transitions.

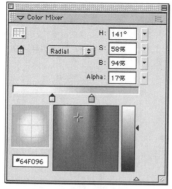

Figure 3.102 When transparent colors make up part of a gradient, grid lines appear in the gradient pointer, the color-proxy window, and the gradient-preview window.

To create a new radial gradient:

1. Open the Color Mixer panel.

2. From the Fill Style menu, choose Radial.

   The tools for defining circular gradients appear. The gradient-definition bar looks the same as it does for linear gradients, but the preview shows your gradient as a set of concentric circles (**Figure 3.101**). The leftmost pointer defines the inner ring; the rightmost pointer defines the outer ring.

3. Follow steps 4 through 8 of "To create a three-color linear gradient" earlier in this chapter to define the color transitions in the radial gradient.

✔ Tips

- Gradients can have transparency. You simply use a transparent color in one or more gradient pointers (see "To define a color's transparency" earlier in this chapter). If a gradient has transparency, a grid shows up in the gradient pointer, in the color-proxy box, and in the transparent part of the gradient in the preview window (**Figure 3.102**).

- Each pointer in a gradient can have a different alpha setting. To create fade effects, try creating a gradient that blends from a fully opaque color to a transparent one.

You can save a new gradient by adding it to the Color Swatches panel.

To add a gradient to the Color Swatches panel:

1. Create a new gradient, using any of the techniques outlined in the preceding sections.

2. In the Color Mixer panel, *do one of the following:*

   ▲ From the Options menu, choose Add Swatch.

   ▲ Position the pointer over the gray empty area of the Color Swatches panel, and when the paint-bucket tool appears, click.

   Flash adds the new gradient to the gradients section of the Color Swatches panel.

Click for Options menu

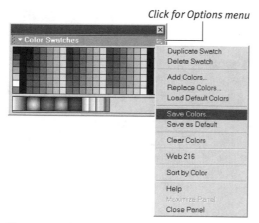

Figure 3.103 The Options menu in the Color Swatches panel offers commands for working with color sets.

Creating Color Sets

Flash stores a default set of colors and gradients in the system color file, but it stores the colors and gradients used in each document with that document. (In Flash 3 and earlier versions, all colors resided in the system color file.)

Flash lets you define what colors and gradients make up the default set. In addition, you can create and save other color sets and load them into the Color Swatches panel. This practice makes it easy to maintain a consistent color palette when you are creating several documents for use in a single movie or on a single Web site.

To access the Color Swatches panel:

◆ If the Color Swatches panel is not open, from the Window menu, choose Color Swatches or press Command-F9 (Mac) or Ctrl-F9 (Windows).

The Color Swatches panel appears.

To define a new set of colors:

1. Define all the colors and gradients you want to use in your special color set (see the "Creating Solid Colors" sections and "Creating New Gradients" earlier in this chapter).

You don't need to define all your colors at the same time, but after you have a set that you want to save, move on to step 2.

2. From the Color Swatches panel's Options menu, choose Save Colors (**Figure 3.103**).

(continues on next page)

The Export Color Swatch dialog box appears (**Figure 3.104**).

3. Navigate to the folder where you want to store your color set.

4. Enter a name for your color-set file in the Name field (Mac OS 9), Save As (OS X), or File Name field (Windows).

5. From the Format (Mac) or Save As Type (Windows) pop-up menu, *choose one of two formats:*

   ▲ To save colors and gradients in Flash's proprietary Flash Color Set (CLR) format, choose Flash Color Set.

   ▲ To save the colors in Color Table (ACT) format, choose Color Table.

   The ACT format saves only colors (not gradients) but allows you to share color sets with other programs, such as Adobe Photoshop and Macromedia Fireworks.

6. Click Save.

Mac OS 9

Mac OS X

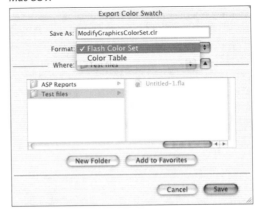

Windows

Figure 3.104 Use the Export Color Swatch dialog box to save a set of colors for reuse.

Mac OS 9

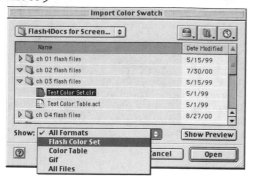

Mac OS X

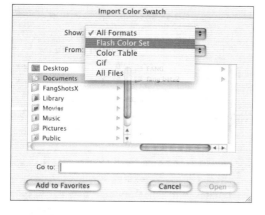

Windows

Figure 3.105 Use the Import Color Swatch dialog box to reload a saved set of colors.

To load a set of colors:

1. From the Options menu in the Color Swatches panel, *choose one of the following:*

   ▲ To add to the color set currently displayed in the Color Swatches panel, choose Add Colors.

   ▲ To replace the entire set currently displayed in the Color Swatches panel, choose Replace Colors.

   The Import Color Swatch dialog box appears (**Figure 3.105**).

2. To determine what types of files to display, from the Show pop-up menu (Mac) or Files of Type (Windows) pop-up menu, choose one of the following:

   ▲ All Formats, which displays CLR, ACT, and GIF files.

   ▲ Flash Color Set, which displays only CLR files.

   ▲ Color Table, which displays only ACT files.

   ▲ GIF, which displays only GIF files.

   ▲ All Files, which displays files of any format.

   Note that the Color Table and GIF formats are for color import only; these formats do not handle gradients. Flash Color Set handles both colors and gradients.

3. Navigate to the file you want to import.

4. Click Open.

CREATING COLOR SETS

To define the default set of colors:

1. From the Options menu in the Color Swatches panel, choose Save As Default. A warning dialog box appears, giving you the chance to cancel the operation at this point (**Figure 3.106**).

2. *Do one of the following:*
   ▲ To cancel the operation, click No.
   ▲ To go ahead and create the new default color set, click Yes.

✔ Tips

■ The Options menu in the Color Swatches panel also offers some handy shortcuts for dealing with color sets. To reload the default color set, choose Load Default Colors. To remove all color swatches from the current panel window, choose Clear Colors. To load the standard Web-safe colors, choose Web 216. To arrange colors by hue, choose Sort by Color. (Note that you cannot undo the color sorting. So be sure to save your current set of colors if there's any chance that you'll want to restore the unsorted order.)

■ To delete a swatch from the current set, in the Color Swatches panel, select the swatch; then, from the panel's Options menu, choose Delete Swatch.

■ To copy a swatch to modify it—to create a transparent version of the color, for example—in the Color Swatches panel, select the swatch. Then, from the panel's Options menu, choose Duplicate Swatch. Or you can position the pointer over the gray area below the swatch set. When the paint-bucket tool appears, click to add a copy of the selected swatch.

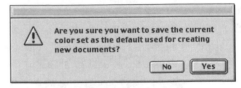

Figure 3.106 This warning dialog box gives you a chance to change your mind after you've chosen Save As Default from the Options menu in the Color Swatches panel. You can't undo this operation.

■ You can also use the Color Swatches panel to select colors for fills and strokes. The key is first to tell Flash where to apply the new color. You do that by clicking the stroke or fill icon in the Colors section of the Toolbox or in the Color Mixer panel (**Figure 3.107**). Then select a color in the Color Swatches panel. Flash puts that color in every fill-color or stroke-color box. In the Colors section of the Toolbox, for example, click the paint-bucket icon and then select blue in the Color Swatches panel. Blue now appears in the fill-color box in the Toolbox, in the Color Mixer panel, and in the Property Inspector.

■ If the swatches in the Color Swatches panel are too small for you, resize the panel. The swatches grow bigger as the window grows wider.

Original color

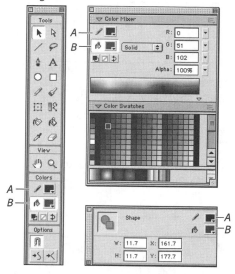

New color

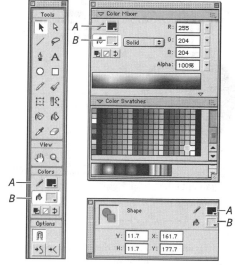

Figure 3.107 Click the stroke icon (A) or fill icon (B) in the Toolbox, Color Mixer panel, or Property Inspector to tell Flash what type of color you are assigning. Then you can select a color in the Color Swatches panel. Flash updates the appropriate color boxes throughout the program.

Putting Gradients to Work

In "Creating New Gradients" earlier in this chapter, you learned how to create color blends. Flash treats gradients just like any other fill. You use the paint-bucket tool to fill outline shapes with a gradient and the brush tool to create freeform swashes of gradient color.

To fill a shape (or replace a solid fill) with a linear gradient:

1. In the Toolbox, select the paint-bucket icon.

2. In the Color Mixer panel, define a new linear gradient.

   or

   From the Color Swatches panel or from the fill-color box in the Toolbox or Property Inspector, choose an existing linear gradient.

3. Click the paint bucket's hot spot (the tip of the drip of paint) somewhere inside the outline shape or within the existing fill (**Figure 3.108**).

   The shape fills with the linear gradient currently displayed in the fill-color boxes.

To fill a shape (or replace a solid fill) with a radial gradient:

1. In the Toolbox, select the paint-bucket tool.

2. In the Color Mixer panel, define a new radial gradient.

or

From the Color Swatches panel or from the fill-color box in the Toolbox or Property Inspector, choose an existing radial gradient.

3. Click the paint bucket's hot spot (the tip of the drip of paint) somewhere inside the outline shape or within the existing fill (**Figure 3.109**).

The shape fills with the radial gradient currently displayed in the fill-color boxes.

To paint with an unlocked gradient:

1. In the Toolbox, select the brush tool.

2. Make sure that the Lock Fill modifier is deselected (**Figure 3.110**).

3. Using one of the methods described in the preceding exercises, choose a gradient.

4. Paint with the brush as described in Chapter 2.

Flash cannot preview the shape you paint with the gradient you chose, as it can do with solid-color fills. The preview shape has a black-and-white pattern.

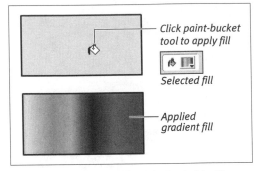

Click paint-bucket tool to apply fill

Selected fill

Applied gradient fill

Figure 3.108 You can use the paint-bucket tool to apply a linear-gradient fill.

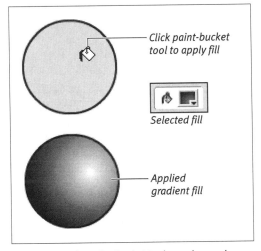

Click paint-bucket tool to apply fill

Selected fill

Applied gradient fill

Figure 3.109 The paint-bucket tool can also apply a radial-gradient fill.

 Figure 3.110 Deselect the Lock Fill modifier to paint with an unlocked gradient.

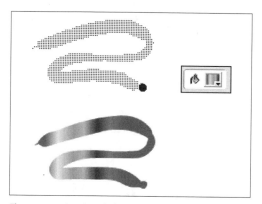

Figure 3.111 A painted shape with a linear-gradient fill.

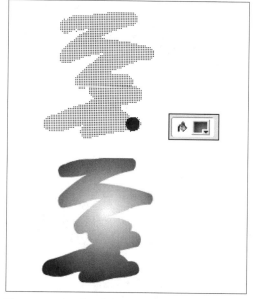

Figure 3.112 A painted shape with a radial-gradient fill.

5. When you finish your brush stroke, release the mouse button.

Flash redraws the painted shape, using the gradient currently selected in the fill-color box. Flash fills the shape's bounding box (an invisible rectangle that's just the right size to enclose the shape) with the gradient. The painted shape reveals portions of that gradient pattern (**Figures 3.111** and **3.112**).

✔ Tip

■ You can also create a single underlying gradient for several shapes on the Stage by using the Lock Fill modifier. With the paint-bucket tool selected, choose a gradient fill. Then click the Lock Fill modifier. Flash creates an underlying hidden rectangle—the same size as the Stage—filled with the locked gradient. Wherever you paint with the locked gradient by using the brush tool (or apply the locked fill to a shape by using the paint-bucket tool), Flash reveals that hidden gradient.

Gradients Add Overhead

Gradients are lovely, but they do increase file sizes and thereby slow the loading of published movies. Each area of gradient fill requires an extra 50 bytes of data that a solid fill doesn't need.

In addition, gradients take processsor power. If you use too many, you may see slower frame rates, or slower animations, in your finished movie.

PUTTING GRADIENTS TO WORK

Modifying Applied Gradients

You can use Flash's fill-transform tool to modify a gradient fill. You can rotate the fill or change its size and center point.

To move a gradient fill's center point:

1. In the Toolbox, select the fill-transform tool (**Figure 3.113**).

   The pointer changes to the fill-transform-pointer.

2. Position the pointer over the graphic element whose gradient you want to modify.

3. Click.

   Handles for manipulating the element appear (**Figure 3.114**).

4. Drag the center-point handle to reposition the center point of the gradient (**Figure 3.115**).

Figure 3.113 The fill-transform tool (left) and the pointer with which you manipulate gradients (right).

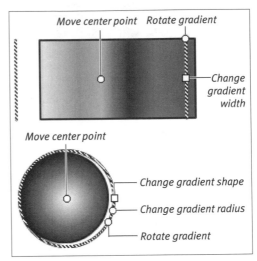

Figure 3.114 Handles for transforming fills appear when you click the fill with the fill transform pointer.

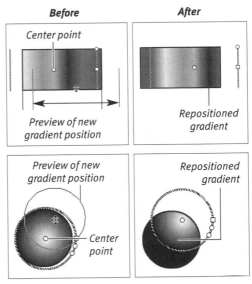

Figure 3.115 Drag the center-point handle to reposition the center of the gradient within your shape.

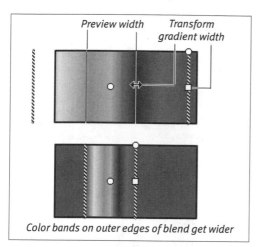

Figure 3.116 With a linear gradient selected, use the fill-transform tool to drag the square handle inward and create a narrower rectangle for a gradient.

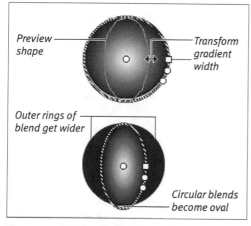

Figure 3.117 With a radial gradient selected, use the fill-transform tool to drag the square handle inward to create a narrower oval for a gradient.

To resize a gradient fill:

1. With the fill-transform tool selected in the Toolbox, click the graphic element that contains the gradient you want to modify.

2. To change the width of a linear gradient, drag the square handle (**Figure 3.116**).

   The pointer changes to a double-headed arrow. Dragging toward the center of your shape squeezes the blend into a narrower space; dragging away from the center of your shape spreads the blend over a wider space.

3. To change the shape of a radial gradient, drag the square handle (**Figure 3.117**).

   The pointer changes to a double-headed arrow. Dragging toward the center of your shape creates a narrower oval space for the blend; dragging away from the center of your shape creates a wider oval space.

   (continues on next page)

MODIFYING APPLIED GRADIENTS

4. To change the radius of a radial gradient, drag the circular handle next to the square handle (**Figure 3.118**).

The pointer changes to a double-headed arrow within a circle. Dragging toward the center of your shape squeezes the blend into a smaller circular space; dragging away from the center of your shape spreads the blend over a larger circular space.

To rotate a gradient fill:

1. With the fill-transform tool selected in the Toolbox, click the graphic element with the gradient you want to modify.

2. To rotate the gradient, *do one of the following:*

▲ To rotate a linear gradient, drag the round handle (**Figure 3.119**).

▲ To rotate a radial gradient, drag the round handle farthest from the square handle.

The pointer changes to a circular arrow. You can rotate the gradient clockwise or counterclockwise.

✔ Tips

■ You can click and drag with the paint-bucket tool to rotate the gradient as you apply it. To constrain the gradient angle to vertical, horizontal, or 45-degree angles, hold down the Shift key as you drag.

■ When you rotate a gradient interactively with the paint-bucket tool, the modified angle remains part of the selected fill even though the color-fill box continues to display the gradient in its vertical position. You can switch to the brush tool, for example, and paint with the rotated gradient. To remove the angle modification, use the paint-bucket tool to modify the gradient again or choose another fill.

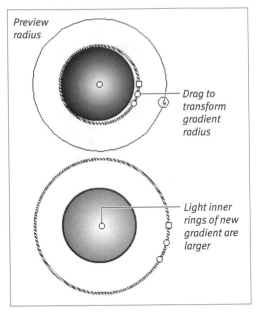

Figure 3.118 With a radial gradient, drag the first round handle outward to create a larger radius.

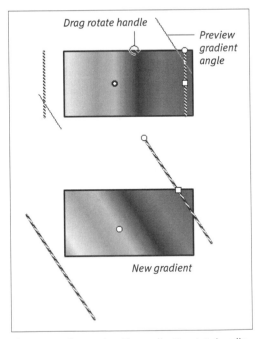

Figure 3.119 As you drag the gradient's rotate handle with the fill-transform tool, you spin the gradient around its center point.

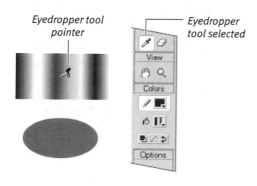

Eyedropper tool pointer

Eyedropper tool selected

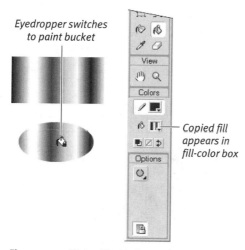

Eyedropper switches to paint bucket

Copied fill appears in fill-color box

Figure 3.120 Click a fill with the eyedropper tool to copy that fill. The paint bucket tool appears; it's loaded with the copied fill. Now click another graphic element to apply the fill.

Applying Attributes of One Graphic Element to Another

To save time, you can copy the fill and stroke attributes of one element and apply them to another element.

To copy fills between graphic elements:

1. In the Toolbox, select the eyedropper tool, or press I.

2. Move the pointer over the Stage.

   The pointer changes to an eyedropper.

3. Position the eyedropper over the fill you want to copy (either a solid color or gradient).

4. Click the fill (**Figure 3.120**).

   Flash switches to the paint-bucket tool automatically. The color or gradient you picked up appears in the fill-color box in the Toolbox and Property Inspector and in the gradient-preview window of the Color Mixer panel. (Clicking the eyedropper tool on a fill activates the paint bucket's locked gradient mode.)

5. Use the paint-bucket tool to apply the copied fill to a different graphic element (see "Modifying Fill Colors" earlier in this chapter).

APPLYING ATTRIBUTES OF GRAPHICS

To copy stroke attributes:

1. In the Toolbox, select the eyedropper tool.

2. Position the eyedropper pointer over a line or outline (stroke) whose attributes you want to copy.

3. Click the line (**Figure 3.121**).

   Flash switches to the ink-bottle tool. The color, stroke height, and style attributes of the line you clicked appear in the Ink Bottle Property Inspector.

   You can use the ink-bottle tool to apply the copied attributes to a different line (see "Modifying Strokes" earlier in this chapter).

✔ Tips

■ To pick up the color of a stroke or fill and use it for both strokes and fills, Shift-click with the eyedropper tool. Flash loads the selected color into the fill- and stroke-color boxes in the Toolbox, the Color Mixer panel, and the Property Inspectors relevant to the selected color.

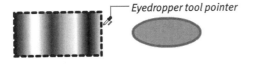

Eyedropper tool pointer

Eyedropper tool selected

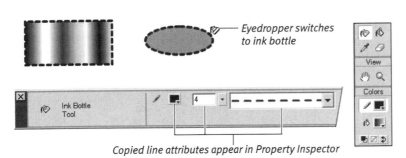

Eyedropper switches to ink bottle

Copied line attributes appear in Property Inspector

Figure 3.121 Clicking a line with the eyedropper tool copies the stroke attributes to the stroke-color box in the Tool-box, the Color Mixer panel, and the Ink Bottle Property Inspector. Use the ink-bottle tool to apply these settings to another line.

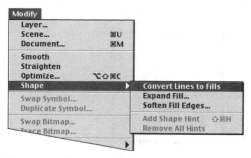

Figure 3.122 Choose Modify > Shape > Convert Lines to Fills to transform strokes into fills.

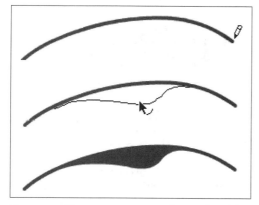

Figure 3.123 You can convert an outline, such as this line drawn with the pencil tool (top), to a fill. The fill then has its own editable outlines (middle and bottom).

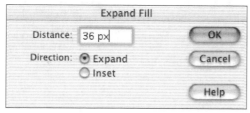

Figure 3.124 The Expand Fill dialog box presents options for resizing a selected fill.

Converting Lines to Fills

Flash lets you convert lines and outlines (strokes) to fills, which you can then edit or fill with gradients. You can expand or contract a shape by a user-specified amount. And you can create soft-edged graphic elements. These conversions increase the number of curves that Flash creates and therefore may increase file size.

To convert a line to a fill:

1. In the Toolbox, select the pencil tool.

2. Draw a simple line on the Stage.

3. Change to the arrow tool, and click the line to select it.

4. From the Modify menu, choose Shape > Convert Lines to Fills (**Figure 3.122**).

   Flash converts the line to a fill shape that looks exactly like the line. You can now edit the "line's" outline (or apply a gradient) as though you were working with a fill created with the brush tool (**Figure 3.123**).

To expand a fill:

1. In the Toolbox, select the oval tool with no stroke.

2. On the Stage, draw an oval shape.

3. Change to the arrow tool, and click the shape to select it.

4. From the Modify menu, choose Shape > Expand Fill.

   The Expand Fill dialog box appears (**Figure 3.124**).

(continues on next page)

5. Enter a value in the Distance field.

6. Choose a Direction option.

Expand makes the shape larger. Inset makes the shape smaller.

7. Click OK.

Flash blows the fill shape up like a balloon or shrinks it (**Figure 3.125**).

To soften the edges of a fill:

1. In the Toolbox, select the oval tool with no stroke.

2. On the Stage, draw an oval shape.

3. Change to the arrow tool, and click the shape to select it.

4. From the Modify menu, choose Shape > Soften Fill Edges.

The Soften Fill Edges dialog box appears (**Figure 3.126**).

5. Enter values for Distance and Number of Steps.

6. Choose a Direction option.

Expand makes the shape larger; Inset makes the shape smaller.

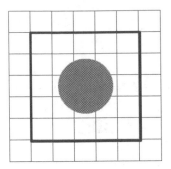

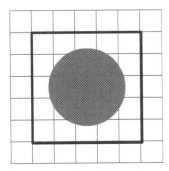

Figure 3.125 Using the Expand Fill command on the selected fill (top) causes its outlines to expand. The grid here is set to 36 pixels.

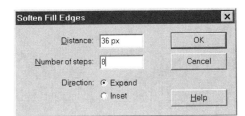

Figure 3.126 The Soften Fill Edges dialog box.

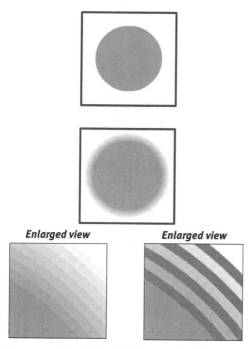

Enlarged view   **Enlarged view**

Figure 3.127 The Soften Fill Edges command creates a purposeful banding effect to give fill shapes a soft edge. The selected circle (top) gets a soft edge in eight steps (middle). Enlarged views show the banding more clearly (bottom left); you can select individual steps of the softened edge (bottom right).

7. Click OK.

Flash divides the expansion or inset value by the number of steps you specified and creates a series of concentric shapes that outline your original shape. The new shapes get progressively lighter in color as they approach the outer edge of the softened shape (**Figure 3.127**).

✔ Tips

■ The Expand Fill and Soften Fill Edges commands work best on plain fill shapes (fills without strokes). Small shapes and shapes with convoluted outlines take a longer time to convert, and the result may not be what you expect.

■ When you use the Modify > Shape commands on fills that also have strokes around them, the stroke doesn't expand or shrink to match the expansion or inset. Depending on how far you expand the fill, it will eat into—or cover—the stroke.

■ If you use one of the Modify > Shape commands to inset the fill of a stroked graphic, you wind up with a blank ring inside the stroke. This effect could be handy should you ever need to create a secondary outline for a shape, but it's usually not the effect you're looking for.

■ The multiple bands created by the Soften Fill Edges command will use processor power during playback. Used too often, the soft-edged effect will slow your final published movie's frame rate.

COMPLEX GRAPHICS ON A SINGLE LAYER

In chapters 2 and 3, you learned to make simple individual shapes from lines (strokes) and fills by using Macromedia Flash MX's drawing tools. You learned to make a single oval and a lone rectangle, for example. In your movies, you'll want to use many shapes together, and you'll need to combine strokes and fills in complex ways. You might combine several ovals and rectangles to create a robot character, for example. To work effectively with complex graphics, you need to understand how Flash shapes interact when they are on the same layer or on different layers. In this chapter, you learn how to work with multiple shapes on one layer. To learn more about the concept of layers, see Chapter 5.

Two of Flash's drawing tools—the brush tool and the eraser—offer special modes for use with multiple fills and strokes on a single layer. In this chapter, unless you are specifically requested to do otherwise, leave both tools at their default settings of Paint Normal (for the brush tool) and Erase Normal (for the eraser).

When Lines Intersect Lines

If you draw several lines on the same layer, they interact. Draw a new line across an existing one, and the new line cuts—or, in Flash terminology, *segments*—the old. Segmentation happens whether the lines are the same color or different colors, but it's easiest to see with contrasting colors.

To see how one line segments another:

1. In the Toolbox, choose the pencil tool.

2. In the Pencil Tool Property Inspector, *do the following*:
   ▲ Set the stroke style to Solid.
   ▲ Set the stroke height to 4 points.
   ▲ Set the color to blue.

3. On the Stage, draw a line.

4. Click the stroke-color box (in the Toolbox or in the Property Inspector), and from the pop-up swatch set, choose a new color, such as red.

5. On the Stage, draw a second line; make it intersect your first line at least once.

   Flash segments the line. To see the segments, select various parts of the line with the arrow tool (**Figure 4.1**).

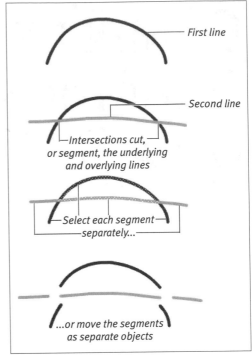

Figure 4.1 When you draw one line across another, every intersection creates a separate segment.

The Mystery of the Stacking Order for Strokes

When drawing one line on top of another, you might expect that the last line drawn would wind up on top, but sometimes, that's not the case. In this exercise about intersecting lines, for example, if you start with a red line and then draw a blue line across it, you'll see that the blue line jumps behind the red one when you release the mouse button.

Flash creates a stacking order for lines based on the hex-color value of the line's stroke-color setting. The higher the hex value of the stroke color, the higher the line sits in a stack of lines drawn on the Stage. A line whose stroke color is set to a hex value of 663399 always winds up on top of a stroke whose color is set to 333399.

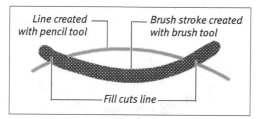

Line created with pencil tool — Brush stroke created with brush tool

Fill cuts line

Figure 4.2 When a fill overlays a line, the fill segments the line. As the selection highlighting shows, the fill remains one solid object.

When Lines and Fills Interact

Even the invisible outlines that describe painted brush-stroke fills can cut other lines. This means that when you draw lines over fills, you can wind up with lots of little segments.

To see how a fill segments a line:

1. In the Toolbox, choose the pencil tool.

2. In the Pencil Tool Property Inspector, *do the following:*
   ▲ Set the stroke style to Solid.
   ▲ Set the stroke height to 4 points.
   ▲ Set the color to blue.

3. On the Stage, draw a line.

4. Return to the Toolbox, and choose the brush tool.

5. Click the fill-color box (in the Toolbox or in the Brush Tool Property Inspector), and from the pop-up swatch set, choose red.

6. On the Stage, paint a brush stroke that intersects your line twice.
   The brush stroke remains one solid object, but the line turns into three separate segments (**Figure 4.2**).

To see how a line segments a fill:

1. In the Toolbox, choose the brush tool.

2. Click the fill-color box (in the Toolbox or the Brush Tool Property Inspector), and from the pop-up swatch set, choose red.

3. On the Stage, paint a brush stroke.

4. Return to the Toolbox, and choose the pencil tool.

5. In the Pencil Tool Property Inspector, *do the following:*

▲ Set the stroke style to Solid.

▲ Set the stroke height to 4 points.

▲ Set the color to blue.

6. On the Stage, draw a line that intersects your brush stroke twice.

The line cuts the brush stroke into three segments; the invisible outline of the brush stroke cuts the line into five separate segments (**Figure 4.3**).

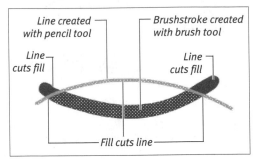

Figure 4.3 When a line overlays a fill, the line cuts the fill, and the fill's invisible outline cuts the line.

How Do Flash's Editable Objects Interact?

You can think of each frame in a Flash movie as being a stack of transparent acetate sheets. In Flash terms, each "sheet" is a layer. Objects on different layers have a depth relationship: Objects on higher layers block your view of those on lower layers, just as a drawing on the top sheet of acetate would obscure drawings on lower sheets.

Imagine that you have two layers in your movie. If you draw a little yellow square on the bottom layer and then switch to the top layer and draw a big red square directly over the yellow one, the little square remains intact. You simply can't see it while the big red square on the top layer is in the way.

On a single layer, however, objects actually interact with one another, almost as though you were painting with wet finger paint. When fills of different colors interact, the newer fill replaces the older one. Take the preceding example: First draw a little yellow square; then switch colors and draw a big red square right on top of the little one in the same layer. The little square disappears for good. The red fill replaces the yellow wherever it overlaps the latter.

If the new fill only intersects the old, it still replaces the part where the two overlap. Imagine, for example, using the brush tool to paint the first stroke of the letter *X*. Now pick up a different color to paint the second stroke of the *X*. Where the second brush stroke overlaps the first, it eats up that first fill color. You wind up with separate segments of the first stroke on either side of the second stroke where the two intersect.

When fills are the same color, the newer fill simply adds to the shape. If you lay down two brush strokes in the same color, the second slightly overlapping the first, the edges of the two brush strokes run together, and you wind up with one wide shape. If you paint both halves of the letter *X* with the same color, you wind up with a single *X*-shape object.

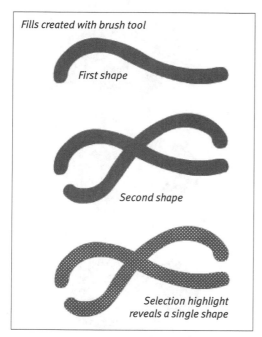

Fills created with brush tool

First shape

Second shape

*Selection highlight
reveals a single shape*

Figure 4.4 When you draw overlapping fills in the same color, Flash puts the two shapes together to create a single shape. (Compare this figure with the overlapping lines in Figure 4.1 that cut one another.)

When Shapes Interact

The interaction of one fill with another can have one of two results; the outcome depends on what color the two fills are. Fills of the same color simply run together and create a new shape. If the fills are different colors, the one you draw second replaces the first in any areas where the two overlap. You can use these interactions to create complex shapes from several simpler ones.

To add to a fill shape:

1. In the Toolbox, select the brush tool.

2. Click the fill-color box (in the Toolbox or in the Brush Tool Property Inspector), and from the pop-up swatch set, choose a color.

3. On the Stage, paint one brush stroke.

4. Using the same color, paint a separate brush stroke that intersects the first one.

   Flash adds the second brush stroke to the first, creating a single new fill shape (**Figure 4.4**).

To subtract one fill from another:

1. In the Toolbox, choose the oval tool.

2. In the Colors section of the Toolbox, click the pencil icon.

   The pencil icon is the stroke control; when it is selected, whatever colors you choose will apply to strokes.

3. Click the No Color button.

   Flash sets the stroke to none. The oval tool now draws a fill without an outline stroke.

4. Click the fill-color box (in the Toolbox or in the Oval Tool Property Inspector), and choose red from the pop-up swatch set.

5. On the Stage, draw a fairly large oval.

6. Back in the Toolbox or the Oval Tool Property Inspector, choose a different fill color for the oval tool.

7. On the Stage, draw a smaller oval in the middle of your first oval to create concentric ovals.

8. Switch to the arrow tool, and select the smaller oval.

As the highlighting indicates, fills of different colors are separate objects (**Figure 4.5**).

9. To delete your selection, press Backspace (Mac) or Delete (Windows).

Removing the smaller oval leaves a hole in the bigger oval, because the fill that overlaps the first fill replaces it (**Figure 4.6**).

✔ Tips

■ Interactions between lines and fills occur not only when you draw a shape, but also when you place a copy of a shape or move a shape. Be careful when placing live shapes and lines on a single layer. You can inadvertently add to or delete part of an underlying shape.

■ If you accidentally change a shape by drawing on top of it with another color, you can restore the original and keep the new shape, too. Select your top shape and press F8 to turn it into a symbol. (For more information on creating and using symbols, see Chapter 6.) Now press ⌘-Z (Mac) or Ctrl-Z (Windows) three times: once to undo the Convert to Symbol command, a second time to undo the selection, and a third time to remove the top shape and restore the bottom shape. Though you undid the conversion of the shape to a symbol, the symbol still lives in the Library. To get back your second shape, you must place an instance of the symbol on the Stage and break it apart (press ⌘-Option-B [Mac] or Ctrl-Alt-B [Windows]).

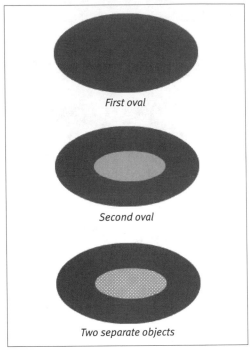

First oval

Second oval

Two separate objects

Figure 4.5 When one fill overlaps another of a different color, the fills don't meld but remain separate. The second oval here replaces the first where they overlap.

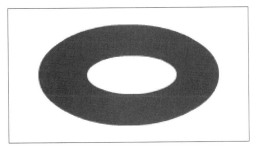

Figure 4.6 Because the smaller oval fill replaces the part of the big oval it covers, deleting the smaller oval leaves a hole in the big one.

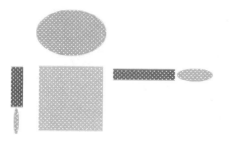

Figure 4.7 The first step in grouping is selecting the objects you want to use in the group.

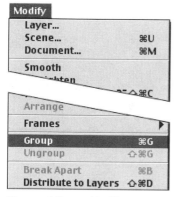

Figure 4.8 Choose Modify > Group to unite several selected objects as a group.

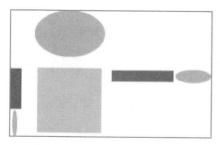

Figure 4.9 When you select the group, a highlighted bounding box appears, surrounding the grouped objects.

Understanding Grouping

Flash does give you ways to force its paint to "dry." When you turn objects into groups (or symbols), they are no longer immediately editable, and they stop interacting with other objects. (You can still edit the contents of groups and symbols, but you must invoke special editing modes to modify them.) If you put several groups (or symbols) on the same layer, they merely stack up, one on top of another. (To learn more about symbols, see Chapter 6.)

To create a group:

1. Select one or more objects on the Stage, using any of the methods discussed in Chapter 3 (**Figure 4.7**).

2. From the Modify menu, choose Group, or press ⌘-G (Mac) or Ctrl-G (Windows) (**Figure 4.8**).

    Flash groups the items, placing them within a bounding box (**Figure 4.9**). The visible bounding box lets you know that the group is selected. When the group is not selected, the bounding box is hidden.

To return objects to ungrouped status:

1. Select the group that you want to return to ungrouped status.

2. From the Modify menu, choose Ungroup, or press Shift-⌘-G (Mac) or Shift-Ctrl-G (Windows).

    Flash removes the bounding box and selects all the items.

✔ Tip

■ If you prefer using a two-key shortcut rather than a three-key shortcut, the command for breaking apart symbols also works to ungroup groups. That command is ⌘-B (Mac) or Ctrl-B (Windows).

Working with Grouped Elements

Grouping is a useful way to prevent shapes from interacting and to keep shapes together as you work with the elements on the Stage.

To prevent interaction between objects on the same layer:

1. In the Toolbox, choose the oval tool.

2. Set the stroke color to no color and the fill color to red.

3. On the Stage, draw a fairly large oval (**Figure 4.10**).

4. In the Toolbox, switch to the arrow tool, and select the oval you just drew.

5. To make the oval a grouped element, from the Modify menu, choose Group (**Figure 4.11**).

Figure 4.10 The oval before grouping.

Figure 4.11 The oval after grouping.

Why Use Grouping?

There are several reasons to use Flash's Group feature:

◆ Grouping makes it easy to reposition a set of shapes whose relationships must stay the same. Imagine that you've created a logo from three triangle shapes. After you've got the triangles arranged just right, turn them into a group so that you can reposition the logo without having to tweak the individual triangle's placement each time.

◆ Grouping prevents individual shapes from interacting with other shapes on the same layer. Suppose that you are drawing shapes that make up a face, with eyes, nose, and mouth. You may want to move the facial features around to get just the right look, and you don't want to leave holes in your basic face oval each time. Grouping each element prevents that result.

◆ Grouping prevents you from editing objects inadvertently. Flash makes it easy to edit lines and fills—you simply grab and drag them with the arrow tool—but it's also easy to reshape an object accidentally when you meant to move it. To edit grouped shapes, you must invoke a special editing mode.

Figure 4.12 Draw a second oval on top of the grouped oval.

Figure 4.13 The ungrouped oval stacks beneath the grouped oval.

Figure 4.14 Drag the grouped oval to make the ungrouped oval visible.

Figure 4.15 Select the small oval.

Figure 4.16 After grouping, the small oval—the most recently created group—pops to the top of the stack.

6. Back in the Toolbox, choose the oval tool and a different fill color.

7. On the Stage, draw a smaller oval in the middle of your first oval (**Figure 4.12**).

When you finish drawing the new oval, it immediately disappears behind the grouped oval (**Figure 4.13**). That's because grouped objects always stack on top of ungrouped objects (see the sidebar "Understanding the Stacking Order of Grouped Shapes" later in this chapter").

8. Switch to the arrow tool, and reposition the large oval so that you can see the small one (**Figure 4.14**).

9. Deselect the large oval, and select the small oval (**Figure 4.15**).

10. To make the small oval a grouped element, from the Modify menu, choose Group (**Figure 4.16**).

Flash puts the small oval in a bounding box and brings it to the top of the stack. Flash always places the most recently created group on the top of the stack. Now you can reposition the two ovals however you like, and they will not interact.

WORKING WITH GROUPED ELEMENTS

To keep multiple items together:

1. Using the drawing tools of your choice, create eight to 10 separate shapes in different locations on the Stage.

2. Select three or four elements that you'd like to keep together (**Figure 4.17**).

3. From the Modify menu, choose Group.

4. In the Toolbox, select the arrow tool, and practice moving and modifying the grouped shapes.

   Every action you take now affects the entire group (**Figure 4.18**). If you click one of the grouped shapes, you select them all. If you drag one, you drag the whole group. Modifications such as duplicating, resizing, or rotating affect the entire group.

✔ Tips

- You can group grouped objects. If you want to position several items on top of one another, group them as individuals first. Position them as you like. Then group all the items to preserve their relationship.

- You can lock groups so that you don't accidentally move or modify them. Select the group that you want to lock. Then, from the Modify menu, choose Arrange > Lock, or press Opt-⌘-L (Mac) or Ctrl-Alt-L (Windows). You can no longer select the item. To make it available again, from the Modify menu, choose Modify > Arrange > Unlock All, or press Opt-Shift-⌘-L (Mac) or Ctrl-Alt-Shift-L (Windows). You cannot unlock locked items selectively.

Figure 4.17 You can group several shapes that you want to manipulate as a group but keep in the same relationship to one another. The eyes and eyebrows in this face are a single group.

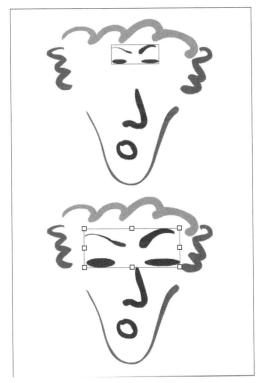

Figure 4.18 It's easy to reposition (top) or resize (bottom) the eyes and eyebrows to create new facial expressions when you've made a group out of them.

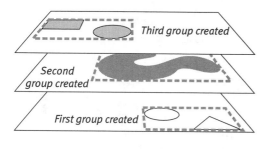

Figure 4.19 This schematic shows Flash's default stacking order for grouped items. The most recently created group is on top. Editable shapes are always on the bottom.

Controlling the Stacking Order

You can change the stacking order of groups via the Modify > Arrange menu. Notice that the stacking order doesn't require that you actually stack objects on top of one another. If you have two groups on opposite sides of the Stage, their stacking order is not visible, but as soon as you drag the objects so that one overlaps the other, the order becomes apparent.

Each grouped object sits on its own sublayer. You can move objects up or down in the stacking order one level at a time, or you can bring an object forward or send it backward through the stack of sublayers. The sublayer containing the live, editable objects is always at the bottom; groups and symbols stack on top of ungrouped elements.

Understanding the Stacking Order of Grouped Shapes

Editable shapes on a single layer always stay on the same layer, cutting one another whenever they inhabit the same space on the Stage. Grouped items (and symbols), however, stack on top of one another. By default, Flash stacks each group that you create on top of the preceding one; the last group created winds up on top of all the others (**Figure 4.19**).

A higher-level group obscures any groups that lie directly beneath it.

To bring an element forward in the stacking order:

1. On the Stage, select a grouped object (**Figure 4.20**).

2. From the Modify menu, choose Arrange > Bring Forward, or press Option-up arrow (Mac) or Ctrl-up arrow (Windows) (**Figure 4.21**).

   Flash brings the selected item up one sublayer in the stacking order (**Figure 4.22**).

To bring an element to the front of the stack:

1. On the Stage, select a grouped object (**Figure 4.23**).

2. From the Modify menu, choose Arrange > Bring to Front, or press ⌘-Shift-up arrow (Mac) or Ctrl-Shift-up arrow (Windows) (**Figure 4.24**).

   Flash brings the selected object to the top of the heap (**Figure 4.25**).

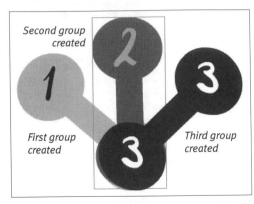

Figure 4.20 Each dumbbell represents a separate group.

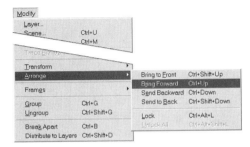

Figure 4.21 Choose Modify > Arrange > Bring Forward to move a selected group up one level in the stacking order.

Figure 4.22 The selected group moves forward in the stacking order one sublayer.

Figure 4.23 Select an item that you want to bring to the very top of the stacking order.

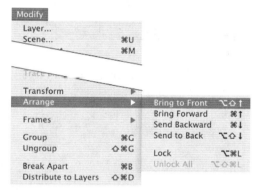

Figure 4.24 Choose Modify > Arrange > Bring to Front to place a selected group on the top of the stack.

Figure 4.25 The selected item comes to the front of the stack, regardless of how many groups (or sublayers) lie on top of the selected group.

To send an element to a lower level of the stack:

1. On the Stage, select a grouped object.

2. From the Modify menu, choose Arrange > Send Backward, or press ⌘-down arrow (Mac) or Ctrl-down arrow (Windows).

   Flash sends the selected item down one sublayer in the stacking order.

To send an element to the bottom of the stack:

1. On the Stage, select a grouped object.

2. From the Modify menu, choose Arrange > Send to Back, or press Option-Shift-down arrow (Mac) or Ctrl-Shift-down arrow (Windows).

   Flash sends the selected item to the bottom of the heap.

Editing Groups

Although you can transform a group as a whole (scale, rotate, and skew it), you can't directly edit the individual shapes within the group, the way that you can edit an ungrouped shape. To edit the shapes within a group, you must use the Edit Selected command.

To edit the contents of a group:

1. In the Toolbox, select the arrow tool.

2. On the Stage, select the group you want to edit.

3. From the Edit menu, choose Edit Selected.

   Flash enters group-editing mode (**Figure 4.26**). The info bar just above the Stage changes to indicate that you are in group-editing mode. The bounding box for the selected group disappears, and Flash dims all the items on the Stage that are not part of the selected group. These dimmed items are not **e**ditable; they merely provide context for editing the selected group.

✔ Tip

- When you have the Property Inspector open, you can see—and change—the height, width, and x and y coordinates of the bounding box of a selected group (**Figure 4.27**).

Movie-editing mode

Click Back button to return to movie-editing mode

Group-editing mode

Selected group being edited

Grayed shapes do not belong to the group that's being edited

Double-click away from the group to return to movie-editing mode

Figure 4.26 These eyes and eyebrows are a selected group that's being edited. The other objects on the Stage are grayed out to indicate that you can't edit them.

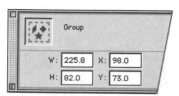

Figure 4.27 The Property Inspector displays the height, width, and *x* and *y* coordinates for the bounding box of a group that you've selected on the Stage. Enter new values to change any of those parameters.

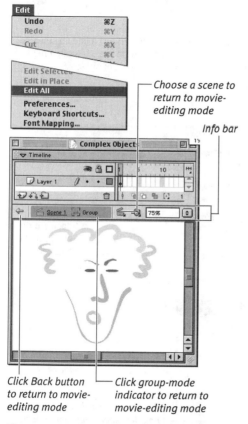

Choose a scene to return to movie-editing mode

Info bar

Click Back button to return to movie-editing mode

Click group-mode indicator to return to movie-editing mode

Figure 4.28 You have several ways to return to movie-editing mode when you are editing a group. From the Edit menu, choose Edit All. Or you can click items in the info bar: the Back button, the scene name, and the Scene pop-up menu all let you resume editing the movie.

To return to movie-editing mode:

Do one of the following:

◆ From the Edit menu, choose Edit All (**Figure 4.28**).

◆ Double-click the Stage or the work area away from the shapes in the group you're editing.

◆ Click the current scene name in the info bar.

◆ Click the Back button in the info bar.

✔ Tips

■ With the arrow tool selected, you can enter group-editing mode quickly by double-clicking a grouped item on the Stage.

■ If in addition to returning to movie-editing mode, you want to work on a different scene, you can simply choose it from the pop-up menu of scenes in the info bar. Flash takes you to the new scene in movie-editing mode. (To learn more about scenes, see Chapter 11.)

Aligning Elements

As you get into the process of animation, you'll discover how important alignment can be. Flash's grids, its guides, and its Snap features (see Chapter 1) help you align objects on the Stage manually. Flash also offers automatic alignment through the Align panel. You can line up selected objects by their top, bottom, left, or right edges or by their centers (**Figure 4.29**). You can align the objects to each other or align them to the Stage—for example, placing the top edge of all selected objects at the top edge of the Stage. Flash can also resize one object to match the dimensions of another—making them the same width, for example.

To access alignment options:

◆ From the Window menu, choose Align, or press ⌘-K (Mac) or Ctrl-K (Windows) (**Figure 4.30**).

The Align panel appears (**Figure 4.31**). You can apply any of the alignment options to selected objects on the Stage.

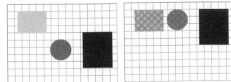

Original object placement Align top edges

Distribute horizontally by right edges Align right edges

Figure 4.29 Flash's Align panel can line up selected objects in various ways. Here are a few alignment choices used on the same set of objects.

Figure 4.30 Choose Window > Align to open the Align panel.

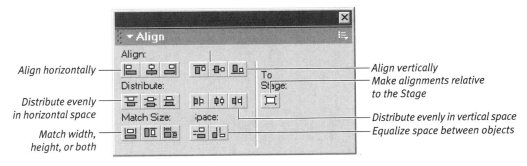

Align horizontally

Distribute evenly in horizontal space

Match width, height, or both

Align vertically

Make alignments relative to the Stage

Distribute evenly in vertical space

Equalize space between objects

Figure 4.31 The Align panel offers options for aligning objects horizontally and vertically, distributing objects evenly in horizontal or vertical space, forcing objects to match each other (or the Stage) in width and height, and creating even spacing between objects.

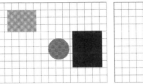

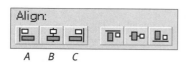

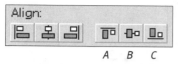

Figure 4.32 You can align objects horizontally by their left edges (A), centers (B), or right edges (C).

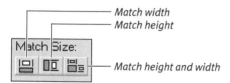

Figure 4.33 You can align objects vertically by their top edges (A), centers (B), or bottom edges (C).

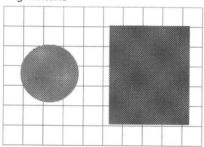

Match width
Match height
Match height and width

Original items

Items after matching height

Figure 4.34 Choosing the Match Height option in the Match Size section of the Align panel changes all selected items to be the same height. Flash makes shorter items grow to match the tallest selected item.

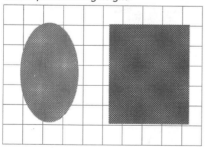

To align items horizontally:

1. On the Stage, select the items that you want to align.

2. In the Align section of the Align panel (**Figure 4.32**), *choose one of the following options:*
   ▲ Align left edge
   ▲ Align horizontal center
   ▲ Align right edge
   Flash rearranges the selected objects.

To align items vertically:

1. On the Stage, select the items that you want to align.

2. In the Align section of the Align panel (**Figure 4.33**), *choose one of the following options:*
   ▲ Align top edge
   ▲ Align vertical center
   ▲ Align bottom edge
   Flash rearranges the selected objects.

To match dimensions of items:

1. On the Stage, select the items that you want to change.

2. In the Match Size section of the Align panel (**Figure 4.34**), *do one of the following:*
   ▲ To expand all items to be the same width as the widest item, choose Match Width.
   ▲ To expand all items to be the same height as the tallest item, choose Match Height.
   ▲ To perform both of the preceding actions, choose Match Width and Height.

ALIGNING ELEMENTS

To make alignment relative to the Stage:

◆ In the Align panel, choose To Stage (**Figure 4.35**).

Flash makes your alignment choices in the Align, Distribute, and Match Size sections relative to the edges of the Stage. Align Bottom Edge, for example, puts all the bottom edges of the selected elements at the bottom of the Stage. Matching height makes selected elements as tall as the Stage.

✔ Tips

■ In addition to aligning items horizontally and vertically, you can create equal horizontal or vertical space among three or more items. The buttons in the Distribute section of the Align panel let you equalize the horizontal space between selected elements' left edges, centers, or right edges or equalize the vertical space between selected items' top edges, centers, or bottom edges.

■ Use the Align panel's Space options to create equal horizontal or vertical space between items' inside edges.

■ You can make a series of alignment adjustments to the same set of elements—for example, aligning all selected items by their left edges and then equalizing the vertical space between them. You can even use the alignment options to pull all selected items into one corner of the Stage.

Shapes after selecting Match Size's Match Height option and To Stage

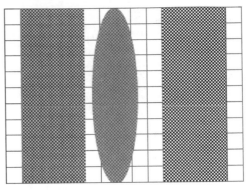

Figure 4.35 Choosing To Stage in the Align panel makes all your alignment choices relative to the edges of the Stage.

Using the Complex Paint Modes with the Brush

In Chapter 3, you learned about using the brush in Normal mode, in which every stroke with the brush lays down a new fill. As you saw earlier in this chapter, when brush strokes overlap, they interact. Flash offers four special brush modes that restrict the way the new brush strokes interact with existing editable lines (strokes) and fills. These special modes make it much easier to work with complex graphics made of multiple fills and lines. You can set the brush to paint over lines without affecting them (the fill winds up behind the lines instead of covering them), to paint only in blank areas of the Stage (existing lines and fills repel the paint), to paint only within a selection (if the brush slips outside the selection, nothing happens), or to paint only within the area where you started your brush stroke (all other areas repel the paint).

To leave lines intact when painting:

1. Create several shapes on the Stage. Use both lines and fills and a variety of colors.

2. In the Toolbox, select the brush tool.

3. Click the fill-color box (in the Toolbox or in the Brush Tool Property Inspector); from the pop-up swatch set, choose a color you haven't used in creating the fills and lines on the Stage.

   Testing the brush modes in a new color makes it easy to see what's happening.

4. From the Brush Mode menu, choose Paint Fills (**Figure 4.36**).

5. Start painting; paint over blank areas of the Stage as well as over the items you created.

   When you release the mouse button, Flash creates the new fill without affecting any lines you may have overlapped. These temporarily obscured lines reappear (**Figure 4.37**).

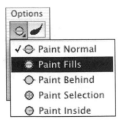

Figure 4.36 The Brush Mode menu lets you choose the way new brushstrokes interact with existing fills and strokes.

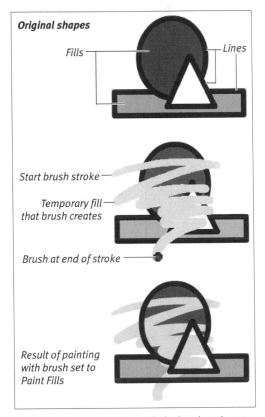

Figure 4.37 When you paint with the brush tool set to Paint Fills, Flash lets you paint over lines without affecting them. Lines pop to the front of the image when you release the mouse button.

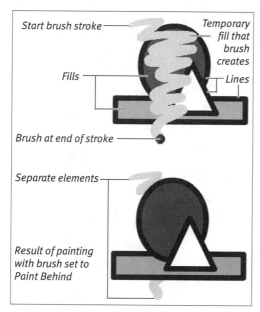

Start brush stroke

Temporary fill that brush creates

Fills

Lines

Brush at end of stroke

Separate elements

Result of painting with brush set to Paint Behind

Figure 4.38 When you paint with the brush set to Paint Behind, Flash lets you paint over lines and fills without affecting them. Existing lines and fills pop to the front of the image when you release the mouse button.

To leave existing lines and fills intact when painting:

1. With a variety of lines and fills already on the Stage, select the brush tool in the Toolbox.

2. From the Brush Mode menu, choose Paint Behind.

3. Start painting; paint over blank areas of the Stage as well as over the elements you created.

When you release the mouse button, Flash creates the fill only in blank areas of the Stage (**Figure 4.38**).

✔ Tip

■ The term *Paint Behind* is a bit misleading. You do not actually create fills that lie behind other fills. Rather, Flash allows existing lines and fills to repel, or cut away, any overlapping portions of the new fill you're creating. When you release the mouse button after painting a new fill, that fill appears to sink down behind the other fills on the Stage. When you use this mode, be sure to remember that any existing lines and fills will segment the new fill you create.

USING COMPLEX PAINT MODES WITH THE BRUSH

To restrict paint to selected fills:

1. With a variety of lines and fills already on the Stage, select one or more of the fills but leave some fills unselected.

2. In the Toolbox, select the brush.

3. From the Brush Mode menu, choose Paint Selection.

4. Start painting; paint over blank areas of the Stage as well as over the elements you've created.

   When you release the mouse button, Flash creates the fill only in areas of the Stage you had highlighted as a selection. Your new brushstroke has no effect on selected lines or on lines and fills that lie outside the selection (**Figure 4.39**).

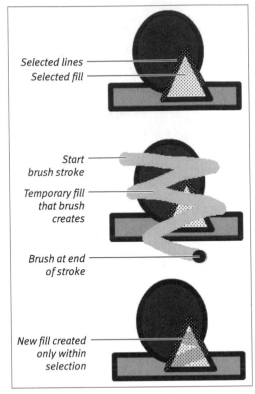

Selected lines
Selected fill

Start brush stroke

Temporary fill that brush creates

Brush at end of stroke

New fill created only within selection

Figure 4.39 When you paint with the brush set to Paint Selection, Flash ignores any brushstrokes you make outside the selection. In this mode, you cannot affect lines, and any unselected fills you accidentally paint over reappear when you release the mouse button.

How Can You Tell What You're Painting?

Flash cannot accurately preview the fills you create in complex paint modes the way it can in Normal mode. In complex modes, as you hold down the mouse button and paint in one continuous brush stroke, Flash displays your new fill in a temporary form. This temporary fill lies on top of every object it overlaps on the Stage and obscures any fills and lines that lie beneath it. When you release the mouse button, Flash calculates and redraws the new fill according to the paint mode you've selected in the Toolbox.

To restrict paint to one area:

1. With a variety of lines and fills already on the Stage, in the Toolbox, select the brush tool.

2. From the Brush Mode menu, choose Paint Inside.

3. Start painting from within one shape, extending your brush strokes to paint outside the shape where you began.

   When you release the mouse button, Flash creates the fill only inside the shape where you first clicked with the brush to begin painting (**Figure 4.40**).

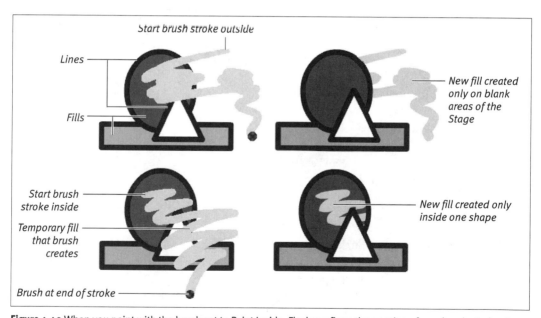

Figure 4.40 When you paint with the brush set to Paint Inside, Flash confines the creation of new brush strokes to the area where you started painting. Painting over lines has no effect, and if your brush slips outside the area in which you started, Flash simply ignores it.

USING COMPLEX PAINT MODES WITH THE BRUSH

Applying Gradients to Multipart Shapes

As the characters and elements in your animations get more complex, you may wind up creating graphics made up of numerous parts. When applying gradients to multipart graphics, you have the choice of filling each part with its own separate gradient (as you learned to do in Chapter 3) or selecting several parts and applying one gradient to all of them.

To apply one gradient separately to multiple fills:

1. On the Stage, create a graphic made of several fills.

2. Select the fills to which you want to apply the same gradient.

3. To choose a gradient fill, *do one of the following:*

   ▲ Click any fill-color box (in the Toolbox, the Property Inspector, or the Color Mixer panel), and from the pop-up swatch set, select a gradient.

   ▲ In the Color Swatches panel, select a gradient.

   Flash applies the fill to each selected shape separately (**Figure 4.41**). The full range of the gradient appears within each shape.

✔ Tip

■ You can also use the paint-bucket tool to apply separate gradients. Make sure that the Lock Fill modifier is deselected, choose the gradient you want, and then click the shapes to which you want to apply the gradient fills.

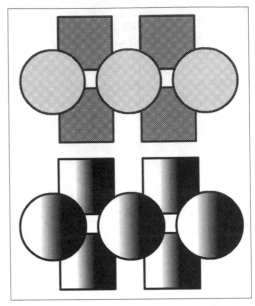

Figure 4.41 With several shapes selected (top), when you choose a gradient from a fill-color box or from the Color Swatches panel, Flash applies the gradient to each shape separately (bottom). The full range of the gradient fits within each shape.

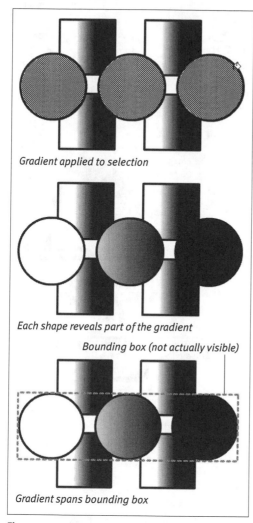

Gradient applied to selection

Each shape reveals part of the gradient

Bounding box (not actually visible)

Gradient spans bounding box

Figure 4.42 When you use the paint-bucket tool to apply a gradient to multiple selected shapes, none of the selected objects contains the entire color range of the gradient. Each object opens a window onto part of the gradient within a behind-the-scenes bounding box that contains a single gradient.

To spread one gradient across multiple fills:

1. On the Stage, create an object made of several fills.

2. On the Stage, select the fills to which you want to apply the gradient.

3. In the Toolbox, select the paint bucket.

4. Deselect the Lock Fill modifier.

5. Choose a gradient fill.

   Flash applies the gradient to each shape separately.

6. On the Stage, use the paint bucket to click any of the selected fills.

   Flash spreads a single gradient across all the selected fills (**Figure 4.42**).

✔ Tip

■ You can also spread a single gradient across unselected fills using the paint-bucket tool. In the Toolbox, select the paint bucket's Lock Fill modifier. Click each unselected fill on the Stage. Flash spreads the gradient across the entire Stage). Each shape you click reveals the portion of the gradient that corresponds to that location in the frame.

Using the Eraser Tool with Multiple Shapes

Just as the brush has complex modes for interacting with live fills and lines, the eraser tool offers complex interaction modes. (For a review of the eraser's normal mode, see Chapter 3.)

Flash's eraser has four special modes that let you select what to erase; in each mode, the eraser interacts differently with lines and fills. In Erase Fills mode, the tool ignores any lines you drag over. In Erase Lines mode, the reverse occurs: The tool ignores fills and removes only lines. Erase Selected Fills mode ignores lines but also ignores any areas of fill you haven't selected. Erase Inside restricts you to erasing within a single fill: the one where you started erasing.

To erase only fills, leaving lines intact:

1. Create several shapes on the Stage, using both lines and fills and a variety of colors.

2. In the Toolbox, select the eraser.

3. From the Eraser Mode pop-up menu, choose Erase Fills (**Figure 4.43**).

4. From the Eraser Shape pop-up menu, choose a shape for your eraser.

5. To erase, click and drag over the objects on the Stage.

   When you release the mouse button, Flash removes only the erased fills. Any lines that you erased over reappear (**Figure 4.44**).

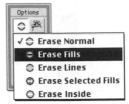

Figure 4.43 The Eraser Mode pop-up menu lets you choose how the eraser interacts with lines and fills.

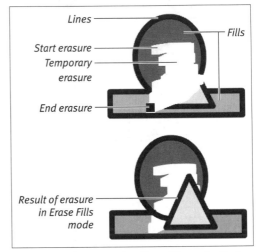

Figure 4.44 When you select Erase Fills mode, Flash lets you run the eraser over lines without affecting them. The "erased" lines reappear when you release the mouse button.

How Can You Tell What You're Erasing?

Flash cannot accurately preview erasures in complex erase modes the way it can in Normal mode. In complex modes, as you hold down the mouse button and erase in one continuous stroke, Flash temporarily obliterates everything you dragged the eraser over. When you release the mouse button, Flash redraws the erasure according to the Erase mode you have selected in the Toolbox.

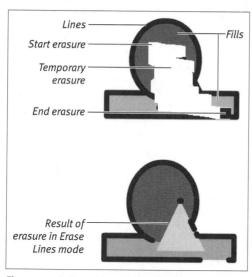

Figure 4.45 In Erase Lines mode, Flash lets you run the eraser over fills without changing them. The "erased" fills reappear when you release the mouse button.

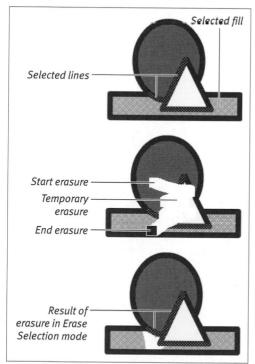

Figure 4.46 When you choose Erase Selected Fills mode, Flash lets you restrict your erasure to fills in selected areas. Any "erased" lines, as well as any "erased" lines and fills that are not part of the selection, reappear when you release the mouse button.

To erase only lines:

1. Create several shapes on the Stage, using both lines and fills and a variety of colors.

2. In the Toolbox, select the eraser.

3. From the Eraser Mode pop-up menu, choose Erase Lines.

4. Click and drag over the objects on the Stage to erase.

   The preview erasure obliterates everything you dragged the eraser over. When you release the mouse button, Flash removes only the erased lines. Any fills you erased pop back up (**Figure 4.45**).

To erase selected fills:

1. With a variety of lines and fills already on the Stage, select one or more fills, making sure to leave some fills unselected.

2. In the Toolbox, select the eraser.

3. From the Eraser Mode pop-up menu, choose Erase Selected Fills.

4. Start erasing; erase over both selected areas and areas you didn't select.

   Flash removes fills only from areas you highlighted as a selection. The eraser has no effect on selected lines or on lines and fills that lie outside the selection (**Figure 4.46**).

USING THE ERASER WITH MULTIPLE SHAPES

197

To restrict erasures to one area:

1. With a variety of lines and fills already on the Stage, select the eraser tool in the Toolbox.

2. From the Eraser Mode pop-up menu, choose Erase Inside.

3. Start erasing within one shape, extending your erasure outside the shape where you began.

   Flash erases only inside the shape where you first clicked with the tool to begin erasing (**Figure 4.47**).

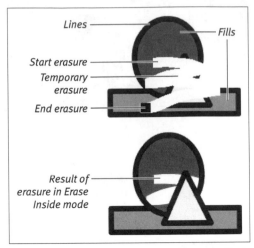

Figure 4.47 When you select Erase Inside mode, Flash lets you restrict your erasure to the fill in which you start erasing. Any other "erased" fills reappear when you release the mouse button.

GRAPHICS ON MULTIPLE LAYERS

Macromedia Flash MX uses two types of spatial organization: (1) the position of elements within the rectangle that is the Stage and (2) the way elements stack up. You create an illusion of three-dimensional depth by overlapping objects. As you learned in Chapter 4, you can create this overlapping effect on one layer by stacking groups and symbols. The more elements your movie contains, however, the more difficult it becomes to manipulate and keep track of the stacking order of items on a single layer. You can use multiple layers to bring that task under control.

You could think of a Flash animation as being a stack of film: a sheaf of long, clear acetate strips divided into frames. Each filmstrip is analogous to a Flash layer. Shapes painted on the top strip of film obscure shapes on lower strips; where the top strip of film is blank, elements from lower strips show through.

When you place items on separate layers, you can easily control and rearrange the way the items stack up. If you have several elements —say, a square, circle, rectangle, and star— each on its own layer, you can play around with which shapes appear to be closer to the viewer by changing the layer order. Placing items on different layers prevents the items from interacting, so you don't need to worry about grouping the items or having one shape inadvertently interact with another.

Touring the Timeline's Layer Features

Flash graphically represents each layer as one horizontal section of the Timeline and provides several controls for viewing and manipulating these graphic representations. Flash layers offer several features that make it easier to work with graphics on layers, such as viewing the items on layers as outlines and assigning different colors to those outlines so you can easily see which items are on which layers. You can lock layers so you don't edit their contents accidentally, and you can hide layers to make it easier to work with individual graphics in a welter of other graphics. You can create special guide layers for help in positioning elements, masks for hiding and revealing layers selectively, and guides for animating motion along a path. (You learn more about motion paths in Chapter 9.) Flash MX now lets you create layer folders for organizing the layers in a movie.

Figure 5.1 offers a road map to the salient layer features in the Timeline.

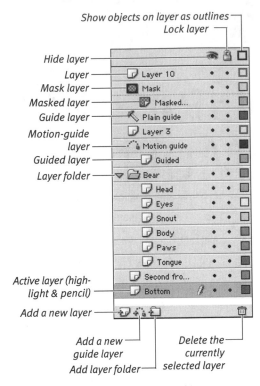

Figure 5.1 The Timeline provides a graphic representation of all the layers in a Flash movie. You can do much of the work of creating and manipulating layers by clicking buttons in the Timeline.

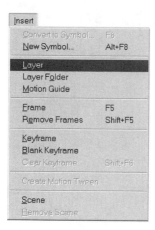

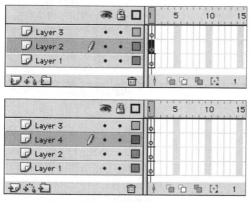

Creating and Deleting Layers

You can add new layers as you need them while creating the ingredients of a particular scene in your movie.

To add a new layer:

1. In the Timeline, select a layer.

   Flash always adds the new layer directly above the selected layer, so be sure to choose the layer that you want to lie directly beneath the new layer. If you want to add a layer beneath the current bottom layer, create it first and then click and drag it to reposition it at the bottom of the stack.

2. *Do one of the following:*

   ▲ From the Insert menu, choose Layer. (**Figure 5.2**).

   ▲ In the Timeline, click the Insert Layer button.

   Flash adds a new layer and gives it a default name—for example, Layer 4 (**Figure 5.3**). Flash bases the number in the default name on the number of layers already created in the active scene of the movie, not on the number of layers that currently exist.

Figure 5.2 Choose Insert > Layer to add a new layer to the Timeline.

Figure 5.3 Select the layer that you want to wind up beneath the new layer (top); Flash inserts a new layer directly above the selected layer and gives the new layer a default name (bottom).

To delete a layer:

1. In the Timeline, select the layer you want to delete.

2. Click the Trash icon (**Figure 5.4**).

   Flash removes that layer (and all its frames) from the Timeline.

✔ Tip

- The contextual menu for layers offers some choices that otherwise are available only via buttons in the Timeline—for example, the Delete Layer command (**Figure 5.5**). To access this menu, Control-click a layer on the Mac or right-click it in Windows.

To delete multiple layers:

1. In the Timeline, select the first layer you want to remove.

2. ⌘-click (Mac) or Ctrl-click (Windows) every layer you want to remove.

   This method of selection allows you to choose multiple layers that are not contiguous (**Figure 5.6**).

3. Click the Trash icon.

   Flash removes the selected layers (and their frames) from the Timeline.

✔ Tips

- To select a range of layers, click the lowest layer you want to delete; then Shift-click the highest layer you want to delete. Flash selects it and all the layers in between.

- You can drag selected layers to the Trash icon to delete them instead of selecting and clicking the Trash icon in two steps.

- You cannot delete all the layers in the Timeline. If you select all the layers and click the Trash icon, Flash keeps the bottom layer and deletes the rest.

Figure 5.4 Click the Trash icon to delete a selected layer.

Figure 5.5 The contextual menu for layers gives you easy access to layer commands, including some that you can otherwise access only via buttons—for example, Delete Layer. To access the contextual menu for layers, Control-click (Mac) or right-click (Windows) the layer icon.

Layers selected for deletion

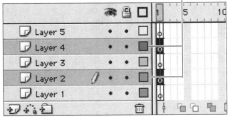

After deletion

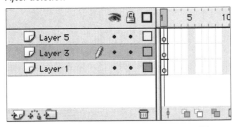

Figure 5.6 To delete noncontiguous layers, ⌘-click (Mac) or Ctrl-click (Windows) the layers you want to add to your selection; then click the Trash icon.

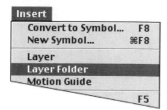

Figure 5.7 Choose Insert > Layer Folder to add a new folder to your Timeline.

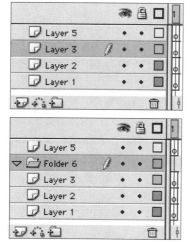

Figure 5.8 Flash places new layer folders above the layer you selected. Flash names new layer folders based on the number of layers and folder layers that have been created in the current scene of the movie.

Creating and Deleting Layer Folders

Complex movies contain dozens of layers. Viewing and navigating such hefty Timelines can get tedious and confusing. Layer folders help keep the Timeline organized. You might want to keep all the layers related to one character or element together in one folder, for example. Flash considers a folder to be another type of layer, and the methods for adding and deleting layer folders are similar to those for adding and deleting layers. Layer folders do not hold content, however, and no keyframes are associated with them in the Timeline.

To create layer folders:

1. In the Timeline, select a layer (or layer folder).

   Flash always adds a new layer folder directly above the selected layer (or folder). Note that the selected layer doesn't wind up inside the new folder, you must place this layer inside the new folder yourself. You'll learn to do that later in this chapter.

2. *Do one of the following:*
   - ▲ From the Insert menu, choose Layer Folder (**Figure 5.7**).
   - ▲ In the Timeline, click the Insert Layer Folder button.

   Flash adds a new layer folder and gives it a default name—for example, Folder 6 (**Figure 5.8**).

   Because Flash considers layer folders to be a type of layer, Flash bases the default name on the number of layers that have been created in the movie.

To delete layer folders:

1. In the Timeline, select the layer folder you want to delete.

2. Click the Trash icon.

   or

   Control-click (Mac) or right-click (Windows) in the *selected* layer.

   The contextual menu for layers appears.

3. Choose Delete Folder.

   A dialog box appears, warning you that deleting the layer folder will also delete all the layers it contains.

4. To delete the folder and its layers, click Yes.

   or

   To cancel the delete operation, click No.

✔ Tip

■ All the instructions and tips for deleting multiple layers work on layer folders as well (see "Creating and Deleting Layers" earlier in this chapter).

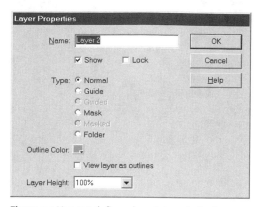

Figure 5.9 You can define a layer's type in the Layer Properties dialog box.

Controlling Layers and Folders

Layer properties are the parameters that define the look and function of a layer. Remember that layer folders are also a type of layer in Flash. You can name layers and folders. You can hide or show layers and folders, lock them to prevent any editing of their contents, and view them in outline form. Flash generally gives you two ways to control the properties of a selected layer or folder: set the property in the Layer Properties dialog box or set the property via button controls located in the Timeline.

To work with the Layer Properties dialog box:

1. In the Timeline, select the layer whose properties you want to define or change.

2. From the Modify menu, choose Layer.

   The Layer Properties dialog box appears (**Figure 5.9**).

3. Name the layer or set other layer properties, or both, as described in the following sections.

4. Click OK.

   Flash applies all the selected settings to the current layer.

Layer Properties Dialog Box versus Timeline-Based Layer Controls

If you just want to set layer visibility, lock layer contents, or view layer elements as outlines, it makes no difference whether you call up the Layer Properties dialog box to do so or click the various layer-property controls in the Timeline. Selecting a property in the dialog box doesn't offer any more permanence than setting that property in the Timeline.

The Layer Properties dialog box does offer functions that lack button equivalents: creating plain guide layers, changing the height of a layer in Timeline view, choosing an outline color, and changing an existing layer from one type to another.

The Timeline offers the capability to create motion guides, whereas the Layer Properties dialog box does not.

Flash divides layers into six types: normal, guide, guided, mask, masked, and folder.

To define the layer type:

1. Select a layer, and open the Layer Properties dialog box.

2. Select one of the following radio buttons (**Figure 5.10**):

   ▲ **Normal.** The default layer type is normal; all the items in a normal layer appear in your final movie.

   ▲ **Guide.** Flash creates two types of guide layers: guides and motion guides. Lines or shapes on plain guide layers serve as reference points for placing and aligning objects on the Stage. A line drawn on a motion-guide layer becomes a path that an animated object can follow (see Chapter 9). You cannot define motion-guide layers directly from the Layer Properties dialog box, you set them from the Timeline or from the contextual menu for layers. Items on guide layers do not appear in the final movie.

   ▲ **Guided.** Guided layers contain the objects that will animate by following the path on a guide layer. You must link the guided layer to the motion-guide layer.

   ▲ **Mask.** A mask layer hides and reveals portions of linked layers that lie directly beneath the mask layer.

   ▲ **Masked.** Masked layers contain elements that can be hidden or revealed by a mask layer.

   ▲ **Folder.** Folder layers allow you to organize layers hierarchically. Setting the layer properties of a folder automatically sets the properties for all the layers within that folder. Collapsing (or expanding) folders hides (or reveals) the frames for all the layers within that folder in the Timeline.

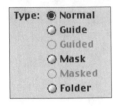

Figure 5.10 There are six types of layers in Flash.

✔ Tip

■ You can change a layer folder's type to Normal, but because layer folders have no frames in the Timeline, the first frame of the resulting layer winds up without a keyframe. If you try to draw on the layer right away, you'll get an error message. To make the layer usable, you need to add a keyframe to frame 1. (For more information on working with keyframes, see Chapter 8.)

Figure 5.11 You can rename a layer by typing a new name in the Name field of the Layer Properties dialog box.

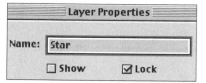

Figure 5.12 You can set a layer's visibility by selecting or deselecting Show in the Layer Properties dialog box.

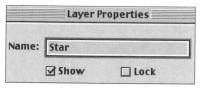

Figure 5.13 You can make the contents of a selected layer uneditable by choosing Lock in the Layer Properties dialog box. Locking a layer folder automatically locks all the layers within that folder.

To name a layer or folder:

◆ In the Name field of the Layer Properties dialog box, type a new name for the layer or folder.

When you call up the dialog box, the Name field is selected; just start typing (**Figure 5.11**).

Although Flash numbers layers and folders, renaming them is a good idea. A movie may have dozens of layers and folders, and you'll never remember that Layer 12 contains your company's name and Folder 4 contains the elements that make up its logo.

✔ Tip

■ Double-clicking the folded-page icon or folder icon in the Timeline opens the Layer Properties dialog box for that layer or folder.

To set the visibility of layer or folder contents:

◆ In the Layer Properties dialog box, check the Show checkbox (**Figure 5.12**).

When the checkbox is checked, the contents of the layer, or of all the layers contained in the folder, are visible on the Stage. When the checkbox is empty, the contents of the layer or folder are hidden during authoring; the content will appear in your final published movie.

To prevent changes in contents of a layer or folder:

◆ In the Layer Properties dialog box, check the Lock checkbox (**Figure 5.13**).

When the checkbox is checked, the layer or folder is locked. Although you can see the elements in that layer, or in all the layers contained in the folder, you can't select or edit those items. When the checkbox is empty, the contents of the layer or folder are available for editing.

To view the contents of a layer as outlines:

1. In the Layer Properties dialog box, click the View Layer As Outlines checkbox (**Figure 5.14**).

   When the checkbox is checked, Flash displays the contents of the layer, or of all the layers contained in the folder, as outlines during authoring.

Using different colors for outlines on different layers makes it easier to edit graphics when you have many layers. Flash assigns default colors to each layer, but you can choose your own.

2. From the Outline Color pop-up swatch set, choose a color for the outlines on the active layer (**Figure 5.15**).

   Flash changes the color swatch to your selected color.

3. Click OK.

   Flash displays the graphics on this layer as outlines, using the color you selected.

✔ Tip

■ When you select the View Layer As Outlines checkbox for a layer folder, Flash displays the contents of all the layers contained in the folder as outlines. Although you can specify an outline color for a layer folder, the color has no effect on what you see on the Stage. When you turn on outline view for the folder, each layer within the folder displays its contents in the outline color set for that layer.

Figure 5.14 Click the View Layer As Outlines box to display the layer's contents on the Stage in outline mode.

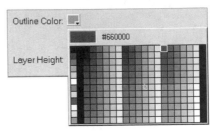

Figure 5.15 Select the color for displaying the outlines of a layer's objects from the pop-up swatch set in the Layer Properties dialog box.

Layer Height pop-up menu

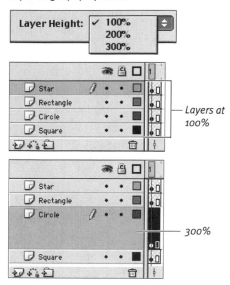

Layers at 100%

300%

Figure 5.16 Choose a larger percentage from the Layer Height pop-up menu in the Layer Properties dialog box to increase the height of a selected layer.

To change the height at which layers or folders display in the Timeline:

◆ In the Layer Properties dialog box, choose a percentage from the Layer Height pop-up menu (**Figure 5.16**).

Flash offers two enlarged layer views. The larger layers in the Timeline are especially useful for working with sounds. The waveform of each sound appears in the layer preview in the Timeline, and some sounds are difficult to see at the 100% setting. (You learn more about sounds in Chapter 14.)

✔ Tip

■ You can change the size of the graphic representation of all the layers in the Timeline by choosing a size from the Frame View pop-up menu, located in the top-right corner of the Timeline. The Preview and Preview in Context options display thumbnails of the contents of each frame in the layers.

Setting Layer Properties via the Timeline

The Timeline represents each layer or layer folder as a horizontal field containing a name and three buttons for controlling the way the layer or folder's contents look on the Stage. You can hide a layer or folder (making all the elements on that layer or within that folder temporarily invisible), lock a layer or folder (making the contents visible but uneditable), and view the items on the layer or within the folder as outlines. These controls are helpful when you are editing numerous items on several layers.

To rename a layer or folder:

1. In the Timeline, double-click the layer or folder name.

Flash activates the name's text-entry field.

2. Type a new name.

3. Press Enter or click anywhere outside the name field.

Contents of
Circle layer
visible

Toggles visibility of
the layer's contents

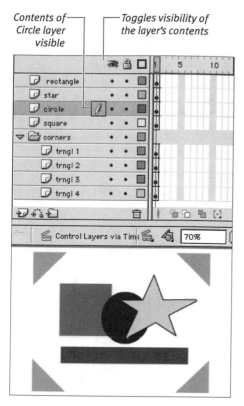

Hide layer contents

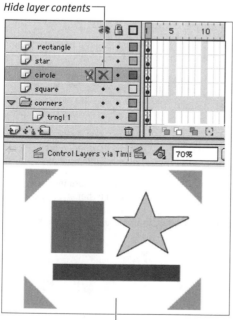

Contents of Circle layer hidden

To hide the contents of a layer or folder:

◆ In the Timeline for the layer or folder that
you want to hide, click the bullet in the
column below the eye icon (**Figure 5.17**).
Flash replaces the bullet with a red *X*,
indicating that the contents of the layer
or folder no longer appear on the Stage.
The invisible setting does not affect the
final movie. When you publish a movie
(see Chapter 16), Flash includes all the
contents of hidden layers and folders.

Hide folder
content

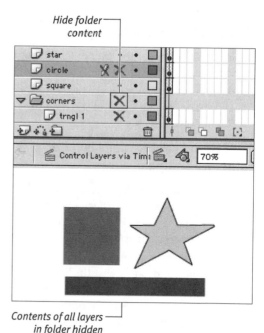

Contents of all layers
in folder hidden

Figure 5.17 The column below the eye icon controls
the visibility of layers. Each of the eight elements
(top) is on a separate layer. The four triangles at the
corners are located within the bottom folder. Hiding
the circle layer makes the circle disappear from the
Stage (middle). Hiding the Corner folder makes the
four triangles disappear as well (bottom).

To show the hidden contents of a layer or folder:

◆ In the Timeline for the layer or folder that you want to show, click the red *X* in the column below the eye icon.

Flash replaces the *X* with a bullet and displays the contents of the layer or folder.

To lock a layer or folder:

◆ In the Timeline for the layer or folder that you want to lock, click the bullet in the column below the padlock icon (**Figure 5.18**).

Flash replaces the bullet with a padlock icon. The contents of the layer or folder appear on the Stage, but you can't edit them. Locking a layer or folder does not affect the final movie.

To unlock a layer or folder:

◆ In the Timeline for the layer or folder that you want to unlock, click the padlock icon.

Flash replaces the padlock with a bullet and makes the contents of the layer or folder editable.

To view the contents of a layer or folder as outlines:

◆ In the Timeline for the layer or folder that you want to view as outlines, click the solid square in the column below the square icon (**Figure 5.19**).

Flash replaces the solid square with a hollow square, indicating that the layer or folder is in outline mode. The contents of a layer appear on the Stage as outlines in the color that the square indicates. The elements on each layer within a folder appear in the outline color associated with their own layer, not in the outline color of the folder. Placing a layer or folder in outline mode does not affect the final movie.

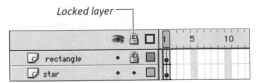

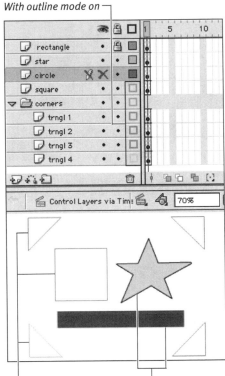

Figure 5.18 The padlock icon indicates that a layer is locked. The contents of a locked layer appear on the Stage, but you can't edit them.

Layer contents appear as outlines   Contents of other layers appear as solid objects

Figure 5.19 A hollow square in the outline-mode column indicates that objects on that layer appear as outlines. Setting a folder to outline mode automatically changes all the layers within it to outline mode.

SETTING LAYER PROPERTIES VIA THE TIMELINE

Figure 5.20 Clicking the hollow square in the outline-mode column returns you to viewing the contents of that layer or folder as solid objects.

To view the contents of a layer or folder as solid objects:

◆ In the Timeline for the layer or folder whose contents you want to view as solid, click the hollow square (**Figure 5.20**).

Flash replaces the hollow square with a solid square, indicating that the layer or folder is no longer in outline mode. The contents of the layer or folder appear on the Stage as solid objects.

Working with Layer-View Columns

Flash provides several shortcuts for working with the three layer-view columns in the Timeline. The following tips describe hiding and showing layer content; the controls in the Timeline for locking and unlocking layer contents and for viewing layer contents as outlines work the same way.

◆ To hide the contents of several layers or folders quickly, click the bullet in the column below the eye icon and drag through all the layers or folders you want to hide. As the pointer passes over each bullet, Flash changes it to a red X.

◆ To show numerous layers or folders quickly, click a red X in the eye column and drag through all the layers or folders whose contents you want to show.

◆ To hide the contents of all layers or folders but one, Option-click (Mac) or Alt-click (Windows) the bullet in the eye column of the layer or folder you want to see. Flash puts an X in all the other layers or folders.

◆ To hide the contents of all the layers and folders, ⌘-click (Mac) or Ctrl-click (Windows) the eye column of any layer or folder, or click the eye icon in the column header. Flash puts an X in all the layers. To show the contents of all the layers and folders, simply ⌘-click or Ctrl-click an X or click the eye icon again.

Controlling Layer Visibility in the Timeline

In addition to controlling the visibility and editability of the contents of a layer or folder, when you organize layers in folders, you gain control of which layers appear in the Timeline. When you close a folder, layers within it disappear from the Timeline; making it much easier to view and navigate. Closing the layer folder has no effect on the contents of each layer within it, however. All the elements on those layers continue to display on the Stage in whatever mode you chose for them before closing the folder.

When you create new layer folders, they are open by default.

To close layer folders in the Timeline:

◆ In the Timeline, click the triangle to the left of the open folder icon (**Figure 5.21**).

The triangle rotates to the closed position, and the icon changes to a closed folder. Flash hides all the layers contained within the layer folder in the Timeline.

To open layer folders in the Timeline:

◆ In the Timeline, click the triangle to the left of the closed folder icon.

The triangle rotates to the open position, and the icon changes to an open folder. Flash displays all the layers contained within the layer folder.

✔ Tip

■ You can open or close all the folders in a movie at the same time via the contextual menu. Access the menu by Control-clicking (Mac) or right-clicking (Windows) any Timeline layer. Then choose Expand All Folders or Collapse All Folders (**Figure 5.22**).

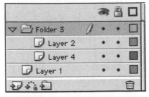
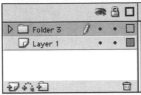

Figure 5.21 Clicking the triangle to the left of the folder icon toggles between open (top) and closed (bottom) folder views.

Figure 5.22 To open all folders at the same time, Control-click (Mac) or right-click (Windows) a layer to access the contextual menu for layers. Then choose Expand All Folders.

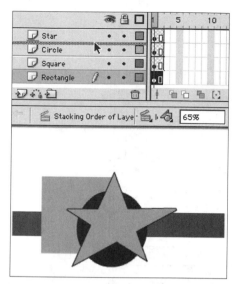

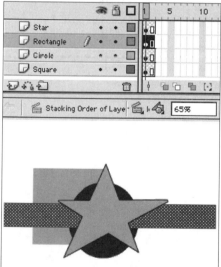

Figure 5.23 The gray line (top) represents the new location for the Rectangle layer you are dragging. Release the mouse button to drop the layer into its new position. Flash selects the layer and its contents (bottom).

Controlling the Stacking Order of Layers

As you add more layers to your document, you may need to rearrange them so that the objects that should appear in the foreground actually cover objects that appear in the background.

Layers make it easy to change the stacking order of numerous elements at the same time. You can, for example, bring all the elements on one layer to the top of the stack simply by dragging that layer to the top of the list in the Timeline. Doing so brings those elements to the front of the Stage (overlapping any items on other layers) in every frame of the movie.

To reorder layers:

1. Create a movie with several layers.

2. In the Timeline, position the mouse pointer over the layer you want to move.

3. Click and drag the layer.

   Flash previews the layer's new location with a thick gray line.

4. Position the preview line in the layer order you want (**Figure 5.23**).

5. Release the mouse button.

   Flash moves the layer to the new location and selects it in the Timeline.

✔ Tip

■ If you accidentally release the mouse button as you move a layer, and your layer winds up in the wrong location, you can choose Edit > Undo or press ⌘-Z (Mac) or Ctrl-Z (Windows) to return to the original layer order. It takes two undo commands to do so, however. The first command undoes the selection of the layer in its new location; the second undoes the dragging action.

Organizing Layers in Folders

After you have created folders, you can drag existing layers into the folders to organize the Timeline. Repositioning a folder in the Timeline changes the stacking order of all the layers within that folder. You can even nest folders within folders to create hierarchical structures. You can also create new layers or folders within existing folders directly.

To move existing layers into folders:

1. Create a movie with several layers, and include at least one folder.

2. In the Timeline, position the mouse pointer over the layer you want to place in a folder.

3. Click and drag the layer.

   Flash previews the layer's new location with a thick gray line.

4. Drag the layer over the folder where you want to place it.

   The folder icon highlights, turning gray (**Figure 5.24**).

5. Release the mouse button.

   Flash moves the layer into the folder, indents the layer name in the Timeline, selects the layer in the Timeline, and selects the layer's contents on the Stage.

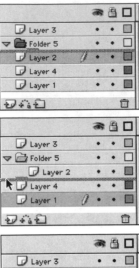
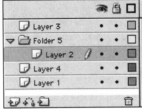

Figure 5.24 When you drag a layer over a folder layer, the folder icon turns gray (top). Release the mouse button to drop the layer into that folder. Flash selects the layer and its contents (bottom).

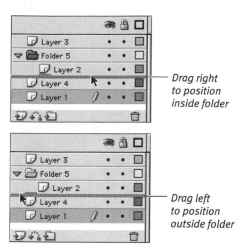

Drag right
to position
inside folder

Drag left
to position
outside folder

Figure 5.25 When you position layers at the bottom of a folder, you need to let Flash know whether you want the layers to wind up inside or outside the folder. The bump on top of the preview bar for the layer indicates where the layer will go.

✔ Tips

- After you've added layers to a folder, you no longer need to drag new layers on top of the folder layer. Positioning a layer's preview line beneath any of the layers in a folder (the indented ones) places the layer you are repositioning in that folder, in the highlighted location.

- Dragging a layer to a closed folder positions the layer at the top of the stack inside the folder.

- Positioning layers beneath an open folder containing layers is a bit tricky. When you position a layer's preview line after the last layer in the folder, Flash defaults to adding the layer to the folder. You can close the folder, to prevent putting the layer inside the folder. Or, with the folder open, watch the layer's preview line carefully as you drag. With the layer in position beneath the last layer in the folder, drag slightly to the left. The gray bump on the top of the preview bar moves over to the left (**Figure 5.25**). Release the mouse button, and the layer winds up outside the folder.

- If you drag a layer whose contents are visible into a folder that's set to hide elements (a red *X* appears above the folder's eye column), the contents of the newly included layer remain visible (a bullet appears in that layer's eye column).

ORGANIZING LAYERS IN FOLDERS

To change folder order:

1. Create a movie with layers and folders.

2. In the Timeline, position the mouse pointer over the folder you want to move.

3. Click and drag the folder.

   Flash previews the folder's new location with a thick gray line.

4. Position the preview line where you want the folder to reside in the Timeline (**Figure 5.26**).

5. Release the mouse button.

   Flash moves the folder to the new location and selects the folder layer in the Timeline. The contents of the layers in the folder are not selected on the Stage.

To create a nested folder:

◆ Using the steps in the preceding exercise, drag one existing folder into another.

   or

   In the Timeline, select a layer within a folder and, *do one of the following:*

   ▲ From the Insert menu, choose Layer Folder.

   ▲ In the Timeline, click the Insert Layer Folder button.

   Flash adds a new indented layer folder.

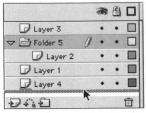

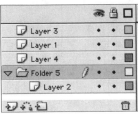

Figure 5.26 You reposition folder layers the same way you reposition other layers. Drag the folder, preview the location (top), and release the mouse button to place the folder (bottom).

Active layer

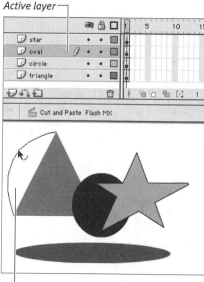

Use arrow tool to modify
shape on inactive layer

No change in active layer

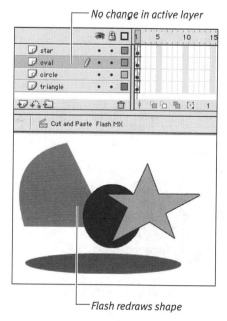

Flash redraws shape

Figure 5.27 Selecting the oval makes the Oval
layer the active layer. You can still edit objects
on inactive layers by reshaping their outlines
with the arrow tool.

Working with Graphics on Different Layers

Unless you lock shapes, or lock or hide layers,
the graphics on all layers are available for
editing.

To edit shape outlines on inactive layers:

1. Create a document that has four layers.

2. Place a different shape on each layer.
   For this example, place a triangle on
   Layer 1, a circle on Layer 2, an oval on
   Layer 3, and a star on Layer 4.

3. In the Toolbox, select the arrow tool.

4. On the Stage, click the oval.
   Flash selects the oval and makes its layer
   active (the pencil icon appears to the
   right of the layer name in the Timeline).

5. Click a blank area of the Stage.
   Flash deselects the oval but keeps its
   layer active.

6. On the Stage, position the pointer over
   the outline of the triangle.
   The curve or corner-point icon appears.

7. Drag the triangle's outline to reshape it.

8. Release the mouse button.
   Flash redraws the shape (**Figure 5.27**).
   Oval is still the active layer. Flash switches
   active layers only if you select a shape.

For the next exercise, continue using the document that you created for the preceding task; make sure that the current layer is still the oval layer.

To edit fills across layers:

1. In the Toolbox, select the paint-bucket tool.

2. Click the fill-color box (in the Toolbox, Color Mixer panel, or Property Inspector), and choose a color you haven't used for any of the shapes on the Stage.

3. Position the paint bucket over the star shape, and click.

   Flash fills the star with the new color (**Figure 5.28**), but the Oval layer remains the active layer.

✔ Tip

- To be safe, get into the habit of putting each graphic you create on a separate layer. That way, if you need to tweak the stacking order, you can. Having more layers doesn't increase the file size of your final movie significantly.

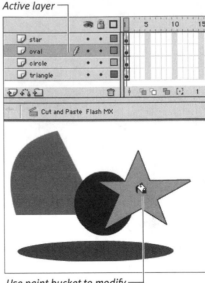

Active layer

Use paint bucket to modify fill on inactive layer

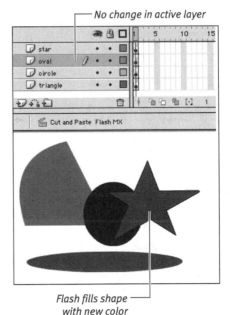

No change in active layer

Flash fills shape with new color

Figure 5.28 Use the paint-bucket tool to change a fill color on an inactive layer.

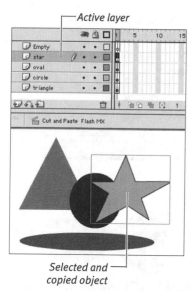

Active layer

*Selected and
copied object*

Select new active layer

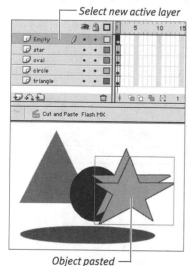

*Object pasted
onto new layer*

Figure 5.29 Copying a shape from one layer to another involves selecting the shape (top), copying it, selecting the target layer, and then pasting the copy there. The Paste command (middle) positions the pasted shape in the center of the window (bottom).

Cutting and Pasting Between Layers

Flash allows you to create and place graphics only on the active layer of a movie. But you can copy, cut, or delete elements from any visible, unlocked layer. You can select items on several layers, cut them, and then paste them all into a single layer. Or you can cut items individually from one layer and redistribute them to separate layers.

To paste across layers:

1. Create a document that contains several layers.

2. Place at least one element on all but one layer.

   Make a document with five layers, for example. Put a triangle on one layer, an oval on another, a circle on a third, a star on a fourth, and leave the fifth layer empty. To make the items easier to work with, group each one.

3. Name each layer according to its contents.

   Adding the names Star, Circle, Triangle, and so on makes it easier to remember which layer contains which items. It also makes it easier for you to see what's going on as you practice moving items across layers in this exercise.

4. On the Stage, select the star.

   Notice that Flash highlights the star's layer in the Timeline.

5. From the Edit menu, choose Copy.

6. In the Timeline, select the empty layer.

7. From the Edit menu, choose Paste.

   Flash pastes the copy of the star in the empty layer, in the middle of the window (**Figure 5.29**). Now you can move the star to a new position, if you want.

To use the Paste in Place command across layers:

1. Using the same document as in the preceding exercise, select the triangle.

2. Using the techniques that you learned in Chapter 3, add the oval and the circle to your selection.

3. From the Edit menu, choose Cut.

   Flash removes the three selected shapes (**Figure 5.30**).

4. In the Timeline, select the empty layer.

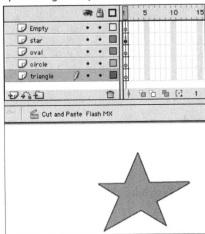

The active layer is the layer of the item last selected

Selected shapes from several layers

After cutting the objects

Figure 5.30 The first step in consolidating items from several layers on a single new layer involves selecting all the items and cutting them. Later, you'll paste them into the new active layer.

Two Ways to Paste

Flash offers two pasting modes: Paste and Paste in Place. Paste puts elements in the center of the Flash window. Paste in Place puts an element at the same x and y coordinates it had when you cut or copied it. Paste in Place is useful for preserving the precise relationships of all elements in a scene as you move items from one layer to another.

CUTTING AND PASTING BETWEEN LAYERS

Figure 5.31 Choose Edit > Paste in Place to paste items back into their original positions, but on a new layer.

Objects after pasting in place

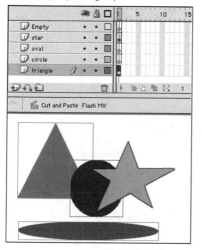

— *Click to hide layer*

— *Layer containing the objects is now hidden*

Figure 5.32 The Paste in Place command positions the pasted items in the new layer. Each shape occupies the same coordinates it had on its former layer, but now all the shapes are together in the new layer. Hide the new layer to make sure that you did move the elements from their old layers.

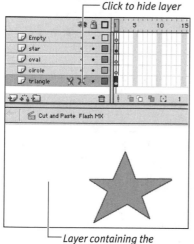

5. From the Edit menu, choose Paste in Place (**Figure 5.31**).

Flash pastes all three shapes back into their original locations on the Stage but on a different layer (**Figure 5.32**). Try hiding the empty layer temporarily; you should no longer see those three objects.

✔ Tips

- You've already learned that selecting an object on the Stage causes Flash to select that object's layer in the Timeline. As you move objects between layers, it helps to know that selections work the other way around, too. When you select a layer in the Timeline, Flash selects all the elements for that layer on the Stage.

- The process of cutting elements and using the Paste in Place command is, obviously, time-consuming, because you have to keep selecting new layers as you place the elements. To automate the process, use the Distribute to Layers command (see "Distributing Graphic Elements to Layers" later in this chapter).

Where Do Pasted Objects Go?

A Flash document can have only one layer active at a time. Any new shapes you create wind up on the currently selected or active layer. The same is true of placing copies of shapes or instances of symbols; if you copy and paste an element, Flash pastes the copy on the active layer. When you drag a symbol instance from the Library window, it winds up on the active layer.

Distributing Graphic Elements to Layers

As you draw elements for your movie, you may not always remember to create a new layer for each one. Using the Cut and Paste in Place commands can get tedious. Flash's Distribute to Layers feature automates the process, putting each element of a selection on a separate layer. This feature comes in handy when you start creating a type of animation called *motion tweening,* in which each element being animated must be on its own layer. (You'll learn more about motion tweening in Chapter 9.)

To place selected elements on individual layers:

1. Open a new file, and on the Stage, create several separate shapes on a single layer.

2. Choose Edit > Select All.
   Flash highlights all the shapes.

3. From the Modify menu, choose Distribute to Layers, or press Shift-⌘-D (Mac) or Ctrl-Shift-D (Windows) (**Figure 5.33**).
   Flash creates a layer for each shape and adds the new layers to the bottom of the Timeline. Each shape winds up in the same location on the Stage, but on a separate layer.

✔ Tips

■ Distribute to Layers works with selected groups and symbols as well as with selected raw shapes. (You learn about symbols in Chapter 6.) Flash distributes each selected group or symbol to its own layer; the separate elements of the group or symbol remain joined.

■ When you use Distribute to Layers, any unselected elements remain on their original layer. Only the selected shapes move to new layers.

Layers set to Preview in Context

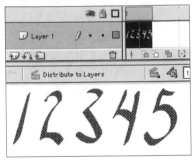

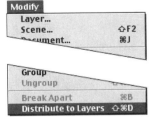

Figure 5.33 Selecting elements on the Stage and choosing Modify > Distribute to Layers automatically cuts each element and pastes it in place in a new layer. The new layers follow the order in which you placed the elements on the Stage originally. In this series of numbers, the numeral 1 was drawn first, so it winds up at the top of the section of new layers.

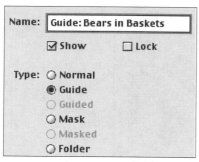

Figure 5.34 Select Guide as the layer type in the Layer Properties dialog box to change a normal layer to a guide layer.

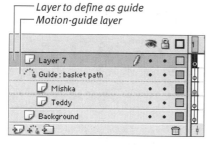

Figure 5.35 Select a layer (top) and define it as a guide layer. In the Timeline, Flash identifies the guide layer with a T-square icon; compare that with the icon for the motion-guide layer (bottom).

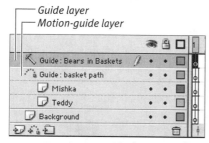

Working with Guide Layers

Flash offers two types of guide layers: guides and motion guides. Plain old guides can contain any kind of content: lines, shapes, or symbols. The contents of a regular guide layer merely serve as a point of reference to help you position items on the Stage. Flash doesn't include such guide layers in the final exported movie.

Motion guides, however, do make up part of the final movie. Motion-guide layers contain a single line that directs the movement of an animated object along a path. (To learn more about creating and animating with motion guides, see Chapter 9.) Another distinction to remember is that Flash creates motion guides by adding a new layer directly to the Timeline. To create plain guides, you must redefine an existing layer as a guide layer.

To create a plain guide layer:

1. *Do one of the following:*
   - ▲ To create a new layer, in the Timeline, click the Insert Layer button. Flash selects the new layer.
   - ▲ Select a layer that already exists.

2. From the Modify menu, choose Layer to display the Layer Properties dialog box.

3. In the Type section, click Guide (**Figure 5.34**).

   You can rename the layer to identify it as a guide, if you want.

4. Click OK.

   Flash turns the selected layer into a guide layer and places a little T-square icon before the layer name (**Figure 5.35**).

   (continues on next page)

WORKING WITH GUIDE LAYERS

5. From the View menu, choose Guides >
Snap to Guides (**Figure 5.36**).

Flash forces items that you draw or drag
to snap to the lines or shapes on guide
layers.

✔ Tips

■ You can create a guide layer quickly by
Control-clicking (Mac) or right-clicking
(Windows) the layer you want to define
as a guide. Choose Guide from the pop-
up contextual menu that appears.

■ When you've placed guide elements
where you need them for a certain scene,
lock the guide layer so that you don't
move the guides accidentally as you draw
on other layers.

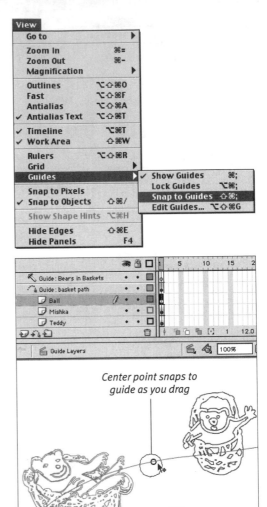

Figure 5.36 Choose View > Guides > Snap to Guides
(top) to force items that you draw on layers beneath
a guide layer to snap to the lines or shapes on the
guide layer (bottom).

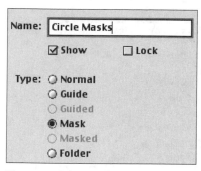

Figure 5.37 Select Mask as the layer type in the Layer Properties dialog box to define a layer as a mask.

Figure 5.38 The mask-layer icon imitates the masking effect with a dark mask shape over a checkerboard pattern.

Working with Mask Layers

Mask layers are special layers that allow you to hide and show elements on underlying layers. Shapes on the Mask layer are holes that allow items on linked layers to show through.

To create a mask layer:

1. *Do one of the following:*

   ▲ To create a new layer, in the Timeline, click the Insert Layer button. Flash selects the new layer.

   ▲ Select a layer that already exists.

   In general, you should create (or select) a layer directly above the layer containing content you want to mask, although you can always create the mask separately and link the masked layers to it later.

2. From the Modify menu, choose Layer to display the Layer Properties dialog box.

3. In the Type section, click Mask (**Figure 5.37**).

   You can also rename the layer to identify it as a mask, if you want.

4. Click OK.

   Flash turns the selected layer into a mask layer and places a mask icon before the layer name (**Figure 5.38**).

To link layers to the mask:

1. In the Timeline, select a layer that contains content you want to mask.

2. From the Modify menu, choose Layer to display the Layer Properties dialog box.

3. In the Type section, click Masked.

   You can rename the layer to identify it as a masked layer, if you want.

4. Click OK.

   Flash links the selected layer to the mask layer directly above it and places a masked icon before the name (**Figure 5.39**). Flash indents the icon and layer name to indicate that the mask above this layer controls it.

5. Repeat steps 1 through 4 to create more linked layers.

   One mask can affect many linked layers.

✔ Tips

■ To create new linked layers, in the Timeline, select the layer directly beneath the mask; then follow the steps for creating a new layer. To link existing layers to a mask layer quickly, simply drag them in the Timeline so that they sit directly below the mask itself or one of its linked layers.

■ Positioning a layer beneath a list of masked layers can be tricky. When you position a layer's preview line after the last layer in the masked set, you have the choice of adding the layer to the masked set or placing it at the main level of the Timeline. Use the preview line's subtle clues to place the layer where you want it. Position the layer directly beneath the last masked layer. To add the layer to the masked set, drag slightly to the right; the bump on the top of the preview bar moves over to the right. To add the layer to the main level of the Timeline drag slightly to the left; the bump follows suit.

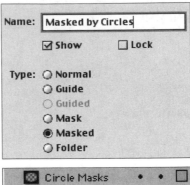

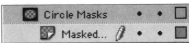

Figure 5.39 Set the Masked layer type in the Layer Properties dialog box (top). The checkerboard pattern on the layer icon in the Timeline indicates that the layer is masked (bottom).

WORKING WITH MASK LAYERS

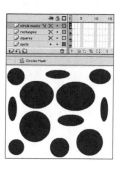 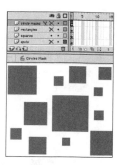

When you define this layer as a mask...

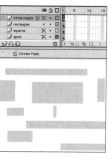 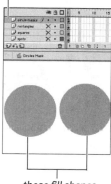

...these fill shapes become the mask

Figure 5.40 The content for the layers that the mask will reveal is just like any other content. You create the holes in the mask from filled shapes. All the mask elements must be on the same sublevel of the layer. In other words, you must either use only editable shapes or combine all your shapes into a single group or symbol.

To create the mask:

1. Create one or more layers containing graphic elements you want to reveal only through a mask.

2. Create a mask layer above your masked-content layers, and make sure that it's selected, visible, and unlocked.

   The layer should be highlighted in the Timeline, and the eye and padlock columns should contain bullets (not *X* or padlock icons).

3. Use the paintbrush, oval, or rectangle tool to create one or more fill shapes (**Figure 5.40**).

   Flash uses only fills to create the mask and ignores any lines on the mask layer. The mask may consist of several shapes on the mask layer, but they must all be on the same sublayer. (For more information on how sublayers within a layer work, see Chapter 4.)

   You can use several editable shapes, or you can create one group or symbol that contains all the shapes. If you combine editable shapes and a group or symbol, Flash uses just the editable shapes to create the mask. If you have two or more groups or symbols, Flash uses just the bottom-most group or symbol. (For more details on stacking order for groups and symbols, see Chapter 4.)

✔ Tip

■ To convert a particular layer into a mask and link the layer beneath it in one step, use the contextual layer menu. Control-click (Mac) or right-click (Windows) the layer you want to be the mask. From the pop-up contextual menu, choose Mask. Flash automatically defines the layer as a mask, links the layer beneath the selected layer to the mask, and locks both layers so that masking is in effect.

To see the mask's effect:

1. Lock the mask layer and all linked layers.

   or

   Control-click (Mac) or right-click (Windows) a mask (or masked) layer.

2. From the contextual menu, choose Show Masking (**Figure 5.41**).

   Flash automatically locks the mask layer and all the layers linked to it.

   In movie-editing mode, you must lock the mask layer and any masked layers beneath it to see the mask effect (**Figure 5.42**). You can see the effect without locking the layers in one of Flash's test modes (see Chapter 13).

To edit a mask:

1. In the Timeline, select the mask layer.

2. Make sure that the layer is visible and unlocked.

3. Use any of the techniques you learned in preceding chapters to create and edit fills.

✔ Tips

- If you want to break the connection between a mask and its linked layers, you can simply redefine the layer type for the masked layer in the Layer Properties dialog box.

- If you delete a mask layer, Flash redefines all the layers linked to it as normal layers.

- Keep in mind that masks use processor power. Using too many masks can slow the frame rate in your final movie.

Figure 5.41 The Show Masking command in the contextual menu for layers locks all layers linked to the selected mask.

Masking not on

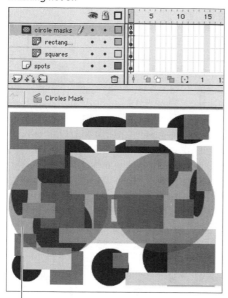

Transparent fill helps you
see what mask will reveal

Masking turned on

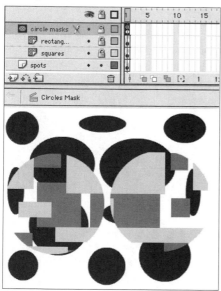

Figure 5.42 After defining the mask and masked layers, you must lock them to see the mask in effect in movie-editing mode.

The Mystery of Masks

A mask layer is like a window envelope (the ones you get your bills in). There may be whole sheaves of papers covered with numbers inside that envelope, but the outside presents a blank white front with just a little window that lets you see the portion of the bill showing your name and address. The mask layer is the window envelope, and the linked, or masked, layers are the papers inside.

In Flash, you create the window in the envelope by drawing and painting on a mask layer. (As you'll learn in Chapter 11, you can animate that window to create special effects.) Any filled shape on the mask layer becomes a window in the final movie. That window reveals whatever lies on the linked (or masked) layers inside the envelope. Within that envelope, you can have several layers that act just like any other Flash layers.

Here's where it gets a bit tricky. Any areas of the envelope (the mask layer) that you leave blank hide the corresponding areas of all the layers inside the envelope (the masked layers). But the same blank areas of the envelope allow all unlinked layers outside and below the envelope to show through.

SAVING AND REUSING GRAPHIC ELEMENTS

Library Terminology

The general term for an item stored in a Flash library is an *asset*. More specifically, graphics created with Flash's drawing tools and stored in a library are called *symbols*; fonts stored in a library are called *font symbols*; and sounds, video clips, and bitmaps (which are always stored in a library) are just called *sounds, video clips,* and *bitmaps*. Flash refers to each copy of a library asset that you actually use in a movie as an *instance* of that asset.

In the previous chapters, you learned to create and edit static graphics. Your ultimate goal will be to use those graphics in animated movies. And to reach that goal, you're likely to want to use items over again. You may want an element to appear several times in one movie, or you may want to use the same element in several movies. Macromedia Flash MX provides a container for storing graphics that makes it easy to do both. This container is called a *library*.

Every Flash document has its own library, where you can store the elements that go into a movie: text, sounds, video clips, animations, rollover buttons, bitmapped graphics, and vector graphics.

Flash's shared libraries let you share assets (including fonts) among movies. Sharing assets helps reduce the amount of material that must be downloaded to a user's system before he or she can view your Flash movies.

In this chapter, you learn to work with libraries and to create symbols that are static graphics. You also learn about shared libraries and font symbols. In later chapters, you learn about creating animated symbols and buttons (see Chapters 11 and 13), working with bitmapped graphics (see Chapter 7), and adding sounds and video (see Chapter 14).

Understanding the Library Window

The Library window offers several ways to view a library's contents and allows you to organize hierarchically the symbols, sounds, video clips, fonts, and bitmaps in folders. The Library window provides information about when an item was last modified, what type of item it is, and how many times the movie uses it. The Library window also contains shortcut buttons and menus for working with symbols. Flash has shortcuts for creating new folders, for renaming elements, and for deleting items quickly. Flash even remembers whether you had the Library window open during your last work session with a file. If so, it opens the Library window for you next time you open that file.

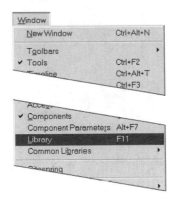

Figure 6.1 Choose Window > Library to open the library of the current Flash document.

To open the library of the current movie:

◆ From the Window menu, choose Library, or press F11 or press ⌘-L (Mac) or Ctrl-L (Windows) (**Figure 6.1**).

The Library window appears on the desktop (**Figure 6.2**).

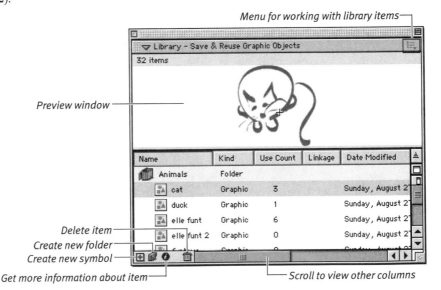

Figure 6.2 The Library window lists the assets assigned to the current document.

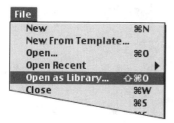

Figure 6.3 Choose File > Open As Library to access symbols from the library of another file.

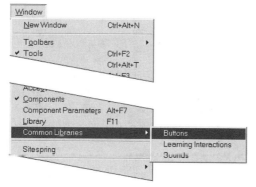

Figure 6.4 The Common Libraries menu gives you quick access to the libraries of Flash documents located inside the Libraries folder (You'll find it inside the First Run folder within the Flash application folder.)

What Are Common Libraries?

Flash makes a set of libraries available from the menu bar—a sort of library of libraries. Flash MX ships with three libraries, but you can add your own to the list. The Common Libraries menu makes it easy for you to access libraries of symbols, sounds, and bitmaps. The libraries in the Common Libraries menu are simply Flash files that live in the Libraries folder. (The Libraries folder is one of the folders in the First Run folder, which is inside the Macromedia Flash MX application folder.) Any files you add to the Libraries folder appear in the Common Libraries menu when you restart the application (**Figure 6.4**). Choosing an item from the Common Libraries menu opens only the library, not the file itself.

To open the library of another movie:

1. From the File menu, choose Open As Library, or press Shift-⌘-O (Mac) or Shift-Ctrl-O (Windows) (**Figure 6.3**).

   The Open As Library dialog box appears.

2. Navigate to the file whose library you want to open, select it, and click Open.

   The Library window appears on the desktop making those symbols available for use in other movies (see "Copying Symbols Between Movies" later in this chapter).

   You can add, delete, or modify elements only in the current movie; when you open another file as a library, you cannot modify the contents of that library. Flash grays out the background, shortcut icons, and most of the Options-menu choices in the Library window of a file that's not open.

✔ Tips

- The variety of menus from which you can open a library of some sort can be daunting at first. Here's the short rundown. To open a library window for the current movie, use Window > Library; to open the library of another file, use File > Open As Library; to open a library from your library of libraries, use the Window > Common Libraries menu (see the sidebar "What Are Common Libraries?" in this section).

- One handy way to keep all the symbols, sounds, video clips, and bitmaps you're using on a project accessible from the menu bar is to create a special My Project file. As you create symbols or import sounds, video clips, and bitmaps, add a copy of each item to My Project. Make the file one of your common libraries. On the Mac, you can put an alias of the file in the Library folder. When you choose the My Project alias from the Window > Common Libraries menu, Flash opens the library containing all your project's items.

UNDERSTANDING THE LIBRARY WINDOW

Understanding Library-Window Views

You can resize the Library window as you would any window, or toggle wide and narrow window views. In its wide state, the Library window displays up to five columns of information about each element (its name, what kind of object it is, how many times it appears in the movie, whether it's exported or imported as a shared asset, and the last modification date).

To view the wide Library window:

◆ In the open Library window, click the Wide Library View button (**Figure 6.5**).

Flash widens the window to accommodate all columns.

To view the narrow Library window:

◆ In the open Library window, click the Narrow Library View button.

Flash narrows the window to accommodate just the first column.

To resize Library columns:

1. In the Library window, position the pointer over a column-head divider.

The pointer changes to a double-arrow divider-moving icon.

2. Click and drag the divider (**Figure 6.6**).

✔ Tips

■ You can't change the order of the columns in the Library window, but you can hide any middle column you don't need to see. Try hiding the Kind column to save space. (The icon preceding each item indicates what type of asset it is.) Drag the divider on the right side of the Kind header until it's almost on top of the left divider. To reveal the column again, drag the divider back to the right.

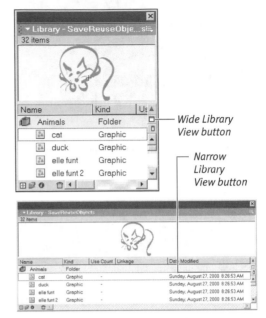

Wide Library View button

Narrow Library View button

Figure 6.5 Click the Wide Library View button to open a wide Library window. Click the Narrow Library View button to open a narrow one.

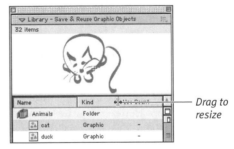

Drag to resize

Figure 6.6 Drag the divider between column headers to resize a column.

■ Flash tracks how many times you use a symbol instance, but, the Use Count column doesn't display the latest number automatically. To change that setting, from the Library window's Options menu, choose Keep Use Counts Updated. (This setting can slow Flash.) To update use counts periodically, choose Update Use Counts Now as needed.

Figure 6.7 From the Options menu in the Library window, choose New Folder to create a library folder.

Understanding Library Hierarchy

Flash lets you store library elements hierarchically within folders, which makes it easy to organize the elements of movies that contain numerous reused elements. To further aid you in organizing the Library window, Flash allows you to sort items by column.

To create a library folder:

1. Open the Library window.

2. To select a location, *do one of the following*:
   ▲ To add a root-level folder, select an item at the root level.
   ▲ To add a subfolder, select an item within the folder where you want to add the new subfolder.

3. To create the new folder, *do one of the following*:
   ▲ From the pop-up Options menu in the top-right corner of the window, choose New Folder (**Figure 6.7**).
   ▲ At the bottom of the window, click the New Folder button (**Figure 6.8**).
   Flash creates a new folder, selects it, and activates the text entry field.

4. Type a name for your folder.

5. Press Enter.

Select root-level item · To add root-level folder

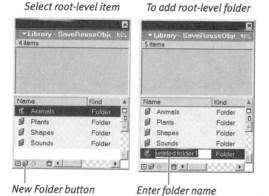

New Folder button · Enter folder name

Select item within a folder · To add subfolder

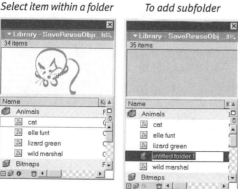

Figure 6.8 To create new folders and subfolders, click the New Folder button.

To open one library folder:

1. In the Library window, select a closed folder.

2. To open the folder, *do one of the following:*

   ▲ Double-click the folder icon.

   ▲ From the Library window's Options menu, choose Expand Folder.

   The folder's contents appear in the Library window (**Figure 6.9**).

To close one library folder:

1. In the Library window, select an open folder.

2. To close the folder, *do one of the following:*

   ▲ Double-click the folder icon.

   ▲ From the Library window's Options menu, choose Collapse Folder.

✔ Tip

■ To open all library folders at the same time, from the Library window's Options menu, choose Expand All Folders. To close all folders, choose Collapse All Folders.

Figure 6.9 Open folders in the Library window to display their contents.

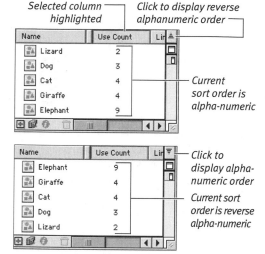

Selected column highlighted

Click to display reverse alphanumeric order

Current sort order is alpha-numeric

Click to display alpha-numeric order

Current sort order is reverse alpha-numeric

Figure 6.10 Click the Sort button to sort library items by data in the selected column.

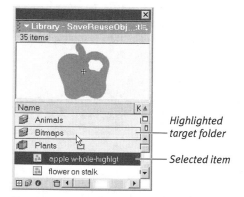

Highlighted target folder

Selected item

Figure 6.11 In the Library window, you can simply drag items between folders. (Windows users will see the target folder highlight; Macintosh users won't.)

To sort library items:

◆ In the Library window, click the heading of the column you want to sort by.

   To sort items by name, for example, click the Name column header. Flash highlights the chosen column header and sorts the Library window by the items in that column.

✔ Tip

■ To change the sort order, click the Sort button, which toggles between alphanumeric and reverse alphanumeric order (**Figure 6.10**).

To move items between library folders:

1. In the open Library window, select the item you want to move.

2. Drag the selected item over the icon of the destination folder.

   In Windows, Flash highlights the target folder (**Figure 6.11**). In the Macintosh operating systems, Flash provides no feedback about the destination folder, so be careful to position the item directly over the folder you want.

3. Release the mouse button.

   Flash moves the item into the new folder.

✔ Tip

■ To move an item to a new folder quickly, from the Library window's Options menu, choose Move to New Folder. A dialog box for naming the new folder appears.

UNDERSTANDING LIBRARY HIERARCHY

Converting Graphics to Symbols

Not all graphics in a Flash movie are symbols; you need to take special steps to define the items you create as symbols. You can turn graphics you've already created into symbols, or you can create a symbol from scratch in the symbol editor. After you do, the symbol resides in the library of the document in which you created the symbol. You can copy a symbol from one document to another or from one library to another; the symbol then resides separately in each document's library. (You can also define shared symbols that reside in shared libraries; see "Creating Shared Libraries" later in this chapter.)

The standard library of a Flash document contains all the symbols used in that document; it can also contain unused symbols and pointers to symbols in shared libraries.

The following exercise covers creating static graphic symbols. But you can also turn graphics into symbols that are animations (see Chapter 11) or buttons (see Chapter 13).

What Is Symbol Behavior?

In Flash, you must specify a behavior for each symbol. Symbols have three behaviors: graphic, button, and movie clip.

Graphics are, as you might expect, graphic elements, but they can also be animated graphic elements. The feature that distinguishes one symbol behavior from another is the way the symbol interacts with the Timeline of the movie in which it appears. Graphic symbols operate in step with the Timeline of the movie in which they appear. If you have a static graphic symbol, it takes up one frame of the movie in which you place it (just as any graphic element would). A three-frame animated graphic symbol takes up three frames of the movie (see Chapter 11).

Buttons have their own four-frame Timeline; a button sits in a single frame of a movie but displays its four frames as a user's mouse interacts with it (see Chapter 13).

Movie clips have their own multiframe Timeline that plays independently of the main movie's Timeline (see Chapter 11).

Figure 6.12 Choose Insert > Convert to Symbol to turn an existing graphic into a symbol.

To turn an existing graphic into a symbol:

1. On the Stage, select the graphic you want to convert to a symbol.

   Flash highlights the graphic.

2. From the Insert menu, choose Convert to Symbol (**Figure 6.12**), or press F8 on the keyboard.

   The Convert to Symbol dialog box appears (**Figure 6.13**). Flash gives the symbol a default name—for example, Symbol 16—based on the number of symbols created for the library.

3. If you don't want to use the default, type a name for your symbol.

4. Choose Graphic as the behavior for your symbol.

   (continues on next page)

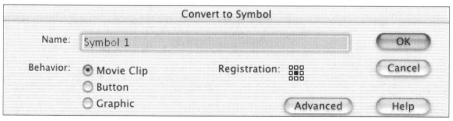

Figure 6.13 The Convert to Symbol dialog box lets you name your symbol, define its behavior, and set its registration point. You can expand the box to set linkages for sharing and import/export by clicking the Advanced button.

CONVERTING GRAPHICS TO SYMBOLS

5. To set the symbol's registration and center point to something other than centered, click one of the squares on the perimeter of the registration proxy diagram.

By default, Flash selects the central square in the proxy, placing the center point and registration mark at the center of the element's bounding box. You can place these elements on any of the corners or sides by selecting another point in the proxy.

6. Click OK.

Flash adds the symbol to the library. The graphic on the Stage becomes an instance of the symbol. The selection highlight no longer appears directly over the graphic itself, but on the symbol's bounding box. A crosshair within a circle appears, indicating location of the registration mark and center point of the symbol (**Figure 6.14**). You can no longer edit the item directly on the Stage; you must open it in one of Flash's symbol-editing modes.

✔ Tips

■ To convert a graphic element to a symbol quickly, select the element on the Stage and drag it to the lower half of the movie's Library window. The Convert to Symbol dialog box appears. Name and define your symbol as described in the preceding exercise.

■ The center point and the registration mark coincide within the master symbol in the library. For individual instances of the symbol, you can reposition the center point by using the free-transform tool. Select the symbol on the Stage; then drag the center-point circle to a new location. (The registration crosshair remains where it was.)

Selected object

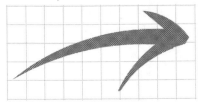

Converted to a symbol

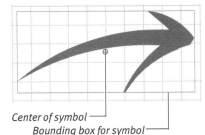

Center of symbol ⎯⎯
Bounding box for symbol ⎯⎯

Figure 6.14 A selected graphic element on the Stage is highlighted with dots. When you convert the graphic to a symbol, the bounding box is the only item that gets highlighted. A crosshair in a circle indicates where the symbol's registration mark and center point are.

Registration Mark Versus Center Point

The symbol's registration mark (the small crosshair) is the point that Flash considers to be the 0,0 point for the symbol. Flash uses that point to register the symbol in ActionScript operations. The registration mark stays the same for all instances of the symbol.

The center point (the small circle) is the point that you can use for snap-to-guide or snap-to-grid operations. It is the stable reference point Flash uses for transforming the symbol. When you rotate a symbol by using the free-transform tool in Rotate and Skew mode, for example, the center point is the pivot around which the symbol spins. You can redefine the center point of individual symbol instances by using the free-transform tool.

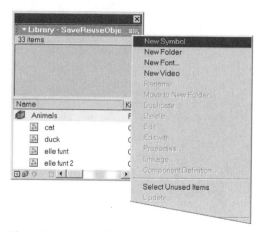

Figure 6.15 From the Library window's Options menu, choose New Symbol to create a symbol from scratch.

New Symbol button

Figure 6.16 Click the Library window's New Symbol button to create a symbol from scratch.

Creating New Symbols from Scratch

You can avoid the conversion process described in the preceding section by creating graphics directly in symbol-editing mode. This practice makes all the tools, frames, and layers of the Flash editor available, but Flash defines the element you are creating as a symbol from the start.

To create a new symbol:

1. To enter symbol-editing mode, *do one of the following:*

   ▲ From the Insert menu, choose New Symbol, or press ⌘-F8 (Mac) or Ctrl-F8 (Windows).

   ▲ From the Library window's Options menu, choose New Symbol (**Figure 6.15**).

   ▲ In the bottom-left corner of the Library window, click the New Symbol button (**Figure 6.16**).

   The Create New Symbol dialog box appears.

   (continues on next page)

2. Type a name for your symbol.

3. Choose Graphic as the behavior for your symbol.

4. Click OK.

   Flash enters symbol-editing mode. Flash displays the name of the symbol you are creating in the info bar above the Stage and places a crosshair in the center of the Stage (**Figure 6.17**). The crosshair indicates the symbol's center and acts as a registration mark.

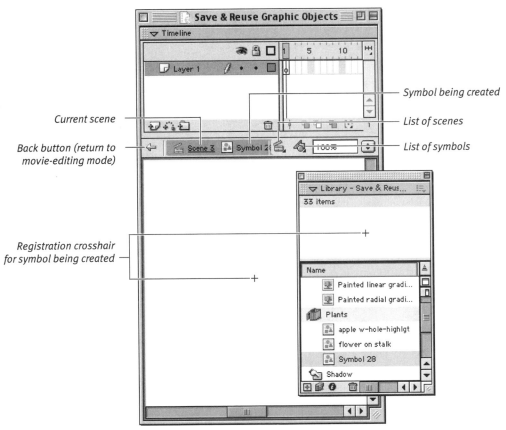

Figure 6.17 In symbol-editing mode, the name of the symbol being worked on appears in the info bar just above the Stage.

Figure 6.18 Click the Back button or the Current Scene button to return to movie-editing mode.

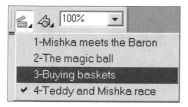

Figure 6.19 Choose a scene from the Edit Scene pop-up menu to return to movie-editing mode.

5. Create your graphic on the Stage of the symbol editor as you would in the regular editing environment.

6. To return to movie-editing mode, *do one of the following*:

   ▲ From the Edit menu, choose Edit Document. Flash returns you to the current scene.

   ▲ In the info bar above the Stage, click the Back button or the Current Scene button (**Figure 6.18**). Flash returns you to the current scene.

   ▲ From the Edit Scene pop-up menu in the info bar, choose a scene (**Figure 6.19**). Flash takes you to that scene.

✔ Tip

■ When you enter symbol-editing mode, the central crosshair registration mark may be outside the current viewing area. To bring the registration mark to the center of your window, choose View > Magnification > Show Frame.

Where Am I?

When you edit symbols, Flash simply switches the current window to symbol-editing mode. It's easy to get confused about whether you're editing the main movie or a symbol. Learn to recognize the following subtle visual cues; they are the only indication that you are in symbol-editing mode.

In symbol-editing mode, Flash displays the name of the scene and symbol you are editing in the info bar above the Stage. Also, a small crosshair, which acts as a registration point for the symbol, appears on the Stage. Apart from these changes, the Timeline, the Stage, and the tools all appear and work just as they do in the Flash editor.

Using Symbol Instances

A *symbol instance* is a pointer to the full description of the symbol. Symbols help keep file sizes small. If you converted a graphic on the Stage to a symbol, you already have one symbol instance on the Stage. If you want to use the symbol again, or if you created your symbol from scratch in symbol-editing mode, you'll need to get a copy out of the library and onto the Stage.

To place a symbol instance in your movie:

1. In the Timeline, select the layer and keyframe where you want the graphic symbol to appear.

   Flash can place symbols only in keyframes. If you are currently in a blank frame, Flash places the symbol in the preceding keyframe. (To learn more about keyframes, see Chapter 8.)

2. Open the library that contains the symbol you want to use.

3. In the Library window, navigate to the symbol you want to place on the Stage, and click it to select it.

   Flash highlights the chosen symbol and displays it in the preview window.

4. Position your pointer over the preview window.

5. Click and drag a copy of the symbol onto the Stage.

   Flash previews the symbol's location on the Stage with a rectangular outline (**Figure 6.20**).

6. Release the mouse button.

   Flash places the symbol on the Stage and selects it.

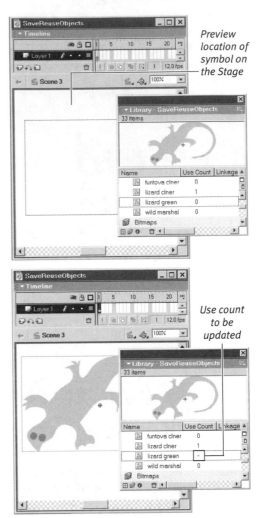

Preview location of symbol on the Stage

Use count to be updated

Figure 6.20 When you drag a symbol from the Library window to the Stage (top), Flash places the symbol on the Stage, selects it, and updates that symbol's use count (bottom). When you are not keeping use counts updated constantly, the dash in the Use Count column indicates a change. To see the actual figure, choose Update Use Counts Now from the Library window's Options menu.

Why Use Symbols?

Symbols help you keep file sizes small. You've already learned how Flash uses vectors to hold down file size: Each vector shape is really just a set of instructions—a recipe for creating the shape. So you could duplicate a vector graphic that you want to reuse, and it would be smaller than a bitmapped version of the same graphic. But symbols are even more efficient than duplicate vector shapes.

A symbol is a master recipe. Imagine a busy restaurant that serves three kinds of soup—chicken noodle, cream of chicken rice, and chicken with garden vegetables—and each pot of soup has its own cook. The head chef could go over with each cook all the steps required to make chicken broth, but that would involve a lot of repetition and take a lot of time.

If the restaurant has a master recipe for chicken broth, the chef can simply tell all the cooks to make a pot of chicken broth and then tell each cook just those additional steps that distinguish each dish—add noodles for chicken noodle; add rice and cream for cream of chicken rice; and add potatoes, carrots, and peas for garden vegetable.

Symbols act the same way in your movie file. The full recipe is in the library. Each instance on the Stage contains just the instructions that say which recipe to start with and how to modify it—for example, use the recipe for the red rectangle but make it twice as large, change the color to blue, and rotate it 45 degrees clockwise. Because symbols can themselves contain other symbols, it really pays to break your graphic elements into their lowest-common-denominator parts, make each individual part a symbol, and then combine the parts into larger symbols or graphics.

Modifying Symbol Instances

You can change the appearance of individual symbol instances without changing the master symbol itself. As with any other element, you can resize and reposition an instance (for example, scale and rotate it) by using Toolbox tools, panels, and the Property Inspector (see Chapter 3).

You can also change a symbol instance's color and transparency, but the method differs from that for assigning colors to raw shapes. You modify the color, intensity, and transparency of a symbol instance via the Color menu in the Property Inspector.

To access the Property Inspector:

◆ If the Property Inspector is not currently open, from the Window menu, choose Properties.

The Property Inspector opens (**Figure 6.21**).

To change an instance's brightness:

1. On the Stage, select the symbol instance you want to modify.

2. From the Property Inspector's Color menu, choose Brightness.

   A field for entering a new brightness percentage appears (**Figure 6.22**).

3. Enter a value in the Brightness field.

   A value of –100 makes the symbol black; a value of 0 leaves the symbol at its original brightness; a value of 100 makes the symbol white (**Figure 6.23**).

4. Press Enter.

   Flash applies the brightness setting to the selected symbol on the Stage.

Figure 6.21 Select a symbol instance on the Stage, and the Property Inspector becomes the gateway to modifying that symbol instance. You can alter the height, width, location, and behavior of the selected symbol by entering new values in the corresponding fields. You can apply color effects from the inspector's Color menu.

Figure 6.22 Use the Brightness settings in the Property Inspector to change the intensity of a symbol instance.

–100 percent brightness setting

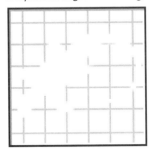

100 percent brightness setting

Figure 6.23 At its extremes, the Brightness setting lets you turn a symbol instance completely black or completely white.

✔ Tip

■ To place a symbol instance quickly, you can drag the symbol name directly from the Library window to the Stage without using the previewed image.

Tint amount ⌐
Tint color ⌐

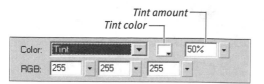

Figure 6.24 Use the Tint settings in the Property Inspector to change the color of a symbol instance.

Color: Alpha ▼ 100% ▼

Figure 6.25 Use the Alpha settings in the Property Inspector to change the transparency of a symbol instance.

To change the instance's color:

1. On the Stage, select the symbol instance you want to modify.

2. From the Property Inspector's Color menu, choose Tint.

   Tint-modification parameters appear (**Figure 6.24**).

3. To choose a new color, *do one of the following*:

   ▲ In the Red, Green, and Blue fields, enter new RGB values.

   ▲ Click the tint-color box, and choose a color from the swatch set that appears.

4. Type a percentage in the Tint Amount field.

   The tint percentage indicates how much of the new color to blend with the existing colors. Applying a tint of 100 percent changes all the lines and fills in the symbol to the new color. Applying a lesser percentage mixes some of the new color with the existing colors in the symbol. It's almost like placing a transparent film of the new color over the symbol.

5. Press Enter.

   Flash applies the tint settings to the selected symbol on the Stage.

To change the instance's transparency:

1. On the Stage, select the symbol instance you want to modify.

2. From the Property Inspector's Color menu, choose Alpha (**Figure 6.25**).

3. Enter a new value in the Alpha field.

   A value of 0 makes the symbol completely transparent; a value of 100 makes the symbol completely opaque.

4. Press Enter.

   Flash applies the alpha setting to the selected symbol on the Stage.

MODIFYING SYMBOL INSTANCES

249

To change the instance's tint and alpha simultaneously:

1. On the Stage, select the symbol instance you want to modify.

2. From the Property Inspector's Color menu, choose Advanced.

   A Settings button appears to the right of the menu in the Property Inspector.

3. Click the Settings button.

   The Advanced Effect dialog box appears (**Figure 6.26**). This dialog box contains sliders and text boxes for changing red, green, blue, and alpha values.

4. Adjust the values to fine-tune the color and transparency of the symbol instance.

5. To apply the color effect, click OK.

✔ Tips

- Instead of pressing Enter to confirm a value you enter in one of the Property Inspector's fields, you can just click elsewhere in the Property Inspector or click the Stage.

- To preview new color values interactively, click and drag the triangle to the right of an entry field. Flash updates the symbol on the Stage as you drag the slider lever. When you release the slider, Flash confirms the change; you don't need to press Enter.

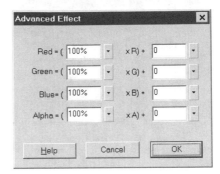

Figure 6.26 Click the Advanced Settings button in the Property Inspector (top) to access the Advanced Effect dialog box (bottom). Enter new values to change the color and transparency of a symbol instance.

The Mystery of Advanced Effect Settings

The Advanced Effect settings allow you to change the RGB values and alpha values for a symbol instance simultaneously. The sliders in the left-hand column control what percentage of the RGB and alpha values that make up the colors in the original symbol will appear in the symbol instance. The sliders on the right add to or subtract from the red, green, blue, and alpha values of the original colors.

Imagine a symbol with three ovals. One is pure red, one is pure green, and one is pure blue. The alpha setting is 50 percent. Changing the percentage of the red slider (the column on the left) affects only the red oval. The green and blue ovals contain no red at all; doubling the amount of red in a pure green doesn't change the green. Changing the slider in the right-hand column affects the amount of red in everything, including the green and blue ovals. These ovals now start to change color.

Swap button

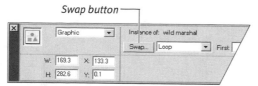

Figure 6.27 The Swap button in the Property Inspector lets you replace a selected symbol instance with an instance of a different symbol from the same document. (Choose Window > Properties to access the inspector if it is not already open.)

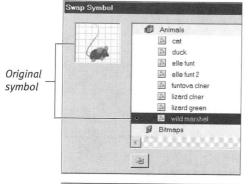

Original symbol

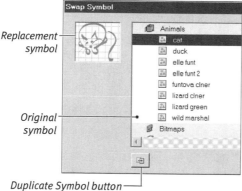

Replacement symbol

Original symbol

Duplicate Symbol button

Figure 6.28 Select a replacement symbol from the list in the Swap Symbol dialog box, and click OK to exchange one symbol for another.

Swapping One Symbol Instance for Another

Flash allows you to replace one symbol instance with another while retaining all the modifications you've made in the symbol instance. If, for example, you want to change the look of a logo in certain places in your site but not everywhere, you can create the new logo as a separate symbol and swap it in as needed. (If you want to change the look for every instance, you could edit the master logo symbol directly, as you learn to do in "Editing Master Symbols" later in the chapter.) You perform symbol swapping in the Property Inspector (**Figure 6.27**).

To switch symbols:

1. On the Stage, select the symbol instance you want to change.

2. In the Property Inspector, click the Swap Symbol button.

   The Swap Symbol dialog box appears, listing all the symbols in the current document's library (**Figure 6.28**). In the Windows operating systems, Flash highlights the name of the symbol you're modifying and places a bullet next to its name in the Symbol list.

   (continues on next page)

3. From the Symbol list, select the replacement symbol.

The original symbol remains bulleted; Flash highlights the new symbol and places it in the preview window.

4. Click OK.

Flash places the new symbol on the Stage, locating the new object where the old one was located and applying any modifications you previously made for that instance (**Figure 6.29**).

✔ Tips

- To swap symbols quickly, double-click the new symbol in the Swap Symbol dialog box. Flash replaces it and closes the dialog box.

- The Duplicate Symbol button in the Swap Symbol dialog box allows you to make a copy of whatever symbol is selected in the list. If you know you need to tweak the master version of the replacement symbol for this instance but also want to keep the current version, create a duplicate and select it as the replacement. You can edit the duplicate's master symbol later.

Unmodified instance of mouse

Unmodified instance of cat

Instance of mouse scaled and rotated before swapping

After swapping: scaling and rotation applied to cat

Figure 6.29 When you swap symbols, any modifications you have made for the selected instance you're swapping apply to the replacement instance.

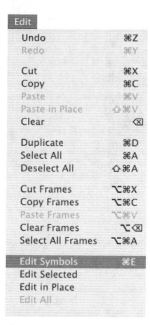

Figure 6.30 Choosing Edit > Edit Symbols takes you from movie-editing mode to symbol-editing mode. If you have selected a symbol on the Stage, choosing Edit > Edit Selected also takes you to symbol-editing mode.

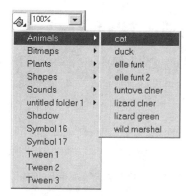

Figure 6.31 Choosing a symbol from this pop-up list of symbols in the info bar takes you into symbol-editing mode.

Editing Master Symbols

After you create a symbol, you can refine and modify it in symbol-editing mode. Unlike modifications of a symbol instance, which affect just that instance on the Stage, leaving the master symbol in the library unchanged, modifications made in symbol-editing mode affect the master symbol and all instances of that symbol in your movie.

You can enter symbol-editing mode in several ways.

To enter symbol-editing mode from the Stage:

1. On the Stage, select the symbol you want to edit.

2. To open the symbol editor, *do one of the following:*

   ▲ From the Edit menu, choose Edit Symbols, or press ⌘-E (Mac) or Ctrl-E (Windows) (**Figure 6.30**).

   ▲ From the Edit menu, choose Edit Selected.

   ▲ From the pop-up list of symbols in the info bar, choose the symbol you want to edit (**Figure 6.31**).

   Flash opens the symbol editor in the current window.

✔ Tip

■ To enter symbol-editing mode quickly, double-click a symbol instance on the Stage.

To enter symbol-editing mode from the Library window:

1. In the Library window, select the symbol you want to edit.

2. To bring up the symbol editor, *do one of the following:*

   ▲ From the Options menu, choose Edit.

   ▲ Double-click the icon next to the selected symbol name.

   ▲ Double-click the symbol in the preview window.

   Flash opens the symbol editor in the main window of the current movie (**Figure 6.32**).

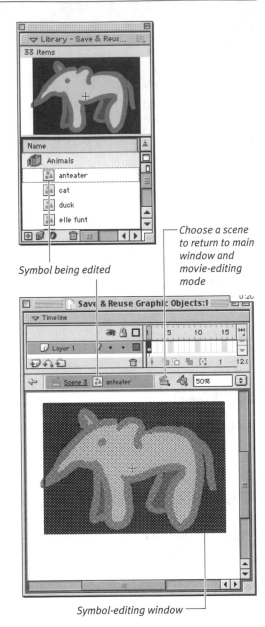

Symbol being edited

Choose a scene to return to main window and movie-editing mode

Symbol-editing window

Figure 6.32 Double-clicking a symbol in the Library window (top) opens that symbol in symbol-editing mode in the main window of the active movie (bottom).

Symbol being edited

Figure 6.33 The Edit in Place command allows you to see your symbol instance in context with other items on the stage. The symbol instance appears in full color; the other elements on the Stage are grayed out. In this mode, changes made to the instance affect the master symbol and all the instances in the movie.

✔ Tips

- After you've placed an instance of a symbol on the Stage, you may want to change the master symbol to make it fit with the items around it. The Edit in Place command allows you to edit your master symbol in context on the Stage with all other items grayed out (**Figure 6.33**). To evoke the Edit in Place command, choose Edit >. Edit in Place. Or Control-click (Mac) or right-click (Windows) the symbol instance you want to edit, and from the contextual menu that appears, choose Edit in Place. Any changes you make affect all instances of that symbol.

- You can edit a symbol in a separate window from your movie. Select an instance of the symbol on the Stage; Control-click (Mac) or right-click (Windows) to access the contextual menu; and choose Edit in New Window. To return to movie-editing mode, close the window.

Duplicating Master Symbols

Although you can always modify the instances of a symbol on the Stage, if you need to use one variation of a symbol over and over, you can duplicate the original master symbol and then modify the duplicate to create a new master symbol with those variations.

To create a duplicate symbol:

1. In the Library window, select the symbol you want to duplicate.

2. From the Options menu, choose Duplicate (**Figure 6.34**).

   Flash opens the Duplicate Symbol dialog box, giving the duplicate symbol a default name (**Figure 6.35**).

3. If you want, type a new name for your symbol.

4. Choose Graphic as the behavior for your symbol.

5. Click OK.

   Flash adds the new symbol to the library at the same level in the hierarchy as the original (**Figure 6.36**). The duplicate doesn't link to the original symbol in any way. You can change the duplicate without changing the original, and vice versa.

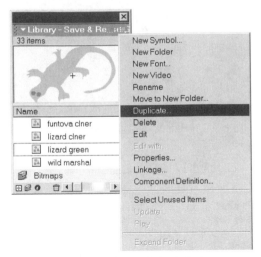

Figure 6.34 From the Library window's Options pop-up menu, choose Duplicate to make a copy of the selected symbol.

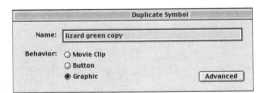

Figure 6.35 The default duplicate name for a symbol in the Duplicate Symbol dialog box is the original name plus the word copy.

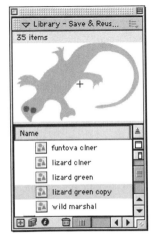

Figure 6.36 Flash puts duplicated symbols at the same library level as the original.

Delete selected item

Figure 6.37 Click the trash can icon to delete a selected library item.

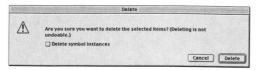

Figure 6.38 Deleting items in the Library is not undoable. Flash gives you a chance to change your mind with this warning dialog box.

Deleting Master Symbols

Deleting symbols can be a little trickier than deleting raw shapes or grouped shapes on the Stage. Deleting one instance of a symbol from its place on the Stage is easy; just use the methods for cutting or deleting graphics discussed in Chapter 3. Deleting symbols from the Library is not difficult but does require some thought, because instances of the symbol may still be in use in your movie. Flash gives you the option to delete all traces of the symbol from the movie or to delete just the graphic portions while keeping a placeholder for the instance, which you can replace with another symbol later.

To delete one symbol from the library:

1. In the Library window, select the symbol you want to remove.

2. To delete the symbol, *do one of the following*:

   ▲ At the bottom of the window, click the Delete button (the trash-can icon) (**Figure 6.37**).

   ▲ From the pop-up Options menu in the top-right corner of the window, choose Delete.

   Flash displays a dialog box, warning that you can't undo the delete operation and giving you the option of deleting all symbol instances in your movie (**Figure 6.38**).

3. To delete all instances of the symbol from the movie completely, check the Delete Symbol Instances checkbox.

   or

   To delete the graphic portion of all instances of the symbol but preserve placeholders for each one, uncheck the Delete Symbol Instances checkbox.

   (continues on next page)

4. To complete the deletion, *do one of the following:*

▲ To stop the operation, click Cancel.

▲ To continue, click Delete.

Deleting permanently removes the symbol from the library. If you check the Delete Symbol Instances option, Flash also removes all instances of the symbol from the Stage completely. If you do not choose that option, Flash retains a small square placeholder—equivalent to the center point of the symbol—for each instance of the symbol on the Stage (**Figure 6.39**).

✔ Tip

■ The instance placeholder for a deleted master symbol retains all the attributes of the instance (**Figure 6.40**). You can select that placeholder and swap in another symbol instance. Any changes you made in the original instance's tint, height, or width, for example, apply to the new symbol instance (see "Swapping One Symbol Instance for Another" earlier in this chapter).

To delete a folder of symbols from the library:

1. Select the folder you want to remove.

2. Follow steps 2 through 4 of the preceding exercise.

Flash removes the folder and all the symbols it contained from the library.

If you chose Delete Symbol Instances in step 3, Flash also removes any instances of those symbols in use in the movie.

If you left the Delete Symbol Instances checkbox unchecked in step 3, Flash retains placeholders in the movie for each deleted symbol instance.

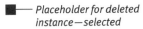

Placeholder for deleted instance—not selected

Figure 6.39 In the Delete dialog box, when you do not select Delete Symbol Instances (top), Flash keeps a symbol-instance placeholder in the movie for every symbol instance that you used (bottom). Choose Delete Symbol Instances to make Flash fully delete all instances of the selected symbol.

Placeholder for deleted instance—selected

Figure 6.40 This deleted-symbol placeholder retains information about modifications made to the instance it stands for. When you select the placeholder (top), that information appears in the Property Inspector (bottom). Use the Swap button to bring in a new symbol; Flash makes the same modifications to the new symbol.

✔ Tip

■ Always carefully check the usage numbers before you delete library items. You don't want to delete a symbol that you're currently using in a movie, which is especially easy to do if you've nested symbols within symbols. Some earlier versions of Flash would warn you when you tried to delete an item that was in use in a movie. All you get now is the warning that you can't undo deletions from a library.

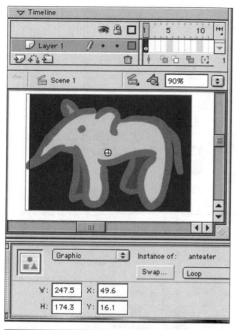

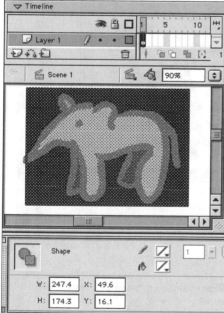

Figure 6.41 The Property Inspector reveals that the selected graphic is a symbol instance (top). To break the link with its master symbol, choose Modify > Break Apart. The Property Inspector reveals that the selection now consists of shapes; it's no longer a symbol instance (bottom).

Converting Symbol Instances to Graphics

At times, you'll want to break the link between a placed instance of a symbol and the master symbol. You may want to redraw the shape in a specific instance but not in every instance, for example. To convert a symbol back to an independent shape or set of shapes, break it apart, just as you break apart grouped shapes (see Chapter 4).

To break the symbol link:

1. On the Stage, select the symbol instance whose link you want to break.

2. From the Modify menu, choose Break Apart, or press ⌘-B (Mac) or Ctrl-B (Windows) (**Figure 6.41**).

   Flash breaks the link to the symbol in the library and selects the symbol's elements. The Property Inspector no longer displays information about the instance of the symbol; it displays information about the selected shapes, groups, and/or symbols.

   If you grouped any of the original elements, they remain grouped after you break the link; ungrouped elements stay ungrouped. Any symbols that existed within the original symbol remain as instances of their respective master symbols. Now you can edit these elements as you learned to do in previous chapters.

Copying Symbols Between Movies

It's easy to reuse symbols. You can transfer symbols via the Clipboard, copying or cutting symbols from one movie and using one of the paste commands to place them in another movie. You can also transfer symbols by dragging them from one movie or library to another, or you can import an entire library of symbols directly into the library of an open movie file.

To transfer symbols to another movie:

1. Open the destination file (the movie in which you would like to reuse existing symbols), or create a new file.

2. Open the source file (the movie containing symbols that you want to reuse).

3. Open the Library window for each file.

   Be sure to size and position the movie-editing and Library windows so that all four are visible on your screen at the same time.

4. To transfer a symbol, *do one of the following:*

   ▲ On the Stage of the source file, select a symbol and drag it to the Stage of the destination file (**Figure 6.42**).

   ▲ On the Stage of the source file, select a symbol and drag it to the lower portion of the Library window of the destination file.

   ▲ In the Library of the source file, select a symbol and drag it to the Stage of the destination file.

   ▲ In the Library of the source file, select a symbol and drag it to the lower portion of the Library window of the destination file.

   When you drag a symbol to the Stage, Flash places the symbol at the root level of the library hierarchy. You can also drag the symbol directly into a folder.

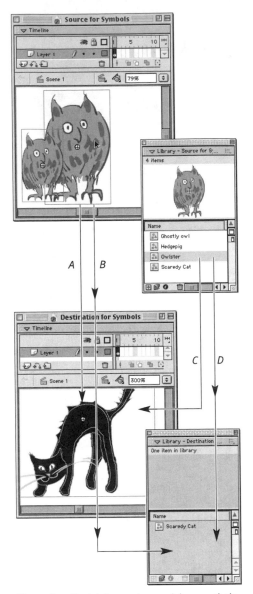

Figure 6.42 Flash lets you drag and drop symbols from Stage to Stage (A), Stage to Library window (B), Library window to Stage (C), or Library window to Library window (D).

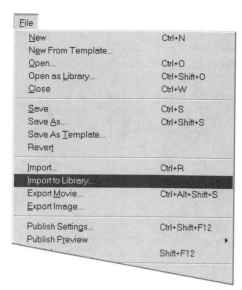

Figure 6.43 Choose File > Import to Library to bring a whole library of symbols and assets into the open movie's library.

✔ Tips

■ If you drag a symbol to the Stage, and a symbol with that name already exists in the root level of the destination file's library (or if you try to place that "duplicate" symbol in a folder containing a symbol with that name), Flash displays a warning dialog box. You can cancel the transfer or replace the existing symbol with the one you are transferring, rename the source file's symbol, create a new folder in your destination library and drag the symbol directly to that folder. Then you can rename the symbol in your destination file.

■ You don't have to open the source file to drag symbols from its library. Choose File > Open As Library to open just the Library window. Select a symbol and drag it to the destination Stage or Library window.

You can also import all the symbols from one movie directly to another's library.

To import an entire library:

1. Open or create the destination file.

2. From the File menu, choose Import to Library (**Figure 6.43**).

   The Import to Library dialog box appears.

3. Navigate to the source file.

4. Click Open.

   Flash brings all the assets from the selected source file's library into the destination file's library.

✔ Tip

■ You can use the File > Import to Library command to bring other individual asset files—such as video clips, sounds, and bitmaps—into your movie as well. (You'll learn more about importing non-Flash graphics in Chapter 7; Chapter 14 covers importing sounds and video.)

Creating Shared Libraries

Flash provides two ways to share library assets. In *author-time sharing,* Flash authors can grab symbols (or other assets) from centralized source files and use those symbols in the movies they are creating. In *run-time sharing,* symbols (and other assets) used in one or more movies reside in a central location, from which the Flash Player downloads the symbols for playback.

For the following exercises, create two movies. Name them for their functions—for example, ItemsToShare.fla and UsingSharedItems.fla. In the file ItemsToShare, create one symbol named Square and another named Rectangle, and place an instance of each symbol on the Stage. In the file UsingSharedItems, create one symbol named Circle and another named Oval, and place an instance of each symbol on the Stage. Save both files in the same folder; call it SharingTest.

To access a shared symbol while authoring:

1. In the destination file (UsingSharedItems.fla), select the symbol named Circle in the Library window.

2. From the Options menu in the top-right corner of the Library window, choose Properties.

   The expanded/advanced version of the Symbol Properties dialog box appears (**Figure 6.44**).

3. In the Source section of the dialog box, click the Browse button.

   The Open dialog box appears.

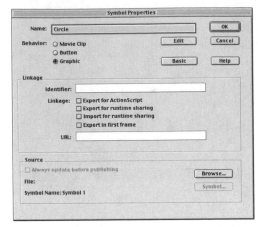

Figure 6.44 The expanded Symbol Properties dialog box contains all the advanced symbol properties, such as linkage to source files for authoring and export/import of symbols for run-time sharing.

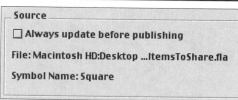

Figure 6.45 In the Select Source Symbol dialog box, select a "super" master symbol to be shared while authoring a destination file (top). Flash automatically enters the pathway to the source file in the Source section of the Symbol Properties dialog box (bottom).

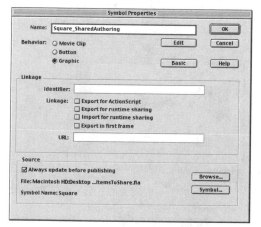

Figure 6.46 With author-time shared symbols you can simply bring a shared symbol into your destination fill; and create no further link to the source file; or you can create a link, so that changes made to the shared symbol in its source file also get made in the destination file when it's published. Check Always Update Before Publishing if you want to incorporate new changes into the source symbol when you publish your movie.

4. Navigate to the source file (ItemsToShare.fla), select it, and click Open.

   The Select Source Symbol dialog box appears, listing the symbols in the source file (**Figure 6.45**).

5. Select the symbol named Square.

6. Click OK.

   Flash returns you to the Symbol Properties dialog box. The Source section now lists the symbol name and the path to the source file.

7. In the Name field, enter a new name for the symbol, such as Square_SharedAuthoring.

   Flash makes no obvious indication in either the source or destination library that a symbol is linked. For your own tracking, you may want to alter the names of linked symbols to remind you of that fact.

8. In the Source section of the dialog box, check the Always Update Before Publishing checkbox (**Figure 6.46**).

   When you choose this setting, Flash takes the content of the latest version of the symbol from the source file and uses it to update the linked symbol in the destination file any time you publish or test the destination movie.

   (continues on next page)

9. Click OK.

In the library of the destination movie (UsingSharedItems.fla), Flash replaces the content of the master symbol named Circle with the content of the source symbol named Square. Any instances of Circle in use in the destination movie get updated as well (**Figure 6.47**). All instances retain their individual positioning, sizing, and color effects.

Now any changes you make in the Square symbol in the source file get incorporated into the destination file when you publish the destination file.

✔ Tip

■ Earlier in this chapter, you learned to swap symbols within a single movie while retaining individual instance modifications. You can use author-time sharing as a sort of super symbol swap, bringing in a symbol that's not currently part of your document. Follow the steps in the preceding exercise, but omit step 8. Flash replaces the content of your selected symbol just once; future changes to the symbol in the source file will not affect the destination file.

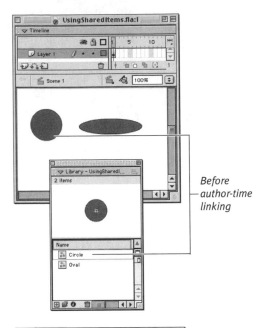

Before author-time linking

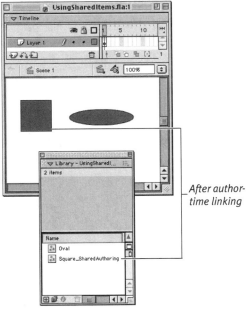

After author-time linking

Figure 6.47 When you link the symbol named Circle to the author-time shared symbol named Square (top), Flash replaces the circle with the square. Unless you've renamed the Circle symbol, it's still called Circle in the destination file. You can give the symbol a name that indicates it's linked to another symbol (bottom).

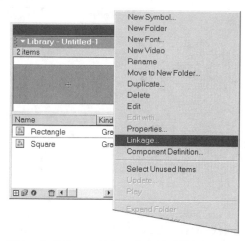

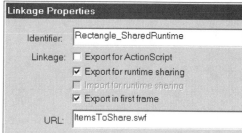

Figure 6.48 Choose Linkage from the Library window's Options menu to define a shared symbol.

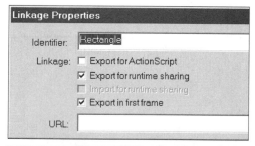

Figure 6.49 In the Linkage Properties dialog box, select Export for Runtime Sharing to make a symbol available for sharing in other Flash movies (top). Fill in the identifier and URL for the symbol (bottom). Flash uses that information to locate and control the symbol. (The identifier must not contain any spaces. The URL is the pathway to the location of the source movie's Player file.)

To define symbols as shared for run time:

1. Open the source file (ItemsToShare.fla).

2. Open the Library window.

3. From the list of symbols, select the symbol to be shared: Rectangle.

4. From the Options menu in the top-right corner of the Library window, choose Linkage (**Figure 6.48**).

   The Linkage Properties dialog box appears.

5. From the list of linkage options, select Export for Runtime Sharing (**Figure 6.49**).

   The name of the selected symbol appears in the Identifier field.

6. Enter an identifier for this shared symbol, such as `Rectangle_SharedRuntime`.

   Do not include spaces in the identifier.

7. In the URL field enter the pathname for the published version of the source file. For this exercise, enter `ItemsToShare.swf`.

   Because for this exercise, the source and destination files live in the same folder— and their Player (.swf) files will live there too (see the following exercise)—you can simply enter the name of the source Player (.swf) file. In real life, you will need to enter the path to the location where you will post the .swf file of shared symbols.

8. Click OK.

9. Save the file.

✔ Tip

■ You can define a symbol's linkage as Export for Runtime Sharing when you create the symbol. When you choose Insert > Create New Symbol or Insert > Convert to Symbol, the Symbol Properties dialog box appears. The Export linkage options are available in the expanded view of the dialog box. Click the Advanced button if those options are not visible.

CREATING SHARED LIBRARIES

After creating and saving shared symbols in the Flash (.fla) file, you must create a Player (.swf) version of the file to make the shared items available for use in other movies.

To make shared symbols available to other movies during playback:

1. Open the source file from the preceding exercises (ItemsToShare.fla).

2. From the File menu, choose Publish Settings.

   The Publish Settings dialog box appears.

3. Click the Formats tab.

4. Check the Flash (.swf) checkbox (**Figure 6.50**).

   For the purpose of creating shared libraries, this checkbox is the only one that must be checked. To learn more about the various publishing options and settings, see Chapter 16.

5. Click the Publish button.

   Flash exports the movie to a Flash Player file (ItemsToShare.swf) that contains the shared library and puts it in the same folder as the original file (SharingTest).

6. Click OK.

✔ Tip

■ To create a Flash Player file quickly, without going through the publishing process, all you need to do is test your movie. Choose Control > Test Movie. Flash creates a Player file, using default settings, and puts it in the same location as the .fla file.

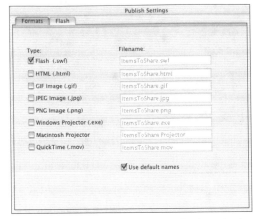

Figure 6.50 In the Publish Settings dialog box, check the Flash (.swf) checkbox to publish a .swf file that contains the shared library items.

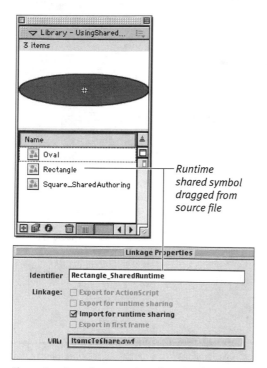

Runtime shared symbol dragged from source file

Figure 6.51 Dragging a run-time shared symbol into a destination file (top) creates the appropriate linkage automatically. Access the Linkage Properties dialog box, and you can see that Flash has filled in the identifier and URL for the shared symbol automatically (bottom).

To add shared run-time symbols to your movie:

1. Open both the source file (ItemsToShare.fla) and the destination file (UsingSharedItems.fla).

2. Open the Library window for each file.

3. Drag the Rectangle symbol from the source's Library window to the Library window of the open destination document.

   The shared symbol becomes part of the destination document's library. Flash automatically sets the symbol's linkage properties to Import for Runtime Sharing and enters the same identifier and URL that you entered when you originally made the symbol available for export as a shared symbol.

✔ Tips

- To verify that the shared symbol made it into the document with the correct links, open the library for the destination file. Select the symbol. From the Library window's Options menu, choose Linkage. In the Linkage Properties dialog box, the symbol name should already appear, and the Import for Runtime Sharing checkbox should already be checked (**Figure 6.51**).

- You don't actually have to open the source file itself. You can use the File > Open as Library command to open the source's library and then drag the symbol(s) you need to your destination library.

CREATING SHARED LIBRARIES

To link existing symbols in destination files to shared run-time symbols in source files:

1. With the destination file (UsingShared Items.fla) active, open the Library window.

2. Select the symbol named Oval (or any symbol that you want to replace with a shared run-time symbol).

3. From the Options menu in the top-right corner of the Library window, choose Properties.

   The Symbol Properties dialog box appears.

4. In the Linkage section of the dialog box, select Import for Runtime Sharing.

5. In the Identifier field, enter the identifier of the symbol you want to use—in this case, Rectangle_SharedRuntime.

   You create the link to a particular shared symbol by entering the same identifier you used when you set linkage properties in the source file.

6. In the URL field, enter the pathname to the published Player file for the source symbol: ItemsToShare.swf.

   This step completes the link for playback.

7. Click OK (**Figure 6.52**).

8. Choose Control > Test Movie.

   Flash publishes the movie and opens the .swf file in the Player. You should now see the linked shared rectangle in the place where the oval symbol was originally.

✔ Tip

- You can define a symbol's linkage as Import for Runtime Sharing when you create the symbol. When you choose Insert > Create New Symbol or Insert > Convert to Symbol, the Symbol Properties dialog box appears. The Export linkage options are available in the expanded view of the dialog box. Click the Advanced button if those options are not visible.

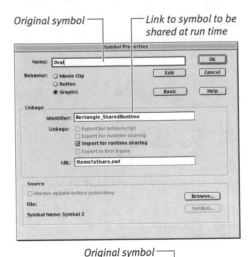

Original symbol ⌐ ⌐ *Link to symbol to be shared at run time*

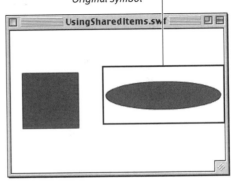

Original symbol ⌐

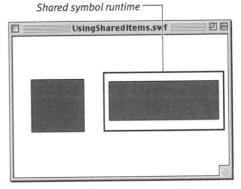

Shared symbol runtime ⌐

Figure 6.52 To define run-time symbol linkage manually from within a destination file, select the master symbol in the destination file's library, access the Linkage Properties dialog box, specify Import for Runtime Sharing, and enter the identifier and URL for the run-time symbol in the source file. When you publish your movie, the linked symbol appears.

CREATING SHARED LIBRARIES

They'll Thank You for Sharing

Why use sharing? First, author-time sharing can help you control the consistency of elements and ensure that the most up-to-date versions of elements wind up in your finished movie. This practice is especially important when several people work on the same project. Imagine a project with five designers. If you create centralized files with the latest approved versions of all the graphic elements needed for the project, anyone working on the project can grab their symbols from the shared file. As updates get made—when the client wants to change the logo from red to blue, for example—the changes need to be made only in the shared source file. At publication time, Flash automatically updates all the instances of that shared logo symbol in all the files that linked to it.

You can think of author-time shared assets as being super symbols; the library of the shared source document becomes, in a sense, the library for all the documents containing symbols linked to it. Just as for individual .fla files, changes to a master symbol in a library update instances of that symbol in that movie; changes to shared symbols in a source file's library update instances of those symbols in all the movies containing links to those symbols. In both cases, the individual instances retain whatever color effects, positioning, or resizing you (or your colleagues) applied to them.

For regular libraries and their symbols, the updates take place immediately. For linked shared symbols, the updates take place on publication. But when you update the shared file, you update all the documents using instances of that symbol.

Note that the actual assets for a symbol linked for authoring purposes reside in each individual library file, whereas all the assets for symbols linked for run time stay in the one source file.

Symbols that are linked for sharing at run time can streamline movie playback/download for the end users who view your movies. These shared symbols are associated with a Flash Player file posted at a specific location accessible to the end user. Any number of published movies (.swf files) can then retrieve the linked symbols from that location.

For run-time sharing, you must create symbol links in two directions. In the file that acts as the source of shared symbols, you must give Flash permission to export the symbol at run time; in the file that links to those shared symbols, you must give Flash permission to import the symbol at run time. In both cases, you must specify the URL (the pathway to the source file's location) and the identifier for the symbol you want to use.

Using Font Symbols

Normally, Flash embeds the fonts you use within each published Flash movie. To avoid embedding the same font in multiple movies, you can create a special type of shared library element: the *font symbol*. Shared font symbols help you keep movie files smaller and make download times faster for your users.

The first step in setting up a shared font is creating a font symbol in a library; then you set the symbol's linkage properties just as you would for any other shared asset.

To create a font symbol:

1. Open the file containing symbols that you defined as shared in the preceding exercises (ItemsToShare.fla).

2. Open the file's Library window (choose Window > Library).

   The Library—ItemsToShare.fla window opens.

3. From the Options menu in the top-right corner of the Library window, choose New Font (**Figure 6.53**).

   The Font Symbol Properties dialog box appears. Flash gives the symbol a default name—for example, Font 1 (**Figure 6.54**).

4. Enter a new name for the font if you want.

5. To specify which font is to be shared, *do one of the following:*

   ▲ In the Font field, enter the name of the font you want to be able to share.

   ▲ Click the triangle to the right of the field and choose a font from the drop-down menu.

6. Click OK.

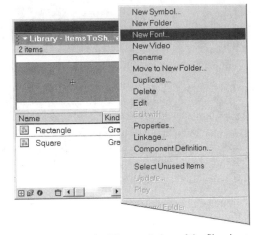

Figure 6.53 From the Library window of the file where you are defining shared assets, choose Options > New Font to create a new font symbol.

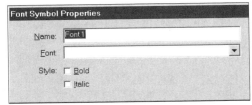

Figure 6.54 Flash assigns a default name to Font symbols in the Font Symbol Properties dialog box (top). You rename the font symbol and select a font for it (bottom).

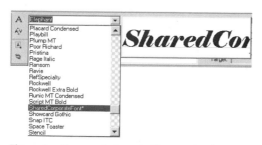

Figure 6.55 To use a font symbol in a movie, choose it from the Font menu in the Property Inspector. The asterisk following a name in the font list indicates that the font is a font symbol.

As with other shared library symbols, you define a font symbol as a shared asset by setting its linkage properties and by publishing the library in a .swf file.

To define a font symbol as a shared asset:

1. Open the source movie containing the font symbol you want to use (ItemsToShare.fla).

2. To set linkage properties for a font symbol, follow steps 2 through 9 in "To define symbols as shared for run time" earlier in this chapter, using the font symbol as your selected symbol.

3. To publish the library in a .swf file, follow the steps in "To make shared symbols available to other movies during playback" earlier in this chapter.

To use a font symbol in another movie:

1. Follow steps 1 through 3 in "To add shared run-time symbols to your movie" earlier in this chapter, using the font symbol as your selected symbol.

2. Make the destination file (UsingShared Items.fla) the active movie.

3. In the Toolbox, select the Text tool.

4. Access the Text Tool Property Inspector. If the Property Inspector is not open, choose Window > Properties.

5. From the inspector's Font menu, choose the name of the shared font symbol (**Figure 6.55**).

   In font lists, an asterisk follow the name of a font symbol.

6. On the Stage, using the Text tool, create new text in the shared font.

USING NON-FLASH GRAPHICS

7

Macromedia Flash MX's drawing tools provide a lot of power, but that doesn't mean you have to abandon all other sources of graphic material. You may already be using another vector graphics program—Macromedia FreeHand or Adobe Illustrator, for example—and feel more comfortable with its tools or want to take advantage of some advanced features it offers. Or you may want to include scanned photos or other bitmaps in your Flash movie, or use a body of artwork that you created outside Flash. Don't despair; you can import those graphics into Flash.

Importing Non-Flash Graphics

Flash imports vector art and bitmapped graphics either through the Clipboard or via the Import command. When you import graphics from FreeHand versions 7 through 10, you can also drag and drop elements directly between files.

To import a FreeHand file:

1. From the File menu, choose Import.
   The Import dialog box appears (**Figure 7.1**).

2. From the Show (Mac) or Files of Type (Windows) menu, choose the format of the file you want to import.

3. Navigate to the file on your system.

4. Select the file.

5. Click Open.
   The FreeHand Import dialog box appears (**Figure 7.2**).

6. In the Mapping section, to convert the FreeHand file's pages and layers to Flash format, *do one of the following*:

   ▲ To create a new scene from each FreeHand page, in the Pages section, choose Scenes.

   ▲ To create a new keyframe from each FreeHand page, in the Pages section, choose Key Frames.

   ▲ To create a new layer from each FreeHand layer, in the Layers section, choose Layers.

   ▲ To create a new keyframe from each FreeHand layer, in the Layers section, choose Key Frames.

   ▲ To combine multiple FreeHand layers into one layer, in the Layers section, choose Flatten.

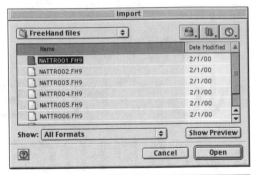
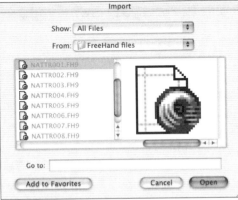
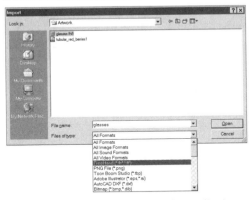

Figure 7.1 Bring graphics created in other applications into your Flash movie through the Import dialog box: Mac OS 9 (top), Mac OS X (middle), Windows (bottom).

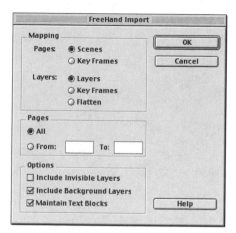

Figure 7.2 When you import files from FreeHand versions 7 through 10, you have greater control of how the elements appear in the Flash document.

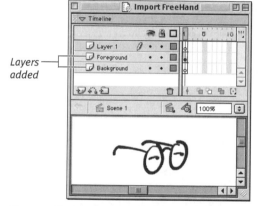

Layers added

Figure 7.3 Flash imports files from FreeHand versions 7 through 10 according to the settings in the FreeHand Import dialog box. Here, the import options were set to include the background layer.

■ Flash supports only eight-color gradient fills. If you import FreeHand objects that have gradients with more colors, Flash adds clipping paths to simulate the gradient, which increases the file size. For best results, when creating FreeHand gradient fills, restrict yourself to eight color changes.

7. In the Pages section, to select the pages to import, *do one of the following:*

▲ To import the entire FreeHand file, choose All.

▲ To import a range of pages from the FreeHand file, choose From/To and then enter the first and last page number.

8. In the Options section, *do one of the following:*

▲ To import any hidden layers from the FreeHand file, choose Include Invisible Layers.

▲ To import the background layer of the FreeHand file, choose Include Background Layers.

▲ To have Flash create editable text blocks from any FreeHand text blocks, choose Maintain Text Blocks. Otherwise, Flash imports the text characters as grouped shapes.

9. Click OK.

The Importing External File dialog box appears, with a Stop button for canceling the operation. Flash imports the FreeHand graphics. Your Flash document now displays the imported graphics arranged according to the options you selected (**Figure 7.3**).

✔ Tips

■ If your FreeHand file contains a set of overlapping objects on a single layer, those elements will segment themselves, just as they would in Flash. To keep objects distinct, be sure to place them on multiple layers in FreeHand; then, when importing, choose Mapping: Layers: Layers in Flash's FreeHand Import dialog box.

■ If you import a FreeHand file containing objects that have transparent lens fills, Flash sets the imported objects' transparency to re-create the transparent effect.

To import an Adobe Illustrator file:

1. Follow steps 1 through 5 in the preceding exercise.

   The Illustrator Import dialog box appears.

2. In the Convert to Layers section, *do one of the following:*

   ▲ To re-create the layers in the original file, choose Layers.

   ▲ To convert the layers to keyframes, choose Key Frames.

   ▲ To place all the graphics on one layer, choose Flatten.

3. To import any invisible layers, check the Include Invisible Layers checkbox .

4. Click OK.

To import other vector files:

◆ Follow steps 1 through 5 of the first exercise in this section.

   Flash imports the file and places the content of the file on the Stage as a grouped element. If you ungroup the element (choose Modify > Ungroup), you can work with the ungrouped shape (or any grouped shapes that were united in that group) as you would with any vector shape created in Flash.

   When you import files in Adobe Illustrator format, Flash presents a dialog box with options for converting layers; you can re-create the layers in the original file, convert the layers to keyframes, or flatten the layers. You can also choose to import invisible layers or leave them behind.

Figure 7.4 Flash stores an imported bitmap in the library and places a copy on the Stage.

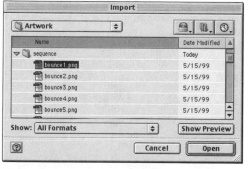

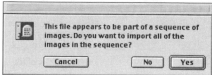

Figure 7.5 When you import one file in a series of numbered files (top), Flash asks whether you want to import the whole series (bottom).

To import a bitmapped graphic:

◆ Follow steps 1 through 5 of the first exercise in this section.

Flash imports the bitmaps you selected into your document, storing them in the library and placing a copy on the Stage in the active layer (**Figure 7.4**).

✔ Tips

■ You can edit an imported bitmap in its creator program, if that program is installed on your system; or you can use any installed bitmap-editing program. Select the bitmap in the Library window, Control-click (Mac) or right-click (Windows) the bitmap icon, and choose Edit With from the contextual menu. (If the creator program is present, it will appear as a menu choice.) In the window that opens, navigate to an editing program and click Open to launch it. The selected bitmap opens in the external program. When you save the bitmap file, Flash updates the imported image in your library.

■ If you use a program other than Flash to create a series of images that will be keyframes in a movie (a set of FreeHand files, for example), Flash can expedite the import process if the file names end in a series of sequential numbers. (To learn more about keyframe animation, see Chapter 8.)

To import a series of graphics files:

1. Follow steps 1 through 5 of the first exercise in this section.

A dialog box appears, asking whether you want to import what looks like a series of sequential images (**Figure 7.5**). Flash recognizes files that form a sequence if they are all within a single folder and have file names that differ only in the number at the end of the file name—for example, Bouncing 1, Bouncing 2, and Bouncing 3.

(continues on next page)

2. In the dialog box, click Yes.

Flash places each image in a separate keyframe on the active layer (**Figure 7.6**).

Flash also allows you to import graphics directly to the library without placing a copy of the graphic on the Stage.

To import graphics to the library:

1. From the File menu, choose Import to Library (**Figure 7.7**).

The Import dialog box appears.

2. Follow steps 2 through 5 of the first exercise in this section.

If you are importing FreeHand or Illustrator files, select the import option as described in the previous exercises.

3. Click OK.

Flash adds the imported graphic to the library of the current movie.

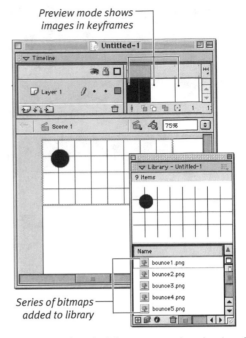

Preview mode shows images in keyframes

Series of bitmaps added to library

Figure 7.6 When Flash imports a numbered series of files, it places each one in a separate keyframe in the movie.

The Flash/FreeHand Partnership

Although not all features of other vector programs translate directly into Flash, Macromedia has strengthened the ties between Flash and Macromedia FreeHand versions 7 through 10. You can import the full FreeHand file, copy selected FreeHand content via the Clipboard and paste it on the Stage in Flash, and drag content from an open FreeHand file directly onto the Stage in Flash.

When you choose File > Import, the Free-Hand Import dialog box appears, giving you a chance to control the way that content appears in the Flash document. In addition, if you are importing FreeHand 9 and 10 files that contain symbols, Flash automatically adds those symbols to the Flash document's library.

Figure 7.7 Choose File > Import to Library to bring graphics directly into the library of the current movie.

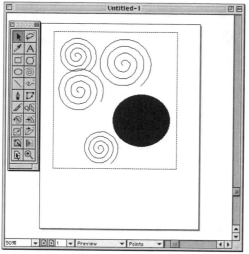

Figure 7.8 Select and copy non-Flash vector graphics (top). In Flash, choose File > Paste (middle). Flash brings each item onto the Stage as a separate group (bottom).

Using the Clipboard to Import Graphics

You can bring bitmaps and vector graphics into Flash via the Clipboard. The process is not always reliable, however. Vector graphics in particular may lose something in translation when they go through the Clipboard. If you have trouble using the Clipboard with a particular item, try saving the file that contains the graphic in one of the formats that Flash imports and then bringing the whole file in with the Import command. You can always delete any portions of the file you don't want to use in Flash.

To paste graphics through the Clipboard:

1. Open the application used to create the graphic you want to bring into Flash.

2. Open the file containing the graphic.

3. Select and copy the graphic, using the procedures appropriate to the creator application.

4. Open the Flash document in which you want to put the graphic.

5. From the Edit menu, choose Paste.

    If the graphic is a bitmap, Flash pastes it on the Stage as a group; Flash also places it in the library. If the graphic is a vector, Flash places it on the Stage as a grouped element. When you import multiple items, Flash brings each one in as a separate group (**Figure 7.8**). Flash does not add imported vectors to the library.

✔ Tip

- To preserve individual text boxes from FreeHand versions 7 through 10 as editable text when importing through the Clipboard, choose Edit > Preferences; in the Preferences dialog box, click the Clipboard tab; in the FreeHand Text section, choose Maintain Text As Blocks (**Figure 7.9**). Otherwise, Flash imports each character in a text block as a grouped shape and groups those groups.

What Graphics Formats Does Flash Import?

Flash imports a variety of bitmapped and vector-graphic file formats. For bitmaps, Flash accepts files in GIF, animated GIF, PNG, JPEG, and BMP (Windows) formats. For vector graphics, Flash accepts files from FreeHand versions 7 through 10 and Illustrator version 8.0 and earlier. Flash also accepts files in PICT (Mac) and in WMF and EMF (Windows).

When Flash imports graphics in a format that includes transparency, Flash preserves the transparency. Transparent areas of a GIF image, for example, have an alpha value of 0 when imported into Flash. When it imports PICTs or PNGs with alpha channels, Flash correctly reads the transparency values of the alpha channel.

Flash can also import AutoCAD DXF files from version 10.

Flash can work with Apple's QuickTime 4 (or a later version) to import additional file formats. Both Mac and Windows users who have the Flash MX/QuickTime 4 combination can import files in Photoshop, QuickTime Image, QuickTime Movie, Silicon Graphics, TGA, TIFF, and MacPaint formats. In addition, Windows users can import PICT files as bitmaps.

Options for export via Clipboard

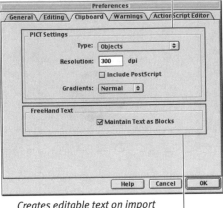

Creates editable text on import

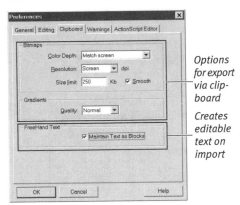

Options for export via clipboard

Creates editable text on import

Figure 7.9 Flash's Clipboard (Mac, top; Windows, bottom) preferences allow you to preserve editable text imported from FreeHand.

Figure 7.10 Choose Modify > Trace Bitmap to convert a bitmap to a group of vector shapes.

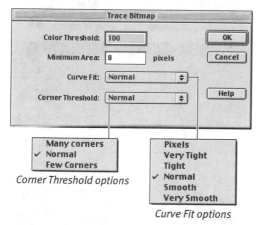

Corner Threshold options

Curve Fit options

Figure 7.11 The Trace Bitmap dialog box controls how Flash converts bitmaps to vectors.

Turning Bitmaps into Vector Graphics

After you've imported a bitmap into a Flash file, you can trace the bitmap to turn it into a set of vector shapes that look like the bitmap. Flash offers several parameters to help you strike a balance between the accurate rendering of the various color areas in the bitmap and the creation of too many curves and small vectors within one object, which increases the file size.

To trace a bitmap:

1. Place a copy of the bitmap on the Stage.

2. Select the bitmap.

3. From the Modify menu, choose Trace Bitmap (**Figure 7.10**).

   The Trace Bitmap dialog box appears (**Figure 7.11**).

4. Enter values for the four parameters in the dialog box: Color Threshold, Minimum Area, Curve Fit, and Corner Threshold.

   The parameters in this dialog box control how closely the vector image matches the bitmapped image. Flash creates the vectors by examining the pixels that make up the bitmap, lumping together contiguous pixels that are the same color and making a vector object out of that clump.

   Color Threshold (a number between 1 and 500) tells Flash how to decide when one pixel is the same color as its neighbor. The higher the threshold, the broader the range of colors Flash lumps together. A sky made up of light and dark blue pixels in three slightly different shades, for example, might wind up as one vector object if you set a high-enough threshold but might wind up as dozens of separate objects if you set a low threshold.

(continues on next page)

TURNING BITMAPS INTO VECTOR GRAPHICS

Minimum Area (a number between 1 and 1,000) determines how many neighbor pixels to include in calculating the color.

Curve Fit tells Flash how smoothly to draw the outlines around the vector shapes it creates.

Corner Threshold tells Flash whether to create sharp corners or smoother, more rounded ones.

5. Click OK.

The Tracing Bitmap dialog box appears, with a progress bar and a Stop button. (To cancel the tracing process, click Stop.)

Flash replaces the bitmap with filled vector shapes that imitate the image (**Figure 7.12**).

✔ Tips

■ For tracing bitmaps that are scans of photographs, Macromedia recommends settings of 10 for Color Threshold, 1 for Minimum Area, Pixels for Curve Fit, and Many Corners for Corner Threshold. These settings can result in really huge files, however.

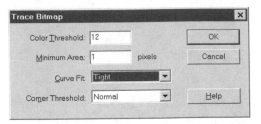

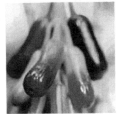

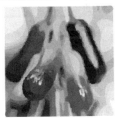

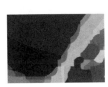

Figure 7.12 These tracings use different settings. The top one closely imitates the original bitmap; the bottom one has a posterized effect but ends up at a much smaller file size.

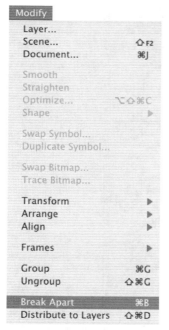

Converted to editable bitmap

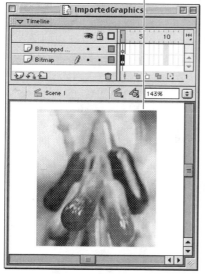

Figure 7.13 Select a bitmap; then choose Modify > Break Apart (top). Flash converts the bitmap to an editable bitmap (bottom). The editable bitmap acts like a gradient fill in that it's not a single color, but the various color areas are not vector shapes.

Editing Bitmaps with Flash's Tools

You can always edit bitmaps with an external bitmap editor, but Flash also lets you create a version of a bitmap that you can edit (to a certain degree) within Flash. First, you break the image apart; next, use the magic-wand tool to select a region of color within the image; and finally, use Flash's drawing tools to edit that region.

To create a bitmap that you can edit in Flash:

1. Create a new Flash document.

2. Import a bitmapped graphic, using the procedures in "Importing Non-Flash Graphics" earlier in this chapter.

   An instance of the bitmap appears on the Stage, and Flash adds the bitmap to the library.

3. Select the bitmap instance on the Stage.

4. From the Modify menu, choose Break Apart (**Figure 7.13**).

   Flash converts the bitmap to a special type of graphic and selects it. Flash doesn't have a specific name for this type of graphic, but let's call it an *editable bitmap*. An editable bitmap is no longer a collection of individual pixels, each with its own color value; neither is it a collection of tiny vector shapes.

   A bitmap you've broken apart acts more or less like a single vector shape with a gradient fill. (Macromedia describes this state as being a number of discrete color areas.) If you click any area of the image now, you select the entire image.

   Try selecting the paint bucket tool and setting the fill color to solid red; click the image, and it becomes a red rectangle. Don't forget to undo your experiment.

To select a range of colors within an editable bitmap:

1. Following the steps in the preceding exercise, create an editable bitmap.

2. Deselect the editable bitmap.

3. In the Toolbox, select the lasso tool.

4. Select the Magic Wand Properties modifier (**Figure 7.14**).

   The Magic Wand Settings dialog box appears.

5. In the dialog box, enter the settings for Threshold and Smoothing.

   The Threshold setting works the same way as the Color Threshold setting in the Trace Bitmap dialog box (described earlier in this chapter). Smoothing works similarly to the Curve Fit setting of the Trace Bitmap dialog box; it determines how smooth a vector path Flash draws when the magic wand makes a selection.

6. Click OK.

7. On the Stage, position the pointer over the editable bitmap.

   The pointer changes to a magic-wand icon. The tool's hot spot is the transparent area in the center of the starburst (**Figure 7.15**).

8. Click a pixel in the region you want to select.

   Flash selects that pixel and all the surrounding pixels that fall within the threshold you chose.

✔ Tip

- If the magic wand fails to grab the full range of colors you wanted, change Threshold to a higher number and try again. You can also add to the selection by clicking (or Shift-clicking, depending on your Preferences setting) the missed pixels.

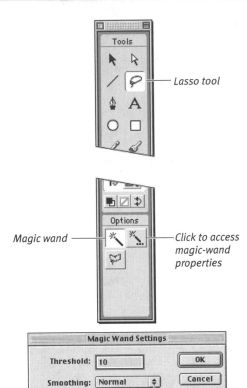

Figure 7.14 The Magic Wand modifier of the lasso tool allows you to select regions of color within an editable bitmap.

Magic-wand hot spot

Click to Select

Selection with threshold of 10

Selection with threshold of 55

Selection with threshold of 155

Figure 7.15 Click with the magic wand's hot spot to select a region of color. The Threshold setting in the Magic Wand Settings dialog box determines how large a color range the magic wand grabs.

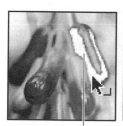

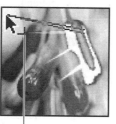

Selection filled with solid color

Editing the vector shape created

Figure 7.16 Filling the selection with a solid fill reduces the full range of colors to a single color. This figure uses white, because it shows up well in this grayscale image. That part of the editable bitmap then becomes an editable vector shape.

To create areas of solid color within an editable bitmap:

1. Make a selection within the editable bitmap.

   You can use any of the selection tools (arrow, lasso, or magic wand). The most precise way to select regions of the image is by color, using the magic wand as described in the preceding exercise.

2. In the Toolbox, select the paint bucket.

3. Select a new fill color.

   Choose one from any fill-color box's pop-up swatch set (for example, in the Toolbox or Property Inspector), or from the Color Swatches panel, or define a new color in the Color Mixer panel.

   Flash fills the selection with the selected color. This solid-color area is a vector shape, which you can edit just like any other shape in Flash (**Figure 7.16**).

✔ Tip

■ You can use the magic wand to reduce the number of colors in an editable bitmap. Keep selecting regions of similar colors and filling them with solid color until the entire bitmapped fill consists of vector shapes filled with solid colors. Use higher Threshold settings to gather more colors in each selection. If you were to select and convert all the color regions in the editable bitmap to vector shapes, the result would be something like tracing a bitmap. The difference is that you can use this version as a tiling fill pattern; you cannot use a traced bitmap as a fill.

Using Bitmaps As Fills

You can create bitmap fills in two ways: by using the bitmaps that live in the library or by using editable bitmaps. When you select a bitmap as a fill, Flash turns it into a repeating, or *tiling*, pattern within the area it fills.

You can use bitmap fills with any of the drawing tools that create fills: the oval, rectangle, pen, paintbrush, and paint bucket tools.

To apply a bitmap fill from the Color Mixer:

1. Open a new Flash document.

2. On the Stage, create a shape with a solid fill, using the oval, rectangle, pen, or paintbrush tool.

3. Access the Color Mixer panel.

   If the panel is not already open, choose Window > Color Mixer.

4. From the Fill Style menu, choose Bitmap.

   Flash replaces the panel's color-definition bar with a window displaying thumbnails of all the bitmaps in the open movie's library.

5. Position the pointer over one of the thumbnails.

   The pointer changes to the eyedropper tool (**Figure 7.17**).

6. Click the bitmap thumbnail you want to use.

   In the Toolbox, Flash makes the bitmap the current fill selection. You are ready to use it as you would any other fill color.

7. In the Toolbox, select the paint bucket; position the paint bucket over the shape you created in step 2; then click.

   Flash fills your shape with a tiling pattern made from the bitmap you selected (**Figure 7.18**).

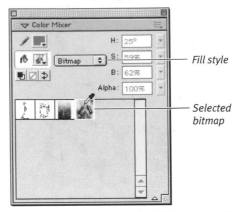

Figure 7.17 Select Bitmap in the Fill Style menu of the Color Mixer panel to see bitmap thumbnails.

Fill style

Selected bitmap

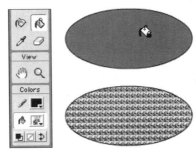

Figure 7.18 With the bitmap fill selected as the fill color, click the item you want to fill with the bitmap pattern (top). Flash fills the shape with repeating tiles of the bitmap (bottom).

The Mystery of the Magic Wand

With the magic wand tool, clicking a pixel within a bitmap that's been broken apart selects that pixel and any pixels of the "same" color that touch it.

The magic wand's Threshold setting determines how different two colors can be and still have Flash consider them to be the same color.

After you've made a magic wand selection, you can fill that selection with a single color. The filled region becomes an editable vector shape.

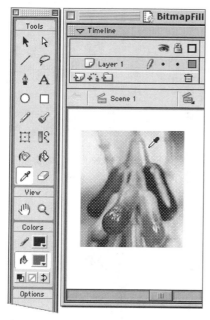

Figure 7.19 Use the eyedropper tool to pick up the editable bitmap.

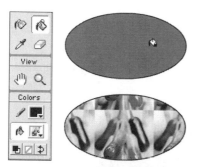

Figure 7.20 When you sample an editable bitmap with the eyedropper tool, Flash makes the bitmap the current fill color and selects the paint bucket tool. Click the item you want to fill with the bit-mapped pattern (top). Flash fills the shape with repeating tiles of the editable bitmap (bottom).

8. In the Toolbox, select the paintbrush tool, and use it to paint a shape on the Stage.

The brushstrokes you create are filled with the tiling pattern. You can use the filled oval, rectangle, and pen tools this way, too.

To apply an editable-bitmap fill:

1. On the Stage, create a shape with a solid fill, using the oval, rectangle, pen, or paintbrush tool.

2. Create an editable bitmap, following the steps in "Editing Bitmaps with Flash's Tools" earlier in this chapter.

3. Deselect the bitmap.

4. To choose the editable bitmap as your fill color, in the Toolbox, select the eyedropper tool.

5. Position the eyedropper over the editable bitmap on the Stage (**Figure 7.19**).

6. Click anywhere within the editable bitmap.

In the Toolbox, Flash makes the bitmap the current fill selection and selects the paint bucket tool.

7. Position the paint bucket over the shape you created in step 1; then click.

Flash fills your shape with a tiling pattern made from the editable bitmap (**Figure 7.20**).

8. In the Toolbox, select the paintbrush tool, and use it to paint a shape on the Stage.

The brushstrokes you create are filled with the tiling pattern. You can use the filled oval, rectangle, and pen tools this way, too.

Modifying Bitmap Fills

You can modify—scale, rotate, and skew—bitmap fills the same way you would modify gradient fills.

To move a bitmap fill's center point:

1. Following the steps in the preceding exercises, create a shape and assign a fill to it, either from the Color Mixer or by sampling an editable-bitmap.

2. In the Toolbox, select the fill-transform tool (**Figure 7.21**).

   The pointer changes to the fill-transform arrow.

3. Position the pointer over the shape with the bitmap fill you want to modify.

4. Click.

   Handles for manipulating the fill appear around one tile of the fill (**Figure 7.22**).

5. Drag the center-point handle to reposition the center point of the fill (**Figure 7.23**).

   Repositioning the center point changes the way the tiling pattern fits within your shape.

✔ Tip

- When you choose a bitmap fill from the Color Mixer panel, the resulting tiles can be quite small. When you select one with the fill-transform tool, the transform handles stack up one on top of another, making it difficult to modify the tile. To make the handles more accessible, choose a larger magnification for viewing the Stage.

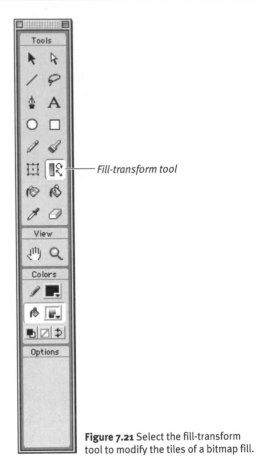

— Fill-transform tool

Figure 7.21 Select the fill-transform tool to modify the tiles of a bitmap fill.

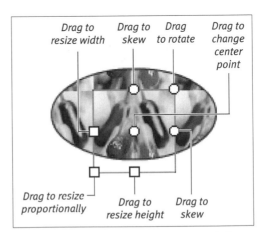

Drag to resize width Drag to skew Drag to rotate Drag to change center point

Drag to resize proportionally Drag to resize height Drag to skew

Figure 7.22 Clicking the bitmap fill pattern with the fill-transform tool brings up handles for modifying the tiles.

MODIFYING BITMAP FILLS

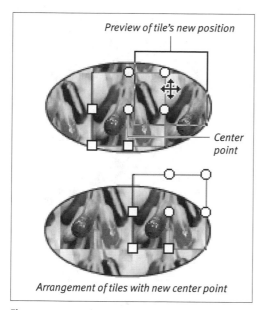

Preview of tile's new position

Center point

Arrangement of tiles with new center point

Figure 7.23 Drag the center point of the selected tile to change the way the tiling pattern fits within the object.

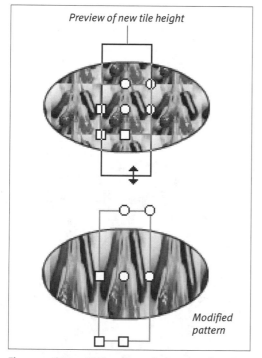

Preview of new tile height

Modified pattern

Figure 7.24 Drag the handle on the bottom edge of the tile to make the tile taller or shorter.

To resize a bitmap fill:

1. Follow steps 1 through 4 of the preceding exercise.

2. To change the height of the bitmap tiles, drag the square handle at the bottom edge of the tile (**Figure 7.24**).

   The pointer changes to a double-headed arrow. Dragging toward the center of the tile makes all the tiles shorter; dragging away from the center of the tile makes all the tiles taller.

3. To change the width of the bitmap tiles, drag the square handle on the left side of the tile.

   The pointer changes to a double-headed arrow. Dragging toward the center of the tile makes all the tiles narrower; dragging away from the center of the tile makes all the tiles wider.

4. To change the size of the bitmap tiles proportionally, drag the square handle at the bottom-left corner of the tile.

   The pointer changes to a double-headed arrow. Dragging toward the center of the tile makes all the tiles smaller; dragging away from the center of the tile makes all the tiles larger.

MODIFYING BITMAP FILLS

To rotate and skew a bitmapped fill:

1. With the fill-transform tool selected, click the shape whose bitmap fill you want to modify.

2. To rotate the bitmap fill, drag the round handle in the top-right corner (**Figure 7.25**).

   The pointer changes to a circular arrow. You can rotate the tiles clockwise or counterclockwise.

3. To skew the bitmap fill, drag the round handle on the right side or top edge (**Figure 7.26**).

   The pointer changes to a double-headed arrow indicating the direction of the skew.

✔ Tip

- If you skew, scale, and/or rotate an editable bitmap (a bitmap that you've broken apart), instead of skewing and scaling tiles within the filled shape, you can save your modifications for later use. Select the modified bitmap; then choose Insert > Convert to Symbol. When you need that fill again, drag an instance of the symbol to the Stage, break it apart, and sample it again with the eyedropper tool. Flash makes that fill the active one in the fill-color box.

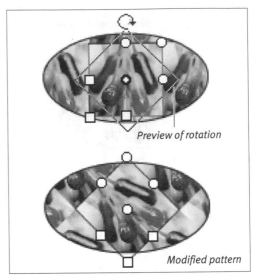

Preview of rotation

Modified pattern

Figure 7.25 Drag the round corner handle to rotate the fill pattern.

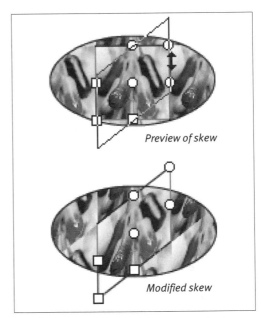

Preview of skew

Modified skew

Figure 7.26 Drag a round side handle to skew the fill pattern.

FRAME-BY-FRAME ANIMATIONS

8

Frame-by-frame animation was the traditional form of animation used before the days of computers. Live-action movies are really a form of frame-by-frame animation. The movie camera captures motion by snapping a picture every so often. Animation simulates motion by showing drawings of objects at several stages of a motion.

Traditional animators, such as those who worked for the early Walt Disney or Warner Bros. studios from the 1930s through the 1960s, had to create hundreds of images, each one slightly different from the next, to achieve every movement of each character or element in the cartoon. To turn those drawings into animations, they captured the images on film, putting a different image in each frame of the movie.

Traditional animators painted individual characters (or parts of characters) and objects on transparent sheets called *cels*. They stacked the cels up to create the entire image for the frame. (Notice the similarity with how Flash works.) The cel technique allowed animators to save time by reusing parts of an image that stayed the same in more than one frame.

In Macromedia Flash MX, you, too, can make frame-by-frame animations by placing different content in different frames. Flash calls the frames that hold new content *keyframes*.

Using the Timeline

In the Timeline, you have five size options for viewing frames and two options for previewing thumbnails of frame contents. A Flash movie may contain hundreds of frames; the Timeline's scroll bars enable you to access frames not currently visible in the Timeline window. You can also undock the Timeline so that it floats as a separate window and resize it to show more or fewer frames. **Figure 8.1** shows the Timeline for a movie with one layer and 20 frames.

To resize the Timeline's area:

1. Open a new Flash document.

   The default Timeline appears.

2. Click the textured area on the left side of the title bar at the top of the Timeline, and drag away from the document window.

   A dotted line represents the Timeline window's position.

3. With the Timeline in its new location, release the mouse button.

   The Timeline turns into a separate resizable window.

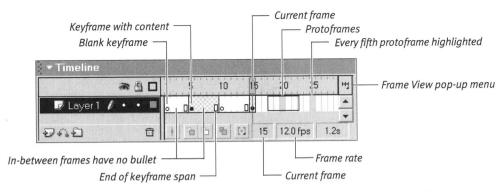

Figure 8.1 Similar to an interactive outline, the Timeline represents each frame of your movie. Click any frame, and Flash displays its contents on the Stage.

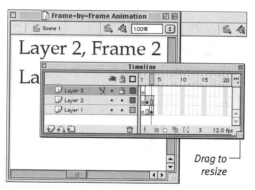

Drag to resize

Figure 8.2 After undocking the Timeline, you can resize it to show more frames.

The Mystery of Timeline Display

When you create a new Flash MX document, the Timeline displays a single layer with hundreds of little boxes. The first box has a solid black outline and contains a hollow bullet; the rest of the boxes are gray outlines. Every fifth box is solid gray. The box with the black outline and hollow bullet is a keyframe; the gray boxes are placeholder frames, or *protoframes*.

When you define a range of live frames by adding keyframes (see "Creating Keyframes" later in this chapter), the outline for the range of frames changes to black in the Timeline.

For a blank a keyframe (one that has no content on the Stage), the Timeline displays a hollow bullet. For a keyframe that has content, the Timeline displays a solid bullet.

Any in-between frames that follow a keyframe that has content display that content on the Stage. In the Timeline, the last in-between frame of a span contains a hollow rectangle. If you've set Frame View to Tinted Frames (the default), the in-between frames with content also have a tinted highlight in the Timeline.

4. Drag the bottom-right corner of the Timeline window to resize it as you would any other window (**Figure 8.2**).

You can make the Timeline wider than your open window showing the Stage to make more frames available without scrolling.

✔ Tips

■ To redock the Timeline, reverse the procedure. Click inside the title bar at the top of the Timeline window, and drag toward the top of the document window. Position the Timeline at the top of the document window or over the info bar at the top of the Stage, and release the mouse button. The Timeline redocks.

■ For those who like a floating Timeline window, it can be a challenge not to redock the Timeline accidentally as you move windows around your desktop. You can force the Timeline to stay undocked. Choose Edit > Preferences to open the Preferences dialog box; in the General tab, select Disable Timeline Docking.

To view frames in the Timeline at various sizes:

◆ In the Timeline, from the Frame View menu, choose a display option (**Figure 8.3**).

Flash resizes the frame representations in the Timeline to reflect your choice. **Figure 8.4** shows some of the frame views available.

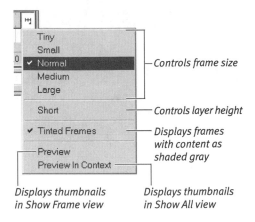

Controls frame size

Controls layer height

Displays frames with content as shaded gray

Displays thumbnails in Show Frame view

Displays thumbnails in Show All view

Figure 8.3 The Timeline's Frame View pop-up menu lets you control the display of frames in the Timeline.

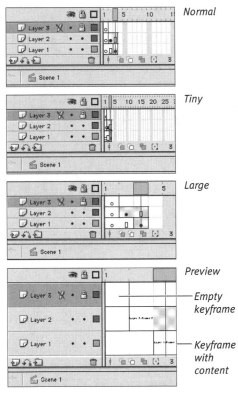

Normal

Tiny

Large

Preview

Empty keyframe

Keyframe with content

Figure 8.4 Flash can display the frames in the Timeline in a variety of sizes, from Tiny to Large. You can also preview the contents of each frame in the Timeline.

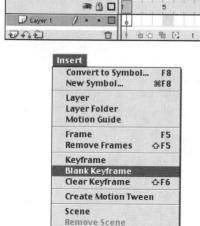

Selected frame

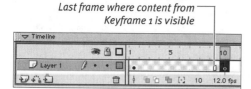

Last frame where content from
Keyframe 1 is visible

Figure 8.5 Select a frame in the Timeline (top) and then choose Insert > Blank Keyframe (middle) to add a new blank keyframe (bottom).

Creating Keyframes

Flash offers two commands for creating keyframes. Insert Blank Keyframe defines a keyframe that's empty, and Insert Keyframe defines a keyframe that duplicates the content of the preceding keyframe in that layer. Use the Insert Blank Keyframe command when you want to change the contents of the Stage completely. Use Insert Keyframe when you want to duplicate the content of the preceding keyframe.

✔ Tip

- The following tasks access frame-related commands from the main menu bar, but all the relevant commands for working with frames are available from the contextual frame menu as well. You can Control-click (Mac) or right-click (Windows) a frame in the Timeline to bring up the contextual frame menu.

To add a blank keyframe to the end of your movie:

1. Create a new Flash document.

   The new document by default has one layer and one blank keyframe at Frame 1.

2. In the Timeline, click the protoframe for Frame 10 to select it.

3. From the Insert menu, choose Blank Keyframe (**Figure 8.5**).

   Flash revises the Timeline to give you information about the frames you've defined. A hollow rectangle appears in Frame 9, and a black line separates Frame 9 from Frame 10. This line indicates where the content for one keyframe ends and the content for the next keyframe begins. Flash replaces the gray bars separating Protoframes 2 through 9 with gray tick marks and removes the gray highlight that appeared in every fifth frame of the undefined frames.

To create a blank keyframe in the middle of your movie:

1. Follow the steps in the preceding section to create a single-layer, 10-frame movie.

2. In the Timeline, click Frame 1 to select it.

3. Place an object on the Stage (use the drawing tools to create something new, copy something from another document, or bring in an instance of a symbol from a library).

   Flash updates the Timeline, adding a solid bullet to Frame 1 (**Figure 8.6**).

   With Tinted Frames selected in the Frame View menu (Flash's default setting), Flash shades Frames 1 through 9 with gray. The shading indicates that Keyframe 1 has content that remains visible until Frame 10 in this layer. A hollow rectangle appears in Frame 9, indicating the end of the span of in-between frames that displays the content of Keyframe 1.

   Frame 10 still contains a hollow bullet, meaning that it has no content. (Try clicking Frame 10 to see that the Stage is blank.)

In-between frames that will display content from Frame 1

Blank keyframe

Keyframe with content

Figure 8.6 When you place content in a keyframe, Flash displays that frame in the Timeline with a solid bullet. The gray tint on the frames between keyframes indicates that content from the preceding keyframe appears during these frames. The hollow square indicates the end of the span of in-between frames displaying the same content.

Display content from preceding keyframe

Current frame

4. In the Timeline, click the number 5 or drag the playhead to position it in Frame 5.

Flash displays Frame 5 on the Stage. Notice that this in-between frame continues to display the content of the preceding keyframe, Frame 1.

5. From the Insert menu, choose Blank Keyframe.

Flash converts the selected in-between frame to a keyframe and removes all content from the Stage in that frame (**Figure 8.7**).

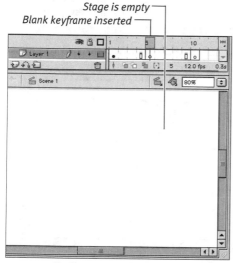

Stage is empty

Blank keyframe inserted

Figure 8.7 When you convert an in-between frame that displays content to a blank keyframe, Flash removes content from the Stage for that frame. Frames 6 through 9 are tinted when they display the content of Frame 1 (top). When you add a blank keyframe at Frame 5 (bottom), the tint disappears, because these frames now display the content of the most recent keyframe, Frame 5, which is empty.

To duplicate the contents of the preceding keyframe:

1. Create a single-layer, 10-frame movie with keyframes at 1, 5, and 10 and content only in Frame 1.

2. In the Timeline, position the playhead in Frame 3.

3. From the Insert menu, choose Keyframe.

   Flash creates a new keyframe, duplicates the contents of Frame 1 in Frame 3, and places a solid bullet in the Timeline at Frame 3 and a hollow rectangle in Frame 4 (**Figure 8.8**). The content of frames 1 and 3 is totally separate. Try selecting Frame 1 and making changes—move the graphic or delete it. Now select Frame 3 again; it remains unchanged.

✔ Tips

- The word *insert* used in connection with keyframes is a bit misleading. When you use the Insert Keyframe command, Flash *adds* frames to your movie only if you've selected a protoframe. If you select an existing in-between frame, the Insert Keyframe command converts the selected frame to a keyframe and leaves the length of the movie as it was. The Insert Frame command, however, always adds frames to your movie.

- The fact that Flash doesn't truly insert keyframes means that you cannot add a keyframe between two back-to-back key-frames. If you have keyframes in frames 5 and 6, and you select Frame 5 and choose Insert > Blank Keyframe, Flash moves the playhead to Frame 6; Flash doesn't add a new blank keyframe. With Frame 5 selected, you must first choose Insert > Frame. Flash creates an in-between frame at Frame 6. Now you can select Frame 5 or Frame 6 and choose Insert > Blank Keyframe; Flash converts Frame 6 to a keyframe.

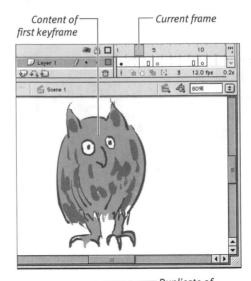

Content of first keyframe — Current frame

Duplicate of first keyframe

Figure 8.8 The Insert > Keyframe command creates a keyframe that duplicates the contents of the preceding keyframe in that layer.

Keyframe Mysteries: Insert versus Convert

In addition to the Insert > Keyframe and Insert > Blank Keyframe commands, Flash offers commands for converting frames to keyframes. Choose Modify > Frames > Convert to Keyframes (or press F6) or choose Modify > Frames > Convert to Blank Keyframes (or press F7). These conversion commands are also found in the contextual menu for frames—Control-click (Mac) or right-click (Windows) a frame in the Timeline to access the menu.

Whether you should insert or convert keyframes depends on how many frames you have selected when you issue the command and how many frames you want to create. The Insert commands create a single keyframe regardless of how many frames you have selected; the Modify > Convert commands create multiple keyframes, one for each selected frame.

With a single frame selected, the Insert > Keyframe command and the Modify > Frames > Convert to Keyframe command work identically. If you select one protoframe or in-between frame, both commands transform that frame to a keyframe and duplicate the content of the preceding keyframe (if there is one). If you select a keyframe that is followed by an in-between frame or protoframe, both commands transform that following frame to a keyframe with the same content as the selected frame. Neither command has any effect on a selected keyframe that is followed by another keyframe.

With multiple protoframes or in-between frames selected, the Insert > Keyframe command creates a single keyframe, usually in the same frame as the playhead (if you select frames at the end of your movie, the playhead can't actually move beyond the last defined frame, but Flash places the new keyframe in the last selected frame). The remaining selected frames become in-between frames.

With multiple protoframes or in-between frames selected, the Modify > Frames > convert to Keyframes command creates a keyframe in every selected frame.

The commands for blank keyframes work similarly. Insert > Blank Keyframe creates one keyframe in the same frame as the playhead; the remaining frames become in-between frames. Modify > Frames > Convert to Blank Keyframe creates a blank keyframe in all the selected frames.

Creating In-Between Frames

The frames that appear between keyframes are in a sense tied to the keyframe that precedes them. They display its content and allow you a space in which to create tweened animation (see Chapters 9 and 10). Flash makes the connections between these frames clear by highlighting them and placing a hollow rectangle at the end of the keyframe span.

To add in-between frames:

1. Create a new Flash document with keyframes and content in Frame 1 and Frame 2.

2. In the Timeline, position the playhead in Frame 1.

3. From the Insert menu, choose Frame, or press F5 on the keyboard.

   Flash adds an in-between frame (**Figure 8.9**). Your movie now contains a keyframe at Frame 1, an in-between frame at Frame 2, and another keyframe at Frame 3.

Timeline before evoking Insert > Frame

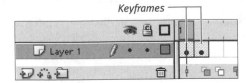

Keyframes

Timeline after evoking Insert > Frame

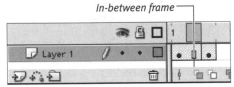

In-between frame

Figure 8.9 The Insert > Frame command adds an in-between frame after the selected frame. Unlike Insert > Keyframe and Insert > Blank Keyframe, which merely convert a selected in-between frame or protoframe to a keyframe, the Insert > Frame command actually adds a new frame to your movie.

What Are Keyframes and In-Between Frames?

In the early days of animation, it took veritable armies of artists to create the enormous number of drawings that frame-by-frame animation requires. To keep costs down, the studios broke the work into various categories based on the artistic skill required and the pay provided. The work might start with creating spec sheets for each character. Then came storyboards that outlined the action over the course of the animation. Eventually, individual artists drew and painted hundreds of cels, each slightly different, to bring the animation to life.

To make the process manageable, animators broke each movement into a series of the most crucial frames that define a movement, called *keyframes*, and frames that incorporate the incremental changes necessary to simulate the movement, called *in-between frames*.

Keyframes define a significant change to a character or object. Imagine a 25-frame sequence in which Bugs Bunny starts out facing the audience and then turns to his right to look at Daffy Duck. This scene requires two keyframes—Bugs in a face-on view and Bugs in profile—and 23 in-between frames.

In the early days, some artists specialized in creating keyframes. Other artists—usually lower-paid—had the job of creating the frames that fell in between the keyframes. These in-betweeners (or tweeners, for short) copied the drawings in the keyframes, making just the slight adjustments necessary to create the intended movement in the desired number of frames while retaining the continuity of the character. In Chapters 9 and 10, you learn how to turn Flash into your own personal wage slave. The program takes on the drudgery of in-betweening for certain types of animation.

In Flash, you must use keyframes to define any change in the content or image, no matter how large or small the change. Flash doesn't use the term *in-between frames;* it simply uses the term *frame* for any frames that are not defined as keyframes. For clarity, the exercises in this book use the term *in-between frames* to refer to any defined frames that are not keyframes.

Selecting Frames

Flash MX offers two styles for selecting frames in the Timeline. The default selection style, frame-based selection, treats every frame as an individual. The span-based style treats frames as members of a *keyframe span*—the keyframe plus any in-between frames that follow it and display its content. In the span-based selection style, clicking one frame in the middle of a span selects the entire span. When you understand the way each style works, you can choose one style (or change between styles) to take advantage of the different selection capabilities.

Except where noted, the examples in this book use Flash's default selection style.

To choose a selection style:

1. From the Edit menu (Mac OS 9 and Windows) or from the Flash application menu (Mac OS X), choose Preferences. The Preferences dialog box appears.

2. Click the General tab (**Figure 8.10**).

3. In the Timeline Options section, *do one of the following*:
   - ▲ To manipulate individual frames in the Timeline, uncheck the Span Based Selection checkbox.
   - ▲ To manipulate keyframe spans in the Timeline, check the Span Based Selection checkbox.

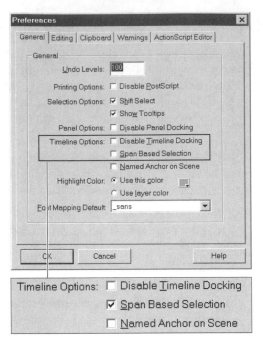

Figure 8.10 Choose the way frame selection works in the Timeline from the General tab of the Preferences dialog box.

To work in frame-based selection mode:

In the Timeline, *do one of the following:*

◆ To select one protoframe, click it.

◆ To select two protoframes and all the frames between them, Shift-click the two protoframes.

◆ To select a keyframe, click it.

◆ To select the last frame in a keyframe span, click it.

◆ To select just a middle frame in a keyframe span, click that frame.

◆ To select an entire keyframe span, double-click a middle frame in the keyframe span.

◆ To add frames to your selection, Shift-click the frames. Flash selects all the frames between the already-selected frames and the frame you Shift-click.

◆ To select a range of frames, click and drag through the frames.

To work in span-based selection mode:

In the Timeline, *do one of the following:*

◆ To select one protoframe, click it.

◆ To select two protoframes and all the frames between them, Shift-click the two protoframes.

◆ To select a keyframe, click it.

◆ To select the last frame in keyframe span, click it.

◆ To select one in-between frame, ⌘-click (Mac) or Ctrl-click (Windows) that frame.

(continues on next page)

SELECTING FRAMES

- To select an entire keyframe span, click a middle frame in the keyframe span.

- To select an entire keyframe span, Shift-click the first or last frame in the span.

- To add other spans to your selection, Shift-click the spans. The selection can include noncontiguous spans (**Figure 8.11**).

- To select a range of frames in the Windows operating system, Ctrl-drag through the frames.

✔ Tips

- In both selection styles, you can select all the frames in a layer by clicking the layer name. In span-base selection style, you can also select all the frames in a layer by double-clicking any frame.

- In both selection styles, you can select noncontiguous frames by ⌘-clicking (Mac) or Ctrl-clicking (Windows) each frame that you want to include.

- Can't remember what selection style you've got set in the Preferences dialog box? Here's an easy way to check. In span-based selection style, when hovering over a keyframe or the last frame of a span, the pointer is a double-headed arrow. Over an in-between frame, the pointer is an arrow with a small square. In individual-frame selection style, when hovering over a keyframe or end-of-span frame, the pointer is an arrow with a square; over an in-between frame, the pointer is just an arrow (**Figure 8.12**).

Figure 8.11 With Flash's span-based frame-selection style, you can Shift-click to select keyframe spans that are not contiguous.

Span-based

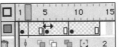 A

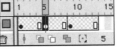 B

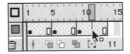 C

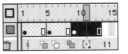 D

Frame-based

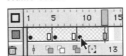 E

 F

 G

Figure 8.12 In span-based selection style, the pointer becomes a double-headed arrow when it's over a keyframe or end-of-span frame (A). Clicking selects that frame individually (B). Over an in-between frame, the pointer changes to an arrow with a square (C); clicking selects the whole keyframe span (D). In frame-based selection style, the pointer is the plain arrow when it's over a keyframe (E) or end-of-span frame; clicking selects that frame. Over an in-between frame, the pointer is a plain arrow (F); clicking selects just that frame (G).

Figure 8.13 To practice moving frames around, create a document with keyframes at frames 3, 5, and 9. Each keyframe contains a text box with the number of the frame.

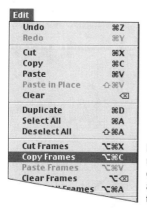

Figure 8.14 Flash's Edit menu provides special commands for copying and pasting frames in the Timeline.

Manipulating Frames in One Layer

You cannot copy or paste frames by using the standard Copy and Paste commands that you use for graphic elements. Flash's Edit menu provides special commands for copying and pasting frames. Flash also lets you drag selected frames to new locations in the Timeline.

For the following exercises, open a new Flash document. Create a 10-frame movie with keyframes at frames 1, 3, 5, and 9. Using the text tool, place a text box in each keyframe, and enter the number of the frame in the text box; this technique makes it easy to tell what frame winds up where as you practice. Your document should look like **Figure 8.13**.

To copy and paste a single frame:

1. In the Timeline, select Frame 3.

2. From the Edit menu, choose Copy Frames, or press Option-⌘-C (Mac) or Ctrl-Alt-C (Windows) (**Figure 8.14**). Flash copies the selected frame to the Clipboard.

3. In the Timeline, click Frame 4 to select it as the location for pasting the copied frame.

(continues on next page)

MANIPULATING FRAMES IN ONE LAYER

4. From the Edit menu, choose Paste Frames, or press Option-⌘-V (Mac) or Ctrl-Alt-V (Windows).

   Flash pastes the copied frame into Frame 4 (**Figure 8.15**).

5. Paste another copy into Frame 5 (**Figure 8.16**).

   Flash replaces the contents of Keyframe 5 with the content of Keyframe 3.

6. Paste another copy into Protoframe 12.

   Flash extends the movie to accommodate the pasted frame.

✔ Tips

- You can copy and paste multiple frames; in step 1 of the preceding exercise, select a range of frames.

- To copy and paste the content of a keyframe, copy an in-between frame that displays that content. When you paste, Flash creates a new keyframe.

- Warning: Flash always replaces the content of the selected frame with the pasted frame (or, for multiple-frame pastes, with the first pasted frame). If you're not careful, you might eat up the content of keyframes you intended to keep. To be safe, always paste frames into in-between frames or blank keyframes. You can always delete an unwanted keyframe separately.

- You cannot paste frames between back-to-back keyframes in a single step. You must first create an in-between frame (press F5) between the two, select the new frame, and paste the copied frames into the new frame.

Copy Keyframe 3 —

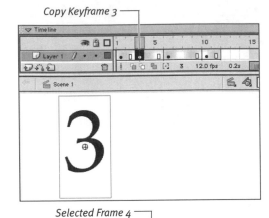

Selected Frame 4 — for pasting

Flash pastes copied — Keyframe 3 into Frame 4

Figure 8.15 When you paste a frame with new content into an in-between frame, Flash converts the frame to a keyframe.

Flash replaces content of Keyframe 5...

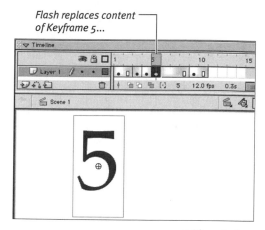

...with pasted Keyframe 3

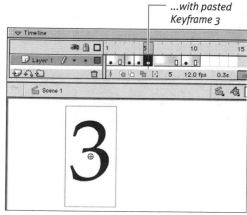

Figure 8.16 When you paste a frame with new content into a keyframe, Flash replaces the keyframe's content.

To move frames using drag and drop:

1. In the Timeline of your practice document, select the keyframe span that starts with Frame 5 and ends with Frame 8.

2. Position the pointer over the selected frames.

   The pointer changes to an arrow with a square.

3. Click and drag the selected frames.

   Flash further highlights the selection with a rectangle of hatched lines. Flash uses this rectangle to preview the new location for the selected frames as you drag in the Timeline.

   (continues on next page)

4. To move the selected frames to the end of your movie, drag the rectangle past the last defined frame and into the area of proto-frames, and release the mouse button.

Flash adds frames to the end of the movie; these frames display the content from Frame 5. In frame-based selection style, Flash completely removes the content from frames 5 through 8 and adds those frames to the preceding span. In span-based selection style, Flash removes the content but keeps a keyframe at Frame 5 (**Figure 8.17**).

5. To move the selected frames to the beginning of your movie, drag the selected frames to Frame 1 and release the mouse button.

The dragged frames replace the content of frames 1 through 4.

✔ Tips

- To drag a copy of selected frames in the Timeline, hold down Option (Mac) or Alt (Windows) as you drag.

- In span-based selection mode, if you select a span that consists of a keyframe and one in-between frame, you never get the arrow-with-square pointer; you only get the double-headed arrow. That means you can't drag the span to move it. To move such spans, switch to frame-based selection, or Option-drag (Mac) or Alt-drag (Windows) a copy of the span; then remove the original.

- No matter which frame-selection style you use, pressing the ⌘ key (Mac) or Ctrl key (Windows) lets you access some of the functionality of the other style temporarily. In frame-based selection, the modifier lets you access the double-headed arrow pointer for extending keyframe spans. In span-based mode, the modifier gives you the arrow pointer for selecting individual frames.

Select and drag: either selection style
Selected frames
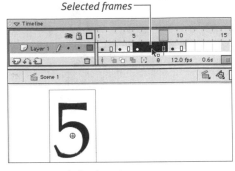

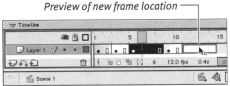
Frames ready for dragging

Preview of new frame location
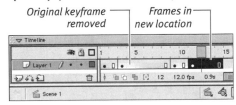

After drop: frame-based selection style
Original keyframe removed   Frames in new location
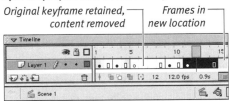

After drop: span-based selection style
Original keyframe retained, content removed   Frames in new location

Figure 8.17 The process of dragging and dropping frames in the Timeline to relocate them is the same in Flash's two frame-selection styles (top). The results, however, are quite different (bottom). The frame-based selection style removes selected keyframes from their original location, leaving only in-between frames. The span-based style retains the original keyframes but removes their content.

The Trick to Extending Keyframe Spans

In span-based selection style, the pointer becomes a double-headed arrow when it hovers over a keyframe or an end-of-span frame. Use this pointer to drag that frame to the right or the left to increase or decrease the length of the span.

Resizing a span in the middle of other spans gets a bit tricky. Flash won't let your expanding span eat up the content of other keyframes. Your expansion can reduce the length of a neighboring span, however. In your practice document, for example, using span-based selection, position the pointer over the end of the span that runs from Frame 3 to Frame 4. With the double-headed arrow pointer, drag Frame 4 to the right. When you get to Frame 7, you can drag no further. Release the mouse button. The span that starts at Frame 3 now extends through Frame 7. The content that was originally in Keyframe 5 still exists, but Flash has pushed it into Frame 8.

To increase the length of a span without affecting the length of neighboring spans, select the span or any frame within it; then choose Insert > Frame or press F5. Flash adds an in-between frame to the selected span and pushes all subsequent spans to the right in the Timeline.

When you reduce the size of a span by dragging, Flash creates blank keyframe spans to cover any gaps between the end of the span you are resizing and the beginning of the neighboring span.

Removing Frames

Just as Flash has two kinds of frames and separate commands for creating each type, it has two commands for removing frames: Clear Keyframe and Remove Frames. The commands can be a little confusing at first. To choose the correct command, ask yourself in what sense you want to remove a frame. Do you want to eliminate it and reduce the length of the movie or just remove its status as a keyframe, keeping the same total number of frames?

Flash's Clear Keyframe command removes keyframe status from a selected frame or range of frames. Clear Keyframe changes keyframes into in-between frames and deletes the keyframes' content from the movie. Clear Keyframe has no effect on the number of frames in the movie.

Remove Frames removes frames (and their content, if they are keyframes) from the movie. Remove Frames reduces the number of frames in the movie.

For the following exercises, use the same practice document you created for working with the exercises in "Manipulating Frames in One Layer."

To remove keyframe status from a frame:

1. In the Timeline, select Keyframe 5.

2. From the Insert menu, choose Clear Keyframe, or press Shift-F6 on the keyboard. Flash removes the bullet from Frame 5 in the Timeline (indicating that the frame is no longer a keyframe) and removes the graphic element it contained. Frame 5 becomes an in-between frame, displaying the contents of the keyframe at Frame 3 (**Figure 8.18**). The total number of frames in the movie remains the same.

Before clearing the keyframe

Selected keyframe is Frame 5

Content of selected keyframe

After clearing the keyframe

Frame 5 becomes an in-between keyframe

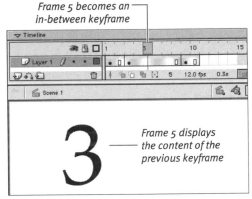

Frame 5 displays the content of the previous keyframe

Figure 8.18 The Clear Keyframe command removes the contents of the selected keyframe from the Stage and converts the keyframe to an in-between frame. The Clear Keyframe command doesn't change the overall length of the movie.

✔ Tip

■ You cannot use the Clear Keyframe command to remove content from the first keyframe in a movie. To "clear" the keyframe manually, select it in the Timeline, choose Edit > Select All, and then press Backspace or Delete on the keyboard. Flash clears the stage and leaves a blank keyframe in Frame 1.

The Indelible Keyframe

The Remove Frames command appears to go haywire sometimes. This happens when you try to delete a keyframe without deleting the in-between frames that make up the whole keyframe span and when the content of the keyframe you are trying to remove differs from the content of the preceding keyframe.

In-between frames don't really have content, but Flash gives them virtual content because they show the graphic elements of the preceding keyframe. Any change in content requires a keyframe. If you try to delete a keyframe without deleting its associated in-between frames, a change in content seems to occur because of the left-over in-between frames. After removing the selected keyframe, Flash deals with the seeming change in content by transforming the next frame (originally, an in-between frame) into a keyframe using the virtual content. You wind up reducing the span by one frame, but the span still starts with a keyframe displaying the content you were trying to remove (**Figure 8.19**).

To avoid the problem, *do one of the following:*

◆ Select all associated in-between frames with any keyframes you want to delete.

◆ With the keyframe selected, delete the entire contents of the Stage before using the Remove Frames command.

◆ Use the Clear Keyframe command and then the Remove Frames command to reduce the number of in-between frames.

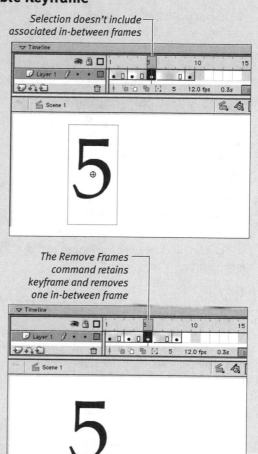

Selection doesn't include associated in-between frames

The Remove Frames command retains keyframe and removes one in-between frame

Figure 8.19 The Remove Frames command won't delete a keyframe's content fully unless you've selected all of its associated in-between frames.

To delete a single frame from a movie:

1. With your practice file in its original state (keyframes at 1, 3, 5, and 9), select Frame 4 in the Timeline.

   Frame 4 is an in-between frame associated with the keyframe in Frame 3.

2. From the Insert menu, choose Remove Frames, or press Shift-F5 on the keyboard.

   Flash deletes Frame 4, reducing the overall length of the movie by one frame (**Figure 8.20**).

3. Now select the keyframe at Frame 3 and choose Insert > Remove Frames again.

   Flash deletes the selected keyframe and its content, and reduces the length of the movie by one frame.

✔ Tip

- Flash doesn't allow you to use Clear Keyframe to remove keyframe status from the first frame of a movie, but you can delete it. If you select all the frames in the movie and choose Insert > Remove Frames, Flash removes all the defined frames in the Timeline, leaving only protoframes. You must add back a keyframe at Frame 1 to place any content in the movie.

Selected in-between frame

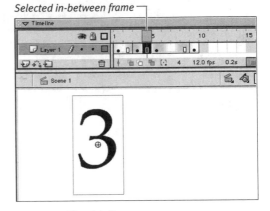

After deleting

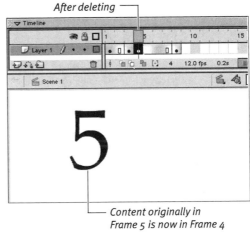

Content originally in Frame 5 is now in Frame 4

Figure 8.20 The Remove Frames command removes frames from the movie and reduces its length.

REMOVING FRAMES

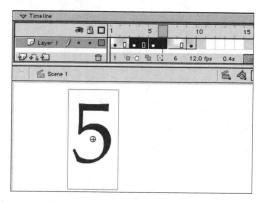

Figure 8.21 The Insert > Remove Frames command can delete a selected range of frames. Because an entire keyframe span (frames 3 and 4) are included in the selection (top), Flash not only reduces the number of frames, but also removes the content of that keyframe span (middle). Where only part of a span was selected, the span gets shorter, but the content remains the same (bottom).

To delete a range of frames:

1. Using your practice file, in the Timeline, select frames 3 through 6.

2. From the Insert menu, choose Remove Frames.

   Flash removes all the selected frames (**Figure 8.21**).

✔ Tips

- With frame-based selection style active, you can replace the contents of one keyframe with those of another quickly. Select an in-between frame that displays the contents you want to copy. Drag that source frame over the keyframe whose contents you want to replace. Flash copies the contents of the target keyframe with the contents of the source keyframe.

- To avoid the multiple-step process of copying a series of frames, pasting them in a new location, and then deleting the originals, you can cut the frames. With frames selected, choose Edit > Cut Frames, or press Option-⌘- X (Mac) or Ctrl-Alt-X (Windows). Flash removes the frames and copies them to the Clipboard, ready for pasting.

Making a Simple Frame-by-Frame Animation

In traditional cel animation or flip-book animation, you create the illusion of movement by showing a series of images, each slightly different from the rest, simulating snapshots of the movement. When you create each of these drawings and place them in a series of keyframes, that process is called *frame-by-frame animation*. When you create only the most crucial snapshots and allow Flash to interpolate the minor changes that take place between those changes, you're creating *tweened animation*. You learn more about tweening in Chapters 9 and 10.

A classic example of frame-by-frame animation is a bouncing ball. You can create a crude bouncing ball in just three frames.

To set up the initial keyframe:

1. Create a new Flash document, and name it something like Frame-by-Frame Bounce.

   By default, Flash creates a document with one layer and a keyframe at Frame 1. Choose View > Grid > Show Grid to help you reposition your graphics in this exercise.

2. In the Timeline, select Frame 1.

   Use the Frame View pop-up menu to set the Timeline to Preview in Context mode. This setting makes it easy to keep track of what you do in the example.

3. In the Toolbox, select the oval tool.

4. Set stroke color to No Color.

5. Near the top of the Stage, draw a circle (**Figure 8.22**).

   This circle will be your ball. Make it fairly large.

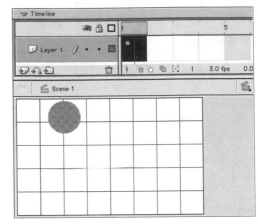

Figure 8.22 In Keyframe 1, draw a circle near the top of the Stage. This circle will become a bouncing ball.

Selected Frame 2

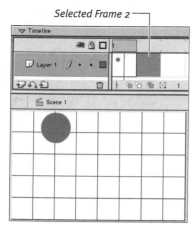

To create the second keyframe:

1. In the Timeline, select Frame 2.

2. Choose Insert > Keyframe.

   Flash creates a keyframe in Frame 2 that duplicates your ball from Frame 1.

3. In Frame 2, select the ball and reposition it at the bottom of the Stage (**Figure 8.23**).

Inserted keyframe

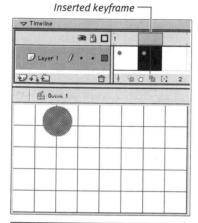

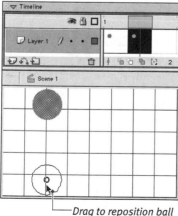

Drag to reposition ball

Figure 8.23 Use the Insert > Keyframe command to duplicate the ball from Frame 1 in Frame 2. Then you can drag the ball to reposition it.

To create the third keyframe:

1. In the Timeline, select Frame 3.

2. Choose Insert > Keyframe.

   Flash creates a keyframe in Frame 3 that duplicates your ball from Frame 2.

3. In Frame 3, select the ball and reposition it in the middle of the Stage (**Figure 8.24**).

   That's it. Believe it or not, you have just created all the content you need to animate a bouncing ball. To see how it works, in the Timeline, click Frames 1, 2, and 3 in turn. As Flash changes the content of the Stage at each click, you see a very crude animation.

Selected Frame 3

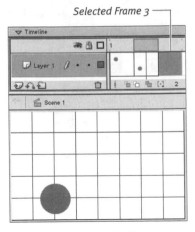

Inserted keyframe

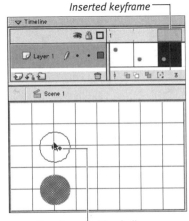

Drag to reposition ball

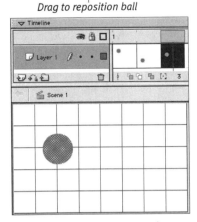

Figure 8.24 Use the Insert > Keyframe command to duplicate the ball from Frame 2 in Frame 3. Drag the ball to reposition it again.

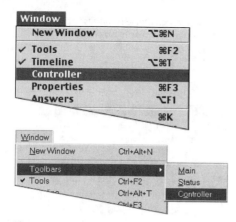

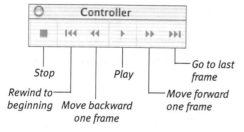

Figure 8.25 To access the Controller, from the Window menu choose Controller (Mac) or Toolbars > Controller (Windows).

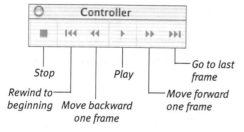

Figure 8.26 The Controller window contains VCR-style buttons for controlling playback of Flash movies.

Previewing the Action

Though you can click each frame to preview a movie, Flash provides more sophisticated ways to see your animation. The Controller window offers VCR-style playback buttons. The Control menu has commands for playback. You can also have Flash export the file and open it for you in Flash Player via the Test Movie command. (For more details about Test Movie, see Chapter 13.)

To use the controller:

1. From the Window menu, choose Controller (Mac) or Toolbars > Controller (Windows) (**Figure 8.25**).

   Flash opens a window containing standard VCR-style buttons.

2. In the Controller window, click the button for the command you want to use (**Figure 8.26**).

✔ Tip

■ For those who prefer not to clutter the desktop with more floating windows, the Control menu in the main menu bar duplicates the Controller's functions.

To step sequentially through frames:

1. In the Timeline, select Frame 1.

2. From the Control menu (**Figure 8.27**), choose Step Forward, or press the period (.) key.
   Flash moves to the following frame.

3. From the Control menu, choose Step Backward, or press the comma (,) key.
   Flash moves to the preceding frame.

✔ Tip

■ You can *scrub* (scroll quickly back and forth) through the movie. Drag the playhead backward or forward through the frames in the Timeline. Flash displays the content of each frame as the playhead moves through it.

To play through all frames in the Flash editor:

◆ To play through the frames once, from the Control menu choose Play, or press Enter.
   Flash displays each frame in turn, starting with the current frame and running through the end of the movie. The Play command in the Control menu changes to a Stop command, which you can use to stop playback at any time.

✔ Tip

■ To play through the frames repeatedly, from the Control menu, choose Loop Playback (**Figure 8.28**). Now whenever you issue a Play command, Flash plays the movie repeatedly until you issue a Stop command.

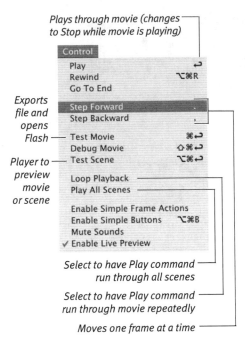

Plays through movie (changes to Stop while movie is playing)

Exports file and opens Flash

Player to preview movie or scene

Select to have Play command run through all scenes

Select to have Play command run through movie repeatedly

Moves one frame at a time

Figure 8.27 The Control menu offers commands for previewing your Flash movie.

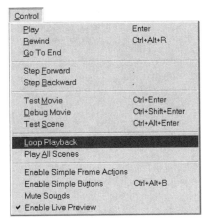

Figure 8.28 Choosing Control > Loop Playback sets Flash to show your movie repeatedly when you subsequently issue a play command from the Controller, the Control menu, or the keyboard.

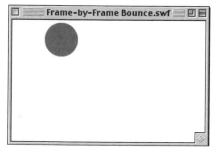

Figure 8.29 Choose Control > Test Movie (top) to see your movie in action in Flash Player (bottom).

To play frames in Flash Player:

◆ Choose Control > Test Movie (**Figure 8.29**). Flash exports your movie to a Flash Player (.swf) file and opens it in Flash Player. Flash stores the .swf file at the same hierarchical level of your system as the original Flash file. The .swf file has the same name as the original, except that Flash appends the .swf extension.

✔ Tip

■ Warning: When you choose Control > Test Movie, Flash doesn't ask whether you want to replace an earlier version of the file that has the same name; it just replaces the file. The down side to that convention is that Flash may replace a file you don't intend it to replace. When you export a Flash movie yourself, it's tempting just to add the .swf extension to the original file name. Unfortunately, the Test Movie command will replace that file if it's in the same folder as the original movie. To be safe, always change the name of your movie when you export it yourself.

Smoothing the Animation by Adding Keyframes

The three-frame bouncing ball you created in the preceding exercise is crude; it's herky and jerky and much too fast. To smooth out the movement, you need to create more snapshots that define the ball's position in the air as it moves up and down. This means adding more keyframes and repositioning the ball slightly in each one.

In the preceding exercise, the ball moves from the top of the stage to the bottom in one step. In the following exercise, you expand that first bounce movement to three steps.

To add keyframes within an existing animation:

1. In the Timeline of the three-frame bouncing ball animation, select Frame 1.

2. Choose Insert > Frame; then choose Insert > Frame again.

   Flash creates new in-between frames at frames 2 and 3, and relocates the keyframes that show the ball at the bottom and middle of the stage to frames 4 and 5 (**Figure 8.30**).

New in-between frames

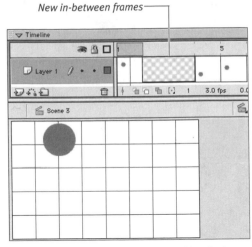

Figure 8.30 With Frame 1 selected, invoking the Insert Frame command twice inserts two new in-between frames after the first frame and pushes the original Keyframe 2 (the ball at the bottom of the Stage) to Frame 4.

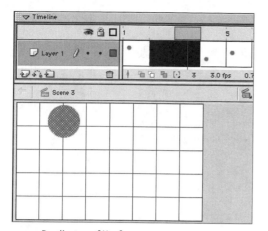

Duplicates of Keyframe 1 ⎤

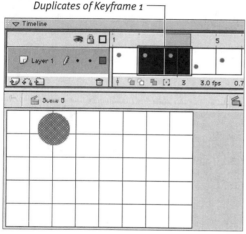

Figure 8.31 Modify > Frames > Convert to Keyframes changes the in-between frames to keyframes containing the content of the preceding keyframe.

3. In the Timeline, select frames 2 and 3.

4. Choose Modify > Frames > Convert to Keyframes.

Flash converts the in-between frames to keyframes that duplicate the content of Keyframe 1 (**Figure 8.31**).

5. In the Timeline, select Frame 2 and reposition the ball on the Stage.

You can use the grid line to help you visualize where to place the ball; you want to position it about a third of the distance between the top and bottom of the Stage.

(continues on next page)

6. In the Timeline, select Frame 3 and reposition the ball on the Stage (**Figure 8.32**).

   Position the ball about two-thirds of the distance between the top and bottom of the Stage.

7. Preview the animation, using any of the methods described in the preceding section.

   The initial bounce movement is smoother. You can repeat these steps to add even more frames with incremental movement to the first half of the bounce. You can also add frames to make the second half of the bounce smoother.

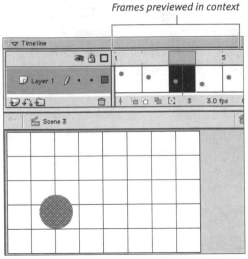

Figure 8.32 You can reposition the ball in keyframes 2 and 3 to make the first bounce smoother.

The Pitfall of Frame-by-Frame Animation

With frame-by-frame animation, the more frames you add, the smaller you can make the differences between frames and the smoother the action will be. Adding keyframes, however, also adds to your final movie's file size, which in turn affects the download time for people viewing your movie over the Web. Your goal is to strike a happy medium.

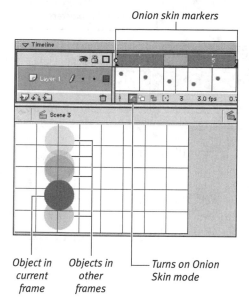

Onion skin markers

Object in current frame

Objects in other frames

Turns on Onion Skin mode

Figure 8.33 In Onion Skin mode, Flash displays the content of multiple frames but dims everything that's not on the current frame. The onion skin markers in the Timeline indicate how many frames appear at the same time.

Using Onion Skinning

In the preceding section, you repositioned a circle to try to create smooth incremental movement for a bouncing ball. To make this task easier, Flash's onion skinning feature lets you see the circle in context with the circles in surrounding frames.

Onion skinning displays dimmed or outline versions of the content of surrounding frames. You determine how many of the surrounding frames Flash displays. The buttons for turning on and off the various types of onion skinning appear at the bottom of the Timeline, in the Timeline's status bar.

To turn on onion skinning:

◆ In the status bar of the Timeline, click the Onion Skin button.

The content of all the frames included in the onion skin markers appears in a dimmed form (**Figure 8.33**). You cannot edit the dimmed objects—only the full-color graphics in the current frame.

To turn on outline onion skinning:

◆ In the status bar of the Timeline, click the Onion Skin Outlines button.

The content of all the frames included in the onion skin markers appears in outline form (**Figure 8.34**). You cannot edit the outline graphics —only the solid graphics that appear in the current frame.

To adjust the number of frames included in onion skinning:

1. In the Timeline, click the Modify Onion Markers button.

A pop-up menu appears, containing commands for setting the way the onion skin markers work (**Figure 8.35**).

2. To see frames on either side of the current frame, *do one of the following:*

   ▲ To see two frames on either side of the current frame, choose Onion 2.

   ▲ To see five frames on either side of the current frame, choose Onion 5.

   ▲ To see all the frames in the movie, choose Onion All.

Flash moves the onion skin markers around in the Timeline as you move the playhead. Flash always includes onion skins (either solid or outline) for objects in the selected number of frames before the current frame and after it.

✔ Tip

■ You can drag onion markers in the Timeline to include more frames or fewer frames in the onion skin view.

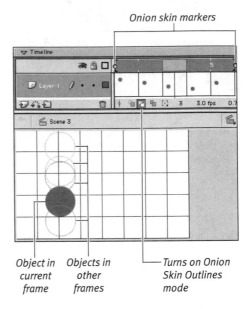

Onion skin markers

Object in current frame   *Objects in other frames*   *Turns on Onion Skin Outlines mode*

Figure 8.34 In Onion Skin Outlines mode, Flash displays the content of multiple frames, but it uses outlines for everything that's not in the current frame. Notice that two of the outlines appear very close together in this example of the bouncing ball. Using that visual cue, you can reposition the ball in Frame 4 to make the spacing (and, thereby, the movement) more even.

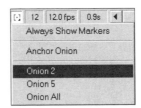

Figure 8.35 The Modify Onion Markers pop-up menu gives you control over the number of frames that appear as onion skins.

Anchored onion skin markers

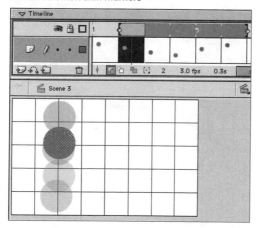

Moving playhead doesn't change markers

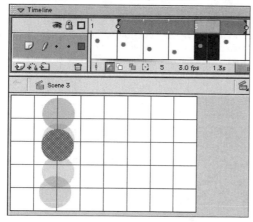

Figure 8.36 When you select Anchor Onion, Flash keeps the onion skin markers in place instead of moving them to follow the playhead. You can select any frame within the marked set and see the same set of onion skinned elements.

To display onion skins for a fixed set of frames:

◆ From the Modify Onion Markers menu, choose Anchor Onion.

Flash stops moving the onion skin markers when you move the playhead and simply displays as onion skins the frames currently within the markers. As long as you keep the playhead inside the anchored range, that set of frames stays in onion skin mode (**Figure 8.36**). This feature lets you work on frames within the set without constantly repositioning the onion skin markers.

Editing Multiple Frames

If you decide to change the location of an animated element, you must change the element's location in every keyframe in which it appears. Repositioning the items one frame at a time is not only tedious, but also dangerous. You might forget one frame, and you could easily get the animated elements out of alignment. Flash solves this problem by letting you move elements in multiple frames simultaneously. The same markers that indicate the frames to include in onion skinning indicate the frames you are allowed to edit simultaneously in Edit Multiple Frames mode.

To relocate animated graphics on the Stage:

1. Open your frame-by-frame animation of a bouncing ball.

2. In the status bar, choose Edit Multiple Frames (**Figure 8.37**).

   Flash displays all graphics in all frames within the onion skin markers and makes them editable.

3. From the Modify Onion Markers menu, choose Onion All.

   Now you can see the ball at each stage of its bounce, and you can edit each of these stages.

4. In the Toolbox, select the arrow tool.

5. Draw a selection rectangle that includes all the visible balls on the Stage (**Figure 8.38**). Flash selects them all.

Frames available for editing

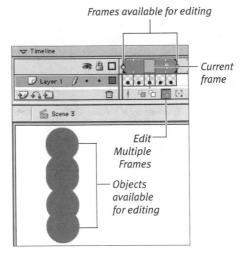

Current frame

Edit Multiple Frames

Objects available for editing

Figure 8.37 In Edit Multiple Frames mode, Flash displays and makes editable all the graphics in the frames that the onion skin markers indicate. This feature makes it possible to move an animated graphic to a new location in every keyframe at the same time.

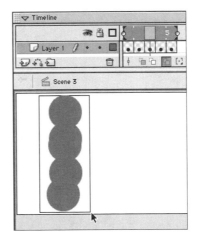

Figure 8.38 In Edit Multiple Frames mode, you can use a selection rectangle to select graphics in any of the frames enclosed in the onion skin markers.

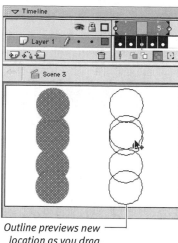

Outline previews new
location as you drag
selected objects

Figure 8.39 In Edit Multiple Frames mode, you can relocate an animated graphic completely, moving it in every keyframe with one action.

6. Drag the selection to the opposite side of the Stage (**Figure 8.39**).

With just a few steps, you've relocated the bouncing ball. (Imagine how much more work it would have been to select each frame separately, move the ball for that frame, select the next frame, line the balls up precisely in the new location, and so on.)

✔ Tip

■ When you select Edit Multiple Frames, Flash no longer displays onion skinning. If you find it confusing to view solid objects in multiple frames, turn on Outline view in the layer-properties section of the Timeline (**Figure 8.40**).

Outline-mode
toggle

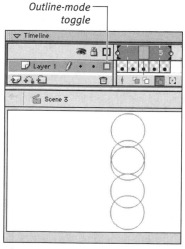

Figure 8.40 Select Outline mode to make it easier to work with graphics in multiple frames.

EDITING MULTIPLE FRAMES

Understanding Frame Rate

The illusion of animation relies on the human brain's ability to fill in gaps in continuity. When we see a series of images in very quick succession, our brain perceives a continuous moving image. In animation, you must display the sequence of images fast enough to convince the brain that it's looking at a single image.

Frame rate controls how fast Flash delivers the images. If the images come too fast, the movie turns into a blur. Slow delivery too much, and your viewers start perceiving each frame as a separate image; then the movement seems jerky. In addition, when you're working in Flash, you're most likely planning to deliver the movie over the Web, and you may not be able to get the precise control you'd like to have to deliver a fast frame rate. The standard rate for film is 24 frames per second (fps). For animation that's going out over the Web, 12 fps is a good setting.

In Flash, you can set only one frame rate for the entire movie. You set the frame rate in the Document Properties dialog box.

To set the frame rate:

1. To access the Document Properties dialog box, *do one of the following:*

   ▲ From the Modify menu, choose Document, or press ⌘-J (Mac) or Ctrl-J (Windows).

   ▲ In the Timeline's status bar, double-click the frame-rate number (**Figure 8.41**).

2. In the Document Properties dialog box, enter a value in the Frame Rate field (**Figure 8.42**).

3. Click OK.

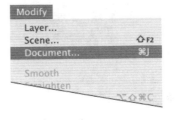

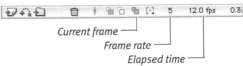

Current frame ⎤

Frame rate ⎤

Elapsed time ⎤

Figure 8.41 To call up the Document Properties dialog box, choose Modify > Document (top) or double-click the frame-rate number in the Timeline's status bar (bottom).

Frame rate ⎤

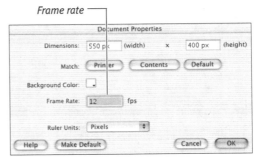

Figure 8.42 Enter a new value in the Frame Rate field. Flash's default frame rate is 12 fps.

UNDERSTANDING FRAME RATE

Varying the Speed of Animations

Though the frame rate for a movie is constant, you can make any particular bit of animation go faster or slower by changing the number of frames it takes to complete the action. You can lengthen a portion of an animation by adding more keyframes or by adding in-between frames. In the bouncing-ball example, you might have the ball drop down slowly (say, over the space of five frames) but have it rebound more quickly (over the space of three frames, for example). To make the smoothest animation, each of those keyframes would show the ball in a slightly different position. Adding keyframes, however, increases file size. Sometimes, you can get away with simply adding in-between frames to slow the action. In-between frames add little to the exported movie's file size.

To add in-between frames:

1. Open (or create) a five-frame bouncing-ball movie.

   Frame 1 is a keyframe showing the ball at the top of the Stage, frames 2 and 3 are keyframes showing the ball at two places in its descent, Frame 4 shows the ball at the bottom of the Stage, and Frame 5 shows the ball bouncing halfway back up. (For step-by-step instructions, see the exercises in "Smoothing the Animation by Adding Keyframes" earlier in this chapter.)

2. From the File menu, choose Save As, and make a copy of the file.

   Give the file a distinguishing name, such as Bounce Slower.

(continues on next page)

3. In the copy's Timeline, select Frame 1.

4. From the Insert menu, choose Frame (or press F5 on the keyboard).

Flash inserts an in-between frame at Frame 2 and pushes the keyframe that was there to Frame 3 (**Figure 8.43**).

5. Repeat steps 3 and 4 for the second and third keyframes in the movie.

You wind up with keyframes in frames 1, 3, 5, 7, and 8 (**Figure 8.44**).

6. From the Control menu, choose Test Movie.

Flash exports the movie to a .swf file and opens it in Flash Player. You can see that the action in the movie with added in-between frames feels different from the action in the one in which one keyframe directly follows another.

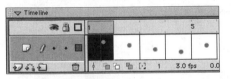

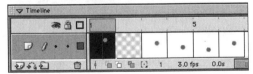

Figure 8.43 Select a frame and press F5 (top); Flash inserts an in-between frame directly after the selected frame (bottom).

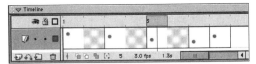

Figure 8.44 With in-between frames separating the initial keyframes, the first part of the animation moves at a slower pace than the second.

✔ Tip

- Keep in mind that this example serves to illustrate a process. In most animations, you would not want to overuse this technique. If you simply add many in-between frames, you'll slow the action too much and destroy the illusion of movement.

ANIMATION WITH MOTION TWEENING

Frame-by-frame animation has two drawbacks: First, it's labor-intensive; second, it creates large files. Macromedia Flash MX offers a way to mitigate both problems with a process called *tweening*. In Chapter 8, you created a three-frame animation of a bouncing ball by changing the position of the ball graphic in each of the three keyframes. Then you learned how to stretch out the animation by adding in-between frames that simply repeated the contents of the preceding keyframe. With tweening, you create similar keyframes, but Flash breaks the keyframe changes into multiple steps and displays them in the in-between frames.

To tween a graphic, Flash creates a series of incremental changes to that graphic; these changes are simple enough that Flash can describe them mathematically. Flash performs two types of tweening: motion tweening and shape tweening. This chapter covers motion tweening; Chapter 10 covers shape tweening.

Both types of tweening follow the same basic pattern. You give Flash the beginning and end of the sequence by placing graphic elements in keyframes. Then you tell Flash to spread the change out over a certain number of steps by placing that number of frames between the keyframes. Flash creates a series of images with incremental changes that accomplish the action in the desired number of frames.

Creating a Bouncing Ball with Motion Tweening

Flash provides a special command, Create Motion Tween, that helps you through the steps of making a motion tween. The Create Motion Tween command makes sure that you have symbols in your tweens and a keyframe at both the beginning and end of the tween sequence.

To use the Create Motion Tween command:

1. Create a new Flash document, and name it something like Motion Tween Bounce.

   By default, Flash creates a document with one layer and a keyframe at Frame 1.

2. In the Timeline, select Frame 1.

3. In the Toolbox, choose the oval tool, and set the stroke to No Color.

4. Near the top of the Stage, draw a circle. This circle will be the ball. Make it fairly large.

5. With Frame 1 still selected, from the Insert menu, choose Create Motion Tween (**Figure 9.1**).

   Flash creates a symbol from the graphics on the Stage. Flash gives the symbol a default name based on the number of tweening graphics already created in the movie. In this case, Flash turns the ball into a symbol named Tween 1 (**Figure 9.2**). You can rename the symbol by using the techniques described in Chapter 6.

6. In the Timeline, select Frame 5.

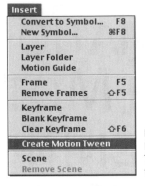

Figure 9.1 Choose Insert > Create Motion Tween to start the tweening process.

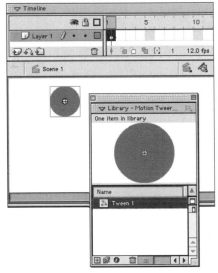

Figure 9.2 The Create Motion Tween command turns an editable shape on the Stage in the selected frame into a symbol and names the symbol Tween 1, Tween 2, and so on.

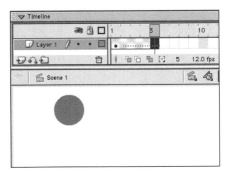

Figure 9.3 Adding frames to the motion tween results in a temporarily broken tween, indicated by the dotted line in the Timeline.

CREATING A MOTION TWEEN

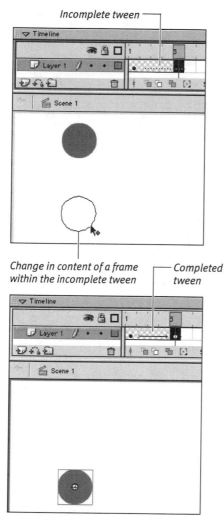

Incomplete tween

Change in content of a frame within the incomplete tween

Completed tween

Figure 9.4 After you create a motion tween over a range of frames, repositioning the content of a frame (top) causes Flash to create a new keyframe in the current frame and complete the tween (bottom).

7. Choose Insert > Frame.

Flash adds frames containing a dotted line (**Figure 9.3**). The dotted line indicates that these frames are set to contain a motion tween, but something is wrong, and Flash cannot complete the tween. In this case, the keyframe that describes where the ball should be at the end of this animation sequence is missing.

8. In Frame 5, move the circle to the bottom of the Stage to create the downward bounce of the ball.

Flash creates a keyframe in Frame 5 with the symbol located at the bottom of the Stage. Then Flash updates the Timeline to give you information about the tween. In the in-between frames that contain the motion tween, Flash replaces the dotted line with an arrow, indicating that tweening takes place in these frames (**Figure 9.4**). These in-between frames are still "empty," in the sense that they have no content on the Stage that you can edit. They no longer display the content of the preceding keyframe, but they display the incrementally changed content that Flash creates.

9. In the Timeline, select Frame 10.

10. Choose Insert > Frame.

Flash extends the motion-tween tinting to Frame 10. A dotted line indicating an incomplete tween appears in Frames 6 through 10.

(continues on next page)

11. In Frame 10, move the circle to the top of the Stage to create the upward bounce of the ball.

Flash creates a new keyframe to contain the changed content and puts the tweening arrow over the in-between frames (**Figure 9.5**).

12. From the Control menu, choose Play to preview the animation.

You've created another simple bouncing ball. You created new content for just three frames, yet this tweened animation is much smoother than the three-keyframe animation you created with the frame-by-frame technique in Chapter 8. That's because you've actually created a 10-frame animation; you're just letting Flash do the work of repositioning the ball in the in-between frames.

Which Frames Contain Tweening?

As your road map of the movie, the Timeline provides visual cues about which frames contain tweens. Flash draws an arrow across a series of frames to indicate that those frames contain a tween.

Flash color-codes frames in the Timeline to distinguish motion tweens from shape tweens. With Tinted Frames active (choose it from the Frame View pop-up menu at the right end of the Timeline), Flash applies a light bluish-purple shade to the frames that contain a motion tween. If Tinted Frames is inactive, the frames are white, but Flash changes the arrow that indicates the presence of a tween from black to red. Flash indicates shape tweens by tinting frames light green (if Tinted Frames is active) or by changing the tweening arrow to light green (if Tinted Frames is inactive).

Last frame is selected

Added frames; incomplete tween

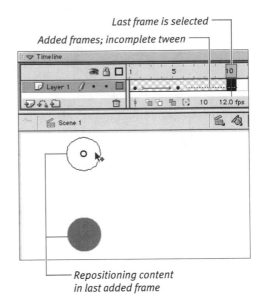

Repositioning content
in last added frame

Completed tween

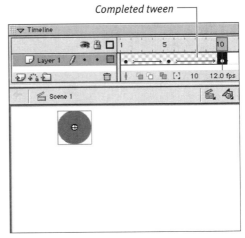

Figure 9.5 Adding frames to the end of a motion tween extends the tween. Repositioning the ball in the last frame of the tween completes the tween (top). Flash creates a new keyframe for the repositioned ball (bottom).

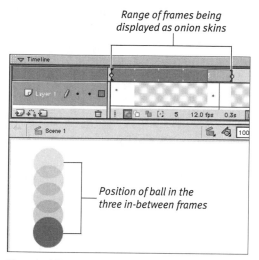

Range of frames being
displayed as onion skins

Position of ball in the
three in-between frames

Figure 9.6 Turn on onion skinning to preview the positions of the tweened object on the Stage.

✔ Tips

- When you choose Preview or Preview in Context from the Frame View pop-up menu (at the right end of the Timeline), you can't see the incremental steps Flash creates for the tween. But if you turn on onion skinning, you can see all the in-between frames in position on the Stage (**Figure 9.6**).

- If you choose Insert > Keyframe in steps 7 and 10 of the preceding exercise, you will not see the broken-tween line in the Timeline. That's because that command duplicates the content of the preceding keyframe, and Flash considers the tween to be complete when it finds an ending keyframe with content. Nevertheless, your tween will still seem to be broken until you go into the ending keyframe of the sequence and change its content.

Motion Tweening or Shape Tweening?

The key to deciding whether to use motion tweening or shape tweening is to ask yourself whether you could make this change via a dialog box, Property Inspector, or another panel. If the answer is yes, Flash can make the change with motion tweening. If the answer is no— if the change requires redrawing the shape of a vector object—Flash must use shape tweening.

Another important distinction between motion tweening and shape tweening is that motion tweening works only on groups and symbols, whereas shape tweening works only on editable shapes. Sometimes, you can arrive at the same tweening effect with either a motion tween or a shape tween. (In fact, you do that with the bouncing-ball example in the preceding section and in the next chapter.)

If you want to tween a multipart graphic— say, a robot constructed of many shapes—and you don't want to tween each shape separately, you'll need to make that graphic a group or symbol. When the graphic is a symbol, you can tween it only with motion tweening. If you want to create morphing effects—transforming a pumpkin into a magic coach, for example—you must use shape tweening. In addition, if you want Flash to move a tweened graphic around the Stage along a curving path (as opposed to a straight line), you must use motion tweening.

Setting the Tween Property

To have a working motion tween, you need three things: a beginning keyframe containing a group or a symbol, in-between frames defined as motion tweens, and an ending keyframe containing the same group or symbol to which you've made some kind of change.

The Create Motion Tween command helps ensure that you have all the ingredients in the correct places. You can also create motion tweens manually by setting up the beginning and ending keyframes and then defining the frame sequence as a motion tween in the Frame Property Inspector.

To access the Frame Property Inspector:

◆ With the Property Inspector open, select a Frame in the Timeline.

The Property Inspector displays information about the selected frame (**Figure 9.7**). (If the Frame Property Inspector is not open, choose Window > Properties.)

You can use motion tweening to create the same bouncing ball as in the preceding exercise, but in a slightly different way.

To define motion tweens via the Frame Property Inspector:

1. Create a new document with a ball near the top of the Stage in Frame 1.

   (For more detailed instructions, follow steps 1 through 4 of the preceding exercise.)

2. Select the ball, and from the Modify menu, choose Group.

   Flash can make motion tweens only from groups or symbols. The Create Motion Tween command creates a symbol if you use it on editable shapes. When you define the motion tween yourself, you must create the group or symbol yourself.

Keyframe selected in Timeline

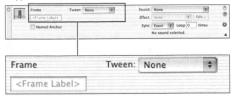

Protoframe selected in Timeline

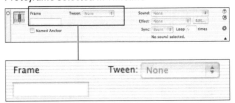

Figure 9.7 When you select a frame in the Timeline, the Property Inspector displays information about that frame.

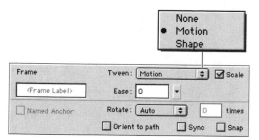

Figure 9.8 Choose Motion from the Frame Property Inspector's Tween pop-up menu to access the parameters for motion tweens.

3. In the Timeline, select Frame 5, and choose Insert > Keyframe.

The Insert > Keyframe command makes a new keyframe that contains the same elements as the preceding keyframe.

4. Select Frame 10, and choose Insert > Keyframe.

5. Select Frame 5, and drag the ball to the bottom of the Stage.

You have just re-created the same keyframes you wound up with in the preceding exercise. In Frame 1, the ball is at the top of its bounce; in Frame 5, the ball is at the bottom of its bounce; and in Frame 10, the ball is back up at the top.

6. To define the motion tween for the first half of the ball's bounce, in the Timeline, select any of the frames in the first keyframe span (1, 2, 3, or 4).

Note that Flash automatically selects the ball graphic. When you define a motion tween, the graphic to be tweened must be selected.

7. From the Frame Property Inspector's Tween pop-up menu, choose Motion.

The parameters for the motion tween appear (**Figure 9.8**). You learn more about using these parameters in the following exercises.

Flash defines frames 1 through 4 as a motion tween. The tweening arrow and color coding appear in the Timeline, just as they do when you use the Create Motion Tween command.

(continues on next page)

8. To define the motion tween for the second half of the ball's bounce, in the Timeline, select any of the frames in the second keyframe span (5, 6, 7, 8, or 9).

9. Repeat step 7.

Flash creates the second half of the ball's bounce with another motion tween (**Figure 9.9**). Note that in this exercise, you never see the broken line indicating an incomplete tween. That's because you defined the changes to the ball in the three keyframes before you told Flash to do the tweening.

✔ Tips

■ You can access the Frame Property Inspector from the contextual menu for frames. Control-click (Mac) or right-click (Windows) a frame in the Timeline to bring up the contextual menu.

■ Here's another way to select the proper frames for defining a motion tween. Position the playhead within the keyframe span that you want to tween; then, with the arrow tool, select the grouped graphic or symbol on the Stage. Flash selects the keyframe span in the Timeline as well.

Selected frame in keyframe span

Ball in position for bottom of bounce

Motion tween for frames 5 through 9

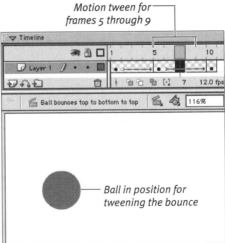

Ball in position for tweening the bounce

Figure 9.9 Defining a motion tween via the Frame Property Inspector for Frame 7 creates a motion tween for the entire Keyframe 5 span (frames 5 through 9).

SETTING THE TWEEN PROPERTY

Tween created with Create Motion Tween command — *Broken tween*

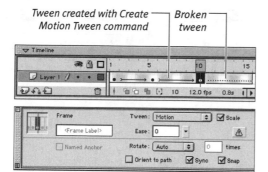

Figure 9.10 When you use the Create Motion Tween command, the final keyframe of the tween has its Tween property set to Motion. If you add frames after that keyframe, Flash tries to continue the tween (note the broken tween line).

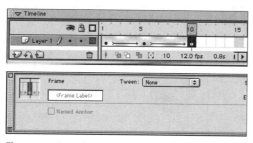

Figure 9.11 To end a series of tweens created with the Create Motion Tween command, select the last keyframe of the series (top). Then, in the Frame Property Inspector, set the Tween property of the frame to None (bottom).

Ending a Motion Tween

When you use the Create Motion Tween command as described in the first exercise of this chapter, the final frame (Keyframe 10) has tween status. If you select that frame and check the Frame Property Inspector, you can see that the Tween property is set to Motion. That property tells Flash to create a motion tween between Keyframe 10 and the next keyframe. If you add new frames after Keyframe 10, Flash defines the new frames as motion tweens, too (**Figure 9.10**). To end a motion-tween sequence, you must set the Tween pop-up menu to None in the Frame Property Inspector.

When you create a motion tween as described in the second exercise in this chapter, only the first keyframe and the in-between frames have tween status. The final keyframe has a Tween property of None. Any frames you add after the end of that sequence will have the default Tween property of None.

To remove tween status from a frame:

1. Create a new Flash document, and use the Create Motion Tween command to set up a series of tween sequences as you did in the first exercise in this chapter.

2. In the Timeline, select the last keyframe in the series of tweens.

   Flash tweens from one keyframe up to the next. Removing tween status from the final keyframe doesn't affect the previous tween sequence. Removing tween status from any frame in the tweened keyframe span, however, kills the tween.

3. From the Frame Property Inspector's Tween pop-up menu, choose None (**Figure 9.11**).

   Flash removes the color coding that indicates tweening from the selected frame.

Adding Keyframes to Motion Tweens

After you create a motion tween (either with the Create Motion Tween command or via the Frame Property Inspector), Flash creates new keyframes for you when you reposition a tweened object in an in-between frame. You can also add new keyframes by choosing Insert > Keyframe.

To add new keyframes to a motion tween:

1. Create a 10-frame motion tween of a bouncing ball, following the steps in the one of the preceding two exercises.

2. In the Timeline, select Frame 3.

   On the Stage, you see the ball in one of the in-between positions Flash created.

3. In the Toolbox, select the arrow tool.

4. Drag the ball to a new position—slightly to the right of its current position, for example.

   Flash inserts a new keyframe at Frame 3 and splits the preceding five-frame tween into separate tweens (**Figure 9.12**).

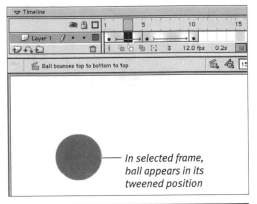

In selected frame, ball appears in its tweened position

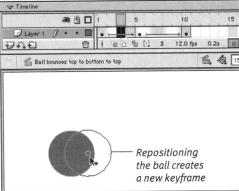

Repositioning the ball creates a new keyframe

Turn on onion skinning

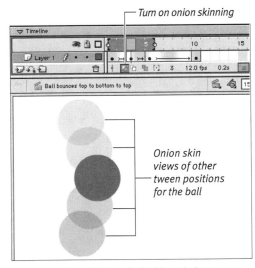

Onion skin views of other tween positions for the ball

Figure 9.12 Repositioning the ball in an in-between frame that's part of a tween creates a new keyframe and a revision of the tweened frames.

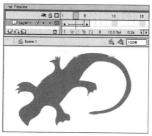

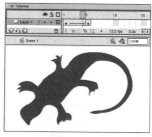

Figure 9.13 You can change the color of a symbol rather than its position in a motion tween. Flash creates transitional colors for each in-between frame.

Animating Color Effects

Tweening is not just about changing the position of an item on the Stage. You can also tween changes in the color of symbol instances.

To change a symbol's color over time:

1. Create a new Flash document.

2. On the Stage, place a symbol in Frame 1.

3. In the Timeline, select Frame 5, and choose Insert > Keyframe.

   Flash duplicates the contents of Frame 1 in a new keyframe.

4. With Frame 5 as the current frame, select the symbol and change its color.

   (To change the color of a selected symbol, set new parameters in the Color section of the Property Inspector. For detailed instructions on editing symbols, see Chapter 6.)

5. Select any of the frames in the first keyframe span (1, 2, 3, or 4), and choose Insert > Create Motion Tween.

   Flash recolors the object in three transitional steps—one for each in-between frame (**Figure 9.13**).

✔ Tip

- You can tween a change in an object's transparency to make that object appear to fade in or out.

Animating Graphics That Change Size

Flash can tween changes in the size of a graphic. To tween graphics that grow or shrink, you must check the Scale checkbox in the Frame Property Inspector.

To tween a growing and shrinking graphic:

1. Create a new Flash document.

2. On the Stage, create a new object in Frame 1.

3. With Frame 1 selected, choose Insert > Create Motion Tween.

   Flash turns your graphic into a symbol.

4. To create a keyframe that defines the end of a growing sequence, in the Timeline, select Frame 5; then choose Insert > Keyframe.

   Flash duplicates the symbol from Frame 1 in the new keyframe. The motion-tween arrow and color coding now appear in frames 2 through 4.

5. With Frame 5 being the current frame, select your graphic and make it bigger.

   (For detailed instructions on resizing graphics, see Chapter 3.)

6. In the Timeline, select any of the frames in the first keyframe span (1, 2, 3, or 4).

7. In the Frame Property Inspector, make sure that the Tween property is set to Motion.

8. Check the Scale checkbox.

   Flash increases the size of your graphic in equal steps from Frame 1 to Frame 5 (**Figure 9.14**).

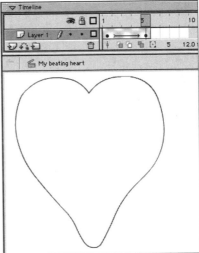

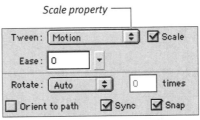

Figure 9.14 To tween a growing graphic, the graphic in the first keyframe of the sequence (top) must be smaller than the graphic in the end keyframe of the sequence (middle). To make the graphic grow in equal steps, set the Tween property of the frames in the tweened span to Motion, and choose the Scale property. You set the properties for a selected frame in the Frame Property Inspector (bottom).

ANIMATING GRAPHICS THAT CHANGE SIZE

Figure 9.15 To tween a shrinking graphic, make it smaller in the end keyframe of the sequence. Turn on onion skin mode to see the size of the graphic Flash creates for each in-between frame.

9. To add an ending keyframe for a shrinking sequence, in the Timeline, select Frame 10; then choose Insert > Keyframe.

   Flash duplicates the symbol from Frame 5 in the new keyframe. The motion-tween arrow and color coding now appear in frames 6 through 9. All the motion-tween parameters you set in the Frame Property Inspector continue in force.

10. With Frame 10 being the current frame, select your graphic and make it smaller.

   Flash creates a tween that shrinks your graphic in five equal steps (**Figure 9.15**).

✔ Tip

■ As long as you don't change the settings in the Frame Property Inspector, the Scale checkbox remains checked, and Flash updates the tween any time you change the content in one of the keyframes in this series. You don't even have to have the Frame Property Inspector open to fine-tune the size of your scaling graphic.

Rotating and Spinning Graphics

You cannot create tweens of rotating and spinning graphics quite as simply as you create the types of tweens presented in the preceding exercises, because you can't describe rotation accurately with just two keyframes.

Imagine, for example, trying to rotate the pointer of a compass 180 degrees so that it turns from pointing north to pointing south. The initial keyframe contains the pointer pointing up; the ending keyframe contains the pointer pointing down. But how should the pointer move to reach that position?

Flash gives you three choices: rotate the pointer clockwise, rotate it counterclockwise, or simply flip it upside down. Trying to describe the pointer spinning all the way around the compass in just two keyframes would be even less informative, because the beginning and ending keyframes would be identical.

To clarify the motion, you could create a series of keyframes, rotating the pointer a few degrees in each one. That method is tedious, however, and adds to the file size of the final exported movie. Fortunately, Flash's Frame Property Inspector lets you provide extra information about tweens so that Flash can create rotational tweens with just two keyframes.

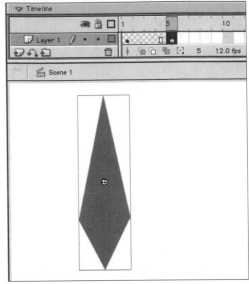

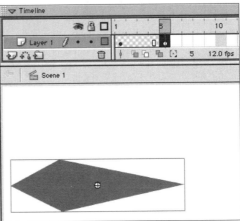

Figure 9.16 To prepare a rotational tween, rotate the item to be tweened.

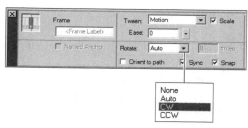

Figure 9.17 The Rotate menu in the Frame Property Inspector lets you tell Flash the direction in which to rotate a tweened object.

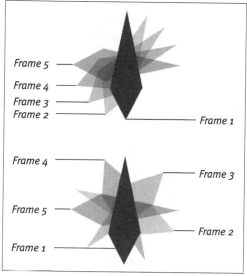

Figure 9.18 To create a tween that involves rotation, you can specify the direction of the rotation as clockwise or counterclockwise. You can also let Flash pick the direction that involves the smallest change, which allows Flash to create the smoothest motion. Compare the degree of change in each frame between rotating an arrow clockwise from 12 o'clock to 3 o'clock (top) versus rotating the arrow counterclockwise to reach the same position (bottom).

To rotate a graphic less than 360 degrees:

1. Create a new Flash document.

2. On the Stage, in Frame 1, create a new graphic (or place a symbol instance).

   Be sure to use something that will look different at various stages of its rotation.

3. If you've created a new graphic, select it and then choose Modify > Group or Insert > Convert to Symbol.

   Flash can create motion tweens only from grouped items or from symbols.

4. In the Timeline, select Frame 5, and choose Insert > Keyframe.

   Flash duplicates the symbol from Frame 1 in the new keyframe.

5. On the Stage, in Frame 5, rotate your graphic 90 degrees clockwise (**Figure 9.16**).

   (For detailed instructions on rotating objects, see Chapter 3.)

6. In the Timeline, select any of the frames in the first keyframe span (1, 2, 3, or 4).

7. From the Frame Property Inspector's Tween pop-up menu, choose Motion.

   The parameters for motion tweening appear in the panel.

8. From the Rotate menu (**Figure 9.17**), *choose one of the following options:*

   ▲ To rotate the graphic in the direction that requires the smallest movement, choose Auto (**Figure 9.18**).

   ▲ To rotate the graphic clockwise, choose CW.

   ▲ To rotate the graphic counterclockwise, choose CCW.

   Flash tweens the graphic so that it rotates around its center point. Each in-between frame shows the graphic rotated a little more.

To spin a graphic 360 degrees:

1. Follow steps 1 through 4 of the preceding exercise to create a five-frame movie with identical keyframes in Frame 1 and Frame 5.

   You don't need to reposition your graphic, because the beginning frame and ending frame of a 360-degree spin should look exactly the same.

2. In the Timeline, select any of the frames in the first keyframe span (1, 2, 3, or 4).

3. From the Frame Property Inspector's Tween pop-up menu, choose Motion.

   The parameters for motion tweening appear in the panel.

4. From the Rotate menu, choose a direction of rotation.

5. In the Rotate field, to the right of the Rotate menu, enter the number of rotations that you want to use (**Figure 9.19**).

   The value that you enter in the Rotate field determines how Flash tweens the graphic. Flash creates new positions for the graphic to rotate it completely in the given number of in-between frames. Flash tweens the graphic differently depending on the number of rotations you choose (**Figure 9.20**).

   Flash tweens the item so that it spins the number of times you indicated over the span of frames that you defined as the motion tween.

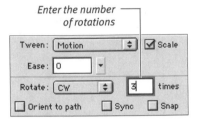

Enter the number of rotations

Figure 9.19 In the Frame Property Inspector, you can set the number of times a tweened item should spin.

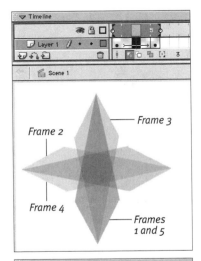

Frame 2
Frame 3
Frame 4
Frames 1 and 5

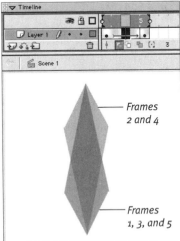

Frames 2 and 4
Frames 1, 3, and 5

Figure 9.20 Compare a single rotation (top) with a double rotation (bottom) in the same number of frames.

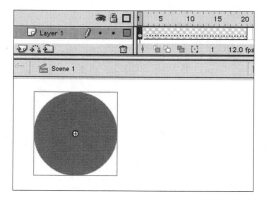

Figure 9.21 The dotted line in the Timeline indicates that these 20 frames contain a motion tween, but a broken one. The final keyframe is missing.

Moving Graphics in Straight Lines

In the preceding exercises, you created an animation of a well-behaved bouncing ball—one that simply moves up and down. You can make that ball bounce all around the Stage like a crazy Ping-Pong ball, if you like. Simply add more keyframes and position the ball in a variety of locations. The ball moves in a straight line from one position to the next, but the effect can be one of much livelier movement.

If you move the ball a great distance and then tween the motion in a small number of in-between frames, you'll get frenetic bouncing. If you move the ball a short distance or use a larger number of in-between frames, you'll slow the action.

To move an item from point to point:

1. Create a new Flash document.

2. On the Stage, in Frame 1, use the oval tool to create a solid circle that represents the ball.

3. Select the ball, and choose Modify > Group or Insert > Convert to Symbol.

   Flash can create motion tweens only from grouped objects or from symbols.

4. In the Timeline, select Frame 20, and choose Insert > Frame.

   Flash creates 19 in-between frames.

5. In the Timeline, select Frame 1.

6. From the Insert menu, choose Create Motion Tween.

   Flash defines frames 1 through 20 as a motion tween but with a broken line, indicating that the tween is not yet complete (**Figure 9.21**). You need to create keyframes that describe the ball's motion.

(continues on next page)

MOVING GRAPHICS IN STRAIGHT LINES

7. In the Timeline, position the playhead in Frame 5.

8. On the Stage, drag the ball to a new position.

   Try moving the ball a fair distance. Flash creates a new keyframe in Frame 5 and completes a tween for frames 1 through 5.

9. In the Timeline, position the playhead in Frame 10.

10. On the Stage, drag the ball to a new position.

    Flash creates a new keyframe in Frame 10 and completes a tween for frames 5 through 10.

11. Repeat this repositioning process for frames 15 and 20.

    You now have a ball that bounces around wildly (**Figure 9.22**).

12. To add more frames, select Frame 30 or Frame 40 and then choose Insert > Frame.

    Flash extends the motion tween, and you can add keyframes by following the procedure described earlier in this exercise. Just be sure to make the last frame in the series a keyframe.

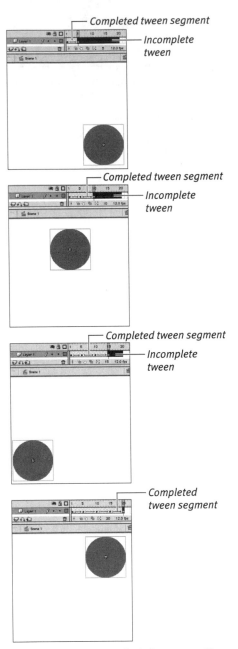

Figure 9.22 As you move the ball to new positions in different frames within the motion tween, Flash creates keyframes and completes the tween between one keyframe and the next.

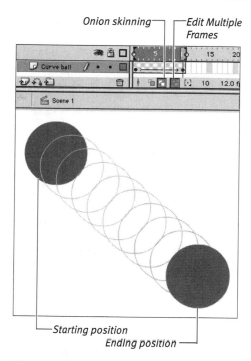

Onion skinning — Edit Multiple Frames

Starting position
Ending position

Figure 9.23 The first step in creating a tweened graphic that follows a path is defining a motion tween with the graphic in the beginning and ending positions you want to use. Here, the graphic moves from the beginning to the end in a straight line. (Onion skinning and Edit Multiple Frames are selected to show all the tween's components.)

Moving Graphics Along a Path

The preceding exercise showed how you can make graphics move all over the Stage in short, point-to-point hops. For a ball that bounces off the walls, ceiling, and floor, that's appropriate. But for other things, you want movements that are softer—trajectories that are arcs, not straight lines. You could achieve this effect by stringing together many point-to-point keyframes, but Flash offers a more efficient method: the motion guide.

A *motion guide* is a graphic you create on a special separate layer. The motion guide defines the path for a linked, tweened graphic to follow. One motion-guide layer can control items on several layers. The motion-guide layer governs any layers linked to it. The linked layers are defined as guided layers in the Layer Properties dialog box.

If you want different elements to follow different paths, you can create several motion-guide layers within a single Flash document. Each motion guide governs the actions of objects on its own set of linked layers.

To add a motion-guide layer:

1. Create a new Flash document containing a 10-frame motion tween.

   In the first frame, place a circle in the top-left corner of the Stage. In the last frame, place a circle in the bottom-right corner of the Stage. Your document should resemble **Figure 9.23**.

2. Select the layer that contains the tweened graphic you want to move along a path.

3. At the bottom of the Timeline, click the Add Motion Guide button.

Flash adds the motion-guide layer directly above the layer you selected and gives it a default name of Guide:, followed by the name of the layer you selected (**Figure 9.24**). The motion-guide icon appears next to the layer name. Flash also indents the layer linked to the motion-guide layer.

4. With the motion-guide layer selected, use the pencil tool to draw a line on the Stage showing the path you want the graphic to take (**Figure 9.25**).

5. In Frame 1, drag the circle to reposition its center point (the small white circle inside the graphic) directly over the beginning of the motion path.

For Flash to move an item along a motion path, the center point of the item must be centered on the path.

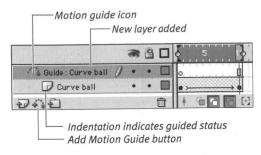

Motion guide icon

New layer added

Indentation indicates guided status

Add Motion Guide button

Figure 9.24 The Add Motion Guide button inserts a new layer, defined as a *motion-guide layer*, above the selected layer in the Timeline. The default name for the motion-guide layer includes the name of the layer selected when you created the motion-guide layer. The layer containing the tweened graphic is indented and linked to the motion-guide layer. Flash defines the linked layer as a *guided layer*.

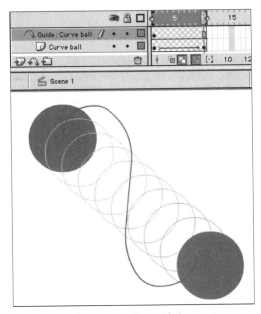

Figure 9.25 A line on a motion-guide layer acts as a path for the tweened graphic on a linked layer to follow.

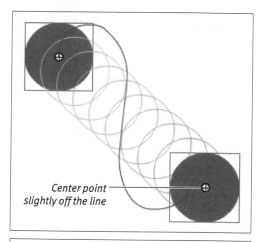

Center point
slightly off the line

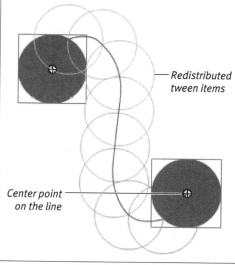

Redistributed
tween items

Center point
on the line

Figure 9.26 To follow the path, tweened items must have their center point (indicated by a small white circle within the selected graphic) sitting directly on the line.

6. In Frame 10, drag the circle to reposition its center point directly over the end of the motion path.

Flash redraws the in-between frames so that the circle follows the motion path (**Figure 9.26**). Flash centers the tweened item over the motion path in each in-between frame. In the final movie, Flash hides the path.

✔ Tips

- After you draw the motion path, lock the motion-guide layer to prevent yourself from editing the path accidentally as you snap the graphic to the path.

- In the Frame Property Inspector, check the Snap checkbox to have Flash assist you in centering keyframe graphics over the end of the guide line.

- You can use any of Flash's drawing tools—line, pencil, pen, oval, rectangle, and brush—to create a motion path.

- In many graphics, the center point (indicated by a small white circle) and registration mark (indicated by a small crosshair) are in the same spot. It's possible to move the center point to a different location by using the free-transform tool. If you do, it's still the center-point circle that you must snap to the motion guide.

If you want to have several items follow the same path, you need to put them on separate layers linked to the motion-guide layer.

To create a second guided layer:

1. In the Flash file you created in the preceding exercise, select the guided layer—the one containing the circle.

2. To add a new layer, *do one of the following*:
   ▲ From the Insert menu, choose Layer.
   ▲ In the Timeline, click the Insert Layer button.

   Flash adds a new indented (guided) layer above the selected layer (**Figure 9.27**). Tweened items on this layer follow the motion guide when you position them correctly.

If you want to have items following different paths, you need to create multiple motion-guide layers, each with its own set of guided layers.

To add a second motion-guide layer:

1. Create a Flash document with at least one normal layer containing a motion tween, and one motion-guide layer with a linked guided layer containing a motion tween.

2. In the Timeline, create or select the normal layer containing the motion tween.

3. Click the Add Motion Guide button.

   Flash adds a motion-guide layer above the selected layer and links the selected layer to it. Follow the steps in the preceding exercises to draw the motion path and position the tweened item.

4. Play the movie.

   The two tweened graphics follow their own motion paths simultaneously.

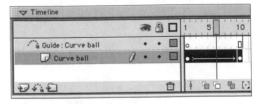

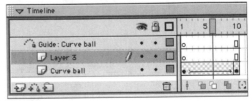

Figure 9.27 When a guided layer is selected (top), clicking the Insert Guide Layer button creates another guided layer below the motion-guide layer (bottom).

✔ Tip

■ To convert an existing layer to a guided layer quickly, drag it below the motion-guide layer or any of its linked layers.

Orienting Graphics to a Motion Path

Imagine a waiter carrying a full tray through a crowded room, raising and lowering the tray to avoid various obstacles but always keeping the tray level so as not to spill anything. That's how the animation you created in the preceding exercise works. Flash moved the circle in each in-between frame to snap its center point to the motion guide, but it did not rotate the circle at all.

With a circle, that procedure results in a natural-looking motion, but with other objects, the result is very unnatural. Imagine animating a lizard following a path: If the lizard graphic snaps to different spots along the motion path, never changing the way that it's oriented in space, the lizard appears to be in the grip of some invisible force, not moving forward of its own volition.

To create more-natural movement, Flash gives you the option of forcing a tweened graphic to orient itself parallel to the path in each frame of the tween.

To match a graphic's orientation to the path:

1. Create a 10-frame motion tween of an item that follows a motion guide, using the steps in the first exercise in "Moving Graphics Along a Path" earlier in this chapter.

   This time, however, don't use a circle; draw a small animal or create a simple noncircular graphic. An arrow or triangle works well.

2. Turn on onion skinning to see how the item moves along the path without orientation.

3. In the Timeline, in the layer containing the tweened graphic, select Frame 1.

4. In the Frame Property Inspector, check the Orient to Path checkbox (**Figure 9.28**).

   Flash redraws the tween. In the in-between frames, Flash rotates the tweened item to align it with the path more naturally (**Figure 9.29**).

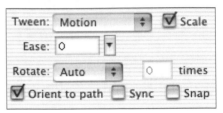

Figure 9.28 With Motion tweening selected in the Frame Property Inspector, check Orient to Path to make Flash rotate a tweened item to "face" the direction of movement.

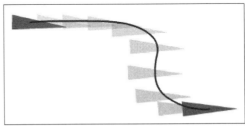

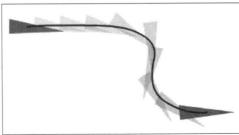

Figure 9.29 The arrow in the top tween is not oriented to the path; it stays parallel to the bottom of the Stage and moves to various points along the path. The bottom tween is oriented to the path. The arrow rotates to align better with the path.

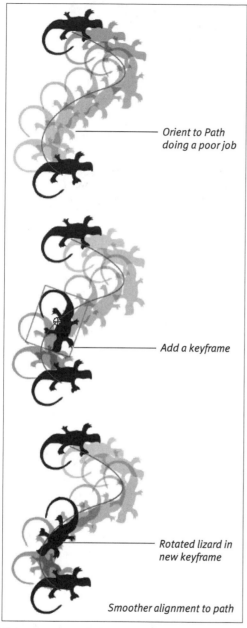

Orient to Path
doing a poor job

Add a keyframe

Rotated lizard in
new keyframe

Smoother alignment to path

Figure 9.30 Here, Flash could be doing a better job of aligning this lizard with the path (top). Creating a new keyframe and rotating the lizard manually in the seventh frame (middle) helps the Orient to Path feature do its job (bottom). (Tweaking the orientation of the lizard in the first and last keyframes would further improve this tween.)

✔ Tips

- The Orient to Path option does not always create the most natural positions for your graphic. Step through the tween one frame at a time. When you get to a frame where Flash positions the graphic poorly, you can fix it. In the Timeline, select the in-between frame, and choose Insert > Keyframe. In the new keyframe that Flash creates, select the graphic and rotate it manually to align it with the motion guide. Flash redraws the in-between frames (**Figure 9.30**).

- Turn on onion skinning as you follow the preceding tip. That way, you can see how your adjustments affect the orientation of your graphic in each frame of the tween.

- Sometimes, moving the center point of your graphic will help it orient to the path in a more lifelike manner. The center point of the lizard in **Figure 9.30** coincides with the center point of the graphic's bounding box. Because the lizard has a huge curved tail, that point is not even inside the lizard body. Moving the center point to the middle of the lizard's body lets the Orient to Path setting create more lifelike movement. (You can use the free-transform tool to reposition the center point of a grouped graphic or a symbol instance.)

ORIENTING GRAPHICS TO A MOTION PATH

Changing Tween Speed

In Chapter 8, you learned to make an animated item appear to move slowly or quickly by adjusting the number of in-between frames. When you create an animation with tweening, that method no longer works, because Flash distributes the motion evenly over however many in-between frames you create. You can, however, make an animation slower at the beginning or end of a tween sequence by setting an Ease value in the Frame Property Inspector.

You can use easing to create a more natural look in animations of objects that gravity affects. In an animation of a bouncing ball, for example, you might want the bouncing to start quickly but slow toward the end to simulate the way that entropy in the real world slows a bouncing ball.

To make the animation start slowly and accelerate (ease in):

1. Create a 10-frame motion tween of a graphic that follows a motion guide, using the steps in the first exercise in "Moving Graphics Along a Path" earlier in this chapter.

2. In the Timeline, select any of the frames in the keyframe span (frames 1 through 9).

3. In the Frame Property Inspector, enter a negative number in the Ease field (**Figure 9.31**).

   The word *In* appears next to the field. Easing in makes the animation start slow and speed up toward the end. The lower the Ease value, the greater the rate of acceleration.

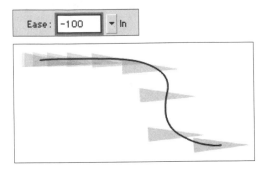

Figure 9.31 A negative Ease value (top), makes changes in the initial frames of the tween smaller and changes toward the end larger (bottom). The animation seems to start slowly and then speed up.

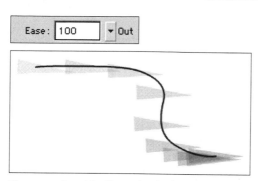

Figure 9.32 A positive Ease value (top), makes changes at the end of the animation smaller and changes in the initial frames larger (bottom). The animation seems to start quickly and then slow down.

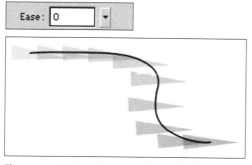

Figure 9.33 With an Ease value of 0 (top), Flash distributes the tweening changes evenly across the in-between frames (bottom). The effect is that of animation at a constant rate.

To make the animation start quickly and decelerate (ease out):

1. Follow steps 1 and 2 of the preceding exercise.

2. In the Frame Property Inspector, enter a positive number in the Ease field.

   The word *Out* appears next to the field. Easing out makes the animation start quickly and slow toward the end (**Figure 9.32**). The higher the Ease value, the greater the rate of deceleration.

✔ Tips

- An Ease value of 0 causes Flash to display the whole animation at a constant rate (**Figure 9.33**).

- For easy entry of Ease values, click the triangle to the right of the Ease field. A slider pops open. Drag the slider's lever to choose a value between –100 and 100. Click away from the slider in the panel or on the Stage to confirm your entry.

- For even quicker changes, click and drag the slider triangle. When you release the slider's lever, Flash confirms the new Ease value; you don't need to click anywhere.

ANIMATION WITH SHAPE TWEENING

In shape tweening, as in motion tweening, you define the beginning and ending graphics in keyframes. Macromedia Flash MX creates the in-between frames, redrawing the graphic with incremental changes that transform it. The important difference between motion tweening and shape tweening is that motion tweening works on groups and symbols, and shape tweening requires editable graphics.

Shape tweening doesn't restrict you to changing the graphic's shape. You can change any of the graphic's properties—size, color, location, and so on—as you would in motion tweening. Though it's possible to shape-tween graphics that move in straight lines, the other automated-motion features are not available. You cannot instruct Flash to rotate a shape-tweened item, for example.

Flash can shape-tween more than one graphic on a layer, but the results can be unpredictable. When you have several shapes on a layer, there is no way to tell Flash which starting shape goes with which ending shape. By limiting yourself to a single shape tween on each layer, you tell Flash exactly what to change.

You define shape tweens by setting the tweening parameters in the Frame Property Inspector. For the exercises in this chapter, keep the Frame Property Inspector open on your desktop.

Creating a Bouncing Ball with Shape Tweening

Although shape tweens can animate changes in many properties of graphics—color, size, location—the distinguishing function of shape tweens is to transform one shape into another. In this chapter, however, you start by using a shape tween to create another simple bouncing-ball animation. This exercise demonstrates the similarity between the two types of tweens and shows how you can achieve the same result by using different tween commands.

To define shape tweens via the Frame Property Inspector:

1. Create a new Flash document, and name it something like Shape Tween Bounce.

   Flash creates a document with one layer and a keyframe at Frame 1 by default.

2. In the Timeline, position the playhead in Frame 1.

3. In the Toolbox, choose the oval tool.

4. Set the stroke to No Color.

5. Near the top of the Stage, draw a circle. This circle will be the ball. Make it fairly large.

6. In the Timeline, select Frame 5, and choose Insert > Keyframe.

   The Insert > Keyframe command makes a new keyframe that contains the same elements as the preceding keyframe.

7. Select Frame 10, and choose Insert > Keyframe.

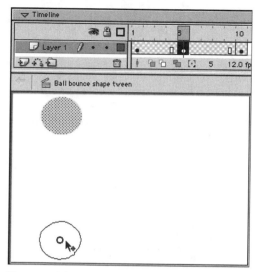

Figure 10.1 When you reposition an editable graphic, for the purposes of shape tweening Flash considers the change in location to be a change in shape. In the middle keyframe of this figure, you relocate the ball to create the bottom of the bounce.

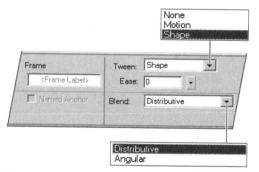

Figure 10.2 Choosing Shape from the Tween pop-up menu in the Frame Property Inspector displays the shape-tween parameters.

8. In Frame 5, select the ball, and drag it to the bottom of the Stage (**Figure 10.1**).

Now you have the keyframes necessary to make a simple bouncing ball like the one in the motion-tween exercise. In Frame 1, the ball is at the top of its bounce; in Frame 5, the ball is at the bottom of its bounce; and in Frame 10, the ball is back up at the top.

9. To define the shape tween for the first half of the ball's bounce, in the Timeline, select any of the frames in the first keyframe span (1, 2, 3, or 4).

Note that the ball is selected automatically. When you define a shape tween, the element to be tweened must be selected.

10. From the Frame Property Inspector's Tween pop-up menu, choose Shape.

The parameters for the shape tween appear (**Figure 10.2**).

Flash creates a shape tween in frames 1 through 4 and color-codes those frames in the Timeline. With Tinted Frames active (choose it from the Frame View pop-up menu at the end of the info bar), Flash applies a light green shade to the frames containing a shape tween. If Tinted Frames is inactive, the frames are white, but Flash changes the arrow that indicates the presence of a tween from blue to green.

(continues on next page)

SHAPE TWEENING A BOUNCING BALL

11. In the Ease field, *do one of the following:*

   ▲ To make the bounce start slowly and speed up, enter a negative value.

   ▲ To make the bounce start quickly and slow down, enter a positive value.

   ▲ To keep the bounce constant, enter **0**.

12. From the Blend menu, *choose one of the following options:*

   ▲ To preserve sharp corners and straight lines as one shape transforms into another, choose Angular.

   ▲ To smooth out the in-between shapes, choose Distributive.

13. To define the motion tween for the second half of the ball's bounce, in the Timeline, select any of the frames in the second keyframe span (5, 6, 7, 8, or 9).

14. Repeat steps 10 through 12.

Flash creates the second half of the ball's bounce with another shape tween (**Figure 10.3**).

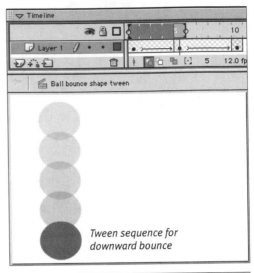

Tween sequence for downward bounce

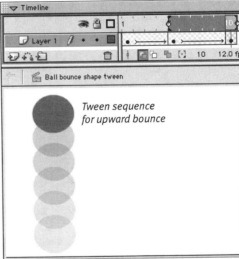

Tween sequence for upward bounce

Figure 10.3 With onion skinning turned on, you can see the in-between frames Flash creates for the tween. In this case, because you changed only the position of the object, it looks just like the bouncing ball created with a motion tween.

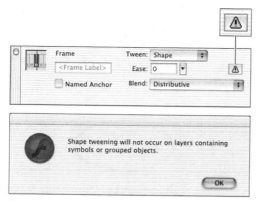

Figure 10.4 A warning button appears in the Frame Property Inspector when there are groups or symbols in frames you are defining as shape tweens (top). Click the exclamation-sign button to see the warning dialog box (bottom).

✔ Tip

- Flash doesn't prevent you from defining shape tweens for frames that contain grouped shapes or symbols. Flash does warn you by placing the broken-tween dotted line in the relevant frames in the Timeline. When you select such frames, a warning button appears in the Frame Property Inspector (**Figure 10.4**). When you see these warnings, go back to the Stage and reevaluate what's there. If the item you want to tween is a group or symbol, you could use motion tweening. Or, to use shape tweening, you could break the group or symbol apart (select the shape or symbol and then choose Modify > Break Apart). If there's a symbol or group on the same layer as the editable shape you want to tween, move the extra item to its own layer (select it and choose Modify > Distribute to Layers).

Shape-Tween Requirements

To have a working shape tween, you need three things: a beginning keyframe containing one or more editable shapes, in-between frames defined as shape tweens, and an ending keyframe containing the new editable shape.

For motion tweens, the Create Motion Tween command helps you combine those ingredients correctly. No equivalent command is available for shape tweens. You must create all shape tweens manually by setting up the beginning and ending keyframes and then defining the in-between frames as shape tweens in the Frame Property Inspector.

Morphing Simple Lines and Fills

In the bouncing-ball example, you worked with a fill shape but merely changed its location. The true work of a shape tween is to transform one shape into another. Flash can transform both fill shapes and lines. In this section, you try some truly shape-changing exercises with both types of shapes.

To transform an oval into a rectangle:

1. Create a new Flash document.

2. On the Stage, in Frame 1, draw an outline oval (**Figure 10.5**).

3. In the Timeline, select Frame 5, and choose Insert > Blank Keyframe.

    Flash creates a keyframe but removes all content from the Stage.

4. On the Stage, in Frame 5, draw an outline rectangle (**Figure 10.6**).

    Don't worry about placing the rectangle in exactly the same location on the Stage as the oval; you'll adjust the position later.

    In the Timeline, select any of the frames in the Keyframe span (1, 2, 3, or 4).

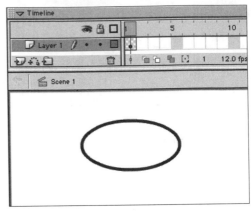

Figure 10.5 Draw an oval in the first keyframe of your shape tween.

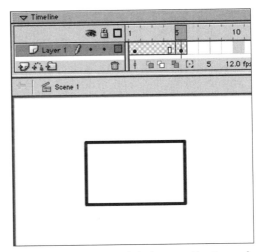

Figure 10.6 Draw a rectangle in the second keyframe of your shape tween.

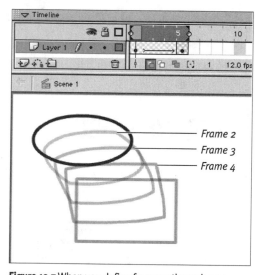

Figure 10.7 When you define frames 1 through 4 as shape tweens, Flash creates the three intermediate shapes that transform the oval into a square. Turn on onion skinning to see the shapes for the in-between frames.

5. From the Frame Property Inspector's Tween pop-up menu, choose Shape.

Flash transforms the oval into the rectangle in three equal steps—one for each in-between frame (**Figure 10.7**).

6. To align the oval and rectangle, in the Timeline status bar, click the Onion Skin or Onion Skin Outlines button.

Flash displays all the in-between frames.

7. In the Timeline, position the playhead in Frame 1.

8. On the Stage, select and reposition the oval so that it aligns with the rectangle (**Figure 10.8**).

The oval transforms into a rectangle, remaining in one spot on the Stage.

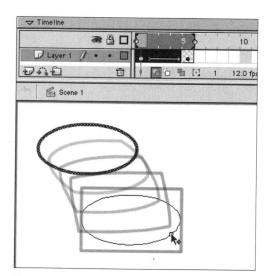

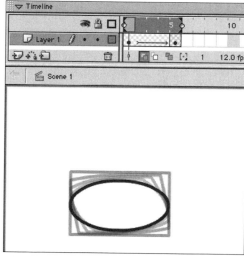

Figure 10.8 Use onion skinning to help position your keyframe shapes. Here, with Frame 1 selected, you can drag the oval to center it within the rectangle. That makes the oval grow into a rectangle without moving anywhere else on the Stage.

MORPHING SIMPLE LINES AND FILLS

To transform a rectangle into a freeform shape:

1. Create a new Flash document.

2. On the Stage, in Frame 1, draw a rectangular fill.

3. In the Timeline, select Frame 5, and choose Insert > Blank Keyframe.

4. On the Stage, in Frame 5, use the brush tool to paint a free-form fill.

   Don't make the fill too complex—just a blob or brush stroke with gentle curves.

5. In the Timeline, select any of the frames in the Keyframe span (1, 2, 3, or 4).

6. From the Frame Property Inspector's Tween pop-up menu, choose Shape.

   Flash transforms the rectangle into the fill in three equal steps—one for each in-between frame (**Figure 10.9**).

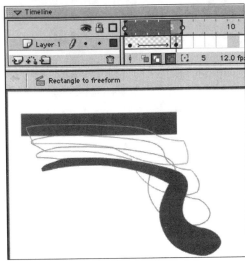

Figure 10.9 Flash transforms a rectangle into a free-form brush stroke with shape tweening.

Shape-Tweening Multiple Shapes

In motion tweening, Flash limits you to one item per tween, meaning just one item per layer. In shape tweening, however, Flash can handle more than one shape on a layer. The drawback is that you may get some very strange results if you try to tween several shapes on a layer. The simpler and fewer the shapes you use, the more reliable your multishape tweens will be. For the most predictable results, limit yourself to one shape per layer.

You may want to keep both shapes on the same layer for a fill with an outline, however. As long as the transformation is not too complicated, Flash can handle the two together.

(continues on next page)

When Multiple Shape Tweens on a Single Layer Go Bad

If you are shape-tweening stationary objects, you probably can get away with having several on the same layer. But if the objects are in motion, Flash can get confused about which shape goes where. Though you may intend the paths of two shapes to cross, Flash creates the most direct route between the starting object and the ending object. **Figure 10.10** illustrates the problem.

All objects on one layer

All objects on one layer

Light circle and arrow on one layer

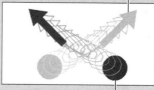

Dark circle and arrow on another layer

Figure 10.10 Tweening multiple shapes whose paths don't cross in a single layer works fine. In the top image, both objects are on the same layer, and the light circle transforms into the light arrow without a hitch. In the middle image, both objects are on the same layer, but Flash transforms the light circle into the dark arrow and the dark circle into the light arrow because that's the most direct path. If you want to create diagonal paths that cross, you must put each object on its own layer, as in the bottom image.

To shape-tween fills with strokes (outlines):

1. Follow the steps in the preceding exercises to create a shape tween of an outline oval transforming into a rectangle.

2. Fill each shape with a different color.

   Flash tweens the fill and the stroke together and tweens the change in color (**Figure 10.11**).

3. In the Toolbox, choose the ink bottle, and select white for the stroke color.

4. In Frame 5, click the rectangle with the ink-bottle tool.

   The rectangle's stroke changes to white (the same as the background).

   Flash tweens the shape, and the color changes as well, creating a "disappearing" stroke (**Figure 10.12**).

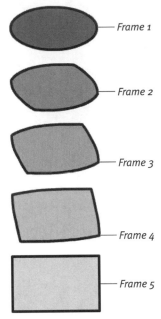

Frame 1

Frame 2

Frame 3

Frame 4

Frame 5

Figure 10.11 Here, Flash transforms a shape with a stroke in five frames. The shape tween changes not only the graphic's shape, but also its color (from dark to light).

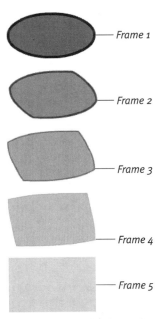

Frame 1

Frame 2

Frame 3

Frame 4

Frame 5

Figure 10.12 In this five-frame shape tween, the stroke color changes to match the movie's background, making the stroke disappear.

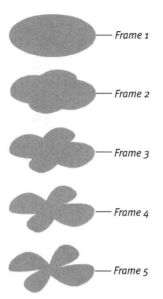

Frame 1

Frame 2

Frame 3

Frame 4

Frame 5

Figure 10.13 Flash handles the tween from an oval to a simple flower shape without requiring shape hints.

Transforming a Simple Shape into a Complex Shape

The more complex the shape you tween, the more difficult it is for Flash to create the expected result. That's because Flash changes the shapes by changing the mathematical description of the graphic. Flash does not understand how the forces of gravity, light, and so on affect the ways humans see; therefore, it doesn't always choose to make a change in a way that preserves the illusion you want. You can help Flash tween better by using *shape hints*—markers that allow you to identify points on the original shape's outline that correspond to points on the final shape's outline.

To shape-tween a more complex shape:

1. Create a new Flash document.

2. On the Stage, in Frame 1, draw an oval with no stroke.

3. In the Timeline, select Frame 5, and choose Insert > Keyframe.

   Flash duplicates the contents of Keyframe 1 in Keyframe 5.

4. In the Timeline, select any of the frames in the Keyframe span (1, 2, 3, or 4).

5. From the Frame Property Inspector's Tween pop-up menu, choose Shape.

6. In the Timeline, position the playhead in Frame 5.

7. Using the arrow tool or the pen and sub-selection tools, drag four corner points in toward the center of the oval to create a flower shape.

   For more detailed instructions on editing shapes, see Chapter 3.

8. Play the movie to see the shape tween.

   Flash handles the tweening for this change well (**Figure 10.13**). It's fairly obvious what points of the oval should move in to create the petal shapes.

If you modify the shape further, however, it gets harder for Flash to know how to create the new shape. That's when you need to use shape hints.

To use shape hints:

1. Using the animation you created in the preceding exercise, in the Timeline, select Frame 10, and choose Insert > Keyframe.

   Flash duplicates the flower shape in a new keyframe.

2. In Frame 10, edit the flower to add a stem. Reshape the outline with the arrow tool or the pen and subselection tools, or add a stem with a brush stroke in the same color as the flower.

3. Define a shape tween for frames 5 through 9.

4. Play the movie.

   The addition of the stem to the flower makes it hard for Flash to create a smooth tween that looks right (**Figure 10.14**).

5. To begin adding shape hints, position the playhead in Frame 5 (the initial keyframe of this tweening sequence).

6. From the Modify menu, choose Shape > Add Shape Hint, or press Shift-⌘-H (Mac) or Ctrl-Shift-H (Windows) (**Figure 10.15**).

   Flash places a shape hint—a small red circle labeled with a letter, starting with *a*—in the center of the object in the current frame. You need to reposition the shape hint to place it on a problem point on the shape's outline.

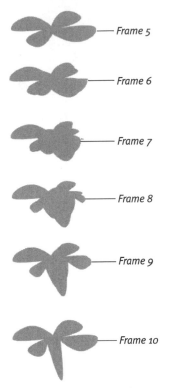

Frame 5

Frame 6

Frame 7

Frame 8

Frame 9

Frame 10

Figure 10.14 The addition of a stem to the flower overloads Flash's capability to create a smooth shape tween. Frames 7 and 8 are particularly bad.

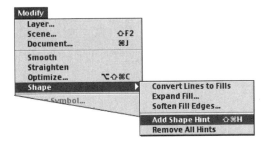

Figure 10.15 Choose Modify > Shape > Add Shape Hint to activate markers that help Flash make connections between the original shape and the final shape of the tween.

———— Areas of change

Figure 10.16 Start adding shape hints in the first keyframe of a tween sequence. Flash places the hints in the center of the tweened object (top). You must drag the hints into position (middle). Distribute the hints in alphabetical order around the outline of the object, placing them on crucial points of change (bottom). Here, the three points with hints a, b, and c define the points from which the stem of the flower will grow.

Figure 10.17 To complete the placement of shape hints, you need to select the second keyframe of your tween sequence. Flash stacks up hints corresponding to the ones you placed in the preceding keyframe (top). You must drag them into the correct final position (bottom).

7. With the arrow tool, drag the shape hint to a problem point on the edge of the shape.

   Don't worry about getting the shape hint in exactly the right spot; you can fine-tune it later.

8. Repeat steps 6 and 7 until you have placed shape hints on all the problem points of your shape in Frame 5 (**Figure 10.16**).

   Each time you add a shape hint, you get another small red circle labeled with a letter. You cannot place the hints at random; you must place them so that they go in alphabetical order around the edge of the shape. (Flash does the best job when you place shape hints in counterclockwise order, but you can also place them in clockwise order.)

9. In the Timeline, position the playhead in Frame 10.

   Flash has already added shape hints to this frame; they all stack up in the center of the shape.

10. With the arrow tool, drag each shape hint to its position on the new shape.

    Keep them in the same order (counterclockwise or clockwise) you chose in step 8 (**Figure 10.17**).

11. To evaluate the improvement in tweening, play the movie.

    (continues on next page)

SIMPLE SHAPES INTO COMPLEX SHAPES

12. To fine-tune the shape hints' positions, select one of the tween's keyframes, and turn on onion skinning.

Set the onion markers to include all the frames of the tween. Where the onion skins reveal rough spots in the tween, you may need to match the hint position better from the first keyframe to the last one (**Figure 10.18**). Repositioning the shape hints changes the in-between frames.

You may need to adjust the shape hints in both keyframes. If you still can't get a smooth tween, try adding more shape hints.

✔ Tips

■ To remove a single shape hint, make the initial keyframe the current frame. Select the shape hint you want to remove, and drag it completely off the Stage.

■ To remove all the hints at the same time, with the initial keyframe current, choose Modify > Shape > Remove All Hints.

■ Onion skins don't always update correctly when you reposition shape hints. Clicking a blank area of the Stage forces Flash to redraw them.

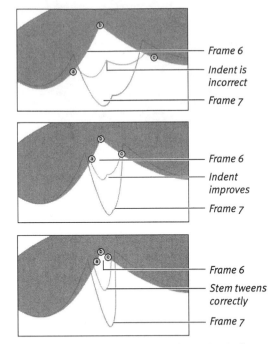

Frame 6
Indent is incorrect
Frame 7

Frame 6
Indent improves
Frame 7

Frame 6
Stem tweens correctly
Frame 7

Figure 10.18 It can be difficult to match up points in the two keyframes exactly when you first place the shape hints. When you've positioned the hints in the beginning and ending keyframes of a sequence, turn on onion skinning to see where you need to adjust the placement of your hints. With the initial placement, Flash starts the stem growing with an indent at the bottom (top). Moving the points closer together improves the tween (middle). When the onion skins reveal a smooth tween, you're done (bottom).

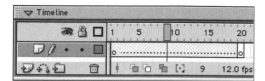

Figure 10.19 To save yourself numerous trips to the Frame Property Inspector's Tween pop-up menu, you can assign the shape-tween property to a range of frames and add keyframes and shapes later. Flash defines a shape tween even though there's no content to tween yet.

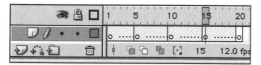

Figure 10.20 When you insert keyframes into a long tween sequence, Flash breaks it into smaller tween sequences. Until you place content in the keyframes, the Timeline will display the dotted line in each span to indicate a broken tween.

Creating Shapes That Move As They Change

You cannot create shape tweens that follow a path, but you can move shapes around the Stage in straight lines. You simply reposition the elements on the Stage from one keyframe to the next.

To shape-tween a moving graphic:

1. Create a new Flash document.

2. On the Stage, select Frame 20, and choose Insert > Keyframe.

   Flash adds a blank keyframe at Frame 20 and blank in-between frames at frames 2 through 19.

3. In the Timeline, select any frame from 1 to 19.

   Note that you must click the frame to select it; you cannot just position the playhead in the frame.

4. From the Frame Property Inspector's Tween pop-up menu, choose Shape.

   Even though you have no shapes on the Stage to tween yet, Flash gives the frames the shape-tween property. In the Timeline, the frames contain a dotted line, indicating that the tween is incomplete (**Figure 10.19**). Now you can add keyframes and shapes.

5. In the Timeline, insert a blank keyframe at frames 5, 10, and 15.

   Flash creates four shape-tween sequences (**Figure 10.20**).

   (continues on next page)

6. In each keyframe, draw a different shape; place each one in a different corner of the Stage.

In Frame 1, for example, draw a circular fill in the bottom-left corner of the Stage. In Frame 5, draw a rectangular fill in the top-right corner of the Stage. In Frame 10, draw a flattened oval in the bottom-right corner of the Stage. In Frame 15, draw a star in the top-left corner of the Stage. And in Frame 20, duplicate Frame 1's circle in the bottom-left corner of the Stage. For extra variety, give each object a different color. As you add content to keyframe, Flash fills in the spans in the Timeline with tween arrows.

7. Play the movie.

You see a graphic that bounces around the Stage, morphing from one shape to the next (**Figure 10.21**).

✔ Tip

■ Although shape-tweened objects cannot follow a path the way motion-tweened objects can, you can make Flash do the work of creating the separate keyframes you need to animate shape tweens that move on curved paths. First, create your shape tween. In the Timeline, select the full range of frames in the tween sequence. From the Modify menu, choose Frames > Convert to Keyframes. Flash converts each in-between frame (with its transitional content) into a keyframe. Now you can position each keyframe object anywhere you like. To simulate a motion guide, create a regular guide layer, and draw the path you want your morphing shape to follow. Choose View > Guides > Snap to Guides. Reposition the shape in each keyframe. When you drag a shape close to the line on the guide layer, Flash snaps the shape to the line.

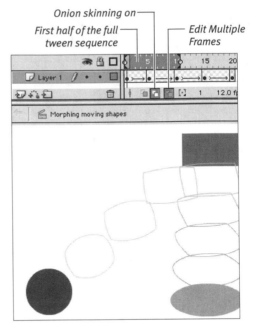

Onion skinning on ─
First half of the full ─ tween sequence
Edit Multiple Frames

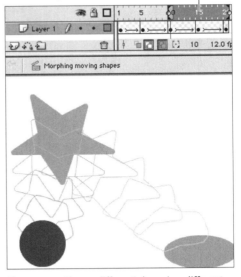

Second half of the full tween sequence ─

Figure 10.21 Place a different shape in a different location in each keyframe. Flash creates the intermediate steps necessary to transform the shapes and move them across the Stage. Play through the movie or turn on onion skinning to examine the motion and shape changes on the in-between frames. (Here, Edit Multiple Frames is also on, making it easy to see the keyframe shapes.)

MORE-
COMPLEX
ANIMATION TASKS

So far, you've learned to manipulate shapes and animate them one at a time, in a single layer. In some cases, those techniques are all you need, but Macromedia Flash MX is capable of handling much more complicated animation tasks. To create complex animated movies, you're going to need to work with multiple shapes and multiple layers. You may even want to use multiple scenes to organize long animations. In this chapter, you learn to work with multiple layers in the Timeline, stack animations on the various layers to create more-complex movement, and save animations as reusable elements for easy manipulation—either as animated graphic symbols or as movie-clip symbols. With these techniques, you can really start to bring your animations to life.

Understanding Scenes

In the metaphor of the Timeline's being the table of contents for the "book" of your movie, scenes are the equivalent of chapters. Scenes help you organize the contents of a long movie. So far, you've worked with 5-, 10-, and 20-frame movies, but in real life, your movie may run to hundreds of frames. You can get pretty tired of scrolling around the Timeline, trying to keep track of where you are, if the movie has hundreds of frames. But you can break the animation into reasonable chunks and deal with each set of frames separately by creating scenes.

In your final published movie, Flash plays through the scenes in order unless you use the interactivity features to provide instructions for moving through the scenes in a different order. (To learn more about interactivity in Flash movies, see Chapters 12 and 13.)

Flash's Scene panel makes it easy to see what scenes exist in your movie, create new scenes, delete scenes, and reorganize them.

To access the Scene panel:

◆ If the Scene panel is not open, from the Window menu, choose Scene (**Figure 11.1**). The Scene panel appears.

In a new Flash document, the Scene panel lists only the default Scene 1. When you add scenes to a movie, the Scene panel lists all the movie's scenes in order (**Figure 11.2**).

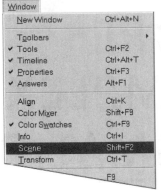

Figure 11.1 Choose Window > Scene to access the Scene panel.

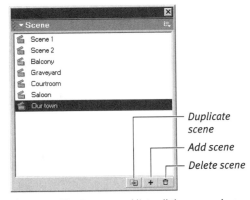

Figure 11.2 The Scene panel lists all the scenes in a movie. It also provides buttons for adding, duplicating, and deleting scenes.

Scene panel's Add Scene button

Figure 11.3 To add a new scene to your Flash document, choose Insert > Scene (top) or, in the Scene panel, click the Add Scene button (bottom).

To add a scene:

Do one of the following:

◆ From the Insert menu, choose Scene (**Figure 11.3**).

◆ In the Scene panel, click the Add Scene button.

Flash adds another scene, giving it the default name Scene 2.

✔ Tip

■ Flash bases default scene names on the number of scenes you have ever added, not on the number of scenes currently in the movie. If you add Scenes 2 and 3 and then delete Scene 2, Flash names the next scene that you add Scene 4 .

To select a scene to edit:

Do one of the following:

◆ From the Edit Scene pop-up menu in the info bar at the top of the Stage, choose the scene that you want to edit.

◆ From the scrolling list in the Scene panel, select the scene that you want to edit.

Flash displays the selected scene on the Stage, putting its name in the current-scene box in the middle of the info bar and placing a check next to that scene's name in the Edit Scene pop-up menu (**Figure 11.4**).

To delete a selected scene:

1. *Do one of the following:*

◆ From the Insert menu, choose Remove Scene (**Figure 11.5**).

◆ In the Scene panel, click the Delete button.

A dialog box appears, warning you that you can't undo this operation.

2. Click OK.

Flash deletes the scene, removing it from the Edit Scene pop-up menu in the Timeline as well as from the scrolling list in the Scene panel.

✔ Tip

■ If you don't want to see the warning dialog box when you delete a scene, ⌘-click (Mac) or Ctrl-click (Windows) the Delete Scene button in the Scene panel.

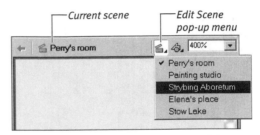

Current scene   *Edit Scene pop-up menu*

Figure 11.4 The info bar displays the name of the current scene. Choose a scene from the Edit Scene pop-up menu to switch scenes quickly.

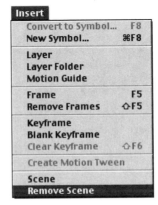

Scene panel's Delete Scene button

Figure 11.5 To delete a scene, choose Insert > Remove Scene (top) or click the Scene panel's Delete Scene button (bottom).

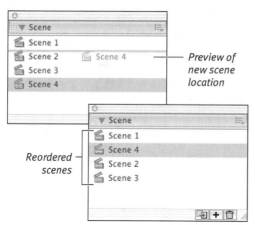

Figure 11.6 As you drag a selected scene, the clapper icon and scene name come along for the ride. In addition, a highlighted bar previews the new location for the scene. When the bar is between the scenes where you want to place the selected scene, release the mouse button.

To change scene order:

◆ In the Scene panel, drag a selected scene name up or down in the list.

Flash moves the clapper icon and scene name and previews the new location for the scene with a highlighted line (**Figure 11.6**).

To rename a scene:

1. In the Scene panel, double-click the name of the scene that you want to rename.

2. Type the new name in the Name field.

The Pitfalls of Using Scenes

In Flash, each scene is like a self-contained movie. The fact that each scene is, in a sense, a new beginning can make it difficult to keep the continuity of actions between scenes. For some types of movies—ones with interactivity that requires variables or preloading—scenes are inappropriate. In such cases, you may need to stick to a single long movie or use separate movies to organize your animation, stringing them together with interactivity features such as the loadMovie action. (See Chapter 15 to learn about this Action-Script item.)

Manipulating Frames in Multiple Layers

As your movie gets more complex, you will need to add layers. You can perform editing operations on selected frames and layers, for example, by copying, cutting, and pasting frames across multiple layers. You can also insert frames, keyframes, and blank key-frames into selected frames and layers.

To select and copy frames in several layers:

1. Open a new Flash document.

2. Add two layers—for a total of three layers in the movie—and insert 20 frames into each layer.

   Place content in the layers to help you see what's going on as you work with the various frames and layers. Use the text tool, for example, to place the frame number in every other frame of Layer 1 and to place a text block with the name of the layer in layers 2 and 3.

3. In the Timeline, in Layer 3, in frame-based selections mode click and drag as though you were drawing a selection rectangle around frames 5 through 10 in all three layers. In span-based selection mode; ⌘-click (Mac) or Ctrl-Click (Windows) and drag to select a range of frames or reversal layers.

   Flash highlights the selected frames (**Figure 11.7**).

4. From the Edit menu, choose Copy Frames. Flash copies the frames and layer information to the Clipboard.

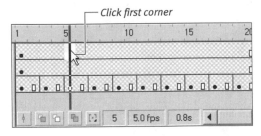

— Click first corner

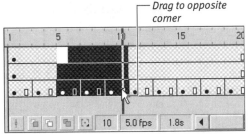

— Drag to opposite corner

Figure 11.7 In frame-based mode click and drag across frames and layers to select frames in those layers (bottom).

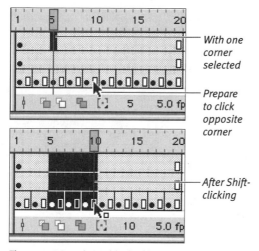

With one corner selected

Prepare to click opposite corner

After Shift-clicking

Figure 11.8 To select a block of frames, in frame-based selection style, click one corner of the block; then Shift-click the opposite corner to define the block. In span-based selection style, ⌘-click (Mac) or Ctrl-click (Windows) the first corner and then ⌘-Shift-click (Mac) or Ctrl-Shift-click (Windows) the opposite corner of your selection block.

✔ Tip

- To select a block of frames that spans several layers without dragging, in frame-based selection style, click a frame at one of the four corners of the block. Then Shift-click the frame at the opposite corner. Flash selects all the frames in the rectangle that you've defined (**Figure 11.8**). In span-based selection style, ⌘-click (Mac) or Ctrl-click (Windows) one corner and then ⌘-Shift-click (Mac) or Ctrl-Shift-click (Windows) the opposite corner to make your selection.

To replace the content of frames with a multilayer selection:

1. Continuing with the document that you created in the preceding exercise, select frames 15 through 20 on all three layers.

2. From the Edit menu, choose Paste Frames.

   Flash pastes the copied frames 5 through 10 into frames 15 through 20 in each of the three layers. The numbers on the Stage in Layer 1 now start over with 5 at Frame 15, 7 at Frame 17, and 9 at Frame 19.

To paste a multiple-layer selection into blank frames:

1. Using the document that you created in the preceding exercise, select Frame 21 on all three layers.

2. From the Edit menu, choose Paste Frames.

   Flash pastes the copied frames 5 through 10 into protoframes 21 through 26 in each of the three layers (**Figure 11.9**). Layer 1 now displays the number 5 at Frame 21, 7 at Frame 23, and 9 at Frame 25.

To paste a multiple-layer selection into a new scene:

1. Using the document that you created in the preceding exercise, insert a new scene, following the instructions in the first section in this chapter.

   By default, the new scene has one layer and one frame.

2. Select Frame 1.

3. From the Edit menu, choose Paste Frames.

   Flash pastes the copied selection from the first scene (frames 5 through 10 on layers 1 through 3) into the new scene. Flash adds layers 2 and 3 and creates frames 1 through 6 in each layer (**Figure 11.10**). Layer 1 now displays the number 5 at Frame 1, 7 at Frame 3, and 9 at Frame 5.

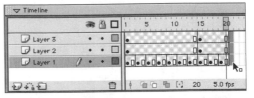
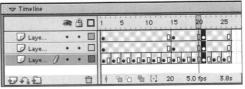

Figure 11.9 Pasting a multiple-layer, multiple-frame selection at the end of a movie (top) extends the movie to accommodate the new frames and layers (bottom).

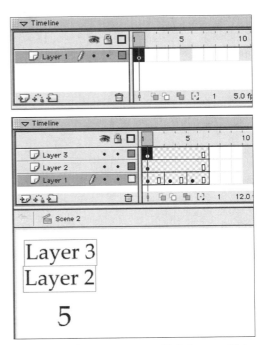

Figure 11.10 When you paste a multiple-layer, multiple-frame selection into a new scene (top), Flash creates new layers and frames to hold the contents of the Clipboard (bottom).

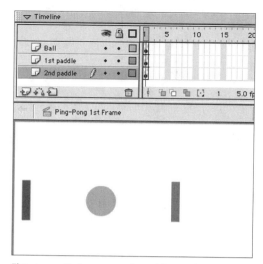

Figure 11.11 To have several graphics motion-tween simultaneously, you must place each one on a separate layer. Here, each item is on a separate layer. The descriptive layer names help you keep track of what goes where.

Animating Multiple Motion Tweens

As you learned in Chapter 9, Flash can motion-tween only one item per layer. You can tween multiple items simultaneously; you just have to put each one on a separate layer. You can use Onion Skin and Edit Multiple Frame modes to make sure that all the elements line up in the right place at the right time. To get a feel for tweening multiple items, try combining three simple motion tweens to create a game of Ping-Pong. One layer contains the ball; the other layers each contain a paddle.

To set up the three graphics in separate layers:

1. Open a new Flash document, and add two new layers.

2. Rename the layers.

   Name the top layer Ball, the next layer 1st Paddle, and the bottom layer 2nd Paddle. Naming the layers helps you keep track of the elements and their locations.

3. Create the graphics.

   On the Stage, in the Ball layer, use the oval tool to create a ball; in the layer named 1st Paddle, use the rectangle tool to create a paddle; and then copy the paddle and paste the copy into the layer named 2nd Paddle. Give each shape a different color. Your file should look something like **Figure 11.11**.

To set up the tween in all layers with one command:

1. Using the document that you created in the preceding task, in the Timeline, select Frame 1 in all three layers.

2. From the Insert menu, choose Create Motion Tween.

   Flash turns each shape into a symbol (naming the symbols Tween 1, Tween 2, and Tween 3) and gives all the frames the motion-tween property (**Figure 11.12**).

3. In the Timeline, select Frame 20 in all three layers.

4. From the Insert menu, choose Frame.

   Flash extends the motion tween through Frame 20 on all three layers, placing a dotted line across the frames to indicate that they are part of an incomplete motion tween. You need to reposition the symbols and create keyframes to complete the tweens.

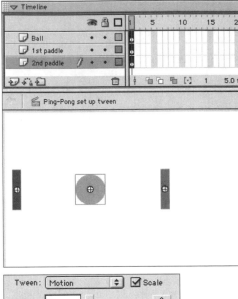

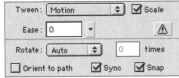

Figure 11.12 By using the Create Motion Tween command with frames selected on all three layers, you create three motion tweens with one command. The Frame Property Inspector reveals their status as motion tweens (bottom).

Animating Multiple Motion Tweens

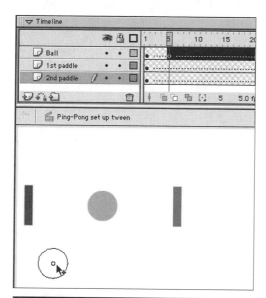

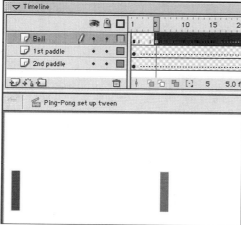

Figure 11.13 Moving a graphic in a frame that's defined as part of a motion tween causes Flash to make the layer containing the graphic the active layer (top). Flash creates a keyframe in that layer for the graphic's new position, completing one tween sequence (bottom).

To adjust the positions of the tweened items:

1. Using the document that you created in the preceding task, in the Timeline, position the playhead in Frame 5.

2. On the Stage, drag the ball to the approximate location where it should connect with one of the paddles for the first hit.

   Flash makes Ball the active layer and creates a keyframe (in Frame 5) for the ball in its new location (**Figure 11.13**). Flash completes the motion tween between Frame 1 and Frame 5 of the Ball layer and leaves the broken-tween line in all the other frames.

   (continues on next page)

3. On the Stage, reposition the first paddle graphic so that the paddle connects with the ball for the first hit.

Flash makes 1st Paddle the active layer and creates a keyframe (in Frame 5) for the paddle in its new location (**Figure 11.14**).

4. In the Timeline, position the playhead in Frame 10.

5. On the Stage, drag the ball to the approximate location where you want it to connect with a paddle for the second hit.

Flash makes Ball the active layer and creates a keyframe (in Frame 10) for the ball in its new location. Flash completes the motion tween between Frame 5 and Frame 10 of the Ball layer.

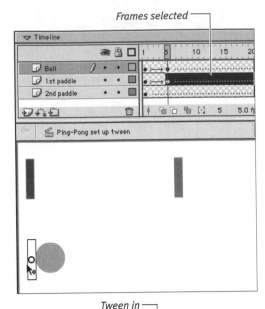

Frames selected

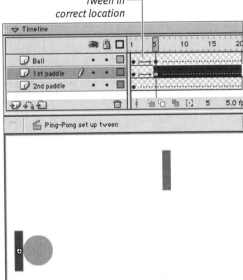

Tween in correct location

Figure 11.14 As you reposition the paddle (top), Flash appears to be selecting the wrong set of frames, but when you release the mouse button, Flash correctly tweens frames 1 through 4 (bottom).

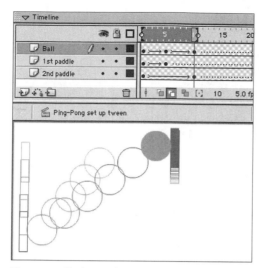

Figure 11.15 Moving an element in another frame creates another tween. Here, the paddle on the right side appears to move more slowly than the paddle on the left side, because Flash is creating a 10-frame tween for the right paddle, while the left paddle tweens in 5 frames.

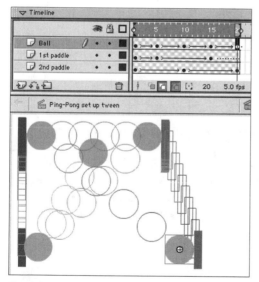

Figure 11.16 Selecting Onion Skin Outlines and Edit Multiple Frames makes fine-tuning the location of objects easier. Here, the paddle on the right doesn't move in a straight line. If you want it to do so, reposition the paddle graphics in the first and final frames so that one lies directly above the other; then reposition the ball so that it comes into contact with both paddles.

6. On the Stage, reposition the second paddle so that it connects with the ball for the second hit.

Flash makes 2nd Paddle the active layer and creates a keyframe (in Frame 10) for the paddle in its new location (**Figure 11.15**).

7. Repeat steps 1 through 6, using keyframes 15 and 20, to make the ball connect with each paddle one more time.

8. Play the movie to see the animation in action.

9. Select Onion Skin Outlines and Edit Multiple Frames, and reposition objects as necessary to fine-tune the motion (**Figure 11.16**).

✔ Tips

■ After you define a set of frames as tweens, any slight change you make to an object causes Flash to create a new keyframe. Even simply double-clicking an object causes Flash to insert a keyframe. So that you don't change objects' positions or create new keyframes accidentally, lock or hide the layers that you're not working on.

■ To position items on the Stage with greater precision than dragging allows, select an item and use the Property Inspector or the Info panel to set the item's *x* and *y* coordinates.

ANIMATING MULTIPLE MOTION TWEENS

387

Motion-Tweening Text

You can use the multiple-motion tween idea to animate individual characters within a piece of text. After you create the text that you want to animate, select it and choose Modify > Break Apart. That command places each character in its own text box. Next, with each character of the text selected, choose Modify > Distribute to Layers. Each character winds up on its own layer. Now use any of the animating techniques you learned in chapters 9 and 10, or in earlier exercises in this chapter, to animate the individual text characters (**Figure 11.17**).

Broken-apart text; one character per text box

Text distributed to layers

Each letter is a separate motion tween

Figure 11.17 Using Flash's Modify > Break Apart command in conjunction with the Modify > Distribute to Layers command, you can set up tweens quickly to animate individual text characters. Each letter in this animated text is a motion tween.

If you want to transform the shapes of the letters, you'll need to use shape tweening. That means converting the letters from editable text elements to editable graphics. Select one or more text boxes containing individual letters and choose Modify > Break Apart. The letter-forms will look the same, but now they are raw shapes that you can modify with the drawing tools and use in shape tweens.

ANIMATING MULTIPLE MOTION TWEENS

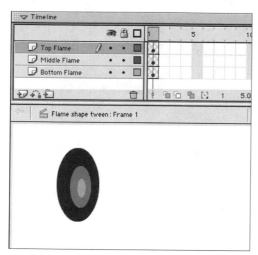

Figure 11.18 Create each part of a multiple-element shape tween on a separate layer. Name the layers to help you track what goes where.

Animating Shape Tweens in Multiple-Shape Graphics

An important thing to remember about complex shape tweens is that Flash deals most reliably with a single shape tween on a layer. In the following exercises, you create a multipart, multilayer graphic and shape-tween the whole package simultaneously.

To create shape tweens on separate layers:

1. Open a new Flash document, and add two new layers.

2. Rename the layers Top Flame, Middle Flame, and Bottom Flame.

   Naming the layers helps you keep track of the objects and their locations.

3. Create the shapes.

   On the Stage, use the oval tool to create three concentric oval shapes. In the Bottom Flame layer, create a large oval; in the Middle Flame layer, create a medium oval (center it over the first oval); in the Top Flame layer, create a small oval (center it over the medium oval). Give each oval a different color. Your file should look something like **Figure 11.18**.

4. Select Frame 5 in all three layers.

5. From the Insert menu, choose Keyframe.

   Flash creates a keyframe with the same content as Frame 1 for each layer.

6. In the Timeline, select any of the frames in the Keyframe 1 span (1, 2, 3, or 4) in all three layers.

   (continues on next page)

When Should One Element Span Several Layers?

Often, an element that you think of as a single entity actually consists of several shapes in Flash. A candle flame is a good example. To simulate the flickering of a lighted candle, you might create a flame with three shades of orange and then animate changes in the flame shape and colors.

One natural way to do this is to draw each flame segment in the same layer so that you can see the interaction of the shapes immediately. Unfortunately, Flash has trouble tweening shapes that you create that way. You'll be better off creating a rough version of each segment in a separate layer and then fine-tuning that version. That way, Flash has to tween only one shape per layer, and the result will be cleaner.

7. From the Frame Property Inspector's Tween menu, choose Shape.

   Flash gives the shape-tween property to frames 1 through 4 on all three layers (**Figure 11.19**). To create flickering flames, you need to reshape the ovals in Frame 5.

8. In the Timeline, position the playhead in Frame 5.

9. On the Stage, edit the ovals to create flame shapes.

10. Play the movie to see the animation in action.

    Flash handles the shape-tweening of each layer separately. For comparison, try creating the oval and flame shapes on a single layer and then shape-tweening them (**Figure 11.20**).

11. Select Onion Skin Outlines and Edit Multiple Frames; then reposition the flame objects as necessary to fine-tune the motion.

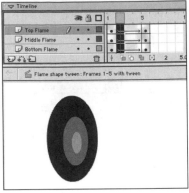

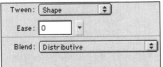

Figure 11.19 When you select multiple frames, you can set the tweening property for those frames simultaneously by choosing a property from the Tween pop-up menu in the Property Inspector.

Figure 11.20 With the three colors of flames on separate layers (left), Flash does a reasonable job of tweening even when you don't add shape hints. With the three flame shapes on a single layer (right), Flash has great difficulty creating the tweens.

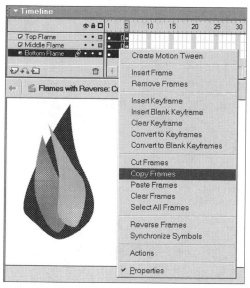

Figure 11.21 The contextual menu for frames lets you copy all selected frames with a single command.

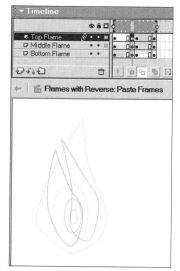

Figure 11.22 After you paste the copied selection, you have two tween sequences ending with the tall, flickering flame.

Reversing Frames

Sometimes, you can save work by creating just half the animation that you need and letting Flash do the rest of the work. Think of the candle flame that you created in the preceding section. You might want the flame to grow larger and then shrink back to its original size. The shrinking phase is really just the reverse of the growing phase. You can make a copy of the growing-flame animation and then have Flash reverse the order of the frames.

To reverse the order of frames:

1. Open the document that you created in the preceding section.

   This movie spans five frames on three layers. The first keyframe shows the flame as three concentric oval shapes; the final keyframe shows the flame in a taller, flickering configuration.

2. In the Timeline, select all five frames on all three layers.

3. In one of the selected frames, Control-click (Mac) or right-click (Windows) to access the frame-editing contextual menu; then choose Copy Frames (**Figure 11.21**).

4. In the Timeline, select Frame 6 in all three layers.

5. In one of the selected frames, Control-click (Mac) or right-click (Windows) to access the frame-editing contextual menu, and choose Paste Frames from that menu.

   Your movie now contains two back-to-back animation sequences of the growing flame (**Figure 11.22**).

(continues on next page)

6. In the Timeline, select frames 6 through 10 on all three layers.

7. From the Modify menu, choose Frames > Reverse (**Figure 11.23**).

Flash reverses the tween in the second sequence so that the flame starts out tall and flickery, and winds up in its original oval configuration in the final keyframe (**Figure 11.24**).

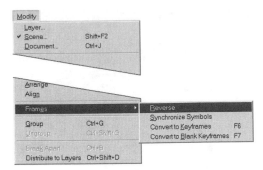

Figure 11.23 Choosing Modify > Frames > Reverse rearranges the order of selected frames. Use this command to make a selected tween run backward.

Figure 11.24 After you reverse the frames, the second tween sequence ends with the oval flame.

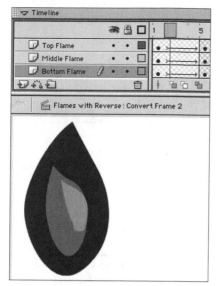

Figure 11.25 Flash's shape tween in Frame 2 leaves something to be desired.

Combining Tweening with Frame-by-Frame Techniques

Especially with shape tweening, you cannot rely on Flash to create the in-between frames that capture the exact movement you want. You can combine Flash's tweening with your own frame-by-frame efforts, however, letting Flash do the work whenever it can. Or let Flash create the broad outlines of your animation and then add keyframes to refine the movement. Flash helps with the process by allowing you to convert those intangible in-between frames to keyframes that you can edit and refine yourself.

In the preceding section, you created a crude version of a flickering flame. In the following exercises, you refine it.

To convert in-between frames to keyframes:

1. Open the Flash document that you created in the preceding section.

2. In the Timeline, position the playhead in Frame 2.

   The first step in this tween is not particularly effective: The central flame portion seems to be a bit too far to the side (**Figure 11.25**). Because Frame 2 is an in-between frame, however, you can't edit it. You can try to improve the motion by adding shape hints, or you can create a new keyframe to refine the animation.

3. To convert the in-between frame to a keyframe, in the Timeline, select Frame 2 in all three layers.

(continues on next page)

COMBINING TWEENING FRAME-BY-FRAME

4. From the Modify menu, choose Frames > Convert to Keyframes, or press F6 (**Figure 11.26**).

Flash converts Frame 2 from an in-between frame to a keyframe; then it creates the contents of Keyframe 2 from the transitional shapes that it created for the shape tween at that frame. Now you are free to edit the contents to improve the tweening action (**Figure 11.27**). If you want to create a smoother motion, expand the tween between Keyframe 1 and Keyframe 2.

5. To add more in-between frames, position the playhead in Frame 1.

6. From the Insert menu, choose Frame, or press F5.

Flash adds new in-between frames in all layers. You can repeat the Insert > Frame command to add as many frames as you like. These frames inherit the shape-tween property that you defined for Frame 1. Now you can examine Flash's tweening for the new frames and repeat the process of converting any awkward tween frames to keyframes and editing them.

✔ Tips

- You can convert multiple in-between frames of a shape or motion tween by selecting them and then choosing Modify > Frames > Convert to Keyframes.

- Flash limits you to one color change per tween sequence. To speed the process of making several color changes, set up one long tween (either motion or shape) that goes from the initial color to the final color. Then selectively convert in-between frames to keyframes so that you can make additional color changes.

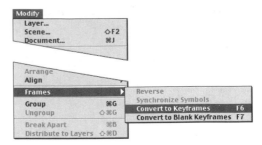

Figure 11.26 Choose Modify > Frames > Convert to Keyframes to add a keyframe for adjusting your multi-layer tween.

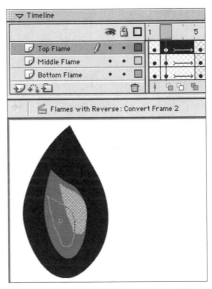

Figure 11.27 After you convert Frame 2 from an in-between frame (part of a tween) to a keyframe, you can edit the flame objects.

COMBINING TWEENING FRAME-BY-FRAME

Figure 11.28 You set a new symbol's behavior in the Create New Symbol dialog box. Movie clips operate from their own independent Timeline. Animated graphic symbols share a Timeline with the main movie that contains them. One frame of the main movie displays one frame of the symbol.

Symbols Reduce Layer Buildup

In general, for tweened animations, you need to place each shape on a separate layer. To animate a person, for example, create separate layers for the head, the torso, each arm, and each leg. For complex motion, you might even create separate layers for eyes, mouth, fingers, and toes. Add some other elements to this character's environment, and you wind up dealing with many layers.

Turning an animation sequence into a symbol in effect collapses all those layers into one object. The process is a bit like grouping. On the Stage, the symbol exists on a single layer, but that layer contains all the layers of the original animation.

Saving Animations As Graphic Symbols

One great thing about symbols is that they allow you to use the work you do over and over. In Chapter 6, you learned to save work and keep file sizes small by using symbols. Flash lets you do the same thing with entire multiple-frame, multiple-layer animation sequences. You can save such sequences either as an animated graphic symbol or as a movie-clip symbol. You can use these symbols repeatedly with a much smaller hit on file size than if you simply re-create the animation by using graphic-symbol instances within separate animations. Additionally, for complex animations, symbols help keep down the number of frames and layers that you have to deal with at any time.

To convert an animation to a graphic symbol:

1. Open the document that you created to make the Ping-Pong animation in "Animating Multiple Motion Tweens" earlier in this chapter, or create your own multiple-layer animation.

   The Ping-Pong animation is a three-layer, 20-frame animation.

2. In the Timeline, select all 20 frames in all three layers.

3. From the Edit menu, choose Copy Frames.

4. From the Insert menu, choose New Symbol, or press ⌘-F8 (Mac) or Ctrl-F8 (Windows).

   The Create New Symbol dialog box appears (**Figure 11.28**).

   (continues on next page)

5. In the Create New Symbol dialog box, type a name for your symbol—for example, Ping-Pong Animation.

6. Choose Graphic as the behavior type.

In Flash, a symbol's behavior identifies what kind of symbol it is: graphic, button, or movie clip.

7. Click OK.

Flash creates a new symbol in the library and switches you to symbol-editing mode, with that symbol selected.

The name of your symbol appears in the info bar above the Timeline. The default Timeline for your new symbol consists of just one layer and a blank keyframe at Frame 1.

8. In the symbol Timeline, select Frame 1, and choose Edit > Paste Frames.

Flash pastes the 20 frames and three layers that you copied from the original Ping-Pong movie into the Timeline for the Ping-Pong Animation symbol (**Figure 11.29**). If you want to make any adjustments in the animation sequence, you can do so at this point.

9. To return to movie-editing mode, click the Back button at the left end of the info bar.

✔ Tip

■ In the list of symbols in the Library window, an animated graphic symbol looks the same as a static graphic; both have the same icon, and both are listed as Graphic in the Kind column (**Figure 11.30**). The animated graphic, however, has Play and Stop buttons in the top-right corner of the Library window; static graphics do not. You can preview an animated symbol by clicking the Play button.

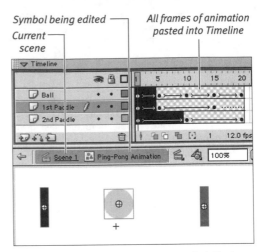

Symbol being edited — All frames of animation pasted into Timeline
Current scene —

Figure 11.29 When you create a new symbol, Flash switches to symbol-editing mode, making the new symbol's Timeline available for editing. You must paste all the frames of your animation into the symbol's Timeline to create the animated symbol.

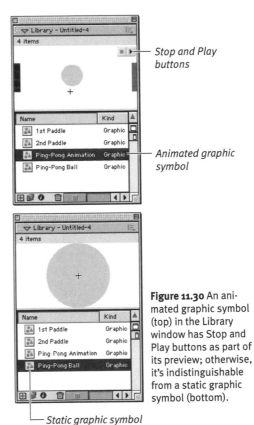

Stop and Play buttons

Animated graphic symbol

Figure 11.30 An animated graphic symbol (top) in the Library window has Stop and Play buttons as part of its preview; otherwise, it's indistinguishable from a static graphic symbol (bottom).

Static graphic symbol

How Do Animated Graphic Symbols Differ From Movie-Clip Symbols?

Flash provides for two kinds of animated symbols: graphic symbols and movie clips. The difference is a bit subtle and hard to grasp at first. An animated graphic symbol is tied to the Timeline of any movie in which you place the symbol, whereas a movie-clip symbol runs on its own independent Timeline.

You can think of animated graphic symbols as being a slide show. Each frame of the symbol is a separate slide. When you move to the next frame in the animated graphic symbol, you must move to another frame in the hosting movie. Also, there's no sound track. Even if you have sounds or interactivity functions in a movie, when you convert it to a graphic symbol, you lose those features.

A movie-clip symbol is like a film loop. You can project all its frames one after another, over and over, in a single frame of the hosting movie. Movie clips do have a sound track and do retain their interactivity. (To learn more about interactivity, see Chapters 12 and 13.)

One more thing to know about the two symbol types is that movie clips, because they run on their own Timeline, do not appear as animations in the Flash editing environment. You see only the first frame of the movie as a static object on the Stage. Animated graphic symbols, which use the same Timeline as the main movie, do display their animation in movie-editing mode.

Using Animated Graphic Symbols

To put an animated graphic symbol to work, you must place an instance of it in your main movie. The layer containing the movie must have enough frames to display the frames of the symbol. You can use instances of an animated graphic symbol just as you would any other symbol—combine it with other graphics on a layer; motion-tween it; modify its color, size, and rotation; and so on.

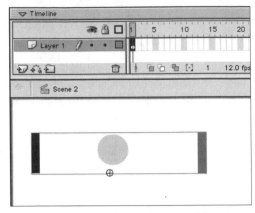

Figure 11.31 When you drag an instance of the animated graphic to the Stage, you see the symbol's first frame with its graphics selected. You must add frames to allow the full animation of the symbol to play in the main movie.

To place an instance of an animated graphic symbol:

1. Using the movie and symbol that you created in the preceding section, from the Insert menu, choose Scene to create a new scene.

   Flash displays the new scene's Timeline—a single layer with a blank keyframe in Frame 1. The Stage is empty.

   Adding a new scene gives you a blank Stage to work with and makes it easy to compare the two animations: the original (created directly in the main movie) and the instance of the graphic symbol placed in the movie.

2. Access the Library window.

   If it's not open, choose Window > Library.

3. In the Library window for your document, select the Ping-Pong Animation symbol.

   The first frame of the animation appears in the preview window.

4. Drag a copy of the selected symbol to the Stage.

   Flash places the symbol in Keyframe 1. At this point, you can see only the first frame of the animation (**Figure 11.31**). The animation is 20 frames long, so you need to add least 20 frames to view the symbol in its entirety.

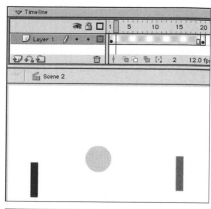

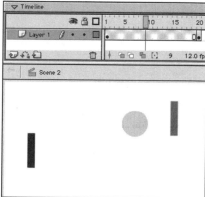

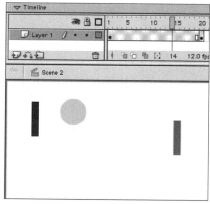

Figure 11.32 Frames 1 through 20 have a tweening property of None, but they still display animation. Flash displays the 20 tween frames of the graphic symbol that you placed in Keyframe 1. It's as though the symbol is a tray of slides, and Flash is projecting one image per frame in the main movie. If the main movie is longer than the slide show, Flash just starts the slide show over.

5. In the Timeline, select Frame 20, and choose Insert > Frame.

Flash adds in-between frames 2 through 20.

6. Play the movie.

Now Flash can display each frame of the animated graphic symbol in a frame of the movie. Frame 2 of the symbol appears in Frame 2 of the movie, Frame 5 of the symbol appears in Frame 5 of the movie, and so on (**Figure 11.32**). If you place fewer than 20 frames in the movie, Flash truncates the symbol and displays only as many frames of the symbol as there are frames in the movie. If you place more than 20 frames, Flash starts playing the graphic symbol over again in Frame 21.

✔ Tip

■ To create complex motion, you can use animated graphic symbols in motion tweens in your main movie. You can create, for example, an animated graphic symbol of a bug whose legs move to simulate walking. Place an instance of the bug symbol in keyframes at frames 1 and 5. You can motion-tween the bug symbol in your main movie and add a motion guide layer to make the wiggly bug follow a path.

Saving Animations As Movie-Clip Symbols

The procedure that you use to save an animation as a movie-clip symbol is the same as for saving an animated graphic symbol, except that you define the symbol as a movie clip in the Create New Symbol dialog box.

To convert an animation to a movie-clip symbol:

1. Open the document that you created to make the Ping-Pong animation in "Animating Multiple Motion Tweens" earlier in this chapter, or create your own multiple-layer animation.

   The Ping-Pong animation is a three-layer, 20-frame animation.

2. In the Timeline, select all 20 frames in all three layers.

3. From the Edit menu, choose Copy Frames.

4. From the Insert menu, choose New Symbol, or press ⌘-F8 (Mac) or Ctrl-F8 (Windows).

   The Create New Symbol dialog box appears.

5. In the Name field, type a name for your symbol—for example, Ping-Pong Clip.

   Flash remembers what behavior you selected for the last symbol you created and selects that behavior for you again when you choose Insert > New Symbol.

6. Select Movie Clip as the behavior for your symbol (**Figure 11.33**).

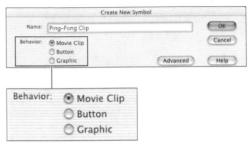

Figure 11.33 Selecting Movie Clip in the Behavior section of the Create New Symbol dialog box defines a symbol that has an independent Timeline. The entire movie-clip symbol runs in a single frame of the main movie that contains that symbol.

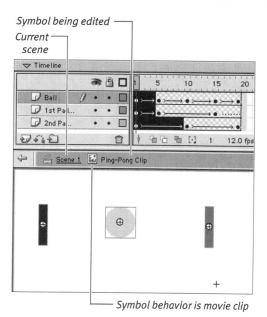

Symbol being edited ─┐
Current ─┐
scene

Symbol behavior is movie clip

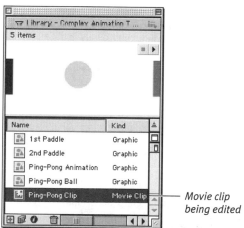

Movie clip
being edited

Figure 11.34 After you name the symbol and define its behavior in the Create New Symbol dialog box, Flash switches to symbol-editing mode. The icon that precedes the name of the symbol indicates that this symbol has movie-clip behavior. Now you can paste the animation frames into the symbol's Timeline.

7. Click OK.

Flash creates a new symbol in the Library window and switches you to symbol-editing mode, with that symbol selected.

The name of your symbol appears in the info bar above the Stage. The default Timeline for your new symbol consists of just one layer and a blank keyframe at Frame 1.

8. In the symbol Timeline, select Frame 1, and choose Edit > Paste Frames.

Flash pastes all 20 frames and three layers that you copied from the original Ping-Pong movie into the Timeline for the Ping-Pong Clip symbol (**Figure 11.34**). If you want to make any adjustments in the animation sequence, you can do so at this point.

9. To return to movie-editing mode, click the current scene name in the info bar at the top of the Stage.

✔ Tip

■ If you want to make a movie clip that contains exactly the same frames as an existing animated graphic symbol (as you did in the preceding exercise), you can duplicate that symbol and change its behavior. Select the animated graphic symbol in the Library window. From the Library window's Options menu, choose Duplicate. The Duplicate Symbol dialog box appears, allowing you to rename the symbol and give it Movie Clip behavior.

SAVING ANIMATIONS AS MOVIE-CLIP SYMBOLS

Using Movie-Clip Symbols

You put movie-clip symbols to work by placing an instance of the symbol on the Stage in your Flash document. Unlike animated graphic symbols, movie-clip symbols have their own Timeline. A movie clip plays continuously, like a little film loop, in a single frame of the main movie. As long as the movie contains no other instructions that stop the clip from playing—a blank keyframe in the Timeline for the layer containing the movie clip, for example—the clip continues to loop.

As you work on your Flash document, you can see only the first frame of a movie clip. To view the animation of the movie-clip symbol in context with all the other elements of your movie, you must export the movie (by choosing one of the test modes, for example). You can preview the animation of the movie-clip symbol by itself in the Library window.

To place an instance of a movie clip:

1. With the movie that you created in the preceding exercises open, in the Scene panel, click the Add Scene button.

   Flash creates a new scene and displays in its Timeline a single layer with a blank keyframe in Frame 1. The Stage is empty.

2. Access the Library window.

   If it's not open, choose Window > Library.

3. Select the Ping-Pong Clip symbol.

   The first frame of the animation appears in the preview window.

4. Drag a copy of the selected symbol to the Stage.

   Flash places the symbol in Keyframe 1 (**Figure 11.35**). You don't need to add any more frames to accommodate the animation, but you must export the movie to see the animation.

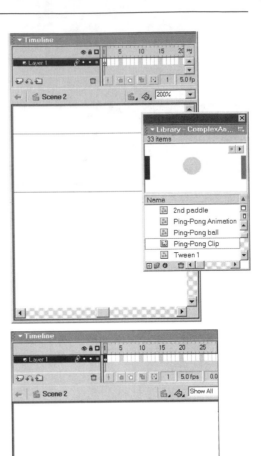

Figure 11.35 Drag an instance of your movie clip from the Library window to the Stage (top). Flash places the instance in Keyframe 1 (bottom).

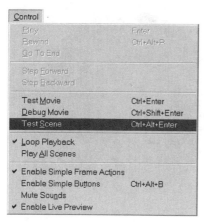

Figure 11.36 Choose Control > Test Scene to preview the animation of just one scene in a movie.

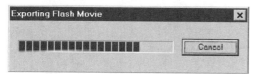

Figure 11.37 The Exporting Flash Movie dialog box contains a progress bar and a button for canceling the export.

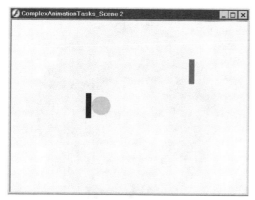

Figure 11.38 Flash Player displays your movie in a regular window. To exit the Player, close the window.

To view movie-clip animation in a movie:

1. Continuing with the movie that you created in the preceding exercise, from the Control menu, choose Test Scene (**Figure 11.36**).

   Flash exports the movie to a Flash Player format file, adding the .swf extension to the file name and using the current publishing settings for all the export options. (For more information on using the Publish Settings dialog box, see Chapter 16.) During export, Flash displays the Exporting Flash Movie dialog box, which contains a progress bar and a Stop (Mac) or Cancel (Windows) button for canceling the operation (**Figure 11.37**).

   When it finishes exporting the movie, Flash opens the .swf file in Flash Player so that you can see the movie in action (**Figure 11.38**).

2. When you have seen enough of the movie in test mode, click the movie window's Close box (Mac OS 9 and Windows) or Close button (Mac OS X) to exit Flash Player.

   Flash returns you to the editing environment.

Using Animated Masks

In Chapter 5, you learned about Flash's capability to create mask layers that hide and reveal objects on lower layers. Sometimes, the best way to create the illusion of movement is to animate a mask so that it gradually hides or reveals objects.

Imagine a line that starts at the left edge of the Stage and goes all the way to the right edge. If you create a mask that reveals the line bit by bit, you create the illusion of a line that draws itself. Reverse the process, and you have a line that gradually erases itself.

Creating rotating and shape-tweened mask graphics can give you some interesting effects. The more familiar you are with using animated masks to reveal stationary items, the better sense you'll have of when to use this technique. For practice, try animating a mask that creates a growing rainbow.

To create a stationary graphic and a moving mask that reveals it:

1. Open a new Flash document, and add a second layer.

2. In the Timeline, rename the bottom layer Rainbow, and rename the top layer Rotating Rectangle.

3. In Frame 1 of the Rainbow layer, on the Stage, use the oval tool to draw a perfect circle with a radial-gradient fill.

   To create a rainbow effect, use a gradient that has distinct bands of color.

4. Erase the bottom half of the circle (**Figure 11.39**).

   What's left is your rainbow graphic. For safety, convert the graphic to a symbol (select the graphic, choose Insert > Convert to Symbol, Choose Graphic behavior, name the symbol, and click OK) so that you'll have a copy of the rainbow in case you accidentally delete the original.

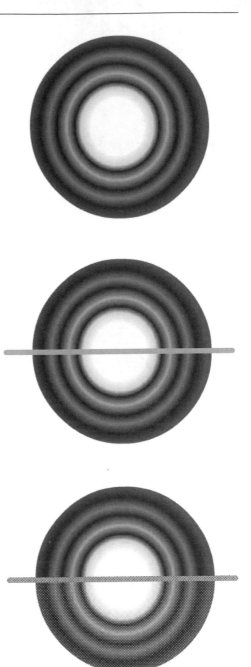

Figure 11.39 An easy way to create a rainbow object is to fill a circle with a multiple-color radial gradient and then delete the bottom half of the circle. Here, bisecting the circle by drawing a line through it (middle) makes deletion easy; just select the line and the bottom half of the circle (bottom), and press Delete.

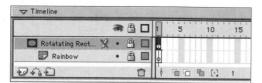

Figure 11.40 When you create a mask layer, Flash automatically links the layer directly below the mask layer in the Timeline and locks both layers.

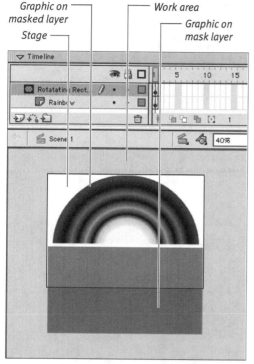

Figure 11.41 To create a mask that reveals the entire rainbow, draw a rectangle that's wider and taller than the rainbow graphic. Positioning the rectangle below the rainbow graphic hides the rainbow completely.

5. In the Timeline, Control-click (Mac) or right-click (Windows) the Rotating Rectangle layer.

The contextual menu for layers appears.

6. Choose Mask.

Flash converts the layer to a mask, links the Rainbow layer to the mask, and locks both layers (**Figure 11.40**).

7. In the Timeline, click the padlock icons in the Rotating Rectangle and Rainbow layers to unlock them.

8. On the Stage, in Frame 1 of the Rotating Rectangle layer, use the rectangle tool to draw a rectangle just below the bottom of the rainbow (**Figure 11.41**).

The rectangle is your mask. Any items that lie below the rectangle on a linked layer appear; everything else is hidden.

Make the rectangle a bit larger than the rainbow so that the mask covers the whole rainbow. Using a transparent fill color lets you see the rainbow graphic through the mask graphic and helps you verify the mask's position. (To make the rectangle's fill color transparent, select it and then, in the Color Mixer panel, assign it a low Alpha percentage.)

✔ Tip

■ You can use any of the three types of animation on a mask layer: frame-by-frame, motion tweening, or shape tweening. You can also use ActionScript to tell one movie clip symbol to mask another. (You'll learn about using ActionScript to manipulate objects in Chapters 13 and 15.)

USING ANIMATED MASKS

To prepare the mask for rotational animation:

1. Select the rectangle, and choose Insert > Convert to Symbol.

   Because you want to create rotational animation, you must use a motion tween for the mask, which means that the mask graphic must be a symbol or a grouped element.

   The Convert to Symbol dialog box appears.

2. In the Name field, enter a name for the symbol; then click OK.

3. Using the free-transform tool, select the rectangle on the Stage, and position the pointer over the white circle that indicates the center point of the object.

   A small white circle appears next to the arrow pointer, indicating that you can move the selected object's center point.

4. Drag the center-point circle straight up until it rests in the middle of the top edge of the rectangle (**Figure 11.42**).

   Now you can rotate the rectangle so that it swings up and over the rainbow.

To complete the rotating-mask animation:

1. In the Timeline, in the Rainbow layer, select Frame 15, and choose Insert > Frame.

2. In the Timeline, in the Rotating Rectangle layer, select Frame 15, and choose Insert > Keyframe.

3. In Frame 15, with the rectangle selected on the Stage, use the Rotate and Skew modifier of the free-transform tool to reposition the rectangle; click and drag the bottom-left corner of the rectangle and rotate it so that the rectangle completely covers the rainbow.

   The mask that covers the rainbow in authoring mode will reveal the rainbow in the final movie.

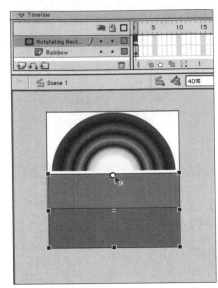

Figure 11.42 Use the free-transform tool to reposition the point around which a symbol (or grouped item) rotates. Drag the circle that indicates the center point to a new position. A small circle previews the new center-point location.

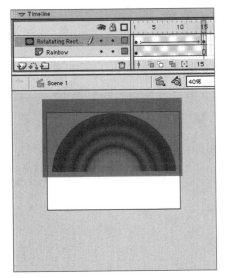

Figure 11.43 In the final keyframe with the completed motion tween for the mask object, the mask covers the rainbow. Giving the mask a transparent fill lets you see the objects to be revealed through it as you work. The transparency of objects on the mask layer doesn't appear in the final movie.

USING ANIMATED MASKS

Play movie;
layers unlocked

Play movie,
layers locked

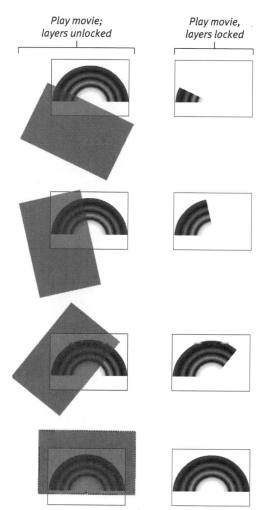

Figure 11.44 As you play the movie with the layers unlocked (left), you can see the in-between positions of the mask graphic. When you lock the layers (right), you see the masking as it will appear in the final exported movie.

4. In the Timeline, in the Rotating Rectangle layer, select any of the frames in the Keyframe 1 span (frames 1 through 14).

5. From the Frame Property Inspector's Tween pop-up menu, choose Motion.

6. From the Rotate pop-up menu, choose CW.

7. Enter 0 in the Times field.

   This step sets up the motion tween that rotates the rectangle, swinging it up and over the rainbow until it fully covers the rainbow (**Figure 11.43**).

To preview the animation:

◆ Choose Control > Test Movie or Control > Test Scene.

   or

◆ In the Timeline, click the lock icon to lock both layers; then play the movie.

   If the rainbow is not fully revealed during the tween, you may need to enlarge or reposition the rectangle. Unlock both layers, and move the playhead through the movie to see where the rectangle is in each in-between frame (**Figure 11.44**).

✔ Tip

■ To make the rainbow appear to fade in gradually, create a keyframe for it in Frame 15 and tween a change in transparency for the rainbow symbol. In Frame 1, select this instance of the rainbow symbol and use the Property Inspector to modify it. From the Color menu, choose Alpha; in the Value field, enter a low percentage.

USING ANIMATED MASKS

INTERACTIVITY WITH SIMPLE FRAME ACTIONS

By default, Macromedia Flash MX plays the scenes and frames of a movie sequentially. The movie opens with Scene 1, plays all those frames in order, moves to Scene 2, plays all those frames, and so on. Sometimes, that's appropriate. But you can also instruct Flash to jump around in a movie, playing scenes and frames in any order you choose.

You tell Flash what to do by assigning actions to frames, buttons, and movie clips. Actions are commands, or *statements*, that you string together to make Flash perform certain...well, actions, such as replaying Scene 2 at the end of every other scene or repeatedly displaying the first five frames of a movie until all the other frames in the movie have loaded. Actions can add efficiency and a degree of intelligence or interactivity to your movie.

Flash provides a full-fledged scripting language called ActionScript for adding actions to movies. You create ActionScripts in the Actions panel, which provides various levels of scripting assistance.

In this chapter, you get acquainted with the Actions panel by assigning simple actions to frames, using Flash's most-assisted scripting mode: Normal. To learn about creating buttons and attaching actions to buttons and movie clips, see Chapter 13. To learn about more-complex actions, see Chapter 15.

Touring the Actions Panel

The Actions panel is a whole scripting environment in a box. It is filled with windows, buttons, fields, and message areas. The two items that dominate the panel are the Actions Toolbox and the Script pane.

The Actions Toolbox contains most of the "words" (actions) that make up the Action-Script language; these snippets of code appear in lists that are arranged hierarchically under folderlike category icons. The Script pane is a text window where you assemble your scripts.

The Actions panel has two scripting modes: Normal and Expert. In both modes, you can choose actions from the Actions Toolbox or the Add pop-up menu. Both modes let you import scripts or pieces of scripts from an external file, such as one created with a stand-alone text editor. In addition, in Expert mode, you can use the Script pane as a text editor and enter scripts manually.

Figure 12.1 shows the various elements of the Actions panel in Normal mode.

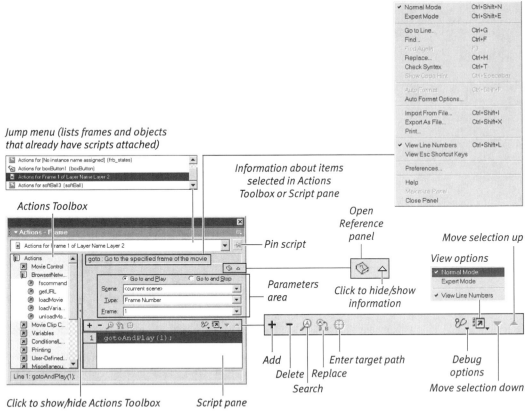

Figure 12.1 The Actions panel offers two modes for entering ActionScripts. Normal mode (shown) gives you the most assistance. Expert mode allows you to type scripts directly in the Script pane; this method can be much faster for users who become familiar with the ActionScripting language. The Actions-Frame panel in Normal mode has three main areas: the Actions Toolbox, where you choose actions; the Script pane, where Flash assembles the ActionScript; and the parameters area, where Flash presents items that require you to fill in more information.

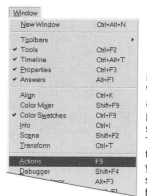

Figure 12.2 Choose Window > Actions to access the Actions panel. When you select a frame in the Timeline, the panel's title bar indicates that you are creating a script for the selected frame.

To access the Actions panel:

If the Actions panel is not active, *do one of the following:*

◆ From the Window menu, choose Actions (**Figure 12.2**).

◆ Press F9.

◆ In the Timeline, Control-click (Mac) or right-click (Windows) a frame, and choose Actions from the contextual menu for frames.

The Actions-Frame panel opens.

(continues on next page)

Two Types of Actions

Flash uses two basic types of scripts: scripts that attach to frames and scripts that attach to objects.

Frame-based scripts are sets of actions attached to a keyframe. They require no input from the person watching your movie. In the final exported movie, when the playhead reaches a frame that contains a script, Flash carries out the script's instructions.

Object-based scripts are sets of actions attached to buttons or movie clips. Actions attached to buttons require input from someone who is viewing the movie. In a text-heavy frame, for example, you could make Flash pause the movie until the user clicks a button that instructs Flash to resume playback.

Actions attached to movie clips can also respond to user input. If your text-heavy frame contains a movie clip, for example, you could attach an action to the movie clip that pauses playback until the user clicks anywhere in the same frame. Movie-clip actions can also be triggered without user intervention. You might, for example, have Flash stop playing all sounds when a movie clip first appears. Attaching that action to the movie clip instead of the frame containing the movie clip lets you tie the soundtrack more precisely to the movie clip's appearance.

In addition, advanced ActionScripters can create scripts that target text fields, performing operations that modify them or retrieve information from them. Text fields on their own, however, cannot have attached scripts.

✔ Tips

■ The Actions panel's title bar reveals what type of item the script you are creating will attach to: a frame, movie clip, or button. If, while working on a script for the current frame, you happened to click a movie clip or button on the Stage, the title bar changes. To return to the Actions panel for frames, click the frame in the Timeline, or click an empty area of the Stage or work area. You learn about attaching scripts to movie clips and buttons in Chapter 13.

■ To prevent Flash from displaying or starting a different script as you click different items, you can pin a script. *Pinning* forces Flash to continue displaying the pinned script even if you select a different frame or object. Pinning allows you to examine a variety of elements and situations in your movie as you create your scripts. To pin a script, choose the script from the Jump menu, or select the frame or object that the script is attached to (which makes the script active in the Script pane). Now click the pushpin icon in the top-right corner of the Actions panel. The icon changes to a more upright version of a pushpin. When you're ready to view other scripts, click the upright-pushpin icon.

To close the Actions panel:

◆ Repeat any of the actions in the preceding exercise.

   or

◆ Click the Actions panel's close box (Mac OS 9 and Windows) or close button (Mac OS X).

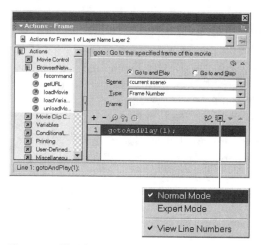

Figure 12.3 The View Options pop-up menu gives you fast access to the two scripting modes.

Choosing a Scripting Mode

Flash offers two modes for scripting in the Actions panel: Normal and Expert. Normal mode offers you the highest level of assistance with the complex task of scripting. The following exercises teach you how to switch modes. But after completing this practice session, unless you are directed otherwise, keep the Actions panel set to Normal mode for the exercises in this book.

To set the Actions panel to Normal mode:

◆ In the Actions panel, from the Options menu in the top-right corner, choose Normal Mode.

   or

◆ In the Actions panel, from the View Options pop-up menu, choose Normal Mode (**Figure 12.3**).

To set the Actions panel to Expert mode:

◆ In the Actions panel, from the Options menu in the top-right corner, choose Expert Mode.

   or

◆ In the Actions panel, from the View Options pop-up menu, choose Expert Mode.

✔ Tip

■ The Options menu in the top-right corner of the Actions panel lists keyboard shortcuts for switching between Normal and Expert modes. These shortcuts are available only when you have actually selected something in the Actions Toolbox.

Only Experts Make Mistakes

Because Normal mode is for less experienced scripters, it does everything it can to ensure that the scripts you create are entered correctly and ready to run. Therefore, in Normal mode, any scripts that you import from an external source (such as a text editor) must be in perfect shape. If the script contains any errors of syntax, a dialog box appears, warning you that you must import the script in Expert mode. In Expert mode, you are free to make as many mistakes as you like; Flash highlights the errors in red for you to fix.

Normal and Expert Modes Compared

In Normal mode, when you choose actions in the Actions Toolbox, information about the action appears in the parameters area of the Actions panel; in the Script pane, and in the line-by-line display below the Script pane. If you have selected Show Tooltips in the General tab of the Preferences dialog box, you will also see tooltips information when you position the pointer over an action or category in the Actions Toolbox.

In Normal mode, Flash helps you complete action statements that require parameters that the scripter must supply. When you select such an action in the Script pane, Flash displays text fields for entering any parameters associated with that action (**Figure 12.4**). (If there are no parameters for a selected action, Flash lets you know that, too.) This method of completing the action statements makes it easier to know when parameters must be entered. Flash takes the information you provide in the parameters area and places it in the script, using the correct ActionScript syntax.

In Expert mode, you can choose actions from the Actions Toolbox or simply type them in the Script pane. In this mode, you must enter any required parameters yourself.

Both Normal and Expert modes let you use code hinting. Code hints prompt you to fill in parameters and properties in the correct syntax; in Expert mode, code hints also help you with the scripting for events. The hints appear as tooltips or pop-up menus.

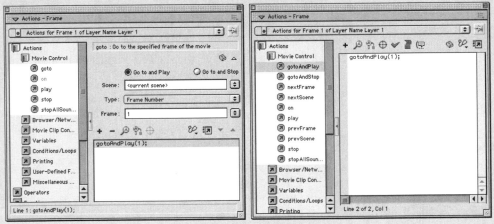

Figure 12.4 The Actions Toolbox presents different options in Normal and Expert mode. In Normal mode (left), the stop and play parameters that complete the goto action appear in the parameters area along with the other parameters that direct Flash to a new location. Flash helps you fill in these parameters accurately in the script. In Expert mode (right), you must select the action you want (gotoAndPlay or gotoAndStop) and complete its parameters yourself.

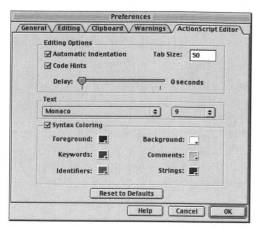

Figure 12.5 In the Preferences dialog box, the Action-Script Editor tab contains settings for customizing the way Flash displays your scripts. You can also turn on code hints—tooltips with explanations of items listed in the Actions Toolbox.

Customizing the Actions Panel

The Actions panel takes up a good deal of room on your screen. You can resize the panel, collapse some of its panes, and make other adjustments. You can customize the way that scripts appear in the Script pane to make them appear in the smallest typeface you can read, for example (or, if you've spent long hours staring at tiny onscreen type, to make scripts display in nice large letters). You can choose settings for font and type size; you can set Flash to highlight different types of script elements in different colors; you can control the number of spaces Flash uses to indent with each tab you type; and you can turn on or off code hints.

To set preferences for the Actions panel:

1. From the Edit menu (Mac OS 9 and Windows) or from the Flash menu (Mac OS X), choose Preferences.

   or

   From the Options menu in the top-right corner of the Actions panel, choose Preferences.

   The Preferences dialog box appears (**Figure 12.5**).

2. Click the ActionScript Editor tab.

   The various settings for working with statements in the Script pane of the Actions panel appear.

3. Change any of the settings as described in the following exercises.

4. Click OK.

   Flash applies your preferences settings immediately.

To get scripting help from code hints:

1. Access the ActionScript Editor tab of the Preferences dialog box.

2. In the Editing Options section, check the Code Hints checkbox.

3. Move the lever of the Delay slider to set the amount of time your pointer must hover over an item before Flash displays the hint.

To choose the font for writing scripts:

1. Access the ActionScript Editor tab of the Preferences dialog box.

2. In the Text section, *do the following:*

   ▲ From the pop-up menu of installed fonts, choose a font.

   ▲ From the pop-up menu of sizes, choose a type size.

   The Actions panel can display scripts in text as small as 8 points and as large as 72 points.

Taming the Unwieldy ActionScript Panel

The Actions panel is quite large. You can resize and collapse the entire the panel as you would any other panel and dock it with other panels—or, in the Windows world, dock it to the application window. You can also resize or hide certain portions of the panel to keep the window more manageable. Try these techniques:

Resize the Actions Toolbox. Position the pointer to the right of the Actions Toolbox's scroll bar. The pointer changes to the double-headed arrow icon. Click and drag the edge of the Actions Toolbox to resize it.

Hide/show the Actions Toolbox. Click the triangle between the Actions Toolbox pane and the Script pane to close the toolbox completely. To show it again, click the triangle to the left of the Script pane.

Hide/show the information area. Click the triangle to the right of the Reference Book icon to toggle between showing and hiding the information that Flash provides about selected statements in Normal mode. This action doesn't change the size of the panel, but it does keep the panel from being so cluttered.

To color-code script items:

1. Access the ActionScript Editor tab of the Preferences dialog box.

2. Check the Syntax Coloring checkbox.

3. From the pop-up sets of color swatches, *choose new colors for the following:*

   ▲ **Foreground.** The basic text color for your scripts.

   ▲ **Background.** The color against which your script displays in the Script pane.

   ▲ **Keywords.** Words reserved for special purposes in ActionScript, such as var (which sets up local variables).

   ▲ **Identifiers.** The names of things, such as the names of objects, variables, and functions.

   ▲ **Comments.** Text that Flash ignores when it reads the script; used to make notes about what's going on in the script.

   ▲ **Strings.** Series of characters (letters, numbers, and punctuation marks).

✔ Tips

■ You may want to color-code only certain parts of your scripts. If, for example, you want your comments to appear in a different color but nothing else, set the color boxes of Keywords, Identifiers, and Strings to match the color you choose for Foreground.

■ Flash's default settings for keywords, identifiers, and strings are all similar shades of blue. For these exercises, try setting them to wildly different colors—say, pink, orange, and brown. This technique will help you learn to recognize these different parts of ActionScript speech.

■ In addition to color-coding the various parts of speech in the Script pane, Flash color-codes problem areas of your script. Flash highlights syntax errors in red; deprecated actions (those whose use is being discouraged, and which may one day be phased out) appear in green. If you have set your publishing options to create .swf files for an earlier version of Flash Player, any actions introduced in Flash 6 that would break in the earlier Player appear in yellow in the Script pane.

Organizing Actions

Flash identifies each keyframe that has attached actions by putting a little letter *a* in that keyframe in the Timeline (**Figure 12.6**). But can you imagine scrolling through dozens—or hundreds—of layers, looking for little letter *a*'s when you want to edit a movie's actions? That's a recipe for eyestrain. Create a layer just for actions so that you'll know exactly where the actions are at any point in the Timeline. Also, with a separate layer for actions, you won't accidentally assign actions to two different layers at the same point in the Timeline, which could cause problems if you reorder the layers at some point.

To create a separate layer for actions:

1. In the Timeline, add a new layer.

(For detailed instructions on adding layers, see Chapter 5.)

2. Rename the layer Actions.

3. Drag the layer to the top or bottom of the Timeline.

With a separate Actions layer as the top or bottom layer, you'll always know where to find the frames that contain actions when you need to modify or add to them (**Figure 12.7**).

✔ Tip

- To prevent yourself from adding any graphics to the Actions layer accidentally, lock it (by clicking the bullet in the padlock column). Locking keeps you from making changes in the elements on the Stage for that layer, but it doesn't prevent you from adding actions to frames.

Figure 12.6 Keyframes that contain actions display the letter *a* in the Timeline.

Figure 12.7 When you assign actions to many layers (top), it's harder to find them, and you might accidentally assign actions to the same frame number on different layers. Adding a separate layer just for actions (bottom) makes it easy to find them all and to see whether a certain frame does contain an action.

The Pitfall of Placing Actions on Multiple Layers

At each point in the Timeline, Flash implements the actions in the highest-level frame that contains an action. Imagine a three-layer movie. Frame 2 of the top layer contains no actions. In Frame 2 of the middle layer, an action tells Flash to skip to Frame 5. In Frame 2 of the bottom layer, an action tells Flash to skip to Frame 10. When you play this movie, and the playhead hits Frame 2, Flash looks in the top layer for actions and finds none. Flash moves to the next layer down. There, it finds an instruction and follows it. Flash whisks you away to Frame 5; it never has a chance to get to the instruction in the bottom layer. But if you reorder the layers so that the bottom layer is on top, Flash whisks you to Frame 10 instead of Frame 5! This situation could cause havoc with your movie.

Figure 12.8 The hierarchical Add pop-up menu lists actions to choose among.

Choosing Actions

In Normal mode, the Actions panel provides several ways for you to select action statements to include in an ActionScript: You can choose items from the Add pop-up menu; you can choose items from a scrolling list in the Actions Toolbox; and you can copy and paste items from a separate panel, the Reference panel (you'll learn more about using it later in this chapter). In both the menu and list form, Flash organizes statements hierarchically in categories and subcategories. In the Actions Toolbox, the categories can be collapsed and expanded just like nested folders.

To use the Add menu:

1. Open a Flash document, and make sure that the Actions panel is open.

2. In the Timeline, select the frame to which you want to add actions.

   The name Actions-Frame appears in the title bar of the Actions panel.

3. In the Actions-Frame panel, click the Add button (the one with a plus sign).

   A menu of action-statement categories appears.

4. Choose a category.

   Some categories break down further into subcategories. In that case, a submenu of action-statement subcategories appears, and you must choose a subcategory as well.

5. Choose a subcategory, if appropriate.

   A submenu of actions appears (**Figure 12.8**).

6. Choose an action.

   Flash adds the chosen action to the Script pane.

✔ Tips

- The Add menu is always available. Use it to create ActionScripts when you've configured the Actions panel to hide the Actions Toolbox.

- With so many categories and subcategories, it can be hard to remember exactly which category holds a particular action. The Index category shows all the actions from the other categories in a single alphabetical list.

The Mystery of Action Categories

In early versions of Flash, you put together scripts by choosing English-like statements from a single menu. As the ActionScript language has evolved, however, the statements have become less like English, and their numbers have increased. Scrolling through one long list of actions has become less practical. In an attempt to make the list more manageable, the Actions Toolbox organizes actions in eight main categories, each with its own subcategories. Until you become familiar with ActionScripting, however, trying to remember which category contains the action you are looking for can be difficult. You may find it easier to look for action statements directly by name. A ninth category, Index, lists all ActionScript items in one huge alphabetical list.

Here's a brief overview of the Actions Toolbox categories.

◆ **Actions.** This category includes actions for controlling movie playback; controlling Web browsers and networks; manipulating movie clips, working with variables; creating more sophisticated, subtle controls (such as testing whether certain conditions are true and creating logical loops); printing from within Flash Player; setting up actions; and miscellaneous actions.

◆ **Operators.** This category includes actions for calculating values from variables and expressions. One subcategory, Arithmetic Operators, is fairly easy to grasp. Arithmetic Operators basically are familiar mathematical symbols, such as the plus sign (+). You can use the + operator to add a series of numbers, for example.

Operators can do more than math, however. You might have operators perform a "math operation" on text elements—"adding" a series of words to form a message, for example. Or you might use operators to assign values to variables. The equal sign in the expression $p = w$, for example, puts the value of the variable on the right side of the equal sign (in this case, w) into the variable on the left side (p). Again, that value might be numbers, or it might be letters and words.

You can also use operators to compare items—to see whether the variables on either side of the operator have the same value, for example.

◆ **Functions.** Functions are predefined chunks of ActionScript. Just as macros in a word processor encapsulate the necessary code for repetitive typing, formatting, and so on, functions in ActionScripts encapsulate bits of ActionScript that perform frequently used operations.

The Mystery of Action Categories (continued)

◆ **Constants.** Constants are reserved words whose value is always the same, such as the Boolean expressions `true` and `false`.

◆ **Properties.** Properties define the characteristics of objects. You often include properties actions in scripts that control objects—to set the transparency (`_alpha`) or screen position (`_x` and `_y`) of a movie-clip instance, for example.

◆ **Objects.** Objects are collections of predefined properties (characteristics of an object), methods (sets of instructions for carrying out operations involving the object), and events. The Movie Clip object, for example, includes predefined properties such as `useHandCursor` and `hitArea`; methods such as `prevFrame`, `nextFrame`, `play`, and `stop`; and events such as `onLoad` and `onMouseDown`.

◆ **Deprecated.** Deprecated actions are actions that were available in earlier versions of Flash but that are being phased out (see the sidebar "More about Deprecated Actions," later in this chapter).

◆ **Flash UI Components.** This category contains actions for creating your own reusable elements. Flash comes with several prefabricated components, such as scroll boxes and radio buttons. You can access these items from the Components panel.

◆ **Index.** This category contains an alphabetical listing of all the items located in the other category folders.

✔ Tip

■ Can't recall what category holds the action you want? Select the action in the alphabetized list in the Index category of the Actions Toolbox. Control-click (Mac) or right-click (Windows); then, from the contextual menu, choose Show Original. Flash pops open the right category and subcategory folders and selects the action in the Actions Toolbox.

To use the Actions Toolbox:

1. In the Actions Toolbox, on the left side of the Actions panel, click a category icon.

   The icon expands, and a list of subcategories and/or actions appears.

2. If appropriate, click a subcategory icon to access the action you need.

3. To add an action to the Script pane, *do one of the following:*

   ▲ Double-click the action.

   ▲ Drag the action from the Actions Toolbox to the Script pane (**Figure 12.9**).

   ▲ Control-click (Mac) or right-click (Windows) the action to access the contextual menu; then choose Add to Script.

   Flash places the appropriate text in the Script pane and displays any parameters associated with the statement in the Parameters area, located just above the Script pane (**Figure 12.10**).

✔ Tip

■ If you prefer, you can enter actions with keyboard shortcuts. All shortcuts for adding actions to scripts begin with the Esc key. To view these shortcuts in the Actions Toolbox, from the Options menu in the top-right corner of the Actions panel, choose View Esc Shortcut Keys. Flash displays the shortcut within square brackets immediately following the action to which it's assigned.

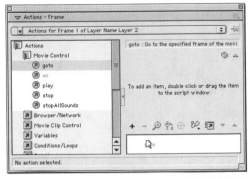

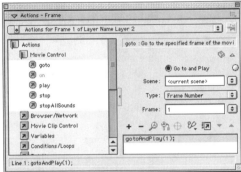

Figure 12.9 When you drag a statement from the Actions Toolbox to the Script pane, the dog-eared pointer helps you position the action (top). Release the mouse button to place the action in your ActionScript (bottom).

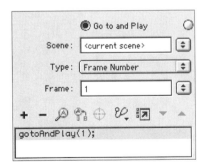

Figure 12.10 When you add an action to the Script pane, any parameters or properties that further define the action appear in the parameters area.

More about Deprecated Actions

As any language evolves, new words and expressions become standard and old terms fall out of everyday use. You can continue to speak and write with the older words, but as time passes those antiquated words become unintelligible to modern speakers. The same is true for scripting languages, where the term *deprecated* is used to designate "words," pieces of code, that still work but are superceded by more recent code. In the Actions Toolbox, the deprecated actions are gathered together in the Deprecated category.

In the development of Flash's scripting capabilities, major changes occurred between Flash versions 4 and 5. Version 5 introduced the full-fledged scripting language Action-Script. Many deprecated actions (such as the ones found in the Deprecated > Actions category of the Actions Toolbox) are left over from a time when Flash attempted to use easy-to-understand, English-like action statements to make scripting as easy as possible for novices.

Here's an example of a situation where you might have used a deprecated action: controlling playback of a movie clip with a button. Imagine you have an instance of a movie clip of a kitten playing (the name of the movie clip instance is *cat*). In English, you might think, "At this point in my Flash movie, I want people to be able to make the cat be still. I must create a button that *tells* the cat to *stop* playing." In Flash 4, you might have created a script for the button like this

```
on (release){
    tellTarget ("cat"){
        stop();
    }
}
```

In Flash MX you can accomplish the same thing with *dot syntax* using a much more compact statement (you'll learn more about dot syntax in Chapter 15).

```
on (release){
    cat.stop();
}
```

The difference is subtle. The deprecated action is a bit longer and more English-like. Telling a target item (the thing in parentheses) to do the action that follows is a fairly easy concept for scripting novices. Simply using a period to connect an object to the action you want to perform on that object is more abstract. It may take a bit of practice to feel comfortable with the new syntax if you are making the transition from earlier versions of Flash.

Ultimately, relying on deprecated actions will stand in the way of your learning scripting. You'll soon reach the place where you want to try more adventuresome scripts, and you'll have to switch the way you think about putting those scripts together. So it makes sense to learn to use the new ActionScript right now.

In order to allow Flash MX designers to create documents that are compatible with earlier versions of Flash Player, Flash MX continues to support the deprecated actions, and they are compliant with ECMA-262—a set of specifications for the JavaScript language developed by the European Computers Manufacturers Association (ECMA). A day may come, however, when that's no longer true.

Adding Actions to a Frame

You can assign actions to just one keyframe at a time, but a keyframe can contain multiple actions. Flash executes the actions in the order in which they appear in the Script pane. To change a selected action's place in the script, click the Up and Down buttons. To get a feel for working with the Actions panel, practice adding, moving, and deleting actions. Don't worry about filling in any parameters that may appear; this exercise is strictly for familiarizing yourself with the mechanics of the Actions Toolbox and Script pane. You will learn more about how the actions and parameters operate in later exercises.

Figure 12.11 Click a category icon to reveal subcategories and/or individual actions in the Actions Toolbox.

Because you will be creating actions that involve moving from frame to frame, it will be useful to create a multiframe document that has identifying text in each frame.

To set up a document for testing frame actions:

1. Open a new Flash document, and create two layers: Contents and Actions.

2. In the Contents layer, create keyframes in frames 1 through 5.

3. Add text that identifies each keyframe (Scene 1·Frame 1, Scene 1·Frame 2, and so on).

4. Save the document as a template for use throughout this chapter, and name it FrameActions Template.

   (For detailed instructions for saving documents as templates, see Chapter 1.)

To add one action to a keyframe:

1. Open a new copy of the FrameActions Template document you created in the preceding exercise (choose File > New from Template).

Figure 12.12 When an action has no parameters, Flash tells you so.

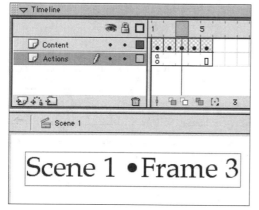

Figure 12.13 The letter *a* in Keyframe 1 indicates that actions are assigned to that frame.

2. In the Timeline for Scene 1, in the Actions layer, select Keyframe 1.

3. In the Actions-Frame panel, in the Actions Toolbox, click the category icon for Actions.

   The category expands to reveal a list of actions subcategories (**Figure 12.11**).

4. Click the subcategory icon for Movie Control.

   A list of actions for controlling movie playback appears.

5. Double-click the action `stopAllSounds`.

   Flash adds `stopAllSounds ();` to Line 1 in the Script pane for Keyframe 1.

   The message *No Parameters* appears in the Parameters area (**Figure 12.12**). If an action has parameters, those parameters appear above the Script pane when you select the action in the Actions Toolbox.

   (The `stopAllSounds ();` action turns off any event sounds that were initiated by earlier frames and that are still playing. To learn more about sounds, see Chapter 14.)

6. In the Timeline, deselect Keyframe 1.

   A small letter *a* now appears in Keyframe 1 of the Actions layer, indicating that this frame contains actions (**Figure 12.13**).

✔ Tips

- You must attach scripts to keyframes, but you don't have to select a keyframe to do so. Select any frame within a keyframe span, and Flash assigns the script to the keyframe that begins the span.

- The line number for selected actions in the Script pane always appears in the line-by-line display at the bottom of the Actions panel. To display line numbers inside the Script pane, from the Action panel's Options menu, choose View Line Number; press Shift-⌘-L (Mac) or Shift-Ctrl-L (Windows); or from the View Options pop-up menu, choose View Line Numbers.

To add multiple actions to a keyframe:

1. Continuing with the file that you created in the preceding exercise, in the Timeline for Scene 1, select Keyframe 1.

   This frame should already contain the stopAllSounds (); action.

2. In the Actions-Frame panel in Line 1 in the Script pane, select the stopAllSounds (); action.

3. From the Actions-Frame panel's Add menu, choose Actions > Browser/ Network > getURL.

   Flash adds getURL (""); to Line 2 in the Script pane, below stopAllSounds ();. The parameters for this action appear in the parameters area.

   (The getURL (""); action tells the Web browser to open a URL; the action's para- meters define what kind of window to open the URL in and whether or not to send variables. You'll learn more about this action in Chapter 15.)

4. With getURL (""); selected in Line 2 in the Script pane, from the Add menu, choose Actions > Movie Control > stop.

   Flash adds stop (); to Line 3 in the Script pane, below the getURL (""); action. The message *No Parameters* appears in the parameters area (**Figure 12.14**).

   (The stop action makes the movie pause in the current frame until another instruc- tion tells Flash to resume playback.)

✔ Tip

- If you want to add an action to a particu- lar spot in the Script pane, drag the action from the Actions Toolbox to the Script pane. You get the dog-eared page icon with the name of the action you are dragging attached. A highlighted line indicates where in the script the new action will go (**Figure 12.15**).

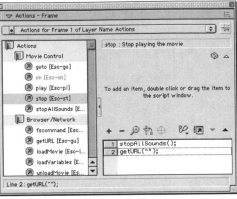

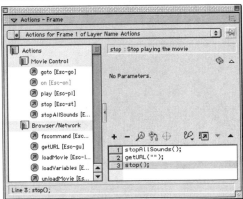

Figure 12.14 As you choose additional actions in the Actions Toolbox or from the Add menu (top), Flash adds them below whatever action was selected in the Script pane for that frame (bottom).

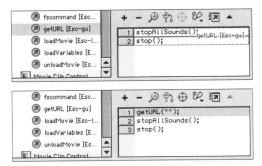

Figure 12.15 When you drag an action from the Actions Toolbox (top), you can scroll the Script pane and position the action where you want it (bottom).

Moves selected action —
down one line

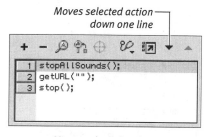

Moves selected action —
down another line

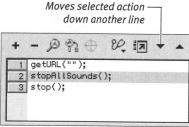

Moves selected —
action down again

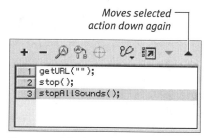

Figure 12.16 The Up and Down buttons let you change the order of the actions in the script. Select an action and then click the Down button (top) to move the action down one line (middle). Click the Down button again to move the selected action again (bottom).

Editing the Script

Flash plays the actions for a frame in the order in which they appear in the Script pane. The Up and Down buttons let you change the order of the actions that you've selected. The Delete button lets you remove actions from the script.

For these exercises, use the file that you created in the preceding exercise. Your movie should contain two scenes, each of which contains a bottom layer named Actions and a top layer named Content. Each Content layer contains keyframes in Frames 1 through 5. The Actions layer of Frame 1 of Scene 1 contains the following three lines of code:

```
stopAllSounds ();
```

```
getURL ("");
```

```
stop ();
```

To change the order of actions:

1. In the Timeline for Scene 1, select Keyframe 1 of the Actions layer.

2. In the first line of the Actions-Frame panel's Script pane, choose stopAllSounds ();.

3. To send the action down one level in the Script pane, click the Down button.

   The stopAllSounds (); action is on Line 2 now.

4. To send the action down another level in the Script pane, click the Down button again.

   The stopAllSounds (); action is on Line 3 now (**Figure 12.16**).

✔ Tip

■ To reorder items in the Script pane quickly, click and drag the item you want to reposition it. The dog-eared page pointer appears, and you can scroll through the script to position the item.

To remove an action from the list:

1. Continuing with the file that you created in the preceding exercises, in the Timeline for Scene 1, select Keyframe 1 in the Actions layer.

2. In the Actions-Frame panel, in Line 2 in the Script pane, select the **stop** (); action.

3. To remove the action from the Script pane, *do one of the following:*

   ▲ Click the Delete button (the one with the minus sign).

   ▲ Press Delete.

   The Script pane now contains just two actions (**Figure 12.17**).

✔ Tip

■ To remove a script from a frame, you must delete each line in the Script pane. To select the whole script quickly, click the first line of the script; Shift-click the last line of the script; then click the Delete button or press Delete.

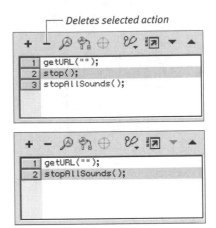

Deletes selected action

Figure 12.17 Click the Delete button (top) to remove the selected action from the list (bottom).

Figure 12.18 Enter text in the Frame field of the Frame Property Inspector to label a selected keyframe.

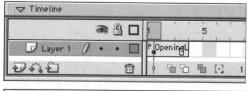

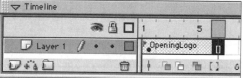

Figure 12.19 A red flag in the Timeline indicates a keyframe that has a label. Flash displays as much of the label as fits in the keyframe span.

Assigning Frame Labels and Comments

Some actions call for you to specify a frame of your movie—when you want Flash to jump to a new location or to get information from a keyframe, for example. You can always refer to keyframes by number, but it's often safer to refer to them by label. That way, if you later add or subtract frames or move them around, you won't have to respecify the keyframe number; Flash will always find the keyframe by its label name. (You cannot label in-between frames, however; you must specify those frames by number.)

For keyframes that are not the target of an action, it may be more useful to add a comment that describes what's going on at this point in the movie. You can label a keyframe or attach a comment to it, but not both. You add labels and comments through the Frame Property Inspector.

To label a keyframe:

1. In the Timeline, select the keyframe (or any frame within its span) that you want to label.

2. Access the Frame Property Inspector.

   If it is not open, choose Window > Properties.

3. In the Frame field, type a name for this keyframe (**Figure 12.18**).

   Do not include spaces in frame labels.

4. In the Timeline, deselect the keyframe.

   A little red flag appears in the labeled keyframe. If there's room before the next keyframe, the text of the label appears as well (**Figure 12.19**).

To add comments to a keyframe:

1. In the Timeline, select the keyframe (or any frame within its span) to which you want to add a comment.

2. Access the Frame Property Inspector.

3. In the Frame Label field, type two slashes, followed by the comment for this keyframe (**Figure 12.20**).

   Two slashes tell Flash to interpret this text as a comment instead of a label.

4. In the Timeline, deselect the keyframe.

   Two green slashes appear in the keyframe that has a comment. If there's room before the next keyframe, the text of the comment appears as well (**Figure 12.21**).

✔ Tips

- If you see a red flag or green slashes in the Timeline, but the label or comment is cut off by the next keyframe or because it's the end of the movie, turn on tooltips (for detailed instructions, see Chapter 1). When you position the pointer over a keyframe span, the tooltips window displays as many as 80 characters of the keyframe's label or comment.

- Frame labels are important parts of a movie's interactivity, and frame-label text gets exported with the other movie data when you publish a Flash Player file. Keeping frame labels short helps keep file sizes small. Comments do not get exported with the final movie, so they can be as long as you like.

- If you wish you could add frame comments to frames that have labels, just add a special comments layer. Place keyframes where you need comments and add your notes there. Similarly, you could place the frame labels on their own layer.

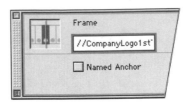

Figure 12.20 You enter comments in the Frame Label field of the Frame Property Inspector. Start the label with two slashes. Flash interprets the text as a comment.

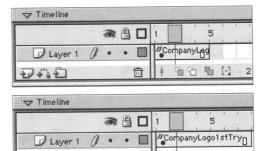

Figure 12.21 Two green slashes identify a keyframe with comments. Flash displays as much comment text as fits in the keyframe span.

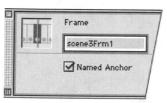

Figure 12.22 Checking the Named Anchor checkbox makes it possible to publish a movie with the proper HTML coding for anchor tags. These tags allow some browsers in the Windows world to navigate through the anchor frames when the user clicks the browser's Back and Forward buttons.

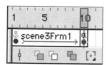

Figure 12.23 Anchors must be placed in keyframes. The anchor icon in the Timeline indicates that the keyframe is a named anchor.

The Limitations of Named Anchors

Although you can create named anchors in the authoring environment on both the Mac and Windows platforms, not every browser that can display Flash Player 6 content will be able to take advantage of the named-anchor feature. Named anchors require Internet Explorer 5 or later or Netscape 4.x with Live Connect enabled. And even with these browsers installed, some users—especially those in the Macintosh world—may have difficulty using the browsers navigation arrows with named anchors.

Creating Named Anchors

In previous versions of Flash, it was difficult to make Flash sites that allowed viewers to use their browser's navigation methods (Back and Forward buttons) to move through the Flash movie. Because each .swf file appeared to the browser to be a single page, you had to create separate movies for each "page" that you wanted the browser to be able to find. Flash MX allows you to integrate browser navigation with Flash's keyframe navigation for some browsers on the Windows platform.

You choose which points in your movie constitute new "pages." Then you set up keyframes at those points and assign to them a special form of frame label called the *named anchor*. Qualified browsers will be able to find these anchors, thereby allowing viewers to navigate your movie with the browser's Back and Forward buttons. When you publish your movie, Flash creates the HTML coding necessary for the anchor tags.

To assign anchor status to a keyframe:

1. In the Timeline, select the keyframe that you want to contain an anchor tag.

2. Access the Frame Property Inspector.

3. In the Frame field, type a name for this frame.

4. Check the Named Anchor checkbox below the Frame Label field (**Figure 12.22**).

5. In the Timeline, deselect the keyframe.

    A little anchor icon replaces the red label flag in the labeled keyframe. If there's room within the keyframe span, the text of the label appears as well (**Figure 12.23**).

    To see how the anchors work in a browser, you must publish your movie by using the HTML template called Flash with Named Anchors. You will learn about publishing movies with templates in Chapter 16.

Controlling Movie Playback

Some of the most basic scripting tasks involve frame actions for controlling movie playback: making your movie stop and start and jump from place to place. Of course sophisticated scripts that do complicated things (such as sending instructions that manipulate objects and gathering and reusing human input) can be attached to frames; and scripts attached to objects can also control movie playback and navigation. But let's start by attaching two movie-control actions—stop and goto—to frames. These actions live in the Actions Toolbox in the Actions > Movie Control category. Both actions are easy to use, and they'll introduce you to working with actions and parameters, as well as viewing the playback of actions.

When you export a movie (covered in Chapter 16) as a Flash Player (.swf) file or as a stand-alone projector, the movie is set to play as soon as your audience opens it. You can override that default setting by placing a stop action in the first frame of your movie.

To set the movie to pause at startup:

1. Open a new copy of the FrameActions Template document you created in "Adding Actions to a Frame" earlier in this chapter (choose File > New from Template.)

2. In the Actions layer, select Keyframe 1.

3. In the Actions-Frame panel, in the Actions Toolbox, click the icon for the Actions category.

   A list of subcategories appears.

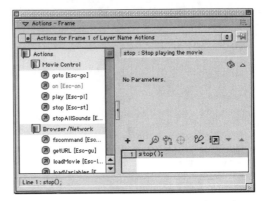

Figure 12.24 In Actions > Movie Control in the Actions Toolbox, double-clicking stop adds stop (); to the current frame's script.

More About stop, goto, and play

Think of the stop action as being like the Pause button on a VCR remote control. You can add a stop action to any keyframe in a movie. The stop action makes the playhead pause in the current frame until another instruction tells the playhead to resume playback. You might want to pause in Frame 10 while the script attached to Frame 10 carries and adds new movie clips to the Stage. Or you might want a movie to pause in Frame 10, because the user must make choices or enter text there.

If you don't need user input, you could add the play action to the end of the script in Frame 10. If you want your user to be able to control playback of the movie, use an object-based script to trigger the play action. You might, for example, attach a script containing a play action to a button or movie clip in the frame where the user enters text. You can set up the object-based script to respond to mouse or keyboard input by issuing the instruction to resume playback of the movie.

The goto action works more like a TV's remote control; you punch in some numbers, and the remote whisks you away to a new channel. An added feature of goto is that you can pause the show when you get there (by using gotoAndStop) or move to the new channel and have it play immediately (by using gotoAndPlay).

Although you could use the goto action by itself in frames in the Timeline (simply as a way to organize the order in which things play back in your movie), goto works best in combination with other actions. You learn more about complex forms of interactivity in Chapters 13 and 15.

4. Click the icon for the Movie Control subcategory.

   A list of actions appears.

5. Double-click stop.

   Flash adds stop (); to Line 1 in the Script pane for Keyframe 1. The stop action has no additional parameters (**Figure 12.24**).

6. In the Timeline, deselect Keyframe 1.

   A small letter *a* now appears in Keyframe 1 of the Actions layer, indicating that this frame has actions. When you export the movie to a Flash Player file (or create a stand-alone projector) and open the movie, it will not play until it receives further instructions that tell it to do so.

A goto action has parameters that you must fill in to make the action work. The parameters identify a specific scene and frame in your movie and tell Flash either to pause there or start playback from there. Playing around with goto is a good way to familiarize yourself with the way the parameters area helps you enter parameters in your script.

To use actions to jump to a new location:

1. Open a new copy of the FrameActions Template document you created in "Adding Actions to a Frame" earlier in this chapter (choose File > New from Template.)

2. Add one or more new scenes to the movie (choose Insert > Scene), and place identifying text in them.

3. In the Timeline in the Actions layer for Scene 1, create a keyframe in Frame 3 or in another frame where you want to stop the movie's sequential playback and make Flash jump to a new location in the Timeline.

(continues on next page)

CONTROLLING MOVIE PLAYBACK

4. In the Actions-Frame panel, in the Actions Toolbox, click the icon for the Actions category.

5. Click the icon for the Movie Control category.

A list of actions appears.

6. Double-click goto.

Flash adds the action gotoAndPlay (1); to Line 1 in the Script pane and displays parameters that direct Flash to a particular frame (**Figure 12.25**). By default, the parameters for goto tell Flash to start playing the new frame immediately.

The default target scene is the current scene, and the default target frame is Keyframe 1. In other words, the default parameters direct Flash to the first frame of the scene that you're in right now. You can change these parameters to make Flash go somewhere else.

7. To make Flash pause after switching to a new location, click the Go To and Stop button in the Parameters area (**Figure 12.26**).

8. To tell Flash which scene to jump to, *do one of the following*:

   ▲ In the Scene field, type the name of the scene (Scene 2, for example).

   ▲ From the Scene pop-up menu, choose the scene.

   Flash lists all the current scenes by name in this pop-up menu, along with the descriptive choices <current scene>, <next scene>, and <previous scene> (**Figure 12.27**).

Parameters for goto action

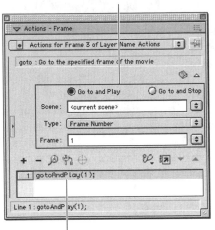

Default action added to script

Figure 12.25 Adding goto to a frame's script brings up parameters for the target frame.

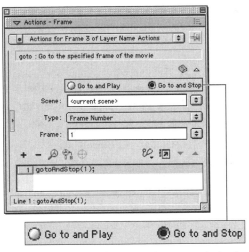

Figure 12.26 The default goto action starts playback immediately after switching to a new location in the Timeline. To have Flash pause in the new location, click Go To and Stop.

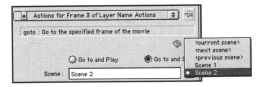

Figure 12.27 You define the target scene by typing its name or choosing it from the list of scenes.

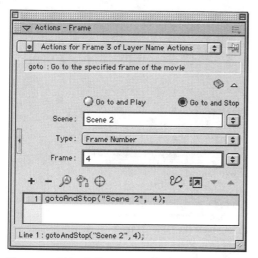

Figure 12.28 You define a target frame by choosing one of the frame types and then, as needed, entering a frame number or label in the Frame field.

9. To specify the frame that Flash should jump to in the finished movie, *do one of the following:*

   ▲ From the Type pop-up menu, choose Number, and type the target frame number in the Frame field (**Figure 12.28**).

   ▲ From the Type pop-up menu, choose Frame Label, and enter the target frame's label in the Frame field.

   ▲ From the Type pop-up menu, choose Expression, and enter an expression in the Frame field that describes the target frame.

   ▲ From the Type pop-up menu, choose Next Frame.

   ▲ From the Type pop-up menu, choose Previous Frame.

10. Choose Control > Test Movie. Play with this exercise, specifying different scenes and frames in steps 8 and 9. Try setting the goto action to play when it reaches its new destination (step 7).

    When the playhead reaches the frame containing the goto action, it jumps to whatever scene and frame you specified.

✔ Tips

■ When you resize the Actions panel to make it narrower, the triangles indicating pop-up menus for the Scene, Type, and Frame fields may disappear. To access these menus, make the window wider.

■ You can enter the name of a scene or frame as the target even if that scene or frame doesn't exist yet. If you have created a storyboard or outline for your movie, and you know for sure what you will name the crucial scenes and frames that will be targeted by actions, you can go ahead and type the names as you create the actions. When Flash encounters an action that tells it to go to a frame or scene that doesn't exist, Flash simply ignores the goto action.

Terminology: Expressions

One of the frame-type choices—Expression—may be mysterious to anyone who's not used to scripting. *Expressions* are formulas that allow Flash to calculate numeric values or enter text strings based on external information, such as information that users type in text boxes. Expressions can also test whether certain conditions are true, such as whether the playhead is in Frame 5. (To learn more about expressions and variables, see Chapter 15.)

Previewing Actions in Action

As you can imagine, it would be difficult to work in the Flash authoring environment if the actions that you added to frames were continually sending you to new locations in the Timeline. The default movie-editing mode disables frame actions. To see frame actions at work when you play your movie in the authoring environment, you must enable them via the Enable Simple Frame Actions command.

To enable frame actions:

1. Open the Flash file whose frame actions you want to preview.

2. From the Control menu, choose Enable Simple Frame Actions.

   Flash places a check next to the Enable Simple Frame Actions command in the menu (**Figure 12.29**). When you play the movie now, Flash follows the instructions in the Script pane.

To disable frame actions:

1. Open the Flash file that has frame actions enabled.

2. From the Control menu, choose the checked Enable Simple Frame Actions.

   Flash removes the check next to the Enable Simple Frame Actions command in the menu to indicate that frame actions are disabled (**Figure 12.30**). When you play the movie now, Flash ignores any instructions in the Script pane and plays the movie frames sequentially.

✔ Tip

■ You can also preview your actions by playing the movie in a test mode. From the Control menu, choose Test Scene or Test Movie. Frame actions are always enabled in these test modes. (For more details about test modes, see Chapter 13.)

Figure 12.29 When a check precedes the Enable Simple Frame Actions command in the Control menu, frame actions are enabled. Enable frame actions when you want to preview them in the Flash authoring environment.

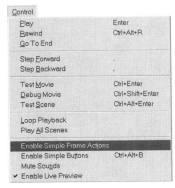

Figure 12.30 When no check precedes the Enable Simple Frame Actions command in the Control menu, frame actions are disabled.

PREVIEWING ACTIONS IN ACTION

INTERACTIVITY WITH OBJECTS

As you learned in the preceding chapter, Macromedia Flash MX's actions attached to frames give you control over a movie's playback, but actions attached to objects let you put viewers in the driver's seat, giving them the power to interact directly with a Flash movie. You can create ActionScripts for two kinds of objects: buttons and movie clips.

Buttons can be simple, displaying static graphics that change slightly as you roll over them and click them. Or buttons can be wild and animated, using movie clips and sounds.

Movie clips can also become vehicles for controlling interactivity, responding to user input, Timeline-related cues, and input from variables. This flexibility makes movie clips a key way of controlling interactivity for advanced ActionScripters.

In this chapter, you discover some basic ways to add interactivity to your movies. You learn to create buttons and attach simple Action-Scripts to buttons and movie clips. You also learn one approach to making movie clips behave like buttons. To get a taste of more-complex interactivity, check out Chapter 15.

Previewing Button and Movie-Clip Actions in Test Mode

Before you dive into creating buttons, take a moment to learn about testing. Flash's test mode is the only place in the authoring environment where you can check the full interactivity of your buttons and movie clips. Test mode is really just an abbreviated form of publishing a movie. (For more information about publishing your final movie, see Chapter 16.) You will want to use test mode to get live feedback from the elements you create in this chapter. Test mode fully enables a button's rollover capabilities, button actions, any movie-clip animation that you've placed in your button, and any actions that you've attached to movie-clip instances in your movie.

To test fully enabled elements:

1. Open the Flash document containing the elements you want to test.

2. From the Control menu, choose Test Scene or Test Movie (**Figure 13.1**).

   Flash exports the scene or movie to a Flash Player file, adding the .swf extension to the file name and using the parameters currently assigned in the Publish Settings dialog box. (For more information on Publish Settings, see Chapter 16.) During export, Flash displays the Exporting Flash Movie dialog box, which contains a progress bar and a button for canceling the operation (**Figure 13.2**).

   When it finishes exporting the movie, Flash opens the .swf file in Flash Player so that you see the movie in action. The buttons and movie clips in the test window are all live, so you can see how they interact with mouse actions by the viewer.

Figure 13.1 To test the full animation and interactivity of buttons, you must export your movie. To export only the current scene, choose Control >Test Scene.

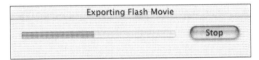

Figure 13.2 The Exporting Flash Movie dialog box appears during export.

3. When you finish testing, click the movie window's close box (Mac OS 9 and Windows) or close button (Mac OS X) to exit the Player.

Flash returns you to the movie-editing environment.

✔ Tips

■ Warning: When you choose Control > Test Movie, Flash creates a test Player file and appends .swf to the file's name. Flash doesn't ask whether you want to replace earlier versions of the file that have the same name; it just assumes that you do. The downside of that convention, however, is that Flash may replace a file that you don't intend to replace. When you export a Flash movie yourself, it's tempting to use the file name and just add the .swf extension to differentiate your original Flash file from your exported .swf file. Unfortunately, Flash can't tell the difference between .swf files that you create and .swf files that it creates in test mode. As a result, the Test Movie command replaces your file. To be safe, always change the name of your movie when you export it yourself.

■ When you choose Control > Test Scene, Flash appends the name of the scene to the file, as well as .swf, when it creates the Player file. This situation can make the file name exceed the number of allowable characters. If Test Movie worked fine with your file, but Test Scene brings up the warning dialog box, that's probably the problem. Try shortening the scene name.

Creating a Basic Rollover Button

A button is a movie clip that has just four frames in its Timeline. Flash labels these frames Up, Over, Down, and Hit. In the Up state, you create a graphic that looks like a static, unused button. This graphic appears whenever the pointer lies outside the active area of the button. In the Over state, create the graphic as it should look when the pointer rolls over the button. Usually, you want some kind of visual change to alert your viewer that the pointer is now on a live button. In the Down state, create the graphic as it should look when someone clicks the button.

In the fourth frame, which is called the Hit frame, create a graphic that defines the boundary of the button. Any filled shape in this frame becomes a place where mouse movements trigger the button in the final movie.

To create the most basic button, choose a simple geometric shape and use it throughout the button states; just change its color or add or modify internal elements for the button.

To create a button symbol:

1. Open a new Flash document, or open an existing Flash document to which you want to add buttons.

2. From the Insert menu, choose New Symbol, or press ⌘-F8 (Mac) or Ctrl-F8 (Windows) (**Figure 13.3**).

   The Create New Symbol dialog box appears.

Figure 13.3 Choose Insert > New Symbol as the first step in creating a button.

CREATING A BASIC ROLLOVER BUTTON

Figure 13.4 To make a button, you must create a new symbol and assign it button behavior in the Create New Symbol dialog box. You can also name the button.

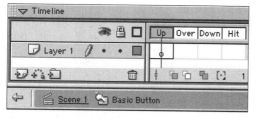

Figure 13.5 The Timeline for every button symbol contains just four frames: Up, Over, Down, and Hit. Flash automatically puts a keyframe in the Up frame of a new button symbol.

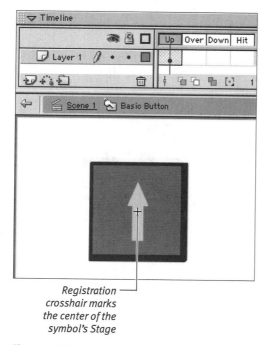

Registration crosshair marks the center of the symbol's Stage

Figure 13.6 When a button is waiting for your viewer to notice and interact with it, Flash displays the contents of the Up frame.

3. Type a name in the Name field, choose Button in the Behavior section, and click OK (**Figure 13.4**).

Flash creates a new symbol in the Library window and returns you to the Timeline and Stage in symbol-editing mode. The Timeline for a button symbol contains the four frames that you need to define the button: Up, Over, Down, and Hit.

By default, the Up frame contains a keyframe (**Figure 13.5**). You must add keyframes to the Over, Down, and Hit frames and place the graphics in each frame of the button. To give users feedback about the button—so that they can tell when they're on a live button and sense the difference when they actually click it—use a different graphic in each frame.

To create the Up state:

1. Using the file from the preceding exercise, in the Timeline, select the Up frame.

2. On the Stage, create a new graphic or place a graphic symbol (**Figure 13.6**).

This graphic element becomes the button as it's just sitting onstage in your movie, waiting for someone to click it. In symbol-editing mode, the crosshair in the middle of the Stage serves as the central point for registering your graphic symbols.

To create the Over state:

1. Using the file from the preceding exercise, in the Timeline, select the Over frame.

2. From the Insert menu, choose Keyframe.

   Flash inserts a keyframe that duplicates the contents of the Up keyframe. Now you can make minor changes in the Up graphic to convert it to an Over graphic. You might enlarge an element within the button, for example (**Figure 13.7**). Duplicating the preceding keyframe makes it easy to align all your button elements so that they don't appear to jump around as they change states.

To create the Down state:

1. Using the file from the preceding exercise, in the Timeline, select the Down frame.

2. From the Insert menu, choose Keyframe.

   Flash inserts a keyframe that duplicates the contents of the Over keyframe. Now you can make minor changes to convert the Over graphic to a Down graphic. You might change the button color, for example, and reverse the shadow effect so that the button looks indented (**Figure 13.8**).

   After you create graphics for the three states of your button, you need to define the active area of the button.

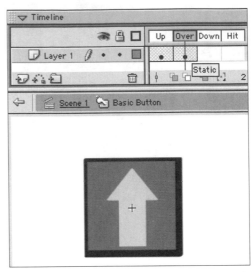

Figure 13.7 When the viewer's pointer rolls (or pauses) over the button, Flash displays the contents of the Over frame.

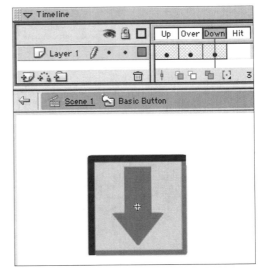

Figure 13.8 When the viewer clicks the button, Flash displays the contents of the Down frame.

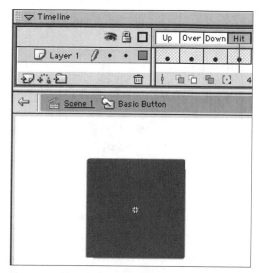

Figure 13.9 The Hit-frame graphic doesn't need to be a fully detailed image of the button in any state; it just needs to be a silhouette of the button shape. Flash uses that shape to define the active button area. This Hit frame contains a copy of the Down frame that has been filled with dark gray.

To create the Hit state:

1. Using the file from the preceding exercise, in the Timeline, select the Hit frame.

2. From the Insert menu, choose Keyframe to duplicate the contents of the Down keyframe.

   When you use a graphic with the same shape and size for all three phases of your button, you can safely use a copy of any previous frame as the Hit-frame graphic.

3. If you want, using the paint-bucket tool, fill the Hit-frame graphic with a single color (**Figure 13.9**).

   This step is not required, but it helps remind you that this graphic is not the one that viewers of your movie will actually see.

The Mystery of Hit-Frame Graphics

Though it never appears in a Flash movie, the Hit frame's graphic content is vital to a button's operation. The sole purpose of the Hit-frame graphic is to define the button's boundaries. This graphic doesn't need to be detailed; it's just a silhouette that defines the button shape. Any painted area in the Hit frame becomes an active part of the button. In the final movie, when the viewer moves the pointer into that area, the Over frame of the button appears; when the user clicks that area, the Down frame appears.

For the clearest, most user-friendly buttons, make sure that your Hit-frame graphic is large enough to cover all the graphics in the first three frames of the button. To be safe, make your Hit-frame graphic a little larger than the other graphics.

If your button is something delicate, such as a piece of type or a line drawing, make your Hit-frame graphic a geometric shape —say, a filled rectangle or oval—that completely covers the Up, Over, and Down graphics. That way, your viewers will have no trouble finding and clicking the button.

When you've completed all four frames, your button is ready to use. Return to movie-editing mode, and drag a copy of the button symbol from the Library window to the Stage.

To place the newly created button in your movie:

1. Continuing with the file from the preceding exercise, from the Edit menu, choose Edit Document, or click the Back button in the info bar at the top of the Stage.

   Flash returns you to the main Timeline. Now you can use the button symbol in your movie just as you would use any other symbol.

2. Drag an instance of the button from the Library window to the Stage.

   You can modify the instance to change its size, rotation, and color. (For more information on modifying symbol instances, see Chapter 6.)

✔ Tips

■ To create a consistent look on a Web site, you might want to use a set of buttons over and over. You can even reuse buttons in several projects with only slight changes. To save time, try devoting one whole document to buttons and always create your button symbols there. Then you can copy a button from this master button file to your current Flash movie file and tweak the button in that file. You can also create a shared library of buttons (see Chapter 6).

■ Always fill your Hit-frame silhouette with the same color—say, light gray or neon blue. That way, the silhouette becomes another visual cue that you are in the Hit frame of a button, in symbol-editing mode.

The Mystery of Buttons

In Flash, you create a button by creating a symbol and then assigning it button behavior. Buttons are actually short—four frames, to be precise—interactive movies. When you select button behavior for a symbol, Flash sets up a Timeline with four keyframes. The first three keyframes display the three ways a button can look; the fourth keyframe (never shown to the viewer) defines the active area of the button.

Any changes you make in the appearance of the graphic elements in the keyframes create the illusion of movement. In other Flash animation sequences, changes occur over time as the playhead moves through the frames. In Flash buttons, however, changes occur when the user moves the pointer over a specific area of the screen.

You can include movie clips within each frame of a button to create buttons that are fully animated, and you can attach actions to buttons to give your viewers more control of the movie.

Figure 13.10 Choose Control > Enable Simple Buttons to test rollover buttons in Flash's movie-editing mode.

Previewing Buttons in Movie-Editing Mode

By default, Flash disables the rollover capabilities of buttons in movie-editing mode. If buttons were always active, you could never reposition them or work with them on the Stage. Every time you tried to grab the button, it would simply display its Over and Down frames. To view a button's operation in movie-editing mode, you must enable buttons.

To enable buttons on the Stage:

◆ Using the file from the preceding exercise, from the Control menu, choose Enable Simple Buttons, or press Option-⌘-B (Mac) or Ctrl-Alt-B (Windows) (**Figure 13.10**).

Any buttons on the Stage now act live. As you move the mouse over a button, Flash displays the Over frame; when you click within the button's active area, Flash displays the Down frame.

✔ Tips

■ You can preview the Up, Down, and Over frames of a button by selecting the button in the Library window and then clicking the Play button in the preview window. Flash displays each frame in turn.

■ The Enable Simple Buttons command allows you to see only the most basic button actions in movie-editing mode. If your enabled buttons behave unexpectedly in movie-editing mode, try viewing them in test mode to verify all their functionality. (Choose Control > Test Movie or Control > Test Scene to enter test mode.)

Creating Buttons That Change Shape

You can use Flash to create buttons more exotic than the simple geometric shapes you'd find on a telephone or calculator. Button graphics can emulate real-world switches or toggles. You can disguise buttons as part of a movie's scenery—making the blinking eye of a character a button, for example. That situation often happens in games; finding the hot spots or buttons is part of the fun. When the exterior shape of the button changes in Up, Over, and Down modes, however, creating an effective Hit-frame graphic can be a bit tricky.

To create Up, Over, and Down states with various graphics:

1. Open a new Flash document, or open an existing Flash document to which you want to add buttons.

2. From the Insert menu, choose New Symbol. The Create New Symbol dialog box appears.

3. Enter a name in the Name field, choose Button in the Behavior section, and click OK.

   Flash creates a new symbol in the Library window and returns you to the Timeline and Stage in symbol-editing mode. The Timeline for a button symbol contains the four frames necessary for defining the button: Up, Over, Down, and Hit.

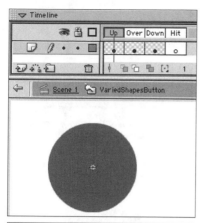

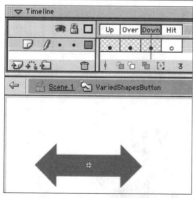

Figure 13.11 You can create fanciful buttons that change shape when a user rolls over or clicks them. In this example, the inactive button is a simple circle (top). When the pointer rolls over the button, the circle changes to a star (middle). When the user clicks the button, it changes to a double-headed arrow.

4. In the Timeline, select the Over, Down, and Hit frames.

5. From the Modify menu, choose Frames > Convert to Blank Keyframes.

   Now you have a blank keyframe in every frame of your button, and you're ready to place various graphics in each frame.

6. With the Up frame selected in the Timeline, on the Stage, create a new graphic, or place the graphic symbol that you want to use for the button's Up state.

7. Repeat step 6 for the Over and Down frames.

   For this exercise, use graphics that have different shapes—a circle, a star, and a double-headed arrow, for example (**Figure 13.11**).

When the Up, Over, and Down frames of your button contain graphics of different shapes and sizes, you need to create a graphic for the Hit state that covers all of them.

To create the Hit state for graphics of various shapes:

1. Using the file that you created in the preceding exercise, in the Timeline, select the Hit frame.

2. To create the Hit-frame graphic, *do one of the following:*

   ▲ Draw a simple geometric shape large enough to cover all areas of the button. Turn on onion skinning so that you can see exactly what you need to cover (**Figure 13.12**).

   ▲ Use Flash's Edit > Copy and Edit > Paste in Place commands to copy the graphic elements from the first three frames of the button and paste them into the Hit frame of the button one by one.

   The graphics stack up in the Hit frame, occupying the exact area needed to cover the button in any phase of its operation (**Figure 13.13**).

✔ Tips

- When you use the copy-and-paste-in-place technique to create your Hit-frame graphic, it's a good idea to expand the resulting graphic slightly—by using the Modify > Shape > Expand Fill command, for example. Making the Hit graphic slop over the edges of the active button areas ensures that your viewers will easily activate the button.

- Use a transparent color (one with an alpha value less than 100 percent) for your Hit-frame graphic. The other graphics will show through the Hit-frame graphic in onion-skin mode, making it easy to see how to position or size the Hit-frame graphic to cover the graphics in the other frames.

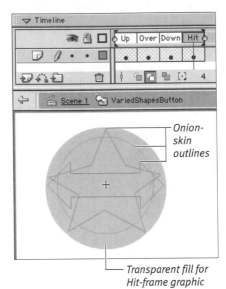

Figure 13.12 The Hit-frame silhouette needs to encompass all possible button areas in all three button modes. If, for example, you duplicate only the circle as your Hit frame for this button, you exclude the tips of the star. A user who clicked those tips in the Over phase would be unable to activate the button. If you duplicate only the star, the user could roll over several areas of the circle and never discover that it's a button.

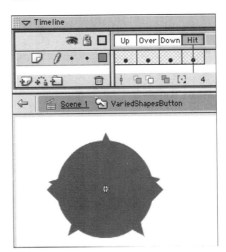

Figure 13.13 By copying the graphic in each of the button modes and using the Paste in Place command to place them in the Hit frame, you wind up with a perfectly positioned silhouette that incorporates all the possible button areas.

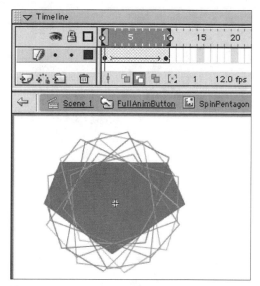

Figure 13.14 Onion skinning reveals all the frames of the spinning pentagon (a motion tween) that appear when the fully animated button is in the Up state.

Figure 13.15 The Preview mode of the Timeline shows the animation of the clip that appears when the pointer rolls or rests over the button area.

Creating a Fully Animated Button

The buttons that you created in the preceding exercises are animated in the sense that they change as the user interacts with them. Flash also allows you to create buttons that are fully animated—a glowing light bulb, for example, or a little ladybug that jumps up and down, saying, "Click me!" The trick to making fully animated buttons is placing movie clips in the frames of your button. Because the movie clips play in their own Timeline, animated buttons remain animated even when you pause the movie.

To animate a rollover button:

1. Create a new Flash document, or open an existing Flash document to which you want to add buttons.

2. Choose Insert > New Symbol.
   The Create New Symbol dialog box appears.

3. Name your button, choose Button in the Behavior section, and click OK.

4. In the Timeline, select the Over, Down, and Hit frames of the button, and choose Modify > Frames > Convert to Blank Keyframes.
   Flash creates blank keyframes for the button's Over, Down, and Hit frames.

5. In the Timeline, select the Up frame, and create a movie-clip symbol or import one from an existing movie.
   For this example, the Up-frame clip contains a spinning pentagon (**Figure 13.14**).

6. In the Timeline, select the Over frame, and create a movie-clip symbol or import one from an existing movie.
   In this example, the Over-frame clip contains a pentagon that turns into a star (**Figure 13.15**).

(continues on next page)

7. In the Timeline, select the Down frame, and create a movie-clip symbol or import one from an existing movie.

For this example, the Down-frame clip contains a star that flies apart (**Figure 13.16**).

8. In the Timeline, select the Hit frame, and create a graphic that covers all the button areas for the three button states (Up, Over, and Down).

A large oval works well for this purpose (**Figure 13.17**). This graphic creates an active button area that's larger than the spinning pentagon. As your viewer's pointer nears the spinning graphic in the final movie, the button switches to Over mode. In Over mode, the oval is big enough to encompass all points of the star, and in Down mode, the user can let the pointer drift a fair amount and still be within the confines of the button.

9. Return to movie-editing mode by clicking the name of the current scene in the Info bar at the top of the Stage.

10. Drag a copy of your button from the Library window to the Stage.

✔ Tips

■ You can place a movie clip in the Hit frame of your button, but only the visible graphic from the clip's first frame determines the hit area.

■ With buttons enabled, in movie-editing mode, Flash previews the Up, Over, and Down frames of your button but not its complete animation. For each frame, you see only the first frame of the movie clip. To view the fully animated button, you must export the movie and view it in Flash Player (by choosing Control > Test Movie, for example).

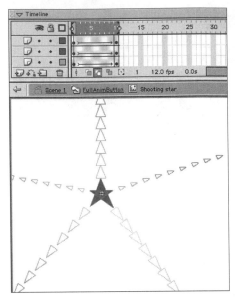

Figure 13.16 Onion skinning reveals the animation of the clip that appears when the viewer clicks inside the button area.

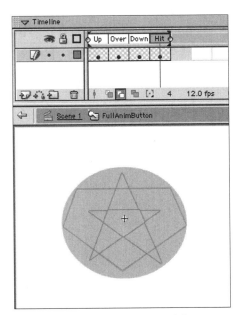

Figure 13.17 When you're creating a Hit-frame graphic, use onion skinning to see the first frame of the movie clip in each button frame. Here, the Hit-frame graphic is a transparent fill, which also helps you position the graphic to cover the graphics in the other frames.

Adding Actions to Buttons

All Flash buttons have certain actions built in. By default, when you move the mouse into the button area, Flash jumps to the Over frame; when you click the button, Flash takes you to the Down frame. To create more interactivity or to refine the way a button responds to a user's mouse movements, you attach ActionScripts to an instance of a button. The process is similar to adding frame actions (see Chapter 12).

Throughout the rest of this chapter, you'll be working with actions that make Flash move from frame to frame; therefore, it will be useful to create a multiframe document that has identifying text in each frame.

To set up a document for testing actions:

1. Open a new Flash document, and create two layers (Contents and Actions).

2. In the Contents layer, create keyframes in frames 1 through 5.

3. Add text that identifies each keyframe (Scene 1·Frame 1, Scene 1·Frame 2, and so on).

4. In the Actions layer, add a **stop** action to Keyframe 1 so that the movie doesn't loop through the frames on playback.
   (For more-detailed instructions on adding actions to frames, see Chapter 12.)

5. In the Timeline, select Keyframe 1 in the Contents layer.

6. Create a button symbol, or copy one from an existing movie.

7. Place an instance of the button symbol on the Stage.

8. Save the document as a template for use throughout this chapter, and name it ObjectActions Template.

The Mystery of ActionScript Terminology

Entering the world of ActionScripting is like visiting a foreign country where you encounter a whole new language. You can't expect to gain native fluency immediately, but you can get around and have a good time if you learn a few key words and phrases—*Hello. Where is the train station? How much does this cost? Please. Thank you. Good bye.* Teaching the full power and beauty of the ActionScript language is a task beyond the scope of this book. Still, the following definitions introduce some important ActionScript terms and concepts. Think of it as your travel-guide phrasebook. Look for other Terminology sidebars throughout the rest of the book for introductions to important ActionScript concepts.

ActionScript is an *object-oriented scripting language*. The name of the object-oriented game is organization. You want to assemble and organize pieces of code for efficiency. When you write documents in a word processor, you use containers and tools to help make your writing fast and efficient. You can create files and folders, templates and boilerplate text, macros and mail merges, to name a few such tools.

In writing scripts, you also use a variety of containers and tools for storing and reusing pieces of code. By nesting containers within containers and stringing them together, you wind up with a whole set of building blocks for creating interactivity in Flash movies.

The largest ActionScript container is a *class*—a group of items that are similar in some way. The items themselves are referred to as *objects* or *instances* of the class. Objects can be concrete graphical elements (*buttons* and *movie clips*) or abstract containers that merely hold data and never appear on the Stage (*variables*).

Objects have two aspects: form and function. In scripting, the two aspects are called *properties* and *methods*. (You could also think of these two aspects as *characteristics* and *behaviors*.)

Consider a concrete example. Imagine Ball, a class of items defined as spherical things. One particular *object* in this class is a movie clip called tennisBall. The *properties* of tennisBall (its form or characteristics) might be the color neon green, a rough surface, and a 3-inch diameter; its *methods* (functions or behaviors) might be bounce, roll, and spin. A second object in this class, softBall, might have such properties as the color white; a smooth surface; a 16-inch diameter; and such methods as fly, roll, and spin.

Each property and method is defined by *actions* (also called *statements* by programmers). Actions are pieces of code that tell Flash how to manipulate a target object at any point in your movie.

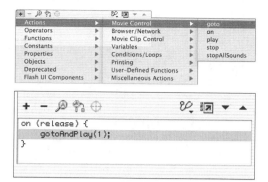

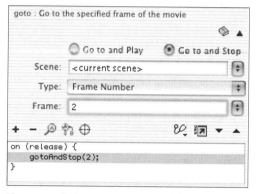

Figure 13.18 In Normal mode, when you select an action for a button (top), Flash embeds that action in an event handler in the Script pane (bottom). The default handler for buttons makes your action take place when the user clicks and releases the mouse button within the active area of your button.

Figure 13.19 In the parameters area of the Actions-Button panel, set any parameters required for your actions. For goto, for example, define the destination frame by entering your choices for the Scene, Type, and Frame parameters. To pause playback at your destination frame, choose Go to and Stop.

✔ Tip

■ You may find it helpful to compare the script you just created with a script that you will create in the next section. To do so, save the changes you made to this file and then save a second copy of this file with a slightly different name. Name the files GoToButton and GoToButton Compare, for example.

To add an action to a button instance:

1. Open a new copy of the ObjectActions Template that you created in the preceding exercise (choose File > New from Template).

2. On the Stage, select the button.

3. Access the Actions panel.

   The title bar indicates what type of object you have selected and, therefore, what type of object the script you are creating will attach to. This panel's title bar reads Actions-Button.

4. From the Add menu, choose an action (Actions > Movie Control > goto, for example).

   When you have the Actions panel set to Normal mode, Flash adds an *event handler* (see the sidebar, "Terminology: Event Handler" on the next page) and appropriate statements for the action to the Script pane (**Figure 13.18**).

5. In the parameters area of the Actions-Button panel, define any parameters necessary for the action that you chose.

   For the goto action, for example, *do the following:*

   ▲ Select the radio button named Go to and Stop.

   ▲ In the Scene field, enter <current scene>, or choose it from the pop-up menu.

   ▲ From the Type pop-up menu, choose Frame Number.

   ▲ In the Frame field, enter **2** (**Figure 13.19**).

6. From the Control menu, choose Enable Simple Buttons, and test the action of your button.

   When you click the button, Flash moves the playhead to Frame 2 in the Timeline and stops playback of the movie.

Terminology: Event Handler

The Movie Control subset of the Actions category contains an action that is available only for buttons and movie clips, not frames. That action—on—is called an *event handler* because it responds to things that happen (events) and uses that incoming information to decide (handle) when and how to run a chunk of ActionScript.

An event handler must be present at the beginning of all ActionScripts attached to buttons and movie clips. In Normal mode, whenever you choose an action from the Actions Toolbox, Flash checks to make sure that there is a handler in the Script pane. If there is no handler, Flash embeds your action in the default handler. The default handler for buttons differs slightly from the one for movie clips (**Figure 13.20**).

If you have a button selected on the Stage, and you choose an action from the Add menu, the default handler that Flash adds to the Script pane is on. If you have a movie clip selected on the Stage, the default handler is onClipEvent.

on and onClipEvent indicate the start of the handler. You can also use the on handler with movie clips to make them act like buttons.

What follows the handler in parentheses— (release)or (load), for example—indicates the condition under which the handler tells the script to run (in these examples, when the mouse button is released or when the movie appears). The statement inside the parentheses is called an *event*. In Normal mode, you choose (from the parameters area of the Actions panel) new events for a handler that you've selected in the Script pane.

The other items that get added to your script when you set up event handlers are curly braces.

{ indicates the beginning of the list of actions that are to be triggered by the specified event.

} indicates the end of the list of the actions that are to be triggered by the specified event.

All actions between the two braces take place when the triggering event occurs.

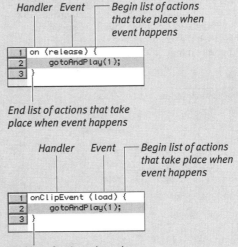

Figure 13.20 The default event handler for buttons, on (release), tells Flash to run the ActionScript after the user has clicked inside a button and released the mouse button. The rest of the ActionScript—the part that tells the button what to do—goes between the opening and closing curly-brace symbols in the Script pane. The default event handler for movie clips, onClipEvent (load), tells Flash to run the ActionScript after the movie clip has been created and appears in the Timeline.

Preparing to add stopAllSounds

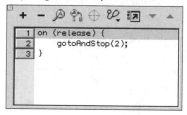

Preparing to add getURL

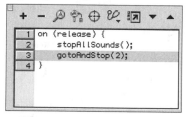

Final script

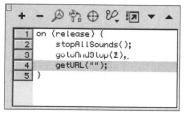

Figure 13.21 You can add multiple actions within one set of curly braces. Flash adds new actions directly below the selected line in the Script pane. In the bottom script, releasing the mouse button stops all sounds, sends the movie to Frame 2, and opens a new browser window. One mouse event triggers all the actions.

To add multiple actions to a button instance:

1. Continuing with the file that you created in the preceding exercise, in Keyframe 1, select the button.

2. Access the Actions-Button panel.

   The Script pane contains the event handler in Line 1 and the gotoAndStop (2) action.

3. To add more actions to the script, *do one of the following:*

   ▲ To add an action before the gotoAndStop (2) action, select on (release) in Line 1 in the Script pane and then choose another action from the Add menu (or double-click an action in the Actions Toolbox).

   Flash adds the new action to the Script pane and displays the action's parameters.

   ▲ To add an action after the gotoAndStop (2) action, select gotoAndStop (2) in Line 2 in the Script pane and then choose another action from the Add menu (or double-click an action in the Actions Toolbox).

   Flash adds the new action to Line 3 in the Script pane (**Figure 13.21**) and displays the action's parameters.

✔ Tip

■ When you choose Actions from the Add menu (or double-click an action in the Actions Toolbox), Flash adds the new action directly below whatever line is selected in the Script pane. You can also drag actions directly from the Actions Toolbox and place them where you want in the Script pane.

Choosing a Button's Event Handler

When you click a basic Flash button, pressing the mouse button down is what actually triggers Flash to display the Down frame. When you attach ActionScript to a button, the script adds to the button's built-in actions. In Normal mode, when you attach an action to a button instance Flash automatically adds the default event handler, on (release), to the Script pane. That code makes the release of the mouse button trigger the actions attached to the button. You can change that behavior by selecting a different event parameter for the handler.

In the preceding exercise, you let Flash add the event handler automatically when you chose an action. This time, try choosing the event-handler action yourself.

To choose the triggering mouse events:

1. Open a new copy of the ObjectActions Template that you created in "To set up a document for testing actions" earlier in this chapter (a movie with five keyframes and a **stop** action in Frame 1).

2. In Keyframe 1, select the button instance on the Stage.

3. Access the Actions-Button panel.

4. From the Add menu, choose Actions > Movie Control > on (**Figure 13.22**).

   Flash adds the event handler—on (release) and a pair of curly braces—to the Script pane. The parameters governing mouse events appear in the parameters area. These parameters specify the exact mouse event that will trigger any actions that you add between the handler's curly braces.

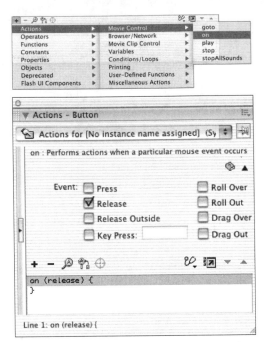

Figure 13.22 The on action allows you to define a button's triggering mouse event.

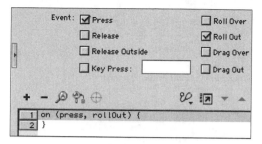

Figure 13.23 With the on action selected in the Script pane, you can select one or more triggering mouse events for a button in the parameters area of the Actions panel.

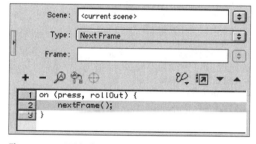

Figure 13.24 With this script, in which Press and Roll Out are selected as the event parameters, your viewers can trigger the nextFrame action in two ways: by clicking inside the button area or by rolling the pointer into and then out of the active button area.

5. In the Event section of the parameters area, uncheck the Release checkbox.

6. Check one or more of the other Event checkboxes (Roll Out, for example).

Flash updates the Script pane, adding the specified mouse events within the parentheses. To set multiple parameters for a mouse event—such as making the button respond to a click within the button area (On Press) as well as to the user's rolling the pointer out of the button area (On Roll Out)—check more than one checkbox (**Figure 13.23**).

7. With on (press, rollOut) { selected in Line 1 in the Script pane, from the Add menu, choose Actions > Movie Control > goto.

8. In the parameters area, from the Type pop-up menu, choose Next Frame.

Flash adds nextFrame (); to the Script pane between the curly braces (**Figure 13.24**).

The Go To and Play and Go To and Stop radio buttons are grayed out. The nextFrame action instructs the button to take the viewer to the next frame and then stop playback.

You're ready to see the button in action.

9. Choose Control > Test Movie.

Flash exports the movie and opens it in Flash Player. The button responds to the pointer's rolling into and then out of the button area by taking you to Frame 2 of the movie. Flash also responds to a downward press of the mouse button within the button area by taking you to Frame 2.

(continues on next page)

✔ Tips

- Compare the two processes you've used for adding ActionScript to a button. In the first exercise, you started your script by choosing a goto action; because you are working in Normal mode, Flash assisted you by adding the necessary event handler to your script. In the second exercise, you chose the event handler on your own and also chose the action. In addition, you modified the handler so that the button would respond to different user activities. Compare the resulting scripts. They are quite similar; only the Event parameters of the handler differ (**Figure 13.25**).

- You do not have to choose the event handler from the Actions Toolbox or Add menu to change its parameters. When you are using Normal mode and select an action, Flash adds the handler for you. Simply select the handler in the Script pane. The parameters area displays the Event choices.

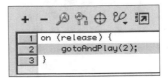

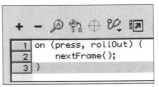

Figure 13.25 Whether you let Flash assist you with adding event handlers or you select them yourself, the resulting scripts will carry out the same instructions. The top script was created by selecting the goto action and setting its parameters. The bottom script was created by selecting the on action, changing the Event parameters of the on action, and then selecting a goto action and setting its parameters.

Terminology: Mouse Event Parameters

Buttons can respond to eight different events. Because all but one of these events involve user input with a mouse (or equivalent device), they are called *mouse events*. You can choose which mouse event triggers your button's script.

Press refers to the downward part of a click when the pointer is located within the hit area of a button.

Release refers to the upward part of a click (the user presses and then releases the mouse button) when the pointer is located within the hit area of a button. A Release event lets users click and then change their minds—and avoid activating the button—by dragging away before releasing the mouse button. This is the way most buttons in professional programs work.

Release Outside happens when the user clicks inside the button area, holds down the mouse button, and moves the mouse outside the active button area before releasing the mouse button.

Key Press happens any time the user presses the specified keyboard key while the Flash button is present. The user doesn't have to use the mouse to interact with the button for this event to trigger an action.

Roll Over occurs any time the pointer rolls into the button's hit area when the mouse button has not been pressed.

Roll Out happens any time the pointer rolls out of the button's hit area when the mouse button has not been pressed.

Drag Over works in a slightly unexpected way. A Drag Over event occurs when the user clicks and holds down the mouse button within the button's hit area, rolls the pointer outside the hit area, and then rolls the pointer back into the hit area.

Drag Out happens when the user clicks within the button's hit area, holds down the mouse button, and rolls the pointer out of the hit area.

Using Multiple Mouse Event Handlers

You can make a single button respond differently to different mouse events by placing several handlers in the button's ActionScript. You could, for example, create one action set that jumps Flash to the next scene when the user clicks and then releases the mouse button within the active button area. You could create a second action set that opens a new movie with help information in a separate window if the user clicks within the button area but then drags the pointer out of the button area before releasing the mouse button. And you could deliver yet another action if the user presses a key on the keyboard, such as jumping to a frame that displays the message "You must click the button to move to the next question."

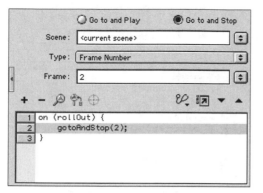

Figure 13.26 This set of actions tells Flash to jump to Frame 2 if the user rolls the pointer into and then out of the active button area.

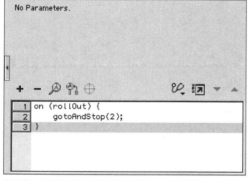

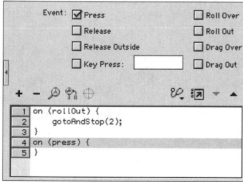

Figure 13.27 To add a second set of actions with a different mouse-event trigger, in the Script pane, select the closing curly brace of the first handler (top). From the Add menu, choose Actions > Movie Control > on, and select a new event (bottom).

To vary a button's response to different mouse events:

1. Open a new copy of the ObjectActions Template that you created earlier in this chapter (a movie with five keyframes and a stop action in Keyframe 1).

2. In Keyframe 1, select the button on the Stage.

3. Access the Actions-Button panel.

4. From the Add menu, choose Actions > Movie Control > on.

5. In the Event section of the parameters area, uncheck the Release checkbox, and check the Roll Out checkbox.

6. From the Add menu, choose Actions > Movie Control > goto.

7. In the parameters area, *do the following:*
   ▲ Choose the radio button named Go to and Stop.
   ▲ From the Type pop-up menu, choose Frame Number.
   ▲ Enter 2 in the Frame field.

   Flash adds gotoAndStop (2); to Line 2 in the Script pane between the curly braces of the event handler (**Figure 13.26**).

8. In the Script pane, select the closing curly brace (Line 3).

9. Repeat steps 4 and 5, this time choosing the mouse event Press.

   Flash adds a second handler—on (press) and a second set of curly braces—to the bottom of the Script pane (**Figure 13.27**).

   (continues on next page)

10. With on (press) selected, from the Add menu, choose Actions > Movie Control > goto.

11. In the parameters area, *do the following:*

   ▲ Choose the radio button named Go to and Stop.

   ▲ From the Type pop-up menu, choose Frame Number.

   ▲ Enter **3** in the Frame field.

Flash adds gotoAndStop (3); to Line 5 in the Script pane, placing the action between the second set of curly braces (**Figure 13.28**).

You're ready to see the button in action.

12. Choose Control > Test Movie.

Flash exports the movie and opens it in Flash Player. If you move the mouse so that the pointer rolls into and then out of the active button area, Flash jumps to Frame 2. If you click within the active button area, Flash immediately jumps to Frame 3, even before you release the mouse button.

✔ Tip

■ Remember that the button you see when you jump to Frame 3 or Frame 2 has no script attached. To try both types of events, you must choose Control > Rewind to return to Frame 1.

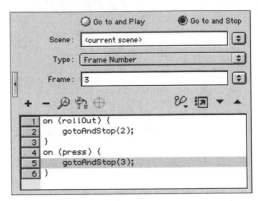

Figure 13.28 The second set of actions in the Script pane tells Flash to jump to Frame 3 if the user clicks within the active button area.

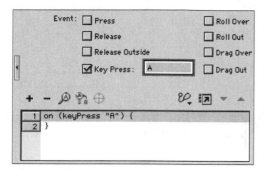

Figure 13.29 When you select Key Press as the Event parameter for an on action, you must specify the triggering key by typing it in the text field.

Triggering Button Actions from the Keyboard

The On keyPress mouse event allows viewers to trigger actions from the keyboard by pressing a specified key. Although you assign it to a button, on (keyPress) affects the entire range of frames in which it resides. The button's Hit-frame graphic need not cover the whole Stage, and the user need not position the pointer over the button before pressing the specified key. Whenever the button is in the currently displayed frame, pressing the specified key triggers the assigned actions.

To set up an action triggered by a key press:

1. Open a new copy of the ObjectActions Template that you created in "To set up a document for testing actions," earlier in this chapter (a movie with five keyframes and a stop action in Keyframe 1).

2. In Keyframe 1, select the button on the Stage.

3. Access the Actions-Button panel.

4. From the Add menu, choose Actions > Movie Control > on.

5. In the Event section of the parameters area, *do the following:*
   - ▲ Uncheck the Release checkbox
   - ▲ Check the Key Press checkbox.
   - ▲ Type **A** in the text field (**Figure 13.29**).

   Flash places on (keyPress "A") and a set of curly braces in the Script pane. In the final movie, pressing the letter *A* on the keyboard triggers whatever actions you specify in this script.

   (continues on next page)

6. With on (keyPress "A") { (Line 1) selected in the Script pane, from the Add menu, choose Actions > Movie Control > goto.

7. In the parameters area, *do the following:*

   ▲ Choose Go to and Stop.

   ▲ From the Type pop-up menu, choose Frame Number.

   ▲ Enter **2** in the Frame field.

   Flash adds gotoAndStop (2); to Line 2 in the Script pane between the curly braces (**Figure 13.30**).

   You're ready to see the button in action.

8. Choose Control > Test Movie.

   Flash exports the movie and opens it in Flash Player. No matter where the pointer is, when the button is on-screen and you press *A* on the keyboard, Flash jumps to Frame 2 of the movie.

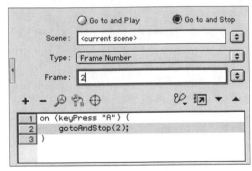

Figure 13.30 This script makes Flash jump to Frame 2 when the user presses *A* on the keyboard at a time when this button is being displayed in the movie.

✔ Tip

■ In some cases, assigned key-press actions fail to work in a published movie. (Browsers, for example, often intercept all key presses, assuming that the user wants to enter a new URL.) When a user clicks a button in a Flash movie, Flash sets the key-press focus—the capability to intercept all key presses. To ensure that your key-press actions always work, include a button for users to click before they can enter a part of the movie that uses key presses.

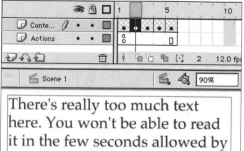

Figure 13.31 Your practice file should look something like this: a five-frame, two-layer movie with lots of text in the Content layer's first frame and a stop action in the first frame of the Actions layer.

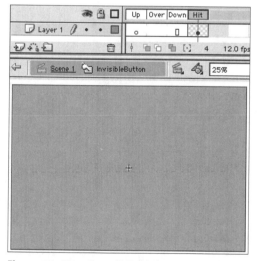

Figure 13.32 To make an invisible button, create a button symbol that has nothing in the Up, Over, and Down frames. Here, the Hit frame contains a filled rectangle large enough to cover the Stage.

Creating an Invisible Button

You don't actually have to place a graphic in every frame of a button. The only frame that must have content is the Hit frame, because it describes the active button area. Buttons without content in the Up, Over, and Down frames are invisible in the final movie. A common use for an invisible button is to resume playback of a movie that pauses on a frame that contains lots of text. Make an invisible button with a Hit-frame graphic that covers the whole Stage, and give the button a **play** action; then place the button in the paused movie frame. When viewers finish reading your text, they can click anywhere in the frame to resume playback of the movie.

To create an invisible button:

1. Open a new copy of the ObjectActions Template that you created earlier.

2. In the Contents layer, in Keyframe 1, delete all the items on the Stage.

3. Using the text tool, place a long text block in Keyframe 1 of the Contents layer (**Figure 13.31**).

4. With Frame 1 selected, choose Insert > New Symbol.
   The Create New Symbol dialog box appears.

5. Type a name for your button, choose Button in the Behavior section, and click OK.

6. In symbol-editing mode, in the Timeline for your button, select the Hit frame.

7. Choose Insert > Blank Keyframe.

8. Use the rectangle tool to create a filled rectangle large enough to cover the entire Stage (**Figure 13.32**).
   This solid rectangle turns the whole Stage into an active button, but because no graphics are associated with the button, it will be invisible to the user.

(continues on next page)

9. Return to movie-editing mode, and drag a copy of your button to the Stage.

Flash shows a transparent object that previews the hot-spot area. If necessary, you can reposition (or resize) the button so that it covers the Stage fully (**Figure 13.33**).

10. On the Stage, select the hot-spot preview.

11. Access the Actions-Button panel.

12. Assign a play action to your button instance (as described in "Adding Actions to Buttons" earlier in this chapter).

You're ready to see the button in action.

13. Choose Control > Test Movie.

Flash exports the movie and opens it in Flash Player. Playback pauses on Frame 1—the one with lots of text (**Figure 13.34**). But as soon as you click within the current frame in the Player window, Flash moves to Frame 2 and plays through the rest of the frames in the movie.

✔ Tips

- In symbol-editing mode, the Stage is a fixed size (20 inches by 20 inches), and it's not necessarily the same size as the Stage in your current movie. To make sure that your Hit-frame rectangle covers the whole Stage in the movie, select the rectangle and access the Info panel. In the Width and Height fields, enter values that are slightly larger than the dimensions of your movie.

- For frames that contain movie clips, you can skip creating an invisible button and attach an ActionScript that responds to mouse events to the movie clip itself (see "Adding Actions to Movie Clips" later in this chapter).

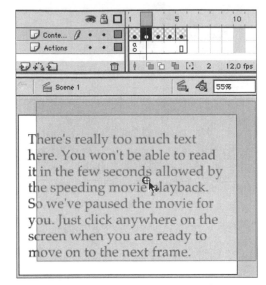

Figure 13.33 When the Up frame of a symbol is empty, Flash displays a transparent version of the Hit-frame graphic to help you position your invisible button in movie-editing mode.

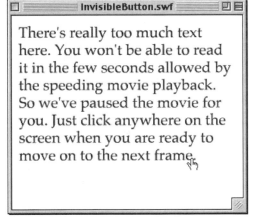

Figure 13.34 This movie is paused on a frame with a stop action and an invisible button that covers the entire Stage. The index-finger pointer indicates the presence of the button. Clicking takes the user to the second frame and resumes playback of the movie.

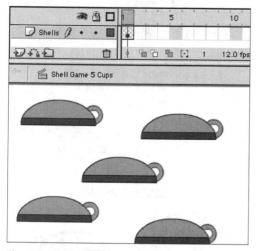

Figure 13.35 On the Stage, create the picture for which you want to activate multiple hot spots. Here, five cups are part of a shell game. One cup hides an item; the others are empty. You can use one button with multiple hot spots to display the same message when the user clicks any of the empty cups.

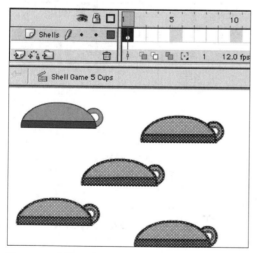

Figure 13.36 Copy the empty cups on the Stage.

Creating a Button with Multiple Hot Spots

Part of the fun of buttons is that you can use them for anything. You don't have to simulate buttons or switches. Flash buttons are versatile in part because each frame of a button can have quite different content. The Hit-frame graphic, for example, need not coincide with any of the graphics of the previous frames: It can be a separate graphic that creates hot spots in various areas of the Stage.

Imagine an animated shell game in which your viewer must determine which cup is hiding a bean. You could create a separate button that displays the message "Nope, guess again!" for each empty cup, or you could create one button that displays the message and put a graphic for each empty cup in the Hit frame of that button.

To create multiple hot spots for a single button:

1. Create a new Flash document with a simple illustration of five cups in Frame 1 (**Figure 13.35**).

2. On the Stage, use the arrow tool to select four of the cups, and choose Edit > Copy (**Figure 13.36**).

3. Choose Insert > New Symbol.
   The Create New Symbol dialog box appears.

(continues on next page)

4. Type a name, choose Button in the Behavior section, click OK.

5. In symbol-editing mode, in the Timeline for your button, select the Hit frame.

6. Choose Insert > Blank Keyframe.

7. Choose Edit > Paste.

   Flash pastes copies of the four cups in the center of the Stage (**Figure 13.37**). You can fill these graphics with a solid color if you want to remind yourself that users will not see them.

8. In the Timeline, select the Down frame.

9. Choose Insert > Blank Keyframe.

10. On the Stage, create the message that you want people to see when they click an empty cup (**Figure 13.38**).

11. Return to movie-editing mode, and drag a copy of your button to the Stage.

    Flash shows transparent previews of the hot-spot area.

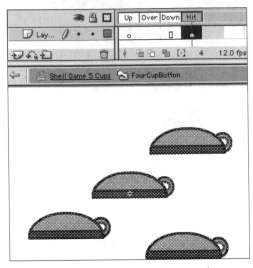

Figure 13.37 In symbol-editing mode, paste the Clipboard contents (the empty cups) into the Hit frame of your invisible button.

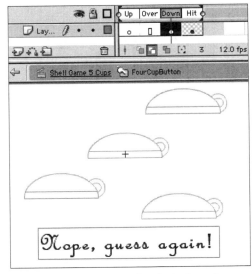

Figure 13.38 Whatever you place in the Down frame appears whenever someone clicks one of the hot-spot areas that you created for the Hit-frame graphic. Here, onion skinning is turned on to help with positioning the message text.

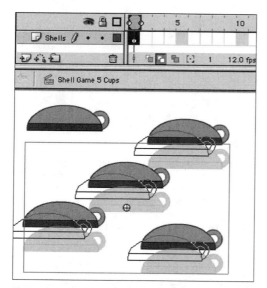

Figure 13.39 When a button contains no images in the Up frame, Flash displays a transparent version of the Hit-frame graphic. You can use the arrow tool or the arrow keys to position the button so that the preview graphics precisely cover the graphic elements on the Stage.

12. Use the arrow tool or the arrow keys to reposition the hot-spot cups to coincide with the cups in Frame 1 of your movie (**Figure 13.39**).

    You're ready to see the button in action.

13. Choose Control > Test Movie.

    Flash exports the movie and opens it in Flash Player. When you click one of the four empty cups, Flash displays the message that you created for the Down frame of your button.

✔ Tip

- If you were creating a real game, you'd want to be sure to create another, separate button to place over the fifth cup. Not only might you want to display a winner's message (or start an animation or jump to another frame) when someone clicks this cup, but you also would want to be sure that the pointer would change to the pointing finger consistently, so as not to give the game away.

Adding Actions to Movie Clips

Just as you can attach ActionScripts to button instances, you can attach ActionScripts to movie-clip instances. Movie-clip ActionScripts have a default handler—onClipEvent —that encompasses its own set of event parameters. The onClipEvent handler can respond to mouse events (such as pressing the mouse button or moving the mouse), keyboard activity (such as pressing a certain key), the activity of the movie clip itself (such as loading into the main Timeline), and the receipt of data (from variables).

To add an event handler to a movie-clip instance:

1. Open a new document.

2. In Frame 1, place an instance of a movie-clip animation on the Stage.

3. Select the movie-clip instance.

4. Access the Actions panel.

   The panel's title bar changes to Actions-Movie Clip.

5. From the Add menu, choose Actions > Movie Clip Control > onClipEvent.

   Flash places the default movie-clip handler onClipEvent (load); and a pair of curly braces in the Script pane (**Figure 13.40**).

   The default movie-clip event handler tells Flash to implement the ActionScript within the braces as soon as the movie clip loads into the frame containing it (in this case, Frame 1) during playback of the movie.

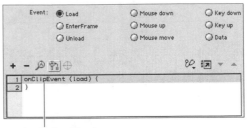

Movie-clip handler

Figure 13.40 With a movie clip selected on the Stage, when you choose Actions > Movie Clip Control > onClipEvent from the Actions panel's Add menu, Flash adds the default movie-clip event handler onClipEvent (load) to the Script pane. This handler causes the script to trigger when the clip loads.

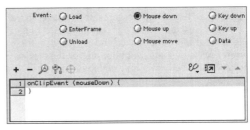

Figure 13.41 Selecting Mouse Down as the triggering event changes the ActionScript. Now the script will trigger whenever someone clicks anywhere in the playback window while the movie clip is present.

Terminology: Clip Event Parameters

The onClipEvent action has nine parameters. The parameters tell Flash when to run the ActionScript that falls within the curly braces of the movie-clip handler statement. Some parameters are pairs of opposite events, such as Load and Unload; others require further scripting to create a precise event trigger. If you want to trigger an ActionScript with a particular key, for example, you must add to the Key Press statement other actions that test to see what key the user has pressed.

Load triggers the ActionScript when the playhead reaches the first frame in the Timeline containing that movie clip and the clip appears. Unload triggers when the playhead reaches the first frame that no longer contains that movie clip.

Enter Frame triggers the ActionScript when each new frame of the movie clip appears.

Mouse Down/Mouse Up triggers the ActionScript when the user presses/releases the mouse button anywhere in a frame that contains the movie clip.

Mouse Move triggers the ActionScript when the user moves the mouse anywhere in a frame that contains the movie clip.

Key Down/Key Up triggers the ActionScript when the user presses/releases a key on the keyboard while a frame that contains the movie clip appears.

Data triggers the ActionScript when the script of another object or movie passes variables to the current movie.

You can change the movie clip's handler so that it responds to another event.

To change the movie-clip handler:

1. Continuing with the file you created in the preceding exercise, in the Script pane, select the movie-clip event handler (Line 1).

   The event parameters for the onClipEvent action appear in the parameters area.

2. Click the Mouse Down radio button.

   The first line of code in the Script pane updates to reflect the new event parameter. It now reads onClipEvent (mouseDown){ (**Figure 13.41**).

   In the final published movie, this script will trigger whenever this movie clip is in the current frame and someone clicks the mouse button anywhere in the movie-display area.

You're ready to make your clip script do something.

To add an action to be triggered by the movie-clip's event handler:

1. Continuing with the file from the preceding exercise, with the movie clip selected on the Stage, from the Add menu, choose Actions > Movie Control > stop.

   Flash places stop (); in Line 2 in the Script pane. You're ready to test your movie.

2. From the Control menu, choose Test Movie.

   The move opens in Flash Player, displaying the animation contained in the movie clip. When you click anywhere in the Flash Player window, Flash stops the animation cold.

Note that when you use onClipEvent, the triggering mouse event doesn't have to happen inside the area occupied by the movie clip. To tie the mouse input to the location of the movie clip, you need to use the on event handler. The next section shows you how.

Making Movie Clips Act Like Buttons

In the preceding exercise, you created a script for a movie clip in which the location of the pointer during the triggering event (the downward click of the mouse button) did not have to coincide with the movie clip's location. You can use actions to create a script that ties the mouse input directly to the movie clip's physical location, so that the movie clip acts just like a button.

To create a movie-clip button:

1. Open a new document.

2. In Frame 1, place an instance of a movie-clip animation on the Stage.

3. Select the movie clip.

4. Access the Actions panel.

   The panel's title bar changes to Actions-Movie Clip.

5. From the Add menu, choose Actions > Movie Control > on.

   Flash places the default event handler on (release) in Line 1 in the Script pane (**Figure 13.42**).

   The default event tells Flash to implement the ActionScript as soon as the mouse button is clicked and then released while the pointer is within the image area of the movie clip. As you did for buttons earlier in this chapter, you can change the event parameter of the handler so that other mouse actions or keyboard input will trigger the movie-clip button's script.

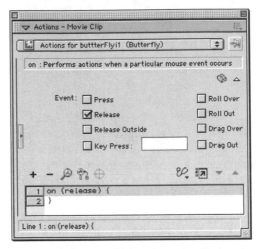

Figure 13.42 You can add the on event handler to movie clips as well as to buttons. Then this handler responds to mouse clicks only when they are directly over the movie clip itself.

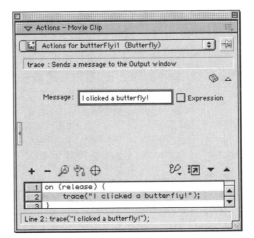

Figure 13.43 The trace action lets you post messages to the Output window to track which part of your script is executing. You can also use trace to test small sections of code as you build your script.

Figure 13.44 In Flash Player, the pointer changes to the pointing-finger icon as it passes over a movie clip whose script starts with the event handler on.

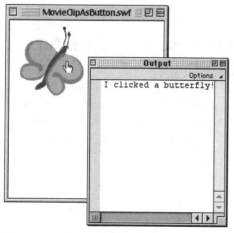

Figure 13.45 The Output window displays whatever message you created for a trace action.

6. In the Script pane, select Line 1.

7. From the Add menu, choose Actions > Miscellaneous > trace.

   Flash adds trace (""); to Line 2 of the script.

8. With Line 2 selected, in the parameters area of the Actions-Movie Clip panel, enter text in the Message field—for example, **I clicked a butterfly** (**Figure 13.43**).

9. Choose Control > Test Movie to try out your button movie clip.

10. In the Flash Player window, position the pointer over various areas of the Stage.

   As it moves over the image area of the movie clip, the pointer changes from an arrow to the pointing-finger icon (**Figure 13.44**). When you click the movie clip, Flash enters the trace message in the Output window (**Figure 13.45**).

Terminology: trace

The trace action is very useful both for learning scripting and for finding problems with your script as you start to do more complex things. When you run the movie in test mode during authoring, any time a script contains the trace action, Flash opens a special window named Output and displays whatever message you created in your trace action. By placing trace messages at strategic points in your script, you can narrow down the point in the script where problems are occurring. You can also use trace as a sort of shorthand for "all the rest of the actions," which allows you to script incrementally and test each additional chunk of interactivity without having to create the full script.

Buttons Versus Movie Clips Acting as Buttons

Now that you know the basic way to make a movie clip act like a button, why would you? Consider some differences between them.

Button symbols come with built-in frames for the Up, Over, Down, and Hit stages of a button. Each frame contains its own form of scripting that detects how the mouse is interacting the button. This built-in functionality makes it easy to create buttons that work as users expect them to.

With buttons, you decide what content appears in each phase; you must create the Hit-frame graphic that Flash uses to detect the interaction of the mouse with the button. For movie-clip symbols used as buttons, that detecting capability is built in. You don't have to (and don't get to) define what constitutes the active area of the button; Flash uses whatever graphic image the movie clip is displaying as the hit area.

With buttons, you can enhance the feedback to the user about the fact that the button is live by creating content in the Over frame. With movie-clip buttons, you rely on the pointer's changing to the pointing-finger icon when it rolls over the active area of a movie-clip button to indicate that the user has found a live button.

But this is Flash, remember? That means there's always more than one way to approach your problem. The movie-clip-as-button procedures that you learn in this chapter are just the beginning of the story. Advanced ActionScripters can override some of this default activity for movie-clip buttons, for example, by assigning button-state properties to frames within a movie clip, thereby creating their own animated Up, Down, and Over frames without nesting movie clips within the button. You can also define your own functions to describe what happens when a viewer interacts with your movie-clip button in certain ways, such as rolling over it.

ADDING
SOUND AND VIDEO

It's amazing how much a classic silent film conveys with just moving pictures and text, but that era is history. Audio is a vital feature of today's Web sites. In Macromedia Flash, movies can incorporate sound, either as an ongoing background element or as a synchronized element that matches a particular piece of action—say, a slapping sound that accompanies a pair of hands clapping.

Adding yet another tool for bringing realism to your movies, Flash MX introduces the capability to embed video clips for playback directly in Flash Player. Sorenson Media's Spark codec, which is built into Flash MX, handles the compression of video for import into Flash's authoring environment and decompression of the video data during playback of the published movie. This system allows you to include short video clips in your Flash movies and still keep file sizes manageable. You also have the option of linking video clips to your movie during authoring and then exporting the movie to QuickTime, where all the Flash animation takes place on a separate track from the video.

Using Sounds in Flash

To add sound to Flash movies, you must import the sound clips to the library and then attach instances of the sound clips to keyframes. You access sounds and control synchronization of sounds via the Frame Property Inspector. You can also call up Flash's simple sound-editing tools through the Frame Property Inspector.

To access the Frame Property Inspector:

◆ If the Frame Property Inspector is not currently active, from the Window menu, choose Properties (**Figure 14.1**).

The Frame Property Inspector opens or comes to the front if other panels are on top of it (**Figure 14.2**).

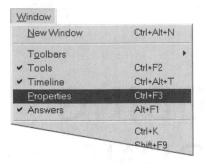

Figure 14.1 To access Flash's sound tools, choose Window > Properties.

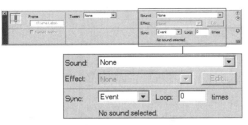

Figure 14.2 Using the Frame Property Inspector, you can attach sounds to keyframes, set synchronization, and perform simple sound-editing operations. Some sound tools are always visible on the right side of the panel. To view all the sound tools, click the triangle in the bottom-right corner of the Property Inspector to expand the panel.

Flash Sound Features

Flash deals only with *sampled* sounds—those that have been recorded digitally or converted to digital format. Flash imports AIFF-format files for the Mac OS, WAV-format files for Windows, and MP3-format files for both platforms. In addition, with the combination of Flash MX and QuickTime 4, users on both platforms can import QuickTime movies containing sounds and Sun AU files. Mac users can also import WAV, Sound Designer II, and System 7 sounds. Any sounds you import or copy into a movie reside in the movie file's library.

Flash offers a limited form of sound editing. You can clip the ends off a sound and adjust its volume, but you must do other kinds of sound editing outside Flash.

When you publish your finished movie, pay attention to the sampling rate and compression of sounds to balance sound quality with the file size of your finished movie. You learn more about these considerations in Chapter 16.

Figure 14.3
Choose File >
Import to bring
sounds into your
Flash file.

Figure 14.4 The
Import dialog box
lets you import
sound files into
Flash. Choose the
sound-file type
that is appropriate
for your platform
from the pop-up
menu of file types.

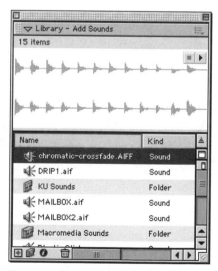

Figure 14.5 Flash keeps sound files in the
library, giving each file a separate sound-file
icon. You can see the waveform for a selected
sound in the preview window. Click the Play
button to hear the sound.

Importing Sounds

The procedure for importing sounds is just like
the procedure for importing bitmaps or other
artwork: You use the File > Import command.
Flash brings the sound file into the library for
the current movie, and you drag a copy of the
sound from the Library window into that movie.

To import a sound file:

1. Open the file to which you want to add
sounds.

2. From the File menu, choose Import or
press ⌘-R (Mac) or Ctrl-R (Windows)
(**Figure 14.3**).

The standard file-import dialog box
appears (**Figure 14.4**).

3. From the Show pop-up menu (Mac) or the
Files of Type pop-up menu (Windows),
choose the format of the sound file that
you want to import.

Flash imports AIFF files for the Mac, WAV
files for Windows, and MP3 files for both
platforms.

4. Navigate to the sound file on your system.

5. Select the file.

6. Click Open.

Flash imports the sound file that you
selected, placing it in the library. Flash
displays the waveform of the sound in the
Library preview window (**Figure 14.5**).

✔ Tips

- You can hear a sound without placing it in
  a movie. Select the sound in the Library
  window. Flash displays the waveform in the
  preview window. To hear the sound, click
  the Play button in the preview window.

- Not sure what sound formats are available to you? You don't have to choose a
  specific one; you can choose All Sound
  Formats from the pop-up menu of file
  types in the Import dialog box.

Organizing Sounds

Nothing prevents you from adding sounds in layers that contain other content, but your movie will be easier to handle—and sounds will be easier to find for updating and editing—if you always put sounds in separate layers reserved just for your sound track. Flash can handle multiple sound layers.

To add a layer for sound:

1. Open a new Flash document, or open an existing one to which you want to add sound.

2. In the Timeline, select a layer.

3. *Do one of the following:*

   ▲ From the Insert menu, choose Layer (**Figure 14.6**).

   ▲ In the Timeline, click the Add Layer button.

   Flash always adds the new layer directly above the selected layer.

4. Drag the layer to the desired position in the layer stacking order.

   The position in the stacking order of layers has no effect on the playback of sounds in the movie, but you may find it helpful to place all your sound layers at either the bottom of the layers or at the top so that you can find them easily.

5. Rename the layer.

   For detailed instructions on working with layers, see Chapter 5.

✔ Tips

■ After you've placed sounds in a layer, you can lock the layer—to prevent yourself from adding graphics to it accidentally—by clicking the bullet in the column below the padlock icon.

■ If you will be working with numerous sound layers, add a layer folder, and name it Soundtracks. Drag every sound layer into the Soundtracks folder (**Figure 14.7**).

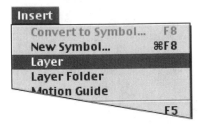

Figure 14.6 It's best to keep sounds in separate layers from the graphics and actions in your movie. To add a new layer, choose Insert > Layer.

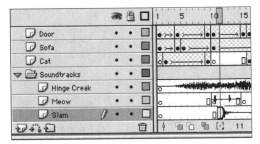

Figure 14.7 To organize multiple sound layers, place them in a separate layer folder.

Figure 14.8 Choose Modify > Layer to access the Layer Properties dialog box, where you can change a layer's height.

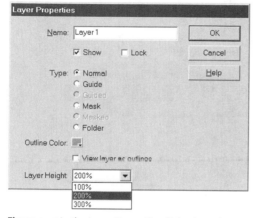

Figure 14.9 In the Layer Properties dialog box, choose 200% or 300% from the Layer Height pop-up menu to enlarge the layer view in the Timeline and make any sound wave attached to the layer easier to view.

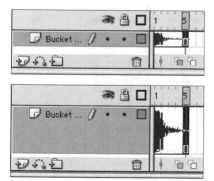

Figure 14.10 Compare a five-frame sound wave at normal layer height (top) with the same sound wave in a 300 percent layer (bottom).

Adjusting Sound-Layer Height

As a default, Flash displays layers at 100 percent, but you can bump the layer display up to 200 or 300 percent. It can be helpful to make the sound layers larger so that you can see the waveform (a graphic image of the sound) for that layer better. You change layer size in the Layer Properties dialog box.

To adjust the layer height for sound:

1. In the Timeline, select the sound layer that you want to enlarge.

2. To access the Layer Properties dialog box, *do one of the following:*

   ▲ From the Modify menu, choose Layer (**Figure 14.8**).

   ▲ Double-click the layer icon of the selected layer.

   The Layer Properties dialog box appears.

3. From the Layer Height pop-up menu, choose the desired percentage (**Figure 14.9**).

   Choose 200% or 300% to make the layer taller.

4. Click OK.

   Flash returns you to the Timeline. The selected layer is taller, and the waveform in it is larger and shows a bit more detail (**Figure 14.10**).

Adding Sounds to Frames

You can assign a sound to a keyframe the same way that you place a symbol or bitmap: by selecting the keyframe and then dragging a copy of the sound from an open Library window (either that movie's or another's) to the Stage. You can also assign any sound that resides in the movie's library to a selected keyframe by choosing the sound from the Sound pop-up menu in the Frame Property Inspector.

To assign a sound to a keyframe:

1. Open a Flash file to which you want to add sound.

   The Ping-Pong animation that you created in Chapter 11 makes a good practice file. The movie contains four keyframes, in which a ball connects with a paddle. Adding sound can heighten the reality of that contact: You can make the sound realistic (say, a small *thwock*) or make it humorous, if the sound is unexpected (a wolf's howl, for example).

2. Add a new layer for the sounds in your movie.

   (For more detailed instructions, follow the steps in "Organizing Sounds" earlier in this chapter.)

3. Name the layer Sound.

4. In the Timeline, select your new Sound layer, and add keyframes at frames 5, 10, 15, and 20.

   These four keyframes match the keyframes in the animation in which the ball hits one of the paddles (**Figure 14.11**).

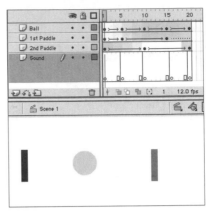

Figure 14.11 Create a separate layer for the sounds in your movie. In that layer, add a separate keyframe at each place where you want a sound to occur. Here, the keyframes correspond to the keyframes in which the ball makes contact with a paddle.

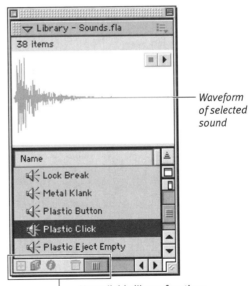

Waveform of selected sound

Unavailable library functions

Figure 14.12 Flash comes with a library of sounds for you to use in your movies. Choosing Window > Common Libraries > Sounds opens Flash's built-in library of sounds without opening its parent movie. This method makes sounds available for copying to other movies but prevents you from changing them accidentally in the original movie. Plastic Click makes a good Ping-Pong-ball sound.

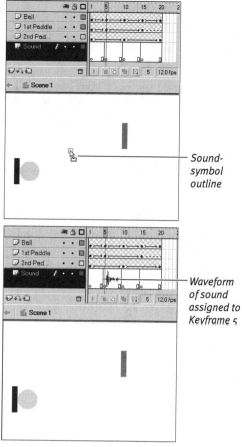

Sound-symbol outline

Waveform of sound assigned to Keyframe 5

Figure 14.13 When you drag a sound from the Library window to the Stage, you see the symbol outline (top). A sound has no visible presence on the Stage, but Flash displays the sound's waveform in the Timeline (bottom).

5. From the Window menu, choose Common Libraries > Sounds.

   The Library-Sounds window opens (it's one of the libraries that Macromedia provides with Flash). The library's background and editing functions are grayed out because you haven't opened the Sound file—just its library. But you can drag sounds to your own Flash file.

6. In the Library-Sounds window, choose the sound named Plastic Click (**Figure 14.12**).

   Its waveform appears in the preview window.

7. In the Timeline, select Keyframe 5 of the Sound layer.

   This is the first frame in which the ball and paddle connect.

8. Drag a copy of the Plastic Click sound from the Library window to the Stage of your movie.

   Although sounds have no visible presence on the Stage, you must drag the sound copy to the Stage. As you drag the sound, you see the outline of a box on the Stage. When you release the mouse button, Flash puts the sound in the selected keyframe and displays the waveform in that keyframe and any in-between frames associated with it (**Figure 14.13**).

9. In the Timeline, select Keyframe 10 of the Sound layer.

   This is the second frame in which the ball and paddle connect.

(continues on next page)

10. Access the Frame Property Inspector.

11. From the Sound pop-up menu, choose the sound named Plastic Click.

All the sounds in the movie's library are available from the Frame Property Inspector's Sound pop-up menu (**Figure 14.14**). You don't have to drag a copy of the sound to the Stage each time you want to turn that sound on in a keyframe.

For now, leave the other settings in the Frame Property Inspector alone. You learn more about them in later tasks.

12. Repeat steps 7 and 8 (or 9, 10, and 11) for keyframes 15 and 20.

After adding the sound to the four keyframes, you are ready to play the movie and check out the sounds (**Figure 14.15**). As each paddle strikes the ball, Flash plays the Plastic Click sound, adding a level of realism to your simple Ping-Pong animation.

✔ Tip

- Can't remember what sound that little squiggly waveform is? With tooltips active (choose the option in the General tab of the Preferences dialog box), let the mouse pointer hover over the waveform in the Timeline. Flash displays the name of the sound.

Figure 14.14 In the Frame Property Inspector, the Sound pop-up menu lists all the sounds that are in the movie. From this menu, you can choose a sound that you want to assign to the keyframe that's currently selected in the Timeline.

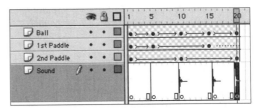

Figure 14.15 For each spot in the movie where a sound should occur, add a sound to a keyframe in the sound layer.

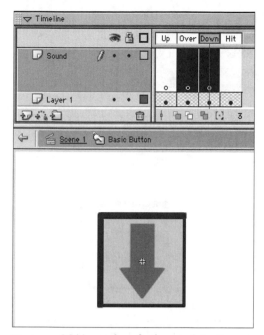

Figure 14.16 Add a new layer for the sounds in a button, and create keyframes at the points where you plan to assign sounds.

Adding Sounds to Buttons

Auditory feedback helps people who view your movie interact with buttons correctly. For buttons that look like real-world buttons, adding a click sound to the Down frame provides a more realistic feel. For more fanciful buttons or ones disguised as part of the scenery of your movie, adding sound to the Over frame lets users know that they've discovered a hot spot.

To enhance buttons with auditory feedback:

1. Open a Flash file containing a button to which you want to add sound.

   (To learn how to create buttons, see Chapter 13.)

2. Open the file's Library window (choose Window > Library), and select the button symbol that you want to modify.

3. From the Options menu, choose Edit.

   Flash opens the button in symbol-editing mode.

4. In the Timeline, add a new layer (click the Add Layer button), and name it Sound.

5. In the Sound layer, select the Over and Down frames, and choose Modify > Frames > Convert to Blank Keyframes (**Figure 14.16**).

(continues on next page)

6. Using the techniques described in "Adding Sounds to Frames" earlier in this chapter, assign a sound to the Over frame and a different sound to the Down frame.

Flash displays as much of the waveform as possible in each frame. When you add sounds to buttons, it makes sense to increase the height of the layer that contains sounds (**Figure 14.17**).

7. Return to movie-editing mode.

Every instance of the button in the movie now has sounds attached.

8. To hear the buttons in action, choose Control > Enable Simple Buttons.

When you move the pointer over the button, Flash plays the sound that you assigned to the Over frame. When you click the button, you hear the sound that you assigned to the Down frame.

✔ Tip

■ The most common frames to use for button feedback are the Over and Down frames, but you can add sounds to any of the button frames. Sounds added to the Up frame play when the pointer rolls out of the active button area. Sounds added to the Hit frame play when you release the mouse button within the active button area.

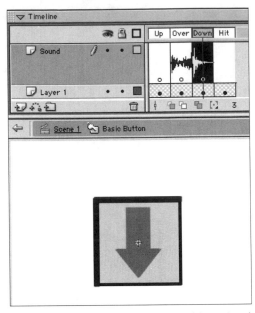

Figure 14.17 Flash displays the waveform of the assigned sound in the keyframe. Unlike movie Timelines, button Timelines have no in-between frames that can contain part of the waveform. Increasing the layer height for a button's sound layer enlarges any waveforms in the button's frames, letting you see more detail.

Independent Sounds Versus Synchronized Sounds

Unsynchronized sound clips play independently of the frames in a movie and can even continue playing after the movie ends. Flash starts these *event sounds* at a specific frame, but thereafter, event sounds play without relation to specific frames. On one viewer's computer, the sound may take 10 frames to play; on a slower setup, the sound may finish when only 5 frames have appeared.

Flash can also synchronize entire sound clips with specific frames. Flash breaks these *streaming sounds* into smaller pieces and attaches each piece to a specific frame. For streaming sounds, Flash forces the animation to keep up with the sounds. On slower setups, Flash draws fewer frames so that important actions and sounds stay together.

Using Event Sounds

One of the sound parameters available in the Frame Property Inspector is Sync. The Sync setting determines the way that Flash synchronizes the sounds in your movie. Sync has four settings: Event, Start, Stop, and Stream. The default is Event.

Event sounds play in their own Timeline. Flash synchronizes the beginning of an event sound with a specific keyframe in a movie, but then the event sound plays until Flash reaches the end of the sound clip or encounters an instruction to stop playing either that specific sound or all sounds. If it's long enough, an event sound continues to play after the movie ends. If your movie loops, every time the playhead passes a frame containing an event sound, Flash starts another instance of that sound playing.

To understand the way sound synchronization works in Flash, it is helpful to work in a document that has identifying text in keyframes.

To set up a file for testing sounds:

1. Create a 20-frame, 3-layer Flash document.

2. Label the layers Objects, Sound 1, and Sound 2.

3. In all layers, insert keyframes into frames 1, 5, 10, 15, and 20.

4. In the Object layer, place identifying text on the Stage for each keyframe.

5. Import into the movie's library several sounds of different lengths.

   This example uses a 15.8-second sound clip of a musical-scale passage, the Bucket Hit sound from Flash's common library of sounds, a wolf's howl, and some crickets chirping.

6. Save the document as a template for use throughout this chapter, and name it SoundSync Template.

   For detailed instructions on saving documents as templates, see Chapter 1.

To make an assigned sound an event sound:

1. Open a new copy of the SoundSync Template that you created in the preceding exercise. (Choose File > New From Template.)

2. In the Timeline, select Frame 5 of the Sound 1 layer (**Figure 14.18**).

3. In the Frame Property Inspector, from the Sound pop-up menu, choose the sound named Scale (**Figure 14.19**).

4. From the Sync pop-up menu, choose Event (**Figure 14.20**).

   The Scale sound is assigned to Keyframe 5 of the Sound 1 layer.

5. Position the playhead in Frame 1, and play your movie (choose Control > Play).

   In a movie that has a standard frame rate of 12 fps, the 15.8-second Scale sound continues to play after the end of the movie.

✔ Tip

■ To understand better how Flash handles event sounds, choose Control > Loop Playback. Now play the movie again, and let it loop through a couple of times. Each time the playhead enters Frame 5, Flash starts another instance of the Scale sound, and you start to hear not one set of notes going up the scale, but a cacophony of bad harmonies. When you stop the playback, each sound instance plays out until its end—an effect sort of like people singing a round.

Figure 14.18 Select the keyframe to which you want to assign a sound. Settings that you create in the Frame Property Inspector get applied to the selected keyframe.

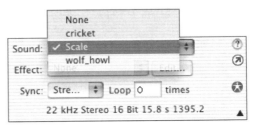

Figure 14.19 In the Frame Property Inspector, choose a sound from the Sound pop-up menu.

Figure 14.20 From the Sync pop-up menu, choose Event to make the assigned sound start in the selected keyframe and play to the end of the sound, without synchronizing with any subsequent frames of the movie.

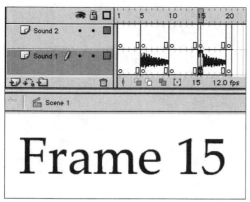

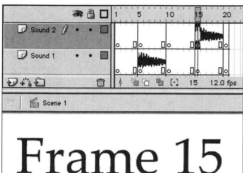

Figure 14.21 You can add a second instance of your sound and make it play on top of the first. Event sounds play in their own Timeline, so you're free to add the second sound to the same layer as the first (top). Alternatively, you can add the second sound to its own layer (bottom).

To play overlapping instances of the same sound:

1. Using the file that you created in the preceding exercise, to assign a sound to a later point in the movie's Timeline, *do one of the following:*

   ▲ Select Frame 15 of the Sound 1 layer.

   ▲ Select Frame 15 of the Sound 2 layer.

   Because Flash starts a new instance of an event sound, even if that sound is already playing, you have the choice of adding a second instance to the same layer as the first or adding it to a different layer.

2. In the Frame Property Inspector, from the Sound pop-up menu, choose the sound named Scale.

3. From the Sync pop-up menu, choose Event.

   The Scale sound is assigned to Keyframe 15 of whichever layer you chose (**Figure 14.21**).

4. Position the playhead in Frame 1, and play your movie one time.

   When the playhead reaches Frame 5, the Scale sound starts. When the playhead reaches Frame 15, another instance of the Scale sound starts, and the two sounds play together (you hear two voices). When the first instance ends, you again hear only one voice.

Within a single layer, each frame can contain only one sound. To make Flash play multiple sounds at the same point in a movie, you must put the sounds in separate layers.

To start different sounds simultaneously:

1. Open a new copy of the SoundSync Template that you created earlier in this chapter. (Choose File > New From Template.)

2. In the Timeline, select Keyframe 5 of the Sound 1 layer.

3. In the Frame Property Inspector, from the Sound pop-up menu, choose Scale.

4. From the Sync pop-up menu, choose Event.

5. In the Timeline, select Keyframe 5 of the Sound 2 layer.

6. In the Frame Property Inspector, from the Sound pop-up menu, choose a different sound.

   You could also import a new sound to your movie's library or open the Library window of another movie containing the sound you want to use and then drag a copy of the sound to the Stage. This example uses the Bucket Hit sound from Flash's common library of sounds.

   Flash places the waveform for the second sound in Keyframe 5 of the Sound 2 layer (**Figure 14.22**).

7. In the Frame Property Inspector, from the Sync pop-up menu, choose Event.

8. Position the playhead in Frame 1, and play your movie one time.

   When the playhead reaches Frame 5, Flash starts playing the Scale sound and the Bucket Hit sound simultaneously.

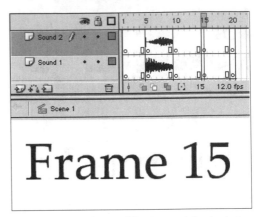

Figure 14.22 To make two different sounds begin playing simultaneously, you must put each sound in a different layer.

✔ Tip

■ All the information required to play an event sound lives in the keyframe to which you assigned that sound. When you play the movie, Flash pauses at that keyframe until all the information has downloaded. It's best to reserve Event Syncing for short sound clips; otherwise, your movie may be interrupted by long pauses for downloading sounds.

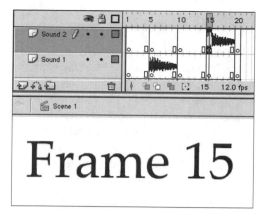

Figure 14.23 To change a sound's Sync setting, select the frame that contains the sound. Then, from the Frame Property Inspector's Sync pop-up menu, choose a new setting.

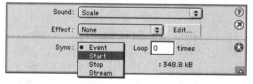

Figure 14.24 To prevent Flash from playing another instance of the sound, if that sound is already playing, choose Start from the Frame Property Inspector's Sync pop-up menu.

Using Start Sounds

Start sounds behave just like event sounds, with one important difference: Flash does not play a new instance of a start sound if that sound is already playing.

To set an assigned sound's Sync to Start:

1. Open the file that you created in "To play overlapping instances of the same sound" earlier in this chapter.

   You should have one instance of the Scale sound in Keyframe 5 and another in Keyframe 15. The second instance is in the Sound 1 or Sound 2 layer, depending on what you did in the earlier exercise.

2. In the Timeline, select the Keyframe 15 that contains the Scale sound (**Figure 14.23**).

3. In the Frame Property Inspector, from the Sync pop-up menu, choose Start (**Figure 14.24**).

4. Position the playhead in Frame 1, and play your movie one time.

   When the playhead reaches Frame 5, the Scale sound starts. When the playhead reaches Frame 15, nothing changes; you continue to hear just one voice as the Scale sound continues playing. When a sound is playing and Flash encounters another instance of the same sound, the Sync setting determines whether Flash plays that sound. When Sync is set to Start, Flash doesn't play another instance of the sound.

✔ Tip

- In movies that loop, the playback of event sounds can get confusing, because they can stack up on each loop. To avoid playing multiple instances of a sound, set the sound's Sync to Start. If the sound is still playing when Flash starts the movie again, Flash lets it play, adding nothing new. If the sound has finished playing, Flash plays the sound again when the playhead enters a keyframe containing the sound.

USING START SOUNDS

Using Streaming Sounds

Streaming sounds are specifically geared for playback over the Web. When Sync is set to Stream, Flash breaks a sound into smaller sound clips. Flash synchronizes these sub-clips with specific frames of the movie—as many frames as are required to play the sound. Flash stops streaming sounds when playback reaches a new keyframe or an instruction to stop playing either that specific sound or all sounds.

Unlike event sounds, which must download fully before they can play, streaming sounds can start playing after a few frames have downloaded. This situation makes streaming the best choice for long sounds, especially if you'll be delivering your movie over the Web.

The Mystery of Streaming Sound

When you choose Stream as the Sync setting for a sound, Flash divides that sound clip into smaller subclips and embeds them in individual frames. The movie's frame rate determines the subclips' size. In a movie with a frame rate of 10 frames per second (fps), for example, Flash divides streaming sounds into subclips that are a tenth of a second long. For every 10 frames, Flash plays 1 second of the sound.

Flash synchronizes the start of each subclip with a specific frame of the movie. If the sound plays back faster than the computer can draw frames, Flash sacrifices some visuals (doesn't draw some frames of the animation) so that sound and images match up as closely as possible. Streaming sound ensures, for example, that you hear the door slam when you see it swing shut—not a few seconds before. If the discrepancy between sound-playback speed and frame-drawing speed gets big enough, however, those dropped frames make the movie look jerky, just as it would if you set a low frame rate to begin with.

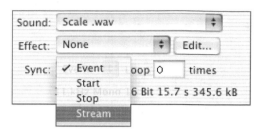

Figure 14.25 To make Flash force a sound to synchronize with specific frames of your movie, choose Stream from the Frame Property Inspector's Sync pop-up menu.

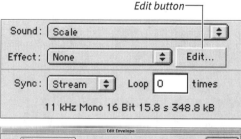

Edit button

Sound will stop playing here

Figure 14.26 When you set a sound's Sync to Stream, you can check how much of the sound will play, given the number of in-between frames your movie has for the sound to play in. Click the Frame Property Inspector's Edit button (top) to open the Edit Envelope window (bottom). This window displays a sound's full waveform in relation to time or to frame numbers.

To make an assigned sound a streaming sound:

1. Open a new copy of the SoundSync Template that you created earlier in this chapter. (Choose File > New From Template.)

2. In the Timeline, in the Sound 1 layer, remove keyframe status from Frame 10 (select it and choose Insert > Clear Keyframe).

3. In the Timeline, in the Sound 1 layer, select Keyframe 5.

4. In the Frame Property Inspector, from the Sound pop-up menu, choose Scale.

5. From the Sync pop-up menu, choose Stream (**Figure 14.25**).

6. To see how the sound fits into the available time in your movie, in the Sound section of the Frame Property Inspector, click the Edit button.

   The Edit Envelope window appears.

   At 15.8 seconds, the Scale sound is too long to play completely in the frames between Keyframe 5 and Keyframe 10. When Sync is set to Stream, Flash plays only as much of the sound as can fit in the frames that are available to it—in this case, slightly less than a second. In the Edit Envelope window, a vertical line indicates where Flash truncates this instance of the sound (**Figure 14.26**).

(continues on next page)

7. To close the Edit Envelope window, click OK or Cancel.

   The truncated waveform appears in frames 5 through 15 (**Figure 14.27**).

8. Position the playhead in Frame 1, and play your movie to hear the sound in action.

   When the playhead reaches Frame 5, the Scale sound starts. When the playhead reaches Frame 15, the keyframe span ends, and Flash stops playback of the Scale sound.

9. Choose Control > Test Movie to hear the sound in looping mode.

   Flash simply repeats the same snippet of sound, stopping it each time the movie reaches Frame 15.

✔ Tips

■ You can hear streaming sounds play as you drag the playhead through the Timeline (a technique called *scrubbing* in audio circles). As the playhead moves over the waveform, you can see how the images and sounds fit together. You can then add or delete frames to better synchronize the sounds with the images on-screen.

■ Shift-click the Timeline to take the playhead to a particular frame (or Shift-drag the playhead to that frame). As long as you hold down the mouse button, Flash repeats the portion of sound that synchronizes with that frame.

■ If you find that your streaming sound is getting cut off too soon, switch the units of measure in the Edit Envelope window to see how many frames you need to add to accommodate the sound (**Figure 14.28**).

Frame 5

Figure 14.27 There is time enough in the 10 frames between Keyframe 5 and Keyframe 15 to play only the first note of the Scale sound. Flash displays just that much of the full 15.8-second waveform in the Timeline.

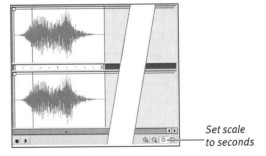

Set scale to seconds

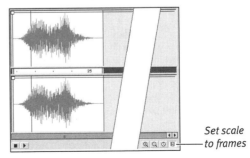

Set scale to frames

Figure 14.28 The scale for the waveform in the Edit Envelope window can be set to seconds (top) or frames (bottom). If you set the scale to frames, you can see exactly how many frames the movie needs to provide enough time for the major parts of the sound to finish. (For this sound, you would need 25 frames.) Usually, you want to make room for the segments of the wave that have the greatest amplitude.

The wolf-howl sound

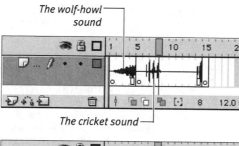

The cricket sound

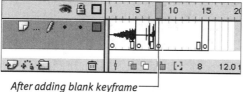

After adding blank keyframe

Figure 14.29 Inserting a new keyframe cuts off your view of the preceding sound's waveform in the Timeline. If the sound is an event sound, however, it continues playing through the keyframe.

Stopping Sounds

Although event sounds normally play to the end, you can force them to stop at a specific keyframe. To issue an instruction to stop a specific sound, you must set that sound's Sync parameter to Stop.

To stop playback of a sound:

1. Create a new 15-frame Flash document with two fairly long event sounds (at least 3 seconds); place one sound in Keyframe 1 and the other in Keyframe 5.

   (For more detailed instructions, see "Adding Sounds to Frames" earlier in this chapter.) In this example, Keyframe 1 contains the sound wolf howl, and Keyframe 5 contains the sound Cricket.

2. In the Timeline, insert a new blank keyframe at Frame 8 (**Figure 14.29**).

   Flash cuts off the waveform at Frame 8 because of the keyframe, but on playback, the event sounds continue to play after Frame 8.

3. Select Keyframe 8.

4. In the Frame Property Inspector, from the Sound pop-up menu, choose wolf_howl.

   (continues on next page)

5. From the Sync pop-up menu, choose Stop (**Figure 14.30**).

Flash uses this instruction to stop playback of the wolf-howl sound at Frame 8.

Flash places a small square in the middle of Keyframe 8 in the Timeline to indicate that the frame contains a stop-sound instruction (**Figure 14.31**).

6. Position the playhead in Frame 1, and play your movie to hear the sounds in action.

The wolf howl starts immediately; the crickets kick in at Frame 5. When the playhead reaches Frame 8, the wolf cuts out, but the crickets continue playing even after the playhead reaches the end of the movie.

✔ Tips

■ The Stop setting and the sound that it stops can be in different layers. The Stop setting stops playback of all instances of the specified sound that are currently playing in any layer.

■ If you want to stop only one instance of a sound, set the Sync parameter of that instance to Stream; then, in the layer containing that instance, put a blank keyframe in the frame where you want that instance of the sound to stop.

■ You can stop all sounds at the same time by adding the frame action stopAllSounds to your movie. For detailed instructions, see Chapter 12.

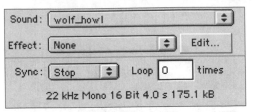

Figure 14.30 To stop a sound's playback at a specific point in a movie, create and then select the keyframe where the sound should stop. From the Frame Property Inspector's Sound pop-up menu, choose the sound you want to stop. From the Sync pop-up menu, choose Stop. Here, the Stop instruction refers to the wolf_howl sound.

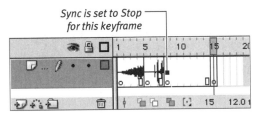

Figure 14.31 In the Timeline, a small square in the middle of a keyframe indicates the presence of the stop-sound instruction.

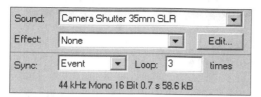

Figure 14.32 Typing a value in the Loop field tells Flash how many times to play the sound.

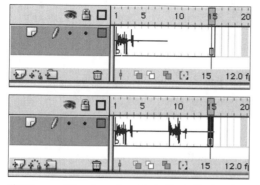

Figure 14.33 When Loop is set to 0, Flash displays just the original waveform in the Timeline (top). When Loop is set to 3, Flash displays as much of the repeated waveform as there is room for (bottom).

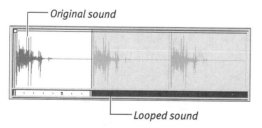

Figure 14.34 You can see a precise waveform for the repeated loops graphed against seconds or frames of your movie in the Edit Envelope window. The grayed-out waveforms are the looped portion of the sound.

Looping Sounds

Flash's sound-looping parameter allows you to repeat sounds without adding another instance of the sound to a frame. Type a value in the Loop field in the sound area (the right side) of the Frame Property Inspector. Flash plays the sound the specified number of times. You can loop event sounds and streaming sounds. The sound's Sync parameter applies to the whole set of repeated sounds.

To set a Loop value:

1. Create a 15-frame Flash document with a short event sound in Keyframe 1.

   This exercise uses the sound called Camera Shutter 35mm SLR from Flash's common library of sounds.

2. In the Timeline, select Frame 1.

3. In the sound area of the Frame Property Inspector, enter **3** in the Loop field (**Figure 14.32**).

   Flash extends the sound's waveform by stringing together three copies of it. In the Timeline, Flash displays as much of the extended waveform as will fit in the available frames (**Figure 14.33**).

✔ Tips

■ To see the extended waveform graphed against seconds or frames, in the Frame Property Inspector, click Edit. The full sound appears in the Edit Envelope window (**Figure 14.34**).

■ Because Flash links the repeated sounds and displays them as a single sound in the Edit Envelope window, you can edit the looping sound. You can change the volume so that the sound gets louder with each repetition, for example. You learn about editing sounds in the following section of this chapter.

Editing Sounds

Flash allows you to make limited changes in each instance of a sound in the Edit Envelope window. You can change the start and end point of the sound (that is, cut a piece off the beginning or end of the waveform) and adjust the sound's volume.

Flash offers six predefined volume edits: Left Channel, Right Channel, Fade Left to Right, Fade Right to Left, Fade In, and Fade Out. These sound-editing templates create common sound effects, such as making a sound grow gradually louder (Fade In) or softer (Fade Out), or (for stereo sounds) making the sound move from one speaker channel to the other.

To assign packaged volume effects:

1. Open the document that you created in the preceding exercise.

   This is a 15-frame movie with an event sound that loops three times in Frame 1.

2. In the Timeline, select Frame 1.

3. In the sound area of the Frame Property Inspector, click the Edit button.

   The Edit Envelope window appears (**Figure 14.35**).

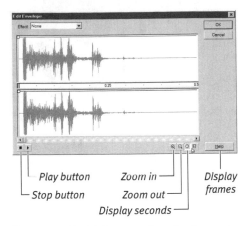

Play button
Stop button
Zoom in
Zoom out
Display seconds
Display frames

Figure 14.35 Flash lets you perform simple sound editing—for length and volume—in the Edit Envelope window.

Figure 14.36 The Effect pop-up menu in the Edit Envelope window offers six templates for common sound effects that deal with volume. You can also choose Custom to create your own effect.

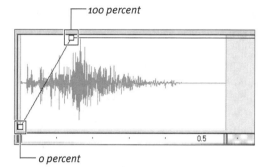

Figure 14.37 The Fade In effect brings the sound's envelope down to 0 percent (the bottom of the sound-editing window) at the start of the sound and quickly raises it to 100 percent (the top of the sound-editing window).

4. From the Effect pop-up menu, choose Fade In (**Figure 14.36**).

Flash adjusts the sound envelope (**Figure 14.37**). When the envelope line is at the top of the window, Flash plays 100 percent of the available sound. When the envelope line is at the bottom of the window, Flash plays 0 percent of the available sound.

5. Click the Play button to hear the sound with its fade-in effect.

The first iteration of the sound starts soft and grows louder. The repetitions play at full volume.

6. Click OK.

Flash returns you to movie-editing mode.

✔ Tip

■ If you don't need to look at your sound's waveform, you can bypass the Edit Envelope window. Just choose an effect from the Effect pop-up menu in the sound area of the Frame Property Inspector.

EDITING SOUNDS

To customize volume effects:

1. Using the movie that you created in the preceding exercise, select Keyframe 1.

2. To access the Edit Envelope window, in the sound area of the Frame Property Inspector, click the Edit button.

3. From the Effect pop-up menu, choose Custom (**Figure 14.38**).

4. In the Edit Envelope window, drag the square envelope handles that appear at the 0-second mark in both channels down to 0 percent.

5. In the right channel (the top section of the window), click the waveform at the 0.5-, 1.0-, and 1.3-second marks.

   Flash adds new envelope handles to both channels.

6. In the right-channel window, at the 0.5 second mark, drag the handle up to the 50 percent volume level (**Figure 14.39**).

7. Repeat step 6 for the left channel.

8. In both channels, drag the 1.0-second mark handles to the 50 percent level and the 1.3-second mark handles to the 100 percent level (**Figure 14.40**).

   You can add as many as eight handles to create a variety of volume changes within one sound.

9. Click the Play button to hear the sound with its fade-in effect.

   Flash fades in the first iteration of the sound, plays the second iteration at half volume, and plays the third iteration at full volume.

10. Click OK.

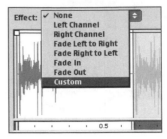

Figure 14.38 To edit the volume of a sound yourself, from the Effect pop-up menu in the Edit Envelope window, choose Custom.

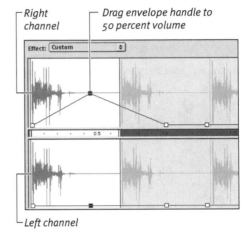

Right channel — Drag envelope handle to 50 percent volume

Left channel

Figure 14.39 Click the waveform in the sound-editing window to add a handle. Drag the handle to adjust the sound envelope. You can make the sound envelope the same or different for both channels. For monaural sounds, both waveforms are identical.

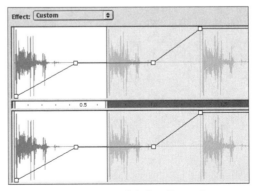

Figure 14.40 You can use eight handles to shape a sound's envelope. By using the zoom tools to view more of the sound in the Edit Envelope window, you can see the sound envelope for all three iterations of the sound. The first fades in, the second plays at 50 percent volume, and the third plays at full volume.

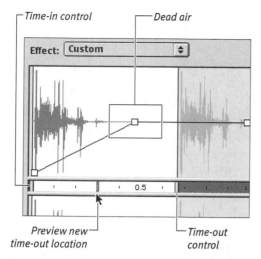

Time-in control · Dead air

Effect: [Custom]

Preview new time-out location · Time-out control

Figure 14.41 Flash lets you trim the beginning and end of a sound in the Edit Envelope window. Here, dragging the time-out control clips off the end of the sound (which is just very soft sound or silence).

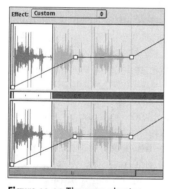

Effect: [Custom]

Figure 14.42 The new, shorter waveform appears in the Edit Envelope window.

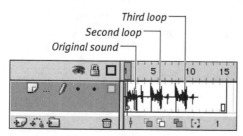

Third loop
Second loop
Original sound

Figure 14.43 After you shorten the sound, all three iterations fit into the 15-frame movie.

✔ Tips

- To remove unwanted envelope handles, drag them out of the sound-editing window.

- When you add a handle to one channel, Flash automatically adds another to the same location in the other channel. To create different volumes from the two channels, however, you can drag the handle to a different level in each channel.

In addition to changing a sound's volume, you can make a sound shorter by instructing Flash to omit some of it at the beginning, the end, or both. The Camera Shutter 35mm SLR sound has a lot of dead air (recorded silence) at the end that you can cut.

To edit sounds for length:

1. Using the movie that you created in the preceding exercise, select Frame 1.

2. To access the Edit Envelope window, in the Frame Property Inspector, click the Edit button.

3. In the Edit Envelope window, drag the time-out control to the 0.3-second mark (**Figure 14.41**).

   Flash shortens the sound in both channels (**Figure 14.42**).

4. Click OK.

   Flash returns you to movie-editing mode. Now all three iterations of the looping sound are visible in the Timeline (**Figure 14.43**).

✔ Tip

- Although you can change the start and end points of a sound in Flash, you still have the whole sound taking up room in your movie file. If you find yourself trimming many sounds in Flash, you should consider investing in a sound-editing program that allows you to leave the excess on the cutting-room floor rather than behind the curtains in Flash.

Importing Video

Before Flash MX, you did not have the ability to embed video clips in a Flash movie. You could simulate video by converting a video clip to a series of bitmap images and placing those images in sequential frames of a Flash movie. Your other option was to bring a linked QuickTime video into your Flash movie during the authoring phase, create Flash animations around it, and export the whole thing as a QuickTime file. This option limited your ability to provide interactivity, however, since QuickTime currently supports only those interactivity features available in Flash 4. (At the time this book was written, Apple had announced that QuickTime 6 will support Flash 5 files.)

You still have the option to work with linked QuickTime video clips, but Flash MX also allows you to embed video clips for playback directly in Flash Player. With embedded video, you can create movies that use all of Flash's animation and interactivity capabilities. In addition, anyone who has the Flash 6 player can play embedded video; there's no need for QuickTime or other plug-ins.

The first step to using video with Flash is to import the video file, just as you would import graphics or sounds from other external sources.

The Mystery of Video-Import Settings

The key to working with video in Flash is Sorenson Media's Spark codec. Spark carries out Flash's video import functions by encoding and decoding (compressing and decompressing) the video data to bring clips into Flash. Your goal—the ever-present juggling act for Web developers—is to balance quality and file size. Here's a quick overview of how Spark's video-import settings help you maintain that balance with video clips.

Keyframe Interval. The term *keyframe* here refers not to the keyframes you set in Flash, but to the crucial frames created as Spark compresses the video clip. To reduce the amount of information in the clip, Spark does not usually encode all the data required to re-create a full-frame image for every frame in the video clip (although you can tell it to do so). Spark encodes the full-frame image only for keyframes. For the other frames, Spark encodes information about how the frame differs from the preceding keyframe and uses that data to create an updated version of the keyframe. The Keyframe Interval setting tells Spark how often to encode a full frame. It's a bit of a brain-twister, but higher numbers here translate to smaller files sizes in your published movie. A higher number means a larger interval between keyframes, which means fewer keyframes, which in turn means that there will be less data to transmit for the finished Flash movie.

Quality. In addition to reducing the amount of video data by not describing each frame fully, Spark applies JPEG-like compression to the image data. A Quality setting of 100 gives you the most faithful rendition of the video information. A setting of 0 gives you a highly pixelated rendition. Here, lower numbers translate into smaller files sizes for the published movie.

Scale. The Scale setting (0 to 100 percent) allows you to reduce the dimensions of the video clip. Spark always retains the original aspect ratio (ratio of width to height) of your video clip. Once again, smaller numbers equal smaller file sizes for your published movie.

Synchronize. Video and Flash animation are both frame-based media, but when the frame rate of an embedded video clip differs from the frame rate of the Flash movie containing it, you can wind up with a situation reminiscent of a goat and a giraffe trying to keep pace with one another: The goat must take several steps to the giraffe's one, or the giraffe must reduce its stride.

When you check the Synchronize . . . checkbox, Spark encodes the video in a way that forces Flash to always preserve the original duration of the embedded video clip. If, for example, you have a 10-second, 10-frames-per-second (fps) clip, with the Synchronize . . . setting, the video lasts 10 seconds, no matter what the Flash movie's frame rate is. In a 5-fps Flash movie, Flash drops enough frames of the video clip so that the clip still takes just

10 seconds to play. In a 20-fps Flash movie, Flash duplicates video-clip frames so that the clip still takes a full 10 seconds to play.

If you uncheck the Synchronize checkbox, the frames go in lock step, but you get to control how the steps interlock by selecting the ratio of video frames to Flash frames. In the Number of Video Frames to Encode per Number of Macromedia Flash Frames section, you can choose from seven different ratios (1:1, 1:2, 1:3, 1:4, 1:8, 2:3, and 3:4). Take a look at importing the 10-second, 10-fps clip; uncheck the Synchronize checkbox . . . and choose a frame-encoding ratio of 1:1 (one video frame for each Flash frame). Placed in a 5-fps Flash movie, the clip takes twice as long to play completely (20 seconds); in a 20-fps Flash movie, the clip takes just half as long (10 seconds).

Import Audio. If your video clip contains audio that's sampled at 44.100Hz, 22.050Hz, 11.025Hz, or 5.50125Hz, you can import the audio together with the video. (Note that Flash does not treat this audio as a sound symbol. You will not see its waveform in the Timeline, and you cannot control its streaming or playback as you learned to do with sounds earlier in this chapter.) You can also choose to import the video without its audio component. If the video clip contains audio sampled at a rate that's not supported, Flash warns you that you cannot import the audio track.

To import links to QuickTime video clips:

1. Create the Flash document in which you want to place the linked video, and select the keyframe in which you want the video to start.

2. From the File menu, choose Import or press ⌘-R (Mac) or Ctrl-R (Windows). The standard file-import dialog box appears.

3. From the Show pop-up menu (Mac) or the Files of Type pop-up menu (Windows), choose QuickTime Movie (**Figure 14.44**). The dialog box displays only QuickTime files.

4. Navigate to a QuickTime file on your system, and select the file.

5. Click Open. The Import Video dialog box appears.

6. Under Import Options, choose Link to External Video File (**Figure 14.45**).

7. Click OK. If the span for the selected keyframe contains fewer frames than the linked video clip, the Macromedia Flash warning dialog box appears, asking whether you want to add enough frames to display the entire linked clip (**Figure 14.46**).

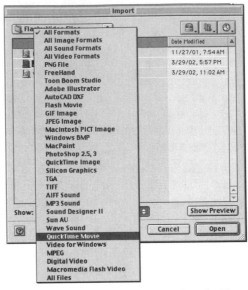

Figure 14.44 Choose QuickTime Movie from the Show (Mac) or Files of Type (Windows) pop-up menu in the Import dialog box to locate QuickTime files for import.

Figure 14.45 The Import Video dialog box gives you the choice of linking a QuickTime video clip or embedding it.

Figure 14.46 Flash can expand the selected keyframe span automatically to accommodate every frame in the video clip that you are importing.

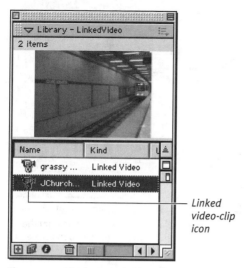

Linked
video-clip
icon

Figure 14.47 The imported video clips live in the library of the active Flash document.

What Video Formats Does Flash Accept?

Flash imports Macromedia Flash Video Format (.flv) files directly. The .flv format is one created by Flash itself and by Sorenson Media's Squeeze codec. (Squeeze is the professional version of Spark and offers more features for manipulating and compressing your video.) To import other video formats, you will need to have a codec or a program that acts as a translator installed on your system. With QuickTime 4 (or a later version) installed on Windows and Macintosh, you can import .mov, .mpg, .mpeg, .dv, and .avi files. On the Windows platform, you can also use DirectX 7 (or a later version) to import .wmv, .asf, .mpg, .mpeg, and .avi files.

8. To enlarge the keyframe span, click Yes. Flash adds enough frames to the span to reveal the entire video clip.

or

To retain the current number of frames in the keyframe span, click No. Flash truncates the video clip to fit in the existing frames.

Flash adds the linked video clip to the active document's library and places an instance of the linked video clip on the Stage. The video frames appear on the Stage within the frames of the keyframe span.

Flash identifies linked video clips by their own icon (a small movie camera with a chain link attached) in the library and lists them as Linked Video in the Kind column (**Figure 14.47**).

✔ Tips

■ Tired of seeing that warning dialog about insufficient frames? Check the Don't Show Me This Message Again checkbox. Then click yes to have Flash always add sufficient frames to display the full video clip. Click no to have Flash truncate imported clips. To restore your choice in the matter, reset the preference for showing or skipping this warning in the Warnings tab of the Preferences dialog box. (Choose Edit > Preferences to access the dialog box.)

■ Even when you refuse to allow Flash to add frames when you place an instance of a video clip on the Stage, the full clip is there. You can add frames to the span later to reveal more of the video clip.

■ To import the video without placing an instance on the Stage, choose File > Import to Library.

To bring embedded video clips into a Flash movie:

1. Follow steps 1 and 2 of the preceding exercise.

2. From the Show pop-up menu (Mac) or the Files of Type pop-up menu (Windows), choose All Video Formats (**Figure 14.48**). Flash displays all the video files that you can import.

3. Navigate to and select the video file on your system.

4. Click Open.

   For QuickTime files, the Import Video dialog box appears. Under Import Options, choose Embed Video in Macromedia Flash Document, and click OK (**Figure 14.49**). The Import Video Settings dialog box appears.

   For all other types of video files, the Import Video Settings dialog box appears immediately (**Figure 14.50**). (To learn more about these settings, see the sidebar "The Mystery of Video-Import Settings" earlier in this chapter.)

5. To optimize compression for the video clip, *do the following:*

   ▲ In the Quality field, enter a value between 0 and 100. The lower the number, the more pixelated the video will appear, but the smaller the published movie will be.

   ▲ In the Keyframe Interval field, enter a value between 0 and 48. Higher values (that is, larger intervals between full video keyframes) translate to smaller file sizes for your published movie but lower quality in the video images.

   ▲ In the Scale field, enter a value between 1 and 100 percent. Reducing the dimensions of the embedded video clip results in smaller file sizes for your published movie.

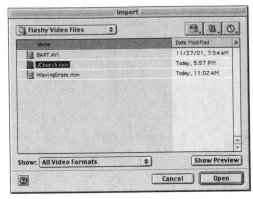

Figure 14.48 To view all the video files available for import by Flash, choose All Video Formats from the Show (Mac) or Files of Type (Windows) pop-up menu in the Import dialog box.

Figure 14.49 When you import QuickTime movies, you have the choice to import a link to the source file or to embed the video clip directly in Flash.

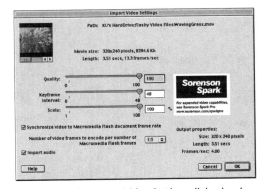

Figure 14.50 The Import Video Settings dialog box is your interface with the Sorenson Spark codec. Spark encodes and compresses the video file on import. Use the Import Video Settings to balance file size and quality.

Figure 14.51 Unlike movie clips, which display only their first frame in movie-editing mode, the changing frames of an imported video clip appear on the Stage in each frame of the span containing the clip.

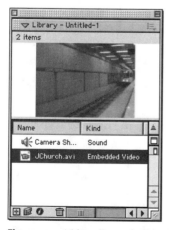

Figure 14.52 Video-clip symbols bear their own identifying icon. Check the Kind column in the Library window to see whether the video is for linking or embedding.

6. To set synchronization between the video clip's frames and the Flash movie's frames, *do one of the following:*

   ▲ To enable Flash to drop or add frames to the video to ensure that it retains its original duration during playback in Flash, check the Synchronize Video to Macromedia Flash Document Frame Rate checkbox.

   ▲ To allow the playback time of the video clip to change, but to retain all of the clip's frames, deselect Synchronize Video to Macromedia Flash Document Frame Rate, and from the pop-up menu, choose a video-to-Flash frame-encoding ratio.

7. To import an audio track (when one is available at a supported sampling rate), check the Import Audio checkbox.

8. Click OK.

   The Importing dialog box appears, displaying a progress bar and a Stop button for canceling the import operation.

   If the span for the selected keyframe contains fewer frames than the embedded video clip, a warning dialog box appears, asking whether you want to add enough frames to display the entire clip.

9. To enlarge the keyframe span, click Yes. Flash adds enough frames to the span to reveal the entire video clip.

   or

   To retain the current number of frames in the keyframe span, click No.

   Flash adds the embedded video clip to the active document's library and places an instance of it on the Stage. The video frames appear on the Stage within the frames of the keyframe span (**Figure 14.51**).

   Flash identifies embedded video clips with their own icon (a small movie camera) in the library and lists them as Embedded Video in the Kind column (**Figure 14.52**).

IMPORTING VIDEO

505

Using Embedded Video Clips in Your Movie

Embedded video clips bear similarities to other symbols, yet they are a distinct and unique type of element. As with bitmaps, you can update video clips, automatically bringing in a new copy of a file you edited with an external editor. Like graphic animation symbols, video clips play within—and must synchronize with—frames within the main movie Timeline. Like sound clips, video clips can contain audio, although you cannot see the sound's waveform in the Timeline. If you place video clips within Flash movie clip symbols, you give the video an independent Timeline, and you gain the full control over the video-clip object that you have over movie-clip objects.

As with any symbol, you place an instance of a video clip by dragging a copy from the Library window to the Stage. The Property Inspector gives you information about selected instances of embedded video clips.

More About Modifying and Animating Video Clips

You can modify the size, shape, and location of the video clip, and even use video clips for motion tweens; you can name the instance and target it with ActionScript. But you cannot change the color or transparency of the clip. To gain control of a video clip's brightness, tint, and alpha properties, you must place the embedded video clip within a movie-clip symbol. You can then manipulate that movie-clip instance to change its color, transparency, and so on.

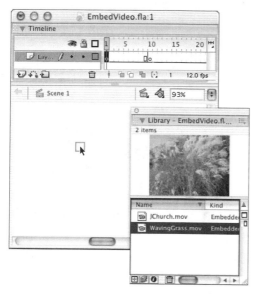

Figure 14.53 To put video clips into action, you must drag an instance from the Library window to the Stage.

To place embedded video clips in your movie:

1. Open the document in which you want to use video clips.

2. Import the video clips as described in the preceding exercise.

3. In the Timeline, select the keyframe in which you want the video clip to start playing.

4. From the Library window, drag a copy of an embedded video clip to the Stage (**Figure 14.53**).

   Unlike movie clips, which play in their own independent Timeline, embedded video clips need to fit their frames into the frames of the Timeline of the movie or movie clip containing them. Each time you drag an instance of the video clip to the Stage, if the span for the selected keyframe contains fewer frames than the embedded video clip, the Macromedia Flash warning dialog box appears, asking whether you want to add enough frames to display the entire linked clip.

5. To enlarge the keyframe span, click Yes.

   Flash adds enough frames to the span to reveal the entire video clip.

   or

   To retain the current number of frames in the keyframe span, click No.

   Flash places the video clip on the Stage, but restricts it to displaying the number of frames in the keyframe span in which you place it.

You can modify a selected instance of a video clip in many (but not all) of the ways that you modify other objects in Flash.

To modify video-clip instances:

1. On the Stage, select the instance of the video clip that you want to modify.

2. To modify the selected instance, *use any of the following methods:*

   ▲ With the arrow tool, reposition the video-clip instance on the Stage.

   ▲ With the free-transform tool, scale, rotate, and/or skew the video-clip instance (**Figure 14.54**). The Distort and Envelope modifiers do not work on video-clip instances.

   ▲ In the Embedded Video Property Inspector, enter new height and width, and/or *x* and *y* values to change the dimensions and location of the video-clip instance (**Figure 14.55**).

   ▲ In the Info panel, enter new height and width and/or *x* and *y* values to change the dimensions and location of the video-clip instance.

   ▲ In the Transform panel, enter new values to scale, rotate, or skew the video-clip instance.

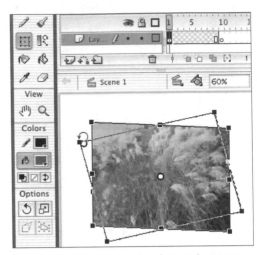

Figure 14.54 Using the free-transform tool, you can scale, rotate, and skew a video-clip instance. The free-transform tool's Distort and Envelope modifiers do not work with video clips.

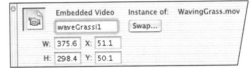

Figure 14.55 When you select an instance of an embedded video clip, the Embedded Video Property Inspector displays information about that clip. Changing values in the Width, Height, *x*, and/or *y* fields modifies the selected clip.

Figure 14.56 To access a video clip's properties, select the clip in the Library window; then choose Properties from the Options pop-up menu.

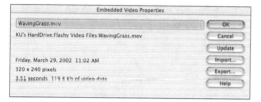

Figure 14.57 To import automatically the latest version of the selected video clip's source file, click the Update button in the Embedded Video Properties dialog box.

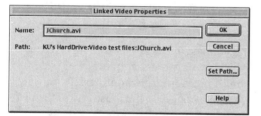

Figure 14.58 The Set Path button in the Linked Video Properties dialog box enables you to enter a new path to a linked video clip by navigating to the file in its current location.

Updating Video Clips

Allthough you cannot edit video clips directly in Flash, you can update embedded video clips that you have edited with external video-editing sofware without going through the full import routine. You can also change the path to linked video clips.

To update embedded video clips:

1. Open the Flash document containing the embedded video clip that needs to be updated.

2. In the Library window, select the embedded video clip.

   If the window is not open, choose Window > Library.

3. From the Options pop-up menu in the top-right corner of the Library window, choose Properties, or double-click the selected clip's name in the Library window (**Figure 14.56**).

   The Embedded Video Properties dialog box appears (**Figure 14.57**).

4. Click the Update button.

   Flash reimports the file.

✔ Tip

- When you follow the steps of the preceding exercise but select a linked video clip in the library, you don't have the choice of updating the clip. You do have the option to change the directory path to the linked file (**Figure 14.58**). To update a linked video clip, select it in the Library window; then, from the Options pop-up menu in the top-right corner of the window, choose Update. A dialog box appears in which you can select the video clip for updating. In addition, Flash automatically updates linked video each time you close and reopen the Flash file containing the linked clip.

You can swap one embedded video clip for another embedded video clip, and you can swap a linked video clip for another linked video clip, but you cannot mix and match linked and embedded clips in a swap, nor can you swap a video clip for a movie clip or any other type of symbol.

To swap video clips:

1. Open a file containing video-clip instances used in the movie.

2. On the Stage, select an instance of a linked video clip.

3. Access the Linked Video Property Inspector.
   If the panel isn't open, choose Window > Properties.

4. Click the Swap button
   The Swap Linked Video dialog box appears (**Figure 14.59**).

5. In the list of available video clips, select the replacement clip.

6. Click OK.
   Flash places an instance of the replacement clip on the Stage.

Figure 14.59 With a video clip selected on the Stage, clicking the Swap button in the Property Inspector lets you substitute a different clip. You can swap one embedded video clip for another embedded clip or one linked clip for another linked clip, but you can't mix and match.

Previewing Video Clips in a Movie

For linked QuickTime video clips, Flash displays only the first frame of the video in the authoring environment. To preview the full video, you must use one of the test modes (choose Control > Test Scene or Control > Test Movie).

Embedded video clips do display their images within the keyframe span that contains the clip during authoring. You can simply play the movie (choose Control > Play) or move the playhead through the Timeline to view the changing video frames. If the embedded audio has an audio track, however, you must use one of the test modes to preview the sound.

INTRODUCING COMPLEX INTERACTIVITY

In Chapters 12 and 13, you created scripts for frames and objects that used simple actions to control the playback of a single Timeline. As you explore the full Actions set, you begin to work with more complex parameters. These complex actions allow you to manipulate objects within the main movie and within movie clips, and control their Timelines; test for the truth of certain conditions; retrieve information from user input, other movies, and other types of files; and control the programs that display your movies.

The ways in which you can combine the elements of a movie with actions are too varied and advanced to cover in this book. But to get you started, this chapter takes you through some of the basic concepts that you need to create complex actions.

Changing the Properties of Objects

An object that you are already familiar with is the movie clip. All its defining characteristics—height, width, transparency, and so on—are called its *properties*. When you are authoring a movie, you can change these characteristics with Flash's drawing tools, but ActionScripts let you modify an object's properties during playback.

To script a button that makes a movie clip invisible:

1. Create a new Flash document, and place an instance of a movie clip and a button on the Stage in Keyframe 1.

2. On the Stage, select the movie clip instance.

3. In the Property Inspector's Instance Name field, enter a name for the instance, such as starMC1 (**Figure 15.1**).

4. On the Stage, select the button instance.

5. In the Property Inspector's Instance Name field, enter hideBTN.

6. In the Actions-Button panel, from the Add menu, choose Actions > Movie Control > on.
   Flash adds the button handler to the Script pane.

7. With the handler (Line 1 of the script) selected, in the Actions Toolbox, double-click Actions > Movie Clip Control > setProperty (**Figure 15.2**).
   Flash adds the setProperty action to Line 2 in the Script pane and displays fields for entering the appropriate parameters.

8. From the Property pop-up menu, choose _visible (Visibility) (**Figure 15.3**).
   The _visible property has two possible states (or values): true (the object is visible) or false (the object is disabled and hidden).

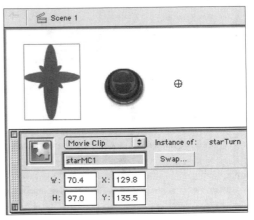

Figure 15.1 To make a movie clip the target of ActionScript, you must give the clip an instance name in the Property Inspector.

Figure 15.2 You can create a button script that will control your movie clip by choosing actions from the Actions > Movie Clip Control category in the Actions Toolbox (shown) or from the Add menu.

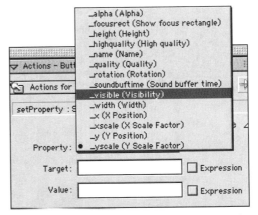

Figure 15.3 In Normal mode, the parameters area of the Actions panel offers a pop-up menu of properties that you can set for movie-clip objects when you add setProperty to a script. Visibility controls whether viewers can see the movie clip.

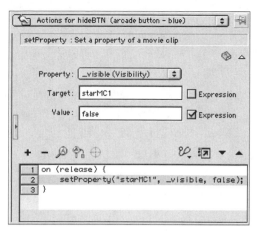

setProperty : Set a property of a movie clip

Property: _visible (Visibility)

Target: starMC1   ☐ Expression

Value: false   ☑ Expression

```
1  on (release) {
2      setProperty("starMC1", _visible, false);
3  }
```

Figure 15.4 By setting the parameters of the setProperty action, you tell Flash which object to manipulate and what to do with it. Here, setting the visibility property of the starMC1 movie clip to false will hide the movie clip.

Terminology: Expressions and Variables

Expressions and variables go hand in hand. If creating ActionScripts were like cooking, expressions would be the recipes, and variables would be the bowls, cups, pans, and other containers. The values would be the ingredients that you place in the containers.

The recipe/expression might say, "Combine the contents of the red bowl and the green bowl, and put it in the blue pan." If you put eggs in the red bowl and milk in the green bowl, you'll get one dish. If you put tomatoes in the red bowl and pasta in the green bowl, you'll get quite another. Although the containers are the same, and although the instructions for combining their contents are the same, the variety of the contents makes for different results.

When you create a movie clip and place it on the Stage, its default visibility is true. To script a button that hides the clip, you must set the clip's visibility to false.

9. In the Target field, enter the instance name of the movie clip, starMC1.

This parameter tells Flash which object you want to perform the action on.

10. In the Value field, enter false, and check the Expression checkbox.

Checking the Expression checkbox tells Flash to interpret what you enter in the Value field as a description of the value, not as a set of the particular letters *f, al, l, s,* and *e* (**Figure 15.4**).

11. Choose Control > Test Movie to try out your button.

When you click the button, the movie clip disappears.

✔ Tips

■ Try duplicating the button, naming it showBTN. The duplicate has the same ActionScript attached. In the Script pane, double-click Line 2 to display the parameters of the _visible property. In the Value field, enter true. Now you have one button that makes the clip disappear and another that brings it back.

■ Play around with the various properties in the pop-up Property menu. Try changing the movie clip's width, height, or alpha setting, for example. If you're not sure what type of value to enter for a given property, look at the property in the Reference panel (choose Window > Reference) to see a description and examples.

■ The letters *MC* in the instance name are not required; they are just a mnemonic device to help you determine what you are dealing with when you see it in the somewhat cryptic context of a script.

Terminology: *Syntax*

ActionScript has its own rules, which are analogous to the rules of grammar and spelling in English. These rules, called *syntax*, govern such things as word order, capitalization, and punctuation of action statements. When you set the Actions panel to operate in Normal mode, Flash enters the statements you choose and handles most of the details of syntax for you. The following list briefly describes common ActionScript punctuation marks.

Dot (.). ActionScript uses *dot syntax*, meaning that periods act as links between objects and the *properties* (characteristics) and *methods* (behaviors) applied to them. In the statement

```
cloneMC._duplicateMovieClip
```

the dot (the period) links the movie clip named cloneMC with the method that creates a copy of the movie clip.

The dot also indicates the hierarchy of files and folders in path names, similar to the way that a slash does in HTML syntax. (Note that Flash 4 used slashes to indicate path names. Flash MX still recognizes this *slash syntax*, but Macromedia recommends using dot syntax, and that's what you'll find in this book.)

Semicolon (;). A semicolon indicates the end of a statement. The semicolon is not required—Flash interprets the end of the line of statements correctly without it—but including it is good scripting practice. The semicolon also acts as a separator in some action statements.

Braces ({}). Braces set off ActionScript statements that belong together. A set of actions that take place after on (release), for example, must be set off by braces.

Note that the action statements within braces can require their own beginning and ending braces. The opening and closing braces must pair up evenly. When you use Normal mode and Basic Actions, Flash enters the pairs of braces for you. You still need to pay attention to where you are adding scripts within the Script pane, however, to ensure that you group the actions as you intend.

Parentheses (). Parentheses group the arguments that apply to a particular statement—defining the scene and frame in a goto action, for example. Parentheses also allow you to group operations, such as mathematical calculations, so that they take place in the right order.

The Mystery of Naming Variables

In naming variables, you must always start with a letter or an underscore character. To make the variable name a sort of mnemonic description of itself, you can use multiple words or word fragments, but you cannot use the space character to separate the words. ActionScript reserves the space character to act as a separator between action statements. Instead, use internal capitalization to make the multi-word names easier to decipher (myVariable, for example). You can also use the underscore character as a separator. All other punctuation, however, is forbidden in variable names.

Instance Names versus Variables for Text Boxes

Flash gives you two ways to name and target a text box, the instance name and the variable name. Usually, you will want to use an instance name. You must use instance names if you want to control the text field itself, using ActionScript to reposition it or change its size or rotation or font, for example. When you give the text box a variable name, the box displays the contents of the variable; by using ActionScript to change the variable's content, you can display new content within the text box. Using ActionScript to change the text property of the text box instance allows you to manipulate and change its contents without using variables.

Creating Scriptable Text Objects

In Chapter 2, you learned to create editable text blocks. But in the published movie, that text is just a graphic element, not an object that ActionScript can interact with. Only text within text boxes whose type is Input or Dynamic can be manipulated with scripts.

To enable ActionScript to recognize the text box and manipulate its properties, you must give the text box an instance name. Although text boxes have different properties than movie clips, the procedures for naming and targeting a text box instance are just like those you learned for targeting movie clip instances earlier in this chapter. You can also give a dynamic or input text box a variable name and use ActionScript to target the variable, thereby manipulating the contents of the text box.

A *variable* is basically a container for storing information. That information could be numbers, letters, or mathematical formulas. The important thing about variables is that they are, well, variable and that ActionScript can put things into them and take things out of them, and generally muck about with their contents.

The container might be represented by an element in your movie, or it might be just an abstract container in Flash's electronic brain. It's easiest to start with the more concrete version. Create a text box into which your viewers can enter information: the input text box. Next, create a text box in which the results of your manipulation of that information will appear: the dynamic text box. (You'll learn about doing the actual manipulation in the next section.)

To create an input text box:

1. Open a new Flash file.

2. In the Toolbox, select the text tool.

3. In the Property Inspector, from the Text Type pop-up menu, choose Input Text. The panel displays the parameters for text boxes that allow users to enter text (**Figure 15.5**).

4. On the Stage, in Keyframe 1, create a text box that contains the word *Age*.

5. To assign a name to the variable, in the Property Inspector's Variable field, enter *age*VAR (**Figure 15.6**).

   Giving the variable a name makes it recognizable to Flash via ActionScript. You use this variable name when you write scripts. You might, for example, tell Flash to retrieve whatever data your movie viewers enter in the text box with this variable name.

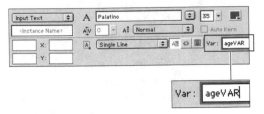

Figure 15.6 To assign a variable name to a text box, enter the new name in the Variable field.

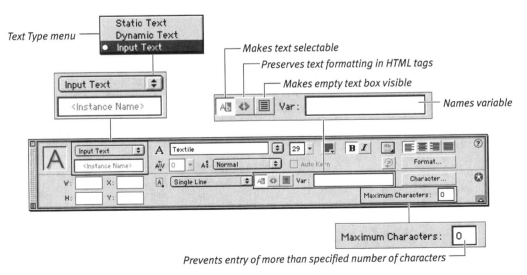

Figure 15.5 To access the parameters for creating text boxes that accept input from your movie's viewers, choose Input Text from the Text Type pop-up menu. The input parameters control the field's appearance and function—giving the text field a border and background, for example, so that the field is visible in the final movie even if it's empty.

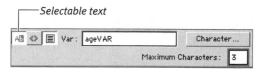

Selectable text

Figure 15.7 To create an input text box that allows end users to select the contents of the text box before entering new text, click the Selectable button in the Property Inspector for text.

6. To make your text box visible in the movie even when the box contains no text, click the Border button.

7. To restrict the length of the text box, in the Maximum Characters field, enter 3.

This setting prevents users from inadvertently typing an impossible age.

8. To allow viewers of your movie to select and replace the word *Age* in the published movie, click the Selectable button (**Figure 15.7**).

9. Leave all other options at their default settings.

✔ Tips

■ To ensure that text boxes in the published movie look exactly as you planned, you can include outlines for rendering all (or part) of the font used in your input text box. Click the Character button in the bottom-right quadrant of the text Property Inspector to access the Character Options dialog box. You can opt to embed font outlines for all characters or various subsets of characters. Or you can skip embedding font outlines altogether.

■ The letters *VAR* in this variable's name are not required; they are just a mnemonic device. As you begin to learn ActionScript, such reminders can help you determine of what type of item you are dealing with when you see it in the somewhat cryptic context of a script.

CREATING SCRIPTABLE TEXT OBJECTS

To create a dynamic text box:

1. Using the file you created in the preceding exercise, with the text tool create a text box that contains the words *Lucky Number.*

2. With the text box still active, access the Property Inspector for text.

3. From the Text Type pop-up menu, choose Dynamic Text.

    The Property Inspector displays the parameters for dynamic text (**Figure 15.8**).

4. In the Variable field, enter LuckyNumVAR.

5. To prevent viewers from typing in this field accidentally, uncheck the Selectable checkbox.

6. Leave all other options at their default settings.

✔ Tip

■ In this example, the text boxes don't contain lengthy text. If you need to, you can make dynamic or input text boxes scrollable either as you create them or via ActionScript. To create scrollable text boxes during authoring, with the arrow tool, select the text box. Then Control-click (Mac) or right-click (Windows) the text box, and from the contextual menu, choose Scrollable.

Figure 15.8 The Dynamic Text parameters are similar to the Input Text parameters.

Manipulating Variables

Figure 15.9 The first step in creating a button that manipulates the text your users input is directing Flash to the variable that holds that text. Choose set variable from the Actions > Variables category.

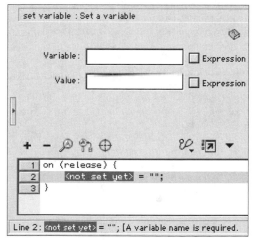

Figure 15.10 The highlighted code in the Script pane indicates a problem in the script. Flash further describes the problem in the parameters area of the Actions panel. The phrase <not set yet> is a placeholder for the name of the variable to be manipulated. You must fill in the variable's name.

You can use ActionScript to manipulate the information contained in variables. You might take the information from an input text box, perform some mathematical operation on it, and then display the result in a dynamic text box. The variable names are what allow you to tell Flash where to get existing information and where to display new information. You do this within an ActionScript by using the set variable action. The process of telling Flash what information to put in a variable is called *assigning* the variable.

To create a button script that manipulates variables:

1. Continuing with the file you created in the preceding exercises, on the Stage, in Keyframe 1, place an instance of a button.

2. With the arrow tool, select the button.

3. Access the Actions-Button panel.

4. In the Actions Toolbox, in the Actions > Variable category, double-click set variable (**Figure 15.9**).

   Flash updates the Script pane to look like **Figure 15.10**.

   Flash highlights the words <not set yet> in red to indicate that you must define the parameters of this action. The parameters for the variable appear in the parameters pane.

5. With Line 2 of the script selected, in the parameters area, in the Variable field, enter the variable name luckyNumVAR.

   This field tells Flash where to put the value that you are about to enter. In this case, the value goes into the dynamic text box containing the words *Lucky Number*.

(continues on next page)

519

6. Check the Expression checkbox to the right of the Value field.

Checking Expression tells Flash that this field contains, not the value itself, but a formula for calculating the value.

7. In the Value field, enter the following:

`Number (ageVAR) + 2`

This code tells Flash to add 2 to the number contained in the `ageVAR` variable that you created in "Creating Scriptable Text Objects" (**Figure 15.11**). The script takes whatever number your viewer types in the *Age* text box and adds 2 to it mathematically. (If the age entered is 76, for example, the result is 78.) Here, `Number` tells Flash to treat the data in the variable as a number, not as a string of characters. If you were to omit `Number` and enter just `ageVAR + 2`, the script would *concatenate* the numbers—that is, join them in one long text string (762, in this example).

8. From the Control menu, choose Test Movie to try out your manipulation script.

9. Type a number in the editable text box containing the word *Age*.

10. Click the button.

Flash adds 2 to the number that you typed and displays the total in the text box that previously contained the words *Lucky Number* (**Figure 15.12**).

✔ Tip

■ You can use the Actions Toolbox to help you enter expressions in the Script pane. With the Value field selected in the parameters area, click the Functions > Conversion Functions category, for example, and then double-click `Number`. Flash enters the word *number,* followed by parentheses, in the Script pane and in the Value field of the parameters area. Click Operators > Arithmetic Operators and then double-click the plus sign to have Flash enter the addition operator.

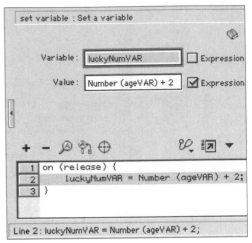

Figure 15.11 This script tells Flash to put the result of the Value-field formula in the variable named in the Variable field, in this case, `luckyNumVAR`, which corresponds to the text box containing the words `Lucky Number`.

Figure 15.12 In Test mode, select the *Age* text box (top), and enter a number. When you click the button, Flash adds 2 to the number you entered and places the result in the Lucky Number text box (bottom).

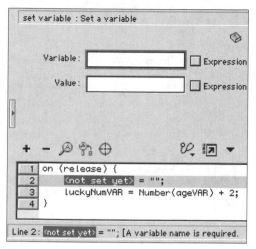

Figure 15.13 To create a variable without a text box, use the set variable action, and fill in the variable name and value.

Creating an Invisible Variable

In the preceding exercise, you set up variables when you created special types of text boxes. These text boxes make the contents of the variable visible, both to you (the Flash author) and the viewers of your movie. You might think of a variable that has no associated text box as being an invisible variable, because neither you nor your target audience will ever see the contents of the variable directly (although as the author, you will see the variable within the script). To create a variable that has no representation on the Stage—a process called *declaring* a variable—you can use the set variable action.

Instead of directing your script to put the result of your mathematical calculations in the Lucky Number text box, you can put the results in an invisible variable where you might perform several calculations before outputting the result.

To declare a new invisible variable:

1. Continuing with the file you created in the preceding exercise, select the button instance on the Stage.

2. In the Actions-Button panel, select Line 1 in the Script pane.

3. From the Add menu, choose Actions > Variables > set variable.

   Flash updates the Script pane to look like **Figure 15.13**. The highlighted words <not set yet> indicate that you must name the variable.

(continues on next page)

4. With Line 2 selected in the Script pane, in the Variable field, enter the variable name holdStuffVAR.

This field tells Flash to put the value that you are about to enter in a variable that exists only in the electronic world of Flash.

5. Check the Expression checkbox to the right of the Value field.

Flash highlights the placeholder <not set yet> in the Value field and in the Script pane (**Figure 15.14**).

6. In the Value field, enter Number (ageVAR) + 2.

7. In the Script pane, select Line 3.

8. In the Value field, enter holdStuffVAR * 2.

This line of the script instructs Flash to take the contents of your invisible variable and multiply it by 2. Your script should look like **Figure 15.15**. Now you're ready to see the script at work.

9. From the Control menu, choose Test Movie to try out your variable-manipulation script.

10. Type a number in the Age text box.

11. Click the button.

Flash adds 2 to the number you entered, temporarily stores the resulting number in the invisible variable, multiplies that number by 2, and places that result in the Lucky Number text box.

✔ **Tip**

■ You don't actually have to use the set variable action to create a new invisible variable. Simply entering a name and using the *assignment operator* (otherwise known as an equals sign) is enough to let Flash know that you are setting up a variable.

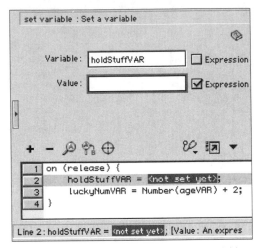

Figure 15.14 When you set the value of your variable to be an expression by checking the Expression checkbox, Flash warns you that you still need to enter the formula for the value by highlighting the placeholder text <not set yet> in the Script pane.

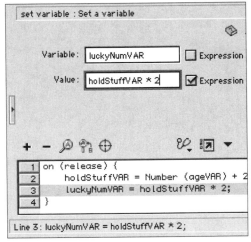

Figure 15.15 This script places the result of your first calculation (adding 2 to the number entered in the Age text box) into an invisible container—the variable named holdStuffVAR. Then Flash multiplies that number by 2 and places the result in the Lucky Number text box.

Using Conditional Actions

Conditional actions allow you to ask certain questions (or test whether conditions have been met) and make Flash carry out another action if the answer is true (or the conditions have been met). You could ask Flash to determine, for example, whether the number that is currently in the variable *ageVAR* is greater than 59. If it is, you could instruct Flash to jump to a frame that describes discounts for senior citizens.

The basic conditional action is if. You use if to test the validity of a given statement. You might, for example, test whether the last frame of your movie loaded. You can use that information in conjunction with a looping teaser animation to tell your viewers that there will be a wait to download information.

To test for download of a frame:

1. Create a 100-frame Flash file, and make every tenth frame a keyframe containing identifying text.

2. In the first 20 frames, create a simple animation that will play while the user waits for the entire file to download.

   You might create a 20-frame animation of a ball moving around a rectangle containing the message "One moment while I get that for you ..."

3. In frames 30 through 100, add a couple of bitmapped graphics, plenty of sounds, and/or video clips to ensure that the file is large.

   The larger the file, the longer it takes to download and the more time you'll have to check your preload message.

   (continues on next page)

4. In the Timeline, add a new layer to contain your actions, and label it Actions.

5. In the Actions layer, select Keyframe 1.

6. In the Actions-Frame panel, in the Actions Toolbox, Actions > Conditions/Loops category, double-click if (**Figure 15.16**).

Flash updates the Script pane with the following code:

```
if (<not set yet>){

}
```

7. In the parameters area, in the Conditions field, enter _framesloaded >= 100.

Flash updates Line 1 of the Script with the condition you enter (**Figure 15.17**). Here, the condition is "Has frame 100 loaded?"

8. With Line 1 selected in the Script pane, from the Add menu, choose Actions > Movie Control > goto.

Flash adds gotoAndPlay(1); to Line 2 in the script pane and displays the goto action's parameters.

Figure 15.16 To create an ActionScript that checks when a frame is loaded, from the Actions Toolbox or the Add menu in the Actions panel, choose Actions > Conditions/Loops > if.

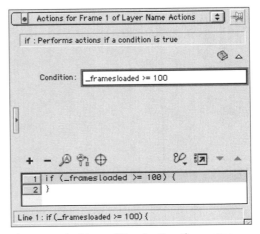

Figure 15.17 In this conditional action, the greater-than-or-equal-to symbol (referred to in ActionScript as a *comparison operator*) tells Flash to check whether the item on its left side is greater than or equal to the item on its right side. In this case, is the number of the frame most recently loaded 100 or greater?

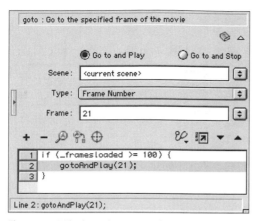

Figure 15.18 Flash carries out any instructions that fall between the curly braces. Adding `gotoAndPlay (21);` instructs Flash to jump to Frame 21 if the test for the presence of Frame 100 proves true.

When Do You Need a Preloader?

If your site contains large or complex animations, you might want to download much or all of the data to the user's computer before allowing the user to explore the site. Waiting until all the data is available locally ensures the smoothest possible playback. To keep users amused (and informed) during the download process, you might create a teaser animation with a small number of frames and fast-loading content (often referred to as a *preloader*) that loops until the last frame of your animation has downloaded to the user's computer.

By combining `if` with the `_framesloaded` property, you can check the user's computer to see whether the data for a certain frame already exists on that computer. If the data is there, Flash follows whatever instruction you include in the conditional test. If the data isn't there, Flash plays the next frame of the movie (or completes the next action, if there is one).

9. In the parameters area, *set the following parameters:*

- ▲ In the Scene field, enter `<current scene>`.
- ▲ From the Type pop-up menu, choose Frame Number.
- ▲ In the Frame field, enter 21.

Flash updates the Script pane to reflect the parameters that you chose (**Figure 15.18**).

In the published movie, Flash checks for Frame 100 before starting to play the movie. If Frame 100 is present on the viewer's computer, Flash jumps to Frame 21 and starts playing from there. If Frame 100 is absent, Flash moves on to Frame 2 of the movie and continues playing the movie.

✔ **Tip**

- You don't have to specify an exact frame number in your conditional action; you can use the `_totalframes` property to make Flash check whether all the frames in the movie have loaded. In step 7 of the preceding exercise, in the Conditions field, enter `_framesloaded >= _totalframes`. If you change the length of your movie, you won't have to remember to go back and change your script.

To make the movie repeat the teaser (the first 20 frames of the movie) until Frame 100 arrives, at the end of the teaser animation, you need to create a loop—that is, tell Flash to start over at Frame 1.

To loop the teaser animation:

1. Using the file that you created in the preceding exercise, in the Actions layer of the Timeline, insert a keyframe at Frame 20 (the last frame of the teaser animation) and select it.

2. In the Actions-Frame panel, from the Add menu, choose Actions > Movie Control > goto.

   Flash adds gotoAndPlay (1); to the Script pane. The default parameters for the goto action are to go to the first frame of the current scene and start playing (**Figure 15.19**).

   When the playhead reaches Frame 20, Flash jumps back to Frame 1. There, the frame actions that you set up in the preceding exercise test for the presence of Frame 100 all over again.

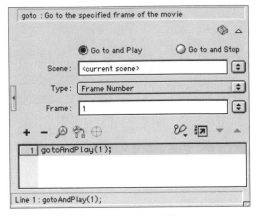

Figure 15.19 Adding gotoAndPlay (1); to the last frame of your teaser animation tells Flash to jump to Frame 1 and start over. This action creates a loop that repeatedly tests to see whether Frame 100 has arrived. If not, Flash plays the teaser again.

The Pitfalls of Conditional Actions

In the following ActionScript, Flash carries out the action between the opening and closing curly braces only when the test result is true:

```
if (_framesloaded >= 100) {
        stopAllSounds;
}
gotoAndPlay (21)
```

Unless that action within the curly braces takes you to another frame, thereby canceling the script, Flash carries out any actions that come after the ending brace, whether the result is true or false. Here, the script would take you to frame 21 even if Frame 100 hadn't loaded yet, thus defeating the purpose of the conditional test. Make sure that all the actions that should take place only when the test result is true are placed *inside* the curly braces.

If you want Flash to carry out one action when the condition is true and a different action when the condition is false, you need to create a *branching condition*. Use if in combination with else or else if. These actions live in the Actions > Conditions/Loops category of the Actions Toolbox.

Figure 15.20 When you are in Flash Player and choose Control > Test Movie, menus offer several commands other than the ones that are available in movie-editing mode. Choose View > Show Streaming to see how your conditional action and preloader animation will work together as your movie streams over the Internet.

You can't view the workings of conditional actions in the movie-editing environment; you must view them in Test mode.

To preview conditional actions:

1. Continuing with the file that you created in the preceding exercise, from the Control menu, choose Test Movie.

   Flash exports the movie and opens it in Flash Player.

2. From Flash Player's View menu, choose Show Streaming (**Figure 15.20**).

   Flash simulates the way that your movie will stream over the Internet. (For more details on simulated streaming, see Chapter 16.) As a result, Frame 100 will not be available for a while, and you'll have a chance to see your teaser animation repeat.

✔ Tips

- Creating a practice file for testing the _framesloaded property can be tricky unless you have a movie that you know will take several seconds to load. If your downloading message doesn't appear or appears too briefly for you to check it, add more sounds, video clips, or bitmaps to frames 30 through 100 of your movie to increase the file size and download time. In a real-world situation, if you have that "problem," you may not need a downloading message at all.

- To ensure that your viewers get to the heart of your movie as soon as possible after the last frame loads, put the conditional test in every frame of the teaser animation.

Conditionals for Error Checking

In the tasks in "Creating Scriptable Text Objects" earlier in this chapter, you restricted the length and selectability of a text box to help ensure that users enter data correctly. As you get more comfortable with scripting, you can use conditional actions (if, else, if else) to test for common user errors.

The following script is similar to the one you created, but it adds an if action to see whether someone accidentally enters letters where there should be numbers. The predefined function isNaN returns a value of true when the tested item contains items that are not numbers. This script catches cases in which users enter letters and displays a message in the text box, reminding them to use numbers:

```
on (release) {
    if (isNAN (ageVAR)) {
        luckyNumVAR = "Use numerals only";
    } else {
        luckyNumVAR = Number (ageVAR) + 2;
    }
}
```

Loading New Files

Flash provides several ways to load new files into your movie or Web site; here are two. The getURL action allows you to find other files and display them in a browser window when you run your movie in a browser. These files might be Flash Player files (with the extension .swf) or HTML pages. You can display the new file in the current browser window or in a new window. If your HTML page uses frames, you can target any frame to display the new file.

The loadMovie action lets you display new movie files within the current movie window. The loaded movie can replace the current movie or stack up on top of the current movie as though it were simply another layer of animation. (An advanced application for the loadMovie and getURL actions is to pass variables from one file to another file.)

To use getURL to open a separate browser window:

1. Create a new Flash document.

2. Place an instance of a button symbol in Keyframe 1 of your movie.
   (For more details on using symbols and buttons, see Chapters 6 and 13.)

3. On the Stage, select the button.

4. In the Actions panel, in the Actions Toolbox's Actions > Browser/Network category, double-click getURL (**Figure 15.21**). Flash updates the Script pane to read as follows:

```
on (release) {
    getURL ("");
}
```

Figure 15.21 From the Actions Toolbox's Actions category, choose getURL to make Flash open another file in the browser.

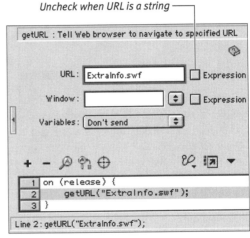

Uncheck when URL is a string

Figure 15.22 For testing on your computer without opening an Internet connection, enter a relative URL in the Actions panel's parameters area. The file you specify as the URL must be in the same folder as the main movie file. To make Flash interpret the URL as an actual file name (a string), uncheck the Expression checkbox.

5. In the parameters area, in the URL field, enter the name or path of the file that you want to appear in a separate window (**Figure 15.22**).

For testing this exercise, enter a relative URL for a file on your computer, such as a file located in the same folder as the Flash file that you created. (Make sure that the Expression checkbox is unchecked. You want Flash to treat the URL as a text string, not a variable or expression.) You can also use an absolute URL in this field, but in that case, you must have an Internet connection open to test the action.

(continues on next page)

The Mystery of URLs

The acronym *URL* stands for *Uniform Resource Locator,* which is a standardized way of handling the addresses of files so that they can be found on the Internet. The conventions of the URL make it possible to decipher the hierarchical structure of the server (or local computer) on which a file is stored, allowing you to maneuver through all the directories, folders, and layers to the specific file that you want.

URLs have two forms: absolute and relative.

An *absolute URL* is a complete address that specifies the protocol your browser should use to open the file (HTTP, or Hypertext Transfer Protocol, is one used to transfer the text and graphics of Web sites), the name of the server on which the file resides, the path name (the nested hierarchy of directories, volumes, folders, and so on), and the name of the file itself.

A *relative URL* is a shorthand version of the full address that lets you describe one file's location in relation to another. In essence, you tell Flash to move up and down the hierarchy of nested files, folders, and directories, starting from the file where you give Flash the getURL instruction. It's like saying, "Look in the folder you're in right now for a file called Fabulous.fla," or "Look in the folder you're in right now for another folder called OtherJunk, and then look inside that folder for the file Fabulous.fla," or "Go up a level to the folder that contains the folder that contains the file you're in right now. In that higher-level folder, look for another folder called ThisJunk. Look in ThisJunk for a file called Abysmal.fla."

Using relative URLs in actions has the advantage of allowing you to test your movies on your computer without opening an Internet connection. Additionally, provided that you keep your files in the same relative positions in the hierarchy, you won't need to rename the files when you transfer them from your local computer to the server where you'll make them available to your viewers.

6. From the Window pop-up menu, choose
_blank (**Figure 15.23**).

The _blank parameter tells Flash to open
the new file in a new window in the
browser. The three other predefined
choices are _self, which opens the new file
in the current browser window; _parent,
which opens the new file in the parent of
the current frame; and _top, which opens
the new file in the top-level frame in the
current browser window. Again, leave the
Expression checkbox unchecked. You can
also type the name of the window or frame
that you want to display the new URL.

7. From the File menu, choose Publish
Preview > HTML (**Figure 15.24**).

Flash exports your movie to a .swf file,
creates an HTML file that plays the file,
and opens that file in whatever browser
you have available. (For more details on
using Flash's publishing features, see
Chapter 16.)

8. In the movie playing in the browser window, click the button that you just created.

Flash opens a new browser window and
displays the file that you specified in the
getURL action.

✔ Tip

■ Instead of scripting a button to link to a
new URL, you can create a text box that
links to it. Using the text tool, create a
text box, and enter the text that you want
to be a hot link. With that text selected,
in the URL field of the Text Property
Inspector, enter the URL of the page to
link to. From the Target pop-up menu,
choose the way you want Flash to open
the new URL; the choices are the same as
those described in step 6 of the preceding
exercise for the getURL action.

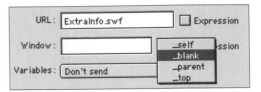

Figure 15.23 Choose _blank from the Window pop-up
menu to make Flash open the new URL in a separate
browser window.

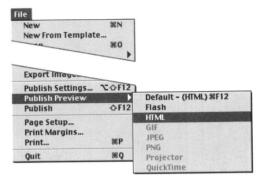

Figure 15.24 Choose File > Publish Preview > HTML to
test the getURL action in your browser.

Figure 15.25 To open a new movie that plays in a different level of your movie, in the Actions Toolbox's Actions category, double-click loadMovie.

To use loadMovie:

1. Follow steps 1 through 3 of the preceding exercise.

2. In the Actions-Button panel, in the Actions Toolbox's Actions > Browser/Network category, double-click loadMovie (**Figure 15.25**).

   Flash updates the Script pane with the following code:

```
on (release){
        loadMovieNum ("",0);
}
```

(continues on next page)

The Mystery of Movie Levels

When you add movie clips to a Flash file or load other movies, the independent Timelines start stacking up. To control them with ActionScript, you need to tell Flash which Timeline you're trying to control. You do this with the target path name, which makes the hierarchical relationships of the nested Timelines clear.

Imagine three family members having lunch: a grandparent, a parent, and child. If you restrict the conversation to the people at the table, the grandparent can talk about "my child," the parent can talk about "my child," and everybody can talk about "my family." The same word can refer to different people because the context is clear; the person saying the word has a known relationship to the person being referred to.

There's a similar phenomenon in creating target paths in ActionScript. Imagine you have a Flash file named Grandma, which contains a movie clip named Mom; the Mom clip contains another movie clip named Kid. A script attached to a frame or object inside the Kid clip can control the Mom clip's Timeline by using the target path _parent. But if you attach a script to an object in the Mom clip using the path name _parent, you'll be controlling the Timeline in the Grandma movie. In other words, which Timeline _parent refers to depends on where the script containing it resides. A path name that always refers to the "founding parent" movie in a set of nested Timelines is _root. No matter where a script lives (in the Kid clip, the Mom clip, or the Grandma movie) when it uses the path name _root, it controls the main movie Timeline—in this example, Grandma.

In addition to having Timelines that stack up within an individual Flash file, in the Flash Player, you can stack up several movies on separate levels. You target these separate movies with the pathname _level plus the number of the level containing the movie (_level1, _level2, and so on). To refer to the main movie Timeline in the bottommost level, use the path name _level0. You determine which level contains which movie when you use the loadMovie action. You can replace the current movie by entering 0 for the Level parameter. If you type a higher number, Flash stacks the loaded movie on top of the current movie.

3. With `loadMovieNum ("",0);` selected in Line 2 of the Script pane, in the parameters area's URL field, enter the name of the Flash Player (.swf) file that you want to load.

4. From the Location pop-up menu, choose Level, and enter 1 in the text field (**Figure 15.26**).

The elements of movies loaded in higher levels obscure elements in movies at lower levels, just as graphics in higher layers of a movie obscure graphics in the lower layers.

5. From the Control menu, choose Test Movie to try out the `loadMovie` action.

When you click the button, Flash loads the second movie on top of the movie that contains the button (**Figure 15.27**).

✔ Tip

■ You can also use actions to unload movies that you've already loaded. The process is similar to the preceding exercise, except that in step 2, you choose Actions > Browser/Network > `unloadMovie,` and you can skip step 3. In step 4, you enter the level number from which Flash should remove a previously loaded movie.

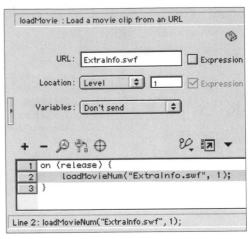

Figure 15.26 Defining the Location parameter as Level, with a number greater than 0, tells Flash to display the loaded movie on top of the current movie. A Level setting of 0 tells Flash to replace the current movie with the loaded movie. (You can also choose to load a movie's variables without displaying or playing any of the movie.)

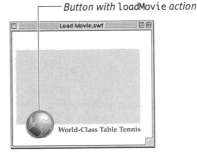
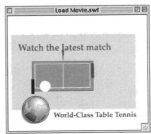

Button with `loadMovie` action

Figure 15.27 The main movie (Load Movie.swf) is playing in Level 0 (top). When you click the globe button, Flash loads another movie (Extra Info.swf) into Level 1. The movie in Level 1 plays as though it were an additional layer of animation sitting on top of the original movie (bottom).

Controlling Nested Timelines

One way to create complex interactions is to use one object to manipulate another. You can use a button to control a movie clip or a movie loaded via ActionScript, for example. The object that you want to manipulate is called the *target*. You point Flash to the target by identifying its *target path* (its address). In Chapter 13, you learned to control the Timeline by creating buttons with the **stop** and **play** actions. In that exercise, you didn't need to tell Flash the path to the Timeline you wanted to stop because there was only one Timeline—the one containing the button. By default, a button's event handler targets the Timeline that contains that button.

As you nest movie clips and buttons within other movie clips, you must tell Flash which of the nested Timelines you want to control. For this purpose, you'll want to learn two shorthand path names: **_parent** and **_root**. The **_parent** is the Timeline of the movie (or movie clip) containing the clip to which you are attaching the script, and the **_root** is the main Timeline containing all your movie's elements.

To control the main Timeline with a clipEvent handler:

1. Create a new Flash document with a layer named Contents that has keyframes in frames 1 through 5, and place identifying text in each keyframe.

   You can open a new copy of the Object-Actions template that you created in Chapter 13 as a basis for this document. Just be sure to remove the **stop** action from Keyframe 1 in the Actions layer.

2. In the Contents layer, in Keyframe 3, place a movie clip instance on the Stage.

3. Access the Actions-Movie Clip panel.

4. In the Actions Toolbox, choose Objects > Movie > _parent, and drag it to the Script pane (**Figure 15.28**).

   Flash updates the Script pane to read:
   ```
   onClipEvent (load) {
   _parent;
   }
   ```
   In the parameters area, **_parent** appears in the Expression field.

5. In the Expression field, place the insertion point after the letter *t*, and enter a period (.).

   If you have code hinting turned on in the ActionScripting tab of the Preferences dialog box, a menu of possible actions pops up in the parameters area (**Figure 15.29**).

Figure 15.28 When you're using a clipEvent handler to control the Timeline of the movie (or movie clip) that contains the movie clip to which the clipEvent script is attached, select _parent.

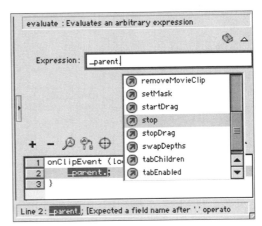

Figure 15.29 When code hinting is turned on, a pop-up menu of possible methods appears when you type the dot (the period character) that connects a method with a target object in ActionScript.

```
1  onClipEvent (load) {
2      _parent.stop();
3  }
```

Figure 15.30 This script tells Flash to stop playback of the Timeline containing this movie clip as soon as the clip loads.

6. From the code-hints menu, choose **stop**, or enter **stop ()**; manually in the field.

Flash updates the script to look like **Figure 15.30**.

You're ready to see the script in action.

7. Choose Control > Test Movie.

When the playhead reaches Frame 3, the movie clip loads, and Flash carries out the instruction to stop playback of the parent Timeline (the Timeline containing the movie clip). The movie clip's Timeline is unaffected; the clip keeps playing.

✔ Tips

■ Try changing the **clipEvent** handler to **unload**. Now when you test the movie, the playback stops on Frame 4—the frame in which the movie clip stops appearing.

■ If you turned off code hinting in the Preferences dialog box, you can turn it on temporarily. In step 5, after entering the period in the Expressions field, from the Options menu in the top-right corner of the Actions-Movie Clip panel choose Show Code Hint. The pop-up menu of actions appears in the parameters area.

Terminology: *Object.Method*

In the script

```
on (release) {
    pongMC1.stop ();
}
```

you used a period to link a method (**stop()**) to a an object (**pongMC1**). As you look at the script, that **object.method** syntax can seem pretty cryptic. Try thinking of the script as speaking with the immediacy of a 2-year-old who points at an object and makes a demand. Imagine a child who wants a snack and points to the cookie jar, saying, "Cookie, give," or who sees the family pet and says, "Kitty, come." The second line of this script is pointing to a movie clip and saying, "Hey, you, movie clip named pongMC1, stop playing!"

You can also use buttons nested in movie clips to control the main movie Timeline. To get a clearer picture of how _parent and _root work together, try creating a set of nested movie clips with buttons that control _parent and _root.

To create a set of basic buttons targeting _parent and _root:

1. Follow step 1 of the preceding exercise.

2. Add a new layer to the movie's Timeline, and name this layer Buttons.

3. In Frame 1 of the Buttons layer, place a button instance on the Stage.

4. With the button instance selected, in the Actions-Button panel, in the Actions Toolbox, double-click Actions > Movie Control > stop.

   Flash updates the script to look like **Figure 15.31**.

5. Place a second button instance on the Stage.

6. With that button instance selected, in the Actions-Button panel, in the Actions Toolbox, double-click the Objects > Movie > parent action.

   Flash adds it to the Script pane and displays the Expressions field in the parameters area.

7. Add .stop(); to the expression (see steps 5 and 6 of the preceding exercise for details).

   Flash updates the script to look like **Figure 15.32**.

8. Repeat steps 5 through 7 for a third button instance; in step 6, choose root.

   Flash updates the script to look like **Figure 15.33**.

9. Duplicate all three buttons and modify their scripts, substituting a play action for the stop action.

10. Create text boxes to label each button to remind you what action each one performs.

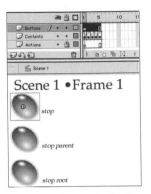

Figure 15.31 The script for the selected button tells Flash to stop playback of the Timeline containing this button.

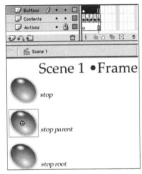

Figure 15.32 This script tells Flash to stop playback of the Timeline one level above the Timeline containing this button.

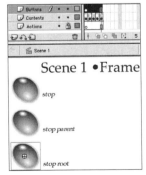

Figure 15.33 This script tells Flash to stop playback of the main movie Timeline, no matter how many levels above this button it is.

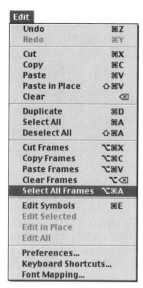

Figure 15.34 Choose Edit > Select All Frames to prepare to copy the set of buttons and animated text that you created.

You can repeat this basic movie in a series of nested movie clips to see how each action works to target different Timelines.

To nest the movie clips:

1. Continuing with the file you created in the preceding exercise, choose Edit > Select All Frames (**Figure 15.34**); then choose Edit > Copy Frames.

2. Choose Insert New Symbol, name the symbol Granddaughter, give it movie clip behavior, and click OK.

    You enter symbol-editing mode.

3. In the Timeline, select Frame 1, and choose Edit > Paste Frames.

    Flash pastes all the frames that you copied from the main movie's Timeline into the symbol's Timeline. Now the symbol has a layer containing your button set and a layer containing five frames, each with identifying text. (If you used the ObjectActions template that you created in Chapter 13 as the basis for your file, you also have a layer for actions, but this layer should be blank.)

4. In the Contents layer, using the text tool, place the word *Granddaughter* near to the numbers that will count up with each frame.

5. In the Library window, select the Granddaughter symbol, and from the Options pop-up menu, choose Duplicate.

    The Duplicate Symbol dialog box appears.

6. Name the copy Daughter, and click OK.

7. In the Library window, double-click the Daughter symbol.

    You enter symbol-editing mode. The symbol already has five frames, with identifying text on one layer and a set of buttons on another layer.

(continues on next page)

CONTROLLING NESTED TIMELINES

8. In the Contents layer, select the word *Granddaughter* and change it to *Daughter.*

9. Add a new layer, name it Granddaughter Clip, select its Keyframe 1, and place a new instance of the Granddaughter symbol on the Stage (**Figure 15.35**).

10. Return to movie-editing mode (by clicking the Back button, for example).

11. Repeat steps 5 through 9, this time naming the duplicate clip Mother (step 6), double-clicking the Mother symbol in the Library window to edit it (step 7), creating a Daughter layer and changing the text label to *Mother* (step 8), and placing an instance of Daughter on the Stage (step 9).

12. Return to movie-editing mode, add a new layer to the Timeline, and name it Mother Clip.

13. In Keyframe 1 of the Mother Clip layer, place an instance of Mother on the stage.

You should see four sets of buttons: the original set created in the main movie Timeline and one set within each movie clip (**Figure 15.36**).

14. Choose Control > Test Movie.

You see four sets of numbers counting from 1 to 5 repeatedly, plus all those button sets. Click the various buttons, and watch which set of numbers stops counting. Any of the **_root** buttons will stop the numbers of the main movie Timeline. But the **stop** and **_parent** buttons will act on different clips, depending on how deeply the button is nested.

In addition to targeting nested Timelines with **_parent** and **_root**, you can target a particular movie-clip instance by name. Targeting names allows you to control objects on the same Timeline, as well as objects that are nested above or below.

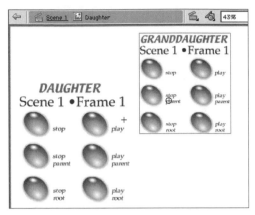

Figure 15.35 Place a copy of the Granddaughter clip in the Daughter symbol. Distribute the elements symmetrically around the registration point to make it easier to work with in movie-editing mode.

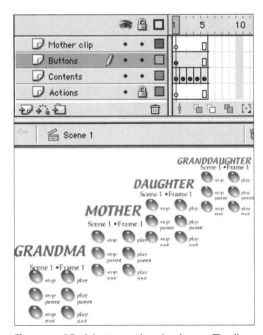

Figure 15.36 Each button set here has its own Timeline. The set labeled *Grandma* is in the main Timeline, and the sets associated with *Mother, Daughter,* and *Granddaughter* are in nested movie-clip Timelines.

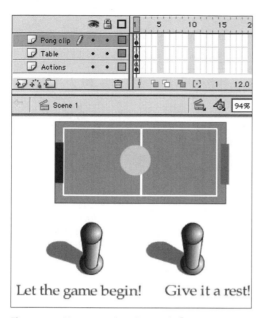

Figure 15.37 You can assign stop and play actions that target a movie clip to buttons. This type of ActionScripting allows users to manipulate the movie clip during playback.

Figure 15.38 To make buttons identifiable to Flash as targets for actions, you must name the button instance in the Property Inspector.

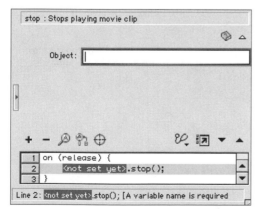

Figure 15.39 In Normal mode, when you add a stop method (from the Objects > Movie, > Movie Clip > Methods category) to the Script pane, Flash prompts you to fill in the path to the object that you are trying to stop.

To control a movie clip with a button handler:

1. Create a new Flash document that contains a movie clip and two buttons in Keyframe 1.

   This example uses the Ping-Pong clip that you created in Chapter 11, plus two buttons that look like switches (**Figure 15.37**). In this exercise, the buttons and the movie clip reside in the same Timeline. You set one of the buttons to stop the action of the Ping-Pong game and the other to start it again. (Add text to identify the button functions, if you want.)

2. On the Stage, select the Ping-Pong movie clip.

3. Access the Property Inspector.

   You must use the Property Inspector to identify the movie clip as the target of your instruction.

4. In the Name field, enter a unique instance name.

   Do not include spaces or punctuation other than the underscore character in this name. Start the name with an underscore or a letter. For this exercise, enter PongMC1 (**Figure 15.38**).

5. On the Stage, select the button that will stop the action.

6. Access the Actions-Button panel.

7. From the Add menu, choose Objects > Movie > Movie Clip > Methods > stop.

   Flash updates the Script pane (**Figure 15.39**) and displays the Object field in the parameters area. You must tell Flash which object you want to affect.

(continues on next page)

8. To get assistance with entering the correct path to your target object, click the Insert Target Path button (**Figure 15.40**).

9. In the Insert Target Path dialog box that appears, *do the following:*

▲ In the hierarchical list of movie elements, click the icon for the movie clip you want to control.

▲ In the Notation section, choose Dots. For Flash versions 5 and later, you should use dot syntax in writing the path name.

▲ In the Mode section, choose Relative. Flash uses a relative path.

10. Click OK.

Flash enters the path in the Object field and updates the Script pane (**Figure 15.41**).

11. On the Stage, select the second button (the one that starts the action again), and repeat steps 6 through 10.

This time, in step 7, choose play.

12. To see your buttons in action, choose Control > Test Movie.

When you click the Stop button, Flash stops playback of the Ping-Pong clip. When you click the Start button, Flash resumes playback of the movie clip.

✔ **Tip**

■ In step 9, to use an absolute path, choose the Absolute radio button.

Find target path

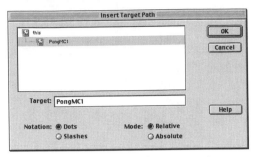

Figure 15.40 In the set of icons above the Script pane, click the Insert Target Path button (top) to open a window that lists possible movie-clip targets (bottom). Click one of the movie-clip icons to enter its name in the path field. When you click OK, Flash enters the target path in the script.

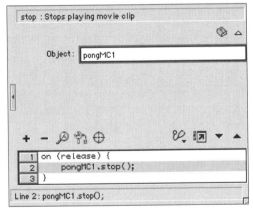

Figure 15.41 This script tells Flash to stop the movie-clip instance named pongMC1 when the button is clicked.

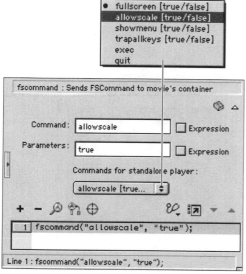

Figure 15.42 The fscommand action allows you to communicate with the program that's running Flash Player, such as your browser or a stand-alone projector.

Figure 15.43 Choose allowscale, and set its parameter to true to make your movie's graphics scale proportionately when viewers resize a projector window.

Using fscommand

The preceding exercises taught you how to control various movie Timelines within Flash. The fscommand action allows you to communicate with and control the program that is running your published movie, such as a browser or a stand-alone projector. (For details about publishing movies, see Chapter 16.) In a movie published as a stand-alone projector, for example, you can set an fscommand action's parameters to make the movie fill the screen, to hide and show the menu bar, and to allow graphics to scale (or prevent them from scaling) when viewers resize the movie's window.

To allow graphics to scale in a projector window:

1. Create a new Flash document.

2. Select Frame 1, and place some graphics on the Stage.

3. With Frame 1 selected, access the Actions-Frame panel.

4. In the Actions Toolbox, open the Actions > Browser/Network category, and drag a copy of fscommand to the Script pane (**Figure 15.42**).

5. In the parameters area, from the Commands for Stand-Alone Player pop-up menu, choose allowscale [true/false].

   Flash enters allowscale in the Command field, enters true (the default value) in the Parameters field, and updates the Script pane (**Figure 15.43**).

(continues on next page)

6. From the File menu, choose Publish Settings.

7. In the Formats tab of the Publish Settings dialog box, check the projector checkbox for the platforms you are working on; leave the Use Default Names box checked, and uncheck all other checkboxes (**Figure 15.44**).

8. Click the Publish button.

Flash creates a projector, using the default name and settings, and places it in the same location as the Flash file from which it derives. (To learn more about publishing, see Chapter 16.)

9. To close the dialog box, click OK or Cancel.

10. To play the movie, navigate to the projector file on your system, and double-click the projector icon.

The stand-alone projector opens in a window. When you resize the window, the graphics scale proportionally to fit within the new window (**Figure 15.45**).

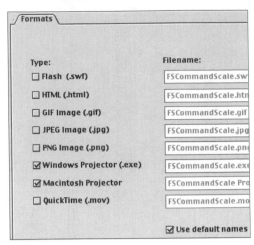

Figure 15.44 To create a projector, check the checkbox for your platform in the Formats tab of the Publish Settings dialog box.

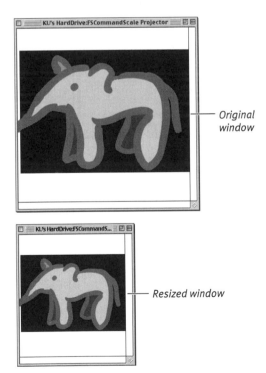

Figure 15.45 With allowscale set to true, graphics shrink when viewers make the projector window smaller.

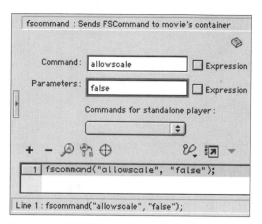

Figure 15.46 Set allowscale to false to keep graphics at a constant size when viewers resize the projector window.

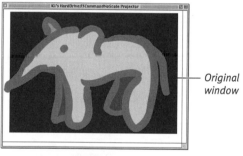

— Original window

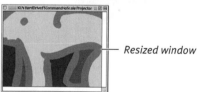

— Resized window

Figure 15.47 With allowscale set to false, graphics remain the same size when viewers make the projector window smaller.

To prevent graphics from scaling in a projector window:

1. Open the Flash document you created in the preceding exercise, and select Frame 1.

2. In the Actions-Frame panel, select Line 1 in the Script pane, which contains the fscommand action.

3. In the parameters area, in the Parameters field, enter false.

   Flash updates the Script pane (**Figure 15.46**).

4. Repeat steps 6 through 10 of the preceding exercise.

   Now when you resize the projector window, the graphic remains the same size. If you make the window smaller, parts of the graphic may be hidden (**Figure 15.47**).

✔ Tip

■ Be aware that creating projectors can trigger any virus-protection software you may have installed.

USING fscommand

Using Components

ActionScripting can be complex and time-consuming. Flash MX provides a way to preserve labor-intensive ActionScripting in reusable, customizable movie clips. This special form of movie clip is called a *component*. (Flash 5 offered a similar item called a *SmartClip*.)

The task of defining your own components is beyond the scope of this book. But Flash comes with seven Component objects that you can play with: CheckBox, RadioButton, ComboBox (a drop-down menu), ListBox, PushButton, ScrollBar, and ScrollPane. You access components from the Components panel. You customize the individual instances of a component—creating the text label for a drop-down selection list, for example—in the Property Inspector or via the Component Parameters panel.

To access the Components panel:

◆ If the panel is not open, from the Window menu, choose Components (**Figure 15.48**).

To create an instance of the ComboBox component:

1. Open a Flash document to which you want to add a drop-down list of items from which to select.

2. Access the Components panel.

3. Drag an instance of the component named ComboBox to the Stage in Keyframe 1.

   Flash adds a folder named Flash UI Components to the Library window. Notice that each component has its own icon, not that of a regular movie-clip symbol (**Figure 15.49**).

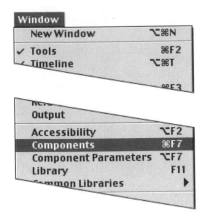

Figure 15.48 Choose Window > Components to open the panel containing Flash's built-in components.

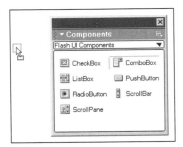

Figure 15.49 When you drag an instance of the ComboBox component from the Components panel to the Stage (top), Flash adds the component and folders containing the global component assets to the library of that document (bottom).

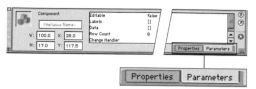

Figure 15.50 The Property Inspector for components looks like the Property Inspector for movie clips, except that it has two tabs. Click the Parameters tab to access the component's parameters.

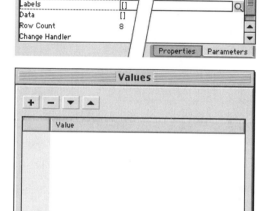

Click to access values

Figure 15.51 When you select the Labels parameter, the magnifying-glass icon appears (top). Click the icon to open the Values dialog box, where you enter the label names (bottom).

To set up the ComboBox instance's choices:

1. With the ComboBox instance selected on the Stage, access the Property Inspector.

   Because the ComboBox is really just a complex movie clip, the Property Inspector lists the component as an instance of a movie clip. Unlike other movie clips, however, components have not only the properties common to movie clips, but also parameters. Therefore, two tabs appear in the bottom-right corner of the Property Inspector (**Figure 15.50**).

2. To access the component's parameters, click the Parameters tab in the Property Inspector.

   Whatever parameters have been set up for the component appear. If you cannot see all the parameters, click the triangle in the bottom-right corner of the Property Inspector to expand the window.

3. Select the second line in the Parameters pane: the line named Labels [].

   A magnifying-glass icon appears at the end of the line.

4. Click the magnifying-glass icon.

   The Values window opens (**Figure 15.51**). By setting the values for the labels, you create the choices that appear in your selection list.

5. To add a label value, click the Add button (the plus sign).

   Flash adds the word *defaultValue* to the label list.

6. To edit a value, click the name *defaultValue*, and enter new text.

   (continues on next page)

7. Repeat the preceding step for as many labels as you want to create.

For this exercise, create three labels, and enter the names Glinka, Borodin, and Shostakovich (**Figure 15.52**).

8. Click OK.

The labels appear in the parameters area of the Property Inspector.

9. Select the fourth line in the Property Inspector's parameters area—the line labeled Row Count.

10. Enter 3.

The row-count number indicates how many items appear in the list. If the number of labels is greater than the row-count number, Flash creates a scroll bar for moving up and down the list.

11. To view your new drop-down selection list, choose Control > Test Movie.

The labels you created appear in a drop-down list. Click the triangle at the right end of the ComboBox to view the choices. The item you select appears as the current choice in the ComboBox in its unexpanded form (**Figure 15.53**).

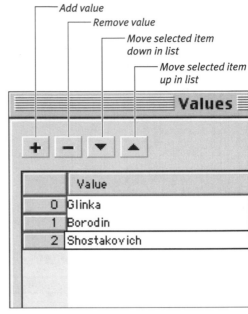

Figure 15.52 Click the plus sign in the Values dialog box to add more labels. Select the word *defaultValue*, and enter your new label name.

Figure 15.53 In your final movie, clicking the ComboBox triangle reveals a list of choices. The choice you select becomes the label for the ComboBox in its closed mode.

✔ Tips

- After you set the parameters for a component instance, Flash displays a placeholder version of the component on the Stage. For the ComboBox, for example, you see a grayed-out line and triangle. To see the instance displaying the first label you created, choose Control > Enable Live Preview (this setting is on by default). To see the full activity of the component, however, you must view the movie in Flash Player.

- You can resize component elements by using the free-transform tool. You can make the ComboBox wider, for example, to display more text in a label.

- Another way to access the parameters for your component instance is through the Component Parameters panel. If the panel is not active, choose Window > Component Parameters.

- To open the Values dialog box quickly, double-click the open and close brackets (or the words within them) to the right of the word *Labels* in the parameters list.

- Use the Tab key to cycle through the labels in the Values dialog box.

- Double-clicking a component in the Components panel puts an instance of that component on the Stage.

At this point, of course, your selection list doesn't actually do anything. To put the list to work, you must create ActionScripts that manipulate the selections your users make. You can create a variable that holds information about those selections.

Figure 15.54 Assigning an instance name to the component allows you to gather information from it via ActionScript.

To create a variable to capture a ComboBox selection:

1. Continuing with the file you created in the preceding exercise, on the Stage, select the ComboBox Component in Frame 1.

2. In the Property Inspector, in the Instance Name field, enter a name, such as yourComposer (**Figure 15.54**).

   Giving the component an instance name allows you to target it with ActionScript and retrieve information about it, such as which label is selected.

3. In Frame 1, place an instance of a button on the Stage, and select the button instance.

4. In the Actions-Button panel, from the Actions Toolbox, choose Actions > Variables > set var, and drag it to the Script pane.

   Flash updates the Script pane and displays the parameters for the set var action.

5. In the parameters area, in the Variable field, enter yourChoice.

   This step sets up a variable that you can use to hold information about your ComboBox instance.

6. In the Value field, enter yourComposer, and with the insertion point in place at the end of your entry, from the Add menu, choose Flash UI Components > ComboBox > Methods > getValue.

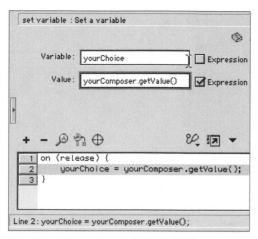

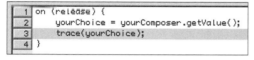

Figure 15.55 This script tells Flash to get the selected label in the ComboBox instance named yourComposer and put that text in the invisible variable yourChoice.

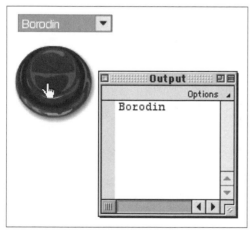

Figure 15.56 To make a quick test of your button script, add a trace action (top). When you select a composer and click the button, Flash writes the selection in the Output window (bottom).

7. Check the Expression checkbox to the right of the Value field.

Flash updates the Value parameter, linking the getValue method to the instance name yourComposer with a dot and updating the Script pane to look like **Figure 15.55**. This line of the Script tells Flash to get the label name currently selected in the ComboBox named yourComposer.

8. With Line 2 of the script selected, from the Add menu, choose Actions > Miscellaneous Actions > trace.

9. In the parameters area, in the Message field, enter yourChoice, and check the Expression checkbox.

Flash updates the Script pane. Line 3 now reads trace(yourChoice);. This code tells Flash to place the contents of the variable named yourChoice (which you set up to contain the name of the label currently showing in the ComboBox instance named yourComposer) in the Output window.

10. Choose Control > Test Movie to try out your menu.

11. From the drop-down list choose Borodin; then click the button.

Flash opens the Output window and enters the word *Borodin* (**Figure 15.56**).

To make the menu fully functional, you must continue adding actions. You might use conditional actions to test which menu choices people make and deal with them accordingly.

To manipulate the ComboBox selection with ActionScript:

1. Continuing with the file you created in the preceding exercise, select the button.

2. In the Actions-Button panel, select Line 3 of the script (the line containing the trace action), and click the Remove button (the minus sign).

3. Select Line 2 in the Script pane, and from the Add menu, choose Actions > Conditions/Loops > if.

4. In the parameters area, in the Condition field, enter yourChoice == "Glinka" (**Figure 15.57**).

   This code sets Flash to check whether the selected label is Glinka. The double equal sign is called the *equality operator*. It checks to see whether the items on either side of it are equal. In this case, it checks whether the label choice is the same as the word *Glinka*. The quotation marks around *Glinka* indicate that Flash should treat the item as a text string—not, for example, as another variable name.

5. With Line 3 selected in the Script pane, from the Add menu, choose Actions > Miscellaneous Actions > trace.

6. In the parameters area, in the Message field, enter Glinka is great!

7. With Line 4 selected in the Script pane, in the Actions Toolbox, select Actions > Conditions/Loops > else if, and drag it to the Script pane (**Figure 15.58**).

8. In the parameters area, in the Condition field, enter yourChoice == "Borodin".

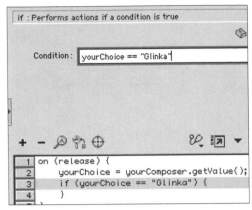

Figure 15.57 Using a conditional action allows you to see which label your user has chosen.

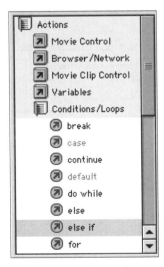

Figure 15.58 The else if conditional allows you to test a number of conditions in a row.

```
1   on (release) {
2       yourChoice = yourComposer.getValue();
3       if (yourChoice == "Glinka") {
4           trace("Glinka is great!");
5       } else if (yourChoice == "Borodin") {
6           trace("Borodin: never boring.");
7       } else {
8           trace("Shostakovich? Serious!");
9       }
10  }
```

Figure 15.59 This script checks to see whether the user has chosen Glinka or Borodin. If neither text string is a match, the user must have chosen Shostakovich. Each match (or the remaining choice) leads Flash to trace a different message.

9. Repeat step 5 (but this time select Line 5) and step 6 (enter a different message to trace, such as Borodin: never boring.).

10. With Line 6 selected in the Script pane, from the Add menu, choose Actions > Conditions/Loops > else.

11. With Line 7 selected in the Script pane, from the Add menu, choose Actions > Miscellaneous Actions > trace, and enter a message for Shostakovich, such as Shostakovich? Serious!.

    Because you have only three choices—and you have already tested for Glinka and Borodin—by the process of elimination, Shostakovich must be the selected label. Therefore, you do not need to test to see whether yourChoice is equal to the text string "Shostakovich". The completed script should look like **Figure 15.59**.

12. To try out your script, choose Control > Test Movie.

    Now the trace action can do more than parrot back the label that's selected. The conditional actions direct Flash to write an appropriate message based on your user's choices.

✔ **Tip**

■ Within the Flash UI Components folder is another folder named Component Skins, within which you'll find yet more folders for the various component elements. The skins are the movie clips that make up the various parts of the components, such as the triangle that indicates the drop-down list in the ComboBox component. You can customize components by modifying these skin movie clips. Modifying a skin movie clip changes all the components that use that skin element.

Using the Movie Explorer

As you add text, graphic symbols, buttons, movie clips, and actions to your movies, the job of tracking where each element resides increases dramatically. The Movie Explorer is a powerful tool for tracking, finding, and modifying the elements in your movies. It also gives you an overview of the whole movie.

The Movie Explorer panel displays the various movie elements hierarchically in a *display list.* You determine which types of elements appear in the list. You can expand and collapse the list levels, similar to the way that you expand and collapse folders as you navigate your hard drive.

To access the Movie Explorer panel:

◆ If the Movie Explorer panel is not open, from the Window menu, choose Movie Explorer (**Figure 15.60**).

To determine the overall content of the display list:

From the Options menu in the Movie Explorer panel's top-right corner (**Figure 15.61**), choose any of the following:

▲ To display all the elements in the movie, choose Show Movie Elements.

▲ To display a list of all the symbols used in the movie (including a display list for the elements that make up each movie clip), choose Show Symbol Definitions.

▲ To display the contents of all the scenes of a movie—not just the current scene—choose Show All Scenes.

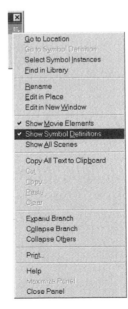

Figure 15.60 To access the Movie Explorer window, choose Window > Movie Explorer.

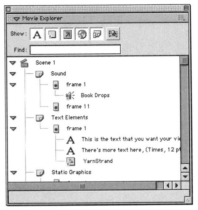

Figure 15.61 The Movie Explorer panel's Options menu lets you choose what elements of your movie appear in the panel's display list and offers commands for editing elements that you've selected in the display list.

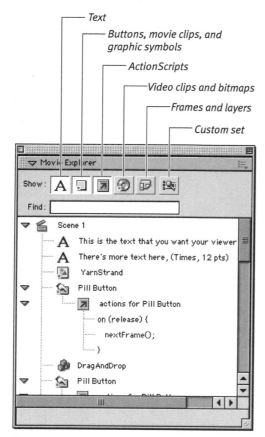

Text

Buttons, movie clips, and graphic symbols

ActionScripts

Video clips and bitmaps

Frames and layers

Custom set

Figure 15.62 Click the buttons in the Show section of the Movie Explorer window to specify which movie elements to display.

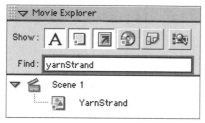

Figure 15.63 To find all instances of a movie-clip symbol, enter the symbol name in the Find field.

To determine which types of elements appear in the display list:

In the Show section of the Movie Explorer panel, *do any of the following:*

▲ To display text elements, click the first button (**Figure 15.62**).

▲ To display buttons, movie clips, and graphic elements, click the second button.

▲ To display ActionScripts, click the third button.

▲ To display video clips, sounds, and bit-mapped graphics, click the fourth button.

▲ To display frame and layer information, click the fifth button.

▲ To create a custom set of elements to display, click the sixth button, and select elements in the window that appears.

To find an element:

In the Find field of the Movie Explorer panel, enter text that identifies the element you want to find (**Figure 15.63**), as in the following examples:

▲ To find one instance of a symbol, enter the instance name.

▲ To find all instances of a symbol, enter the symbol name.

▲ To find all text boxes that use a certain font, enter the font name.

✔ Tips

■ You don't need to press Enter after typing in the Find field; Flash starts searching as soon as you enter any characters.

■ The Movie Explorer panel puts a big drain on your system, because it constantly checks for changes. Even when the panel is just sitting open on your desktop as you work on a file, Flash can slow to a crawl. Keep this panel closed until you're ready to use it.

USING THE MOVIE EXPLORER

To modify elements from the Movie Explorer panel:

1. In the display list, select the element you want to modify.

2. From the Options menu, *choose one of the following options:*

   ▲ To select the object on the Stage, choose Go to Location.

   ▲ To rename an element, choose Rename.

   ▲ To edit a symbol, choose Edit in Place or Edit in New Window.

✔ Tips

■ Double-click an element to modify it quickly. Double-click a scene or a text box, for example, to change the scene's name, or change the contents of the text box directly in the Movie Explorer window (**Figure 15.64**). Double-click a symbol to open it in symbol-editing mode. Double-click an ActionScript to open the Actions panel, where you can update the selected script.

■ You can do a spell check by copying text from the Movie Explorer window, pasting it into a text editor, checking and correcting the spelling, and then reimporting the corrected text.

To print a display list:

1. Set the display list to show the hierarchy levels and contents you want to print.

2. From the Options menu, choose Print.

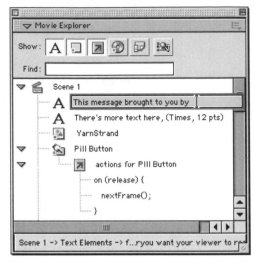

Figure 15.64 Double-click a text item to edit it directly in the Movie Explorer window.

DELIVERING MOVIES TO YOUR AUDIENCE

16

When you finish creating graphics, animation, and interactivity in Macromedia Flash MX, it's time to deliver the goods to your audience. You must export the Flash movie file to another format for playback. You have several formats to choose among. The one that guarantees viewers will see all your animations and take part in all your movie's interactivity is the Flash Player format. Player files end with the extension .swf.

Installing Flash MX also installs version 6 of the Flash Player application. You can view .swf files running directly in Flash Player on your computer. Other programs, such as Web browsers, can control Flash Player, too.

You can export movies as a series of images in either bitmap format (.GIF or .PNG files, for example) or vector format (such as Adobe Illustrator files). Another option for movie delivery is a self-playing file called a projector. Users double-click the projector file to open and play the movie. And you can print your entire movie or individual frames, should you want to give someone a hard-copy version of the movie (for storyboarding, for example). Flash MX also lets you control viewers' ability to print selected frames, or all frames, from Flash Player's contextual menu or from buttons or movie clips via the print action.

Preparing Your Movie for Optimal Playback

When you create movies to show over the Web, you must face the issue of quality versus quantity. Higher quality (smoother animation and better sounds) increases file size. The larger the file, the longer the download time and the slower your movie will be. Things that add to your file's size include lots of bitmaps (especially animated bitmaps), video clips, sounds, lots of keyframes instead of tweening, multiple areas of animation at one time, embedded fonts, gradients, and separate graphic elements instead of symbols and groups.

To help you find out where your movie is bogging down, Flash offers simulated streaming. The Size Report and Bandwidth Profiler reveal which frames will cause hang-ups. You can then rethink or optimize the problem areas.

To use Bandwidth Profiler:

1. Open the Flash document that you want to test for playback over the Web.

2. From the Control menu, choose Test Movie (or Test Scene).

   Flash exports the movie and opens it in Flash Player.

3. From Flash Player's Debug menu, choose the download speed that you want to test.

   The menu lists six speeds, all of which are customizable. To change them, choose Debug > Customize (**Figure 16.1**). By default, Flash lists three common modem speeds—14.4 Kbps, 28.8 Kbps, and 56 Kbps—set to simulate real-world data-transfer rates (**Figure 16.2**).

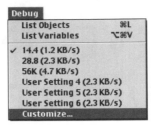

Figure 16.1 To create a custom connection speed for simulating playback over the Web, from the test environment's Debug menu, choose Customize.

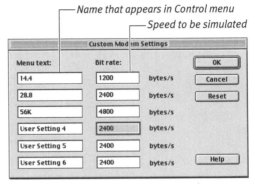

Name that appears in Control menu
Speed to be simulated

Figure 16.2 At its default setting, Flash offers choices for simulating three standard modem speeds. To imitate the real world more accurately, Flash simulates a data-transfer rate of 1.2 KBps for a 14.4 Kbps modem (not the theoretically possible rate of 1.7KBps). Flash simulates 28.8 Kbps and 56 Kbps modems at 2.3 KBps and 4.7 KBps, respectively. You can change the test names and rates in the Custom Modem Settings dialog box.

Figure 16.3 To view a graph of the amount of data in each frame, choose View > Bandwidth Profiler when a Flash Player window is open.

Downloads within set frame rate ⸺

Causes delay in playback ⸺

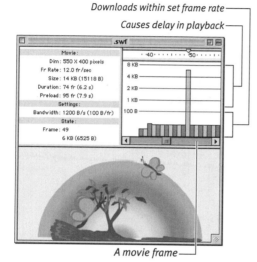

A movie frame ⸺

Figure 16.4 The Bandwidth Profiler graph at the top of the Flash Player window shows you how much data each movie frame contains and where the movie will pause to download data. Each bar represents a frame of the movie.

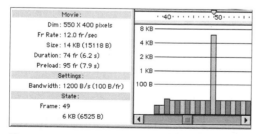

Figure 16.5 In Frame by Frame Graph mode, the height of each bar indicates how much data the frame holds. If the frame extends above the bottom line of the graph, the movie must pause to download the frame. In this movie, Frame 49 will cause a pause in playback.

4. From Flash Player's View menu, choose Bandwidth Profiler (**Figure 16.3**).

At the top of the Test Movie window, Flash graphs the amount of data that is being transmitted against the movie's Timeline (**Figure 16.4**). The bars represent the number of bytes of data per frame. The bottom line (highlighted in red) represents the amount of data that will safely download fast enough to keep up with the movie's frame rate. Any frame that contains a greater amount of data forces the movie to pause while the data downloads.

Flash offers you two ways to view the bandwidth graph.

To view the contents of each frame separately:

1. From the View menu, choose Frame by Frame Graph, or press ⌘-F (Mac) or Ctrl-F (Windows).

Flash presents a single bar for each frame in the Bandwidth Profiler graph. The numbers along the top of the graph represent frames (**Figure 16.5**). The height of the bar represents the amount of data in that frame.

2. Select a bar.

Specifics about that frame and the movie in general appear in the profile window.

To see how frames stream:

1. From the View menu, choose Streaming Graph, or press ⌘-G (Mac) or Ctrl-G (Windows).

   Flash displays the frames as alternating bars of light and dark gray, sized to reflect the time each one takes to download (**Figure 16.6**). The numbers along the top of the streaming graph represent frames as a unit of time based on the frame rate. (In a 12-fps movie, for example, each number represents $1/12$ second.) For frames that contain very little data, you might see several bars in a single time unit in the graph. Frames that have lots of data stretch out over several time units.

2. Select a bar.

   Specifics about that frame and the movie in general appear in the left profile window.

With either type of graph, you can make Flash simulate the time it takes your movie to load at various connection speeds.

To display a download-progress bar:

◆ From Flash Player's Control menu, choose Show Streaming, or press ⌘-Return (Mac) or Ctrl-Enter (Windows).

   As the animation plays in the test window, Flash highlights the numbers of the Timeline in green to show where you are in the download progress.

To exit Bandwidth Profiler:

◆ From Flash Player's View menu, choose Bandwidth Profiler again.

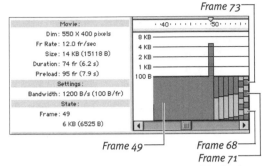
Frame 73
Frame 49
Frame 68
Frame 71

Figure 16.6 In Streaming Graph mode, the width of each bar indicates how long the frame takes to download at the given connection speed and frame rate. In this movie, Frame 49 contains 6KB of data and takes roughly 5 seconds to download at a frame rate of 12 fps over a 14.4 Kbps modem. Each number along the top of the graph is a frame, and at 12 fps, this equals $1/12$ second.

✔ Tips

■ After you set up a test environment incorporating the Bandwidth Profiler, you can open any .swf file directly in test mode. Choose File > Open, navigate to the file that you want to test, and then click Open. Flash opens the movie in a Flash Player window, using the bandwidth profile and other viewing options that you selected.

■ You can get a printed version of the information about the amount of data in each frame. Choose the Generate Size Report option in the Export Flash Player dialog box or the Flash tab of the Publish Settings dialog box (for more information, see "Publishing and Exporting" later in this chapter). During the export or publishing process, Flash simultaneously creates a text file documenting how many bytes of information each frame of the movie contains.

A Note About Accessibility

As you think about the best ways to deliver Flash movies to your audience, you should also consider the fact that some members of that audience may have physical conditions that affect the way they interact with your site. As the Web has become more of a visual medium, it presents challenges to users with visual impairments who want to take advantage of the many resources available there.

Our society is becoming more sensitive to the ways in which activities and resources exclude people with disabilities. Web designers need to think about using Flash not only to make eye-catching Web sites that dazzle with artwork, animation, interactivity, sound, and video, but also to make sites that can convey information to a wide range of people, some of whom are unable to view the site's content.

Flash MX addresses the issue of accessible Web sites by allowing you to make Flash content available to screen-reading software that uses Microsoft Active Accessibility (MSAA) technology. (At the time Flash MX was released, MSAA was available only for Windows.) Screen readers provide audio feedback about a variety of elements on a Web site, reading aloud the labels of buttons, for example, or reading the contents of text fields. Through Flash's accessibility features, you can create descriptions of objects for the screen reader; prevent the screen reader from attempting to describe certain objects (such as purely decorative movie clips); and also assign keyboard commands that let the user manipulate objects by pressing keyboard commands or tabbing through text fields, for example.

The considerations that go into making an effective, accessible site are too numerous and complex to cover in this book. But you can check out the tools for defining accessible objects in the Accessibility panel. Choose Window > Accessibility to open the panel, or click the Accessibility icon in the bottom-right quadrant of the Property Inspector (**Figure 16.7**). The accessibility parameters for selected objects appear in the panel.

Macromedia outlines some of the basic concepts of accessible Web design in an online help file, Using Flash, that comes with Flash MX. More information is available on Macromedia's Accessibility page (*www.macromedia.com/macromedia/accessibility/*).

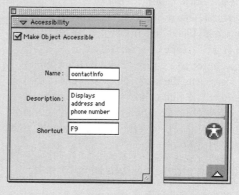

Figure 16.7 Clicking the Accessibility icon (top) in the Property Inspector opens the Accessibility panel (bottom). Use these settings to make selected objects in your movie available (or unavailable) to screen-reader software.

Publishing and Exporting

Flash's Publish function is geared toward presenting animation on the Web. The Publish command can create the Flash Player (.swf) file and an HTML document that puts your Flash Player file in a browser window. The Publish command can also create alternative file formats—GIF, JPEG, PNG, and QuickTime—and the HTML needed to display them in the browser window. Alternative formats let you make some of the animation and interactivity of your site available even to viewers who lack the Flash plug-in. Flash can also create stand-alone projector files.

Flash's Export Movie command exports a movie directly into a single format. In general, the options for exporting from Flash—GIF, JPEG, PNG, and QuickTime—are the same as those for publishing to those formats. The arrangement of some options differs between the export and publish dialog boxes, and some formats have more options in the Publish Settings dialog box. In the Publish Settings dialog box, for example, you have the choice to remove gradients from GIFs (to keep the file size small), whereas in the Export GIF dialog box, you don't have that option. Another difference between publishing and exporting is that Flash stores the publish settings with the movie file for reuse.

Figure 16.8 To access the settings for publishing a movie, choose File > Publish Settings.

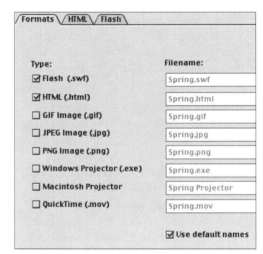

Figure 16.9 The Formats tab of the Publish Settings dialog box allows you to publish your Flash movie in as many as seven formats at the same time. You also can create an HTML document for displaying the published files in a browser.

To set a movie's publishing format:

1. Open the Flash document that you want to publish.

2. From the File menu, choose Publish Settings, or press Option-Shift-F12 (Mac) or Ctrl-Shift-F12 (Windows) (**Figure 16.8**). The Publish Settings dialog box appears.

3. Click the Formats tab (**Figure 16.9**).

Figure 16.10 Choose File > Publish to publish the files.

Figure 16.11 To cancel the publishing process, click the Stop (Mac) or Cancel (Windows) button in the Publishing dialog box.

4. Choose one of the eight format options.

   The formats available are Flash (.swf), HTML (.html), GIF Image (.gif), JPEG Image (.jpg), PNG Image (.png), Windows Projector, Macintosh Projector, and QuickTime (.mov). Choosing HTML automatically selects Flash as well.

5. To set the options for a selected format, choose the tab associated with that format (as outlined in separate exercises later in this chapter).

6. To save these settings with the current file, click OK.

   Flash uses these settings each time you choose the Publish or Publish Preview command for this document. Flash also uses a file's current publish settings when you enter test mode (by choosing Control > Test Movie or Control > Test Scene).

To publish a movie:

1. Open the Flash file that you want to publish.

2. To issue the Publish command, *do one of the following:*

   ▲ From the File menu, choose Publish Settings. The Publish Settings dialog box appears. You can follow the steps in the preceding exercise to set new format options or accept the current settings. Then click the Publish button.

   ▲ From the File menu, choose Publish, or press Shift-F12 (**Figure 16.10**). The Publishing dialog box appears, displaying a progress bar and a button for canceling the procedure (**Figure 16.11**). Flash uses the publish settings that are stored with your Flash document.

   Flash creates a new file for each format that is selected in the Publish Settings dialog box. By default, Flash places the published files in the same location as the original Flash file.

PUBLISHING AND EXPORTING

✔ Tips

- You can open your browser and preview a movie in one step. Choose File > Publish Preview. Flash offers a menu that contains all the formats selected in the Publish Settings dialog box (**Figure 16.12**). Choose a format. Flash publishes the file in that format, using the current settings, and opens the movie in a browser window.

- Flash makes one of the formats the default for Publish Preview. To publish in the default format, press ⌘-F12 (Mac) or Ctrl-F12 (Windows). If you want to do lots of testing in a format other than SWF (if you want to test your animated GIF versions, for example), set your publish settings in only that format. Then that format will be the default, and you can choose it quickly by pressing ⌘-F12 (Mac) or Ctrl-F12 (Windows).

- By default, Flash names the published files by adding the appropriate extension to the file name, adding .gif for a GIF file or .png for a PNG file, for example. To create your own file names, deselect the Use Default Names option in the Filename section of the Publish Settings dialog box (**Figure 16.13**).

- The Publish and Publish Preview commands do not give you a chance to name the published files; they take the names directly from the Publish Settings dialog box. If you want to publish multiple versions of a movie, each with different settings, you must make sure that you don't overwrite the published file. Rename the published file, move that file to a new location, or type a different name in the Formats tab of the Publish Settings dialog box.

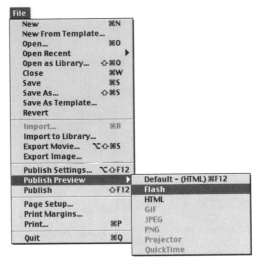

Figure 16.12 The File > Publish Preview submenu displays all the formats that are selected in the Publish Settings dialog box. Flash publishes your movie in the selected format and opens it in your browser.

☑ Use default names

Figure 16.13 To enter your own file names, first deselect Use Default Names in the Filename section of the Publish Settings dialog box. Be sure to enter the .swf extension at the end of the file name.

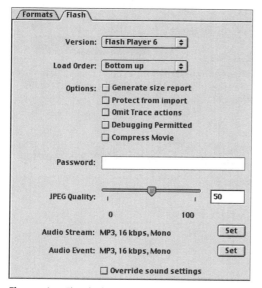

Figure 16.14 The Flash tab of the Publish Settings dialog box offers options for publishing your Flash movie as a Flash Player (.swf) file.

Working with Flash Player Settings

The stand-alone Flash Player is an application file that installs with Flash. The Player opens when you double-click the icon of a file that has the .swf extension. (From within Flash Player, you can use the File > Open command to open and play .swf files.) To prepare a Flash movie for playing in the stand-alone Player, choose either the Export or Publish command in the Flash editor. The options are the same for both commands.

To publish a Flash Player (.swf) file:

1. In the Flash editor, open the Flash file that you want to publish.

2. From the File menu, choose Publish Settings.

   The Publish Settings dialog box appears.

3. Click the Formats tab.

4. In the Type section, select Flash (.swf).

   To enter a file name other than the default, deselect Use Default Names as the Filename option and type a name for your Flash Player. (Be sure to include the .swf extension.)

5. Select the Flash tab (**Figure 16.14**).

6. Set Flash options as described in the following exercises.

7. Click Publish.

To choose a Flash Player version:

- From the Version pop-up menu, choose one of the six versions of Flash Player.

   Your options are Flash Player 1 (formerly known as FutureSplash Animator) through 6. If you publish your file as a version earlier than Flash Player 6, you lose some features specific to Flash MX.

✔ Tip

- Before you start creating any ActionScripts, set the Flash export options in the Publish Settings dialog box to the earliest version of Flash Player to which you plan to export. Any Flash MX actions that won't work in that version appear with yellow highlighting in the Actions Toolbox in the Actions panel.

To control how Flash draws the movie's first frame:

◆ From the Load Order pop-up menu, choose the order in which Flash loads a movie's layers for displaying the first frame of your movie (**Figure 16.15**).

When playback over the Web is slow, Flash starts displaying individual layers as they download. The Top Down setting tells Flash to send (and display) the top layer first and then work its way to the bottom layer. Bottom Up does just the opposite.

To list the amount of data in the movie by frame:

◆ Check the Generate Size Report checkbox (**Figure 16.16**).

Flash creates a separate text file listing the frames of the movie and how much data each frame contains. This report helps you find frames that bog down the movie's playback. You can then optimize or eliminate some of the content in those frames.

To protect your work:

◆ Check the Protect from Import checkbox.

This setting prevents viewers from obtaining the .swf file and converting it back to a Flash movie. This setting is especially important if you plan to make the file available for remote debugging.

To prevent `trace` actions from appearing in the Output window during debugging:

◆ Check the Omit Trace Actions checkbox.

This option strips the `trace` actions from the published movie, allowing you view only non-`trace` debugging items in the Output window. Omitting `trace` actions also reduces file size slightly if your scripts contain lots of trace actions.

Figure 16.15 The Load Order pop-up menu determines the order in which Flash draws the layers of the first frame of your movie.

Options: ☑ **Generate size report**

```
Movie Report
------------

Frame #   Frame Bytes   Total Bytes   Page
-------   -----------   -----------   ----------------
   1          134           134       Scene 1
   2            2           136       2
   3            2           138       3
   4            2           140       4
   5            2           142       5
   6            2           144       6
   7         1586          1730           7
   8            2          1732           8


Page                    Shape Bytes   Text Bytes
---------------------   -----------   ----------
Scene 1                      92            0

Event sounds: 11KHz Mono 16 kbps MP3

Sound Name              Bytes     Format
---------------------   -------   --------
Breaker Switch           1575     11KHz Mono 16 kbps MP3
Book Drops               1575     11KHz Mono 16 kbps MP3
```

Figure 16.16 Choose Generate Size Report (top) to have Flash create a text file that lists the amount of data in your movie (bottom).

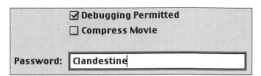

Figure 16.17 When you check the Debugging Permitted checkbox, you can also enter a password to protect movies that are open to remote debugging.

Figure 16.18 To set JPEG compression for any bitmaps in your movie, enter a value in the JPEG Quality field or use the slider. A setting of 0 results in the most compression (worst quality); 100 results in the least compression (best quality).

To debug ActionScripts remotely:

◆ Check the Debugging Permitted checkbox. This option allows you or other users to debug a Flash Player (.swf) file as it plays over the Internet.

✔ Tip

■ When the Debugging Permitted option is selected, you should always enter a password in the Password field (**Figure 16.17**). This password will protect unauthorized individuals from accessing your script but allow authorized personnel to debug the file remotely.

To compress the .swf file (Flash 6 Player):

◆ Choose Flash Player 6 from the Version pop-up menu. Check the Compress Movie option.

The Compress Movie option only becomes active when Flash Player 6 is selected. The best reason to implement movie compression is for text-heavy movies. Movie compression works both on text that appears in the movie and text that's hidden in scripts.

To compress the bitmaps in your movie:

To set JPEG compression, *do one of the following:*

◆ Adjust the JPEG Quality slider.

◆ Enter a specific value in the JPEG Quality field (**Figure 16.18**).

This setting controls how Flash applies JPEG compression as it exports the bitmaps in your movie. A setting of 0 provides the most compression (and the lowest quality, because that compression leads to loss of data).

✔ Tip

■ Flash doesn't apply JPEG compression to GIF images that you've imported into your movie, because Flash defaults to using lossless compression for GIFs.

Flash divides sounds into two types: streaming and event (for more details, see Chapter 14). You must set the compression for each type separately, but the process and options are the same for both.

To control compression and sample rate for all movie sounds:

1. In the Audio Stream section (or the Audio Event section) of the Publish Settings dialog box, click the Set button (**Figure 16.19**).

   The Sound Settings dialog box appears.

2. To set compression parameters, from the Compression pop-up menu (**Figure 16.20**), *choose one of the following*:

   ▲ To make Flash omit sound from the published file, choose Disable.

   ▲ To set compression for movies containing mostly short event sounds, such as handclaps or button clicks, choose ADPCM. (Generally, you'll use this setting in the Audio Event section.) The ADPCM options appear. From the ADPCM Bits pop-up menu, choose 2-Bit for the greatest degree of compression (resulting in the lowest-quality sound); choose 5-Bit for the least compression (resulting in the highest-quality sound). With the ADPCM setting, you can also set a sample rate and convert stereo sound to mono sound.

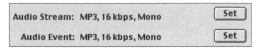

Figure 16.19 You must set the sample rate and compression options for streaming sounds and event sounds separately. Click the Set button to access the options for each type of sound.

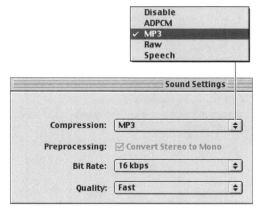

Figure 16.20 Choose a compression method from the Compression pop-up menu. Other options appropriate to the selected method appear. Choose Disable to turn off sound.

Sample-Rate Rule of Thumb

Sample rates are measured in kHz or frequency. Recording for music CDs is done at 44 kHz. For multimedia CD-ROMs, 22 kHz is a standard rate. For music clips in Flash movies played on the Web, 11 kHz is often sufficient. For shorter sounds, including spoken words, you may be able to get away with even lower sampling rates.

Advanced Sound Handling

The sound-compression settings in the Publish Settings dialog box apply to all the sounds in your movie unless you have specified sound settings for individual sounds in the library of the Flash document. A more advanced method of dealing with sound compression is setting compression options and sample rates for sounds individually. Assigning the highest quality to selected sounds helps you keep file size reasonable but still have high-quality sound where you need it.

You set compression options for individual sounds via the Sound Properties dialog box, which you access from the movie's Library window. Control-click (Mac) or right-click (Windows) a sound name in the Library window; then choose Properties from the contextual menu that appears. The Sound Properties dialog box appears, offering the same sound-export settings as the Flash tab of the Publish Settings dialog box.

If some sounds in a movie have individual sound-export settings, Flash uses those settings for those sounds when you choose Publish. Flash uses the sound options that you set in the Publish Settings dialog box for all other sounds in that movie.

If you've used individual compression methods for some sounds in your movie, you can force Flash to ignore them and publish all sounds with the sound options you've chosen in the Publish Settings dialog box. In the Flash tab of the Publish Settings dialog box, choose Override Sound Settings. You might use this feature to make a lower-quality Web version of a movie that you created for CD-ROM.

▲ To set compression for movies containing mostly longer streaming sounds, choose MP3. (Generally, you'll use this setting in the Audio Stream section.) The MP3 options appear. From the Bit Rate pop-up menu, choose one of 12 bit rates for the published sounds. At Bit Rate settings of less than 20 Kbps, Flash converts sounds from stereo to mono; at settings of 20 Kbps and above, you can publish stereo sounds or convert them to mono sounds. From the Quality pop-up menu, choose Fast for movies that will play back over the Web; Medium and Best provide better quality.

▲ To omit sound compression, choose Raw. Raw does allow you to control file size by choosing a sample rate and converting stereo sound to mono.

▲ To set compression for sounds consisting of spoken words, choose Speech. Choose a sample-rate from the pop-up menu of options that appears.

Publishing HTML for Flash Player Files

An *HTML document* is the master set of instructions that tells a browser how to display Web content. The Publish function of Flash creates an HTML document that tells the browser how to display the files that Flash creates when you click the Publish button (in Flash, GIF, JPEG, PNG, or QuickTime format).

The Publish command creates the required HTML by filling in blanks in one of the templates provided with Flash or by using a template that you create. The templates included with Flash contain the basic HTML coding needed to display the formats that are available with the Publish command.

To publish HTML for displaying a Flash file:

1. Open the Flash document that you want to publish for the Web.

2. From the File menu, choose Publish Settings.
   The Publish Setting dialog box appears.

3. Click the Formats tab.

4. In the Type section, choose HTML (.html).
   When you choose HTML, Flash automatically selects Flash (.swf) as well. To use a file name other than the default, deselect Use Default Names as the Filename option, and type the appropriate name for your Flash and HTML files.

5. Select the HTML tab (**Figure 16.21**).
   Flash displays the options for displaying your Flash movie in the browser window. When you publish the current file, Flash feeds your choices into the appropriate HTML tags and parameters in the template of your choice.

Digitally Recorded Sounds

As motion pictures are to movement, digital recordings are to sound. Both media capture slices of a continuous event. By playing the captured slices back in order, you re-create the event. In a movie, the slices are frames of film; in a digital recording, they're slices of sound.

You can think of the recording process as capturing a sound wave by laying a grid over it and copying a piece of the wave at each intersection on the grid. The lines across the horizontal axis are the *sample rate*—how often you capture the sound. The lines up and down the vertical axis are the *bit rate*—how much of the sound wave's amplitude you capture. The greater the frequency and bit rate (the finer the mesh of your recording grid), the greater the realism of your recording during playback. Unfortunately, greater realism translates into larger files.

The sound options in the Publish Settings dialog box give you the flexibility to create different versions of your movie with different sample rates and bit rates without actually changing the sounds embedded in the movie. You might allow yourself larger file sizes and higher-quality sounds for a version being delivered on CD-ROM than for a version being distributed on the Web. As you try different sound options, be sure to actually listen to your published sounds to determine the best balance between sound quality and file size.

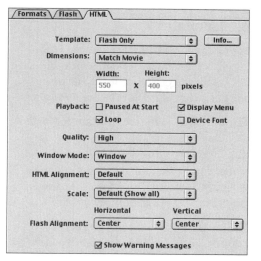

Figure 16.21 The HTML tab of the Publish Settings dialog box displays options for displaying your Flash movie in the browser window.

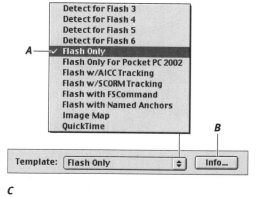

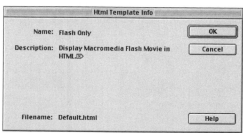

Figure 16.22 Choose Flash Only (A) as the template when you want to create HTML for displaying only a Flash movie, with no other options for alternative images. Click the Info button (B) to see a description of what the template does (C).

To choose an HTML template for Flash only:

◆ From the Template pop-up menu, choose Flash Only (**Figure 16.22**).

This template is the simplest one. It uses the OBJECT and EMBED tags to display your Flash movie for viewers who are properly equipped with the version 6 of Flash Player. Other viewers will be unable to see your movie. (Other template choices create HTML that displays alternative images when the viewer lacks the proper plug-in.)

To choose an HTML template that detects the Flash Player version:

◆ From the Template pop-up menu, choose one of the "Detect for" templates.

The detection templates use JavaScript to check whether a particular version of the Flash Player is installed on a viewer's machine. (Flash MX comes with detection templates for versions 3 through 6 of Flash Player.) If the desired version is not installed, the user can choose to get the Player or view a GIF or JPEG version of your site.

✔ Tip

■ If you can't remember what one of the included HTML templates does, click the Info button next to the Template pop-up menu in the HTML tab of the Publish Settings dialog box. Flash displays a brief description, including instructions about which formats to choose.

The Mystery of HTML Templates

The HTML codes (called *tags*) required for displaying a .swf file in a browser window are OBJECT for Internet Explorer (Windows) and EMBED for Netscape Navigator (Mac and Windows) and Internet Explorer (Mac). (In addition, Flash can use the IMG tag to display a file in another format, such as a JPEG image or an animated GIF. If you have created named anchors in your Flash movie and you choose the Flash with Named Anchors template, Flash can create anchor tags for browser navigation, as well.)

Flash's Publish command works hand in hand with HTML templates—which are fill-in-the-blank recipes—to define the parameters of those tags. These parameters include the width and height of the movie window, the quality of the images (the amount of antialiasing to provide), and the way the movie window aligns with the browser window.

Each option and parameter in the HTML tab of the Publish Settings dialog box has an equivalent template variable. The template variable is a code word that starts with the dollar sign ($). When you choose an option in the Publish Settings dialog box, Flash enters your choice as an HTML tag that replaces the variable in the template document. If you set the width of your movie as 500 pixels in the Publish Settings

dialog box for HTML, for example, Flash replaces the template variable for width ($WI) with the proper coding to display the movie in a window 500 pixels wide.

Flash's HTML templates contain coding not only for displaying your Flash movie, but also for showing the JPEG, GIF, or PNG versions of your movie that you want to make available to viewers who don't have the proper browser player to view Flash.

During the publishing process, Flash saves a copy of the HTML template for your movie, giving it the name of your movie file and adding whatever extension the template file has. (The template files that come with Flash MX use the extension .html, for example.) You can go into a template file as you would any other text file and modify the HTML coding.

You can extend the Publish command's capacity for creating HTML documents by setting up your own HTML templates. To be available to Flash's template menu, the HTML file must include a title (use the code $TT). The HTML file must be inside the HTML folder (Macromedia/Flash MX/Configuration/HTML), which you'll find in the Application Support (Mac) or Application Data (Windows) folder on the drive where you've installed Flash.

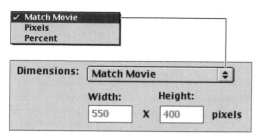

Figure 16.23 Choose a method for sizing the movie-display window (the window in which a browser displays your Flash movie).

Controlling Movie Placement in the Browser

When you publish HTML for displaying movies in a Web page, you need to think in terms of three windows:

◆ The *browser window* contains the entire Web page.

◆ Within the browser window is a *movie-display* window (created by the OBJECT, EMBED, and IMG tags), where the Flash plug-in displays a Flash movie.

◆ Inside the movie-display window is the actual *movie window*.

Each of the three windows has its own dimensions, and you need to tell Flash where to put the windows and how to handle them if their aspect ratios differ, for example, or when a user resizes the browser window.

You instruct browsers on how to deal with these three windows by choosing settings in the HTML tab of the Publish Settings dialog box.

To set the dimensions of the movie-display window:

To set the width and height of the rectangle created by the OBJECT and EMBED tags for displaying your movie in the browser, from the Dimensions pop-up menu in the HTML tab of the Publish Settings dialog box (**Figure 16.23**), *choose one of the following:*

◆ To use the movie's dimensions (specified in the Document Properties dialog box), choose Match Movie.

◆ To specify the dimensions as a percentage of the browser window's dimensions, choose Percent, and type a value between 1 and 100 in the Width and Height fields.

◆ To specify new dimensions, choose Pixels, and type the new values in the Width and Height fields.

MOVIE PLACEMENT IN THE BROWSER

571

When you define a movie-display window with a different width or height from the original Flash movie, you must tell Flash how to scale the movie to fit in that window.

To scale the movie to fit a movie-display window:

From the Scale pop-up menu (**Figure 16.24**), *choose one of the following:*

- To keep the movie's original aspect ratio (width to height) and resize the movie so that it fits completely within the newly specified rectangle, choose Default (Show All) (**Figure 16.25**). (Be aware that the resized movie may not fill the new rectangle: Gaps may appear on the sides or at the top and bottom.)

- To keep the movie's original aspect ratio and resize the movie so that the whole new rectangle is filled with the movie, choose No Border. (Some of the movie may slop over the edges and be cropped.)

- To change the movie's height and width to the new specifications, even if it involves changing the aspect ratio and distorting the image, choose Exact Fit.

- To keep the movie at a constant size, choose No Scale. Resizing the browser window can crop the image.

✔ Tip

- If you define the movie-display window as 100 percent of the width and height of the browser window, in some browser versions, no matter how large your viewer makes the browser window, a scroll bar always appears. Setting the width and height to 95 percent (or lower) ensures that all viewers will be able to enlarge the browser window enough to eliminate the scroll bar.

Figure 16.24 The scale method tells Flash how to fit the Flash movie inside the movie-display window that you define. You need to set the scale only if you define a movie-display window with different dimensions from those of the movie itself—as a percentage of the browser width and height, for example.

Dimensions: Match Movie; Scale: NA

Dimensions: 100 by 50 pixels; Scale: No Border

Dimensions: 100 by 50 pixels; Scale: Exact Fit

Dimensions: 100 by 50 pixels; Scale: Default

Dimensions: % of Window; Scale: Default

Figure 16.25 This 300-by-300 pixel movie looks quite different in the different dimension-and-scale combinations. The movie-display window's dimensions and the scale setting are identified in the examples above.

Horizontal: Left; Vertical: Center

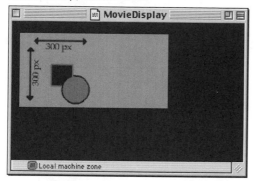

Horizontal: Right; Vertical: Center

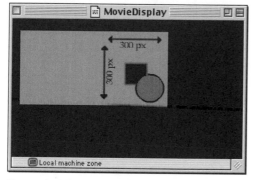

Figure 16.26 The Flash Alignment section's Horizontal and Vertical pop-up menus allow you to position your movie within the movie-display window when the dimensions of that window differ from those of the movie. Compare the results of two different settings for this 300-by-300-pixel movie set inside a 200-by-100-pixel display window. The light-gray rectangle is the display window.

To control placement of the movie window in the movie-display window:

To align the movie window within the movie-display window, in the Flash Alignment section of the HTML tab of the Publish Settings dialog box, *do one of the following:*

◆ From the Horizontal pop-up menu, choose Left, Center, or Right.

◆ From the Vertical pop-up menu, choose Top, Center, or Bottom.

Flash positions the movie within the movie-display window (**Figure 16.26**).

To set playback options:

In the Playback section of the HTML tab of the Publish Settings dialog box, *choose any of the following options:*

◆ To make users begin the movie manually (by clicking a button or by choosing Play from the contextual menu), choose Paused At Start.

◆ To create a contextual menu with playback options that are available to users, choose Display Menu.

◆ To make the movie start over when it reaches the last frame, choose Loop.

◆ To speed playback on Windows systems, choose Device Font. The Device Font option allows Windows systems to substitute aliased system fonts for fonts that are not installed on the user's system. This substitution takes place only in static text blocks where you have enabled device fonts during the authoring phase.

For the best viewing experience, you need to balance the image quality and playback speed of your published movie.

To control antialiasing and smoothing:

From the Quality pop-up menu in the HTML tab of the Publish Settings dialog box (**Figure 16.27**), *choose one of the following options:*

◆ **Low**. Flash keeps antialiasing off.

◆ **Auto Low**. Flash starts playback with antialiasing off, but if it finds that the viewer's computer and connection can handle antialiasing while keeping the movie's specified frame rate, Flash turns antialiasing on.

◆ **Auto High**. Flash turns antialiasing on to start with and turns it off if playback drops below the movie's specified frame rate.

◆ **Medium**. Taking the middle ground, Flash forgoes bitmap smoothing but does do some antialiasing.

◆ **High**. Flash uses antialiasing on everything but smooths bitmaps only if there is no animation.

◆ **Best**. Flash keeps antialiasing on.

On Windows computers running Internet Explorer 4.0 with the Flash ActiveX control, Flash movies can have transparent backgrounds.

To control transparency (Windows only):

From the Window Mode pop-up menu, *choose one of the following options:*

◆ To play the movie in its own window within the Web page, choose Window.

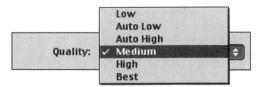

Figure 16.27 The Quality setting for publishing HTML balances image quality against playback speed in a published movie.

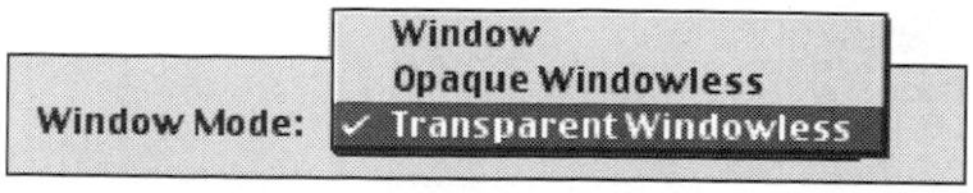

Figure 16.28 For viewers of your movie who use Internet Explorer 4.0 with the ActiveX control on the Windows platform, you can create a transparency effect that reveals Web-page elements beneath any transparent areas of your Flash movie. In the HTML tab of the Publish Settings dialog box, set Window Mode to Transparent Windowless.

Title of template for menu

```
$TTFlash Only
$DS
Display Macromedia Flash Movie in HTML.
$DF

<HTML>
<HEAD>

$CS
<TITLE>$TI</TITLE>
</HEAD>
<BODY bgcolor="$BG">
```

Background-color variable

Title of template for menu

```
$TTFlash Only (BlackBackground)
$DS
Display Macromedia Flash Movie in HTML.
$DF

<HTML>
<HEAD>

$CS
<TITLE>$TI</TITLE>
</HEAD>
<BODY bgcolor="000000">
```

Background-color variable

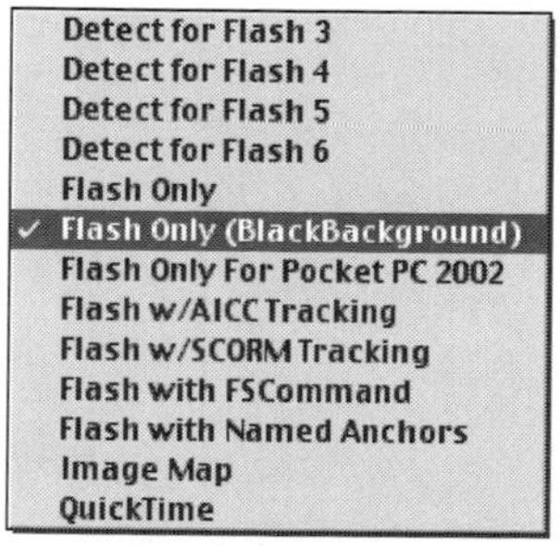

Figure 16.29 The default HTML template picks up the movie's background color as the Web page's background color. You can modify a copy of the template (top). Change the Title tag, and set a specific background color (middle). The new title appears in the Template menu in the HTML tab of the Publish Settings dialog box (bottom).

- To make the transparent areas of your movie block out the background and other elements of the Web page that lie below the Flash movie, choose Opaque Windowless.
- To allow those elements to show through in any transparent areas of your movie, choose Transparent Windowless (**Figure 16.28**).

To alert users to problems with HTML:

- At the bottom of the HTML tab of the Publish Settings dialog box, check the Show Warning Message check box if you want Flash to display error messages when it finds problems with your HTML tags.

✔ Tip

- The default HTML template automatically sets the background color of your Web page to the background color of your movie. If you want to use a different color, try creating a modified template (**Figure 16.29**). Open the default template, and save a copy with a new name. In the first line of code—`$TTFlash Only`—change the title to something like `$TTFlash Only (MyBackground)`, so that Flash recognizes and adds the template to the Template menu. In the `tag <BODY bgcolor="$BG">`, replace `$BG` with the HTML code for a specific hex color (`000000` for a black background, for example). Be sure to place the new template in Flash's HTML folder (Macromedia/Flash MX/Configuration/HTML), which you'll find in the Application Support (Mac) or Application Data (Windows) folder on the drive where you've installed Flash.

Using HTML for Alternative Images

Although most of your viewers will have access to the plug-ins that they need to view your Flash movies, some may not. You can make at least some of your site available to them by providing alternative image files for their browsers to display. If you're using Flash animations for a simple Web banner, for example, you could use an animated GIF to re-create that banner for viewers who lack the Flash plug-in. The other alternative files types are JPEG, PNG, and QuickTime.

To publish HTML for displaying an animated GIF:

1. Open the Flash document for which you want to create an alternative GIF image.

2. Choose File > Publish Settings.
   The Publish Setting dialog box appears.

3. In the Formats tab, choose GIF Image (.gif) and HTML (.html).

4. Set the options for Flash as described in "Working with Flash Player Settings" earlier in this chapter.

5. In the HTML tab, from the Template pop-up menu, choose any of the "Detect for" templates (**Figure 16.30**).

   These templates allow Flash to create an HTML document that uses JavaScript to check the viewer's browser for the specified version of Flash Player. If that version, or a later version, is not available, the HTML calls for a display of the animated GIF that you're about to set up and publish.

6. Set the other HTML options as described in "Publishing HTML for Flash Player Files" earlier in this chapter.

Figure 16.30 All of the "Detect for" HTML templates will display alternative images if your viewer doesn't have access to the specified version of Flash Player. When you choose one of these templates, you must also choose one of the alternative formats, such as GIF.

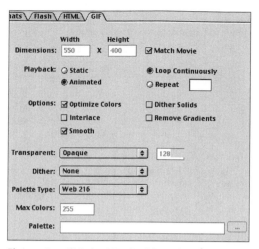

Figure 16.31 Click the GIF tab of the Publish Settings dialog box to access the options for creating a static or animated GIF for your alternative image.

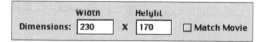

Figure 16.32 Deselect Match Movie to enter the dimensions you want the published GIF image to be, or choose Match Movie to use the movie's dimensions as the dimensions of your GIF image.

Figure 16.33 To preserve the motion of your Flash movie (though not the sound or interactivity) for viewers who lack the Flash plug-in, choose Animated in the GIF tab of the Publish Settings dialog box.

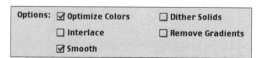

Figure 16.34 The settings in the Options section of the GIF tab help you limit the amount of time that your viewers will spend looking at a blank screen, waiting for an image to appear. (The Remove Gradients option is available only in the Publish Settings dialog box, not in the Export GIF dialog box.)

7. In the GIF tab (**Figure 16.31**), set GIF options as described in the following exercises.

8. Click Publish.

To set the dimensions of the GIF image:

In the Dimensions section of the GIF tab of the Publish Settings dialog box, *do one of the following:*

◆ To keep the GIF images the same size as the original Flash movie, choose Match Movie (**Figure 16.32**).

◆ To create a new size for the published GIF image, deselect Match Movie and enter values in the Width and Height fields.

To make an animated GIF:

1. In the Playback section of the GIF tab of the Publish Settings dialog box, choose Animated (**Figure 16.33**).

   The animation settings become active.

2. Choose Loop Continuously.

   You can also limit the number of times that the animation loops by choosing Repeat and typing a number. (Choosing Static makes Flash export only the first frame of the movie as a single GIF image.)

To balance size, download speed, and appearance:

In the Options section of the GIF tab of the Publish Settings dialog box (**Figure 16.34**), *do one of the following:*

◆ To remove any unused colors from the GIF file's color table, choose Optimize Colors.

(continues on next page)

- To make the GIF appear quickly at low resolution and come into focus as the download continues, choose Interlace. (The Interlace option should be used only for static GIFs.)

- To reduce the size of the file, deselect Smooth. (Select it if you want Flash to create smoothed bitmaps for your animated GIF.)

- To apply the dither method to solids as well as gradients and bitmapped images, choose Dither Solids (see "To control colors that are not in the current color palette" later in this chapter).

- To reduce file size by converting gradient fills to solid fills, choose Remove Gradients. (Flash uses the first color in the gradient as the solid fill color.)

To set a GIF's background transparency:

From the Transparent pop-up menu of the GIF tab of the Publish Settings dialog box (**Figure 16.35**), *do one of the following:*

- To make background areas of the Flash movie opaque in the published GIF, choose Opaque.

- To make the background areas of the Flash movie transparent in the published GIF, choose Transparent.

The Alpha and Threshold settings control not only the background of your movie, but also any shapes with transparent fills within the movie.

Figure 16.35 The Transparent setting (top) determines how the background of a published GIF appears. Choose Opaque to make the background a solid color (middle); choose Transparent to make the background invisible (bottom).

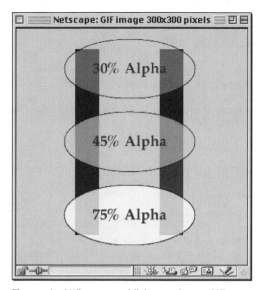

Figure 16.36 When you publish a movie as a GIF, you can make partially transparent graphic elements sitting on the background of the Flash movie look fully transparent in a browser window. Each oval here has the same color fill but a different Alpha value. For this GIF, the Transparent option is set to Alpha with a threshold of 128 (equal to 50 percent Alpha in Flash). The 30 percent and 45 percent ovals are fully transparent where only background lies below them. Where those ovals overlap other graphic elements, however, they are 30 percent and 45 percent transparent, respectively. The 75 percent oval (above the threshold value) retains its partial transparency even over the background.

Figure 16.37 The GIF format has three options for dithering the colors that are not included in the current color table.

To control transparency of Flash fill colors in GIFs:

◆ From the Transparent pop-up menu in the GIF tab of the Publish Settings dialog box, choose Alpha.

The Alpha setting makes the GIF's background transparent and allows you to set a threshold below which partially transparent fills in Flash convert to full transparency in the published GIF. The threshold settings are values from 0 to 255 (the number of possible colors in a GIF image). The default threshold value is 128 (corresponding to an Alpha value of 50 percent in Flash).

✔ Tip

■ The GIF Alpha transparency setting can have unexpected results, especially in animated GIFs. Full GIF transparency appears only where a filled graphic element sits directly on the background of the Flash movie. Wherever the graphic element overlaps (or moves over) another fill, the "invisible" graphic suddenly pops into view again (**Figure 16.36**).

If the graphic elements of your Flash file contain colors that are not part of the current color palette, you must tell Flash how to deal with those colors when creating GIFs for the published movie.

To control colors that are not in the current color palette:

1. From the Dither pop-up menu of the GIF tab of the Publish Settings dialog box (**Figure 16.37**), *choose one of the following options:*

   ▲ To replace the missing color with the closest match from the current palette, choose None.

   ▲ To simulate the missing color by applying a regular pattern of colors from the current palette, choose Ordered.

▲ To simulate the missing color by applying a random pattern of colors from the Web 216 palette, choose Diffusion. (You must also choose Web 216 as your Palette Type in Step 2 for Diffusion to work.)

2. From the Palette Type pop-up menu, choose a color table for use with this GIF (**Figure 16.38**).

   Your choices are Web 216 (the standard 216 Web-safe colors), Adaptive (only colors used in your movie; 256 colors maximum), Web Snap Adaptive (a modified Adaptive palette, substituting Web-safe colors for any near matches to colors in the animation that are not Web safe), and Custom (the color table specified in Step 4).

3. If you chose Adaptive or Web Snap Adaptive as the Palette Type, in the Max Colors field, type the number of colors that you want to use.

   This option allows you to further limit the size of the color table available for the GIF and, thus, reduce file size.

4. If you chose Custom as the Palette Type, load the custom palette (**Figure 16.39**).

   Click the ellipsis (...) button. In the file-import dialog box that appears, navigate to the custom palette, select it, and click Import (Mac) or Open (Windows).

✔ Tip

■ You don't have to turn your entire movie into an animated GIF. You can tell Flash to publish a subset of the movie's frames. Assign the label #First to the first keyframe of the subset; assign the label #Last to the keyframe that ends the subset. Flash creates an animated GIF from that range of frames (**Figure 16.40**).

Figure 16.38 Choose a palette that optimizes colors for the published GIF image. You can create custom palettes or use the Web-safe or adaptive palettes provided by Flash.

Figure 16.39 When you choose Custom from the Palette Type pop-up menu, you must enter a file name in the Palette field. Click the ellipsis button to open a dialog box for locating the file.

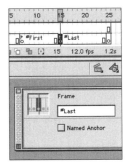

Figure 16.40 Assigning the frame labels #First and #Last allows you to limit the range of frames that Flash publishes as an animated GIF.

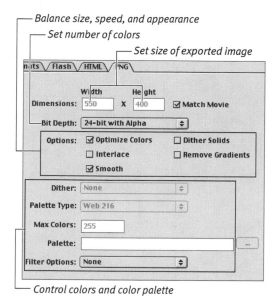

— *Balance size, speed, and appearance*
— *Set number of colors*
— *Set size of exported image*
— *Control colors and color palette*

Figure 16.41 The options for publishing PNGs are similar to those for publishing GIFs (described earlier in this chapter).

Using Other Publish Settings

In the preceding exercises, you learned about the specific publish settings for Flash and GIF files. Flash's Publish Settings dialog box also contains tabs for PNG, JPEG, and QuickTime formats. You can choose an HTML template that publishes GIF and JPEG images as alternatives to Flash for viewers who lack Flash Player.

To publish PNG files:

1. Open the Flash file for which you want to create an alternative PNG image.

2. Choose File > Publish Settings.
   The Publish Settings dialog box appears.

3. In the Formats tab, choose Flash, PNG Image, and HTML.

4. In the HTML tab, from the Template pop-up menu, choose any of the "Detect for" templates.

   If the specified (or later) version of Flash Player is not available, the HTML calls for the viewer's browser to display the PNG you're about to publish.

5. Choose the PNG tab, and set its options (**Figure 16.41**).

6. Click Publish.

To publish JPEG files:

1. Open the Flash file for which you want to create an alternative JPEG image.

2. Choose File > Publish Settings.
   The Publish Settings dialog box appears.

3. In the Formats tab, choose Flash, JPEG Image, and HTML.

4. In the HTML tab, from the Template pop-up menu, choose any of the "Detect for" templates.

   If the specified (or later) version of Flash Player is not available, the HTML calls for the viewer's browser to display the JPEG that you're about to publish.

5. Choose the JPEG tab, and set its options (**Figure 16.42**).

6. Click Publish.

To publish QuickTime 4 files:

1. Open the Flash file for which you want to create a QuickTime movie.

2. Choose File > Publish Settings.
   The Publish Settings dialog box appears.

3. In the Formats tab, choose Flash, QuickTime, and HTML.

4. In the HTML tab, from the Template pop-up menu, choose QuickTime.

   This template allows Flash to create an HTML document that lets the browser display the QuickTime movie you're about to publish.

5. Choose the QuickTime tab, and set its options (**Figure 16.43**).

6. Click Publish.

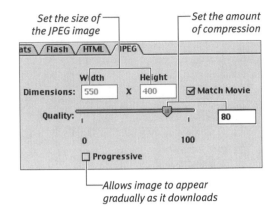

Set the size of the JPEG image

Set the amount of compression

Allows image to appear gradually as it downloads

Figure 16.42 The options for publishing JPEGs help you balance file size (download time) against quality.

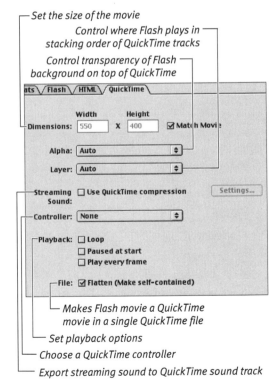

Set the size of the movie

Control where Flash plays in stacking order of QuickTime tracks

Control transparency of Flash background on top of QuickTime

Makes Flash movie a QuickTime movie in a single QuickTime file

Set playback options

Choose a QuickTime controller

Export streaming sound to QuickTime sound track

Figure 16.43 Set the options for publishing QuickTime movies in the QuickTime tab.

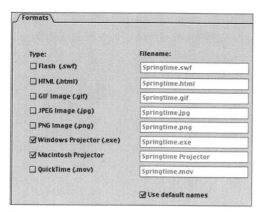

Figure 16.44 To create a run-time version of your movie, choose Windows Projector or Macintosh Projector in the Formats tab of the Publish Settings dialog box. You have no other options for formatting projectors.

Figure 16.45 The projector is a stand-alone run-time file. Double-click the icon to launch the projector.

Playing Macintosh Projectors Created in Windows

When you publish a Macintosh projector on a computer running the Windows operating system, Flash gives the projector the extension .hqx. That extension indicates a file encoded in binhex format. Macintosh users need to translate the file by using a program such as BinHex or StuffIt Deluxe to play the projector on the Mac OS.

Creating Projectors

Projectors are self-sufficient run-time applications. To play a projector file, you simply double-click the projector icon. Projectors are an excellent way to distribute movies directly to people, such as to e-mail a Flash-animated greeting card to a friend. Projectors are platform-specific, but you can make projectors for both platforms from either platform.

To create a projector:

1. Open the Flash movie from which you want to publish a projector.

2. Choose File > Publish Settings.
   The Publish Settings dialog box appears.

3. In the Formats tab (**Figure 16.44**), *choose one of the following options:*
   ▲ To create a projector that runs on a Mac, choose Macintosh Projector.
   ▲ To create a projector that runs in Windows, choose Windows Projector (.exe).

4. Click the Publish button.
   As it creates the projector files, Flash displays the Publishing dialog box, which has a progress bar and a button for canceling the operation. Flash places the projector files in the same location as the original Flash movie. A projector has a distinctive icon (**Figure 16.45**).

✔ Tip

■ If your projector movie includes any loadMovie or getURL actions, you must keep the additional files at the same hierarchical level as the projector. Place the projector and its ancillary files together in one folder; otherwise, the projector can't find the files to load.

Setting MIME Types on Your Server

For browsers to recognize and display Flash files, the server that delivers the Flash Player (.swf) files must tell the browser what type of files it's serving. This information is called the *MIME type*. The intricacies of server administration are beyond the scope of this book, but this section provides a basic description of the MIME types and the Flash suffixes to add to your server's configuration files. (Check out the Macromedia Flash Support Center at */www.macromedia.com/support/flash* for technical notes about setting MIME types on specific servers.)

To identify a MIME type:

To update your server's configuration files, *do one of the following:*

◆ For files published as Flash Player 2 through 6 or exported as Flash Movie, add the MIME type `application/x-shockwave-flash` and the associated suffix `.swf`.

◆ For files published as Flash Player 1 or exported as FutureSplash Player, add the MIME type `application/futuresplash` and the associated suffix `.spl`.

To set additional parameters for Macintosh servers:

1. For servers hosting movies published as Flash Player 2 through 6, *do the following:*
   ▲ Set the Action parameter to `Binary`.
   ▲ Set the Type parameter to `SWFL`.
   ▲ Set the Creator parameter to `SWF2`.

2. For servers hosting movies published as Flash Player 1 or FutureSplash Player, *do the following:*
   ▲ Set the Action parameter to `Binary`.
   ▲ Set the Type parameter to `TEXT`.
   ▲ Set the Creator parameter to `Fspl`.

Click to get MIME type for current URL

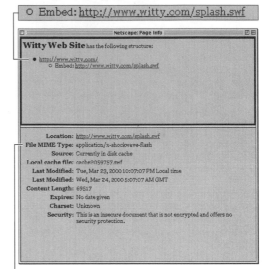

MIME type of the server where this URL is located

Figure 16.46 The View > Document Info (or View > Page Info) command in Netscape Navigator lets you see whether the MIME type has been set correctly on the server where your Web site is located.

✔ Tip

■ You can use Netscape Navigator to check whether the MIME type has been set properly on the server where you're posting your Flash movies. In Navigator, surf to a movie on the server that you want to check. From Navigator's View menu, choose Page Info (or Document Info). In the window that appears, click the Embed link for the .swf file. Navigator lists the MIME type for the Embed URL in the bottom frame of the browser window (**Figure 16.46**). See whether the type displayed there matches the MIME type that you need.

Figure 16.47 To export a single frame of your movie, choose File > Export Image.

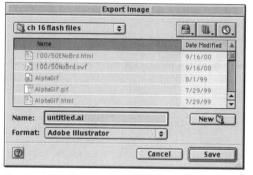

Figure 16.48 The Export Image dialog box allows you to select an export format, name your file, and navigate to the location where you want to save the file.

Exporting Flash to Other Formats

When you export Flash movies, you can export the entire movie or just one frame. Flash exports to a variety of formats that are not included in the Publish Settings dialog box: for both Mac and Windows, Adobe Illustrator, EPS, and DXF; for Mac only, PICT and QuickTime Video; and for Windows only, Enhanced Metafile (EMF), Windows Metafile (WMF), Windows AVI, and WAV. Although the options for the export formats differ, the basic process is always the same. The example used in the following sections exports to Illustrator format, which preserves the vector information from your Flash graphics.

To export a single frame to Illustrator format:

1. Open the Flash file that contains the frame that you want to export to another format.

2. In the Timeline, move the playhead to the frame that you want to export.

3. From the File menu, choose Export Image (**Figure 16.47**).

   The Export Image dialog box appears (**Figure 16.48**).

4. Navigate to the location where you want to save the file.

5. Enter a name in the Name (Mac) or Filename (Windows) field.

6. From the Format (Mac) or Save As Type (Windows) pop-up menu, choose Adobe Illustrator.

   Flash adds the proper extension, .ai, to your file name.

   (continues on next page)

7. Click Save.

The Export Adobe Illustrator dialog box appears (**Figure 16.49**).

Whenever your chosen export format requires you to set further parameters, Flash displays those parameters in a dialog box after you click Save. For Illustrator format, the additional parameter is a version number.

8. Choose the version to which you want to export.

9. Click OK.

Flash displays the Exporting dialog box, which contains a progress bar and a button for canceling the export process.

To export the entire movie to Illustrator format:

◆ Follow the instructions in the preceding exercise, but in step 3, from the File menu, choose Export Movie, or press Option-Shift-⌘-S (Mac) or Ctrl-Alt-Shift-S (Windows) (**Figure 16.50**), and in step 6, choose Adobe Illustrator Sequence.

When you chose Export Movie, Flash creates a separate Illustrator file for each frame of the movie and numbers the files sequentially.

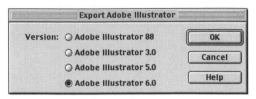

Figure 16.49 Whenever an export format requires additional settings, a dialog box with format-specific options appears when you click Save in the Export Image dialog box. You can export to four versions of Illustrator, for example.

Figure 16.50 To export all the frames of your movie, choose File > Export Movie.

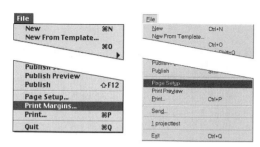

Figure 16.51 To define print settings for frames of your movie, choose File > Print Margins (Mac) or Page Setup (Windows).

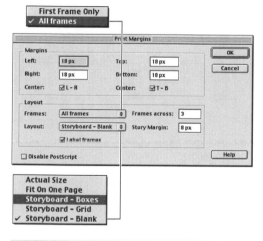

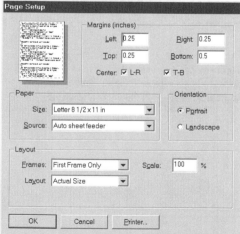

Figure 16.52 The options in the Print Margins (Mac, top) and Page Setup (Windows, bottom) dialog boxes enable you to print the frames of your movie as single pages or as storyboard layouts.

Printing from Flash

In Flash, you can print frames of a movie as individual pages or print several frames per page in a storyboard layout. You choose how many frames each row in the storyboard contains. Flash sizes the frames accordingly. Use the Print Margins (Mac) or Page Setup (Windows) command to choose layout options.

To print a single frame:

1. Open the Flash document from which you want to print.

2. From the File menu, choose Print Margins (Mac) or Page Setup (Windows) (**Figure 16.51**).

   The Print Margins or Page Setup dialog box appears (**Figure 16.52**).

3. From the Frames pop-up menu, choose All Frames.

4. From the Layout pop-up menu, choose Fit on One Page.

5. Click OK.

6. From the File menu, choose Print.
   The Print dialog box appears.

7. Enter the desired frame numbers in the From and To fields.

8. Click Print.

✔ Tip

■ If your Macintosh printer isn't capable of printing PostScript, be sure to check the Disable PostScript checkbox.

To print storyboard thumbnails:

1. Follow steps 1 through 3 of the preceding exercise.

2. From the Layout pop-up menu, *choose one of the following options:*
   ▲ To outline each movie-frame rectangle, choose Storyboard-Boxes.
   ▲ To print the frames in a grid, choose Storyboard-Grid.
   ▲ To print just the graphic elements of each movie frame, choose Storyboard-Blank.

   The layout parameters appear.

3. In the Frames Across field, enter the number of frames that you want to print across the page.

   Flash prints as many as 128 frames in a single storyboard row.

4. In the Story Margin (Mac) or Frame Margin (Windows) field, enter the amount of space that you want to use between frames in your layout.

5. Click OK.

6. From the File menu, choose Print.

   The Print dialog box appears.

7. If you want to print only some pages of your thumbnails, type those page numbers in the From and To fields.

8. Click OK.

   Flash creates the thumbnails, using the options you specified (**Figure 16.53**).

✔ Tip

■ To print the scene and frame number below each frame in the layout, choose Label Frames in the Print Margins (Mac) or Page Setup (Windows) dialog box.

Storyboard boxes

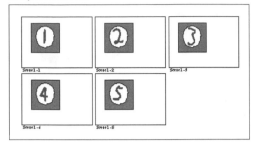

Storyboard grid

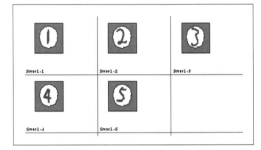

Storyboard blank

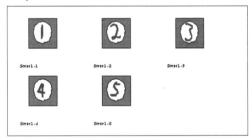

Figure 16.53 The Layout menu of the Print Margins (Mac) or Page Setup (Windows) dialog box offers three storyboard options: movie frames outlined in a box, frames set inside a grid, or each frame alone.

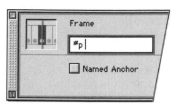

Figure 16.54 To define keyframes that print when viewers choose Print from Flash Player's contextual menu, select the keyframe and enter #p in the Label field of the Frame Property Inspector.

Figure 16.55 In your browser, Control-click (Mac) or right-click (Windows) to access Flash Player's contextual menu. Choosing Print outputs all the pages defined as printable.

Printing from Flash Player

Flash gives you the option of letting your viewers print some or all of a movie directly from Flash Player. You can allow viewers to access a print command from Flash Player's contextual menu. By default, the contextual menu's Print command prints every frame in the movie. You restrict printing to certain frames by labeling them as printable in the original Flash document. You can also create buttons for printing frames of your Flash movie.

To set frames to print from the contextual menu:

1. Create a Flash document with three keyframes.

   Place different content in each frame to make it easy to tell which frames you've actually printed. Add a **stop** action to each keyframe, and add a button with a **play** action so that you can move from frame to frame in the published movie.

2. In the Timeline, select Keyframe 1.

3. Access the Frames Property Inspector.

   If the Frames Property Inspector is not open, choose Window > Properties.

4. To define the selected frame as printable, in the Label field, enter #p (**Figure 16.54**).

5. In the Timeline, select Keyframe 3.

6. Repeat Step 4.

7. Publish your Flash movie, and view the resulting Flash Player file in your browser.

8. To access the contextual menu, Control-click (Mac) or right-click (Windows) anywhere in the movie window.

   The contextual menu appears (**Figure 16.55**).

(continues on next page)

9. Choose Print.

Flash prints the frames you labeled as printable (frames 1 and 3) and skips the frame that doesn't contain the #p label (Frame 2).

✔ Tips

- If there are no frames with the #p label in the movie, the contextual menu's Print command prints each frame in the movie.

- If you define more than one frame as printable by labeling it #p, when you publish the movie, Flash displays a warning message in the Output window, letting you know that there are multiple frames with the same label name. If the only duplicates are #p labels, just ignore the warning.

You can also create buttons that use ActionScript to print selected frames.

To set frames to print from a button:

1. Open the file you created in the preceding exercise.

Keyframes 1 and 3 already contain the frame label #p. Even when you print via ActionScript, you must define the printable frames with this frame label.

2. Place an instance of a button in Keyframe 1.

3. With the button selected on the Stage, access the Actions-Button panel.

4. From the Add menu, choose Actions > Printing > print.

Flash updates the Script pane to look like **Figure 16.56**.

5. In the Script pane, select Line 2.

The parameters for the print action appear in the Parameters area (**Figure 16.57**).

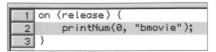

Figure 16.56 Attaching a print action to an instance of a button is another way to give viewers the ability to print the contents of your movie.

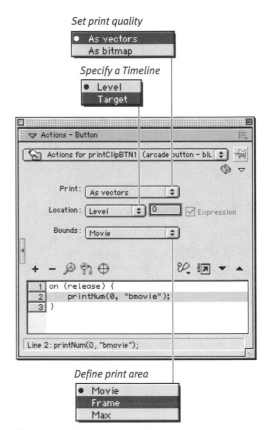

Figure 16.57 The parameters for the print action allow you to control print quality and print area, in addition to targeting a particular Timeline for printing.

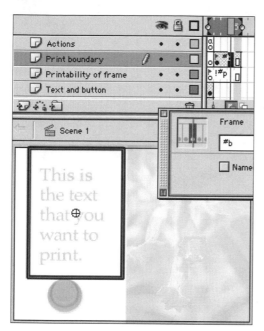

Figure 16.58 The #b frame label tells Flash to use the objects in this frame as the bounding box for printed output. The black rectangle—the only object in the #b frame—defines the print area in the published movie.

6. To set print quality, from the Print pop-up menu, *choose one of the following:*

   ▲ To print at high quality, without transparency, choose As Vector.

   ▲ To preserve transparency effects, choose As Bitmap.

7. To designate which Timeline to print when you have loaded more than one movie (or you want to print a particular movie clip), from the Location menu, *choose one of the following:*

   ▲ Choose Level, and enter the level number of the loaded movie.

   ▲ Choose Target, and enter the target path of the movie clip.

8. To define the print area, from the Bounding pop-up menu, *choose one of the following options:*

   ▲ To use an object in a particular frame as a template for setting the print area, choose Movie. For the Movie option to work, you must also define the template frame. Select the frame containing the template object, access the Frame Property Inspector, and enter #b as the frame label (**Figure 16.58**).

   ▲ To vary the print area to enclose just the objects in each frame and scale those objects to fit the page, choose Frame.

   ▲ To make the print area large enough to print all the objects in all the movie's frames, choose Max.

✔ Tips

■ If you want to give your end users the ability to print items one at a time, instead of printing all the printable frames in your movie each time they choose Print (or click a button with a `print` command in its script), put the printable items in movie clips. You can then use buttons whose scripts target individual movie clips for printing.

■ Using the #b label to create a bounding box for printing can be a bit tricky in a movie with many layers. All the objects in the #b frame—no matter what layer they live in—become part of the print area.

■ The bounding-box object need not be visible in the final movie. Place an instance of a movie clip as your bounding-box object, and use `onClipEvent (load)` to set the instance's `_visible` property to `false`.

PRINTING FROM FLASH PLAYER

591

To disable printing from Flash Player:

1. Open the Flash file for which you want to disable printing.

2. In the Timeline, select any frame.

3. Access the Frame Property Inspector.

4. In the Label field, enter !#p.

   When you publish the file, the Print option is unavailable from Flash Player's contextual menu (**Figure 16.59**).

✔ Tip

- You can remove the contextual menu from your published Flash Player file by unchecking the Display Menu checkbox in the Playback section of the HTML tab of the Publish Settings dialog box (**Figure 16.60**).

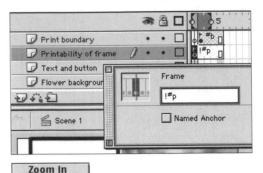

Figure 16.59 Attaching the label !#p to any frame in a movie (top) grays out the Print option in the contextual menu of Flash Player (bottom).

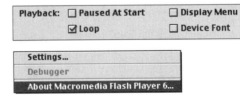

Figure 16.60 Deselecting the Display Menu checkbox in the HTML tab of the Publish Settings dialog box (top) limits the functions of the contextual menu for your published movie and is one way to disable printing from within your movie (bottom). The browser's print functions will still be available, however.

KEYBOARD SHORTCUTS

Shortcuts for Commands

COMMAND	WINDOWS	MACINTOSH	MENU
100% (View)	Ctrl-1	⌘-1	View > Magnification
Accessibility Panel (Show/Hide)	Alt-F2	Option-F2	Window
Actions Panel (Show/Hide)	F9	F9	Window
Add Shape Hint	Ctrl-Shift-H	⌘-Shift-H	Modify > Shape
Align (Objects) Bottom	Ctrl-Alt-6	⌘-Option-6	Modify > Align
Align (Objects) Left	Ctrl-Alt-1	⌘-Option-1	Modify > Align
Align (Objects) Right	Ctrl-Alt-3	⌘-Option-3	Modify > Align
Align (Objects) to Stage (toggle)	Ctrl-Alt-8	⌘-Option-8	Modify > Align
Align (Objects) Top	Ctrl-Alt-4	⌘-Option-4	Modify > Align
Align (Text) Center	Ctrl-Shift-C	⌘-Shift-C	Text > Align
Align (Text) Left	Ctrl-Shift-L	⌘-Shift-L	Text > Align
Align (Text) Right	Ctrl-Shift-R	⌘-Shift-R	Text > Align
Align Panel (Show/Hide)	Ctrl-K	⌘-K	Window
Answers Panel (Show/Hide)	Alt-F1	Option-F1	Window
Antialias Text	Ctrl-Alt-Shift-T	⌘-Shift-Option-T	View
Antialias	Ctrl-Alt-Shift-A	⌘-Shift-Option-A	View
Auto Format	Ctrl-Shift-F	⌘-Shift-F	Actions Panel Options
Bandwidth Profiler (Show/Hide)	Ctrl-B	⌘-B	View (in Test Movie mode)
Bold (Text)	Ctrl-Shift-B	⌘-Shift-B	Text > Style
Break Apart	Ctrl-B	⌘-B	Modify
Bring (Selected Item) to Front	Ctrl-Shift-Up	⌘-Shift-Up	Modify > Arrange
Bring (Selected Item) Forward	Ctrl-Up	⌘-Up	Modify > Arrange
Center Horizontal (Objects)	Ctrl-Alt-5	⌘-Option-5	Modify > Align
Center Vertical (Objects)	Ctrl-Alt-2	⌘-Option-2	Modify > Align
Check Syntax	Ctrl-T	⌘-T	Actions Panel Options
Clear Frames	Alt-Backspace	Option-Delete	Edit
Clear (Stage)	Backspace or Delete	Delete or Clear	Edit
Clear Keyframe	Shift-F6	Shift-F6	Insert
Close (File)	Ctrl-W	⌘-W	File
Color Mixer Panel (Show/Hide)	Shift-F9	Shift-F9	Window
Color Swatches Panel (Show/Hide)	Ctrl-F9	⌘-F9	Window

Shortcuts for Commands *(continued)*

COMMAND	WINDOWS	MACINTOSH	MENU
Component Parameters Panel (Show/Hide)	Alt-F7	Option-F7	Window
Components Panel (Show/Hide)	Ctrl-F7	⌘-F7	Window
Continue	F8	F8	Control (in Test Movie Mode)
Convert to Blank Keyframes	F7	F7	Modify > Frames
Convert to Keyframes	F6	F6	Modify > Frames
Convert to Symbol	F8	F8	Insert
Copy (Selection)	Ctrl-C	⌘-C	Edit
Copy Frames	Ctrl-Alt-C	⌘-Option-C	Edit
Cut (Selection)	Ctrl-X	⌘-X	Edit
Cut Frames	Ctrl-Alt-X	⌘-Option-X	Edit
Debug Movie	Ctrl-Shift-Enter	⌘-Shift-Return	Control
Debugger Panel (Show/Hide)	Shift-F4	Shift-F4	Window
Decrease (Tracking)	Ctrl-Alt-Left	⌘-Option-Left	Text > Tracking
Default (Publishing)	Ctrl-⌘, F12	Ctrl-⌘, F12	File > Publish Preview
Deselect All	Ctrl-Shift-A	⌘-Shift-A	Edit
Distribute Heights	Ctrl-Alt-9	⌘-Option-9	Modify > Align
Distribute to Layers	Ctrl-Shift-D	⌘-Shift-D	Modify
Distribute Widths	Ctrl-Alt-7	⌘-Option-7	Modify > Align
Document Properties	Ctrl-J	⌘-J	Modify
Duplicate (Selection)	Ctrl-D	⌘-D	Edit
Edit Grid	Ctrl-Alt-G	⌘-Option-G	View > Grid
Edit Guides	Ctrl-Alt-Shift-G	⌘-Shift-Option-G	View > Guides
Edit Symbols	Ctrl-E	⌘-E	Edit
Enable Simple Buttons	Ctrl-Alt-B	⌘-Option-B	Control
Expert Mode	Ctrl-Shift-E	⌘-Shift-E	Actions Panel Options
Export as File	Ctrl-Shift-X	⌘-Shift-X	Actions Panel Options
Export Movie	Ctrl-Alt-Shift-S	⌘-Shift-Option-S	File
Fast (View)	Ctrl-Alt-Shift-F	⌘-Shift-Option-F	View
Find	Ctrl-F	⌘-F	Actions Panel Options
Find Again	F3	⌘-G	Actions Panel Options
First (Scene)	Home	Home	View > Goto
Frame (Add)	F5	F5	Insert
Frame-by-Frame Graph (Show)	Ctrl-F	⌘-F	View (in Test Movie-Mode)
Go to Line	Ctrl-G	⌘-, [comma]	Actions Panel Options
Grid (Show/Hide)	Ctrl-'	⌘-'	View > Grid
Group (Selected Items)	Ctrl-G	⌘-G	Modify
Guides (Show/Hide)	Ctrl-;	⌘-;	View > Guides
Hide Edges (Show/Hide Selection Highlight)	Ctrl-H	⌘-Shift-E	View
Import	Ctrl-R	⌘-R	File
Import (Text) from File	Ctrl-Shift-I	⌘-Shift-I	Actions Panel Options
Increase (Tracking)	Ctrl-Alt-Right	⌘-Option-Right	Text > Tracking
Info Panel (Show/Hide)	Ctrl-I	⌘-I	Window
Italic (Text)	Ctrl-Shift-I	⌘-Shift-I	Text > Style
Justify (Text)	Ctrl-Shift-J	⌘-Shift-J	Text > Align

Shortcut for Commands *(continued)*

COMMAND	WINDOWS	MACINTOSH	MENU
Last (Scene)	End	End	View > Goto
Library window (Show/Hide)	Ctrl-L, F11	⌘-L, F11	Window
List Objects	Ctrl-L	⌘-L	Debug (in Test Movie Mode)
List Variables	Ctrl-Alt-V	⌘-Option-V	Debug (in Test Movie Mode)
Lock (Group)	Ctrl-Alt-L	⌘-Option-L	Modify > Arrange
Lock Guides	Ctrl-Alt-; (semi-colon)	⌘-Option-; (semi-colon)	View > Guide
Make Same Height	Ctrl-Shift-Alt-9	⌘-Option-Shift-9	Modify > Align
Make Same Width	Ctrl-Shift-Alt-7	⌘-Option-Shift-7	Modify > Align
Movie Explorer Panel (Show/Hide)	Alt-F3	Option-F3	Window
New (File)	Ctrl-N	⌘-N	File
New Symbol	Ctrl-F8	⌘-F8	Insert
New Window	Ctrl-Alt-N	⌘-Option-N	Window
Next (Scene)	Page Down	Page Down	View > Goto
Normal Mode	Ctrl-Shift-N	⌘-Shift-N	Actions Panel Options
Open (File)	Ctrl-O	⌘-O	File
Open as Library	Ctrl-Shift-O	⌘-Shift-O	File
Optimize (Curves)	Ctrl-Alt-Shift-C	⌘-Shift-Option-C	Modify
Outlines (View As)	Ctrl-Alt-Shift-O	⌘-Shift-Option-O	View
Output Panel (Show/Hide)	F2	F2	Window
Panels (Show/Hide, including Toolbox)	F4, Tab	F4, Tab	View, Tab
Paste (Clipboard Contents)	Ctrl-V	⌘-V	Edit
Paste Frames	Ctrl-Alt-V	⌘-Option-V	Edit
Paste In Place	Ctrl-Shift-V	⌘-Shift-V	Edit
Plain (Text)	Ctrl-Shift-P	⌘-Shift-P	Text > Style
Play (Movie)	Enter	Return	Control
Previous (Scene)	Page Up	Page Up	View > Goto
Print	Ctrl-P	⌘-P	File
Properties Panel (Show/Hide)	Ctrl-F3	⌘-F3	Window
Publish	Shift-F12	Shift-F12	File
Publish Preview	Ctrl-F12	⌘-F12	File
Publish Settings	Ctrl-Shift-F12	Option-Shift-F12	File
Quit (Exit)	Ctrl-Q	⌘-Q	File
Redo	Ctrl-Y	⌘-Y	Edit
Reference Panel (Show/Hide)	Shift-F1	Shift-F1	Window
Remove All Breakpoints	Ctrl-Shift-A	⌘-Shift-A	Control (in Test Movie Mode)
Remove Breakpoint	Ctrl-Shift-B	⌘-Shift-B	Control (in Test Movie Mode)
Remove Frames	Shift-F5	Shift-F5	Insert
Remove Transform	Ctrl-Shift-Z	⌘-Shift-Z	Modify > Transform
Replace	Ctrl-H	⌘-Shift-H	Actions Panel Options
Reset (Tracking)	Ctrl-Alt-Up	⌘-Option-Up	Text > Tracking
Rewind	Ctrl-Alt-R	⌘-Option-R	Control
Rotate 90º CCW	Ctrl-Shift-7	⌘-Shift-7	Modify > Transform
Rotate 90º CW	Ctrl-Shift-9	⌘-Shift-9	Modify > Transform
Rulers (Show/Hide)	Ctrl-Alt-Shift-R	⌘-Shift-Option-R	View
Save As	Ctrl-Shift-S	⌘-Shift-S	File

Shortcut for Commands *(continued)*

COMMAND	WINDOWS	MACINTOSH	MENU
Save	Ctrl-S	⌘-S	File
Scale and Rotate	Ctrl-Alt-S	⌘-Option-S	Modify > Transform
Scene Panel (Show/Hide)	Shift-F12	Shift-F12	Modify; Window
Select All	Ctrl-A	⌘-A	Edit
Select All Frames	Ctrl-Alt-A	⌘-Option-A	Edit
Send (selected item) to back	Ctrl-Shift-Down	⌘-Shift-Down	Modify > Arrange
Send (selected item) backward	Ctrl-Down	⌘-Down	Modify > Arrange
Set Breakpoint	Ctrl-Shift-B	⌘-Shift-B	Control (in Test Movie Mode)
Shape Hints (Show/Hide)	Ctrl-Alt-H	⌘-Option-H	View
Show All	Ctrl-3	⌘-3	View > Magnification
Show Code Hint	Ctrl-Spacebar	Control-Spacebar	Actions Panel Options
Show Frame	Ctrl-2	⌘-2	View > Magnification
Snap to Grid	Ctrl-Shift-' (apostrophe)	⌘-Shift-' (apostrophe)	View > Grid
Snap to Guides	Ctrl-Shift-; (semi-colon)	⌘-Shift-; (semi-colon)	View > Guides
Snap to Objects	Ctrl-Shift-/ (slash	⌘-Shift-/ (slash)	View
Step Backward	,	, (comma)	Control (comma)
Step Forward	.	. (period)	Control (period)
Step In	F10	F10	Control (in Test Movie Mode)
Step Out	F11	F11	Control (in Test Movie Mode)
Step Over	F9	F9	Control (in Test Movie Mode)
Stop Debugging	F7	F7	Control (in Test Movie Mode)
Streaming (Show/Hide)	Ctrl-Enter	⌘- Return	View (in Test Movie Mode)
Streaming Graph (Show/Hide)	Ctrl-G	⌘-G	View (in Test Movie Mode)
Test Movie	Ctrl-Enter	⌘-Return	Control
Test Scene	Ctrl-Alt-Enter	⌘-Option-Return	Control
Timeline (Show/Hide)	Ctrl-Alt-T	⌘-Option-T	View
Tools Panel (Show/Hide)	Ctrl-F2	Cmd-F2	Window
Transform Panel (Show/Hide)	Ctrl-T	Cmd-T	Window
Undo	Ctrl-Z	⌘-Z	Edit
Ungroup	Ctrl-Shift-G	⌘-Shift-G	Modify
Unlock All	Ctrl-Alt-Shift-L	⌘-Shift-Option-L	Modify > Arrange
Using Flash (open in browser)	F1	F1	Help
View Line Numbers	Ctrl-Shift-L	⌘-Shift-L	Actions Panel Options
Work Area (View)	Ctrl-Shift-W	⌘-Shift-W	View
Zoom In	Ctrl-= (equals sign)	⌘-= (equals sign)	View
Zoom Out	Ctrl-— (minus sign)	⌘-— (minus)	View

In OS 9, Function Keys (Fkeys) are set by default to act as "Hot Function Keys," that can be defined to start an application, or open a document or other item. You can temporarily disable Hot Function Keys by holding down the Option key (on desktop Macs) or the fn key (on portable Macs) while pressing the Function Key, but keyboard shortcuts that require the use of modifier keys are iffy. To enable the full range of shortcuts defined for F1-F12 in Flash MX, it's best to disable the Hot Function Keys feature: open the Keyboard Control Panel (Apple Menu > Control Panels > Keyboard), then press the Function Keys... button. Remove the check mark from the Enable Hot Function Keys box. Click OK, then close the control panel.

In PowerBooks, F1–F6 are permanently defined as screen brightness, volume, and num lock keys, so you still have to use the fn key. If a modifier key is part of the keyboard shortcut, hold down the modifier, then press fn and the Function Key. For example, to display the Properties window, hold down the Command key, then press fn-F3.

The Hot Function Keys feature is not present in OS X, but on portable Macs you still have to use the fn key to make F1-F6 act like normal (Cool?) Function Keys.

Shortcuts for Accessing Tools and Manipulating Elements

OPERATION/TOOL	WINDOWS	MACINTOSH
Arrow tool (select in Toolbox)	V	V
Arrow tool (temporary access)	Ctrl	⌘
Brush tool (select in Toolbox)	B	B
Constrain (ovals to circles, rectangles to squares, lines and rotation to 45-degree angles)	Shift-drag	Shift-drag
Convert corner point to curve point (subselection tool)	Alt-drag	Option-drag
Create new corner point (arrow tool)	Alt-drag a line	Option-drag a line
Drag a copy of selected element on Stage	Alt-drag	Option-drag
Drag a copy of selected keyframe unit in Timeline	Alt-drag	Option-drag
Dropper tool (select in Toolbox)	I	I
End open path (pen tool)	Ctrl-click	⌘-click
Eraser tool (select in Toolbox)	E	E
Fill Transform tool (select in Toolbox)	F	F
Free Transform tool (select in Toolbox)	Q	Q
Hand tool (select in Toolbox)	H	H
Hand tool (temporary access)	Spacebar	Spacebar
Show/Hide all but one layer	Alt-click active layer's eye column	Option-click active layer's eye column
Ink bottle tool (select in Toolbox)	S	S
Lasso tool (select in Toolbox)	L	L
Line tool (select in Toolbox)	N	N
Lock/unlock all but one layer	Alt-click active layer's padlock column	Option-click active layer's padlock column
Magnifier tool (select in Toolbox)	M, Z	M, Z
Magnifier zoom-in tool (temporary access)	Ctrl-Spacebar	⌘-Spacebar
Magnifier zoom-out tool (temporary access)	Ctrl-Shift-Spacebar	⌘-Shift-Spacebar
Move keyframe unit in Timeline	Click-and-drag	Click-and-drag
Nudge selected element down 10 pixels	Shift-Down arrow	Shift-Down arrow

Shortcuts for Accessing Tools and Manipulating Elements *(continued)*

OPERATION/TOOL	WINDOWS	MACINTOSH
Nudge selected element to the left 1 pixel	Left arrow	Left arrow
Nudge selected element to the left 10 pixels	Shift-Left arrow	Shift-Left arrow
Nudge selected element to the right 1 pixel	Right arrow	Right arrow
Nudge selected element to the right 10 pixels	Shift-Right arrow	Shift-Right arrow
Nudge selected element up 1 pixel	Up arrow	Up arrow
Nudge selected element up 10 pixels	Shift-Up arrow	Shift-Up arrow
Nudge selected element down 1 pixel	Down arrow	Down arrow
Oval tool (select in Toolbox)	O	O
Paint bucket tool (select in Toolbox)	K	K
Pen tool (select in Toolbox)	P	P
Pencil tool (select in Toolbox)	Y	Y
Rectangle tool (select in Toolbox)	R	R
Select multiple layers	Shift-click	Shift-click
Select noncontiguous layers	Ctrl-click	⌘-click
Set fill and stroke color simultaneously	Shift-click with the dropper tool	Shift-click with the dropper tool
Show outlines for all but one layer	Alt-click that layer's outline column	Option-click that layer's outline column
Subselection tool (select in Toolbox)	A	A
Switch magnifier tool temporarily from zoom-in to zoom-out and vice versa	Alt	Option
Text tool (select in Toolbox)	T	T

INDEX

INDEX

INDEX

M

INDEX